'This is a formidable book. The book provides a golden opportunity to learn about how democracy works at the local level. Forty great chapters about electoral systems, electoral participation, party politicization, and descriptive representation in 40 different countries, plus an enlightening introduction and conclusion in which the similarities and amazing variety of patterns are clearly highlighted. This is an absolute must read if you study local politics, and it is fun to read for everyone. You will learn a lot and you will want to study local elections because there are so many intriguing facts and patterns to make sense of'.

André Blais, *University of Montreal, Canada*

'This comprehensive volume on local elections and voting in Europe is truly impressive. It offers a well-conceived theoretical two-dimensional structure which allows the many authors to provide comparable insights on the 40 countries covered, whether large or small, well-known or completely new to the scholarly community. The study of local elections has previously often suffered from a focus on only a few selected jurisdictions, but now presentations and data-access for a huge variety of countries are made available so that a new generation of local election studies can further enrich election studies in general. The editors' effort is very commendable and there is no doubt that this volume is the new must-read for all comparativists working with elections at the local level. But there is also no doubt that even people who still prefer to focus on one country only can also benefit considerably from it'.

Jørgen Elklit, *Aarhus University, Denmark*

'Elections have been called "feasts of democracy". Without any doubt local governments across the globe are the main venue for such democratic feasts. It is therefore hard to believe that local polls have long been a blank spot on the map of our knowledge of democratic elections. This volume – produced by the fine-fleur of international experts in this emerging field of research – makes a giant step forward in charting this largely unknown territory'.

Bas Denters, *University of Twente, The Netherlands*

The Routledge Handbook of Local Elections and Voting in Europe

The Routledge Handbook of Local Elections and Voting in Europe represents the standard reference text and practical resource for everybody who analyzes issues such as local electoral systems, voting behavior, or political representation in Europe.

It provides comprehensive and expert coverage of 40 European countries – organized along the respective local state traditions – and in addressing a wide range of important questions related to local elections and voting, it broadens the scope of existing analyses quantitatively as well as qualitatively. Finally, it affords a more theoretically grounded typology of local elections and voting. Each country chapter is written by a leading expert and follows a rigorous conceptual framework for cross-national comparisons, providing an overview of the local government system, details on the place of local elections within the multilevel political system, specific features of the electoral system, analysis of the main electoral outcomes in recent decades, and, finally, reflective discussion. Representative democracy is as widespread at the local as at the national level, and as the significance of local authorities in Europe has increased in recent decades, local elections represent a crucial area of study.

The Routledge Handbook of Local Elections and Voting in Europe is an authoritative and essential reference text for scholars and students interested in local electoral politics and, more broadly, European studies, public administration, and political science.

Adam Gendźwiłł is Assistant Professor in the Department of Local Development and Policy at the University of Warsaw, Poland.

Ulrik Kjaer is Professor of Political Science in the Department of Political Science at the University of Southern Denmark, Odense, Denmark.

Kristof Steyvers is Associate Professor in the Department of Political Science at Ghent University, Belgium.

The Routledge Handbook of Local Elections and Voting in Europe

Edited by Adam Gendźwiłł, Ulrik Kjaer, and Kristof Steyvers

LONDON AND NEW YORK

Cover image: © Getty Images

First published 2022
by Routledge
4 Park Square, Milton Park, Abingdon, Oxon OX14 4RN

and by Routledge
605 Third Avenue, New York, NY 10158

Routledge is an imprint of the Taylor & Francis Group, an informa business

© 2022 selection and editorial matter, Adam Gendźwiłł, Ulrik Kjaer and Kristof Steyvers; individual chapters, the contributors

The right of Adam Gendźwiłł, Ulrik Kjaer and Kristof Steyvers to be identified as the authors of the editorial material, and of the authors for their individual chapters, has been asserted in accordance with sections 77 and 78 of the Copyright, Designs and Patents Act 1988.

All rights reserved. No part of this book may be reprinted or reproduced or utilised in any form or by any electronic, mechanical, or other means, now known or hereafter invented, including photocopying and recording, or in any information storage or retrieval system, without permission in writing from the publishers.

Trademark notice: Product or corporate names may be trademarks or registered trademarks, and are used only for identification and explanation without intent to infringe.

British Library Cataloguing-in-Publication Data
A catalogue record for this book is available from the British Library

Library of Congress Cataloging-in-Publication Data
Names: Gendźwiłł, Adam, editor. | Kjaer, Ulrik, editor. | Steyvers, Kristof, editor.
Title: The Routledge handbook of local elections and voting in Europe / Adam Gendźwiłł, Ulrik Kjaer and Kristof Steyvers.
Other titles: Handbook of local elections and voting in Europe
Description: Abingdon, Oxon ; New York, NY : Routledge, 2022. | Series: Routledge international handbooks | Includes bibliographical references and index.
Identifiers: LCCN 2021042145 (print) | LCCN 2021042146 (ebook) | ISBN 9780367444334 (hardcover) | ISBN 9781032194882 (paperback) | ISBN 9781003009672 (ebook)
Subjects: LCSH: Local elections—Europe. | Voting research—Europe. | Local government—Europe.
Classification: LCC JS3000 .R68 2022 (print) | LCC JS3000 (ebook) | DDC 320.8094—dc23/eng/20211014
LC record available at https://lccn.loc.gov/2021042145
LC ebook record available at https://lccn.loc.gov/2021042146

ISBN: 978-0-367-44433-4 (hbk)
ISBN: 978-1-032-19488-2 (pbk)
ISBN: 978-1-003-00967-2 (ebk)

DOI: 10.4324/9781003009672

Typeset in Bembo
by Apex CoVantage, LLC

Contents

List of figures	xii
List of tables	xv
List of contributors	xx
Preface	xxviii

PART 1
Introduction 1

1   From perennial bridesmaids to fully fledged spouses: advancing the comparative study of local elections and voting 3
    Adam Gendźwiłł, Ulrik Kjaer, and Kristof Steyvers

PART 2
The Nordic States 19

2   Denmark: how two and a half parties rule within a multiparty system 21
    Ulrik Kjaer

3   Finland: local autonomy, tenacious national parties, and sovereign, but indifferent voters 31
    Siv Sandberg

4   Iceland: where localism prevails 41
    Eva Marín Hlynsdóttir and Eva H. Önnudóttir

5   Norway: local democracy by trial (and error) 51
    Jo Saglie and Signe Bock Segaard

6   Sweden: joint election day, party dominance, and extensive turnout 62
    Anders Lidström

PART 3
The British Isles — 71

7 Ireland: an atypical electoral system for an atypical local government system — 73
   Aodh Quinlivan, Mark Callanan, and Liam Weeks

8 United Kingdom: diversity amid the Cinderella elections? — 84
   Alistair Clark and Alia Middleton

PART 4
The Rhinelandic States — 95

9 Austria: strong participation across federal diversity — 97
   Philipp Umek

10 Belgium: between national barometer and local atmosphere — 114
   Kristof Steyvers

11 Germany: a variety of local elections in a federal system — 126
   Angelika Vetter

12 Liechtenstein: two leading parties in a direct democratic framework — 140
   Wilfried Marxer

13 Luxembourg: toward a thinner relationship between local and national elections? — 151
   Dan Schmit, Raphaël Kies, and Patrick Dumont

14 The Netherlands: increasing responsibilities and nationalized elections — 161
   Henk van der Kolk

15 Switzerland: low turnout but no second-order elections — 174
   Andreas Ladner

PART 5
The Southern European States — 185

16 Andorra: local elections in quasi-federal institutions — 187
   Lluís Medir, Pere Vilanova, and Esther Pano

17	Cyprus: national parties' dominance and the decline of electoral participation *Andreas Kirlappos*	197
18	France: competition only in large cities *Bernard Dolez and Annie Laurent*	209
19	Greece: mayors in the foreground, parties behind the scenes *Nikos Hlepas and Theodore Chadjipadelis*	222
20	Italy: hard-to-decipher local elections and voting *Silvia Bolgherini and Selena Grimaldi*	233
21	Portugal: elections and voting in a dual-tier, local government system *António F. Tavares and Pedro J. Camões*	246
22	Spain: one main system to govern them all? Stable institutions in heterogeneous contexts *Carmen Navarro, Lluís Medir, and Jaume Magre*	258

PART 6
New democracies: the Central and Eastern European States — 269

23	Czech Republic: local elections in a fragmented municipal system *Petr Voda*	271
24	Estonia: the consolidation of partisan politics in a small country with small municipalities *Tõnis Saarts, Georg Sootla, and Kersten Kattai*	282
25	Hungary: the expansion and the limits of national politics at the local level *Gábor Dobos*	293
26	Latvia: electoral drama in local governments *Iveta Reinholde and Malvīne Stučka*	303
27	Lithuania: between a volatile electorate and the revival of nonpartisanship *Aistė Lazauskienė and Jurga Bučaitė-Vilkė*	316

28 Poland: a hyperlocalized system? 327
    Adam Gendźwiłł

29 Slovakia: a gradual weakening of political parties in a stable
    local electoral system 337
    Daniel Klimovský

30 Ukraine: the first experiences with voting in the amalgamated
    territorial communities 347
    Valentyna Romanova

PART 7
New democracies: the Southeastern European States 361

31 Albania: the path to decentralized democratic governance 363
    Naz Feka, Iain Frank Wilson, and Alba Dakoli Wilson

32 Bosnia and Herzegovina: local elections within a weak
    and contested state 374
    Kiran Auerbach

33 Bulgaria: more open local electoral rules 387
    Desislava Kalcheva and Daniela Ushatova

34 Croatia: games of local democracy in the shadow
    of national politics 396
    Mihovil Škarica and Tijana Vukojičić Tomić

35 Kosovo: local elections and ethnic ramifications 408
    Memet Memeti

36 Moldova: party-shifting mayors within a nationalized
    local party system 419
    Ion Beschieru

37 Montenegro: local elections in the shadow of national politics 430
    Olivera Komar and Slaven Živković

38 North Macedonia: local elections and parliamentary
    political dynamics 441
    Veli Kreci and Islam Jusufi

39 Romania: a case of national parties ruling local politics 453
    Cristina Stănuş and Andrei Gheorghiţă

40 Serbia: three phases of local electoral politics after 1990   465
    Aleksandar Marinković and Novak Gajić

41 Slovenia: where strong, nonpartisan mayors are reelected
    many times over   476
    Simona Kukovič and Miro Haček

PART 8
Conclusions   **487**

42 'Happily ever after'? Comparing local elections and voting
    in 40 European countries   489
    Adam Gendźwiłł, Ulrik Kjaer, and Kristof Steyvers

Index   *533*

Figures

2.1	Voter turnout in Danish elections for municipal councils, national parliament, and EU Parliament, 1990–2019	24
2.2	Voter turnout in the 2017 Danish local elections by municipality size	25
2.3	Women's representation among councilors, mayors, and MPs in Denmark, 1990–2019	27
4.1	Voter turnout in local and national elections in Iceland, 1990–2019	45
5.1	Voter turnout in national and municipal elections in Norway, 1987–2019	55
5.2	Voter turnout in the 2019 Norwegian municipal elections by municipality size	56
5.3	Women's representation among councilors, mayors, and deputy mayors in Norway, 1991–2019	57
7.1	Voter turnout for local and general elections in Ireland, 1990–2020	78
8.1	Voter turnout for national and local elections in the United Kingdom, 1990–2019	88
8.2	Voter turnout by size of the electorate in 2017 (Scotland and Wales) and in 2019 (England and Northern Ireland)	89
9.1	Voter turnout in Austria across all levels, 1990–2020	104
9.2	Voter turnout in the Austrian local elections by municipality size	105
10.1	Voter turnout for local and national elections in Belgium, 1990–2020	118
10.2	Voter turnout in the 2018 Belgian local elections by municipality size	119
10.3	Women's representation among councilors in Belgium by region since 1994	122
11.1	Voter turnout for federal and local elections in Germany, 1991–2019	132
11.2	Voter turnout for local council elections in Baden-Wuerttemberg (2019) and North-Rhine Westphalia (2014) by number of eligible voters	133
11.3	Women's representation among German councilors, mayors, and heads of district administrations by state (2019)	135
12.1	Mean number of candidates for local councils in Liechtenstein, 1991–2019	144
12.2	Voter turnout for local and national elections in Liechtenstein, 1990–2019	145
12.3	Average voter turnout for local elections in Liechtenstein by municipality size, 1991–2019	146
12.4	Women's representation among councilors, mayors, and MPs in Liechtenstein, 1991–2019	147
14.1	Voter turnout for Dutch elections and referenda, 1945–2020	166
14.2	Voter turnout in the 2018 Dutch local elections by municipality size	167
14.3	Percentages of votes for local lists not formally connected to national lists from three somewhat different sources, 1970–2020	169

Figures

15.1	Average voter turnout at all three levels in 2017 by municipality size	179
16.1	Size of the electorate and voter turnout for local elections in Andorra, 1995–2019	191
16.2	Voter turnout for local and national elections in Andorra, 1993–2019	192
16.3	Voter turnout and the number of candidatures and preelectoral coalitions in Andorra	193
17.1	Voter turnout for local and national elections in Cyprus, 1991–2016	202
17.2	Voter turnout for local elections by number of enrolled voters in Cyprus, 2016	203
17.3	Women's representation among elected councilors and mayors in Cyprus, 1991–2016	205
18.1	Voter turnout for local and national elections in France since 1990	214
18.2	Voter turnout in the 2017 French local elections according to the number of registered voters (competitive elections in municipalities with more than 1,000 inhabitants; Pearson's r= -0.72)	215
19.1	Voter turnout for local and national elections in Greece, 1990–2019	227
20.1	Average number of competing lists and mayoral candidates in smaller (SM) and larger (LM) municipalities in Italy, 2017–2019	239
21.1	Number of councilors in Portugal municipalities by municipal population size	250
21.2	Voter turnout for local and parliamentary elections in Portugal municipalities of different size	253
22.1	Voter turnout for local and national elections in Spain, 1989–2019	262
22.2	Average voter turnout for local elections in Spain by population tranches, 1990–2015	263
22.3	Total number of independent lists with representation on councils in Spain, by election year	264
23.1	Voter turnout for national, regional, and local elections in the Czech Republic, 1990–2018	276
23.2	Women's representation among councilors in the Czech Republic, 1990–2018	278
26.1	Voter turnout for national and local elections in Latvia, 1993–2018	309
26.2	Voter turnout in the 2017 Latvian local elections by municipality size	310
26.3	Competitiveness in the 2017 Latvian local elections (lists and candidates)	311
28.1	Voter turnout for local and parliamentary elections in Poland, by municipality size	333
32.1	Decentralization in Bosnia and Herzegovina	375
32.2	Voter turnout for local and general elections in Bosnia and Herzegovina, 1996–2016	379
32.3	Voter turnout for the 2016 local elections in Bosnia and Herzegovina by municipality size	380
32.4	Women's representation among councilors and mayors in Bosnia and Herzegovina	382
33.1	Voter turnout for the 2019 Bulgarian local elections by municipality size	392
35.1	Voter turnout for local and national elections in Kosovo, 2000–2017	413
35.2	Voter turnout for local elections in Kosovo by municipality size	413
36.1	Voter turnout for local elections in Moldova in municipalities of different size	424
37.1	Voter turnout for parliamentary and local elections in Montenegro, 2006–2020	435

xiii

Figures

37.2	Average voter turnout in Montenegrin local elections by size of municipality, 2006–2020	436
38.1	Voter turnout for local and parliamentary elections in North Macedonia, 1994–2017	446
38.2	Voter turnout in the 2017 North Macedonian local elections by municipality size	447
42.1	Council size by eligible voters (country averages)	493
42.2	Average turnout in national and local elections	501
42.3	Examples of elections' simultaneity effects on voter turnout: (A) Denmark and (B) North Rhine-Westphalia, Germany	503
42.4	Post-1990 changes in voter turnout in 30 European countries	504
42.5	Share of independent mayors and councilors in local elections	508
42.6	Female councilors by country (% in ascending order)	510
42.7	The legislative-executive gender gap (18 countries with directly elected mayors)	511
42.8	The local-national gender gap	513

Tables

1.1	Countries included in the *Handbook*	9
2.1	Results of the local elections in the 98 Danish municipalities on 21 November 2017	26
3.1	Turnout for local and national elections in Finland, 1991–2019	35
3.2	Participation and performance of national parties in Finnish local elections, 2017	36
3.3	Share of women among elected local councilors and elected members of parliament, 1992–2017, Finland	37
4.1	Number and percentage of municipalities with proportional elections in which national parties presented a list in the 2018 election in Iceland	46
4.2	Proportion of parties' elected council members in the 2018 election in Iceland	47
4.3	Proportion of female councilors and female members of parliament in Iceland, 1990–2018	47
5.1	Party politicization of councils – participation and performance of the parliamentary (national) parties in Norwegian local elections, 2019	56
6.1	Perception of the importance (percent) of different tiers of government in Sweden	63
6.2	Turnout (percent) for parliamentary and municipal elections in Sweden, 1991–2018	66
6.3	Turnout (percent) for the 2018 municipal elections in Sweden in municipalities with different population sizes	67
6.4	Party politicization in the 2018 Swedish municipal elections	67
6.5	Female representation (percent) in the parliament, on municipal councils, and as chairs of executive committees in Sweden	68
7.1	Local election results in Ireland, 2019	80
8.1	Party politicization in United Kingdom local elections in 2017 (Scotland and Wales) and 2019 (England and Northern Ireland)	90
8.2	Percentage of female councilors across the United Kingdom	91
9.1	Timing and provisions for local elections in Austria	101
9.2	Municipal council majorities in Austrian local elections	106
9.3	Political competition in Austrian local elections	107
9.4	Party politicization in recent local elections in Austria	108
9.5	Female representation in recent local elections in Austria	109
10.1	Participation and performance of families of lists in Belgian local elections by region, 2018	121

Tables

11.1	Number and average size of municipalities across the German states, 1991 and 2020	127
11.2	Variations in the electoral systems in 13 German states	131
11.3	Shares of votes for national parties and 'other' parties/local lists in local elections in North Rhine-Westphalia and Baden-Wuerttemberg, 1994–2019	134
12.1	Number of local council and mayoral candidates in 11 municipalities in Liechtenstein, 1991–2019	144
12.2	Participation and performance of parties in local elections in Liechtenstein, 2019	145
12.3	Voter turnout for local elections by gender and age for all municipalities in Liechtenstein, 2019	146
13.1	Voter turnout (percent) for national and local elections in Luxembourg, 2004–2018	155
13.2	Election results for the main parties in the 2017 local elections for 46 communes in Luxembourg (PR system only)	155
13.3	Share (percent) of female candidates and councilors in Luxembourg, 1993–2017	157
13.4	Share (percent) of non-Luxembourgish candidates and voters, 1999–2017	158
14.1	Municipal size, council seats, and aldermen in the Netherlands, 1990 and 2019	162
14.2	Party politicization in Dutch local elections, 2018	168
15.1	Electoral turnout (percent) at all three levels in Switzerland	179
15.2	Aggregate electoral results of the most important parties in the most recent local elections (prior to 2017) in Switzerland	180
15.3	Representation of women in Swiss local government and percentage of executives without women	181
16.1	Political parties in the 2019 local elections in Andorra	193
16.2	Electoral trends in Andorra	194
16.3	Percentage of female councilors and mayors in Andorra	194
17.1	Participation and performance of families of lists in local elections in Cyprus, 2016	204
18.1	Competitiveness in the 2014 French municipal elections according to the electoral system and the number of inhabitants	216
18.2	The level of politicization of French mayors in 2014	217
18.3	Share of women elected as municipal councilors and mayors in France, 1995–2014	218
19.1	Number of council seats by population in Greek municipalities	226
19.2	Turnout and council size in Greece, 2019	228
19.3	Party performance in four different Greek polls, 2019	230
19.4	Incumbency of Greek mayors	231
20.1	Main features of the municipal electoral system in Italy	237
20.2	Turnout for local, regional, and legislative elections in Italy per year	238
20.3	Presence and performance of the main national parties in Italian municipal elections in OSRs, 2017–2019	241
21.1	Municipal council and municipal executive size in Portugal	251
21.2	Parish council and parish executive size in Portugal	252
21.3	Voter turnout (percent) for local and national elections in Portugal since 1990	253
21.4	Share of all seats on municipal executives received by the main (parliamentary) parties in the last local elections in Portugal, 2017	254

21.5	Share of women elected councilors, members of the executive, and mayors in Portugal, 1989–2017	255
22.1	Municipalities and population in Spain, 2018	259
22.2	Councilors from national parties in Spanish local elections, 1991–2019 (percent of municipalities)	264
22.3	Percent of votes for national political parties in local elections in historical regions of Spain, 1991–2019 (Catalunya, Galicia, Euskadi)	265
22.4	Percent of councilors by political party in Spain, 1991–2019	266
23.1	Turnout in 2018 Czech local elections by size of municipality	277
23.2	Participation and performance of families of lists in local elections in the Czech Republic, 2018	277
24.1	Voter turnout (percent) for local and national elections in Estonia	286
24.2	Size of local government and the proportion of votes received by the election winners in Estonia	288
24.3	Female representation in local elections in Estonia	288
24.4	The role of parties in national and local elections in Estonia (percent of all votes)	289
24.5	Incumbency ratio (percent) on the councils among the top three candidates in the Estonian elections	290
25.1	Voter turnout (percent) for local and national elections in Hungary since 1990	296
25.2	Electoral results by electoral subsystems in Hungary, 2019	297
25.3	Share (percent) of women among elected councilors, mayors, and members of parliament in Hungary, 1990–2019	299
26.1	Number of councilors in municipalities in Latvia	308
26.2	Female representation in local and national offices in Latvia	312
27.1	Representation of Lithuanians and national minorities on the local level	319
27.2	Voter turnout (percent) for local and national elections in Lithuania	320
27.3	Number of candidates in local elections in Lithuania, 1995–2019	321
27.4	Share of all seats on local councils received by the main parties in the latest local elections in Lithuania, 2019	322
27.5	Share of women among Seimas members and councilors in Lithuania	323
28.1	Main parameters of the local electoral system in Poland, 1990–2018	330
28.2	Voter turnout (percent) for local and national elections in Poland since 1990	332
28.3	Share of all seats on local councils received by the main (parliamentary) parties in the last local elections in Poland, 2018	334
28.4	Share of women among elected councilors (1990–2018) and mayors (1994–2018) in Poland	334
29.1	Voter turnout (percent) for local and national elections in Slovakia since 1990	341
29.2	Numbers of cases with missing candidates in two recent local elections in Slovakia, 2014 and 2018	342
29.3	Share of independent candidates among elected councilors and mayors in Slovakia, 1990–2018	343
29.4	Comparison of national and subnational electoral results of the selected political parties in Slovakia	344
29.5	Share of women among elected councilors and mayors in Slovakia, 1990–2018	345
30.1	The tiers of administrative and territorial divisions in Ukraine	348

30.2	Number of councilors on local councils elected in the 2015 Ukrainian local elections	350
30.3	Results of the 2015 Ukrainian local elections in nonamalgamated communities	353
30.4	Results of the 2015 Ukrainian mayoral elections in nonamalgamated communities	353
30.5	Results of the 2015 local elections in 159 ATCs in Ukraine	354
30.6	Results of the 2015 mayoral elections in 159 ATCs in Ukraine	354
30.7	Official results of the 2020 local elections in Ukraine	355
30.8	Official results of the 2020 mayoral elections in Ukraine	357
31.1	Number of municipal councilors according to population size in Albania	365
31.2	Voter turnout for local and national elections in Albania since 1992 and 1991, respectively	366
31.3	Number of inhabitants in municipalities (2011 census) and voter turnout (percent) in large and small municipalities for the elections of 2011 and 2015 in Albania in decreasing order of voter turnout in 2011	367
31.4	Votes won by the various party groups in the municipal council and mayoral elections in Albania of 2011 and 2015	369
32.1	Parliamentary parties and 2016 local election results in Bosnia and Herzegovina	381
33.1	Number of municipal councilors by number of residents in a local territorial unit in Bulgaria	390
33.2	Turnout for local and parliamentary elections in Bulgaria during the period 1991–2019	392
33.3	Share of all seats on the local councils won by the main parties in the last local elections in Bulgaria, 2019	393
33.4	Share of female elected mayors (1999–2019) and municipal councilors (2015–2019) in Bulgaria	394
34.1	Voter turnout for local and national elections in Croatia since 1990	400
34.2	Voter turnout in municipalities of different size in Croatia	401
34.3	Number of mayoral candidates and candidate lists in the last three cycles of local elections in Croatia	401
34.4	Share of all seats on local councils received by parliamentary parties in the last local elections (2017) in Croatia	403
34.5	Share (percent) of women among elected councilors (2001–2017) and mayors (2009–2017) in Croatia	404
34.6	Representation of ethnic minorities on municipal councils in Croatia	405
35.1	Party politicization in local elections in Kosovo, 2017	415
35.2	Members of municipal assemblies in Kosovo by ethnicity and gender, compared to proportion of population	416
36.1	Voter turnout (percent) for local and national elections in Moldova since 1990	423
36.2	Aggregate electoral results of the parliamentary (national) parties in the most recent local elections (2019) in Moldova	425
37.1	Percentage of female councilors and mayors in Montenegro	438
38.1	Party politicization in the 2017 local elections in North Macedonia	448
38.2	Female representation at the local and national levels in North Macedonia	449
39.1	Voter turnout for local and national elections in Romania, 1992–2020	458
39.2	Competitiveness of local elections in Romania, 2004–2016	459
39.3	Electoral performance of the parliamentary parties, independent candidates, and nonnational lists in the 2016 local elections in Romania	460

39.4	Electoral success of incumbents in mayoral elections in Romania, 2004–2016	461
39.5	Share of women among elected mayors (2004–2016) and local councilors (2016) in Romania	462
39.6	The electoral success of minority organizations and parties in Romanian municipalities, 2016	462
40.1	Main parameters of the local electoral system in Serbia, 1992–2016	468
40.2	Voter turnout (percent) for local and national elections in Serbia since 1990	469
40.3	Share of all seats on local councils received by the main (parliamentary) parties in the latest local elections (2016) in Serbia	471
40.4	Share of women among elected councilors in Serbia, 1990–2016	473
41.1	Voter turnout (percent) for local elections in the period 1994–2018 with details regarding the size of municipalities in the 2018 local elections in Slovenia	480
41.2	Success of political parties and local lists in the Slovenian 2018 municipal council elections in municipalities with the proportional principle	481
41.3	Number of female mayoral candidates in local elections in Slovenia, 1994–2018	482
41.4	Incumbency of mayors in local elections in Slovenia, 1998–2018	483
42.1	Local council size by country	492
42.2	Local electoral systems by state tradition (synthetic overview)	495
42.3	Directly elected mayors and local state traditions	496
42.4	Electoral systems in mayoral elections	499
42.5	Party politicization and local state traditions	507
42.6	Local elections and voting in Europe: indicators of vertical dissimilarity and horizontal variation	517
42.7	Typology of local elections in Europe: horizontal variation and vertical dissimilarity	519
42.8	Local electoral systems by state traditions (extensive description)	522
42.9	Turnout (gap) for local and national elections by country	527

Contributors

Kiran Auerbach is postdoctoral research fellow in the Department of Comparative Politics at the University of Bergen, Norway. Her research interests include comparative democratization, subnational politics, and political parties. Her work on Bosnia and Herzegovina was recently published in *Party Politics*.

Ion Beschieru is an experienced freelance expert on local government reforms and decentralization. He has worked for the national association of local authorities from Moldova (CALM) and several international organizations, including the Council of Europe, where he managed a regional program on local governance in Eastern Partnership countries. He is also a member of the Group of Independent Experts of the Council of Europe on the European Charter on Local Self-Government.

Silvia Bolgherini is Associate Professor in the Department of Political Science at the University of Perugia, Italy. She has been Senior Researcher at the Eurac Research in Bolzano/Bozen. Her research interests revolve around local government, electoral studies, and comparative political systems.

Jurga Bučaitė-Vilkė is Associate Professor in the Department of Sociology, Faculty of Social Sciences, at the Vytautas Magnus University, Kaunas, Lithuania. Her research interests include local governance, local democracy, and social policy. Her expertise also includes practice-based research on municipalities.

Mark Callanan is a Senior Lecturer in the Whitaker School of Government & Management at the Institute of Public Administration, Dublin, Ireland. His most recent book is *A Research Agenda for Regional and Local Government* (2021, co-edited with John Loughlin). He is also the author of *Local Government in the Republic of Ireland* (2018).

Pedro J. Camões is Assistant Professor and member of the Research Center in Political Science at the School of Economics and Management of the University of Minho, Braga, Portugal. His research interests include local public service delivery arrangements and the adoption of political and administrative institutions. His work has appeared in several journals in the fields of political science and public administration.

Theodore Chadjipadelis is Professor of Applied Statistics in the School of Political Sciences, Aristotle University of Thessaloniki, Greece. His main research interests include applied statistics, electoral and political behavior, urban and regional planning, and e-governance. He coordinates the Greek section of the Comparative Candidates Survey and the Comparative Study of Electoral Systems programs. His main publication are *Mathematics in Political Science*, Ziti (in Greek), 2005 and The Greek Crisis and its Cultural Origins, (with M. Marangudakis), Palgrave Macmillan, 2020.

Alistair Clark is Reader in Politics at Newcastle University, United Kingdom. His research interests include local elections and party politics and issues around electoral integrity and administration. He has written extensively on electoral reform in Scottish local government and is author of *Political Parties in the UK* (Palgrave Macmillan).

Gábor Dobos is a research fellow at the Centre for Social Sciences in Budapest and at the National University of Public Service, Budapest, Hungary. He is primarily interested in local politics and constitutional adjudication. His latest publication is the chapter 'Institutional Changes and Shifting Roles: Local Government Reform in Hungary, 2010–14' in Lackowska et al. (eds.) Local Government in Europe: New Perspectives and Democratic Challenges.

Bernard Dolez is Professor of Political Science at the University Panthéon-Sorbonne, Paris 1, and is a researcher at the European Centre for Sociology and Political Science (CESSP) of Paris 1, France. His research focuses on national and local political institutions, electoral rules and their effects, and electoral behavior.

Patrick Dumont is Professor in the School of Politics and International Relations of The Australian National University in Canberra, Australia. He is also a guest professor at the University of Luxembourg, chair of IPSA's Research Committee on Elites (RC02), and co-convenor of the ECPR Standing Group on Elites and Political Leadership.

Naz Feka lectures in International Relations and Political Sciences at Albanian University, Tirana. His research focuses on electoral processes, geopolitics and security studies in Kosovo and Albania. Naz has been involved for many years in EU and other international organisation developmental projects in the region, including providing support to local security councils with FLAG.

Novak Gajić heads the Political System Department at the Standing Conference of Cities & Municipalities – National Association of Local Authorities in Serbia. His work includes local electoral system. He has a PhD in political science from the University of Belgrade, with a dissertation on the influence of globalization on contemporary ideologies.

Adam Gendźwiłł is Assistant Professor of political science and human geography in the Department of Local Development and Policy at the University of Warsaw, Poland. His research interests comprise local elections, political representation, and territorial reforms.

Andrei Gheorghiță is Associate Professor of Sociology at the Lucian Blaga University of Sibiu, Romania, where he teaches courses on political and electoral sociology and quantitative data analysis. His research interests are related to the personalization of electoral politics in the post-Communist context and the mechanisms of social solidarity.

Selena Grimaldi is Assistant Professor at the Department of Political Science, Law and International Studies at Padova University, Italy. She teaches comparative politics and political science. Her research interests revolve around presidential studies, regional and local elections, and comparative political systems. Her research has been published in journals such as *Local Government Studies*, *Regional and Federal Studies*, and *Political Studies Review*.

Miro Haček is Professor at the University of Ljubljana, Slovenia. He is president of the Central European Political Science Association (CEPSA) and editor-in-chief of *Journal of Comparative Politics*. His main research areas include comparative politics, civil service, local (self-) government, and political management.

Nikos Hlepas is Professor of Regional Administration and Local Self-Government in the Faculty of Political Science and Public Administration, National and Kapodistrian University of Athens, Greece. His current research interests include regional administration, local self-government, and public law. He is past chairman of the National School of Public Administration and Local Government (2010–2012) and is an ordinary member of the Group of Independent Experts, CLRA, Council of Europe (2010–present). His main publication is *The European Charter of Local Self-Government* [Athens: Papazisis (in Greek), 2020].

Eva Marín Hlynsdóttir is Professor in the Faculty of Political Science, University of Iceland, Reykjavik. Her research focuses on various areas of subnational government. Her most recent publications include *Gender in Organizations: The Icelandic Female Council Manager* (2020) and *Subnational Governance in Small States: The Case of Iceland* (2020).

Islam Jusufi is Lecturer in the Political Science and International Relations Department at Epoka University, Tirana, Albania. He is one of the founders of Analytica, a think tank based in Skopje, North Macedonia. He studied politics at the University of Sheffield and international relations in Amsterdam, Bilkent, and Ankara. He is an alternate for the Group of Independent Experts on European Charter of Local Self-Government.

Desislava Kalcheva is a part-time lecturer at Sofia University 'St. Kliment Ohridski', Bulgaria. Her research interests and publications focus on local government, public investment, and regional development.

Kersten Kattai is a Lecturer of Public Administration at Tallinn University, Estonia. His research interests include multilevel governance, decentralization and local autonomy, local government reforms, local democracy, and local government internal institutional structure. He has published a chapter on Estonia in *The Oxford Handbook of Local and Regional Democracy in Europe* (with Georg Sootla). An article of his recently appeared in *Regional and Federal Studies*.

Raphaël Kies is researcher in Political Science at the University of Luxembourg. His research interests and publications are related to e-democracy, democratic innovations, and media studies. He is responsible for the Luxembourgish platform for participatory democracy.

Andreas Kirlappos holds a PhD in Political Science from the University of Cyprus. He is a Special Teaching Personnel and Research Fellow at the Cyprus Center for European and International Affairs and the Department of Politics and Governance at the University of Nicosia, Cyprus. He has published academic articles focusing on local government reforms, the EU and local authorities, and austerity and local government.

Contributors

Ulrik Kjaer is Professor of Political Science in the Department of Political Science at the University of Southern Denmark, Odense. His research interests are local government reforms, local democracy, mayoral leadership, and local elections. He has published in journals such as *Local Government Studies*, *Urban Affairs Review*, and *European Journal of Political Research*.

Daniel Klimovský is Associate Professor in the Department of Political Science, Faculty of Arts, Comenius University, Bratislava, Slovakia. His research is focused on local politics and local governance. He recently co-authored *Where Have All the Women Gone? Women's Political Representation in Local Councils of Czech and Slovak Towns, 1994–2014*.

Olivera Komar is Professor at the Faculty of Political Science, University of Montenegro. Her main research interests include voting behavior, elections, political parties, and gender politics. She is a principal investigator of the Montenegrin National Election Study (MNES). She publishes often on Montenegrin and regional politics and gender topics. Her work featured in many political science outlets, most prominently in *Politics, Journal of Public Affairs, Problems of Post-Communis, East European Politics and Society* and others.

Veli Kreci is Professor and Director of the Max van der Stoel Institute at the South East European University, North Macedonia. He is involved in several major academic research projects. His current research interests include public policy analysis, research methodology, knowledge utilization, and foreign policy analysis. He has recently published in *Local Government Studies*.

Simona Kukovič is Associate Professor at the University of Ljubljana, Slovenia. Her research covers local political leadership, local democracy, and comparative local government systems. She is general editor of *Journal of Comparative Politics* and head of the postdoctoral research project 'Leading Local Community: Bureaucratisation of Politics or Politicisation of Bureaucracy?'

Andreas Ladner is Professor for Political Institutions and Public Administration at the IDHEAP at the University of Lausanne, Switzerland. His areas of research include the quality of democracy, local government, institutional change, political parties, and voting advice applications. He has conducted several major research projects of the Swiss National Science Foundation. His major publications include *Patterns of Local Autonomy in Europe* (2019) and *Swiss Public Administration: Making State Work Successfully* (2019).

Annie Laurent is CNRS Research Director Emerita at the Centre d'études et de recherches administratives politiques et sociales (CERAPS) of the University of Lille, France. Her areas of specialization are political behavior, electoral rules and their effects, and strategic voting, in particular in two-round electoral systems.

Aistė Lazauskienė is Associate Professor in the Department of Public Administration, Faculty of Political Science and Diplomacy, Vytautas Magnus University, Kaunas, Lithuania. She is a member of the Group of Independent Experts at the Congress of Local and Regional Authorities at the Council of Europe. Her research currently focuses on local democracy, local elites, and Lithuanian local government reforms.

Anders Lidström is Professor of Political Science in the Department of Political Science, Umeå University, Sweden. He specializes in local, regional, and urban democracy and governance. His recent publications include *Multilevel Democracy. How Local Institutions and Civil Society Shape the Modern State* (with J.M. Sellers and Y. Bae, Cambridge University Press, 2020).

Jaume Magre is Associate Professor of Political Science in the Department of Political Science, Constitutional Law and Philosophy of Law at the University of Barcelona, Spain. He is principal investigator of GREL and director of Fundació Carles Pi i Sunyer. His research interests focus on mayors, local elections and democracy, and local institutions.

Aleksandar Marinković is the Head of Strategic Planning & Public Policy Department at the Standing Conference of Cities & Municipalities – National Association of Local Authorities in Serbia. His work and research interests include public finance, urban economics, and local and regional development.

Wilfried Marxer is a political scientist and former head of research politics at the Liechtenstein Institute, Bendern. He has published books and articles on the Liechtenstein electoral system at the national and local levels, analyses of voting behavior, direct democracy, and other aspects of Liechtenstein politics and its political system, and numerous surveys on elections and referendums since 1997.

Lluís Medir is Associate Professor of Political Science at the University of Barcelona, Spain. He belongs to the research group on local government, and his research interests include local government, intergovernmental relations, and public policies at the local level. He is coordinator of the master's degree program in advanced public administration. He has published in *Local Government Studies* and *International Journal of Public Sector Management*, among others.

Memet Memeti is a policy making and governance expert with a MPA from Indiana University and a PhD (SEEU) in the area of decision-making process in the local government in the Republic of Macedonia. His interest is good governance, public management, public policies, public administration reform, gender mainstreaming and Gender responsive budgeting, decentralization, leadership, and institutional and human development.

Alia Middleton is Senior Lecturer in Politics at the University of Surrey, United Kingdom. Her research interests include local, regional, and national elections, political leadership, candidates, and election campaign strategies. She has written on a variety of electoral contests and is the author of *Communicating and Strategizing Leadership in British Elections* (Palgrave Macmillan).

Carmen Navarro is Associate Professor in the Department of Political Science at the University Autonoma of Madrid, Spain. Her areas of teaching and research are local government and public policy. She is a member of international research networks for the study of local democracy and local government, and she has published extensively on the results of her research in Spanish and international journals and books.

Eva H. Önnudóttir is Professor in the Faculty of Political Science, University of Iceland, Reykjavik. She has published in journals such as *Party Politics*, *Scandinavian Political Studies*, *West-European Politics*, and *Representation*. She is the principal investigator of the Icelandic National Election Study and serves on the board of the Comparative Candidate Surveys.

Esther Pano is Associate Lecturer in the Department of Political Science at the University of Barcelona, Spain, and a member of several research groups. Since 2001 she has been the coordinator of the Observatory of Local Government Foundation Carles Pi i Sunyer. The center promotes studies aimed at the creation of knowledge, both theoretical and applied, about institutional networks and local government systems.

Aodh Quinlivan is a Lecturer in the Department of Government and Politics at University College Cork, Ireland. He is director of the Centre for Local and Regional Governance (CLRG) and has written eight books on different aspects of subnational government, including *Forgotten Lord Mayor* (2020).

Iveta Reinholde is Associate Professor and head of department in the Department of Political Science at the University of Latvia, Riga.

Valentyna Romanova holds a PhD in political science from the University of Kyiv-Mohyla Academy (UKMA). In 2020, she joined the Japan Association of Russian and East European Studies. Previously she worked as a senior consultant for the Department of Regional Policy at Ukraine's National Institute for Strategic Studies and taught within a joint German–Ukrainian MA program on German and European studies at UKMA.

Tõnis Saarts is Associate Professor of Comparative Politics at Tallinn University, Estonia. His research interests include political parties, elections, regional governance, and democratization in Central and Eastern Europe. He has published with Routledge and Palgrave MacMillan. His articles have recently appeared in *Regional and Federal Studies*, *East European Politics*, and *Problems of Post-Communism*.

Jo Saglie is Research professor at the Institute for Social Research, Oslo, Norway. His research interests include party organizations, local elections and local democracy, and the politics and representation of indigenous peoples. His publications include the volume *Indigenous Politics: Institutions, Representation, Mobilisation* (co-edited with M. Berg-Nordlie and A. Sullivan, 2015).

Siv Sandberg works as university lecturer and project leader in public administration at Åbo Akademi University, Turku, Finland. Her current research interests include longitudinal and comparative studies of the interplay between local politicians and administrators in Finland and the Nordic countries, as well as projects concerning long-term decision-making in multilevel political systems.

Dan Schmit is a PhD candidate at the University of Luxembourg whose research focuses on electoral systems, voting behavior, and politics in Luxembourg. He holds a BA in Philosophy, Politics and Economics from the University of East Anglia and a MPhil in Comparative Government from the University of Oxford.

Signe Bock Segaard is a Senior Research Fellow at the Institute for Social Research, Oslo, Norway. Her research interests include local democracy, elections, representation, and voter behavior. Her recent publications include the article 'When do consultative referendums improve democracy? Evidence from local referendums in Norway' (*International Political Science Review*, 2021, with B. Folkestad, J.E. Klausen, and J. Saglie).

Contributors

Mihovil Škarica is Assistant Professor in the Faculty of Law, University of Zagreb, Croatia, where he teaches public administration and local government. His work is related to the political, institutional, organizational, and developmental issues of local government, decentralization and local democracy, intermunicipal cooperation, local executive, and modernization of local public services.

Georg Sootla is a Professor of public policy at Tallinn University, School of Governance, Law and Society, Estonia. His publications have appeared as chapters in *The Oxford Handbook of Local and Regional Democracy in Europe* and in the other books issued by Palgrave, Edward Elgar, Macmillan, Elsevier, CRC Press, Routledge, Preager. His articles have also appeared in *Journal of Public Administration, Regional and Federal Studies*, and *Baltic Journal of Law and Politics*. His current research interests include multilevel and network governance, comparative local government, and interactive policy analysis.

Cristina Stănuş is Associate Professor of Political Science at the Lucian Blaga University of Sibiu, Romania, where she teaches courses on governance, policy analysis, and research methodology. Her research interests focus on the study of Romanian local government and politics in a comparative context and the governance of public service delivery.

Kristof Steyvers is Associate Professor in the Department of Political Science, Ghent University, Belgium. His research is conducted at the Centre for Local Politics and is concerned with topics such as local elections and voting, local political participation, local political leadership, local government reform, and comparative local politics.

Malvīne Stučka is a PhD candidate in the Department of Political Science at the University of Latvia, Riga.

António F. Tavares is Associate Professor and member of the Research Center in Political Science at the School of Economics and Management of the University of Minho in Braga, Portugal. His research interests include local public service delivery arrangements, land use management, and political participation. His work has appeared in several journals in the fields of political science and public administration.

Tijana Vukojičić Tomić is Assistant Professor of Administrative Science, Faculty of Law, University of Zagreb, Croatia. Her main research interests include local political institutions, forms of political participation of citizens at the local level, and representation of minorities and diversity management.

Philipp Umek is a PhD candidate and Lecturer at the University of Innsbruck, Austria. His research takes a quantitative approach and focuses on voter turnout and political competition at the local level in Austria.

Daniela Ushatova is leader of the expert team 'Local Policies and Finance' at the National Association of Municipalities in the Republic of Bulgaria. She is also a PhD student in the Department of Regional Development, Trakia University, Stara Zagora, Bulgaria. Her main interests are local government and local finance.

Henk van der Kolk is Associate Professor at the University of Twente, the Netherlands. In his PhD research (defended in 1997), he studied differences between municipalities in the 'nationalization' of local elections and its effect on councilors. Between 1998 and 2017, he co-directed several Dutch National Election Studies and was co-director of the Local Election Study of 2016. He co-authored *When citizens decide* (2011), covering three large-scale democratic experiments.

Angelika Vetter is Associate Professor at the Department of Social Sciences, University of Stuttgart, Germany. Her current research interests include local political participation, democratic innovations, and elections. She recently published a chapter on political participation in *Comparative European Politics: Distinctive Democracies, Common Challenges* (Oxford University Press).

Pere Vilanova is Professor Emeritus in Political Science at Universitat de Barcelona, Spain. He has also taught in universities from Europe to America and the Middle East. From 2008 to August 2010, he was director of the Division of Strategic and Security Affairs (DAES) of the Spanish Ministry of Defense. He was head of the expert's commission appointed by the General Council (parliament) for the elaboration of the text of the Constitution of Andorra. From 1993 to 2003, he was magistrate of the Constitutional Court of Andorra, and from 2000 to 2002, he was its president. He has been a member of institutional electoral observation missions in Bosnia and Herzegovina, Palestine, Indonesia, Central Asia, and Haiti.

Petr Voda is Assistant Professor in the Department of Political Science, Masaryk University, Brno, Czech Republic. He conducts research on local politics, public opinion and voting behavior, representation, and electoral systems.

Liam Weeks is Lecturer in the Department of Government and Politics, University College Cork, Ireland. His main research interests are elections and political parties. His most recent (co-authored) book is *The Treaty: Birth of a Nation* (Irish Academic Press, 2021). His first book, co-authored with Aodh Quinlivan, on local elections in Ireland is the only monograph published on this topic.

Alba Dakoli Wilson has contributed for 25 years to decentralization processes in Albania. As FLAG director, team leader, and local government and waste management specialist, she has facilitated and delivered direct support to local and central authorities. Environment and waste management, her post-graduate specialisation, is an area where Alba contributes at local, national and international levels.

Iain Frank Wilson is quality manager for the Foundation for Local Autonomy and Governance, FLAG, and for 16 years has been assisting local governments in Albania and elsewhere in the areas of strategic planning and improvement of service provision. Iain has a PhD in population genetics, has authored some 16 scientific publications, and continues to proofread and edit papers in this area, a role he has also been performing for the UN agencies in Albania for the last 20 years.

Slaven Živković is Research Associate with the Comparative Study of Electoral Systems (CSES) at the GESIS – Leibniz Institute for the Social Sciences, Germany. His research interests include voting behavior, public opinion, election and research methods. He wrote and co-authored several articles/book chapters about Montenegrin politics and behavior of voters around Europe.

Preface

Like many seemingly sensible ideas in (academic) life, the very first draft of this book grew over a beer. This particular one was drafted on a terrace at the Market Square in Wrocław, Poland (in the margin of the ECPR General Conference 2019). After exchanging a cask full of thoughts almost as big as the stated square, we found the piping toward the eventual publication turned out to be a bit less straightforward than the said market.

Mutual stays in Odense and Warsaw had already revealed that the three of us shared a common predilection for niche ingredients as well as local elections and voting. Subsequent paper collaborations rendered a taster of what a wider assemblage could look and savor like. With the residue of our minds, we had already conducted fieldwork on each other's *terroir* toward developing a more advanced comparative sample. Then, the global pandemic required a major revision of online elaboration. Despite the less flowery scene, further discussions blossomed and turned out to be equally fruitful.

Along with the home brewing experiments, we were lucky to add the experience and expertise of excellent contributors from the 40 European countries included in this book. It was a joy to sense their initial enthusiasm for hopping on to this project. Wrestling through our recipe instructions and suggestions for maturation, they managed to strike the proper balance between prompt action and prolonged patience for the final product to filter out. We are deeply indebted to them for their cooperation. After two years of intense fermentation, the joint endeavor of this *Routledge Handbook on Local Elections and Voting in Europe* is now bottled.

We are grateful to Routledge for giving us the opportunity to publish this book as part of their *Handbook* series. In particular, we are grateful to publisher Andrew Taylor for accepting our initial intent and to senior editorial assistant Sophie Iddamalgoda for helping us through the whole process.

This book owes big cheers to those we have elected locally as our fully fledged spouses and the children ultimately represented: Magda, Franek, Tosia, and Dominik; Rikke; and Nele, Lien, and Lauren.

We present this *Handbook* with pride, hoping that our readers will enjoy the degustation.
July 2021

Adam Gendźwiłł, Warsaw
Ulrik Kjaer, Odense
Kristof Steyvers, Ghent

Part 1
Introduction

1

From perennial bridesmaids to fully fledged spouses

Advancing the comparative study of local elections and voting

Adam Gendźwiłł, Ulrik Kjaer, and Kristof Steyvers

Labeling local elections and voting 'the perennial bridesmaids of behavioral research'

Elections and voting are central research objects in political science, but national elections seem to steal the thunder. The focus of attention tends to be on the elections that determine the composition of parliaments and the leader of the country. All other elections, jointly labeled as 'second order' (Reif & Schmitt 1980), have attracted much less scholarly attention. This broad category includes not only supranational elections, such as European Parliament elections, but also elections in subnational units, that is, local and regional governments. The gap in our understanding of electoral behavior in these subnational elections and the peculiarities of the electoral arenas at the lower tiers of government have been noticed but not yet fully addressed. Within the emerging stream of literature that scrutinizes multilevel electoral politics, the local level is still a somewhat missing piece. However, in response to the progress of decentralization in recent decades, more and more studies of local elections are being conducted. In many countries, local governments are becoming (more) important pillars of the public sector, and therefore the representative democratic institution of local elections deserves scrutiny. And the scholarly interest in these important local democratic phenomena – hitherto characterized by fragmented insights in a few countries – should mature into more systematic research.

This handbook aims to contribute to the comparative study of local elections and voting. We argue that going local is not only pertinent in its own right, it is also a means to advance our overall understanding of elections and voting in multilevel political systems (Gendźwiłł & Steyvers 2021). Our knowledge of local electoral systems and insight into the patterns of voting in local elections are surprisingly incomplete. Reviewing existing studies, Marschall (2010: 471) put it this way: 'to say that a field of study of local elections exists would be a bit of an overstatement'. Much of the existing literature is 'rather small and not particularly cohesive', and the 'data collection and methods of analysis are also somewhat primitive' (Marschall et al. 2011: 97). Elsewhere, Kaufmann and Rodriguez (2011: 101) come to a similar but more imaginative conclusion when they state that, 'within contemporary political science, local elections are the perennial bridesmaids of behavioral research'.

A decade later, this continues to hold true despite the persistent function of elections as a key mechanism assuring representative legitimacy and accountability at the level closest to the citizen, where individual electoral participation might have the largest effect (Clark & Krebs 2012; Denters et al. 2015). Some progress in mainstreaming the study of local elections has been reported in the United States (Warshaw 2019). Yet, in the European context it can still be observed that local elections remain somehow in the shadows, despite the increasing importance of the local tier of the multilevel governance structure existing in many European countries (Loughlin et al. 2012; Ladner et al. 2016).

When it comes to the study of local elections and voting, a broad, cross-national comparative perspective is still missing. This remains in contrast with recent endeavors in the field of comparative local government covering other topics (Swianiewicz 2020), such as local autonomy (Ladner et al. 2019), local state-society relations (Sellers et al. 2020; Teles et al. 2021), the role of local politicians (Egner et al. 2013; Heinelt et al. 2018), and local territorial reforms (Kuhlmann & Bouckaert 2016).

Existing relations: lower rank or a different kind[1]

Although relatively underexplored, studies of local elections and voting are, however, not entirely absent in the field. A search of the *Social Sciences Citation Index* based on the topics 'local' and 'elections' or 'voting' returned 1,639 and 924 articles, respectively, in the category political science since the late 1950s. Tellingly, in the most cited (nonmethodological) article, Lijphart (1997) discusses low voter turnout as a democratic problem of equality and influence. This includes how the issue specifically materializes at the local level as being a less salient but not unimportant arena. Implicitly, his contribution points to two of the dominant strands in the field – in most of the existing literature, local elections and voting are seen as either of *lower rank* or of a *different kind*.

The first perspective assumes that local elections are less important and less relevant than national elections. According to this approach, local elections are seen as second-order elections (Rallings & Thrasher 2005; Clark & Krebs 2012). This approach builds on the model developed by Reif and Schmitt (1980) regarding European elections; a field in which this model continues to be considered robust and consistent (Marsh & Mikhaylov 2010; Hix & Marsh 2011). Participation and party choice in local elections, similarly to those held in the other second-order arenas, are said to reflect the first-order arena considerations guiding parties' and voters' behavior. The latter will perceive less impetus to turn out (as less is at stake) but will be more inclined to switch their vote – as they do in European elections (Carrubba & Timpone 2005) – and vote expressively, for example, for small, fringe, and new parties or to punish or reward nationally governing ones. In this respect, a local election is treated as a nationwide event and essentially serves a barometric function, conditional upon the timing, that is, its placement within the first-order electoral cycle (Vetter 2015). This approach highlights the vertical integration of the local level into the national political system. Yet, it assumes that the relation between the local (second-order) and national (first-order) levels is asymmetrical, with the local level being an agent of the center in terms of execution and co-governance.

The second approach acknowledges the heterogeneity of local electoral arenas and claims that local elections and voting are of a different kind (Kaufmann 2004). Given the specific size of local jurisdictions (relatively small population), their scope of authority (comparatively limited constitutive powers with a focus on basic public service delivery), and/or bias (rather redistributive in resources), the local level produces particular electoral features and voting dynamics that differ from those found elsewhere (Oliver et al. 2012). Moreover, a 'different kind' of local electoral politics manifests itself in personal contacts with candidates and elected officials, lower costs of campaigning and generally lower barriers to enter the electoral market, and the widespread presence of amateur politicians. In local elections, place-bound considerations such as the perceived performance of local officeholders or the assessment of issues with deep ties in the community tend to dominate the mental calculus of national party identification, ideological assertions, or social group appeals (e.g., through organized interests). Oliver et al. notice that, in this regard, local elections and voting are more managerial than existential (2012).

Furthermore, size, scope, and/or bias are differentiated between places and polities. Thus, this approach highlights horizontal variation. Not only do local authorities differ substantially from their national counterparts but they also differ from one another. This heterogeneous, place-bound electoral dynamic makes local elections a bundle of local events. Obviously, there is a potential downside to the latter argument. Where localities differ substantially, idiosyncrasies lure. If particularities affect elections and voting across localities, findings from one context are harder to generalize to other contexts. The predominance of local events and circumstances threatens to undermine the feasibility of comparison (Kaufmann & Rodriguez 2011). Therefore, the study of local elections and voting must strike a balance with the factors that are more systemic while acknowledging the politics of places. Evidently, specific configurations can be discerned with a more structural impact on local elections and voting (Hajnal & Trounstine 2014). In jurisdictions that are relatively small and low in bias (think about an archetypal rural municipality), the emergence of civic-minded politicians is more likely. Here, personal connections between voters and candidates will determine electoral outcomes, with low-key campaigns and elections as referenda on the incumbent and his or her performance. In places where these parameters are large and high (as in an urban setting), ambitious candidates tend to run large-scale campaigns, with parties and other organizations active in mobilizing key supporters. Elections center on core issues and group interests (Oliver et al. 2012: 46–50).

A growing body of literature has focused on the regional tier of the subnational political arena (Dandoy & Schakel 2013; Golder et al. 2017). This literature often adopts the second-order framework. The congruence between regional and national elections varies, depending on the scope of regional authority, the strength of regional identity, the presence and/or success of non-statewide parties, and differences between electoral systems (Schakel 2013, 2017). However, the observed focus on regional elections tends to further ignore the peculiarities of the local level, which in most cases is at least as important as the regional one (Loughlin et al. 2012; Ladner et al. 2019). The local level is continuously the missing link in the study of multilevel electoral politics.

A few exceptions do exist. Kjaer and Steyvers (2019) proposed a model of local elections as *second-tier elections and voting*, which includes both vertical and horizontal perspectives. The authors emphasize the relationship with a first-tier national counterpart (which can be relatively weak or strong), while conceding variation among different local authorities (which can be minor or major). This follows from a commentative approach to the predominant perspective on local elections and voting as being of lower rank or a different kind. While there is merit in both, they are equally incomplete. Each accounts for only one of the two defining characteristics of almost any local government setting (and tends to miss the other): the lower rank view clearly incorporates the vertical relation but overlooks the horizontal variation; the different kind approach understands horizontal variation but underestimates the vertical relation (Kjaer & Steyvers 2019).

Within this framework and along these themes, local elections and voting can be located on two main analytical dimensions: vertical integration and horizontal variation. The first makes comparisons between levels, the second between jurisdictions.

Vertical integration follows from the innate and enduring relationship between local and national governance (Wollmann 2006). Whereas substantial variation appears in the balance between both levels (e.g., brought about by specific configurations of intergovernmental arrangements in terms of decentralization or discretion), it ultimately remains asymmetrical as local authorities are nearly universally parts of the state. This implies that we should situate local elections and voting in the contemporary layers of governance. What (if any) is the interconnection between the local and national electoral arenas? What similarities and differences in the concomitant patterns and dynamics follow from this default linkage between tiers? Here, for instance, we could probe the level of congruence between the electoral and/or party system at the local and national levels. This helps us to situate our object of study on a continuum between localization and nationalization. Vertical similarity versus dissimilarity is therefore the first approach to the *localness* of municipal elections and voting in the wider political system.

Horizontal variation stems from the simple admission that even in the smallest of systems with a local government tier, there is more than one place-bound authority. The local level stands for multiple entities with separate political institutions and a concomitant electoral chain of representation and accountability. We tend to focus on comparing the participation in and outcome of one election at a certain level with other elections at a different level and point in time. But each election is a set of contests in many different constituencies, and this applies to about 100,000 electoral races regularly held in European localities (Loughlin et al. 2012). Apart from looking for aggregate trends and tendencies (gauging the overall level of local turnout or success of this or that national party), we should therefore also concede to municipal diversity in terms of formal rules and electoral outcomes. This invites us to examine systematic patterns of contextual influences such as the effect of municipal size, residential density, and socioeconomic diversity on, for instance, voter turnout. The focus on differences between local governments leads to the second approach to the *localness* of municipal elections and voting in the wider political system: the continuum between homogeneity and heterogeneity across places.

The handbook will build on this theoretical groundwork; the dimensions of vertical integration and horizontal variation will guide the country-by-country analyses and the comparative analysis in the summary. However, first we will argue why and what going local adds to our understanding of multilevel elections and voting.

Rationale for further engagement: going local as means and goal

We need more knowledge about local elections and voting; there is still a lack of systematic analyses (Kjaer & Steyvers 2019: 414–415), even though the richness of electoral data allow for a huge variety of further research (Marschall et al. 2011). After all, in most countries, a vast majority of elected officials are local legislators and/or executives. The outcomes of local elections represent a large proportion of political events. Even if not all politics is local, the bulk of all elections and voting are (Trounstine 2009: 612). A thorough concern with the local tier thus has merit as a goal on its own.

The study of the local level speaks to the wider field of electoral studies. It is therefore also a means to a wider purpose. This is due to the methodological advantages brought by local elections: they offer many observations with a considerable variation in local contexts, institutional settings, and electoral outcomes (Clark & Krebs 2012). In particular, the basic parameters of local electoral systems tend to be diversified, some even exotic in comparison with the well-mapped, national electoral systems. The high number of cases and the variation among them allow for more fine-grained analyses and more reliable findings (John 2006). The number and variety of cases also give those with a more qualitative outlook access to a rich universe of cases for a purposeful selection, including extreme configurations of local contextual features. Another advantage of 'going local' is related to the appearance of electoral reforms, which are more frequently observed at the local level. As they are often introduced selectively in only a part of the local jurisdictions (e.g., only in municipalities above a certain threshold of size), there is an opening to apply quasi-experimental designs (e.g., Garmann 2016; Gendźwiłł & Żółtak 2017; Koch & Rochat 2017; Górecki & Kukołowicz 2018).

The local level can also be exploited to conduct multilevel analyses in which the effect of aggregate characteristics (socioeconomic or institutional context) on individual attitudes and behavior can be investigated using a design that accounts for the clustering of individuals in different local contexts and for cross-level interactions (Denters & Mossberger 2006; Oliver & Ha 2007; John 2009; Denters et al. 2015). If local context contributes to the explanation of individual voting behavior, its impact should be visible first and foremost in local elections (Górecki & Gendźwiłł 2021).

The study of local elections and voting enriches electoral studies. It generates different kinds of questions and answers that are likely to be more generally applicable (Trounstine 2009; Harris et al. 2016). The proximity of local politics (with its embeddedness in neighborhood ties and personal interactions and its decision-making processes with readily observable consequences) implies electoral and voting patterns and dynamics, some of which have already been suggested earlier. The patterns of voter turnout in local elections are an exemplar in this respect. Whereas participation in local elections tends to be lower than in their national counterparts, the default 'less-at-stake' explanation does not tell the whole story. It is clear that the difference in turnout varies in time and space. Often, the electoral system, municipal size, and population density appear as key correlates (Cancela & Geys 2016; Van Houwelingen 2017; Tavares & Raudla 2018; Gendźwiłł & Kjaer 2021). The same holds for the degree of local party system nationalization, that is, the similarity between the national and local party systems. Patterns of voting in local elections tend to diverge from patterns in national elections, yet the (in)congruence of voting is also affected by the presence and success of various (non)national lists and/or independent candidates, which vary from municipality to municipality (Kjaer & Elklit 2010; Steyvers & Heyerick 2017).

Ultimately, to espouse local elections to make them more fully fledged in the multilevel study of elections and voting fosters a more comprehensive and integrated understanding. However, not many have embarked on such a path. Obviously, one of the remaining challenges is the lack of comparable, cross-national data sets: 'Students searching for large data sets to mine have few options at the local level' (Trounstine 2009: 65). This argument can be extended beyond the mere availability of numbers for statistical analysis. Many insights and findings taken for granted in parliamentary studies simply do not have local equivalents. In the cross-national study of electoral systems, systematic overviews of formal rules are foundational (Herron et al. 2018). For the local level, even the most basic counterpart is lacking. This is a case in point. Seminal contributions that have attempted to fill this gap are becoming rather outdated, remain narrowly focused, or are confined to particular areas or exemplar cases (Van der Kolk 2007; Cole 2019). The same holds for our understanding of individual voting behavior. Whereas regular national election studies have been conducted systematically for decades (with the Comparative Study of Electoral Systems (CSES) as an 'umbrella' project that affiliates national election studies and serves as a 'gold standard' in survey research), the motives and behavior pertaining to the local vote are only scrutinized in a limited number of countries. A few local election studies based on voter surveys are conducted regularly (Elklit et al. 2017; Jansen & Denters 2018; Dandoy et al. 2020), but their integration and comparability are limited. Still, nothing analogous to the CSES exists for local election studies.

There is thus a substantial and methodological gap on local elections. On an anecdotal basis, this was confirmed by some of the authors in our handbook. In various instances, their contributions are the first to address the patterns and dynamics of local elections and voting in their respective countries for an international readership. For some of the new European democracies, it is even the primary attempt to collect nationwide data on the topic. Therefore, to paraphrase Greenstein (1967), this handbook is also 'an attempt to clear away underbrush'. This is a first step that justifies our approach to address the comparison in a rather traditional, cross-country manner. It also justifies an intensive effort to collect and assemble the basic data describing local electoral systems and election outcomes. Given the overall lack of data on the local level, we have explicitly requested our contributors to provide us with not only some key information to supplement each chapter but also references for the sources of primary data. Consequently, we consider the handbook, along with the related databases, an important guide to students of the field that is necessary but not sufficient to fully close the aforementioned gap. We hope our attempt will provide fruitful soil for further comparative endeavors.

The following sections will set out the selection of units and cases included in this handbook and our comparative framework.

Pairing units and cases: first-tier local government in 40 European countries

To maximize comparability across countries, our handbook concentrates on the first (lowest) tier of local government. This is the local administrative unit that is closest to the citizens and is commonly denoted as the municipality (or its functional equivalent). The units covered thus refer to territorially integrated, multipurpose, and directly elected local authorities (Lidström 1999; Wollmann 2016). In the wider descriptions of their local government system (see the explanation of the comparative framework to follow), the authors of the individual country chapters might mention a possible second tier of local government (Heinelt & Bertrana 2011), potential submunicipal entities (Hlepas et al. 2018), and/or possible functionally differentiated arrangements of intermunicipal cooperation, often with indirectly elected or appointed governing bodies (Teles & Swianiewicz 2018). These are not the focus of the current analysis of local elections and voting in this book. The only exception to this general rule is Portugal, where local governments are traditionally characterized as a dual-tier system with constitutionally embedded municipalities and parishes.

Our handbook covers 40 countries in Europe (Table 1.1; in alphabetical order): Albania, Andorra, Austria, Belgium, Bosnia and Herzegovina, Bulgaria, Croatia, Cyprus, Czech Republic, Denmark, Estonia, Finland, France, Germany, Greece, Hungary, Iceland, Ireland, Italy, Kosovo, Latvia, Liechtenstein, Lithuania, Luxembourg, Moldova, Montenegro, The Netherlands, North Macedonia, Norway, Poland, Portugal, Romania, Serbia, Slovakia, Slovenia, Spain, Sweden, Switzerland, Ukraine, and the United Kingdom. The sheer number and subsequent listing already suggest that we have been able to include a range of countries that is rather exceptional in cross-national studies of local government and politics in general. As in all comparative endeavors, however, the selection of cases stems from a mixture of substantial and pragmatic considerations and, therefore, has obvious limitations.

To organize our handbook, we placed the countries in their respective state traditions (see also the table of contents). These refer to the historically rooted legal basis of the state,

Table 1.1 Countries included in the *Handbook*

Country	State tradition	Local government units
Albania	New democracies – Southeastern	Bashkia (urban)
Andorra	Southern	Parròquies/comuns
Austria (Ländern)	Rhinelandic	Gemeinden
Belgium (regions)	Rhinelandic	Gemeenten, communes, Gemeinden
Bosnia and Herzegovina	New democracies – Southeastern	Opštine, općine
Bulgaria	New democracies – Southeastern	Obshtini
Croatia	New democracies – Southeastern	Gradovi (urban), općine (rural)
Cyprus	Southern	Dímoi (municipalities), koinotites (rural communities)
Czech Republic	New democracies – Central and Eastern	Obcí
Denmark	Nordic	Kommuner
Estonia	New democracies – Central and Eastern	Linnad (urban), vallad (rural)
Finland	Nordic	Kunnat, kommuner
France	Southern	Communes
Germany (Ländern)	Rhinelandic	Gemeinden, kreisfreie Städte
Greece	Southern	Dímoi
Hungary	New democracies – Central and Eastern	Települései
Iceland	Nordic	Sveitarfélögin
Ireland	British Isles	Counties, cities
Italy	Southern	Comuni
Kosovo	New democracies – Southeastern	Komunat, opštine
Latvia	New democracies – Central and Eastern	Novads (rural), republikas pilsēta (urban)
Liechtenstein	Rhinelandic	Gemeinden
Lithuania	New democracies – Central and Eastern	Savivaldybės
Luxembourg	Rhinelandic	Communes
Moldova	New democracies – Southeastern	Municipii
Montenegro	New democracies – Southeastern	Opštine
Netherlands	Rhinelandic	Gemeenten
North Macedonia	New democracies – Southeastern	Opštini
Norway	Nordic	Kommuner
Poland	New democracies – Central and Eastern	Gminy
Portugal	Southern	Municípios, freguesias
Romania	New democracies – Southeastern	Municipii, orașe, comunes
Serbia	New democracies – Southeastern	Opštine (rural), gradovi (urban)
Slovakia	New democracies – Central and Eastern	Obcí
Slovenia	New democracies – Southeastern	Občine

(*Continued*)

Table 1.1 (Continued)

Country	State tradition	Local government units
Spain	Southern	Municipios
Sweden	Nordic	Kommuner
Switzerland (cantons)	Rhinelandic	Gemeinden
United Kingdom (England, Wales, Scotland, Northern Ireland)	British Isles	County councils, district councils, London boroughs, metropolitan boroughs, unitary local authorities
Ukraine	New democracies – Central and Eastern	Hromady

Source: Loughlin et al. (2012), Ladner et al. (2019), and country chapters

state-society relations, the form of political organization and decentralization, and the basis of policy style, and they are likely to affect local elections and voting. State traditions are thus more than just regional clusters and will serve as the basis for our exploration (i.e., the starting point for a more in-depth comparison). The often-cited typology of the *Oxford Handbook of Local and Regional Democracy in Europe* (Loughlin et al. 2012) makes the following classifications: the Nordic Countries, the British Isles, the Rhinelandic States, Southern Europe, and the New Democracies of Central and Eastern Europe (for our purposes divided into Central and Eastern Europe and Southeastern Europe; see also Swianiewicz 2014).

We aimed to extend our reach by incorporating all European countries that have democratically elected local governments. This refers to countries that are members of the European Union or the European Free Trade Association (31 countries).[2] It also involves countries in the wider European sphere, and, here, recent comparative work on patterns of local autonomy was our main source of inspiration (Ladner et al. 2016, 2019). It included most (but not all) of the members of the Council of Europe that have ratified the European Charter of Local Self-Government. In comparison with the publications just mentioned (39 countries), we left out Malta (because of difficulties involved in finding a country expert) and two countries that are geographically only partly in Europe. We added three hitherto uncovered members of the Council of Europe and Kosovo to ultimately arrive at 40 cases.[3] Without claiming to provide an all-encompassing picture, we are confident that this selection offers a rather comprehensive view of the pattern and dynamics of local elections and voting in Europe. Even apart from the topic, for some countries a mere description of their local government system is rare in the international literature. This handbook is an open invitation to complete the list and offers an analytical framework that could easily be extended to other regions of the world.

Comparative framework: from local government system to electoral outcomes

With this selection of units and cases, country chapters are at the heart of our handbook. These are authored by national experts in the field of local government and electoral studies. To select them, we relied on our own academic networks (often rendering a snowball effect of suggestions for other cases) with a keen eye on the group of scholars engaged in the Local Autonomy Index project (Ladner et al. 2019). Where necessary, we also referred to the Group of Independent Experts on the European Charter of Local Self-Government of the Council of Europe.[4]

To assure cross-national comparability, all authors received a template for their chapter that was developed by the editors. It outlined the scope and the substance that each country chapter needed to address. The subsequent points of the common template constitute a comparative framework for the handbook. Additionally, the template specified the requirements to provide country data to be pooled in a common database and to use a shared coding scheme. Both features will be discussed later.

Comparative scope and substance

The handbook is intended as a cross-national exercise. Therefore, authors were generally expected to cover local elections and voting for their entire country.[5] In terms of geographical scope, the emphasis thus has been on the aggregate picture for all municipalities in a state's territory. Of course, structural differentiation within countries exists. Where this affects the features of local electoral systems, the timing of elections, or the distribution of votes, the authors were invited to discuss relevant subsystems. For one thing, it is not unlikely that in federal systems, the states (or equivalent entities) set the constitutive frameworks for the municipalities in their regional jurisdiction. This might invoke pertinent differences in the organization of local elections and voting. This can also be the case in both unitary and federal states, where systemic variation is related to municipal size, urbanization, or legal status. Of course, this renders the drawing of an aggregate picture to be rather straightforward in some cases and almost gruesomely complex in others (to compare the 11 municipalities in unitary Liechtenstein with their 2,202 counterparts in the 26 internally diversified cantons of the neighboring federation of Switzerland). Overall, we aim to compare political (sub)systems pertaining to local elections and voting between and within countries.

The handbook is also more cross-sectional than longitudinal. Therefore, the descriptions of the institutional setups and the election outcomes take the most recent local elections in the country as their primary reference.[6] To include a time perspective, we nevertheless requested that the authors reflect on local elections and voting in their country since 1990 (or later if local democracy was founded only afterward) in the various sections. Therein, substantial changes in pertinent aspects should be noted and interpreted. This includes a consideration of the most likely future reforms.

With this geographical and temporal scope, each chapter comprises five substantial sections together covering the most relevant dimensions and aspects of local elections and voting in the respective country.

Brief overview of the local government system

In the first section of each chapter, a brief overview of the local government system is given. It locates the local level within the structure of multilevel governance with a keen eye on the subnational institutional infrastructure. This involves an assertion of the territorial and functional organization of the municipal tier (Swianiewicz 2014). It starts with the number and level of fragmentation of local units. This is further complemented by situating the municipal tier in the categorical typologies and discrete measures of vertical and horizontal power relations existing in the comparative local government literature. On one dimension, the local level can be placed in terms of intergovernmental relations and concerns or issues such as decentralization or discretion (including asymmetric decentralization, which differentiates functionally local jurisdictions within the country). The authors referred to either the Local Autonomy Index (Ladner et al. 2016, 2019) or the OECD Fiscal Decentralization Database.[7] On another dimension, the intragovernmental arrangements can be estimated according to the relationship between the local legislature and the executive (either a mayor, collegiate body, set of committees, or manager). Here, the primary reference is the typology developed by the European Mayor project (Heinelt & Hlepas 2006; Heinelt et al. 2018).[8] This helps to discern elections and voting for mayors and councilors in the handbook, often entailing different principles and practices (Sweeting 2017). We also gauged for changes in the institutional infrastructure or departures from earlier ideal types.

Overall, the basic analysis of the institutional setting helps to determine the stakes in local elections and voting. Where possible, the authors have included information on the public perceptions of how important the different tiers of government are in their respective countries.

Local elections and their place in the multilevel system

In the subsequent section, the focus sharpens on local elections (for the council and for the mayor, where applicable). These elections are placed against those organized at other tiers, specifically national,[9] but also regional and European (when applicable). This part first probes the timing of the local elections, acknowledging that the placement of local elections within the main electoral cycle is an important part of the institutional setup. The authors explain whether and to what extent these are held at the same time for all municipalities (following the research on regional elections, we label this dimension 'horizontal simultaneity'; Schakel & Dandoy 2014), or whether they occur conjointly with other elections at different tiers (vertical simultaneity).[10] The section subsequently scrutinizes the term of office at the local level: to what extent and how does the duration of the local electoral cycle(s) correspond to the duration at the national level? This part also questions whether the same entity organizes local and national elections. In addition, and where applicable, the section discusses the introduction of directly elected executives – a type of administrative reform that has been widely discussed in recent decades and introduced in many European countries (Sweeting 2017). The authors address whether there are procedural ties between council and mayoral elections (and if and how this affects the chances of unified or divided local government). The section ends with the issue of local recall referenda, the conditions for these to be effective, and possibilities for early local elections.

Features of the local electoral system

This section discusses the characteristics of the local electoral system. It starts out by considering passive and active eligibility. These are also considered against the rules of the national elections. Here, we particularly question the conditions under which noncitizens can potentially execute their vote (e.g., within the EU, following the 1992 Maastricht Treaty, citizens of the member states have the right to participate in municipal elections in their states of residence under the same conditions as nationals; several countries introduced analogous regulations based on the residence status or reciprocity rule). This part also ascertains whether voting is compulsory and with what consequences.

Furthermore, the section goes deeper into the issue of council size. As this tends to vary between municipalities, we scrutinize who decides on the number of seats and what rules (if any) apply (such as population thresholds). Each country chapter indicates the total number of seats filled during the latest local elections (for councilors and/or mayors).

However, most of the section is dedicated to the dimensions and aspects of the local electoral system in the stricter sense. We start by probing the uniformity of that system: is this the same throughout the country or are certain subsystems detected (e.g., by region or type of municipality)? Each electoral (sub)system is then classified into the mainstream families distinguished in the typology developed by the International Institute for Democracy and Electoral Assistance. It makes the key distinction between plurality/majority, proportional, and mixed systems (Reynolds et al. 2005).[11] Authors may also allude to a typology that considers the incentives to cultivate a preference vote and render campaigning more personal than based on party reputation (Carey & Shugart 1995).[12]

Next to the overall situating of the electoral system, this part further outlines its central dimensions. In this respect, we develop the framework proposed earlier by Van der Kolk (2007), who distinguished three core aspects of local electoral systems: electoral formula, district structure, and ballot structure. The *electoral formula* refers to the mechanism by which votes are translated into seats. Apart from distinguishing between majority/plurality, proportional list systems, and mixed systems, the additional conditions of seat distribution are also taken into account. They play a role in proportional representation (PR) list systems: the existence of a legal threshold, the possibility of *apparentement* (in which votes can be pooled for electoral alliances between lists), the exact method of seat allocation (d'Hondt, Sainte-Laguë, Imperiali, etc.), or the significance of preference votes. The second dimension, *district structure*, concerns whether local elections are held at large or whether the municipality is divided into districts (in cases of the latter, the general rules of delimitation and the range of district magnitudes are included). Finally, the *ballot structure* answers how the voter can express his or her preference: whether a vote is cast on a party, a candidate, or both; the number of votes one disposes of; the prospect of *panachage* (in which votes can be split between different lists); cumulative voting; rank ordering, etc.

The section ends by assessing the parameters of candidacy. This concerns the basic rules of entry (such as the registration to stand for an election) as an estimate of the openness of local electoral markets. It also refers to the potential restrictions on candidacy and the effective taking up of a mandate. Specific attention is paid to the local manifestations and implications of *cumul des mandats* (i.e., the possibility to simultaneously occupy elected mandates at different levels in the political system).

Local electoral outcomes

The fourth section of each chapter addresses the local electoral outcomes. First, voter turnout is considered. Starting from the aggregate level in the most recent local elections, a comparison is made with its national counterpart, which makes it possible to estimate the size of the national vs. local turnout gap and subsequently discuss the evolutions therein since the 1990s. Further, the authors reflect on the similarities and differences in the patterns of electoral participation between national and local elections, assessing the differences between municipalities and relating them to municipal size and other relevant contextual variables.

The subsequent part scrutinizes the politicization of local elections. First, the degree of electoral competition is assessed: are there any cases of uncontested seats? What is the average number of contesting lists and/or candidates? Second, the presence of political parties is discussed. Following the literature on local party system nationalization, this part of each chapter reflects on the role played in the local arenas by the national parties (contrasted with their alternatives, local independent lists), as well as the main dissimilarities between the national party system and local party systems.

Finally, this section investigates aspects of descriptive representation. For one thing, this concerns female representation. Where possible, the percentage of elected offices in local government occupied by women is compared between local and national elections, as well as between local councils and executives (where applicable). The authors also reflect on how this indicator of female descriptive representation has evolved since the 1990s. It questions whether gender quotas (either voluntary or imposed by legislation) are applied in local elections and with what effect. Furthermore, it refers to the representation of minorities and people of foreign origin at the local level (in several countries, local electoral systems are precisely designed to resolve local ethnic tensions and incorporate minorities into local decision-making).

Conclusion and discussion

Finally, in the fifth section, insights on local elections and voting in each country are discussed and extended. Following the analytical framework of this handbook, the authors offer a summary of their findings along two main lines. (1) What are the most important similarities and differences between local and national elections? In other words, what makes local elections special compared to other elections? (2) What is the key variation between localities and what are the drivers? In other words, what renders local elections diverse across the municipalities? Also included are an assertion of distinctive features of the local electoral system and the patterns and dynamics of local elections and voting hitherto unmentioned. It also makes references to the currently most relevant academic studies on local elections and voting in the country. The chapter ends with a consideration of (potential) debates for electoral reform and what these debates might entail for the future of local elections and voting.

Comparative data and coding scheme

To complement the substantive analyses made in the sections of the country chapters, we requested the authors to provide us with some reference material and data to fuel the common database supplementing the handbook, which will be accessible online. For each country, the online supplement provides a reference to the current version of the Electoral Code(s), the website of the institution (i.e., national and/or regional electoral commission) responsible for the organization of local elections and voting, and the website (or institution) where the official electoral data at the municipal level can be found and accessed (if available). This information can be found in the online supplement to this book: localelections.eu. Additionally, authors filled in a prestructured database using a common template alongside their chapter.[13] The initial list of variables can also be found in the online supplement.

This framework with two analytical dimensions, vertical integration and horizontal variation, will be the basis for the development of a new typology for describing local elections and voting in Europe in the concluding section. This also offers a brief overview of similarities and differences between different countries – it might be a useful guide for the reader who is willing to selectively explore cases covered in this volume.

Notes

1 This section is based upon and develops the arguments presented in the guest editors' introduction to the special issue of *Local Government Studies*, 'Comparing local elections and voting in Europe' (Gendźwiłł & Steyvers 2021).
2 This includes the United Kingdom as it was an EU member until 2020.

3 In contrast to Ladner et al. (2016, 2019), we left out Georgia and Turkey (geographically only partly in Europe and not EU/EEA members). We added Andorra, Montenegro, and Bosnia and Herzegovina, which are all members of the Council of Europe. The Council also contains Armenia, Azerbaijan, and the Russian Federation (geographically partly in or largely outside of Europe and not EU/EEA members), as well as the microstates of Monaco and San Marino. These enclaves evidently are part of Europe and do have municipalities (1 and 9, respectively). However, as in the case of Malta, we were unable to identify experts able to deliver a chapter on either country.
4 See www.coe.int/en/web/congress/group-of-independent-experts-on-the-european-charter-of-local-self-government-gie-.
5 Yet, there are several exceptions to this general rule, as explained in the respective chapters. For example, the chapter on Finland does not discuss local elections in the autonomous region of the Åland Islands; local elections held in the Faroe Islands and Greenland are not covered by the chapter on Denmark. The chapter on Germany excludes elections in the city states of Berlin, Hamburg, and Bremen. The descriptions of French and Dutch local elections focus on the mainland municipalities (excluding overseas territories).
6 Some exceptions apply due to data availability, elections that have been boycotted by the main parties, or elections postponed due to the COVID-19 pandemic.
7 This index covers 11 variables measured in 39 countries between 1990 and 2014 by means of an expert survey based on a comparative codebook: institutional depth, policy scope, effective political discretion, fiscal autonomy and financial transfer system, financial self-reliance and borrowing autonomy, organizational autonomy, legal protection, administrative supervision, and central or regional access. Alternatively, the authors could look into the OECD Fiscal Decentralization Database; see www.oecd.org/ctp/federalism/fiscal-decentralisation-database.htm.
8 This comparative project collected data on European mayors (in municipalities with more than 10,000 inhabitants) in two waves (around 2003–2004 and 2015–2016) in 17 and 29 countries, respectively. It included the development of a typology with a strong mayor (and a political and executive subtype), a collegiate, or a committee form. It also resulted in an index of mayoral strength based on whether the mayor is directly designated by the citizens, has a term of office that does not correspond to that of the council, usually controls a majority in the council, cannot be recalled, presides over the council, at least co-defines the council agenda, and/or can appoint the municipal CEO and heads of departments.
9 Throughout the handbook, we consider the elections for the lower chamber of the (federal) parliament as the national elections (unless specified otherwise).
10 We compare vertical simultaneity with presidential, parliamentary (lower and/or upper chamber), regional (state, cantonal, province, etc.), and meso-level (upper local such as county assemblies, etc.) elections and nationwide referenda (except parliamentary), if applicable.
11 The plurality/majority family is further divided into first past the post (FPTP), the bloc vote (BV), the party bloc vote (PBV), the alternative vote (AV), and the two-round system (TRS). The proportional family is divided into the list proportional representation (list PR) and the single transferable vote (STV). Mixed systems are divided into mixed member proportional (MMP) and parallel systems. A category with other systems also exists. A regular update on the adoption of the various members of these families in more than 200 countries can be found at www.idea.int/data-tools/data/electoral-system-design.
12 This depends on the extent to which (1) party leaders control access to and rank on the ballots, (2) candidates are elected on individual votes or can draw on a common pool, and (3) voters can cast a single-party, candidate, or multiple vote. This ultimately leads to 13 possible configurations.
13 As the collection was closed by the end of that year, data refer to 2020 or earlier. Here, the unit of analysis was the country (or pertinent subcountry systems). In the case of nonsimultaneous local elections, the focus was on the main wave (with the largest coverage).

References

Cancela, J. & Geys, B. (2016). Explaining Voter Turnout: A Meta-Analysis of National and Subnational Elections. *Electoral Studies*, 42: 264–275.

Carey, J. & Shugart, M. (1995). Incentives to Cultivate a Personal Vote: A Rank Ordering of Electoral Formulas. *Electoral Studies*, 14(4): 417–439.

Carrubba, C. & Timpone, R.J. (2005). Explaining Vote Switching across First-and Second-order Elections: Evidence from Europe. *Comparative Political Studies*, 38(3): 260–281.

Clark, A. & Krebs, T. (2012). Elections and Policy Responsiveness. In K. Mossberger, S. Clarke & P. John (Eds.), *The Oxford Handbook of Urban Politics* (pp. 87–113). Oxford: Oxford University Press.

Cole, M. (2019). Local Electoral Systems. In R. Kerley, P. Dunning & J. Liddle (Eds.), *The Routledge Handbook of International Local Government* (pp. 13–24). London: Routledge.

Dandoy, R., Dodeigne, J., Steyvers, K. & Verthé, T. (Eds.) (2020). *Lokale kiezers hebben hun voorkeur. De gemeenteraadsverkiezingen van 2018 geanalyseerd*. Brugge: Vanden Broele.

Dandoy, R. & Schakel, A. (Eds.) (2013). *Regional and National Elections in Western Europe. Territoriality of the Vote in Thirteen Countries*. London: Palgrave Macmillan.

Denters, B., Goldsmith, M., Ladner, A., Mouritzen, P.-E. & Rose, L. (2015). *Size and Local Democracy*. Cheltenham: Edward Elgar Publishing.

Denters, B. & Mossberger, K. (2006). Building Blocks for a Methodology for Comparative Urban Political Research. *Urban Affairs Review*, 41(4): 550–571.

Egner, B., Sweeting, D. & Klok, P.-J. (Eds.) (2013). *Local Councillors in Europe*. Wiesbaden: VS Verlag für Sozialwissenschaften.

Elklit, J., Elmelund-Præstekær, C. & Kjær, U. (Eds.) (2017). *KV13. Analyser af kommunalvalget 2013*. Odense: University of Southern Denmark Press.

Garmann, S. (2016). Concurrent Elections and Turnout: Causal Estimates from a German Quasi-experiment. *Journal of Economic Behavior & Organization*, 126: 167–178.

Gendźwiłł, A. & Kjaer, U. (2021). Mind the Gap, Please! Pinpointing the Influence of Municipal Size on Local Electoral Participation. *Local Government Studies*, 47(1): 11–30.

Gendźwiłł, A. & Steyvers, K. (2021). Comparing Local Elections and Voting in Europe: Lower Rank, Different Kind . . . or Missing Link? *Local Government Studies*, 47(1): 1–10.

Gendźwiłł, A. & Żółtak, T. (2017). How Single-member Districts are Reinforcing Local Independents and Strengthening Mayors: On the Electoral Reform in Polish Local Government. *Local Government Studies*, 43(1): 110–131.

Golder, S., Lago, I., Blais, A., Gidengil, E. & Gschwend, T. (2017). *Multi-Level Electoral Politics: Beyond the Second-Order Election Model*. Oxford: Oxford University Press.

Górecki, M.A. & Gendźwiłł, A. (2021). Polity Size and Voter Turnout Revisited: Micro-level Evidence from 14 Countries of Central and Eastern Europe. *Local Government Studies*, 47(1): 31–53.

Górecki, M.A. & Kukołowicz, P. (2018). Electoral Formula, Legal Threshold and the Number of Parties: A Natural Experiment. *Party Politics*, 24(6): 617–628.

Greenstein, F. (1967). The Impact of Personality on Politics: An Attempt to Clear Away Underbrush. *American Political Science Review*, 61(3): 629–641.

Hajnal, Z. & Trounstine, J. (2014). What Underlies Urban Politics? Race, Class, Ideology, Partisanship, and the Urban Vote. *Urban Affairs Review*, 50(1): 63–99.

Harris, A., Kao, K. & Lust, E. (2016). The Determinants of Local and National Vote Choice: Evidence from a Conjoint Experiment. *Comparative Democratization*, 16(1): 8–11.

Heinelt, H. & Bertrana, X. (Eds.) (2011). *The Second Tier of Local Government in Europe: Provinces, Counties, Départements and Landkreise in Comparison*. London: Routledge.

Heinelt, H. & Hlepas, N. (2006). Typologies of Local Government Systems. In H. Bäck, H. Heinelt, & A. Magnier (Eds.), *The European Mayor. Political Leaders in the Changing Context of Local Democracy* (pp. 21–33). Wiesbaden: VS Verlag für Sozialwissenschaften.

Heinelt, H., Hlepas, N., Kuhlmann, S. & Swianiewicz, P. (2018). Local Government Systems: Grasping the Institutional Environment of Mayors. In H. Heinelt, A. Magnier, M. Cabria & H. Reynaert (Eds.), *Political Leaders and Changing Local Democracy. The European Mayor* (pp. 19–78). London: Palgrave Macmillan.

Herron, E., Pekkanen, R. & Shugart, M. (Eds.) (2018). *The Oxford Handbook of Electoral Systems*. Oxford: Oxford University Press.

Hix, S. & Marsh, M. (2011). Second-Order Effects Plus Pan-European Political Swings: An Analysis of European Parliament Elections across Time. *Electoral Studies*, 30: 4–15.

Hlepas, N., Kersting, N., Kuhlmann, S., Swianiewicz, P. & Teles, F. (Eds.) (2018). *Sub-Municipal Governance in Europe. Decentralization Beyond the Municipal Tier*. London: Palgrave Macmillan.

Jansen, G. & Denters, B. (Eds.) (2018). *Democratie dichterbij. Lokaal kiezersonderzoek 2018*. Twente: Universiteit Twente.

John, P. (2006). Methodologies and Research Methods in Urban Political Science. In H. Baldersheim & H. Wollmann (Eds.), *The Comparative Study of Local Government and Politics. Overview and Synthesis* (pp. 67–82). Opladen: Barbara Budrich Publishers.

John, P. (2009). Why Study Urban Politics? In J. Davies & D. Imbroscio (Eds.), *Theories of Urban Politics* (pp. 17–24). London: Sage.

Kaufmann, K. (2004). *The Urban Voter: Group Conflict and Mayoral Voting Behavior in American Cities*. Ann Arbor: University of Michigan Press.

Kaufmann, K. & Rodriguez, A. (2011). Political Behavior in the Context of Racial Diversity: The Case for Studying Local Politics. *PS: Political Science and Politics*, 44(1): 101–102.

Kjaer, U. & Elklit, J. (2010). Party Politicization of Local Councils. Cultural or Institutional Explanations for Trends in Denmark (1966–2005). *European Journal of Political Research*, 49(3): 337–358.

Kjaer, U. & Steyvers, K. (2019). Second Thoughts on Second-Order? Towards a Second-Tier Model of Local Elections and Voting. In R. Kerley, P. Dunning & J. Liddle (Eds.), *The Routledge Handbook of International Local Government* (pp. 405–417). London: Routledge.

Koch, P. & Rochat, P.E. (2017). The Effects of Local Government Consolidation on Turnout: Evidence from a Quasi-experiment in Switzerland. *Swiss Political Science Review*, 23(3): 215–230.

Kuhlmann, S. & Bouckaert, G. (Eds.) (2016). *Local Public Sector Reforms in Time of Crisis*. London: Palgrave Macmillan.

Ladner, A., Keuffer, N. & Baldersheim, H. (2016). Measuring Local Autonomy in 39 Countries (1990–2014). *Regional and Federal Studies*, 26(3): 321–357.

Ladner, A., Keuffer, N., Baldersheim, H., Hlepas, N., Swianiewicz, P., Steyvers, K. & Navarro, C. (2019). *Patterns of Local Autonomy in Europe*. London: Palgrave Macmillan.

Lidström, A. (1999). The Comparative Study of Local Government: A Research Agenda. *Journal of Comparative Policy Analysis*, 1(1): 95–115.

Lijphart, A. (1997). Unequal Participation: Democracy's Unresolved Dilemma. *American Political Science Review*, 91(1): 1–14.

Loughlin, J., Hendriks, F. & Lidström, A. (Eds.) (2012). *The Oxford Handbook of Local and Regional Democracy in Europe*. Oxford: Oxford University Press.

Marschall, M. (2010). The Study of Local Elections in American Politics. In J. Leighley (Ed.), *The Oxford Handbook of American Elections and Political Behavior* (pp. 471–492). New York: Oxford University Press.

Marschall, M., Shah, P. & Anirudh, R. (2011). The Study of Local Elections. A Looking Glass into the Future. *PS: Political Science and Politics*, 44(1): 97–100.

Marsh, M. & Mikhaylov, S. (2010). European Parliament Elections and EU Governance. *Living Reviews in European Governance*, 5.

Oliver, E. & Ha, S. (2007). Vote Choice in Suburban Elections. *American Political Science Review*, 101(3): 393–408.

Oliver, E., Ha, S. & Callen, Z. (2012). *Local Elections and the Politics of Small-Scale Democracy*. Princeton: Princeton University Press.

Rallings, C. & Thrasher, M. (2005). Not All 'Second-Order' Contests Are the Same: Turnout and Party Choice at the Concurrent 2004 Local and European Parliament Elections in England. *British Journal of Politics and International Relations*, 7: 584–597.

Reif, K. & Schmitt, H. (1980). Nine Second-Order National Elections. A Conceptual Framework for the Analysis of European Election Results. *European Journal of Political Research*, 8(1): 3–44.

Reynolds, A., Reilly, B. & Ellis, A. (Eds.) (2005). *Electoral System Design: The New International IDEA Handbook*. Stockholm: International IDEA.

Schakel, A. (2013). Nationalisation of Multilevel Party Systems. A Conceptual and Empirical Analysis. *European Journal of Political Research*, 52(2): 212–236.

Schakel, A. (Ed.) (2017). *Regional and National Elections in Eastern Europe. Territoriality of the Vote in Ten Countries*. London: Palgrave Macmillan.

Schakel, A. & Dandoy, R. (2014). Electoral Cycles and Turnout in Multilevel Electoral Systems. *West European Politics*, 37(3), 605–623.

Sellers, J., Lidström, A. & Bae, Y. (2020). *Multilevel Democracy. How Local Institutions and Civil Society Shape the Modern State*. Cambridge: Cambridge University Press.

Steyvers, K. & Heyerick, A. (2017). Fifty Shades of Rokkan? Reconceiving Local Party System Nationalisation in Belgium. *Croatian and Comparative Public Administration*, 17(4): 509–538.

Sweeting, D. (Ed.) (2017). *Directly Elected Mayors in Urban Governance. Impact and Practice*. Bristol: Polity Press.

Swianiewicz, P. (2014). An Empirical Typology of Local Government Systems in Eastern Europe. *Local Government Studies*, 40(2): 292–311.

Swianiewicz, P. (2020). Recent and Contemporary Trends in European Studies of Local Government and Local Politics. In C. Nunes Silva (Ed.), *Contemporary Trends in Local Governance* (pp. 21–44). London: Palgrave Macmillan.

Tavares, A.F. & Raudla, R. (2018). Size, Density and Small Scale Elections: A Multi-level Analysis of Voter Turnout in Sub-municipal Governments. *Electoral Studies*, 56: 1–13.

Teles, F., Gendźwiłł, A., Stănuș, C. & Heinelt, H. (Eds.) (2021). *Close Ties in European Local Governance. Linking Local State and Society*. London: Palgrave Macmillan.

Teles, F. & Swianiewicz, P. (Eds.) (2018). *Inter-Municipal Cooperation in Europe. Institutions and Governance*. London: Palgrave Macmillan.

Trounstine, J. (2009). All Politics Is Local: The Reemergence of the Study of City Politics. *Perspectives on Politics*, 7(3): 611–618.

Van der Kolk, H. (2007). Local Electoral Systems in Western Europe. *Local Government Studies*, 33(2): 159–180.

Van Houwelingen, P. (2017). Political Participation and Municipal Population Size. A Meta-Study. *Local Government Studies*, 43(3): 408–428.

Vetter, A. (2015). Just a Matter of Timing? Local Electoral Turnout in Germany in the Context of National and European Parliamentary Elections. *German Politics*, 24(1): 67–84.

Warshaw, C. (2019). Local Elections and Representation in the United States. *Annual Review of Political Science*, 22(1): 461–479.

Wollmann, H. (2006). The Fall and Rise of the Local Community: A Comparative and Historical Perspective. *Urban Studies*, 43(8): 1419–1438.

Wollmann, H. (2016). Local Government Reforms: Between Multifunction and Single-purpose Organisations. *Local Government Studies*, 42(3): 376–384.

Part 2
The Nordic States

2
Denmark
How two and a half parties rule within a multiparty system

Ulrik Kjaer

The Danish local welfare state

The latest Danish local elections were held simultaneously in the 98 municipalities on 21 November 2017.[1] Local elections are quite important political events in Denmark: the turnout is high (70.8% of eligible voters voted in 2017), the political parties represented in the national parliament (the *Folketing*) are running in most municipalities, and the media coverage (also by the nationwide media) is extensive. The relatively high importance attached (and the attention paid) to local elections in Denmark is probably linked to and reflects the fact that local governments are very significant. Local councils and the councilors elected to them make quite important political decisions. In terms of budgets, Denmark is one of the most economically decentralized countries in the world. According to the most recent figures (2018), local governments account for no less than 63.6% of public expenditures in Denmark, which equals 32.4% of GDP (OECD 2020: Table 4 + 5). This is the highest among the 30 OECD countries for which comparable data exist.

Denmark is also, in more general terms, a very decentralized country. According to the Local Autonomy Index, it is ranked 6th among 39 countries analyzed (in 2014; see Ladner *et al.* 2016). Danish municipalities collect their own income taxes, and they are truly multipurpose with a portfolio including as varied tasks as child care, primary schools, elderly care, planning, housing, social care, integration of immigrants, employment initiatives, the issuing of passports, roads, cultural activities, parks, water, sewage, and waste management. The growth of activities managed by Danish local governments took off with the consolidation of the municipalities in 1970, when a major reform restructured the local government system and reduced the number of municipalities from more than 1,100 to 275. For the past half century, the importance of the municipalities has been growing in tandem with the expansion of the Danish welfare state. Therefore, local governments today are the backbone of the Danish welfare state (Blom-Hansen 2010: 52), and in the Danish case, the term "welfare state" could almost be replaced by the term "welfare municipalities" (Kjaer 2013).

As of 2007, another major structural reform reduced the number of municipalities further from 275 to 98 (Ministry of the Interior and Health 2005).[2] Today, the average size of the municipalities is 58,660 inhabitants, and only seven municipalities have fewer than 20,000 inhabitants. At the same time, the counties were merged into five regional governments, with hospitals and health care as (more or less) their sole task. The regional governments are led by a regional council that is elected in regional elections held on the same day as the municipal elections (see Kjaer 2020a). For a further description of the relations and sharing of tasks between the three levels of government (national, regional, and municipal), see Houlberg and Ejersbo (2020).

In each municipality, a council is elected in the local elections, and the councilors elect a mayor from among themselves (but in formal terms, there is no governing coalition). In formal terms, the mayor is weak with almost no executive power, but in most cases he or she can be a quite powerful person anyway by conducting some version of facilitative leadership (Berg & Kjaer 2009). The formal power to make decisions rests with the council and its committees. However, the mayor is the only politician who is employed full time and has an office at City Hall and the mayor cooperates very closely with the CEO and the administration. Therefore, the Danish system has been denoted a committee-leader form of government by Mouritzen and Svara (2002: 60). It should be mentioned that the 98 Danish municipalities are governed in the same way and under the same legislation, The Local Government Act, although there are minor variations in the form of government across the four largest municipalities, which have a number of paid, full-time deputy mayors (see Berg 2005).

The second-tiered Danish municipal elections

According to the Local and Regional Government Elections Act, subnational elections (municipal and regional) are to be held on the third Tuesday of November every fourth year (so the 2017 elections were preceded by local elections in 2013, 2009, and so forth). Elections to the national parliament have their own electoral cycle of a maximum of four years. The constitution states that a general election should be held no later than four years after the previous one. Even though general elections are nonconcurrent with the local elections, they may coincide (which happened in 2001).

As mentioned, the mayor is indirectly elected from among and by the councilors. The process is quite unregulated; the new council must convene during the first half of December in election years and elect a mayor from among them by a simple majority vote. In most cases, however, the councilors start (and often also conclude) negotiations on election night, when the results of the elections are published late in the evening (the polling stations close at 8:00 p.m., and in most municipalities, the counting of votes takes only a few hours). When the mayor is officially confirmed by the council at the meeting in early December, that person is mayor for the next four years unless he or she voluntarily steps down (which sometimes happens because of health or age). It is almost impossible to unseat the mayor within the term. If a mayor is guilty of dereliction of duty, it can be done by a national electoral board under the Ministry of the Interior or, more recently, by the council through a procedure with votes of confidence supported by at least 9/10 of the councilors (no mayors have yet been removed due to a vote of no confidence). There are no recall options for the citizens.

The Ministry of the Interior is responsible for elections in Denmark, including local ones. However, as with other elections, such as general elections, European Parliament elections, and referenda, the municipalities organize the actual poll: they set up polling stations, administer lists of eligible voters, hand out ballots, and count the votes. This work is led by a local electoral board of 5–7 councilors that is chaired by the mayor in each municipality.

To have their own electoral cycle and to a large extent be in charge of their own elections fits very well with the widespread impression of local government in Denmark as being representative democracy writ small. The geographical area is smaller, but the electoral and political institutions put in place are very similar to those known from the national-level representative democracy. Therefore, Danish municipal elections should not, by default, be categorized as 'second-order elections' (Reif & Schmitt 1980), but rather – as suggested by Kjaer and Steyvers (2019) – as 'second-tier elections': elections that are not ranked second or taken less seriously (see also Chapter 1).

Danes might not be as interested in local politics as in parliamentary politics, but municipal politics is far from neglected. A survey conducted right after the 2017 local elections demonstrated that 36% of Danes find national policy most interesting, 18% municipal policy, 5% regional policy, and 8% foreign policy (33% find policy at the different levels equally interesting) (Kjaer 2020a).

Openness and personalization within a party politicized system

The electorate in local elections in Denmark consists of everyone who (1) is at least 18 years old, (2) has fixed residence in Denmark, and (3) either (a) holds Danish citizenship, (b) holds citizenship in an EU country, (c) holds citizenship from Iceland or Norway, or (d) has resided in Denmark continuously for the previous four years (regardless of citizenship). In parliamentary elections, Danish citizenship is a prerequisite for voting, which means that there are residents in Denmark who can vote in local (municipal and regional) but not parliamentary elections. In the local elections of 2017, about 8% of the persons allowed to vote could not have voted in parliamentary election had it been held the same day (Kjaer 2020b: 384). Voting is not compulsory in Danish elections.

People who are eligible to vote can stand as candidates. The threshold of 25 signatures from eligible voters per list to get on a municipal ballot[3] is quite low compared to the national threshold (which requires more than 20,000 signatures). To run, one needs to form a list of candidates with minimum of one candidate and no more candidates than the number of seats on the council plus four. There are no legal restrictions on candidacy, and therefore *cumul des mandats* is possible but not widespread (not least because the largest party, the Social Democrats, and a couple of minor parties do not allow candidates to hold dual political offices).[4] A list can run under the label of a nationwide party or under a name of its own choosing. All lists will be on the ballot with a 'party identification letter' along with the name of the list. Lists running under the label of one of the nationwide parties registered for participation in parliamentary elections will be identified by the letter of this party. In the 2017 elections, ten parties received a reserved party identification letter to use in the municipalities along with the name of the party for which they were running: the nine parties represented in the *Folketing* at the time plus the newly registered party New Right (*Nye Borgerlige*).[5]

It is for the councils themselves, before the election, to decide the number of seats as long as it is uneven and between 19 and 31. Exceptions apply to the seven smallest municipalities with fewer than 20,000 inhabitants, as they can go as low as nine seats, and to the largest municipality, Copenhagen, which can go as high as 55 seats (which it does). In the 2017 elections, the mean was 25 seats, and a total of 2,432 seats in the councils were filled.

The electoral system is the same for all municipalities,[6] namely, an open-list proportional representation system (Reynolds *et al.* 2005: 60). There are no submunicipal electoral districts – each municipality forms one and only one electoral district. In the voting booth, voters are presented with a list of parties/lists each with the number of candidates listed, and they can cast one and only one vote.[7] They can choose to vote for a party/list or cast a preferential vote for one of the candidates (typically three out of four voters opt for the latter option; 75.1% in the

2017 elections). The translation of votes to seats has two steps. In the first step, seats are distributed between the different parties/lists based on the total number of votes obtained by the list, including votes for the list and preferential votes for individual candidates on the list. D'Hondt's divisor method is applied with no further electoral threshold. *Apparentement* is allowed and is widespread; in 2017, 82% of the lists running participated in an electoral alliance. It should be noted that electoral alliances are not printed on the ballot, where all lists run individually; they are only stipulated by the parties/lists to the local electoral board (43 days before the election) and then made public on a poster at the polling station.

In the second step, the seats obtained by each list are distributed among its candidates. Two different allocation schemes are in function, and the lists can (beforehand) choose between an open-list or a semi-open-list system. In 2017, three out of four lists chose the open-list format, which has a quite simple distribution of seats: those with the most preferential votes among the candidates on a list get the seats obtained by the list. In the semi-open system, preferential votes are also taken into account, but nonpreferential votes cast for the list are distributed among the candidates according to their ranking on the list (candidates at the top of the list will be assigned the nonpreferential votes if they need them to get the number of votes required for a seat) (see also Kjaer 2020b). However, few seats are given to high-ranking candidates at the expense of low-ranking candidates [one study finds that this is the case for fewer than one in 13 candidates elected on semi-open lists; see Kjaer & Krook 2019].

Multiparty system or two and a half party system?

Before we look into whom Danes vote for in the local elections, it should be noted that Danes tend to turn out for elections. However, the type of election matters, and since at least the 1970s, the rule of thumb has been that turnout for national parliamentary elections is 85%, for regional and municipal elections it is 70%, and for European Parliament elections it is

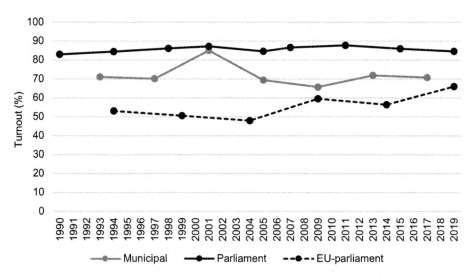

Figure 2.1 Voter turnout in Danish elections for municipal councils, national parliament, and EU Parliament, 1990–2019

Source: Statistics Denmark

55%. Turnout does fluctuate, as shown in Figure 2.1, which depicts turnout for parliamentary, municipal, and European elections since 1990. For example, in 2001, the election days for local elections and parliamentary elections coincided, and the turnout increased by 15 percentage points to more or less the same level as turnout for the parliamentary election (the separate ballots could be filled out during the same visit to the voting booth). In the 2017 municipal elections, turnout was 70.8% (at the coinciding regional elections it was 70.7%, and the two turnout rates are normally close to identical).

However, as stable as the local turnout rates are, this does not mean that voters turn out in the same proportion across the 98 municipalities. In the 2017 elections, the lowest turnout rate was 59.6% and the highest was 85.7%, which is a substantial difference considering that municipalities in Denmark have similar task portfolios, organization, and electoral rules. However, even after the amalgamation reform of 2007, there is still variation in the number of inhabitants of each municipality. The traditional finding is that turnout tends to decrease with increasing municipal size (for an elaboration, see Gendźwiłł & Kjaer 2021). In Figure 2.2, the turnout rates are therefore plotted against the size of the municipalities (a logarithmic scale is used to handle the few, very large municipalities). As expected, Figure 2.2 shows a negative relationship between size and turnout (size can explain 27% of the variation in turnout). This negative relationship remains even after controlling for several variables, including turnout for national elections [for a discussion of why and how to use the national-local turnout gap, see Gendźwiłł and Kjaer (2021)].

Who gets the votes? In Table 2.1, the votes are aggregated across the 98 municipalities, and column four shows that the ten parties represented in the national parliament (or, in the case of the newcomer New Right, being on the ballot for national elections) received most of the votes. Local lists running in only one municipality and smaller nationwide parties running in one or very few municipalities received only 4.2% of the votes. In terms of seats, the parties from the national party system conquered 96% of the 2,432 seats, and the conclusion is that the local party

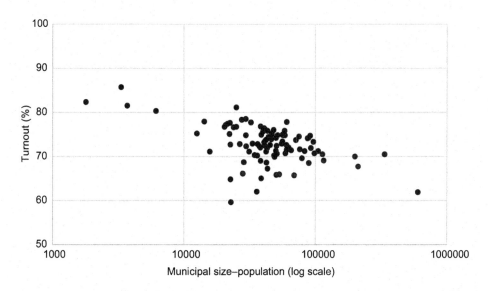

Figure 2.2 Voter turnout in the 2017 Danish local elections by municipality size
Source: Statistics Denmark

Table 2.1 Results of the local elections in the 98 Danish municipalities on 21 November 2017

	% of municipalities where running	% of municipalities where represented	% of seats on local councils	% of aggregate votes	% of mayors affiliated with the party
Social Democrats	100.0	100.0	34.6	32.4	48
Social Liberals	92.9	56.1	3.3	4.6	1
Conservative People's Party	100.0	80.6	9.3	8.8	8
New Right	62.2	1.0	0.0	0.9	0
Socialist People's Party	98.0	80.6	5.2	5.7	1
Liberal Alliance	94.9	24.5	1.1	2.6	0
Danish People's Party	100.0	92.9	9.2	8.8	1
Liberal Party	100.0	98.0	28.3	23.1	38
Red-Green Alliance	88.8	70.4	4.2	6	0
Alternative	84.7	15.3	0.8	2.9	1
Other nationwide parties	} 79.6	} 38.8	0.8	} 4.2	0
Local lists			3.2		2

Source: Statistics Denmark

Note: The Danish names are in parentheses: Social Democrats (*Socialdemokratiet*), Social Liberals (*Radikale Venstre*), Conservative People's Party (*Det Konservative Folkeparti*), New Right (*Nye Borgerlige*), Socialist People's Party (*Socialistisk Folkeparti*), Liberal Alliance (*Liberal Alliance*), Danish People's Party (*Dansk Folkeparti*), Liberal Party (*Venstre*), Red-Green Alliance (*Enhedslisten*), and Alternative (*Alternativet*).

system is very nationalized (Kjaer & Elklit 2010). Table 2.1 also shows that the parliamentary parties ran in almost all municipalities and obtained a large proportion of the seats.

Of the 1,157 lists running, 903 (78%) were branches of one of the ten nationwide parties also running for the national parliament. Among the 655 lists that obtained representation, 607 (93%) were running under the label of one of these ten parties. The nationwide parties nominated 8,503 (89%) of the 9,556 candidates and won 2,335 (96%) of the 2,432 seats.[8] This high level of nationalization of the local party system has been observed ever since the amalgamation reform of 2007. The number of local lists decreased, and the percentage of municipalities where the nationwide parties ran increased. This pattern was also observed after the reform in 1970, but the level has been more or less constant in between amalgamation reforms (Kjaer & Elklit 2010). It should be noted that, even within this very nationalized local party system, three in ten voters vote for a different party in local elections than in national elections (see Kjaer 2020b).

Table 2.1 demonstrates not only that the parliamentary parties are dominating local politics but also that a few of them are particularly dominant. The Social Democrats and the Liberal Party are traditionally the two largest parties in parliament, coming from the left and from the right, respectively, and often alternate being the governing party and supplying the prime minister. In local politics, the same pattern exists; in the 2017 elections, combined they obtained 55% of the votes and 63% of the seats. The pattern is even stronger for the mayoral offices, as the two parties combined won 86 of the 98 mayoralties (88%). For several decades, the Conservatives have won several mayoral offices in the more urban municipalities: eight in 2017. So, even though Denmark is known for its multiparty system (Elmelund-Præstekær et al. 2010), the party system resembles what Blondel called a 'two and a half party system' (Blondel 1968: 185) when it comes to local politics: the mayoral offices in particular are occupied by the Social Democrats and the Liberal Party (the two) and the Conservative Party (the half) (see also Kjaer 2020b).

So, who are the councilors? A total of 1,494 of the 2,432 persons elected in the 2017 local elections were already councilors, which yields an incumbency rate of 61% (similar to the level observed for previous elections). As for sociodemographics, 71% are between 40 and 64 years old, only 6% are under the age of 30, 4% are non-ethnic Danes, 49% have a college degree, 96% are employed, and 59% of these are public employees (Kjaer 2020b). However, the sociodemographic trait that has received the most attention is gender: in the 2017 elections, 31.8% of the candidates were women, and 32.9% of the seats were won by women (against 14% of the mayoral offices). The percentage of female councilors was the highest since women won the right to vote and stand in elections in 1908 (conquering 1.2% of the seats in the first local election in which they could vote and stand in 1909). However, after constant increases in all local elections from 1937 through 1993, female representation decreased (see Figure 2.3) for the first time in more than half a decade in the 1997 elections and has somewhat plateaued ever since [for an explanation of this 'saturation', see Kjaer (1999)]. Contrary to some of its neighboring Scandinavian countries, Denmark is not and has never been a quota country, and this goes for local elections as well. Figure 2.3 demonstrates that, contrary to the traditionally stipulated 'the higher, the fewer' pattern of women's representation, women lag behind at the local compared to the national level. In the present parliament, 38.9% of the MPs are women [for elaborations on this pattern, see Kjaer (2019)].

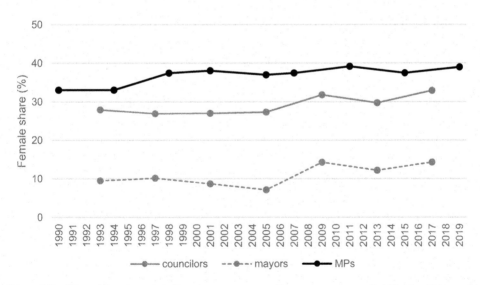

Figure 2.3 Women's representation among councilors, mayors, and MPs in Denmark, 1990–2019

Source: Statistics Denmark

Conclusion: on a trajectory toward party politicization, gender equality, and turnout stabilization?

Local elections in Denmark are important, not least because local governments are important in this highly decentralized country. Local elections in Denmark are also very well researched. First, the major amalgamation reform of 2007 opened up a quasi-experimental setting as some municipalities merged and others did not, and this has been exploited by researchers to study, for instance, interlevel split-ticket voting (Elklit & Kjaer 2009), trust in elected politicians (Hansen 2015), and local party systems (Kjaer & Elklit 2010). Second, for several local elections, an impressive data set with individual-level turnout data for all persons living in Denmark has been built by researchers from the University of Copenhagen, making it possible to map very precisely who votes and who does not (e.g., Bhatti & Hansen 2012). Finally, in the last three elections, The Danish Local Election Study based at the University of Southern Denmark has conducted large voter surveys (4,000–5,000 respondents) in the days right after the local elections and reported the results in edited research volumes on each election (Elklit & Kjaer 2013; Elklit et al. 2017, 2021). These data are available from the author as well as through the Danish Data Archive.

In general, the local electoral system seems to be quite stable. There have been discussions about changing the details of the form of government in the four largest municipalities, removing the remaining specialties of these municipalities, but nothing is likely to happen anytime soon. Directly elected mayors have not been discussed; a reduction in the age of eligibility to 16 years was briefly debated a few years back, but according to the constitution, the local voting age follows the national age (section 86 of the Danish constitution), so that debate died out. Finally, even though Denmark is an extremely digitalized country, debates about electronic voting have been very rudimentary so far.

The most interesting things to follow in the years to come will probably be how three of the patterns described in this chapter will evolve. First, will the turnout level of around 70% stabilize? There have been a few bumps in the road, but unlike in many other countries, it seems that local turnout has the potential to stabilize at a level where seven out of ten voters cast their ballot. Second, will representative gender equality be reached in this otherwise quite gender-equal country? Again, there have been some fluctuations, but after a period of plateau, women's representation seems to be slightly on the rise again. Third, the party politicization initiated by the latest amalgamation reform has created a local party system that is dominated by the parliamentary parties, and it will be interesting to see whether this will stabilize. Traditionally, the takeover of local politics by the nationwide parties has be seen as a process from which there is no going back (Rokkan 1970). The dominance of two and a half of the nationwide parties especially can have consequences for the strong local government system in Denmark with substantial political decentralization. For the two and a half parties making up more than half the seats on the local councils and in the Danish parliament, to take power away from local governments would mean taking power away from their 'own' local people and from their own local power bases.

Notes

1 The Faroe Islands and Greenland are part of the Kingdom of Denmark, which means that, for instance, foreign policy and security are the responsibility of the Danish government. In most matters, the Faroe Islands and Greenland have extended self-rule, and therefore elections for the five Greenlandic and 29 Faroe municipalities are not covered in this chapter.
2 The process had already started in 2003 when five municipalities on the island of Bornholm amalgamated.
3 A total of 150 in the capital of Copenhagen and 50 in the three other large cities.

4 Even though everybody can run, not everybody can take up their seat if they win. Persons who have been committed to psychiatric care, been imprisoned, or had their driving license suspended due to a DUI are excluded from claiming their seat (a 3- to 5-year statute of limitation applies).
5 A special case is the Schleswig Party (*Slesvigsk Parti*), which is the German minority party. The party is, by law, given the right to run in the four municipalities of Southern Jutland that are closest to Germany under the letter S.
6 Only very minor differences exist in the four largest municipalities: there are more indirectly elected deputy mayors, and these positions are quite powerful (they are full-time positions with full pay). Therefore, a few additional rules are specified as to how these deputy mayoralties are distributed.
7 Postal voting is not used in Denmark, but some advance voting is possible if the voter goes to one of the city halls in Denmark in the weeks leading up to the election, or if it is decided that someone can act as a representative for the municipality and take the vote elsewhere (e.g., elderly care facilities, prisons, ships). In the 2017 elections, 5.7% of the votes were cast in advance.
8 In Denmark, all seats are contested.

References

Berg, R. (2005) 'From Cabinets to Committees: The Danish Experience', in Berg, R., & Rao, N. (eds.) *Transforming Local Political Leadership*. Houndmills: Palgrave Macmillan, pp. 85–100.

Berg, R., & Kjaer, U. (2009) 'Facilitation in Its 'Natural' Setting: Supportive Structure and Culture in Denmark', in Svara, J.H. (ed.) *The Facilitative Leader in City Hall: Reexamining the Scope and Contributions*. Boca Raton, FL: CRC Press, pp. 55–72.

Bhatti, Y., & Hansen, K.M. (2012) 'Leaving the Nest and the Social Act of Voting: Turnout among First-Time Voters', *Journal of Elections, Public Opinion, and Parties*, 22 (4), pp. 380–406.

Blom-Hansen, J. (2010) 'Municipal Amalgamations and Common Pool Problems: The Danish Local Government Reform in 2007', *Scandinavian Political Studies*, 33 (1), pp. 51–73.

Blondel, J. (1968) 'Party Systems and Patterns of Government in Western Democracies', *Canadian Journal of Political Science* 1 (2), pp. 180–203.

Elklit, J., Elmelund-Præstekær, C., & Kjaer, U. (eds.) (2017) *KV13. Analyser af kommunalvalget 2013*. Odense: University of Southern Denmark Press.

Elklit, J., Hansen, S.W., & Kjaer, U. (2021) *KV17. Analyser af kommunalvalget 2017*. Odense: University of Southern Denmark Press.

Elklit, J., & Kjaer, U. (2009) 'Split-ticket Voting in Times of Sub-national Government Reorganisation: Evidence from Denmark'. *Scandinavian Political Studies* 32 (4), pp. 422–439.

Elklit, J., & Kjaer, U. (eds.) (2013) *KV09. Analyser af kommunalvalget 2009*. Odense: University of Southern Denmark Press.

Elmelund-Præstekær, C., Elklit, J., & Kjaer, U. (2010) 'The Massive Stability of the Danish Multi-Party System: A Pyrrhic Victory?', in Lawson, K. (ed.) *Political Parties and Democracy: Volume II: Europe*. Santa Barbara: Praeger, pp. 121–137.

Gendźwiłł, A., & Kjaer, U. (2021) 'Mind the Gap, Please! Distilling the Influence of Municipal Size on Local Electoral Participation'. Manuscript under review.

Hansen, S.W. (2015) 'The Democratic Costs of Size: How Increasing Size Affects Citizen Satisfaction with Local Government', *Political Studies*, 63 (2), pp. 373–389.

Houlberg, K., & Ejersbo, N. (2020) 'Municipalities and Regions. Approaching the Limit of Decentralization?', in Christiansen, P.M., Elklit, J., & Nedergaard, P. (eds.) *The Oxford Handbook of Danish Politics*. Oxford: Oxford University Press.

Kjaer, U. (1999) 'Saturation Without Parity: The Stagnating Number of Female Councillors in Denmark', in Beukel, Erik et al. (eds.) *Elites, Parties and Democracy – Festschrift for Professor Mogens N. Pedersen*. Odense: Odense University Press, pp. 149–168.

Kjaer, U. (2013) 'Reforming the Local Welfare State in Denmark – The Geographical Paradox of Amalgamating Municipalities', *Journal of Policy Science*, 7 (1), pp. 33–53.

Kjaer, U. (2019) 'Patterns of Inter-Level Gender Gaps in Women's Descriptive Representation', *Lex Localis – Journal of Local Self-Government*, 17 (1), pp. 53–70.

Kjaer, U. (2020a) 'The 2017 Danish Regional Elections and the Victorious Parliamentary Parties', *Regional & Federal Studies*, 30 (3), pp. 461–473.

Kjaer, U. (2020b) 'Local Elections – Localized Voting Within a Nationalized Party System', Christiansen, P.M., Elklit, J., & Nedergaard, P. (eds.) *The Oxford Handbook of Danish Politics*. Oxford: Oxford University Press, pp. 382–399.

Kjaer, U., & Elklit, J. (2010) 'Party Politicisation of Local Councils: Cultural or Institutional Explanations for Trends in Denmark, 1966–2005', *European Journal of Political Research*, 49 (3), pp. 337–358.

Kjaer, U., & Krook, M.L. (2019) 'The Blame Game: Analyzing Gender Bias in Danish Local Elections', *Politics, Groups, and Identities*, 7 (2), pp. 444–455.

Kjaer, U., & Steyvers, K. (2019) 'Second Thoughts on Second-order? Towards a Second-tier Model of Local Government Elections and Voting', in Kerley, R., Liddle, J., & Dunning, P.T. (eds.) *The Routledge Handbook of International Local Government*. London: Routledge, pp. 405–417.

Ladner, A., Keuffer, N., & Baldersheim, H. (2016) 'Measuring Local Autonomy in 39 Countries (1990–2014)', *Regional & Federal Studies*, 26 (3), pp. 321–357.

Ministry of the Interior and Health (2005) *The Local Government Reform – In Brief*. Copenhagen: Ministry of the Interior and Health (https://english.sim.dk/media/11123/the-local-government-reform-in-brief.pdf).

Mouritzen, P.E., & Svara, J.H. (2002) *Leadership at the Apex: Politicians and Administrators in Western Local Governments*. Pittsburgh: Pittsburgh University Press.

OECD (2020) *OECD Fiscal Decentralisation Database* (www.oecd.org/ctp/federalism/fiscal-decentralisation-database.htm#C_Title).

Reif, K., & Schmitt, H. (1980) 'Nine Second-Order National Elections – A Conceptual Framework for the Analysis of European Election Results', *European Journal of Political Research* 8 (1), pp. 3–44.

Reynolds, A., Reilly, B., & Ellis, A. (2005) *Electoral System Design: The New International IDEA Handbook*. Stockholm: IDEA.

Rokkan, S. (1970) *Citizens, Elections, Parties*. Oslo: Universitetsforlaget.

3
Finland
Local autonomy, tenacious national parties, and sovereign, but indifferent voters

Siv Sandberg

Single-tier system with autonomous and multifunctional local authorities

The Finnish territory comprises mainland Finland (5.5 million inhabitants) and the autonomous Åland Islands (30,000 inhabitants). Finland is a decentralized unitary state with a single-tier, subnational government. As part of major reform of public health care, a new directly elected regional level will be established from 2023. The first regional elections will take place in 2022.

Local government on the Finnish mainland consists of 293 municipalities, ranging in size from 700 to 650,000 inhabitants. The autonomy of the Åland Islands contains legislative powers over matters related to local government, including local and regional elections, involving the region's 16 municipalities.[1] The features of Finnish local government and local elections described in this chapter generally refer to the situation for mainland Finland.

Finnish local government incorporates characteristics typical of the Northern or Scandinavian model of local government (Sellers & Lidström 2007; Heinelt & Hlepas 2006). Municipalities are responsible for a wide range of statutory services, including education, health care, and social services, and they enjoy a considerable degree of discretion in organizing those services. According to comparative rankings, the formal preconditions for local autonomy are good in Finland, placing Finland among the countries with the highest scores on two of the most crucial dimensions, financial autonomy and political discretion (Ladner et al. 2019, 266–267).

Horizontal power relations in Finnish municipalities bear traits of both a collective and a council-manager form of government (Heinelt & Hlepas 2006; Mouritzen & Svara 2002). The council appoints the members of the executive board and other committees, following a principle of political proportionality. All parties in the council are guaranteed representation in proportion to their share of the council seats. The executive board as a collective is the most influential political actor in Finnish municipalities. The 5–15 members of the executive board are appointed from among the members of the council. The council has the right to recall the mandate of the executive board or other committees as a collective if the majority of the council no longer has confidence in the activities of the board or the committee.

On the other hand, the executive functions are firmly in the hands of the professional municipal manager (CEO), a position mandated by law. Traditionally, the strong position of the

CEO has left less room for individual political leaders to maneuver. In a comparative setting, it is important to note that Finland lacks the tradition of having one prominent political leader of the municipality or city, equivalent to a mayor in other European countries. The chairperson of the council and that of the executive board are two different persons. The position of chairperson of the executive board usually ranks as the more influential, while the role of chairperson of the council is more ceremonial. Only a small minority of the leading politicians in Finnish municipalities perform their duties as chairperson on a full-time basis. Each municipality makes its own rules for the remuneration of politicians, but in practice, full-time politicians are common only in municipalities with more than 100,000 inhabitants. A small number of cities have changed, or are about to change, their system of governance by replacing the appointed CEO with a politically elected mayor.

Local and national elections in Finland: separated in time, but connected by people and issues

Finnish citizens have the right to vote in four types of elections: local elections, parliamentary elections, presidential elections, and elections for the EU Parliament. These elections may not take place simultaneously, and Finnish law even restricts the organization of local referenda during local elections. The term of office for local councils, as well as for the Finnish parliament, is four years. Presidential elections take place every sixth year, while members of the EU Parliament are elected for a five-year term.

Regulations concerning local elections are included in three different pieces of legislation: the Constitution (731/1999), the Election Act (714/1998) and the Local Government Act (410/2015).

Only the members of the local councils are directly elected. Each council appoints the members of boards and committees, as well as the chairpersons of the council and the executive board.

Local elections regularly take place on the second Sunday of April,[2] with generous opportunities for voting in advance. Advance voting opens 11 days before and closes 5 days before the main election day. Advance voting is available for all eligible citizens regardless of residence and does not have to take place in one's own municipality. Polling stations for advance voting are located in easily accessible public buildings, such as libraries, shopping malls, post offices, and town halls. In the local elections of 2017, 45% of voters cast their votes in advance.

The most recent reform of the law on elections changed the timing of the local elections from October to April, with the first elections according to the new schedule having been held in April 2017.[3] This reform set local elections to take place exactly midway between two parliamentary elections. In the multilevel political system, local elections play a barometric function with regard to national politics (Borg & Pikkala 2017). Parties utilize local elections to promote national political issues. Party leaders play a prominent role in the media coverage of local elections (Berg & Niemi 2009).

The Ministry of Justice bears the overall responsibility for the organization of general elections. Municipalities are responsible for sustaining the basic infrastructure for all elections, including providing polling stations both on election day and for advance voting. In local elections, the central municipal election board has the ultimate responsibility for approving the candidate lists and confirming the election results. Possible appeals concerning decisions on candidate lists or election results are lodged with the competent administrative court.

Finnish law prohibits recall referenda.

Open-list proportional system with compulsory preferential voting

The general prerequisites for voting in local elections in Finland are age and residence. A person who is at least 18 years old on the day of the election and has been resident in the municipality for at least 51 days is entitled to vote in the local election. Citizens of European Union member states, as well as citizens of Norway and Iceland, are entitled to vote in local elections under the same prerequisites as Finnish citizens. Other foreigners have the right to vote in local elections after a minimum two years' residence in a Finnish municipality.

Persons who are entitled to vote in local elections are also entitled to stand as candidates in local elections, with a few exceptions defined in the Local Government Act. Public servants in the central government who perform supervisory tasks directly concerned with local government administration are not able to take up candidacy in local elections. The same applies for persons employed by a municipality, a joint municipal authority, or a company owned by a municipality, who hold a senior position within an area of responsibility in the local executive. There are no restrictions on the right of members of the Finnish parliament or members of the EU Parliament to run as candidates in local elections. *Cumul des mandats* is very common. About 80% of the 200 members of the Finnish parliament are simultaneously members of a local council.

Voting in local elections in Finland is not compulsory.

The number of councilors to be elected must be decided upon by the preceding municipal council by the end of the November before an upcoming election. The Local Government Act includes provisions on the minimum number of seats in seven categories based on the number of inhabitants in the municipality. A reform in 2015 increased the local degree of freedom regarding council size, changing from defining a fixed number of seats to defining a minimum number of seats, which allows municipalities to elect a larger number of councilors. The minimum legal number of councilors varies from 13 in municipalities with fewer than 5,000 inhabitants to 79 in municipalities with more than 500,000 inhabitants. The most common council size is 27 seats. Before the 2017 local elections, 67% (199) of the municipalities chose to maintain the same number of seats prescribed by the former Local Government Act. Among the minority of 96 municipalities utilizing the new flexible regulation, 94 reduced and two expanded the number of council seats (Pekola-Sjöblom & Piipponen 2017).

In the local elections of 2017, a total of 8,999 councilors were elected, which was 675 fewer councilors than in the elections of 2012 (9,674 councilors). These changes in the number of councilors were due to population changes, municipal amalgamations, and the new regulations concerning council size (Pekola-Sjöblom & Piipponen 2017).

The electoral system for local elections is uniform throughout the country and is similar to the system for parliamentary elections. The Finnish electoral system is an open-list proportional system with compulsory preferential voting. Compulsory preferential voting means that the voter is not given the opportunity to cast his or her vote for a party only; he or she has to pick one of the individual candidates on the party list (Karvonen 2014). Each municipality forms a single constituency in local elections.

A registered political party or a minimum of ten[4] eligible voters who have founded a constituency association may nominate candidates for local elections. Two or more parties may form an electoral alliance by mutual agreement. The number of candidates on each list is restricted to a maximum of the total number of councilors to be elected multiplied by one and a half.

Candidate lists, including a statement of consent from each individual candidate, must be submitted to the central municipal election board for approval 40 days before an election.

The act of voting is simple. The list of candidates, each with an individual candidate number, is displayed in front of the voter. Parties normally list their candidates alphabetically. The voter does not have the opportunity to vote only for a party per se but must select one of the candidates (Karvonen 2010; Sundberg 2002). The ballot paper contains an empty circle in which the voter writes the number of his or her candidate of choice. Preferential voting is popular among Finnish voters. According to a large survey of citizens before the 2017 local elections, voters value the personal qualities of candidates more than party background when casting their vote (Kuntaliitto 2017).

Because the system employs compulsory preferential voting, the election of candidates from the party list is not predetermined; rather, it depends entirely on the number of individual votes cast for each candidate. Accordingly, the system excludes the use of gender quotas or equivalent mechanisms to influence the ranking of candidates. It is not common for parties to name official or unofficial frontrunners on their lists.[5] Given the open nature of the Finnish electoral system and the crucial role of personal votes, discussions about potential candidates for chairpersonships and other influential positions usually take place after election day, not before. The negotiation process following the election result is weakly regulated and surprisingly uncharted, and it varies considerably from one municipality to another. The larger the municipality and the more fragmented the party system, the more common it is for parties to enter into formal agreements concerning the principles for how positions on boards and committees are to be distributed between the parties and individual councilors. One usual ingredient in these agreements is a recognition of the number of personal votes when the most influential positions are distributed.

Compulsory preferential voting fosters intraparty competition between candidates on the same list because candidates depend on their ability to attract voters in order to be elected (Karvonen 2014; von Schoultz & Papageorgiou 2021). One expression of this phenomenon is the widespread use of individual campaigning and fundraising. In local elections, the occurrence of personal campaigning correlates with the degree of competition for council seats. Personal campaign budgets in local elections are considerably larger when the size of the municipality exceeds 50,000 inhabitants (Venho 2015).

Seats are allocated to the lists following the d'Hondt system of party/list proportional representation. The number of seats for each party or constituency association is first calculated on the basis of the total number of votes the list has received. After that, the seats are filled with candidates according to the number of preferential votes they have received. Popular candidates for major parties often help candidates with a more modest number of personal votes to be elected. On the other hand, as the d'Hondt system of allocating seats favors large parties, popular candidates from smaller parties sometimes fail to be elected despite a large number of personal votes (Karvonen 2010, 50).

Tenaciously strong national parties, huge variations between rural and urban areas

Electoral participation in Finland experienced a downward trend in the beginning of the 1990s, with turnout rates in parliamentary and local elections falling below 70%. Turnout in parliamentary elections has since stabilized at a level of 67–68%, while the overall turnout in the last four local elections has been about 10% lower, around 58%.

The decline in electoral participation in local elections is considerable compared to that of the 1970s and 1980s, when turnout rates in local elections were equivalent to or higher than turnout rates in parliamentary elections (see Table 3.1).

Table 3.1 Turnout for local and national elections in Finland, 1991–2019

Local elections		Parliamentary elections	
Election year	Voter turnout (%)	Election year	Voter turnout (%)
1992	70.9	**1991**	68.4
1996	61.3	**1995**	68.6
2000	55.9	**1999**	65.3
2004	58.6	**2003**	66.7
2008	61.2	**2007**	65.0
2012	58.3	**2011**	67.4
2017	58.9	**2015**	66.9
		2019	68.7

Source: Statistics Finland

The average turnout rate hides a variation of more than 30% between the municipality with the lowest (49.3%) and that with the highest (82.6%) level of participation in the 2017 local elections. There has been considerable intermunicipal variation in electoral turnout since the 1980s; however, this does not directly relate to the general decline in electoral participation in the last decades (Borg & Pikkala 2017).

Intermunicipal variation in turnout correlates partly to municipality size and partly to broader geographical and socioeconomic phenomena. Inhabitants of municipalities with a population under 20,000 are somewhat more diligent participants in local elections than inhabitants in larger municipalities. In municipalities with between 20,000 and 100,000 inhabitants, participation in local elections is slightly below the national average. In the largest cities (more than 100,000 inhabitants), electoral participation increased moderately in the 2017 local elections, reaching the same level as Finland as a whole (Borg & Pikkala 2017; Pekola-Sjöblom & Piipponen 2018).

General geographical and socioeconomic patterns of variation in political participation also apply in local elections. Socioeconomic factors related to age, education, occupation, and social class affect voting behavior on an individual level. On the aggregate level, geographical variations in political participation can be observed: turnout is higher in the more prosperous and densely populated southern and western parts of Finland and correspondingly lower in the sparsely populated areas in the east and north (Borg & Pikkala 2017; Pekola-Sjöblom & Piipponen 2017).

The average number of candidates per seat has remained approximately the same since the beginning of the 1990s (Borg & Pikkala 2017). In the local elections of 2017, altogether 33,618 candidates competed for 8,999 council seats. The average number of candidates per seat was 3.7, but with large variations between municipalities. The lowest average number of candidates per seat was 1.4 and the highest was 12.8. Uncontested local elections are extremely rare events in Finland, but in 10% of the municipalities, the number of candidates per seat was below two. Council seats in municipalities with over 50,000 inhabitants are the most contested ones (Pekola-Sjöblom & Piipponen 2018).

Local politics in Finland is highly party politicized. In the local elections of 2017, parties represented in the Finnish parliament won 97.4% of the total number of council seats. Local lists and registered parties without a seat in parliament won only 239 out of 8,999 seats.

Overall, the Finnish party system is characterized by a high degree of fragmentation and by the absence of a party that is decisively larger than its main competitors (Karvonen 2014, 18–19). On a general level, this description is also true for local elections.

The total support for the parties in local elections is usually on the same level as in the parliamentary elections (Borg & Pikkala 2017). In the 2017 local elections, the four largest parties each gathered between 12.5% and 20.7% of the total number of votes cast, illustrating the absence of a dominant party.

The general observation concerning increasing party fragmentation is both true and false on the local level. On average, seven parties or lists run for elections in a Finnish municipality, and, on average, six parties or lists gain at least one seat on the council. Still, the number of groups represented on the council varies between two and ten. In one-third of municipalities, one party is dominant with over 50% of the seats.

In urban areas, like Helsinki, Tampere, and Turku, party fragmentation in local politics has increased over the years, challenging the traditional positions of the conservative National Coalition Party and the Social Democrats as the major political forces in urban politics. The most important phenomenon behind this is the growing influence of the Greens in urban politics since the beginning of the 2000s.

However, the results from these local elections reveal that there are tangible differences in support for the major parties between various types of municipalities (Borg & Pikkala 2017).

Four of the national parties – the Centre Party, the National Coalition Party, the Social Democratic Party, and the Finns Party – are comprehensively represented on local councils throughout the country: the parties run for election in over 90% of the municipalities and have at least one council seat in over 85% of the municipalities (see Table 3.2). The comprehensive presence of the right-wing populist Finns Party in local politics is a relatively recent

Table 3.2 Participation and performance of national parties in Finnish local elections, 2017

	% of municipalities where running	% of municipalities where represented	% of seats on local councils	% of (aggregate) votes in local elections
National Coalition Party (Kansallinen kokoomus)	93.2	86.8	16.6	20.7
Social Democratic Party (Suomen Sosiaalidemokraattinen Puolue)	95.2	91.9	18.9	19.4
Centre Party (Suomen Keskusta)	95.9	94.9	31.4	17.5
Greens (Vihreä liitto)	64.1	51.9	5.9	12.5
Finns Party (Perussuomalaiset)	95.9	85.4	8.6	8.8
Left Alliance (Vasemmistoliitto)	76.2	65.8	7.3	8.8
Swedish People's Party (Svenska folkpartiet i Finland)	17.6	13.9	5.2	4.9
Christian Democrats (Kristillisdemokraatit)	74.6	59.7	3.5	4.1
Registered parties outside parliament	21.0	2.3	0.1	1.4
Independents and nonnational (local) lists	31.5	20.3	2.5	2.1

Source: Statistics Finland

phenomenon. The party experienced a major breakthrough in the parliamentary elections of 2011; since then, the party has been working on strengthening its presence on the local level.

Two parties, the Centre Party (CP) and the Swedish People's Party (SPP), both have a strongly localized electoral base. The Centre Party, with its base in small municipalities in rural areas, won only 17.5% of the total number of votes in the local elections of 2017 but as many as 31.4% of the seats. The support for SPP is geographically concentrated in the bilingual areas in southern and western Finland. The party is a small actor on the national level but is often the dominant party on the municipal level. In the local elections of 2017, CP gained a majority of its own by securing over half of the council seats in 80 municipalities, while SPP gained a majority in 13 municipalities. Other national parties rarely achieve this type of dominant position in Finnish local politics (Pekola-Sjöblom & Piipponen 2018).

On the other hand, parties whose strongholds are in the large cities, especially the Greens and the National Coalition Party, tend to win a considerable share of the votes cast, but a noticeably smaller proportion of the seats. The discrepancy between share of votes and share of seats is utterly remarkable for the Greens, who received 12.5% of the votes but only 5.9% of the seats in the local elections of 2017.

Independent local lists play a marginal role overall, winning only 2.5% of all council seats. There are apparent differences between local lists when it comes to background, policy focus, and stability. In some 15 municipalities, local lists with a broad policy focus have gained considerable support in subsequent local elections. In other municipalities, the presence of local lists is temporary, often channeling protests against the local political establishment. The rise of the Finns Party in the local elections of 2012 consequently reduced the number of local independent lists (Borg & Pikkala 2017, 29).

As Table 3.3 shows, the share of women among elected local councilors has been growing slowly since the 1990s, from 30% to 39%, but it lags behind the increase in the number of women in national politics. Female representation in national politics in Finland experienced a definite breakthrough in the parliamentary elections of 2019, in which 47% of the MPs elected were women, and in the subsequent cabinet formation.

Given the nature of the Finnish electoral system with compulsory preferential voting, the supply of credible female candidates is a basic precondition for reaching an equal representation of men and women in local politics. The electoral system excludes the use of any form of quota mechanisms that could influence the ranking of candidates. In the local elections of 2017, 39%

Table 3.3 Share of women among elected local councilors and elected members of parliament, 1992–2017, Finland

Local elections		Parliamentary elections	
Election year	% female councillors	Election year	% female MPs
1992	30.0	**1991**	38.5
1996	31.5	**1995**	33.5
2000	34.4	**1999**	37.0
2004	36.4	**2003**	37.4
2008	36.7	**2007**	42.0
2012	36.2	**2011**	42.5
2017	39.0	**2015**	41.5
		2019	47.0

Source: Statistics Finland

of the candidates were women, which equals the share of women elected onto the councils (Pekola-Sjöblom & Piipponen 2018). There are considerable geographical variations in the representation of women in local politics in Finland. The share of female councilors is higher in urban areas and correspondingly lower in rural areas.

Persons of foreign origin constitute 5.7% of the electorate in local elections. These groups are underrepresented in local politics, with only 2.2% of the candidates and 0.7% of the elected councilors in the local elections of 2017 originating from countries other than Finland (Tilastokeskus 2017).

Patterns of incumbency and voluntary turnover in Finnish local politics are stable. When facing the choice of running for reelection, about 30% of councilors withdraw voluntarily, while the rest run for reelection. Of the incumbent councilors running for reelection, about 75% are reelected. Among the councilors elected in 2017, 44% were newcomers and 56% were incumbents (Borg & Pikkala 2017, 31; Pekola-Sjöblom & Piipponen 2018).

Discussion

Local elections in Finland are temporally and formally separate from national elections, yet they are firmly integrated into the national political system. In a country with strong and autonomous local government, the primary function of local elections is naturally to maintain and renew the local political system, but local elections also play a barometric role vis-à-vis national politics. Following a general trend of falling participation rates in general elections, turnout for local elections has stabilized at a level approximately 10% lower than for parliamentary elections, which underlines the second-order nature of the local elections.

The position of national political parties in Finnish local politics is solid, holding over 97% of council seats. The tenacious strength of the national parties and, on the other hand, the weak position of local independent groups are linked to a number of institutional factors, including the lack of municipal party funding and the regulations concerning the decision-making bodies in joint municipal authorities, which play an important role in the local Finnish single-tier system. Given the fact that, despite their formal dominance, the ideological importance of political parties varies considerably between municipalities, one could claim that the national parties provide local political activists with handy solutions for organizing local elections: campaign machinery, a party leader who can perform on TV before the election, and access to training and expert knowledge.

Finnish local government is polarized between small, rural local authorities dominated by one strong party – the Centre party – and urban local authorities with a fragmented multiparty system.

Finnish local elections demonstrate the double nature of compulsory preferential voting within the frame of an open-list proportional system. It is relatively easy to become a candidate in Finnish local elections. If one party does not accept a person to be a candidate, he or she can turn to another party or gather ten eligible citizens to establish a constituency association. There is little to no intraparty competition for candidate nominations.

However, the larger the municipality, the more significant the intraparty competition is after the candidate lists have been laid down. Personal campaigning, including individual fundraising of significant sums, affects the campaign and the electoral outcomes in municipalities with over 50,000 inhabitants (Venho 2015). The threshold for becoming a candidate is low, but the more candidates there are, the more each one depends on his or her ability to become visible to the electorate. In the 2017 local elections in Helsinki, the total number of candidates was 1,084, but the ten most popular candidates collected over one-fourth (26.2%) of the total number of votes cast (Statistics Finland 2017).

Recent changes in the power balance between the political and the administrative leadership have the potential to change the nature of local elections, at least in the larger cities. A number of Finnish cities, including the capital city of Helsinki, have replaced, or will soon replace, the traditional council-manager model with a committee-leader model, where the professional chief executive officer is replaced by an appointed political mayor, who chairs the executive board and is responsible for some executive functions (Heinelt & Hlepas 2006, 31). Each municipality sets the rules for how the mayor is appointed, but it has become increasingly common for parties to name their candidate for the office of mayor in advance.

Another reform with potential future consequences for local and regional elections in Finland is the ongoing transformation of public health care and social services. According to the plans, the responsibilities for health care and social services will be transferred from municipalities and joint municipal authorities to a new regional level of government starting in 2023. The new 18–22 regional authorities are set to be governed by directly elected councils with 59–99 members. The regional reform will change the dynamics of subnational politics in Finland, but the main features of the electoral system, including compulsory preferential voting, will remain the same.

Notes

1 The basic features of the electoral system in the Åland Islands are equivalent to those of mainland Finland (open-list proportional system with compulsory preferential voting, distribution of seats according to the d'Hondt method of proportional representation). A number of other features are, however, different: the timing of the elections in the Åland islands is not synchronized with local elections in mainland Finland. Elections for the regional parliament and the local councils are held simultaneously. In addition, the party system in the Åland Islands is unique and not equivalent to the party system in mainland Finland. As far as local elections are concerned, the degree of party politicization is lower than that on the mainland, and (in practice) uncontested elections are more common.
2 The local elections 2021 were postponed from April to June due to the Covid-19 pandemic.
3 Because of the reform, the terms of office for the councilors elected in October 2012 were prolonged by law.
4 In municipalities with under 2,000 inhabitants, the number of voters needed in order to found a constituency association is lower: three persons in municipalities smaller than 1,000 inhabitants and five persons in municipalities with between 1,000 and 2,000 inhabitants.
5 One exception to this general rule is the 2017 local election in Helsinki, where parties nominated their candidates for the position of mayor in advance, which dominated the electoral scene. As large cities gradually change their governance model, this is expected to become more common in the future.

References

Berg, L. & Niemi, M. K. (2009) *Kenen kuntavaalit?* Kunnallisalan kehittämissäätiö. Sastamala: Vammalan Kirjapaino Oy.
Borg, S. & Pikkala, S. (2017) *Kuntavaalitrendit*. Kunnallisalan kehittämissäätiö. Sastamala: Vammalan Kirjapaino Oy.
Heinelt, H. & Hlepas, N.-K. (2006) Typologies of Local Government Systems. In Bäck, Henry, Heinelt, Hubert & Magnier, Annick (eds): *The European Mayor. Political Leaders in the Changing Context of Local Democracy*. Wiesbaden: VS Verlag Für Sozialwissenschaften, pp. 21–42.
Karvonen, L. (2010) *The Personalisation of Politics. A Study of Parliamentary Democracies*. Colchester: ECPR Press.
Karvonen, L. (2014) *Parties, Governments and Voters in Finland. Politics under Fundamental Societal Transformation*. Colchester: ECPR Press.

Kuntaliitto (2017): Kuntalaiskysely 2017.

Ladner, A., Keuffer, N., Baldersheim, H., Hlepas, N., Swianiewicz, P., Steyvers, K. & Navarro, C. (2019). *Patterns of Local Autonomy in Europe*. London: Palgrave Macmillan.

Mouritzen, P. E. & Svara, J. H. (2002). *Leadership at the Apex. Politicians and Administrators in Western Local Governments*. Pittsburgh: Pittsburgh University Press.

Pekola-Sjöblom, M. & Piipponen, S.-L. (2017). *Valtuustokoot Manner-Suomen kunnissa valtuustokaudella 1.6.2017–31.5.2021*. Uutta kunnista 1/2017. Helsinki: Kuntaliitto.

Pekola-Sjöblom, M. & Piipponen, S.-L. (2018): *Kuntavaalit, ehdokkaat ja valitut vuonna 2017*. Uutta kunnista 1/2018. Helsinki: Kuntaliitto.

Sellers, J. & Lidström, A. (2007). 'Decentralization, Local Government, and the Welfare State', *Governance: An International Journal of Policy, Administration, and Institutions*, 20 (4), pp. 609–632.

Statistics Finland (2017): *Ehdokkaiden ja valittujen tausta-analyysi kuntavaaleissa 2017*. Helsinki: Statistics Finland.

Sundberg, J. (2002). 'Finland: Candidate Choice and Party Proportionality', In Reynolds, Andrew & Reilly, Ben (eds): *The International IDEA Handbook of Electoral System Design*. Stockholm: IDEA, pp. 72–75.

Venho, T. (2015). Rahastaa, ei rahasta, rahastaa – suomalaisen vaalirahoituksen seurantatutkimus. Helsingfors: Kunnallisalan kehittämissäätiö.

von Schoultz, Å. & Papageorgiou, A. (2021). "Policy or Person? The Electoral Value of Policy Positions and Personal Attributes in the Finnish Open-list System." *Party Politics*, 27 (4) pp. 767–778.

4
Iceland
Where localism prevails

Eva Marín Hlynsdóttir and Eva H. Önnudóttir

The Icelandic local government system

Iceland is the smallest of the five Nordic states with its 360,000 citizens. There are two levels of government, the national government and the local government, organized into one tier. Until the fall of 2020, the system was fully symmetrical as there was no elected submunicipal government in place. However, a new municipality was established in September 2020, where a partly elected submunicipal government was introduced for the first time. The main aim of these units is to address the negative aspects of large-scale amalgamations. Thus, since September 2020, there are 69 municipalities in Iceland varying in size from 40 to around 130,000 inhabitants. Out of these, more than half of all municipalities have fewer than 1,000 inhabitants, and 21 have fewer than 500. Nevertheless, all local governments have the same responsibilities, as stipulated by the Local Government Act (no. 138/2011). In the early 1990s, a decentralization process of allocating tasks to the local level began with elementary schools being transferred to local governments. Since then, the local government level has been transformed from a passive participant in the provision of welfare services to an active partner in policymaking and implementation across a variety of tasks. Local government is now responsible for around 30% of public spending, which is considerably lower than is typical for a Nordic state (Hlynsdóttir 2018). Local authorities have independent streams of funding, the main sources of which are income tax and real estate tax. Municipalities with a low tax base are compensated through the equalization fund (which is partly state funded and partly funded by the municipalities). Additionally, local authorities do not have independent power to levy taxes, and the percentage allowance of the income tax is regulated by the central government. Local authorities do, however, enjoy a high level of fiscal freedom in the sense that how they use their income is rarely restricted, and earmarked funding is rare.

The existence of local government is protected by the 78th article of the Icelandic constitution. Moreover, in international comparison, Icelandic local governments enjoy a high level of autonomy and discretion (Ladner et al. 2019). This is also the case in a more detailed Nordic comparison (Baldersheim et al. 2019), where Iceland is ranked at the top of the local autonomy index. Likewise, the local government level possesses a high level of trust, with around 60% of citizens expressing high confidence in local government in 2009 compared to 39% of citizens expressing high confidence in the national parliament (Kristinsson 2014; Vilhelmsdóttir 2020).

The local government system in Iceland is characterized by the rule of collective decision making in the council, which means that leadership at the local level falls into the category of a 'collegial leader' (Heinelt & Hlepas 2006). There are, however, important exceptions to this rule in relation to the division of power within individual local governments. The Icelandic system is monistic (Wollmann 2004), with the council being the most important decision-making body within the local government. Traditionally, the leader of the council is normally also the leading politician, someone usually referred to as mayor in English, and is always chosen indirectly from within the council. This is followed by the executive board (or committee), for which members are chosen on a proportional basis from within the council. Recently, it has become more common that the leading politician becomes the leader of the executive board, thereby preceding the position of the council leader in importance. However, only councils with more than five members are permitted to establish an executive committee. The councils are not obliged to do this, though most do. The third source of power is the chief executive, who is responsible for the daily management of local authority.

The horizontal division of power between these different bodies is not clearly defined in the law, and local councils have large discretion in this area. Essentially, there are three different forms of government in place at the local level. These forms are not regulated and may be changed at any time at the will of the local council. The crucial point in deciding which form of government is in place is based on the position of the chief executive. Importantly, the chief executive is appointed by the council and may be hired and fired at the will of the council members. The first and most common form of government is the council manager model, where a council manager is typically hired on a merit basis. In smaller municipalities using the council manager form of government, the most important political position is the council leader, usually referred to as mayor. However, in larger municipalities, the executive board leader is added to the equation; thus, it is not always clear who is the leading politician – the council leader or the leader of the executive board. Following the 2018 elections, two out of three councils used the council manager form of government with or without an executive board (Hlynsdóttir 2018, 2020).

The second form of government is the executive mayor model. In this form of government, the position of the chief executive is taken over by a politician who is simultaneously the political leader as well as the top manager of the administration. The council leadership and the leadership of the executive board are taken over by politicians from the same party as the executive mayor or by the leaders of the coalition party. Following the 2018 elections, 19.4% of councils used this form of government (Hlynsdóttir 2018, 2020).

The final type of government is a remnant of the nineteenth-century organization of local government, where the council leader takes over the management of the municipality. Thus, the council leader is the only leading political figure and s/he also serves as a manager of the council, often working part-time as council leader and manager. Usually, this form of government is found in extremely small municipalities (with fewer than 200 citizens) where there are no clear party lines in the council. Members of those councils are elected through the bloc voting system, meaning that council members are voted by plurality in multimember districts as individual candidates (not from party lists). Following the 2018 elections, 19.8% of councils were using this form of government (Hlynsdóttir 2018, 2020).

The Local Government Act does not include political leaders such as the council leader or the executive board leader with individual discretionary power. Hence, their source of power is first and foremost informal and is based on being supported by the majority in the council. Moreover, the lines between the political and the administrative arms of the local government are not very clear. Icelandic local government is based on the principle of local council members being laymen; thus, although the law stipulates that they should be paid for their services, this is at the discretion of the individual councils. The same rule applies to the political leaders; therefore, some of them work full-time, and some do not. The only exception to this rule is the city council of Reykjavík, where all members are paid full-time (Hlynsdóttir 2018).

The formal features of the Icelandic local electoral system

The Act of Local Government Elections (no. 5/1998) stipulates that local elections must take place every four years on the last Saturday in May that is not the Saturday before Pentecost Sunday. National and local elections never take place at the same time, and there is a two-year cycle between local and presidential elections. However, local election day is sometimes used for voting on referenda, although this is restricted to local referenda. Each council is responsible for its local elections. It elects a voting committee that is responsible for all types of elections within the given municipality. However, in national elections, the counting of votes takes place in a central place within the electoral region. In local elections this is not the case, and each election committee counts the votes and announces the results. It is the Ministry of Justice that is responsible for overseeing all elections on the national and local levels.

As pointed out before, the terms of office are four years without exception. Hence, if the majority coalition in the council falls apart, another coalition must be established without a new election. This is very different from the national parliamentary system, in which elections can take place at any time within an election cycle of four years. Moreover, there is no possibility for a local recall referendum.

Concerning voting rights, all Icelandic citizens 18 years or older are eligible to vote in local elections in Iceland, including citizens of foreign origin who are 18 years or older and who have been living continuously in Iceland for several years. Citizens of the other Nordic counties are eligible to vote after living in Iceland for three years, and citizens of other foreign countries may vote after five years. In the 2018 election, the proportion of the electorate with foreign citizenship was 4.7% (Statistics Iceland 2018c, 2019c). However, there is very little information available concerning the representation of minorities and persons of foreign origin on local councils. All who have the right to vote in local elections are also eligible to run as candidates in local elections. The right to vote is more flexible at the local level than at the national level, where one must be an Icelandic citizen to be able to vote.

Each of the local municipalities forms one electoral district, and the number of council members ranges from 5 to 23. According to Article 11 of the Local Government Act (no. 138/2011), the number of councilors should be 5–7 for municipalities with fewer than 2,000 residents, 7–11 for municipalities with 2,000–9,999 residents, 11–15 for municipalities with 10,000–49,999 residents, 15–23 for municipalities with 50,000–99,999 residents, and 23–31 for municipalities with over 100,000 residents. More than two-thirds of all councils consist of 5–7 members, a handful of councils have 9–11 council members, and only the city of Reykjavík has a city council of 23 members. In the 2018 local elections, 502 council members were elected across Iceland, and for each council, the same number of substitute council members was established by vote. Each council decides on the number of its council members within the range of the law. However, findings have shown that councils more often use the lower rather than the higher limit, and council size tends to increase temporarily following an amalgamation. Kristinsson (2014) suggested that the ruling parties in the councils like to keep the council size small, as it makes it more difficult for new parties to enter the council and functions as an informal threshold.

The special features of the Icelandic electoral system

There are two voting systems in use in local elections in Iceland. The more common system is the proportional party or list-based system, which is used without a legal threshold. The d'Hondt formula is used for distributing the seats among the lists (Act of Local Government Elections no. 5/1998). The party lists must be formally announced no later than three weeks before election day, and they have to fulfill the minimum requirement for the number of candidates and a number of supporting signatures in order to be presented on the ballot. The number of candidates on each party list must be at least the same as the number of elected council members in the municipality and never more than twice that number. The minimum number of voter signatures needed – indicating their support for the party to run in the upcoming election – depends on the size of the municipality, ranging from 10 signatures in municipalities with fewer than 500 inhabitants to at least 160 signatures in municipalities with 50,000 inhabitants or more.

On the ballot, the party lists, with the names and list positions of the candidates, are listed side by side, from left to right. Each party applies for and is allocated an alphabetic letter, and the order of the parties is in an alphabetic sequence depending on the letter each is allocated. Voters can vote for one party only. Moreover, voters can indicate a nonpreference for a candidate of the party they vote for by crossing over his or her name from the ballot, and/or they can change the list order of the candidates of the party. However, for those changes to take effect, more than half of the voters for the party must either indicate a nonpreference for the same candidate or change the list order in exactly the same way. The high proportion of the parties' voters having to make the same change means that the order of the candidates on the ballot has never been changed (we concluded so after a careful search of the available information). Thus, even though the voters can express both a preference and a nonpreference for certain candidates, the ballot structure is effectively a closed party ballot. In the rare cases of only one list being put forward before the election, no voting takes place, and the members of the list automatically become the elected members of the council. In 2018, this was the case for only one municipality (Statistics Iceland 2019b).

The second voting system is a bloc voting system that functions as a personal vote without parties. Under this system, all entitled members of the municipality are eligible for a council seat. Hence, voters write the names of their five preferred councilpersons in their preferred order on the top half of the ballot sheet (the lower half is for the substitutes), and the number (usually five) of persons with the highest number of votes become council members. The five persons obtaining the highest number of votes as preferred councilpersons are elected, and the one who is placed as number one will usually be the leader of the local government. Strictly speaking, people are obliged to take the seat on the council if they are elected. This system used to be the most common voting practice for the majority of the twentieth century, but now it is mostly used in very small municipalities, although there are exceptions to this rule, as one municipality with more than 600 citizens used this type of voting in 2018. In the 2018 local elections, there were 16 municipalities (representing 1% of the Icelandic population) using this type of personal voting system (Statistics Iceland 2019b). The system is uniform, and there is no legal requirement in relation to the size or geographical situation of the municipality.

A dual mandate is allowed; however, it is not very common, and each parliamentary election cycle rarely has more than one or two MPs serving simultaneously as local councilors. Nonetheless, the locality serves as an important breeding ground for future MPs; for instance, in 2016, 44.4% of MPs had a background in local politics (Hlynsdóttir & Önnudóttir 2018).

The 2018 electoral outcomes

Turnout for local elections was generally quite high and similar to turnout for national elections before the turn of the twenty-first century, as seen in Figure 4.1, or more than 80%. Since 2006, local election turnout has experienced a downward trend, while it has stayed more or less the same for national elections with some fluctuations. Figure 4.1 shows that, since 2006, turnout for local elections has decreased gradually from one election to the next, except the 2018 election, for which turnout was similar to that of the previous local election. The most common explanation for the overall decrease in election turnout has been the increasing absence of younger voters (Halldórsson & Önnudóttir 2019), even if it cannot be considered the only factor. In the most recent local elections in 2018, turnout was higher in smaller than in larger municipalities. In municipalities with fewer than 300 inhabitants, the average turnout was 80.5%, whereas it was 80.1% in municipalities with 300–999 people and 67% in municipalities with 1,000 people or more (Statistics Iceland 2018c).

The Icelandic national party system has historically consisted of four main parties: the right-wing Independence Party, the center-right Progressive Party, the left-center Social Democratic Alliance, and the left-socialist Left-Green Movement. In addition to those four parties, there have usually been one or at most two smaller parties represented in the parliament. Those four established parties typically received a combined share of 85–90% of the vote in national elections, but that changed in 2013. In the 2013 election, the established parties received a combined vote of 75%, followed by 63% in 2016, and 65% in 2017, and in that election, eight parties were elected to the parliament (Önnudóttir & Harðarson 2018).

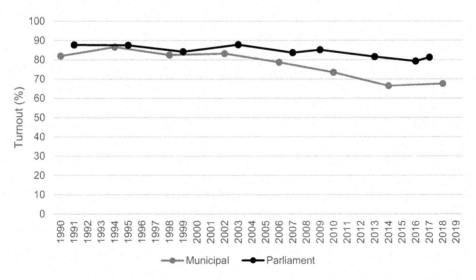

Figure 4.1 Voter turnout in local and national elections in Iceland, 1990–2019
Source: Statistics Iceland (2018b and 2018c)

Usually, the national parties only present lists in larger municipalities, and as can be seen in Table 4.1, there is a large variance in the number of municipalities wherein the parliamentary parties present a party list. In the 2018 local election, the Independence Party was the only parliamentary party that presented lists in over half of the municipalities (60.7%). The presence of the other parliamentary parties in local elections has varied from 1.7% (the People's Party, which offered a list in one municipality) to 42.8% (the Progressive Party). As those numbers indicate, there is considerable room for council members from local lists to get elected. In the 2018 election, 47.6% of council members in municipalities with a proportional election were elected from nonnational lists. Of the national lists, the largest share of elected council members, 28.0%, ran on a local list for the Independence Party. Table 4.2 shows that the national parties mainly run in the local elections of larger municipalities, and again, the Independence Party has the largest presence in municipalities with more than 300 inhabitants.

The turnover of councilors has been on the rise in the past decade. For example, in the 2018 local election, only 41.4% of the elected councilors were incumbents. In the elections before that in 2014, 41.8% were incumbents, 42.5% in 2010, and 44.9% in 2006 (Statistics Iceland 2019a). Findings from a survey conducted in 2017 showed that 50% of councilors were in their first term of office, 26% were in their second term, 12% were in their third term, only 6% were in their fourth term, and the remaining 6% were in their fifth term or more (Hlynsdóttir 2017).

There are no gender quotas in place at the local level, but female representation at the local level is relatively high and has been steadily increasing from 22.2% in the 1990s to its peak in the most recent election in 2018, in which 47.0% of all elected council members were women (see Table 4.3). On the national level, the parties have differed in their approaches to female representation. The left-wing parties, the Left-Green Movement and the Social Democratic Alliance, have long emphasized presenting candidate lists with an equal number of males and females. It has been in the hands of the parties' leadership in the municipalities to decide on how to implement this, whether in the form of strict rules, guidelines, or a general aim. Other

Table 4.1 Number and percentage of municipalities with proportional elections in which national parties presented a list in the 2018 election in Iceland

	% of municipalities where running	% of municipalities where represented	% of seats on local councils	% of (aggregate) votes in local elections	% of mayors affiliated with the party
Left-Green Movement	17.8	10.7	1.9	4.5	0.0
Social Democratic Alliance	23.2	23.2	6.9	16.7	3.5
Progressive Party	42.8	37.5	11.0	8.9	17.8
Independence Party	60.7	58.9	28.3	32.9	32.1
People's Party	1.7	1.7	0.2	1.6	0.0
Pirate Party	8.9	3.5	0.7	4.4	0.0
Centre Party	21.4	17.8	1.9	5.9	0.0
Reform Party	7.1	7.0	1.7	5.3	0.0
Independents and nonnational (local) lists	92.8	92.8	47.4	19.8	46.6

Source: Statistics Iceland (n.d. and authors)

Table 4.2 Proportion of parties' elected council members in the 2018 election in Iceland

	Capital area	Other municipalities with 1,000 or more inhabitants	Other municipalities with 300–999 inhabitants	Other municipalities with fewer than 300 inhabitants
Left-Green Movement	2.8	2.8		
Social Democratic Alliance	19.4	6.0	1.8	
Progressive Party	2.8	18.6	3.5	
Independence Party	47.2	32.1	13.3	
Peoples' Party	1.4			
Center Party	4.2	2.8		
Pirate Party	4.2			
Reform	8.3			
Other lists	9.7	37.7	81.4	100.0
Total	72	215	113	20

Source: Statistics Iceland (2018a)

Table 4.3 Proportion of female councilors and female members of parliament in Iceland, 1990–2018

Year of local election	Female councilors (%)	Female MPs (%)	Difference (%) (f.councilors – f.MPs)
1990	21.8	22.2	−0.4
1994	24.8	25.4	−0.6
1998	28.2	28.6	−0.4
2002	31.5	36.5	−5.0
2006	35.9	36.5	−0.6
2010	39.8	42.9	−3.1
2014	44.0	41.3	2.7
2018	47.0	38.0	9.0

Source: Authors

parties, such as the Progressive Party and the Independence Party, have begun in recent years to advocate that it should be a general aim to present an equal number of males and females on their party lists, but they have not adopted any rules or quotas to ensure that. In 2018, there were 3,482 people running for council, of which 48.4% were women, the highest proportion of female candidates to date. However, findings have shown that it is generally more common for women to be found in the second place rather than the first place on the candidate lists; in the time leading up to the 2018 election, of those listed in first place, men comprised 61% of cases and women comprised 39% of cases. Those listed in second place were women in 63% of cases compared to men's share of 37%. Men were also more frequently in third, fourth, and fifth places on lists. Moreover, there is no local council consisting solely of women, while there is still one with only male members. Additionally, there are more elected women than men on 42% of all local councils, while male members are the majority on 58% of local councils (Statistics Iceland 2019b). As the number of female candidates is almost equal to the number of males, this supports the conclusion that a higher number of female candidates are situated lower on party lists than their male counterparts. The proportion of female councilors was previously close to the proportion of female MPs, but that changed considerably after the 2018 local election, when the proportion of female councilors was 9 percentage points higher than the proportion of female MPs. Moreover, analysis conducted for this chapter shows that as the number of female councilors has increased, the percentage of female mayors has also increased, from 7.9% in 1990 to 34.7% in 2018.

Discussion

Although the Icelandic local government voting system shares many features with those of the other Nordic states, it has several unique qualities. First, there are considerable differences in the presence and success of the national political parties at the local level. Out of the four established parties, the Independence Party has by far the greatest presence in elections at the local level, offering a party list in 63.0% of the municipalities, and 28.1% of local councilors elected represent this party. The Progressive Party follows thereafter, presenting a list in 44.4% of municipalities and winning 11.0% of the local council seats. While there is a lack of research that can shed light on these differences, a number of explanations have been suggested. These differences could be due to variance in the parties' organization and the funding of the national parties. It might be that the Independence Party and the Progressive Party have been better at organizing their outreach and are better funded than the other parties, and thereby they expend more effort to reach voters in smaller municipalities. Another possible explanation could be a difference in the groups and issues upon which parties mobilize. The Progressive Party has historically had strong support from the countryside in national elections as a former agrarian party, while the two established left-wing parties, the Social Democratic Alliance and the Left-Green Movement, have been more successful, at least in national elections, in mobilizing urban voters by advocating for income equality and a strong welfare system (Önnudóttir & Harðarson 2018). Another explanation is that the low presence or absence of national parties at the local level indicates that local elections in most of the municipalities in Iceland are not as concerned with party politics and are more concerned with presenting candidates who are ready to deal with the challenges of running a local municipality.

The second unique feature of Icelandic local elections, and perhaps the most noteworthy, is the presence of an alternative way to vote in contrast to the usual proportional method: the bloc vote. This is, in Iceland, an old method of voting, where all of the citizens in the municipality are running for office. Although usually used in only very small municipalities, there are legally no constraints preventing larger municipalities from implementing this type of voting. Hence, if the city council in Reykjavík decided to use this type of voting, there are no legal restraints to prevent it. This scenario perhaps is not likely to happen, but the legal possibility is an interesting fact. Moreover, there has never been any real attempt to abolish this type of voting, which was still widely used in the early 1990s; however, since then, party politics (usually based on local lists, whether those are local or national parties) has slowly taken over as the tasks of the local government have become more complex, and municipalities have become larger following extensive amalgamation. There is surprisingly limited research available on this system, but it has traditionally been viewed as more conservative, with fewer female council members and fewer female mayors. It is more commonly found in rural municipalities. The system is highly static, as leaders such as mayors tend to be in place for decades. For example, in 2018, one mayor had been an elected member of the local council for 40 continuous years. Moreover, politics in these municipalities tends to take on the shape of 'clan' rivalries, where individuals travel around the community before the election arguing for the votes of certain individuals. In sum, it seems that most people view this type of electoral system as a thing of the past, something that will disappear as more municipalities are amalgamated into larger entities.

Although there is no discussion of changing the local government election system, there is an ongoing effort to introduce elected submunicipal entities. To begin with, it will only take place in one municipality to be selected in the fall of 2020. The main idea behind these changes is to preserve some local decision-making power in a newly established, amalgamated municipality. How this plays out remains to be seen; however, it does constitute a clear break from the otherwise symmetrical approach of the Icelandic local government system.

References

Act of Local Government Elections Pub. L. No 5/1998.
Baldersheim, H., Houlberg, K., Lidström, A., Hlynsdóttir, E.M. & Kettunen, K. (2019) *Local Autonomy in the Nordic Countries*. Universitetet i Agder: Norwegian Association of Local and Regional Authorities.
Halldórsson, E.B. & Önnudóttir, E.H. (2019) 'Kosningaþátttaka ungs fólks á Íslandi, kynslóðabil, áhugi á stjórnmálum og flokkshollusta', *Icelandic Review of Politics & Administration*, 15(2), pp. 229–254.
Heinelt, H. & Hlepas, N.K. (2006) 'Typologies of Local Government Systems', in Bäck, H., Heinelt, H. & Magnier, A. (eds.) *The European Mayor: Political Leaders in the Changing Context of Local Democracy*. Wiesbaden: VS Verlag für Sozialwissenschaften, pp. 21–42.
Hlynsdóttir, E.M. (2017) 'Dutiful Citizen or A Pragmatic Professional? Voluntary Retirement of Icelandic Local Councilors', *Icelandic Review of Politics & Administration*, 13(2), pp. 169–188.
Hlynsdóttir, E.M. (2018) 'Autonomy or Integration: Historical Analysis of the Debate on the Purpose of Icelandic Local Self-government', *Icelandic Review of Politics & Administration*, (Special Issue on Power and Democracy in Iceland), pp. 83–100.
Hlynsdóttir, E.M. (2020) *Gender in Organizations: The Icelandic Female Council Manager*. New York: Peter Lang.
Hlynsdóttir, E.M. & Önnudóttir, E.H. (2018) 'Constituency Service in Iceland and the Importance of the Center-periphery Divide', *Representation*, (Special Issue), pp. 55–68.
Kristinsson, G.H. (2014) *Hin mörgu andlit lýðræðis: Þátttaka og vald á sveitarstjórnarstiginu*. Reykjavík: Háskólaútgáfan.
Ladner, A., Keuffer, N., Baldersheim, H., Hlepas, Paweł Swianiewicz, P., Steyvers, K. & Navarro, C. (2019) *Patterns of Local Autonomy in Europe*. Cham: Palgrave Macmillan.
Local Government Act, Pub. L. No. 138/2011.
Önnudóttir, E.H. & Harðarson, Ó.Þ. (2018) 'Political Cleavages, Party Voter Linkages and the Impact of Voters' Socio-economic Status on Vote-choice in Iceland, 1983–2016/17', *Icelandic Review of Politics & Administration*, (Special Issue on Power and Democracy in Iceland), pp. 101–130.
Statistics Iceland (n.d.) *Local Government Elections*. Available at https://statice.is/statistics/population/elections/ocal-government-elections/ (Accessed: 25 November 2020).
Statistics Iceland (2018a) *Candidates and Representatives in Proportional Voting by Municipality 2018*. Available athttps://px.hagstofa.is/pxen/pxweb/en/Ibuar/Ibuar__kosningar__sveitastjorn__svf_frambj/KOS03307.px (Accessed: 2 July 2020).
Statistics Iceland (2018b) *Participation by Size of Municipality and Election Mode 1990–2018*. Available at https://px.hagstofa.is/pxen/pxweb/en/Ibuar/Ibuar__kosningar__sveitastjorn__svf_yfirlit/KOS03102.px (Accessed: 25 January 2020).
Statistics Iceland (2018c) *Voters on the Electoral Roll, Votes Cast and Participation by Municipality 2018*. Available at https://px.hagstofa.is/pxen/pxweb/en/Ibuar/Ibuar__kosningar__sveitastjorn__svf_urslit/KOS03204a.px (Accessed: 2 July 2020).
Statistics Iceland (2019a) *Elected Representatives by Municipality 2006–2018*. Available at https://px.hagstofa.is/pxen/pxweb/en/Ibuar/Ibuar__kosningar__sveitastjorn__svf_frambj/KOS03303.px (Accessed: 24 November 2020).

Statistics Iceland (2019b) 'Local Government Elections 26 May 2018', *Statistical Series: Elections*, 104(9). Available at www.statice.is/publications/news-archive/elections/local-government-elections-26-may-2018/ (Accessed: 2 March 2020).

Statistics Iceland (2019c) *Participation of Foreign Citizens 2006, 2014 and 2018*. Available at https://px.hagstofa.is/pxen/pxweb/en/Ibuar/Ibuar__kosningar__sveitastjorn__svf_urslit/KOS03216.px (Accessed: 2 July 2020).

Vilhelmsdóttir, S. (2020) *Political Trust in Iceland Determinants and Trends, 1983 to 2018*. Unpublished PhD thesis. University of Iceland.

Wollmann, H. (2004) 'Urban Leadership in German Local Politics: The Rise, Role and Performance of the Directly Elected (Chief Executive) Mayor', *International Journal of Urban and Regional Research*, 28(March), pp. 150–165.

5

Norway

Local democracy by trial (and error)

Jo Saglie and Signe Bock Segaard

The local government system: amalgamation on the agenda

There are three tiers of government in Norway: national, county (regional), and municipal.[1] As of 2020, there are 11 counties and 356 municipalities. They are generalist municipalities with equal status and are responsible for a broad spectrum of public services, including primary education, primary health care, care for the elderly, preschool childcare, and local infrastructure services. All municipalities are located within a larger county except for the city of Oslo, which is both a county and a municipality. Oslo nevertheless also has a three-tier system: it is the only municipality with directly elected submunicipal councils (Klausen 2018).

In this chapter, our focus is on the municipalities. Counties play a less important role in the Norwegian political system, and their importance was further reduced when one of their main tasks – hospitals – was transferred to the state in 2002. Norway's citizens are also less interested in county politics: about 25% found county politics 'somewhat' or 'very' interesting, while the corresponding figures for both municipal and national politics were around 60–70% (Rose & Hansen 2013: 210).

The structure of local government has recently been the subject of considerable changes. One of the main ambitions of the Solberg government, which took office in 2013, was to implement a comprehensive amalgamation reform that merged municipalities as well as counties (Folkestad et al. 2021; Klausen et al. 2021; Saglie 2020). The process was initiated from above, but it also had a bottom-up element: each amalgamation would be locally anchored, and the municipalities themselves should seek and find partners. The final decisions on mergers nevertheless were top down, made by the parliament in June 2017. The parliament followed most of the municipalities' decisions, but eight municipal mergers (and several county mergers) took place despite opposition from one or more of the affected municipalities. The outcome was that the number of counties was reduced from 19 to 11, and the number of municipalities decreased from 428 to 356; these changes went into effect on 1 January 2020. However, many small municipalities remain unmerged, and the size of municipalities in Norway still varies from about 200 inhabitants to more than 690,000 (as of 1 January 2020). Only 4% of municipalities have more than 60,000 inhabitants, whereas 68% have fewer than 10,000. The median is 5,163.[2]

Although Norway is a unitary state, it is fairly decentralized. National regulations, standards, and supervision set limits for municipal discretion, and taxation rights are limited. Norway is, nevertheless, among the highest-scoring countries on Ladner et al.'s (2019) Local Autonomy Index, which covers 39 European countries. Moreover, Baldersheim (2018) found that Norway's score on this index has increased even further since 2014 (when Ladner et al.'s data were collected) due to stronger legal protections for local autonomy (e.g., constitutional recognition of local government).

In most Norwegian municipalities, the municipal council elects an executive committee by proportional representation. Formally, this arrangement corresponds to a consensual model of democracy. In practice, however, informal coalitions in many cases are built to elect a mayor and implement policies, creating a 'governing party or coalition' and an 'opposition' within the executive committee (Martinussen 2004). The alternative model is parliamentary rule, which has been used in three of Norway's largest cities: Oslo (since 1986), Bergen (since 2000), and Tromsø (2011–2016). Here, a majority (or minority) forms a formal governing coalition – a city government – where executive power is concentrated (Bukve & Saxi 2017).

Most typologies of local government systems place Norway within a Nordic model, especially regarding local autonomy (Ladner et al. 2019: 268–269). However, there are some differences within the Nordic model regarding horizontal power relations. Most Norwegian municipalities have a dual leadership. The mayor chairs the council meetings, whereas the CEO is the leader of the municipal administration. This gives Norwegian mayors a less powerful position than, for instance, their Danish counterparts, who also oversee the administration to some degree (Sletnes 2015). However, although the formal powers of Norwegian mayors are limited, they are the undisputed political leaders of their municipality. Mayors are, in most cases, the only full-time politician in their municipality, and they are expected to become involved in matters beyond their formal role (Mikalsen & Bjørnå 2015). Unlike their Swedish and Finnish counterparts, they chair both the council and the executive committee.

In municipalities that choose the *parliamentary model*, however, the leader of the city government is both the political and administrative leader. There is no CEO in this model, and the mayor chairs the council meetings but otherwise has a more ceremonial role.

Local elections within a unitary state

Local elections in Norway – both municipal and county council elections, as well as Oslo submunicipal council elections – are held simultaneously in all municipalities every four years. Parliamentary elections, as well as elections to the Sámi Parliament (the elected assembly for the indigenous Sámi people), also follow a four-year electoral cycle, but are held two years before and after the local elections. None of these elected assemblies can be dissolved before their term expires. Accordingly, the electoral cycle in Norway follows a regular pattern: local elections are always 'midterm elections' seen from a national perspective.

The Norwegian Directorate of Elections organizes both local and national elections, while the municipalities do much of the practical work. The directorate operates and administers the electronic election administration system, in which the municipalities register the election results and other relevant information. The overall responsibility for elections lies with the Ministry of Local Government and Modernization. The tasks of the Directorate of Elections were previously carried out within the Ministry, but the directorate was established in 2016 to create a greater distance between the political leadership and the administration of elections.

Mayors are elected by the municipal council. However, direct election of mayors was tried out in the 1999, 2003, and 2007 elections in 20, 36, and 50 municipalities, respectively (Larsen

2002; Christensen & Aars 2010). One of the stated reasons for holding this trial was that direct election of mayors would stimulate political interest and increase turnout. That did not happen, and the trial was discontinued.

Recall referendums are not used in Norway, but there is a long-standing tradition for local referendums on political issues (Adamiak 2011; Folkestad et al. 2021). For example, the recent local government reform resulted in more than 200 referendums on municipal amalgamation. Local referendums are, however, only consultative, and there is little legal regulation of – or central government involvement in – their administration.

The open-list electoral system[3]

All Norwegian citizens who are or will be 18 years old by the end of the election year and who have been registered in the Population Registry as resident in Norway at some time are qualified to vote in parliamentary elections.[4] For local elections, the electorate is larger. Since 1983, citizens of other countries can vote in local elections if they have been registered in the Population Registry for the last three years prior to the election day. Other Nordic nationals (from Denmark, Finland, Iceland, and Sweden) can vote in local elections without this three-year limit. One must be included in the municipal register of voters in order to vote, but this registration is automatic and based on the Population Registry. Voting is not compulsory.[5]

Election day is always the second Monday of September, but a municipality may decide whether voting for an election may begin the preceding Sunday.[6] Voters can vote in advance from 1 July to the last Friday before election day. Each municipality decides the number and location of voting stations. Advance votes may be cast not only in the municipality holding the election but in any voting station throughout the country. In 2019, 34% of the votes were cast in advance, the highest percentage of votes ever to be cast early.[7] Postal voting is not permitted, except for citizens abroad.

The municipal council itself decides its number of seats, but there is a nationally determined minimum number, ranging from 11 seats in the smallest municipalities (those with a population below 5,000) to 43 in the largest (those with a population above 100,000). A total of 10,621 municipal councilors were elected in the 2015 election; this number dropped to 9,336 in the 2019 election, owing to the large-scale municipal amalgamation mentioned previously.

The electoral system is based on party-list proportional representation, where the whole municipality is a single multimember district. This system is implemented in all municipalities.[8] The distribution of seats between lists follows Sainte-Laguë's modified method (divisors 1.4, 3, 5, 7, and so on), with no threshold.

Norway uses an open-list system that gives both the parties and the voters influence over the distribution of seats within each party (Bergh et al. 2010; Langsæther et al. 2019). Voters first choose a party list, and they may then cast preference votes for one or more candidates. They can vote for an unlimited number of individual candidates on their chosen party list, as well as for a limited number of candidates from *other* lists.[9] Voters are not obliged to cast a preference vote, but preference voting increased steadily until 2015, when 47% of those who voted in elections also cast one or more preference votes (Saglie et al. 2021). In the 2019 elections, this percentage fell slightly to 46% (Saglie et al. 2021: 29–35).

Parties usually rank their candidates. They are also allowed to prioritize a limited number of candidates at the top of their lists.[10] When a party's council seats are allocated to its candidates, these prioritized candidates receive a substantial head start: a number that corresponds to 25% of the votes for the party list is added to his/her number of preference votes. For example, if a prioritized candidate receives 100 preference votes (including those from voters who voted for other parties) and the party list receives 1,000 votes, this candidate will have 350 votes when the party's seats are allocated [100 + (1000 × 0.25)].

This can be said to add a closed element to the system, but the extent to which party branches choose to limit voter influence varies. Some party lists win more seats than their number of prioritized candidates. In these cases, a seat is effectively secured for prioritized candidates, while preference votes are decisive for the remaining candidates. Other party lists win fewer seats than their number of prioritized candidates. In these cases, preference votes decide the election among the prioritized candidates, whereas the nonprioritized are almost never elected. When the number of prioritized candidates equals the number of seats, the prioritized candidates are usually elected.

Highly ranked list candidates are much more likely to get elected, even if we disregard those whose elections are assured (Hellevik & Bergh 2005: 69–70; Christensen et al. 2008: 121–123). Voters tend to vote for highly ranked candidates, presumably because parties place their most popular and well-known candidates at the top of their lists. Voters nevertheless have considerable potential influence. In the most recent elections, approximately one-fourth of the councilors would not have been elected if the list order had been decisive (Bergh et al. 2010: 113–114; Matland & Lilliefeldt 2014). Nonparty actors can organize coordinated campaigns where voters are asked to vote for candidates (from different parties) with a specific position on a local issue. In some cases, this has had a substantial influence on the composition of Norwegian municipal councils (Kvelland 2015; Halsaa 2019).

The legislation on preference voting has been a contested issue. Prior to 2002, voters could also cast *negative* preference votes by striking out names on the list. The right to vote for candidates from other parties was abolished prior to the 1975 elections, but it was reintroduced four years later.

Regarding entry rules, Norwegian legislation distinguishes between registered parties and other groups that field candidates in elections, such as nonpartisan lists (see Saglie & Sivesind 2018). Registration in the national Register of Political Parties requires the party to collect signatures from 5,000 eligible voters (in the whole country). 'Registered party' status is advantageous for two reasons. First, a nonpartisan list must collect a number of signatures (varying according to the size of the municipality) before each new election,[11] whereas a registered party does not need to do so. Second, although a nonpartisan list may receive support for its group in the municipal council, only registered parties receive public funding for their organizations. Even if a nonpartisan list were able to collect enough signatures for registration, it would not last. The Party Act (Section 5) requires that 'when the party has not issued a list of election candidates in any constituency at two consecutive parliamentary elections', it will be deregistered. Local nonparty lists would therefore soon be deregistered, even if they had managed to register.

There are no legal restrictions on *cumul des mandats*, but double mandates do not seem to be widespread. It is not unusual to have elected offices at the county and municipal levels simultaneously, but the municipal-national combination is less common. A large majority of MPs have experience in local office, although they often (but not always) resign from their local council seat when they are elected to parliament. It is, in any case, impossible to be a mayor and an MP at the same time, as both are full-time jobs.

The outcomes of municipal elections

Norwegian voters' participation in elections varies between levels. Turnout is much higher in national elections than in municipal elections, and this turnout difference has been around 15 percentage points during the last three decades (Figure 5.1). The overall trend in municipal

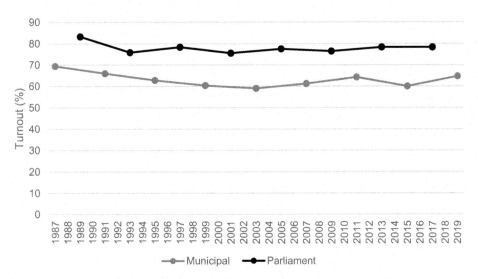

Figure 5.1 Voter turnout in national and municipal elections in Norway, 1987–2019
Source: Statistics Norway, Statbank Tables 08243 and 09475

elections since the 1980s has been one of declining turnout, but there have been exceptions. Turnout in the 2019 election was the highest since 1991, and turnout in 2011 was also relatively high. One reason (among others) for these two exceptions is the relatively strong mobilization of young voters. In 2011, young voters were mobilized due to the terrorist attacks of 22 July on the Norwegian Labor Party's youth organization (Ødegård et al. 2020). In 2019, the relatively high turnout of people younger than 30 (10 percentage points higher than in the 2015 elections; Kleven 2019) may reflect an international climate mobilization of young people. Turnout among nonnationals is low – around 30% in recent elections (Bergh & Christensen 2017).

Voter turnout in municipal elections varies considerably among Norwegian municipalities, from 56.2% to 85.1% in the 2019 election. Turnout has increased over time in the smallest municipalities, which have a higher average voter turnout than larger municipalities (Bjørklund 2013). However, there is also considerable variation among smaller municipalities, with no clear linear correlation between voter turnout and municipal size. Instead, as shown in Figure 5.2, there is a slightly curvilinear relationship with the highest turnout in small municipalities, but also relatively high turnout in the largest cities.

Municipal elections in Norway are relatively competitive. On average, 6.9[12] political parties and lists ran for election in each municipality in the 2019 election, and there was no election with only one list. Nine parties were represented in the national parliament. These parties also dominate municipal politics in terms of both voter support and share of mayors (Table 5.1). The category 'other lists and parties' in Table 5.1 includes so-called joint lists between two or more parties, usually including nationwide parties. Therefore, the role of nationwide parties in local politics may be even stronger than the data presented in Table 5.1 indicate. However, there is also a long tradition of local nonpartisan lists in many Norwegian municipalities, independent of municipal size (Aars & Ringkjøb 2005). Indeed, there was a boom in support for local and minor parties in 2019, as their share of votes increased from 4.1% to 7.5% and they won 7.2% of all seats in local councils. The main reason for this increase was the establishment of lists fighting against road tolls in several cities. These lists did well, and in Bergen, the second-largest city in

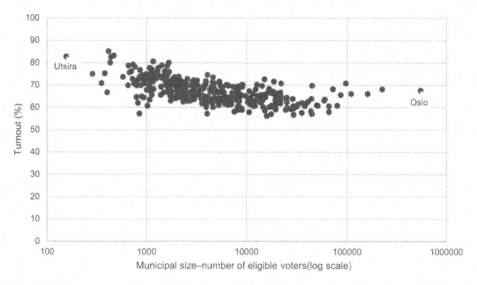

Figure 5.2 Voter turnout in the 2019 Norwegian municipal elections by municipality size
Source: Statistics Norway, Statbank Tables 12758 and 09475

Table 5.1 Party politicization of councils – participation and performance of the parliamentary (national) parties[2] in Norwegian local elections, 2019

	Municipalities where running (%)	Municipalities where represented (%)	Seats on local councils (%)	(Aggregate) votes in local elections (%)	Mayors affiliated with the party (%)
Red Party (R)	39.0	31.5	2.1	3.8	0.0
Socialist Left Party (SV)	67.7	64.3	4.9	6.1	1.7
Labor Party (Ap)	97.8	97.8	27.6	24.9	41.6
Center Party (Sp)	96.3	96.3	24.3	14.5	36.8
Green Party (MDG)	48.9	43.5	3.3	6.8	0.3
Christian Democratic Party (KrF)	62.9	52.8	4.4	4.0	2.5
Liberal Party (V)	62.4	45.5	2.8	3.9	0.6
Conservative Party (H)	87.4	86.8	15.9	20.2	9.6
Progress Party (FrP)	69.9	66.0	7.5	8.3	0.8
Local and other minor lists and parties[1]	53.9	44.1	7.2	7.5	6.2
N	356	356	9,336	2,670,687	356

[1] This category includes national parties not represented in the national parliament, joint lists, or local lists.
[2] The national parties are sorted from left to right.
Source: Statistics Norway, Statbank Tables 09494, 10804, 12705, and 01182

Norway, The People's Action No to More Road Tolls (FNB) received 16.7% of the votes and became the third-largest party in the council.

Norwegian politics has become more fragmented at both the national and local levels. This implies that more parties and lists must collaborate to form a majority and elect a mayor. Such collaborations at the local level may cut across the traditional patterns of coalition formation that dominate national politics. Large parties usually get the mayor, but smaller parties with a pivotal position on the council may use their bargaining strength to obtain positions. The Center Party has a larger share of mayors than their share of the national vote would indicate, because its support is concentrated in small municipalities.

Even though the field of local politics is not strongly regulated by law, and the Election Act does not require any form of gender quotas for electoral lists, norms of equality and nondiscrimination can be said to be prevailing in these areas. Most parties have some kind of internal gender quota rules, and local party branches generally try to produce balanced lists with regard to gender, age, geography, and other characteristics (Segaard & Saglie 2019, 2021). Moreover, for decades national authorities have initiated campaigns to promote gender equality in political representation and have put this issue on the public and political agendas (Halsaa 2019).

Women currently hold 41% of the seats in the national parliament and 40.5% of the municipal council seats after the 2019 elections; furthermore, 35.4% and 41.0% of all mayors and deputy mayors, respectively, are women. Overall, the development in gender representation since the beginning of the 1990s has been in favor of women, but progress is slow and female politicians and mayors are still the minority, as shown in Figure 5.3. There is considerable turnover among local councilors. Usually, less than half of municipal councilors are reelected. The turnover rate was 52% in 2019: 49% for men and 57% for women.[13]

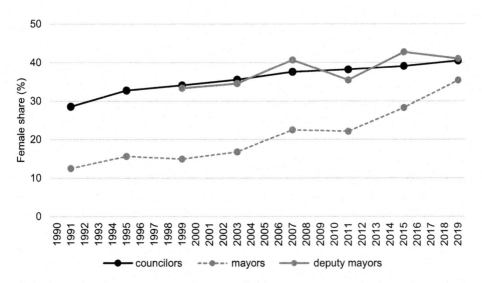

Figure 5.3 Women's representation among councilors, mayors, and deputy mayors in Norway, 1991–2019

Source: Statistics Norway, Statbank Tables 09494, 04774, 04775, and 12872

These overall figures on female representation nevertheless hide considerable variation between municipalities – from 13% to 65% of municipal councilors are women.[14] Moreover, recent research has shown that political representation on local councils is not only gendered – more men than women – but also characterized by a gender-generation gap (Segaard & Saglie 2021). The youngest generation stands out by having slightly more women than men among its elected representatives. In the older generations, the opposite is the case; indeed, the gender gap is pronounced in favor of men. Furthermore, the gender-generation gap in Norwegian local councils depends on municipal size. Both the younger and the older generations of women constitute a larger share of the local councils in larger municipalities compared to smaller units. However, the younger generation of female politicians is benefiting much more from living in a large municipality than the older generation, and the variation in representation depending on municipal size is much greater for younger women than for older.

Persons of foreign origin – that is, from a non-Norwegian background – have held approximately 2–3% of the seats on local councils over the last two decades. However, in municipalities with many immigrants, the share of representatives with non-Norwegian backgrounds is much higher; this is the case in Oslo, Norway's capital, and in Drammen (Kleven & Aalandslid 2016). Indeed, Johannes Bergh and Tor Bjørklund (2011: 134) found that '[g]enerally speaking, minorities are under-represented. However, that general picture is modified by the fact that minorities are over-represented in municipalities where most Norwegian minorities live'.

Trial (and error): the Norwegian approach to local democracy

Debates on electoral reform in Norway tend to lead to experiments that use local government as a testing ground. Trials are held in selected municipalities. The intention of these initiatives is to support and develop local democracy by collecting experiences and learning. The aim has been, in many cases, to find a means of reversing the continuing decline in turnout. These trials are evaluated before final decisions are made, and most do not lead to any permanent change. As mentioned previously, a trial with direct elections of mayors was discontinued. Other experiments include a trial with internet voting in ten municipalities in the 2011 local elections and 12 municipalities in the 2013 parliamentary election (Segaard et al. 2016; Saglie & Segaard 2016), and a trial in which the voting age was lowered to 16 in 20 municipalities in the 2011 and 2015 local elections (Ødegård et al. 2020). Both innovations were implemented quite successfully, but the trials were discontinued due to more fundamental objections – concerns about the secret ballot and about the consistency of voting age and the age of legal adulthood, respectively. In the 2003 election, a municipality was allowed to have a separate election day, three months before the rest of the country. The aim was to have a genuinely local election, without interference from the national election campaign. This aim was achieved, but turnout dropped by 16 percentage points and the trial was not repeated (Skålnes 2005). Only one trial so far has been implemented permanently: a successful trial of voter mobilization by text message and letters in 2015 (Bergh et al. 2021).

Although evaluations of these trials have contributed to Norwegian local electoral research, the most important element has been the Norwegian Local Election Studies (NLES). NLES surveys have been conducted after each election since 1995 . The NLES have been directed by the Institute for Social Research and funded by the Ministry of Local Government and, since 2019, by the Research Council of Norway. This longitudinal data collection enables the study of developments over time.

At first glance, Norway appears to be a strongly integrated country, vertically as well as horizontally. It is a unitary state, where all municipalities have the same status and are responsible for the same tasks. Moreover, the aggregate strength of the parties is almost the same in local and national politics. Before the NLES started, a dominant view in the Norwegian public debate (with some exceptions, e.g., Rommetvedt 1988) was that municipal elections were dominated by national politics. A major contribution of the NLES has been to question this view.

On the one hand, national political trends certainly influence municipal elections. One example is the recent climate mobilization of young voters. Another example is that the national government parties lost votes in the 2019 local election, and their share of mayors was strongly reduced.

On the other hand, surveys describe considerable vertical and horizontal differentiation. Horizontally, although all municipalities perform the same tasks, local politics works differently in large and small municipalities. In small municipalities, local issues and candidates are more important, while party politics matters less. Vertically, municipal elections in Norway should not be perceived merely as second-order elections (Ervik 2012). Local media and local issues are important for the voters. Such local factors tend to be invisible in aggregate statistics, as different developments in different municipalities cancel each other out. For example, whereas net volatility is higher in parliamentary than in municipal elections, survey data show that gross volatility is about the same in the two types of elections (Bergh & Bjørklund 2009). Furthermore, municipal elections even seem to become more local over time, as local issues have become more important for the voters and more voters cast preference votes (Bjørklund 2017). Norwegian local politics is indeed local – and increasingly so.

Notes

1. An earlier version of this chapter was presented at the Norwegian Political Science Conference, Tromsø, 6–8 January 2018. We would like to thank the workshop participants and the editors for useful comments and Øyvin Kleven, of Statistics Norway, for providing data. This work was supported by the Research Council of Norway (grant no. 294597).
2. Statistics Norway, Statbank Table 11342.
3. Parts of this section draw on Segaard and Saglie (2021).
4. Citizens abroad who have not been registered in the Population Registry during the last ten years must formally apply to be registered on the electoral roll.
5. The only legal basis for disenfranchisement is 'entering the service of a foreign power without the consent of the Government' (Article 53 of the Constitution).
6. In 2019, 154 of the 356 municipalities had a two-day election.
7. Statistics Norway, Statbank Table 09475.
8. An alternative procedure exists. If there is no more than one approved list proposal, the election is held by majority ballot: those candidates who receive the most votes are elected. This system was used for the last time in 1999, in a small municipality.
9. A voter can cast *panachage* votes for a number of candidates that corresponds to one-quarter of the council seats, but five *panachage* votes are always allowed, irrespective of council size.
10. The maximum number of prioritized candidates varies from four to ten, depending on the number of council seats. The prioritization must follow the list order. Prioritized candidates are displayed in boldface type on the ballot paper.
11. The number of signatures corresponds to 2% of the number of eligible voters from the previous election but shall in no case be less than the number of municipal councilors. Signatures from 300 persons will in all cases be sufficient.
12. Calculation based on Statistics Norway, Statbank Table 12705.
13. Statistics Norway, Statbank Table 12872.
14. Statistics Norway, Statbank Table 01182.

References

Aars, J. & Ringkjøb, H.-E. (2005). 'Party Politicisation Reversed? Non-partisan Alternatives in Norwegian Local Politics'. *Scandinavian Political Studies*, 28 (2), pp. 161–181.

Adamiak, A.L. (2011). 'Direct Democracy in Local Politics in Norway', in Schiller, T. (ed.) *Local Direct Democracy in Europe*. Wiesbaden: VS Verlag für Sozialwissenschaften, pp. 113–125.

Baldersheim, H. (2018). 'Kommunereform og ny kommunelov: Meir desentralisering?' *Norsk statsvitenskapelig tidsskrift*, 34 (4), pp. 174–187.

Bergh, J. & Bjørklund, T. (2009). 'Lokalvalg og riksvalg: forskjeller og likheter', in Saglie, J. (ed.) *Det nære demokratiet – lokalvalg og lokal deltakelse*. Oslo: Abstrakt, pp. 137–157.

Bergh, J. & Bjørklund, T. (2011). 'Minority Representation in Norway. Success at the Local Level; Failure at the National Level', in Bird, K., Saalfeld, T., & Wüst, A.M. (eds) *The Political Representation of Immigrants and Minorities. Voters, Parties and Parliaments in Liberal Democracies*. Oxon/New York: Routledge, pp. 128–144.

Bergh, J., Bjørklund, T., & Hellevik, O. (2010). 'Personutvelgingen i norske valg'. *Norsk statsvitenskapelig tidsskrift*, 26 (2), pp. 105–131.

Bergh, J. & Christensen, D.A. (2017). 'Hvem er hjemmesitterne? En analyse av valgdeltakelse ved tre påfølgende valg', in Saglie, J. & Christensen, D.A. (eds) *Lokalvalget 2015 – et valg i kommunereformens tegn?* Oslo: Abstrakt, pp. 61–78.

Bergh, J., Christensen, D.A., & Matland, R.E. (2021). 'When is a Reminder Enough? Text Message Voter Mobilization in a European Context'. *Political Behavior*, 43 (3), pp. 1091–1111.

Bjørklund, T. (2013). 'Politisk deltakelse i sentrum og periferi. Kontraster og endringer', in Bergh, J. & Christensen, D.A. (eds) *Et robust lokaldemokrati – lokalvalget i skyggen av 22. juli 2011*. Oslo: Abstrakt, pp. 129–146.

Bjørklund, T. (2017). 'Kommunevalgene fra 1995 til 2015: økt vekt på det lokale', in Saglie, J. & Christensen, D.A. (eds) *Lokalvalget 2015 – et valg i kommunereformens tegn?* Oslo: Abstrakt, pp. 301–329.

Bukve, O. & Saxi, H.P. (2017). 'Institutional Change and System Support – Reforming the Executive in Norwegian Cities and Regions'. *Scandinavian Journal of Public Administration*, 21 (2), pp. 69–88.

Christensen, D.A. & Aars, J. (2010). 'Electing Mayors with the Supplementary Vote Method: Evidence from Norway'. *Local Government Studies*, 36 (6), pp. 823–841.

Christensen, D.A., Midtbø, T., Ringkjøb, H.-E., & Aars, J. (2008). *To valg med ny personvalgordning. Kontinuitet eller endring?* Report 9–2008. Bergen: Uni Rokkansenteret.

Ervik, B. (2012). 'Second-Order Arguments for Second-Order Elections? Measuring "Election Stakes" in a Multilevel Context: The Case of Norway'. *Journal of Elections, Public Opinion and Parties*, 22 (1), pp. 27–50.

Folkestad, B., Klausen, J.E., Saglie, J., & Segaard, S.B. (2021). 'When Do Consultative Referendums Improve Democracy? Evidence from Local Referendums in Norway'. *International Political Science Review*, 42 (2), pp. 213–228.

Halsaa, B. (2019). 'Kampanjer for kvinner i kommunepolitikken'. *Tidsskrift for kjønnsforskning*, 43 (3), pp. 158–176.

Hellevik, O. & Bergh, J. (2005). 'Personutvelgingen. Ny ordning – uendret resultat', in Saglie, J. & Bjørklund, T. (eds) *Lokalvalg og lokalt folkestyre*. Oslo: Gyldendal Akademisk, pp. 58–82.

Klausen, J.E. (2018). 'Sub-Municipal Arrangements in Norway: District System in Oslo', in Hlepas, N.-K., Kersting, N., Kuhlmann, S., Swianiewicz, P., & Teles, F. (eds) *Sub-Municipal Governance in Europe. Decentralization Beyond the Municipal Tier*. Cham: Palgrave Macmillan, pp. 145–165.

Klausen, J.E., Askim, J. & Christensen, T. (2021). 'Local Government Reform: Compromises through Cross-Cutting Cleavages'. *Political Studies Review*, 19 (1), pp. 111–126.

Kleven, Ø. (2019). *Langt flere unge stemte i årets lokalvalg*. Oslo: Statistics Norway. Available at: www.ssb.no/valg/artikler-og-publikasjoner/langt-flere-unge-stemte-i-arets-lokalvalg (Accessed: 21 November 2019).

Kleven, Ø. & Aalandslid, V. (2016). 'Flyktninger og politisk deltakelse – kommunestyrevalget 2015. Deltar flyktningene i lokalpolitikken?' *Samfunnsspeilet*, (4), pp. 54–59. Available at: www.ssb.no/valg/artikler-og-publikasjoner/_attachment/288191?_ts=158fce20a30 (Accessed: 25 November 2019)

Kvelland, E. (2015). 'Når aksjonskanalen møter valgkanalen: Politisk deltakelse i lokalvalg'. *Tidsskrift for samfunnsforskning*, 56 (2), pp. 159–179.

Ladner, A., Keuffer, N., Baldersheim, H., Hlepas, N., Swianiewicz, P., Steyvers, K., & Navarro, C. (2019). *Patterns of Local Autonomy in Europe*. Cham: Palgrave Macmillan.

Langsæther, P.E., Gjerløw, H., & Søyland, M.G. (2019). 'Is all PR Good PR? How the Content of Media Exposure Affects Candidate Popularity'. *Electoral Studies*, 57, pp. 143–152.

Larsen, H.O. (2002). 'Directly Elected Mayors – Democratic Renewal or Constitutional Confusion?', in Caulfield, J. & Larsen, H.O. (eds) *Local Government at the Millennium*. Wiesbaden: VS Verlag für Sozialwissenschaften, pp. 111–133.

Martinussen, P.E. (2004). 'Majority Rule in Consensual Democracies: Explaining Political Influence in Norwegian Local Councils'. *Local Government Studies*, 30 (3), pp. 303–330.

Matland, R.E. & Lilliefeldt, E. (2014). 'The Effect of Preferential Voting on Women's Representation', in Escobar-Lemmon, M. & Taylor-Robinson, M. (eds) *Representation: The Case of Women*. Oxford: Oxford University Press, pp. 79–102.

Mikalsen, K.H. & Bjørnå, H. (2015). 'Den norske ordføreren: begrenset myndighet, mye makt?' in Aarsæther, N. & Mikalsen, K.H. (eds) *Lokalpolitisk lederskap i Norden*. Oslo: Gyldendal Akademisk, pp. 169–195.

Ødegård, G., Bergh, J., & Saglie, J. (2020). 'Why Did Young Norwegians Mobilize: External Events or Early Enfranchisement?', in Eichhorn, J. & Bergh, J. (eds) *Lowering the Voting Age to 16: Learning from Real Experiences to Inform the Debate*. Cham: Palgrave Macmillan, pp. 189–210.

Rommetvedt, H. (1988). *Lokalvalg eller riksgallup?* Oslo: Kommuneforlaget.

Rose, L.E. & Hansen, T. (2013). 'Fylkestingsvalgene: demokratisk milepæl eller demokratisk staffasje?', in Bergh, J. & Christensen, D.A. (eds) *Et robust lokaldemokrati – lokalvalget i skyggen av 22. juli*. Oslo: Abstrakt, pp. 203–221.

Saglie, J. (2020). 'Do Party Organizations Integrate Multi-level States? The Case of the Norwegian Local Government Reform'. *Regional & Federal Studies*, 30 (4), pp. 579–597.

Saglie, J., Bergh, J., Gitlesen, J.P., & Rommetvedt, H. (2021). 'Hva skjedde ved valget? Nasjonale trender og lokale variasjoner', in Saglie, J., Segaard, S.B. & Christensen, D.A. (eds) *Lokalvalget 2019. Nye kommuner – nye valg?* Oslo: Cappelen Damm Akademisk, pp. 27–61.

Saglie, J. & Segaard, S.B. (2016). 'Internet Voting & the Secret Ballot in Norway: Principles & Popular Understandings'. *Journal of Elections, Public Opinion, and Parties*, 26 (2), pp. 155–169.

Saglie, J. & Sivesind, K.H. (2018). 'Civil Society Organizations or Semi-public Agencies: State Regulation of Parties and Voluntary Organizations in Norway'. *Journal of Civil Society*, 14 (4), pp. 292–310.

Segaard, S.B., Baldersheim, H., & Saglie, J. (2016). 'The Norwegian Trial with Internet Voting: Results and Challenges', in Barrat i Esteve, J. (ed.) *El voto electrónico y sus dimensiones jurídicas: Entre la ingenua complacencia y el rechazo precipitado*. Madrid: Iustel, pp. 189–218.

Segaard, S.B. & Saglie, J. (2019). 'Lav kvinnerepresentasjon som demokratisk problem: Lokale partilags arbeid med kjønnsbalanse på valglistene'. *Tidsskrift for kjønnsforskning*, 43 (3), pp. 141–157.

Segaard, S.B. & Saglie, J. (2021). 'A Gender-generation Gap in Political Representation? The Contingent Impact of Preference Voting in Norwegian Municipal Elections'. *Local Government Studies*, 47 (1), pp. 145–165.

Skålnes, S. (2005). 'Uklar diagnose og tvilsam medisin? Erfaringar med eigen valdag i Nittedal i 2003', in Saglie, J. & Bjørklund, T. (eds) *Lokalvalg og lokalt folkestyre*. Oslo: Gyldendal Akademisk, pp. 83–101.

Sletnes, I. (2015). 'Ordførerrollen i Norden i et rettslig perspektiv', in Aarsæther, N. & Mikalsen, K.H. (eds) *Lokalpolitisk lederskap i Norden*. Oslo: Gyldendal Akademisk, pp. 28–68.

6

Sweden

Joint election day, party dominance, and extensive turnout

Anders Lidström

A uniform local government system

The Swedish system of local government consists of two tiers – 290 municipalities and 21 regions (Lidström 2011, 2016). The municipalities are in charge of most of the welfare functions, such as education up to the upper secondary schools, social welfare, and care for the elderly, but they are also responsible for physical planning, local infrastructure, fire services, and cultural and leisure activities. The regions are in charge of health care and regional development policies. Although the municipalities retain the overarching responsibility and provide most of the welfare services, many of these have increasingly been contracted out to private or independent service providers, particularly in the major cities. With only a few exceptions, the distribution of functions between the levels of government is symmetrical.

All municipalities and regions receive most of their revenue from a proportional income tax. Each local authority has full discretion to set the level of its taxation. An equalization system redistributes resources from the wealthy to the neediest local governments. They also receive additional revenue from the state. Swedish municipalities enjoy a high level of autonomy – the fourth highest in Europe according to the Local Autonomy Index (Ladner et al. 2019).

The subnational infrastructure has been relatively stable since 1990, although six new municipalities have been reestablished after having been amalgamated in a comprehensive territorial reform that was completed in 1974. At the second tier, a previous county council structure has been gradually transformed and the counties renamed as regions. Beginning in 1998, five county councils were merged to form two larger regions (*Västra Götaland* and *Skåne*), which also included the transfer of the main responsibility for regional development functions from central government units to these regions. Subsequently, all county councils have been renamed as regions and have been assigned the additional regional development functions but without mergers.

In typologies of local government systems, Sweden is located in a Northern European or Scandinavian group (Sellers et al. 2020). Such groups are generally characterized by extensive responsibilities for welfare services combined with a high level of autonomy and strong traditions of party-based representative democracy.

Table 6.1 Perception of the importance (percent) of different tiers of government in Sweden

Level of government	Most impact on one's living conditions (2008)	Trust in institutions (2018)	Satisfied with democracy (2018)
European Union	2	51	57
Sweden	–	–	74
National government	48	60	–
National parliament	–	73	–
County council or region	}46	}71	64
Municipality			68

Note: For impact, citizens were asked which of the three levels of government had the most impact on their living conditions; trust, % that tend to trust; satisfaction, % very or fairly satisfied.

Sources: European Commission (2008, 2018) and Tipple (2019)

Citizens generally have a high level of trust in public authorities in Sweden, although support varies between levels of government (Loughlin et al. 2011). As indicated in Table 6.1, citizens regard the local and regional levels as having the same importance with regard to their living conditions as the national level. Levels of trust and satisfaction are also fairly similar at both levels of government, although results may vary from one survey to another.

Sweden complies with the committee leader form of local leadership model, according to the Mouritzen and Svara (2002) typology. Within the municipality, power is distributed between the council and committees. The council makes decisions about overarching policy, municipal organization, budget, and tax level. It also appoints members of committees. Of these, the most important is the executive committee, which typically comprises key politicians from each party in proportion to their strength on the council. The executive committee proposes policies to the council and is responsible for the implementation of these decisions. Almost all proposals from the executive committee are confirmed without changes by the council.

In contrast to many other European countries, there are no mayors in Sweden. The closest office to that of mayor is the indirectly elected chair of the executive committee (*kommunstyrelsens ordförande*). This is a full-time political position, usually representing the largest ruling party. Although the position can be strong and important, it has no formal decision-making powers of its own, as all municipal decisions are made collectively, by councils or committees (Lidström 2011). Furthermore, contrary to the case with mayors, the chair is not the leading administrative officer; this function is conducted separately by a professional CEO appointed by the executive committee.

Local elections in a multilevel context

Sweden is the only country in Europe that consistently holds elections to national, regional, and local assemblies on the same day. This format was introduced in 1970 as part of a revision of the Swedish constitution. Since the 2018, the elections have been held on the second Sunday of September, but previously voting was held on the third Sunday of September. Starting 18 days before election day, electors may vote in advance at a reduced number of voting stations in the municipality. Voting by proxy is possible for people with illness or disability.

The overarching responsibility for organizing elections lies with the Swedish Election Authority (*Valmyndigheten*). The central government unit at the regional level – the County

Administrative Board (*Länsstyrelsen*) – is responsible for checking the accuracy of the electoral register, the final counting of votes, and calculating the distribution of seats between parties and candidates in the regional and municipal elections. In each municipality, an appointed municipal committee, the Election Committee, is in charge of conducting and organizing elections within the municipality, for example, by setting up and staffing voting stations.

The term of office in all three elections is fixed and is currently four years. Before 1998, the term was three years, but it was extended to four because a three-year term was considered too brief for governments to be evaluated by the electorate. Since 2017, municipalities have had the ability to hold extraordinary elections between the scheduled election days if such an election is supported by two-thirds of the council. An extraordinary election cannot be held earlier than six months after the first meeting of the newly elected council. The term of office for the new council is the time remaining until the next regularly scheduled election. This provision was introduced as a means for resolving unclear or complicated majority situations on the council, although to date, no extraordinary election has been held in any Swedish municipality.

Swedish local government law allows for local referenda, but recalls of elected members at any level of government are prohibited. Those elected retain their seats for the whole term of office as long as they wish, even if they decide to leave their party. If an elected official leaves his/her seat, an alternate member takes his/her place (see later discussion).

The system of proportional representation

All Swedish citizens and citizens of EU countries, Iceland, and Norway living in the municipality who are 18 years of age or older on the day of the election have the right to vote in municipal and regional elections. Other citizens who have lived in Sweden for at least three years are also allowed to vote in these local elections. In contrast, only Swedish citizens are allowed to vote in national elections. Voting is not compulsory. All citizens eligible to vote are automatically added to the electoral register from the population register by the Election Authority; hence, there is no need for individuals to register in order to have the right to vote.

The number of members to be elected to the council is decided by each local council itself, but it has to comply with minimum requirements as regulated by the Local Government Act. The size requirement varies from 21 (for municipalities with fewer than 8,000 electors) to 101 (in municipalities with more than 600,000 electors). In 2014, the minimum size of the council was reduced from 31, as the smallest municipalities had experienced problems with vacant seats. The total number of seats in the municipal councils in the 2018 elections was 12,700.

If a member cannot attend a meeting, he/she is replaced by an alternate member. The council determines the number of alternate members, which must be at least half the number of seats that the party receives in the election. The alternates are elected at the same time as the regular members and consist of candidates further down on the list below those elected (see later discussion).

The same electoral system is applied in all three types of Swedish elections, and it is also uniform for all sizes of jurisdictions. According to the Institute for Democracy and Electoral Assistance typology of electoral systems worldwide (Reynolds et al. 2008), the system is an *open-list proportional representation* system (OLPR). It is open in the sense that the voters can influence the ordering of the candidates by indicating a specific candidate. If at least 5% of the electors for a party indicate a specific candidate, he/she is moved to the top of the list. In the 2018 municipal elections, 212 candidates, that is, 1.7% of all those elected, would not have had a seat if not for the personal vote.[1] The system was introduced with the 1998 elections, and before that, it was possible to influence the ordering of candidates only by crossing out specific candidates and adding new candidates to the list. There were no cases where these actions had any effect, which means that the system before 1998 was effectively closed. Personal voting has continued to become less common since its introduction, but it is still more common in the municipal than in the national elections and it is most common in European elections (40% in the 2019 elections) (Berg & Oscarsson 2015). In the 2018 elections, 28% of the municipal voters indicated a specific candidate compared to 35% when the system was introduced in 1998.

Sweden's Elections Act stipulates that a municipality may be divided into two or more electoral districts if it has at least 36,000 eligible voters. Such divisions were implemented in 22 of the 48 municipalities that met the size requirement in the 2018 elections.[2] Smaller municipalities form just one district. The division within districts is decided by the municipal council in October of the year before an election at the latest, but it has to be confirmed by the County Administrative Board (*Länsstyrelsen*). All districts are multimember districts and need to have at least 13 seats for distribution.

In the election, political parties provide ballot papers with each party's name and a numbered list of its candidates. Parties can issue several lists in each district. There is a box to the left of each name that is ticked if a personal vote is made. A party label is compulsory, that is, independent candidates are not allowed; however, groups of citizens are free to form new, usually local parties. The party label has to be registered with the National Election Authority. A party symbol may also be added to the list. Each voter has one vote per election. *Apparentement* (pooling the votes for electoral alliances between lists) and *panachage* (splitting votes between lists) are not allowed. In order to make it possible for voters and election officials to distinguish between the different elections, the ballot papers have different colors: white for municipal elections, blue for regional elections, and yellow for parliamentary elections.

Parties may, in addition, register their candidates. Candidates for the municipal elections are usually registered with the County Administrative Board. If all candidates are registered, voters cannot add additional candidates to the list. Most parties register all of their candidates. The candidates must sign a written consent that is usually administered by the party. In practice, in order to stand a chance of being elected, every candidate has to be nominated by a political party.

After the election, the County Administrative Boards calculate and administer the distribution of seats on the municipal councils according to the election results and based on the rules stipulated in the Elections Act. In order to qualify for the distribution of seats, a party needs to have received at least 2% of the votes if the municipality comprises only one district and 3% if the municipality is divided into two or more districts. With districts, 90% of the seats are *permanent constituency seats* and the remaining are *adjustment seats* aimed at ensuring that representation is proportional to the election results in the whole municipality. The permanent constituency seats are allocated first in each district. The adjustment seats are distributed, with the municipality as one district, to the parties that are the closest to receiving additional seats. The system of adjustment seats was introduced with the 2018 elections in order to improve the proportionality of local elections.

The distribution of seats among the parties is regulated in the Elections Act (Section 14:3). A *comparative number*[3] is calculated for each party in the constituency using a modified Sainte-Laguë method, also known as the adjusted odd-number method. The first comparative number for the party is the number of votes in the constituency divided by 1.2. The party that has the highest comparative number receives the first seat. A new comparative number is then calculated for this party by dividing the party's number of votes by 3. The second seat is allocated to the party that now has the highest comparative number. This continues, but the next time, the divisor 5 is used (followed by the next odd number sequentially, i.e., 7, 9, 11, etc.). The procedure continues until all seats are distributed.

In the final stage, candidates are allocated seats within each party. First, seats are given to those who have received at least 5% of the personal votes for the party. If several candidates qualify, they are given seats according to the number of their personal votes. Second, the other candidates are given seats in the order in which they are listed, using the ordinary Sainte-Laguë method (i.e., without any initial division by 1.2), until all seats that the party has won are filled. The personal votes only benefit candidates who otherwise would not have been elected according to the priorities of the party. If several lists are used, the relative weight of each list is determined by the number of votes that it receives. This is followed by the identification of the alternate members, that is, those listed below the individuals who were elected. Members and alternates are officially informed by the County Administrative Boards that they have been elected. If a member of the council decides to leave his/her seat before the end of the term of office, the County Administrative Board conducts a new calculation in order to identify the new member (usually the first alternate member).

There are no rules restricting the simultaneous membership in assemblies at different levels of government (*cumul des mandats*). The Environmental Party is the only party that is, explicitly, hesitant to assemble mandates at different levels. In 1966, about 7% of the municipal councilors were simultaneously members of a regional assembly or the national parliament (Karlsson 2018).

High turnout combined with proportional party and gender representation

Voter turnout in national and local elections is generally high in Sweden compared to other countries with voluntary voting (Lidström 2003). It is also comparatively high in the municipal elections compared to the national elections. This may partly be a consequence of the joint election day, which reduces the need to have to go to the voting station separately for local elections. As indicated in Table 6.2, differences in turnout between national and local elections have been around 2–3% over the last 30 years. Turnout tended to decrease at the beginning of the 2000s, but it has increased again during the last four elections.

As shown in Table 6.3, turnout for the municipal election is more or less identical across municipalities of different sizes, although it is slightly lower in the smaller municipalities.

Local elections in Sweden are highly party politicized, and this includes the smallest municipalities. As mentioned previously, all candidates must represent a political party, which leaves no

Table 6.2 Turnout (percent) for parliamentary and municipal elections in Sweden, 1991–2018

Election date	Parliament	Municipalities
1991-09-15	86.7	84.3
1994-09-18	86.8	84.4
1998-09-20	81.4	78.6
2002-09-15	80.1	77.9
2006-09-17	82.0	79.4
2010-09-19	84.6	81.6
2014-09-14	85.8	82.8
2018-09-09	87.2	84.1

Source: Swedish Election Authority

Table 6.3 Turnout (percent) for the 2018 municipal elections in Sweden in municipalities with different population sizes

Population size	Turnout (%)	N	Std Dev (turnout)
0–9,999	83.2	72	3,9412
10,000–15,999	84.6	73	3,0830
16,000–34,999	84.8	72	2,7102
35,000 or more	84.7	73	3,7425
Total	84.3	290	3,4563

Source: Swedish Election Authority

Table 6.4 Party politicization in the 2018 Swedish municipal elections

Party name	% of municipalities where running	% of municipalities where represented	% of seats on local councils	% of (aggregate) votes in local elections	% of mayors* affiliated with the party
Moderate Party	97.2	97.0	18.9	20.1	30.7
Center Party	99.7	98.3	12.6	9.7	18.6
Liberal Party	93.1	82.4	5.4	6.8	1.4
Christian Democratic Party	91.0	86.6	5.3	5.2	1.7
Environmental Party	86.2	68.6	3.1	4.6	0.0
Social Democratic Party	100.0	100.0	29.5	27.6	43.4
Left Party	97.6	95.9	6.4	7.7	1.0
Feminist Initiative	19.0	4.5	0.2	1.0	0.0
Sweden Democrats	100.0	99.3	14.2	12.7	1.4
Nonnational (local) lists	71.0	48.3	4.4	4.7	1.7

*Refers to the chair of the executive committee.
Source: Swedish Election Authority

room for independent candidates. The eight parties in the national parliament completely dominate the local councils, holding about 95% of all seats, as illustrated in Table 6.4. The major parties have candidates in practically all municipalities, and the Social Democrats and Sweden Democrats are represented in all 290 municipalities. Nonnational lists, that is, parties that run only in specific municipalities, ran in 71% of the municipalities but received seats on only 48% of the councils. There are no uncontested seats in Swedish local elections. Three parties have more seats than their share of votes, but this is mainly a consequence of them being more successful in smaller municipalities, where each councilor represents fewer citizens than in the larger cities. Most of the major leadership positions are held by one of the two largest parties – the Social Democratic Party or the Moderate Party, depending on how the ruling majority is formed. However, the Center Party is strong in many rural areas, which is reflected by a significant number of chairmanships.

In both the national parliament and the local councils, female representation has increased over time, but it has stabilized at about 45% in the national parliament since 2000 and at about 43% on the local councils since 2010 (see Table 6.5). There are no gender quotas, but most parties have mixed lists with a gender representation of 50/50. Female representation is weaker

Table 6.5 Female representation (percent) in the parliament, on municipal councils, and as chairs of executive committees in Sweden

Election year	1991	1994	1998	2002	2006	2010	2014	2018
Members of parliament	33.0	40.4	42.7	45.3	47.3	45.0	43.6	46.1
Municipal councilors	34.1	41.3	41.6	42.4	42.3	43.0	43.7	43.3
Chairs of municipal executive committees	n/a	n/a	n/a	n/a	n/a	n/a	37.0	32.0

Sources: Statistics Sweden and Swedish Association of Local Authorities and Regions

in the topmost positions; for example, only one-third of the chairs of the municipal executive committees are held by women.

Eight percent of the local councilors elected in 2018 had been born abroad. This share has gradually increased; for example, in 1991, 4% were born abroad. The corresponding figure among citizens in 2018 was 19%, which means that the foreign-born population is still underrepresented on the local councils.[4]

The turnover rate among municipal councilors is fairly high, but there is also a minority of long-serving members. Of those elected in 2014, about 40% had no previous councilor experience, whereas 17% had already served at least three terms.[5]

Conclusions: Uniformity, proportionality, and party dominance

The Swedish system for local elections is characterized by its uniformity, emphasis on proportionality, total party politicization, high level of turnout, and extensive female representation. In addition, perhaps its most defining characteristic is the practice of consistently holding national, regional, and municipal elections on the same day, which makes Sweden unique in a European context. Since its introduction, the topic of simultaneous elections has been subject to ongoing debate with recurring suggestions to return to the situation before 1970, when local/regional and national elections were held in different years. However, thus far, there has been no parliamentary majority favoring change.

One reason is probably that local elections have turned out to be more legitimate than originally expected. Split-ticket voting, that is, voting for a different party in any of the three elections, has become increasingly common, up from about 6% in 1970 to 32% in the 2018 elections (Berg et al. 2019). This would suggest that citizens are able to distinguish between the political alternatives in each of the different elections. However, a recent study has also shown that an additional, approximately 38% make separate and independent decisions despite voting for the same party in the local and national elections (Lidström 2020). Hence, almost 60% of the voters would be classified as conscious local voters, which raises questions about previous assumptions that Swedish local elections are subordinate, second-order elections. Local elections can be legitimate despite taking place on the same day as national elections.

The system for local elections has been reformed in several ways over the last 30 years. This includes the introduction of adjustment seats in municipalities divided into two or more districts, a reduction in the size of the smallest councils, and the possibility of holding an extraordinary election. Moreover, in all three elections, the term of office has been extended to four years, and a personal vote has been introduced in addition to the compulsory choice of party. Proposals that have been considered but rejected include reintroducing a separate local election day (Författningsutredningen 2001), reducing the voting age to 16 for local elections (Demokratiutredningen 2016), and allowing electronic voting (Vallagskommittén 2013).

Perhaps surprisingly, research on local elections has been very limited in Sweden. Sweden has a long tradition of national election studies, beginning with the 1956 elections, but the analyses have typically been limited to the national elections. The surveys have recorded party choices in municipal elections since 1994, and this has resulted in a number of publications on split-ticket voting (for example, Berg et al. 2019). Studies of split-ticket voting have also been conducted on the basis of data from the national survey conducted by the SOM Institute at Göteborg University (for example, Johansson 2010; Erlingsson & Oscarsson 2015). However, no separate local election surveys have been implemented. One exception is the study on knowledge, motives, and voting in the three elections conducted in the four northernmost counties in connection with the 2010 elections (Lidström 2020). Hence, there is an obvious need for further and more extensive analyses of the specific characteristics of local voting in Sweden. Sweden is, indeed, a critical case in this respect. If local elections have an independent status, even in a country with a joint election day, they may be relevant elsewhere as well.

Notes

1 Website of the Swedish Election Authority, accessed 17 August 2020: https://data.val.se/val/val2018/statistik/index.html
2 Website of the Swedish Election Authority, accessed 17 August 2020: https://data.val.se/val/val2018/statistik/index.html
3 'Comparative number' is the English term used in official translations of the Swedish Elections Act, but it corresponds to the 'electoral quotient' used in other texts.
4 Data from Statistics Sweden.
5 Information kindly provided by Professor David Karlsson, School of Public Administration, Göteborg University, from the Swedish National Survey of Councilors (KOLFU).

References

Berg, L., Erlingsson, G.Ó. & Oscarsson, H. (2019), 'Rekordhög röstdelning' [Record high split-ticket voting] in *Storm or stiltje [Storm and Lull]*, eds U. Andersson, B. Rönnerstrand, P. Öhberg & A. Bergström, Gothenburg: SOM Institute, pp. 93–105.
Berg, L. & Oscarsson, H. (2015), *20 år med personval [20 Years with the personal vote]*. Report 2015:3. Valforskningsprogrammet, Statsvetenskapliga institutionen, University of Gothenburg.
Demokratiutredningen. (2016), *Låt fler forma framtiden! [Let more shape the future!]*. Parliamentary Commission, SOU 2016:5.
Erlingsson, G.Ó. & Oscarsson, H. (2015), 'Röstdelning i Sverige' ['Split-ticket voting in Sweden'] in *Fragment [Fragments]*, eds A. Bergström, B. Johansson, H. Oscarsson & M. Oskarson, Gothenburg: SOM Institute, pp. 361–376.
European Commission. (2008), *Standard Eurobarometer 70, Autumn 2008. Public opinion in the European Union*. European Union.
European Commission. (2018), *Standard Eurobarometer 90, Autumn 2018. Public opinion in the European Union*. European Union.
Författningsutredningen. (2001), *Skilda valdagar och vårval? [Separate election days and elections in the spring?]*. Parliamentary Commission, SOU 2001:65.
Johansson, F. (ed) (2010), *Kommunalvalet 2010. Väljare och partier i den lokala demokratin [The 2006 local elections: Voters and parties in the local democracy]*. Göteborg: Centrum för forskning om offentlig sektor, Statsvetenskapliga institutionen, University of Göteborg.
Karlsson, D. (2018), 'Finns det ett kommunparti i riksdagen?' ('Is there a municipal party in the parliament?') *Folkets främsta företrädare [The main representatives of the people]*, ed D Karlsson, Gothenburg: University of Gothenburg, pp. 151–170.

Ladner, A., Keuffer, N., Baldersheim, H., Hlepas, N., Swianiewicz, P., Steyvers, K. & Navarro, C. (2019), *Patterns of local autonomy in Europe*. London: Palgrave Macmillan.

Lidström, A. (2003), *Kommunsystem i Europa (Local government systems in Europe)*. Malmö: Liber.

Lidström, A. (2011), 'Sweden – Party dominated sub-national democracy under challenge' in *The Oxford handbook on sub-national democracy in Europe*, eds J. Loughlin, F. Hendriks & A. Lidström, Oxford: Oxford University Press, pp. 261–281

Lidström, A. (2016), 'Swedish local and regional government in a European context' in *The Oxford handbook of Swedish politics*, ed J. Pierre, Oxford: Oxford University Press, pp. 414–428.

Lidström, A. (2020), Who is the local voter? Various faces of localized voting in Sweden. *Local Government Studies*, DOI: 10.1080/03003930.2020.1761338

Loughlin, J., Hendriks, F. & Lidström, A. (eds) (2011), *The Oxford handbook on sub-national democracy in Europe*, Oxford: Oxford University Press.

Mouritzen, P.E. & Svara, J.H. (2002), *Leadership at the apex. Politicians and administrators in Western local governments*. Pittsburgh: University of Pittsburgh Press.

Reynolds, A., Reilly, B. & Ellis, A. (2008), *Electoral system design: The new international IDEA*. Handbook. Stockholm: International IDEA.

Sellers, J.M., Lidström, A. & Bae, Y. (2020), *Multilevel democracy. How local institutions and civil society shape the modern state*, Cambridge: Cambridge University Press.

Tipple, F. (2019), *Svenska demokratitrender 1986–2018. [Swedish democracy trends 1986–2018]*. SOM Report 2019:22, University of Göteborg: SOM Institute.

Vallagskommittén (2013), *E-röstning och andra valfrågor [E-voting and other election matters]*. Parliamentary Commission, SOU 2013:24.

Part 3
The British Isles

7
Ireland
An atypical electoral system for an atypical local government system

Aodh Quinlivan, Mark Callanan, and Liam Weeks

Overview of local government system

Local government in the Republic of Ireland is organized around 31 local authorities of equal status. This has been the situation since 2014 when a Local Government Reform Act reduced the number of local authorities from 114. This was achieved through the complete abolition of the secondary tier of Irish local government, comprising 80 town authorities (75 town councils and five borough councils). In addition, there were mergers involving a selected number of city and county councils. Accordingly, there are now three categories of local authority in Ireland: city councils (3), county councils (26), and city and county Councils (2).

The 2014 reforms also saw a reduction in the number of councilors from 1,627 to 949. The central government justified its decision to abolish the secondary tier of local government on the basis that these councils had 46% of all councilors in the country, while only representing 14% of the population and dealing with a mere 7% of all local government activity. Due to the absence of protection for subnational government in the Irish Constitution, this tier of local government was removed through legislation without the necessity of a referendum. Rationalization of local authorities is not unique to Ireland, and there is an ongoing debate about the optimal size of local government and associated issues such as amalgamations, costs, and economies of scale. International research suggests that there is a weak link between size and costs and that local authority mergers have limited intrinsic efficiency effects and can involve significant transactional costs and, sometimes, dis-economies of scale (see Byrnes & Dollery 2002; Elcock et al. 2010; Martin & Hock Schiff 2011; Callanan, Murphy & Quinlivan 2014).

The roots of the 2014 reforms can be traced back to the deep recession that affected Ireland beginning in 2008, causing a shrinking of the services and staffing of local authorities. A *Report of the Special Group on Public Service Numbers and Expenditure Programmes (2009)* led to the *Report of the Local Government Efficiency Review Group (2010)* and the reports by the *Local Government Efficiency Review Implementation Group (2012 and 2013)*. All advocated a reduction in local government staffing and reform of administration and financing. The local government sector surpassed the recommendations proposed in the 2010 *Report of the Local Government Efficiency Review Group* (NOAC 2016) – local authority staffing decreased by 24.2% nationally in the five years 2008–2013, while gross savings of €839m were achieved in the period 2008–2012. To achieve these savings and efficiencies, while coping with staffing reductions, involved the modification of practices, attitudes, and resource usage, reforms that have had lasting impacts, both positive and negative (Quinlivan 2017).[1] Recent years have been marked by more frequent use of resource sharing, intercouncil cooperation, and shared service approaches, including in areas such as waste management planning, environmental enforcement, and climate action. Once local government stops being local, a democratic deficit is established, and evidence shows that citizen satisfaction with local services tends to be higher in smaller local authorities (see Quinlivan 2017).

Ireland has a population of just under 5 million (4,921,500) with 31 local authorities, so that the average population per council is 158,758. This places Ireland in the 'very large' category of territorial structures alongside the United Kingdom (166,000) and Northern Ireland (164,500).

Historically, local authorities in Ireland have been responsible for a narrow range of functions (see Callanan & MacCarthaigh 2008; Collins & Quinlivan 2010; Loughlin 2011). Irish local authorities have only minor responsibilities in education, primary health care, transport, and policing (Callanan 2018). While the Local Government Reform Act of 2014 did not generally devolve powers from the central to local government, it gave local authorities a more overt role in economic development, based on the unique characteristics and strategic position of councils. Finance is a major restraint on the development of local government in Ireland. The *More Power To You* report produced by the Fórsa trade union in 2019 demonstrates that local government spending as a percentage of general government spending in Ireland is 8.4% (Fórsa 2019), well below the EU average of 23.1%. This reinforces the research of Considine and Reidy (2015: 21), who state that 'very few countries spend less on local government than we do'.

The majority of money spent by local authorities derives from local revenue sources. This is positive from the standpoint of local autonomy, but the rate for some service charges is set nationally, as is the range for changes in the local property tax. The proportion of local government income coming from local taxes is low by international comparative standards.

Given the centralized nature of local government in Ireland, it is hardly a surprise that Ireland ranks 38th out of 39 countries on the Local Autonomy Index (Ladner et al. 2016), which measures the degree of autonomy of local government. Only Moldova has a more centralized form of government. Justifiably, the *More Power To You* report (2019) describes local government as 'the poor cousin' in Ireland's democracy, and it could be argued that local government generally has a relatively low profile in the public consciousness.

One of the defining features of the Irish system of local government is the management system. The law regarding this system recognizes reserved functions (the responsibility of the elected members) and executive functions (the responsibility of the city or county manager, now called the chief executive). Reserved functions tend to be in the policy domain, with executive functions concerned with day-to-day administration. In reality, as the system has evolved, the distinction between reserved and executive functions has become blurred.

Nonetheless, given this delineation of responsibilities between the council and the chief executive in law, Ireland is generally seen as reflecting the council-manager form of typology of horizontal power relations in local government (Heinelt et al. 2018). In this respect, Ireland can be generally said to conform with this model, with executive responsibilities lying with a professional chief executive, the council being responsible for establishing the local policy framework, and a mayor elected by the council and largely fulfilling a ceremonial role.

Local elections

Ireland's 25th set of local elections took place on Friday, 24 May 2019 (see Quinlivan 2020). Since 1999, local elections in Ireland have been held on the same day as European Parliament elections. The elections of 2019 marked the 120th anniversary of Ireland's first local elections held in April 1899, following the passing of the Local Government (Ireland) Act of 1898. 2019 also represented the 20th anniversary of the constitutional amendment passed in 1999 to safeguard the holding of local elections on a five-year cycle. Prior to this, a minority of local elections in Ireland were held in accordance with their original schedule. Between 1923 and 1999, local elections were postponed on 15 occasions, quite often for very flimsy reasons (Weeks & Quinlivan 2009: 33). Since 1999, however, the local council serves a fixed five-year term of office.

For the purpose of local elections, each local authority is subdivided into local electoral areas (LEAs) or constituencies (see Callanan 2018). Some alterations to administrative areas were made following the reports of two Local Electoral Area Boundary Committees in 2018, which specified that, for the 2019 local elections, between five and seven councilors would be elected in most LEAs. In 2014, there were between six and ten councilors elected in each LEA, and this was deemed too large. In total, elections were fought across 166 LEAs in 2019, compared to 137 in 2014.

Separate mayoral elections are not held in Ireland. Rather, the current system is one whereby mayors are elected by the members of the local council to serve a one-year term. That said, the introduction of directly elected mayors has been a recurring theme in debates over local government reform in recent decades, with such debates often couched in references to international trends and examples. In 2019, plebiscites were held in Cork, Limerick, and Waterford on whether to introduce a directly elected mayor in these areas; however, only voters in Limerick approved the proposal. The first election to this new office is currently scheduled to take place in 2021.[2]

Features of the electoral system

The number of seats on each local council is determined by the central government through national legislation. While there are a larger number of seats in more populated council areas and fewer seats on councils in more sparsely populated areas, there is no population threshold between local authorities, and the number of seats on local councils is not strictly proportionate to population. For example, under the last census in 2016, in Ireland's county with the smallest population (Leitrim), there were 18 local council seats, resulting in one councilor for every 1,780 people, while in the largest constituency (Dublin city) with 63 seats, there was one councilor for every 8,802 people. While the Irish Constitution provides for an equitable ratio between population and the number of seats per constituency for *Dáil* elections, no such provision applies for local elections. Thus, a general observation that can be made is that more sparsely populated rural counties have a low councilor per capita ratio, while more populated urban and suburban local authorities have a high councilor per capita ratio (Callanan 2018).

Local councils can, under law, adopt a resolution petitioning the central government to change the number of seats on their council, although the final decision lies with the minister responsible for local government. While such requests are rare, the central government can on its own initiative review the number of council seats within different areas. The 2014 reforms (noted previously) involved the abolition of town and borough councils and the merger of several county and city council areas. The effect of these structural changes was to replace the 883 county and city councilors and the 744 town and borough councilors that had existed prior to 2014, with 949 county and city councilors elected in both the 2014 and 2019 elections.

These changes also entailed a slight redistribution of seats, so that local councils with smaller populations were assigned fewer seats under the reforms, and more populated councils gained some additional seats. For example, some smaller councils saw their number of seats reduced from 20–26 seats down to 18, while larger councils saw increases: for example, Cork county saw an increase from 48 to 55 seats, and Dublin city saw an increase from 52 to 63.

Since independence, Ireland has used proportional representation by means of the single transferable vote (PR-STV) as its electoral system for local elections, as it does for *Dáil*, presidential, and European Parliament elections (Reynolds et al. 2005). The PR-STV system is uniform and used for all local elections across the Republic of Ireland, regardless of size. The operation of multiseat constituencies means that political parties (especially larger parties) can run multicandidate tickets.

Voters rank candidates on the ballot paper in order of preference by writing a '1' beside the name of their first preferred candidate, a '2' beside their second preferred, and so forth. Voters can decide to stop at any stage after registering a first preference, or they can make their way down the full ballot paper so that a number appears after each candidate. Both survey evidence and an analysis of electronic voting data indicate that the average number of preferences cast is between 3 and 4, somewhat independent of the number of candidates on the ballot (Laver 2004). While historically supporters of the larger parties tended to keep their preferences within party, such a tradition has been in decline, with only a bare majority of voters now casting their lower preferences for the same party as that of their first preferred candidate (where the option exists). Indeed, aside from party preference, voters are free to rank candidates on the basis of other criteria, such as geography – for example, where voters might decide to select candidates from their particular locality. Indeed, candidates are listed on the ballot paper alphabetically according to candidate surname rather than party affiliation, although any party affiliation (and party logo) is indicated beside the candidate's name, along with a photo of the candidate.

The counting of votes revolves around the Droop quota, the minimum number of votes that guarantees election (although it is not always necessary to reach this number to be elected). It is calculated by dividing the total valid votes by one more than the number of seats to be filled and adding one, disregarding any fraction. For example, if 60,000 valid votes were cast in a five-seat constituency, the quota would be [60,000/(5 + 1)] + 1, that is, 10,001 votes. Except in the highly unlikely event that the requisite number of candidates filled all of the seats by reaching the quota on the basis of their first preferences alone, the counting process comprises a series of 'counts' or stages, each involving the distribution of the 'surplus' votes (those over and above the quota) of a candidate whose total exceeds the quota or, if no one has reached the quota, the elimination of the lowest placed candidate, all of whose votes are redistributed. If a voter does not express a further preference, his or her vote is discarded, with only transferable votes being examined. The counting continues until all of the seats have been filled. This occurs when a sufficient number of candidates have reached the quota, or when the number of candidates left is one greater than the number of seats to be filled and there are no further surpluses to distribute, at which stage all bar the candidate with the fewest votes are deemed elected.

For further details on the count process under PR-STV in Ireland and illustrative examples, see Farrell and Sinnott (2018) and Weeks and Quinlivan (2009). While the counting of votes can appear complicated with the use of a formula to calculate quotas and the distribution of surpluses and elimination of candidates, from the voter's perspective the task of voting is relatively straightforward – to simply rank candidates on the basis of the voter's preference by placing numbers beside the candidates' names.

As noted previously, in terms of voting districts, each local council is subdivided into electoral districts known as 'local electoral areas' (LEAs), which act as constituencies for the purposes of local elections. While there is no population threshold that exists to determine the number of seats *between* local authorities, the determination of local electoral areas is expected to reflect a balance of population between LEAs *within* local authority areas. In advance of each local election, the boundaries of and number of seats allocated to electoral districts within each local council area are reviewed by independent committees appointed by the minister responsible for local government. The committees are obliged to respect the overall number of seats assigned to each local council under national law, while ensuring a proportionate distribution of seats for each electoral district within the local authority, taking into account population changes and any other criteria determined by government. The work of these committees is usually guided by terms of reference established by the central government specifying criteria the committee should use in making any revisions to LEAs, which may, for example, guide the work of the committees around how big or small electoral districts should be in population terms, or specifying an indicative range of seats for most electoral districts [for an overview of the work of one such committee, see Murphy (2015)].

Eligibility to vote in local elections is the widest in the state. The franchise is more restricted for other types of elections. Only Irish citizens can vote in presidential elections and on constitutional referenda, only Irish and British citizens resident in Ireland can vote in *Dáil* elections, and only Irish and EU citizens resident in Ireland can vote in European Parliament elections. However, in the case of local elections, voting is not linked to citizenship – all residents may vote in local elections. This means that any non-Irish citizen (whether EU or non-EU) legally resident in Ireland who has reached the age of 18 can vote in local elections. The 2019 elections saw a small increase in the number of candidates running and candidates elected to local councils from ethnic minorities (Quinlivan 2020). Compulsory voting does not apply in Ireland.

An individual living in a LEA may either nominate themselves as a candidate, or they may be nominated by a proposer living in the area. Nominations are made during a specified period in advance of local elections, once the date of the election has been fixed. Nominations involve the completion of a short, simple form and, in the case of independent candidates, a small deposit (which is returned to the candidate if the candidate is elected or if the candidate is not elected but he/she has received a number of votes that exceeds one-quarter of the quota). Candidates are also subject to rules on spending limits for the duration of the campaign and on donations. The nomination process is considered to be relatively accessible. Indeed, the large number of candidates running in some recent elections sparked a relatively short-lived debate as to whether the arrangements for running in elections (including deposits) are too 'open'.

National law disqualifies certain categories of persons from serving as a local councilor. This includes members of the lower house of the national parliament (*Dáil*) and the upper house (*Seanad*), MEPs, members of the European Commission, senior local council employees and central government officials, judges, police officers, army personnel, and other specified public servants. Those convicted of specified offenses or undergoing prison terms exceeding 6 months are also disqualified. Before the 2004 local elections, it had been possible for national politicians to also hold a dual mandate as local councilor (the *cumul des mandats*). Earlier restrictions had been introduced in the 1990s providing that national ministers and junior ministers could not hold local council membership and that national politicians could not be elected mayor or deputy mayor of a local council. In 2003, legislation was adopted that abolished the dual mandate in its entirety from the 2004 local elections onward, making national politicians ineligible to serve on local councils while holding office as a member of the *Dáil* or *Seanad*. This practice was relatively common before the 2004 local elections. For example, Weeks and Quinlivan (2009) report that of the 226 members elected to the *Dáil* and *Seanad* in 2002, 138 of these were also members of a local council.

Where councilors cannot serve their full term of office (for example, through death, resignation, or election to national parliament), the vacant seat (known as a 'casual vacancy') is filled by co-option. Where a vacancy is caused by a councilor that is a member of a political party, national law provides that a nominee of that party is chosen to serve for the reminder of the five-year term until the next local election. In the case of nonparty or independent councilors, local arrangements apply, and in most cases independent councilors will have an opportunity to nominate an alternate or replacement to take his or her place should the need arise.

The electoral outcomes

Turnout

As Figure 7.1 indicates, average turnout for general elections is usually 10% greater than for local elections. Given the relative weakness of local government vis-à-vis its national counterpart, this is hardly a great surprise. The trend of turnout at the local level tends to match that at the national level, which was in decline from the 1960s to the 2000s, increased somewhat for a couple of elections, before declining again in the 2010s. The similarity of this pattern is particularly marked when it is considered that there have been a variety of other ballots held occasionally (albeit more frequently now) in conjunction with local elections. European Parliament elections have been held on the same day since 1999, with referendums also coinciding with local elections in 1999, 2004, and 2019.

While we might assume that fewer people vote in local elections because they are less important than the national arena, voters are less discerning when it comes to the type of local election in which they vote, primarily because they take place on the same day. The main source of variation is that between county and city councils, with turnout anything from 5 to 10% lower at the city level. This trend is not particular to Ireland, as turnout is usually higher in rural (our proxy for county councils) vis-à-vis urban areas. Dublin city council, a region comprising the central areas of Ireland's capital, experiences an even lower level of turnout, on average more than 15% lower than that for county councils.

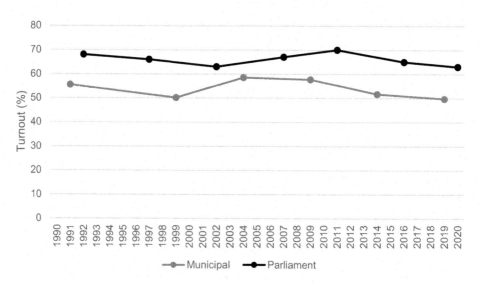

Figure 7.1 Voter turnout for local and general elections in Ireland, 1990–2020

Source: Weeks and Quinlivan (2009) and Quinlivan (2014, 2020)

Representation

The level of competition for local elections is slightly less than for general elections. The mean number of candidates per seat for the latter has been just under three in recent elections, while in local elections it is usually just more than two. In 2019, for example, 1,979 candidates contested the 949 local government seats, equivalent to 2.1 candidates per seat. The mean number of candidates varies across regions, with the most competitive tending to be urban areas (Cork had 2.6 candidates per seat for the 2019 local elections, compared to 4.6 for the 2020 general election) and the least competitive tending to be rural (the predominantly rural constituency of Carlow had 1.7 candidates per seat in 2019, but 2.9 in 2020 as a part of the greater Carlow-Kilkenny *Dáil* constituency). One constituency near the border with Northern Ireland had just six candidates for five seats in 2019, but there has not been an uncontested local election district since 1999. The level of competition can be related to the number of incumbents standing for office, with the ratio of incumbents to seats falling to just under 0.85:1 in recent years. Incumbents' reelection rates were approximately 70% in 2014, down from 78% in 2009 and 76% in 2004.

Historically, there were few differences in the proportions of women contesting local and general elections, both of which were relatively low from a comparative perspective. The adoption of gender quota legislation in 2012 widened this gap, however, as it does not apply to local elections. Gender quotas for *Dáil* elections are not mandatory, but if a party's national list of candidates does not comprise at least 30% of either gender, it loses 50% of its state funding. Consequently, in 2016, the first general election held since the introduction of gender quotas, the proportion of female candidates doubled from the previous election, up from 15% to 30%. In the local elections of 2019, the comparative increase was lower, with women comprising 31% of all candidates, up 6% from 2014.

One noticeable difference, however, is that women used to win a greater proportion of seats in local elections, certainly relative to the number of female candidates running. So, even though women comprised the same proportion of candidates at the 2020 *Dáil* election compared to the 2019 local elections, they won proportionally more seats in the latter, 24% compared to 22% in the *Dáil* election. This has been a consistent pattern for the past few decades, with female candidates more likely to win seats in local government than national parliament. It is not wholly clear why this is the case, but it could be that women face fewer obstacles in local elections with larger multiseat constituencies and smaller electorates. The historically homogeneous construct of Irish society means that minorities and persons of foreign origin are few and far between in local office. Although the new wave of immigration since the 1990s has led to a change in the population, it has not yet resulted in much of a change in political representation. In 2019, there were 53 of what Kavanagh calls 'New Irish' candidates (of a total of close to 2,000), eight of whom won council seats (0.8%). Female 'New Irish' candidates won almost twice as many votes as their male counterparts (Kavanagh 2019; Quinlivan 2020).

Party politicization

There are few differences between the national and local party systems, with the same parties contesting and controlling both levels of government. Traditionally, Ireland had a two-and-a-half-party system, in part a product of civil conflict in the 1920s (Weeks 2018). The two main parties, *Fianna Fáil* and *Fine Gael*, represented opposing sides in the conflict and have dominated politics in the Irish state from its inception in the 1920s until the so-called Great Recession of recent years.

The second-order nature of local elections has the effect that parties and independents outside of the two-and-a-half-party model tend to have greater levels of electoral success in local elections than in *Dáil* elections (see Table 7.1). Parties lose between one-quarter and one-half of their voters in local elections. Compared to the 2011 general election, the government parties of Fine Gael and Labour retained just 52% and 27%, respectively, of their voters in the 2014 local elections. The equivalent figures for the opposition parties were higher – 65% who voted Fianna Fáil in 2011 did so again in 2014, as did 74% of Sinn Féin voters and 59% of Green Party voters (Behaviour and Attitudes 2014). When local and European elections coincide, there is also evidence of split-ticket party voting, most likely a product of the significance of candidate vis-à-vis party in Irish elections.

Voters tend to treat local elections as a midterm contest on the performance of the national government. This gives local elections a national air, which in part is due to the weakness of local government in Ireland but also due to the fact that local elections are important to national parties given their significance as a recruiting ground for future parliamentarians. Approximately 75% of TDs (Teachtaí Dála) have usually been councilors before winning a seat in the *Dáil*; prior to the ban on holding multiple political offices (or dual mandate) introduced in 2004 (see previous discussion), the vast majority of TDs were also county or city councilors. This had the effect that there was no sense of a clear distinction between politicians as councilors and as parliamentarians. Most of the former aspire for a career as the latter, with local office merely a means to an end, while most of the latter fear the emergence of a rival from the former; this explains why TDs (prior to the 2004 ban) traditionally retained their council seat in order to keep a watchful eye on local competition. A consequence of the nationalization of local electoral politics is that parties take the candidate nomination process very seriously. While they want to maximize their representation on local councils, perhaps of greater concern is to produce councilors with a potential of winning *Dáil* seats in future national elections. For this reason, parties might be more inclined to give younger aspirants a nomination or also women, with an eye on the gender quotas in place for *Dáil* elections. One other factor linking the local and national party systems is the method of electing the national upper house of parliament, the *Seanad*. Forty-three (from a total membership of 60) senators in the *Seanad* are chosen by an electorate dominated by councilors, which means that local elections have national consequences.

Outside of the party system, independents are not an unusual presence in Irish elections, sometimes winning more seats to the *Dáil* than the combined total in most other Western parliaments (Weeks 2017). As they are a fairly heterogeneous grouping of candidates [see Weeks

Table 7.1 Local election results in Ireland, 2019

Party/grouping	% of councils where running	% of councils where represented	% of seats on local councils	% of (aggregate) votes in local elections	% of mayors/chairs affiliated with the party
Fine Gael	100.0	100.0	26.9	25.3	32.2
Fianna Fáil	100.0	100.0	29.4	26.9	29.0
Sinn Féin	100.0	80.6	8.5	9.5	3.2
Greens	77.4	54.8	5.2	5.6	9.7
Labour	83.9	67.7	6.0	5.7	0.0
Solidarity/People Before Profit Alliance	71.0	22.6	1.1	2.1	0.0
Social Democrats	51.6	32.2	2.0	2.3	0.0
Independents	100.0	100.0	20.2	20.1	25.8

Source: *Local Elections 2019: Results, Transfer of Votes and Statistics*. Dublin: Department of Housing, Planning and Local Government

(2009) for a detailed typology], most independents at the local and national levels are united in their primarily localistic appeal. This is facilitated in part by the electoral rules, where the threshold for ballot access is relatively low, multiseat constituencies using the single transferable vote are in operation, and there are relatively low numbers of voters per constituency. These features are particularly influential in local elections, where independents can win a seat in an LEA with fewer than 1,000 votes.

Discussion

Local elections in Ireland can certainly be regarded as second-order national elections. In part, this results from the relative weakness of Irish local government vis-à-vis the national government and from the tendency of government parties at the national level to fare poorly in local elections, with some voters using local elections as a means of registering disapproval of the government of the day (both referred to earlier). This is reinforced by a national media narrative that almost exclusively treats local elections as a barometer of national party strength. However, this depiction can be oversimplistic and one-dimensional. Local issues (which might relate to local government service areas or be issues considered especially salient within local communities) can also be influential in voter choices in local elections (Weeks & Quinlivan 2009). So too can the profile and background of local candidates and their involvement in local community organizations and civil society, which for many voters can often be more important than traditional party affiliation or preferences.

Nevertheless, it remains the case that due to a combination of weak institutional powers, overlapping party systems, and personalized politics, local government in Ireland is a subservient level of authority. Such is its weak executive position that local government could probably be more accurately described as local administration, a role that few major political actors have expressed any desire to reform.

Apart from differences between national and local elections, we also observe differences between local authorities themselves, in terms of turnout, level of electoral competition, party representation, and female representation in local government. In this respect, we may draw a broad distinction here between rural local authorities, on the one hand, and more urban and suburban local authorities on the other.

Notes

1 Examples have included improvements in procurement practices and shared contracting arrangements, increased digitization and use of online platforms, and individual initiatives in specific service areas.
2 The precise responsibilities of the directly elected mayor were still being determined at the time of writing, although a consultation document on the issue was published in 2019 (Department of Housing, Planning and Local Government 2019). It seems likely, however, that where the new dimension of a directly elected mayor is introduced, it could be expected to replace the traditional binary horizontal power relationship between council and chief executive with a new trilateral, council-mayor-chief executive set of relationships.

References

Behaviour and Attitudes. (2014). *Behaviour and Attitudes European Election Exit Poll*. Dublin: Behaviour and Attitudes.

Byrnes, J., & Dollery, B. (2002). Do economies of scale exist in Australian local government? A review of research evidence. *Urban Policy and Research*, 20(4), 391–414.

Callanan, M. (2018). *Local Government in the Republic of Ireland*. Dublin: Institute of Public Administration.

Callanan, M., & MacCarthaigh, M. (2008). Local government reforms in Ireland. In B. Dollery, J. Garcea & E. LeSage Jr (Eds.), *Local Government Reform: A Comparative Analysis of Advanced Anglo-American Countries* (pp. 104–132). Cheltenham: Edward Elgar.

Callanan, M., Murphy, R., & Quinlivan, A. (2014). The risks of intuition: Size, costs and economies of scale in local government. *The Economic and Social Review*, *45*(3), 371–403.

Collins, N., & Quinlivan, A. (2010). Multi-level governance. In J. Coakley & M. Gallagher (Eds.), *Politics in the Republic of Ireland* (5th edition) (pp. 359–380). London: Routledge.

Considine, J., & Reidy, T. (2015). Baby steps: The expanding financial base of local government in Ireland. *Administration*, *63*(2), 119–145

Department of Housing, Planning and Local Government. (2019). *Directly-Elected Mayors with Executive Functions: Detailed Policy Proposals*. Dublin: Department of Housing, Planning and Local Government.

Elcock, H., Fenwick, J., & McMillan, J. (2010). The reorganization addiction in local government: Unitary councils for England. *Public Money and Management*, *30*(6), 331–338.

Farrell, D., & Sinnott, R. (2018). The electoral system. In J. Coakley & M. Gallagher (Eds.), *Politics in the Republic of Ireland* (pp. 89–110). London: Routledge.

Fórsa Union. (2019). *More power to you: Democracy works if you let it*. Retrieved from www.forsa.ie/wp-content/uploads/2019/03/MorePowerReport.pdf.

Heinelt, H., Hlepas, N., Kuhlmann, S., & Swianiewicz, P. (2018). Local government systems: Grasping the institutional environment of mayors. In H. Heinelt, A. Magnier, M. Cabria & H. Reynaert (Eds.), *Political Leaders and Changing Local Democracy: The European Mayor* (pp. 19–78). London: Palgrave Macmillan.

Kavanagh, A. (2019). *The 2019 local elections: A geographer's overview*. Retrieved from https://adriankavanaghelections.org/category/new-irish/.

Ladner, A., Keuffer, N., & Baldersheim, H. (2016), Measuring local autonomy in 39 countries. *Regional and Federal Studies*, *26*(3), 321–357.

Laver, M. (2004). Analysing structures of party preference in electronic voting data. *Party Politics*, *10*(5), 521–541.

Local Government Efficiency Review Group. (2010). *Report of the Local Government Efficiency Review Group*. Dublin: The Stationery Office.

Local Government Efficiency Review Implementation Group. (2012). *Report to the Minister for the Environment, Community and Local Government*. Dublin: The Stationery Office.

Local Government Efficiency Review Implementation Group. (2013). *Further Report to the Minister for the Environment, Community and Local Government*. Dublin: The Stationery Office.

Loughlin, J. (2011). Ireland: Halting steps towards local democracy. In J. Loughlin, F. Hendriks & A. Lidström (Eds.), *The Oxford Handbook of Local and Regional Democracy in Europe* (pp. 48–67). Oxford: Oxford University Press.

Martin, L., & Hock Schiff, J. (2011). City-county consolidations: Promise versus performance. *State and Local Government Review*, *43*(2), 167–177

Murphy, G. (2015). 'Residents are fearful that their community will die around them': Some thoughts from inside the 2013 local electoral area boundary committee. *Irish Political Studies*, *30*(4), 555–574.

National Oversight & Audit Commission (NOAC) (2016). *Local Government Efficiency Review Reforms*. NOAC Report no. 5.

Quinlivan, A. (2014). The 2014 local elections in the Republic of Ireland. *Irish Political Studies*, *30*(1), 132–142.

Quinlivan, A. (2017). Reforming local government: Must it always be democracy versus efficiency? *Administration*, *65*(2), 109–126

Quinlivan, A. (2020). The 2019 local elections in the Republic of Ireland, *Irish Political Studies*, *35*(1), 46–60.

Reynolds, A., Reilly, B., Ellis, A. et al. (2005). *Electoral System Design: The New International IDEA Handbook*. Stockholm: International Institute for Democracy and Electoral Assistance.

Weeks, L. (2009). We don't like (to) party. A typology of Independents in Irish political life, 1922–2007. *Irish Political Studies*, *24*(1):1–27.

Weeks, L. (2017). *Independents in Irish Party Democracy*. Manchester: Manchester University Press.
Weeks, L. (2018). Parties and the party system. In J. Coakley & M. Gallagher (Eds.), *Politics in the Republic of Ireland* (pp. 130–156). London: Routledge.
Weeks, L., & Quinlivan, A. (2009). *All Politics is Local: A Guide to Local Elections in Ireland*. Cork: Collins Press.

8
United Kingdom
Diversity amid the Cinderella elections?

Alistair Clark and Alia Middleton

Brief overview of the local government system

The United Kingdom's regular classification as a unitary state misses the multilevel direction that politics has taken in recent decades. Decentralization of power has been asymmetric. Scotland, Wales, and Northern Ireland now have devolved institutions with power over local government. England remains the only part of the UK where the Westminster Parliament has direct authority over local government. There are some intermediate levels of government in England. A London-wide, directly elected mayor was created in 2000 as was a Greater London Assembly, which sits alongside the city's 32 borough councils. Elsewhere, reform of England's local and regional levels of government has been piecemeal. Moves to devolve powers to metro-mayors are ongoing. These mayors lead so-called combined authorities. These are groupings of geographically linked local governments, which are given a range of devolved powers agreed with the central government in specific policy areas.

In 1990, there were 540 councils (Ladner et al. 2019: 57). By December 2018, there were only 418, a reduction of 22.6% from 1990. In 2018, England had 353 local councils. Of these, 27 were county councils, 201 were district councils, and 125 were single-tier councils that included 32 London boroughs and 36 metropolitan boroughs (Sandford 2018). Scotland and Wales both have unitary local authorities, with 32 and 22, respectively. Northern Ireland has 11 district councils, reduced from 26 in a reform in 2015. In late 2018, there were 17,770 councilors in England, 1,224 in Scotland, 1,264 in Wales, and 462 in Northern Ireland. A constant process of council mergers in England means that there were approximately 500 fewer councilors in 2019 than five years earlier (Game 2019). An annual survey by the pollsters IPSOS-MORI consistently shows that councilors are more trusted than politicians generally or government ministers. In 2019, 41% trusted their local councilors, while only 17% trusted government ministers (IPSOS-MORI 2019).

In terms of vertical power relations, central-local relations are a regular theme of UK local government studies, with central government the dominant actor and local government the subordinate (e.g., Saunders 1982; Lowndes 1999). The UK is typically placed at the low end of local government autonomy indices, albeit with variations in different classifications (Ladner & Keuffer 2018; Ladner et al. 2019). Two main themes emerge. Hesse and Sharpe (1991) identify an Anglo group of countries, including the UK and those originating from the Westminster model, where local government has weak legal, constitutional, and political status but is important in delivering public services. Heinelt et al. (2018) also place England in an Anglo-Saxon category of local government. If we use the same index but extend the analysis, this classification rests on the second theme, that the UK can be catalogued differently on different power dimensions. England, Heinelt et al. (2018) indicate, can be categorized as having medium autonomy in relation to municipal spending and, curiously, medium tax autonomy, but only low autonomy on the more institutional and political dimensions of their index. Similarly, Ladner et al. (2019) suggest that, in terms of financial transfers, local government in Britain has low autonomy, although it has medium autonomy on expenditures.

In terms of horizontal power relations, UK councils traditionally were committee based. This changed with the Local Government Act 2000, which forced English councils to choose between new leadership models: 83% chose a cabinet and leader model, which Wollmann (2012: 50) characterizes as 'quasi-parliamentarism', while 14% of smaller councils opted for a revised committee system. The remaining 11 councils (3%) adopted an elected mayor (Lowndes & Leach 2004). The Localism Act 2011 provided for the return to a committee system, although take-up for that was slow. Three councils that opted for directly elected mayors have since moved away from that model, while another three have now adopted such positions (Sandford 2019a).

Local elections and their place in the multilevel system

Local elections are generally held on the first Thursday in May. In Scotland, Wales, Northern Ireland, and London, all seats on all local councils are elected on the same day. While Scotland, Wales, and Northern Ireland are currently on a five-year cycle, in most of England there is a four-year cycle of local elections.[1] Outside London, election timing in England is messy and confusing. A total of 26 county councils have whole council elections every four years, as do 131 district councils and 38 unitary authorities. However, 33 metropolitan district councils elect a one-third of their seats annually, missing every fourth year, as do 54 district councils and 17 unitary authorities. Seven district councils elect by halves every two years (Cabinet Office 2019). Local elections are run administratively by the councils, although their terms of office are determined by parliament. An Electoral Management Board in Scotland and the Electoral Office for Northern Ireland have a role in coordinating and directing the conduct of local elections. England and Wales have no equivalent, and the UK Electoral Commission only has advisory powers over local elections.

Since 2007, Scottish practice has been to hold stand-alone local elections after problems arose with combined local and Scottish parliament elections that year. Wales has also held stand-alone council elections from 2008 onward. Northern Irish and English local elections have, however, been run concurrently with parliamentary or European elections (e.g., Rallings & Thrasher 2005). In both countries, the 2014 local elections were explicitly put back from the start of May to later in the month so that they could be held alongside European Parliament elections. Local elections are typically seen through the lens of national and devolved party politics in each of the UK's four countries. This is even more the case when local elections are held concurrently with those for a higher order institution. There is little coverage of local elections, a situation not helped by the virtual withering away of local newspaper coverage.

In most councils, council leaders are indirectly elected by the full council. While some of the 11 directly elected mayoralties created by the 2000 act were won by mainstream parties, they were often noteworthy because independents and small parties had successfully challenged for the position (Copus 2013). Memorably, one local authority, Hartlepool, elected its local football mascot, who was a political novice, to the post in 2002. He held the position for three successive terms before standing down. Three councils at the forefront of this mayoral initiative, Hartlepool, Stoke-on-Trent, and Torbay, all subsequently voted to abolish the position. Further local referendums were held between 2010 and 2012 in 12 major English cities asking whether voters wanted a directly elected mayor; only three voted in favor – Leicester, Liverpool, and Bristol (Sandford 2019a). Mayoral elections are normally run concurrently with council elections. On very rare occasions they produce a different partisan outcome.

Eight directly elected, so-called metro-mayors have also been elected in England to represent city regions or combined authorities, as part of government moves to devolve power. As of early 2020, four of these posts were held by the Conservatives and four by Labour. Confusingly, they sometimes overlap with the earlier round of directly elected mayors. For example, Liverpool has both an elected mayor and a metro-mayor for the Liverpool city region (Sandford 2019a).

No legal powers exist to permit either councilors or full councils to be recalled.

Features of the electoral system

Different local franchises exist. In England and Northern Ireland, those over 18 who had British, Irish, Commonwealth, or, until the UK left the EU, EU citizenship were entitled to vote. Electors could register in two local authority areas, for example, if they were a student or owned property in different council areas. This differs from the parliamentary franchise, where EU citizens did not have the vote, and voters could only vote once. Scotland and Wales have innovated with the local franchise. This was extended to those 16 and 17 years old in Scotland in 2015 and Wales in 2019. The rationale was to widen the franchise to young people. As yet, however, there have been no studies of the impact of this on local elections. Both countries have also extended the right to vote in local elections to foreign nationals who are legally resident in the country. Voting is not compulsory. There is no overseas voting for local elections.

There is wide variation in the size of populations that councils cover. In mid-2018, Birmingham city council covered a population of around 1.1 million, while the smallest councils covered fewer than 10,000 inhabitants. The average council covered a population of around 177,000.[2] This is large by European standards. Changes to council boundaries have been the result of 'historical contingency' and 'administrative convenience' (Sandford 2019b: 13). Changes historically have resulted from wider reviews into local government. Three rounds of review have been conducted since the 1990s, with recent reviews conducted on an ad hoc basis for individual cases. The trend is toward larger, not smaller, councils (Sandford 2019b: 9–12).

All councils are divided internally into electoral wards. Independent Local Government Boundary Commissions in England, Northern Ireland, Scotland, and Wales carry out periodic reviews of ward boundaries, which determine the number of seats per council.[3] Major cities like Leeds, Liverpool, and Manchester have more than 90 seats, while the remote Isles of Scilly has only 16. The average number of seats on English councils holding elections in 2019 was 47.[4] Around 8,500 seats were contested in the elections.[5]

Variation exists in the type of electoral system. At the time of writing, England and Wales use the single-member plurality, or first past the post (FPTP), system.[6] Scotland and Northern Ireland both use the single transferable vote (STV), with Scotland having moved from FPTP to STV in 2007 (Clark & Bennie 2008). Additionally, the small number of directly elected mayors are elected by supplementary vote (SV). FPTP and SV are both plurality or majoritarian, while STV falls under IDEA's proportional representation category (Reynolds et al. 2005).

Under FPTP and SV, the district magnitude (DM) is 1, meaning that voters are voting for a single representative. STV, however, utilizes multimember wards. Scotland mainly uses either three- or four-member wards, with 54% of wards electing three councilors and the remainder electing four.[7] District magnitude in Northern Ireland ranges between five and seven councilors per ward, with 42.5% of wards electing five councilors, 37.5% electing six, and 20% electing seven.

With FPTP, candidates need only achieve a plurality of votes. With SV, if no candidate achieves 50% of valid votes cast in the first round, all but the first two candidates are eliminated and voters' second and lower preferences are redistributed until one candidate achieves 50% + 1. To be elected under STV, candidates have to achieve a Droop quota, that is, [(number of valid votes cast)/(number of seats to be filled + 1)] + 1. If there are four seats to be filled, the quota is 20% of the valid vote plus one. If no candidate meets quota on the first round of counting, the candidate with the least first preferences is eliminated and their voters' lower preferences are redistributed. This continues until all seats are allocated.

An alternative classification is by ballot structure. Voters under FPTP have a categorical ballot and are required simply to place an 'X' beside the candidate of their choice. With STV and SV, however, the ballot structure is preferential, with voters required to rank as many preferences (1, 2, 3, etc.) as they wish. Where parties offer more than one candidate under STV, electors can choose between both parties and individual candidates and choose to split their preferences should they wish, thereby weakening party control. SV is less permissive. Voters only have a choice of individual party candidates, with preferences transferred between, not within, party options.

Seat distribution under FPTP depends on winning a plurality of votes. Under SV for mayors, preference transfers from other candidates come into play, rewarding candidates who have majority appeal. Preference transfers play a different role under STV and have led to smaller parties such as the Greens being elected to Scottish councils. Nonetheless, it remains crucial to do well in first preferences in order to benefit from transfers and achieve the quota necessary to be elected. In Northern Ireland, preference transfers predominantly remain within the traditional cultural and political blocs.

To contest local elections is straightforward. There is no deposit, candidates need only 10 supporting signatures, and it is free to submit a nomination. Candidates must be over 18, a British, Commonwealth, or (pre-Brexit) an EU citizen and be registered to vote in the council area or have another link to it. There are some disqualifications, which are not particularly onerous (Electoral Commission 2019). Efforts are beginning to be made to address barriers. The Scottish government has introduced a fund to encourage disabled candidates to stand for local office and has proposed allowing residents, not only citizens, to contest local elections. To take up their post, councilors must be sworn in and agree to abide by a code of conduct.

The electoral outcomes

Of the UK's four nations, the highest turnout figures for local elections are recorded in Northern Ireland, largely because of the history of ethnic conflict there. In 2014, both Northern Ireland and England went to the polls on the same day for local elections held concurrently with European elections, but turnout was 16% lower in England at 35.4%[8] compared to 51.3% in Northern Ireland. England consistently records the lowest turnouts for local elections in the United Kingdom, with 30.6% in the 2012 wave and only 32% in 2019.

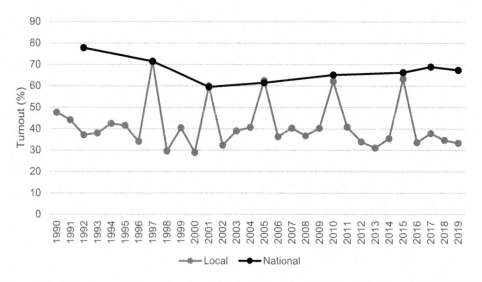

Figure 8.1 Voter turnout for national and local elections in the United Kingdom, 1990–2019

Clear variations in turnout can be observed by comparing local elections with national contests held simultaneously. Since 1990, Figure 8.1 shows that only in the years when national and local elections were held on the same day, between 1997 and 2015, does local election turnout come close to national election turnout. Otherwise, local election turnout has remained stubbornly low. In both 1992 and 2017, local elections took place in the same year as the national elections, albeit on different dates within a month of one another. Here, local turnout was markedly lower than when both contests took place on the same day. This provides some evidence in support of first- and second-order effects (Heath et al. 1999), with turnout lower in local elections than in national contests.

Figure 8.2 demonstrates that turnout in the most recent waves of local elections is low, even when correlating turnout with the size of the electorate. Although the relationship between electorate size and turnout is marginally negative, it is close to zero (Person's correlation coefficients = −.06) and not statistically significant.

A continuing, albeit declining feature of local elections are uncontested seats, where competition for the standing candidate is absent.[9] However, the electoral system in use may reduce noncompetition. Since the local electoral system changed in Scotland, uncontested seats have been reduced substantially to single figures and were eliminated entirely in 2007 and 2012; in Northern Ireland (which also uses STV), uncontested seats were eliminated in 2014.

The UK has historically had a two-party system, with national power shifting over the twentieth century between the Conservatives and Labour. However, since 2005, there has been considerable volatility, resulting in the growth of support for smaller parties and regional parties in national elections. Alongside the statewide British parties, Scotland and Wales each have non-statewide parties [the Scottish National Party (SNP) and Plaid Cymru, respectively], and Northern Ireland has a largely separate party system (Clark 2018).

The statewide parties are heavily represented in local elections, assisted by the FPTP electoral system in England and Wales, which is also utilized for UK parliamentary elections, ensuring

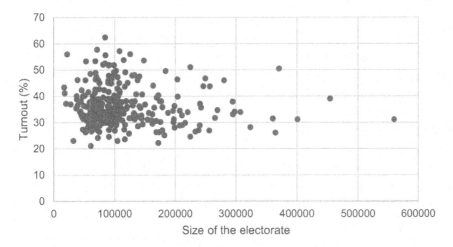

Figure 8.2 Voter turnout by size of the electorate in 2017 (Scotland and Wales) and in 2019 (England and Northern Ireland)

Note: R^2 linear = 0.004

that there is a local presence for parties in most areas (see Table 8.1). The Liberal Democrats have tended to prioritize local 'community politics' as a step toward national representation (Cutts 2006), with some success. However, whereas national parties typically stand in as many seats as possible in parliamentary elections, in local elections, there is a tendency to be more selective, partly because of weak organization. In May 2019, for example, the Liberal Democrats offered candidates for just over half of the council seats in England up for election, yet for the parliamentary election in December 2019 they stood for over 90% of Westminster seats. Northern Ireland has a distinctive party system. Northern Irish parties typically stand in all 11 council areas, incentivized by the multimember STV wards. In both Scotland and Wales, the presence of the SNP and Plaid Cymru enhances electoral choice.

A key feature of local elections in England, however, is the presence of independent candidates, resident associations, and hyperlocal political groupings. Despite predictions that the local government reforms of the 1970s would eradicate independent candidates, they are part of an upward trend in English local elections (Copus et al. 2009; Rallings et al. 2005; Tighe & Bounds 2019). Their appeal lies in their attention to local matters and issues – a key and important feature of what voters in the UK want from local representatives. Their relative success has also been enhanced by not being associated with national agendas or political issues. After the 2019 English council elections, over 1,000 councilors (equivalent to 11.5%) were from resident associations or were otherwise independent. Independent candidates differ elsewhere in the United Kingdom with respect to their success. In the 2017 Welsh local elections, independent candidates received over 22.5% of the vote, second only to Labour, although their share of the vote had declined marginally since the 2014 contest. In Scotland, independent candidates received just over 10% of first preference votes, again. In Northern Ireland, independent candidates represented just 5% of councilors in 2019.

Table 8.1 Party politicization in United Kingdom local elections in 2017 (Scotland and Wales) and 2019 (England and Northern Ireland)

	% of municipalities where running	% of municipalities where represented	% of seats on local councils	% of (aggregate) votes in local elections
England				
Conservatives	96.0	95.2	42.0	31.4
Labour	77.0	79.0	24.0	26.6
Liberal Democrats	53.0	75.4	16.0	16.8
Green Party	30.0	39.5	3.0	9.2
UKIP	16.0	11.3	0.0	4.5
Independents and nonnational (local) lists	99.2	74.2	11.5	11.4
Northern Ireland				
Democratic Unionist Party	100.0	100.0	26.0	24.1
Sinn Fein	100.0	99.1	23.0	23.2
Ulster Unionist Party	100.0	100.0	16.0	14.1
SDLP	100.0	100.0	13.0	12.0
Alliance	91.0	99.1	11.0	11.5
Independents and nonnational (local) lists	100.0	100.0	10.0	11.0
Scotland				
Conservatives	96.9	93.8	22.0	25.3
Labour	90.6	81.3	21.0	20.2
Liberal Democrats	78.1	46.9	5.0	6.8
Scottish National Party	93.8	96.9	35.0	32.3
Green	87.5	21.9	1.0	6.8
Independents and nonnational (local) lists	100.0	71.9	16.0	10.5
Wales				
Conservatives	100.0	36.4	15.0	18.8
Labour	100.0	100.0	38.0	30.4
Liberal Democrats	90.9	27.3	5.0	6.8
Plaid Cymru	95.5	27.3	16.0	16.5
Green	81.8	4.5	0.1	1.3
Independents and nonnational (local) lists	100.0	100.0	26.0	26.1

Gender representation in local politics is often patchy and reflects patterns of national representation (see Table 8.2). Research by the Fawcett Society (2019) demonstrates that 96% of English councils are male-dominated, and movement to improve gender representation is slow. In England, 35% of councilors elected in 2019 were female, comparable to the 34% of female MPs elected in the national election of the same year. The representation of female candidates in direct mayoral elections has been irregular, enhanced by nonsimultaneous elections. In 2013, for example, mayoral elections in Doncaster and North Tyneside were both won by female candidates, yet in 2019 all winners of the six mayoral contests taking place were male. Of the councilors elected in Scotland in 2017, 26% were female with all parties advancing female representation, apart from the Scottish Conservatives who saw a 6% decrease in gender representation, below all other major parties.[10] Northern Ireland has comparatively lower levels of gender equality in politics at all levels. Descriptive representation of women in Northern Irish politics has been restricted by a concentration on ethnonational politics (Thomson 2019). In the 2019 local elections, the proportion of female candidates increased overall to 28%, despite the Democratic Unionist Party having fewer female candidates. For those councilors elected in 2019, 26% were female, an increase of 2% over 2014. The SDLP, Alliance Party, and Greens were the only parties to come close to gender parity in the councilors elected.

There is little representation of minorities at the local level, with 96% of councilors in England describing themselves as white (Local Government Association 2019). Some limited progress in representation has been made since 2014, with the proportion of minorities represented at the local level increasing. There are, however, some large disparities between black and minority ethnic (BAME) representation on councils and in the local population: For example, 11.7% of the members of the City of Westminster Council were from a minority background versus 38.8% of the population the council covers.[11] There are some councils with high proportions of BAME councilors – notably Birmingham, where one-third of the council is from minority backgrounds. In Scotland and Wales, 2% and 1.9% of councilors are from non-white backgrounds, respectively.[12]

Additional controversies

Local government and elections continue to be subordinate to the national political picture and needs. Local elections tend to be Cinderella affairs, of interest mainly as midterm insights into the state of the main parties. This approach, however, belies a diversity that exists in UK local elections. This diversity involves electoral systems, patterns of party competition, nonpartisan candidates, and new forms of mayoralties for the UK. There are nonetheless similarities between them. Local turnout tends to be the lowest for any institutional level, for example, while there are difficulties with descriptive representation in all four constituent countries' local governments.

Table 8.2 Percentage of female councilors across the United Kingdom

Election year	2012	2013	2014	2015	2016	2017	2018	2019
England	32	27	35	32	37	28	38	35
Scotland	24					29		
Wales	26					28		
Northern Ireland			25					26

One recent controversy has seen local elections become central to debates about electoral integrity. At the start of 2020, Northern Ireland was the only part of the United Kingdom that required voters to produce identification when casting a vote. However, English local elections have provided a testing ground for the wider potential introduction of identification (ID) requirements since 2018. The claim has been that this would stamp out very rare incidences of electoral fraud. To ask voters to supply identification before voting to prevent fraud has been controversial, as it is seen as a solution to a nonexistent problem (James & Clark 2020). Pilot ID trials were conducted in five councils in 2018 and extended to ten areas during the 2019 English local elections, with approximately 750 people unable to cast their vote. There are concerns that the reforms would disproportionately affect certain sections of the community, with resultant partisan effects.[13]

Most of the research on local elections has been based on the painstaking collection of aggregate-level data (ward-level or council-level) from councils themselves (e.g., Rallings et al. 2005). There is no individual-level local election study in the UK. This means that individual local voting behavior remains a major lacuna in UK political science, with much research required to understand this better vis-à-vis local government.

Debates on electoral reform at the local level have been sporadic. The tendency, however, has been for diversity and a move away from one model. Scotland underwent countrywide local electoral reform in 2007, while Wales is tentatively trying to introduce STV. Electoral reformers have identified local government as a key area to push their aims in England.[14] However, among the Britain-wide parties, there appears to be little appetite to introduce such reforms. The Conservative Party continues to push for directly elected mayors and for metro-mayors leading combined authorities.[15] The ultimate destination of such piecemeal reform in England is unclear. It looks to many like divide and rule being imposed on councils from the central government. Local government will, however, continue to provide some diversity, not only in electoral and institutional reform but also in the nonpartisan element that continues to survive in local elections.

Notes

1. The most recent Scottish and NI local elections were in 2017 and 2019, respectively.
2. Data are from the Office for National Statistics (2020). *Estimates of the population for the UK, England and Wales, Scotland and Northern Ireland* at www.ons.gov.uk/peoplepopulationandcommunity/populationandmigration/populationestimates/datasets/populationestimatesforukenglandandwalesscotlandandnorthernireland (8/1/2020).
3. District Electoral Areas Review in Northern Ireland. In late 2019, Scotland proposed moving to rolling reviews.
4. Author's calculations,
5. *Daily Telegraph* (2019). 'Local Elections 2019: How many councils are taking part and when will we know the results?' www.telegraph.co.uk/politics/2019/05/02/local-elections-2019-candidates-results/ (8/1/2020).
6. A Welsh government bill [the Local Government and Elections (Wales) Bill] introduced to the Welsh Assembly in late 2019, however, proposed giving local authorities the ability to choose whether they would prefer to adopt STV.
7. Moves were subsequently made to permit remote island communities to elect only one councilor, while in late 2019 the Scottish government proposed permitting DMs of either two or five in addition to the more widely used three and four.
8. Average across London borough elections, county councils, metropolitan councils, and district councils.
9. House of Commons Library (2019). *Uncontested Elections: Where and Why do they Take Place?* https://commonslibrary.parliament.uk/insights/uncontested-elections-where-and-why-do-they-take-place/ (8/1/2020).

10 Duncan, P and Busby, M. (2019). 'UK Elects Record Number of Female MPs', *The Guardian*, 13th December, www.theguardian.com/politics/2019/dec/13/uk-elects-record-number-of-female-mps (8/1/2020).
11 Operation Black Vote (2019). *Local councils failing BAME communities: How's yours performing?* www.obv.org.uk/news-blogs/local-councils-failing-bame-communitieshows-yours-performing (8/1/2020).
12 Welsh Government (2018). *Local Government Candidates Survey 2017*, https://gov.wales/local-government-candidates-survey-2017 (8/1/2020); Improvement Service (2018). *Scotland's Councillors 2017–22* at www.improvementservice.org.uk/documents/research/scotlands-councillors-2017-22.pdf (12/1/2020).
13 Palese, M. (2019). 'Five things we have learnt about England's voter ID trials in the 2019 local elections', *LSE British Politics and Policy Blog*, https://blogs.lse.ac.uk/politicsandpolicy/five-things-we-have-learnt-about-englands-voter-id-trials-in-the-2019-local-elections/ (20/2/2020).
14 Mortimer, J. (2019). *Local elections: How voters in England were cheated by a broken voting system*, Electoral Reform Society, www.electoral-reform.org.uk/local-elections-how-voters-in-england-were-cheated-by-a-broken-voting-system/ (10/1/2020).
15. In late-2021, the Conservative government were attempting to replace the Mayoral electoral systems using SV, described above, with first-past-the-post in a controversial Elections Bill which also sought to introduce photographic voter ID more widely.

References

Cabinet Office (2019). Election timetable in England, https://assets.publishing.service.gov.uk/government/uploads/system/uploads/attachment_data/file/792138/Election_Timetable_in_England_2019.pdf [5/12/2019].

Clark, A. (2018). *Political Parties in the UK* (2nd edition). London: Palgrave Macmillan.

Clark, A., & Bennie, L. (2008). Electoral reform and party adaptation: The introduction of the single transferable vote in Scotland. *Political Quarterly*, 79(2), 241–251.

Copus, C. (2013). *Leading the Localities: Executive Mayors in English Local Governance*. Manchester: Manchester University Press.

Copus, C., Clark, A., Reynaert, H., & Steyvers, K. (2009). Minor party and independent politics beyond the mainstream: Fluctuating fortunes but a permanent presence. *Parliamentary Affairs*, 62(1), 4–18.

Cutts, D. (2006). 'Where we work we win': A case study of local liberal democrat campaigning. *Journal of Elections, Public Opinion and Parties*, 16(3), 221–242.

Electoral Commission (2019). *Local Elections in England and Wales: Guidance for Candidates and Agents Part 1*. London: Electoral Commission.

Fawcett Society (2019). New data reveals that women's representation in local government "at a standstill", www.fawcettsociety.org.uk/news/new-fawcett-data-reveals-that-womens-representation-in-local-government-at-a-standstill

Game, C. (2019). Local elections 2019: Gone missing – 500 councillors. *Democratic Audit*, www.democraticaudit.com/2019/05/02/local-elections-2019-gone-missing-500-councillors/ [27/11/2019].

Heath, A., McLean, I., Taylor, B., & Curtice, J. (1999). Between first and second-order: A comparison of voting behavior in European and local elections in Britain. *European Journal of Political Research*, 35(3), 389–414.

Heinelt, H., Hlepas, N., Kuhlmann, S., & Swianiewicz, P. (2018). Local government systems: Grasping the institutional environment of mayors. In H. Heinelt, A. Magnier, M. Cabria & H. Reynaert (Eds.), *Political Leaders and Changing Local Democracy: The European Mayor* (pp. 19–78). London: Palgrave Macmillan.

Hesse, J. J., & Sharpe, L. J. (1991). Local government in international perspective: Some comparative observations. In J. J. Hesse & L. J. Sharpe (Eds.), *Local Government and Urban Affairs in International Perspective. Analyses of Twenty Western Industrialised Countries* (pp. 603–621). Baden-Baden: Nomos.

IPSOS-MORI (2019). *IPSOS-MORI Veracity Index 2019: Trust in Professions Survey*. London: IPSOS-MORI.

James, T., & Clark, A. (2020). Electoral integrity, voter fraud and voter id in polling stations: Lessons from English local elections. *Policy Studies*, 41(2/3), 190–209.

Ladner, A., & Keuffer, N. (2018). Creating an index of local autonomy – theoretical, conceptual and empirical issues. *Regional and Federal Studies, 31*(2), 209–234.

Ladner, A, Keuffer, N., Baldersheim, H., Hlepas, N., Swianiewicz, P., Steyvers, K., & Navarro, C. (2019). *Patterns of Local Autonomy in Europe*. London: Palgrave Macmillan.

Local Government Association (2019). *National Census of Local Authority Councillors 2018*. London: Local Government Association.

Lowndes, V. (1999). Rebuilding trust in central-local relations: Policy or passion? *Local Government Studies, 25*(4), 116–136.

Lowndes, V., & Leach, S. (2004). Understanding local political leadership: Constitutions, contexts and capabilities. *Local Government Studies, 30*(4), 557–575.

Rallings, C., & Thrasher, M. (2005). Not all 'second-order' contests are the same: Turnout and party choice at the concurrent 2004 local and European parliament elections in England. *British Journal of Politics and International Relations, 7*, 584–597.

Rallings, C., Thrasher, M., & Denver, D. (2005). Trends in local elections in Britain, 1975–2003. *Local Government Studies, 31*(4), 393–413.

Reynolds, A., Reilly, B., & Ellis, A. (2005). *Electoral System Design: The New International IDEA Handbook*. Stockholm: International IDEA.

Sandford, M. (2018). *Local Government in England: Structures*. London: House of Commons Briefing Paper 07104.

Sandford, M. (2019a). *Directly Elected Mayors*. London: House of Commons Briefing Paper 05000.

Sandford, M. (2019b). *Where Do You Draw the Line? Local Administrative Boundaries in England*. London: House of Commons Briefing Paper 08619.

Saunders, P. (1982). Why study central-local relations? *Local Government Studies, 8*(2), 55–66.

Thomson, J. (2019). Feminising politics, politicizing feminism? Women in post-conflict Northern Irish politics. *British Politics, 14*(1), 181–197.

Tighe, C., & Bounds, A. (2019). Britain's independent councillors face challenges of success. *Financial Times*, May 14th, www.ft.com/content/62c2dc50-72af-11e9-bf5c-6eeb837566c5 [9/10/20].

Wollmann, H. (2012). Local government reforms in (seven) European countries: Between convergent and divergent, conflicting and complementary developments. *Local Government Studies, 38*(1), 41–70.

Part 4
The Rhinelandic States

9
Austria
Strong participation across federal diversity

Philipp Umek

Institutions of local government in Austria

The federal Republic of Austria has a long-standing tradition of local autonomy. Local government is organized in small municipalities (*Gemeinden*), most of them with fewer than 2,500 inhabitants. The local tier was first established by a provisional law in 1849 (Stelzer 2011: 148) in the wake of the March Revolution of 1848. The arrangement was adopted by the First Republic of Austria in 1919. At that time, there were over 4,000 municipalities. After a series of mergers in the 1960s, their number dropped to 2,353 across nine federal states (*Bundesländer*) in the reference year of 1990. Since then, the number of municipalities has fallen further. A municipality reform in Styria in 2015 cut its number from 539 to just 287 municipalities. The reform was opposed by small municipalities out of fear of being underrepresented and marginalized in the enlarged local councils. Austrian municipalities remain small: about 65% of them have 2,500 or fewer residents. Currently, there are 2,095 municipalities in Austria, of which 15 are statutory cities that also take on the administrative tasks of a subregional district (*Bezirk*). Moreover, the federal capital of Vienna is a hybrid local and regional government unit. Vienna is also a *Land*, and the municipal council assumes the functions of a regional parliament, with the mayor also being the Land governor (*Landeshauptmann*). Thus, municipal elections in Vienna are at the same time regional elections, complemented by additional city district elections that are comparable to the local elections in the rest of Austria.

Intergovernmental relations are determined by the federal constitution and by regional laws. The autonomous competences of the municipalities cover local spatial planning, schools, road construction and maintenance, culture, local social services, and administration of the municipal finances. The largest financial expenditure is general services (30%), followed by education and sports (16%), representation and general administration, social welfare (11% each), roads and transport (8%), and health care (7%). In these policy areas, the decision-making bodies of municipalities are not bound by other state authorities, except for legal supervision. Although mayors are in principle the local executive branch, they also exercise delegated competences in additional areas, where they are bound by the instructions of Länder authorities. Austria is characterized by great institutional depth, but rather low effective political discretion and policy autonomy (Ladner et al. 2019). OECD indicators of local fiscal autonomy reveal low (and slightly declining) autonomy, while other studies rank Austria from near average (Lane & Ersson 1999; Vetter et al. 2016) to high (Goldsmith & Page 2010; Ladner et al. 2016; Hooghe & Marks 2001) in terms of local autonomy among European and OECD countries. Intergovernmental relations correspond to the Northern and Middle European type (Hesse & Sharpe 1991) with the greatest degree of local autonomy.

Intragovernmental relations are determined by the type of mayoral elections. The gradual introduction of direct mayoral elections in six Länder,[1] starting in 1991, elevated mayors to a strong executive position, while mayors who are not directly elected are characterized as collegial leaders (Mouritzen & Svara 2002). An executive board (*Gemeindevorstand*), headed by the mayor and assisted by the deputy mayor(s) and a number of additional council members, prepares and/or executes the decisions of the municipal council. In line with a consociational political tradition in Austria, the major parties are proportionally represented (d'Hondt) and involved in the decision-making process by the local executive board, where each list appoints the member(s) for the board.

Cooperation between municipalities and cities is optional and typically initiated directly by mayors. European partnerships have existed for many years, and, according to the Austrian Association of Municipalities (*Gemeindebund*),[2] 900 municipalities claim a formal partnership or cooperation with other European municipalities. This association, along with the Association of Cities (*Städtebund*),[3] promotes cooperation, supports municipalities, and represents their interests vis-à-vis the federal government. A study by the Association of Municipalities found that mayors enjoy by far the most trust among politicians in Austria.[4]

Local elections: intersecting electoral cycles and ease of voting

Elections and referenda are always held on Sundays in Austria. Due to the federal structure, not a single year goes by without some type of election being held somewhere in Austria. It is not unusual to have four or more elections coming up in any one year. In addition to presidential elections (every six years), national parliamentary elections (*Nationalrat*, every five years), and European Parliament elections (five years), every Land holds elections for the regional parliament (*Landtag*, five to six years) and local councils (five to six years).[5] Local offices are mostly on five-year terms, except for Carinthia, Upper Austria, and Tyrol, where terms last six years.

Until 2009, three Länder traditionally held concurrent regional and local elections: Salzburg, Upper Austria, and Vienna. Carinthia held simultaneous elections in 2009 because the regional (five years) and the local-term cycles (six years) intersected that year. After Salzburg called a snap election in 2009 in the wake of a financial scandal involving the regional government, only Upper Austria and Vienna remain on the same election cycle. Notably, Vienna is a special case of hybrid regional and local elections (the 100 members of the Vienna city council are also members of the regional parliament, and the mayor of Vienna is also the governor of the Land). Vienna holds concurrent district elections (*Bezirksvertretungswahlen*) at the sublocal tier to compensate for the larger organizational structure. Most Land capitals hold local elections on the same day as the rest of the municipalities, but some large cities have chosen separate dates: Graz (the capital city of Styria and second most populous city in Austria) and Innsbruck (capital of Tyrol). In Lower Austria, the capital city of Sankt Pölten and other statutory cities (Krems an der Donau, Waidhofen an der Ybbs) also have separate election dates.

All citizens are automatically enrolled on the electoral register. Eligible voters receive postal messages informing them of administrative details for the upcoming elections and a request form for voting by postal ballot. The mailer gives the location and opening hours of one's assigned polling station. The administrative tasks for elections at all levels are handled by a local electoral authority (*Wahlbehörde*) created by the municipalities, with the mayor as the chairman (*Wahlleiter*) overseeing the process. The municipal council sets the electoral precincts (*Wahlsprengel*) and their respective opening hours in such a way that an average number of 70 voters per hour in each precinct will not be exceeded. These precincts are for administrative purposes only and do not constitute electoral districts. A major electoral reform at the federal level in 2007 brought about some changes to the local tier in Austria. The active voting age was lowered from 18 to 16 years, and the minimum age for candidacy was lowered from 19 to 18 years (only candidates for federal president must be at least 35 years old). The option of postal voting was expanded to local elections and operates via the request for voting cards (*Wahlkarten*). These voting cards may be sent in by post (thus enabling early voting) or handed in at a polling station by a trusted person on election day. In Burgenland, Carinthia, and Styria, early voting[6] in local elections has been allowed since 2005 on one assigned day before the regular election date.

Direct mayoral elections were introduced in six Länder between 1991 (Carinthia) and 2000 (Vorarlberg). The reasons given for introducing direct mayoral elections in Austria were similar to those in other European countries: to cultivate a livelier political competition (through personalization of local elections) and to increase the accountability and transparency of decisions (Caciagli 2013). However, this created a risk of 'divided loyalties' (Fallend et al. 2006) for the mayors between representing the party and representing the specific interests of the municipalities. Mayoral elections are held concurrently with local council elections, using separate ballot papers. Only Vorarlberg used a single ballot paper for both elections until 2020, which was heavily criticized by the opposition as it lacked the character of two separate elections for council and mayor (thus degrading council elections to secondary status and benefiting the dominant ÖVP). In Länder with direct mayoral elections, a candidate for mayor has to be ranked first on a council election list and that list must win at least one seat. Three Länder abstain from direct mayoral elections: Lower Austria and Styria (both dominated by the ÖVP at local level) and Vienna (dominated by the SPÖ). Here the local council elects the mayor from among its members by simple majority. Lower Austria employs a liberal system of preferential voting that somewhat compensates for the lack of direct elections (Karlhofer & Pallaver 2013b: 15). A recall of directly elected mayors is possible by means of a referendum, after the municipal council has decided on it by a two-thirds supermajority (Caciagli 2013: 236). In Tyrol, mayors and the municipal council can be recalled by the regional government if the council is 'permanently incapable of taking decisions'.[7] After a mayor has been voted out of office, the local council is newly elected for the rest of the term until the next regular election date.[8]

Local electoral system(s): common features and unique characteristics

The local electoral systems vary greatly. Cumulative cleavage structures in Austria manifested themselves early on in the two traditionally dominant parties, the *Österreichische Volkspartei* (ÖVP) and the *Sozialdemokratische Partei Österreichs* (SPÖ). Historically, power sharing between these two created successful grand coalitions and an influential federal structure. Most of the Länder have been dominated for the postwar period by one of the two parties, and the electoral systems therefore often reflect the distinct preferences of these parties. However, elections share three common elements. First, all Länder use an open-list proportional representation system with preferential voting for council elections (Reynolds et al. 2008: 60). Mandatory use of proportional representation for seat allocation is set by the federal constitution (RIS 2020). Second, citizens aged 16 or older are eligible to vote. Third, all council seats are allocated via the d'Hondt method. These three features also apply to elections at the regional and national levels.

Local elections are always held at large, without any districting. The council size (between 9 and 45 seats) varies with the size of the municipality, and therefore there are substantial differences in the number of citizens represented per mandate.

In six Länder, mayoral elections are held using a two-round system (Reynolds et al. 2008: 52). If no candidate wins more than 50% of the vote, a runoff election between the two leading candidates is scheduled two weeks later. If only one candidate is running for mayoral office, five Länder with direct mayoral elections (except Tyrol) include a designated 'no' option on the ballot paper. A candidate is elected mayor if he or she receives the majority of valid votes. Otherwise, the municipal council elects a mayor from among its members. Exceptional provisions are summarized in Table 9.1 and will be discussed later.

In all Länder, except for Vienna, European Union citizens who are permanent residents may cast their votes in local elections after registering in the municipality. In 2002, the Viennese parliament, with the votes of the Social Democrats (SPÖ) and the Greens, extended the right to vote for local level offices to all foreign residents. For the first time in Austria, third-country nationals were granted voting rights if they had a main residence registered in Vienna for five consecutive years. The federal government challenged the foreigners' right to vote in Vienna in February 2003, urging the Viennese parliament to pass a preserving resolution (*Beharrungsbeschluss*) soon thereafter. Arguing that Austrian citizenship is an absolutely necessary condition for exercising the right to vote, the Constitutional Court annulled the right to vote for foreigners in 2004. The case was highly controversial because of the large share of immigrants in the population, with 28% of voting-aged residents in Vienna having non-Austrian citizenship (Stadlmair 2018). European Union citizens still can vote in the Vienna city district elections, but not in the municipal election.

Compared to other levels of government, voting rights are most liberal in Austria at the local level. In Burgenland and Lower Austria, holders of secondary residences (e.g., weekend retreats) are granted voting rights after registration. The practice is not widely used in Burgenland, but some municipalities in Lower Austria have more registered voters than residents because the electoral register is not cross-checked for duplicate entries. Media reports have suggested that this practice helps the ruling Christian Democrats (ÖVP) in Lower Austria to preserve their majority in some municipalities. In the large Land of Lower Austria, geographically located around Vienna, the option is frequently used by ordinary voters and political officials alike. The registration of secondary homes is not scrutinized, which allows some voters to cast a ballot in two different local elections.

The voting age was first lowered to 16 (from 18) for local elections in Burgenland and Carinthia (in 2000), followed by Vienna (2002), and then Salzburg and Styria (both in 2004). An electoral reform at the federal level in 2007 reduced the voting age for the entire country (Wagner et al. 2012). Until 1982, voting in presidential elections was compulsory in Austria. Thereafter, some Länder retained mandatory voting for parliamentary elections. In 1918, the Christian Social Party (CSP, predecessor of the ÖVP) demanded mandatory voting[9] in exchange for agreeing to the introduction of women's suffrage. The CSP feared that conservative women would not exercise their right to vote as much as social democratic women and that such behavior might change the fragile balance of power between the two main parties. Styria, Tyrol, Vorarlberg, and later Carinthia introduced a corresponding regional law for mandatory voting. National electoral reform in 1992 repealed mandatory voting at the federal level. Tyrol and Vorarlberg did not abandon mandatory voting for local elections until 2004.

Preference votes to reorder the parties' candidate lists for local council elections exist in all Länder. Salzburg and Styria allow only one preferential vote, while others grant two (Tyrol, Vienna) or more. Burgenland permits the cumulation of two of the three preferential votes on

Table 9.1 Timing and provisions for local elections in Austria

	Burgenland	Carinthia	Lower Austria	Upper Austria	Salzburg	Styria	Tyrol	Vorarlberg	Vienna
Municipalities	171	132	573	438	119	287[1]	279	96	1
Election cycle (years)	5	6	5	6	5	5	6	5	5
Simultaneous regional elections		in 2009		Yes	Until 2009				Yes
Direct mayoral elections	Since 1996	Since 1991		Since 1997	Since 1994		Since 1994	Since 2000	
Mayoral runoff elections	Yes	Yes		Yes	Yes		Yes	No	
'No option' in case of only one mayoral candidate	Yes	Yes		Yes	Yes			Yes	
Recall of mayor	Council supermajority & referendum	Council supermajority & referendum	Council supermajority	Council supermajority & referendum	Council supermajority & referendum	Council supermajority	Dissolution of council	Council majority & referendum	Council majority
Council seats	9–25	11–35	13–45	9–37	9–25	9–31	9–21	9–36	100
Min population per seat	250	1,000	500	400	800	1,000	200	750	
Max Population per seat	3,000	20,000	30,000	7,300	5,000	10,000	10,000	15,000	
Preferential votes	3	3	many	3	1	1	2	5	2

(Continued)

Table 9.1 (Continued)

	Burgenland	Carinthia	Lower Austria	Upper Austria	Salzburg	Styria	Tyrol	Vorarlberg	Vienna
Cumulation of preferential votes	2 votes per candidate							2 votes per candidate	
Apparentement (List coupling)							Yes		
Voting at age 16 since	2000	2000	2007	2007	2004	2004	2007	2007	2002
Early voting day(s)	Yes	Yes				Yes			
Compulsory voting until		1998				1998	2004	2004	
Special features[2]	BGL		LA				T	V	
Party dominance[3]	SPÖ	ÖVP	ÖVP	ÖVP			ÖVP	ÖVP	SPÖ

[1] 539 municipalities before the 2015 mergers.
[2] Abbreviations: BGL, secondary residence holders may also vote;
LA, nonofficial ballot papers (even prefilled, mailed forms), preference votes 'person before party', secondary residence holders may also vote;
T, list-coupling option for mandate allocation (wasted votes go to coupled partisan-alike lists);
V, special form of 'majority voting' in small municipalities without lists, councilors are chosen by names handwritten on the ballot paper. [3] Party won the last four regional elections.

one candidate, while Vorarlberg allows two cumulations of two votes out of five preferential votes in total. Lower Austria has a very generous preferential voting system with unlimited preferential votes for one party, so that one list can accommodate twice as many candidates as there are seats to be awarded. Generally, *panachage* is not possible. The vote for the party list is counted instead of a diverging preferential vote given to a candidate from another party, except for in Lower Austria, where the reverse principle applies and 'candidate trumps party'. Another unique arrangement in Lower Austria is that nonofficial ballot papers are allowed for local elections. One of the consequences of this is that prefilled ballot papers are sent out by parties during the campaigns, with the request that these ballots should be used on election day. Furthermore, very small municipalities in Vorarlberg can hold elections without official ballot papers if no party has forwarded a list of candidates. In such a case, Vorarlberg allows a special form of 'majority voting' (*Mehrheitswahl*): voters elect their councilors by simply writing names of persons living in the municipality[10] on a paper slip. The councilor collecting the most references is elected mayor. This system was used in 12–16 municipalities (out of 96 in total) for recent local elections.

The Land of Tyrol allows *apparentement* – pooling the votes for electoral alliances between lists – called list-coupling (*Listenkopplung*). This is quite a common feature and was mainly used in the past by the pivotal Christian Democrats (ÖVP). The party consists of several leagues (*Bünde*)[11] that represent different socioeconomic and demographic groups and compete on separate lists with well-known candidates to appeal to a larger segment of the electorate (Müller & Steininger 1994). The ÖVP regulates the coupling of lists in its party statutes. Lists must be coupled if more than one league runs in the local election. List coupling leads to more seats won. In the first round of mandate allocation, coupled lists are treated as one list, awarding a greater share of seats by the d'Hondt method (also used to distribute seats within alliances), with fewer residual votes lost to competitors. Although this practice is not decisive, it is also not irrelevant for the dominance of the ÖVP in Tyrol (Karlhofer 2013: 136). In about 25–30% of the Tyrolean municipalities, coupled lists are registered, which subsequently collaborate in the municipal council. They usually do not compete against each other with separate mayoral candidates. Strikingly, most lists there do not include a clear reference to their party affiliation in the list name (e.g., by including the party abbreviation). Tyrol and Vorarlberg, both dominated by the ÖVP, are the only Länder where 'party brand' cues in list names are often missing. In most recent elections, the ÖVP was running by its official name in only 16% of all municipalities in Tyrol and 34% in Vorarlberg. Even if a reference to the ÖVP is missing, these lists are mostly partisan lists. Voters in both Länder may assume that they are affiliated with the party or one of its leagues.

In general, entry to local elections – for lists and candidates – is very open because of the small size of the communities. This applies to the entry rules[12] as well as to the electoral threshold for the council. Because of the relatively large size of the councils, even in small communities, new lists have a decent chance of winning at least one seat. There are no provisions for incompatibility (*cumul des mandats*); indeed, about 20% of members of the regional parliaments (Karlhofer & Pallaver 2013b: 20) and 9% of the *Nationalrat* also hold a mayoral office.

Outcomes: traditional party dominance and strong electoral participation

Voter turnout is traditionally quite high in Austria, as Figure 9.1 shows. Recent national parliamentary elections have seen a 75% turnout, which is more than 10% above the European average (IDEA 2020). These general elections normally yield the highest rates of participation, although

Philipp Umek

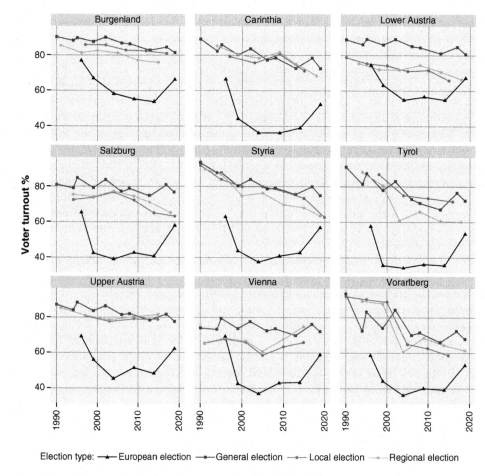

Figure 9.1 Voter turnout in Austria across all levels, 1990–2020

regional and local elections come quite close. European Parliament elections achieved near general election turnout rates for the first election in 1996, then fell sharply, and have recently recovered in all Länder. Local elections have been held simultaneously with regional elections in Upper Austria, Salzburg (until 2009), Carinthia (only once, in 2009), and in Vienna by design. However, turnout for the two levels is highly correlated and not only where local and regional elections are held on the same day. Only in regional elections in Tyrol and Styria is turnout lower than in local elections. The two western Länder, Tyrol and Vorarlberg, generally have seen lower turnout since the abolishment of compulsory voting there, whereas citizens in the eastern Länder of Burgenland and Lower Austria tend to turn out in higher numbers (Jenny 2007).

Voter turnout correlates negatively with the size of the municipality, as numerous comparative studies have shown (Stockemer 2017; Cancela & Geys 2016; Blais 2006). Figure 9.2 reveals the same pattern for the most recent local elections in Austria. This also holds true for all eight Länder and past elections. The black dots on the figure represent municipalities with only one list on the ballot. Unitary single lists with generic names are quite common in small municipalities in Tyrol and Vorarlberg. These run uncontested in 15% of municipalities in Tyrol and

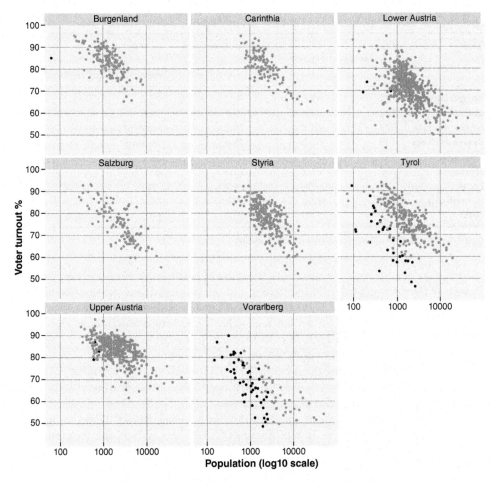

Figure 9.2 Voter turnout in the Austrian local elections by municipality size

Note: Black dots represent uncontested elections

70% in Vorarlberg, and they exhibit an even stronger negative correlation to municipality size for turnout. The two western Länder are major electoral strongholds of the ÖVP and therefore deviate in terms of political competition. In the rest of Austria, the two largest parties, ÖVP and SPÖ, run for elections in almost all municipalities. The same effect of population size on turnout also applies to mayoral elections (not shown). As population size decreases, there is less political competition. On average, only 2.2 candidates run for office, with little variation over time. Uncontested mayoral elections, however, are more common, with 27% municipalities having only one candidate on the ballot. Only in Burgenland does the ÖVP contest the dominance of the SPÖ in nearly all municipalities on a regular basis.

As is typical of small local governments with proportional electoral systems, nearly three-quarters of all municipalities are governed by a dominant list with an absolute majority of seats on the council. Table 9.2 presents Carinthia as an outlier, which is due to major shifts in the political landscape of the Land. Until 2103, Carinthia was dominated by the far-right

Table 9.2 Municipal council majorities in Austrian local elections

Land	Number of municipalities	% of absolute majorities	% of recurring majorities	% of mayoral incumbents running	% of mayoral incumbents reelected
Burgenland	171	83.6	70.2	72.2	65.7
Carinthia	132	50.8	9.1	74.0	62.6
Lower Austria	573	87.1	78.2	no DEM	
Upper Austria	438	63.0	48.6	missing*	
Salzburg	119	75.6	47.1	68.6	66.1
Styria	287	81.2	28.6	no DEM	
Tyrol	279	62.7	24.7	70.7	65.2
Vorarlberg	96	69.8	49.0	46.9	39.6
Total	2,095	74.0	50.0	68.3	61.8

*Candidate names are missing in official data for Upper Austria.

Freiheitliche Partei Österreichs (FPÖ) and its later spin-off the *Bündnis Zukunft Österreich* (BZÖ). Jörg Haider, governor and head of the BZÖ, died in a traffic accident in 2008. His party dominated the Land government and was also responsible for numerous malversations and a large financial scandal involving the Hypo-Alpe-Adria bank (Jenny 2014). Since then, the SPÖ has been able to regain its strength in its former stronghold and won local elections in 2015; consequently, the share of recurring majorities in Table 9.2 is much lower in Carinthia. The lower rates for recurring majorities in Styria can be explained by the numerous mergers in 2015 and those in Tyrol by lists frequently changing their names.

The competitive situation for recent local elections is summarized in Table 9.3. It shows again that noncompetitive elections were almost exclusively held in Tyrol and Vorarlberg (also due to the *Mehrheitswahl* for very small municipalities). Although *apparentement* inflates the number of competing lists for Tyrol because the ÖVP runs with more than one list, they still remain below average. In the other Länder, three lists were most common. The six Länder with direct mayoral elections feature mostly two candidates, except for the Burgenland, where three candidates run in over 45% of all cases. Mayors in office run for reelection in almost 70% of all cases, and over 60% of incumbents are reelected. Only in Vorarlberg are incumbents less likely to be reaffirmed because fewer than half of them run again in the first place.

The Christian Democrats (ÖVP), who have been continuously in coalition governments since 1987 at the federal level, have party strongholds in the western Länder of Vorarlberg and Tyrol and in Lower and Upper Austria. The Social Democrats (SPÖ) are the second most prominent party in terms of presence in governing coalitions at the state level. The SPÖ has a large part of its voter base in the eastern parts of Austria, particularly in the federal capital of Vienna and in Burgenland. The far-right Freedom Party (FPÖ) has gained constant voter support at the national level but plays a marginal role in local elections, as Table 9.4 demonstrates. The only exceptions are Carinthia (as mentioned before) and the capital of Vienna, where the FPÖ's front runner Heinz-Christian Strache, who successfully mobilized voters with his xenophobic campaigns, enjoyed popular support back then. In all other Länder, the FPÖ lacks the necessary local party structures. The scarcity and weakness of community-based organization are also problematic for the Greens (*Die Grünen Österreich*). Although the party now co-governs at the federal level and in five regional governments, as well as backing the federal president, it has been unsuccessful in local elections except in Vienna and Innsbruck.

Table 9.3 Political competition in Austrian local elections

Land		None	Uncon-tested	Two	Three	Four	Five or more
Burgenland	Lists		0.6%	29.4%	44.1%	18.8%	7.1%
	cum. %			30.0%	74.1%	92.9%	100.0%
	Candidates		4.1%	40.6%	45.3%	7.1%	2.9%
	cum. %			44.7%	90.0%	97.1%	100.0%
Carinthia	Lists			2.3%	39.7%	38.2%	19.8%
	cum. %				42.0%	80.2%	100.0%
	Candidates			25.2%	36.6%	26.7%	11.5%
	cum. %				61.8%	88.5%	100.0%
Lower Austria	Lists		0.7%	29.5%	38.2%	17.0%	14.6%
	cum. %			30.2%	68.4%	85.4%	100.0%
	No DEM						
Salzburg	Lists			6.8%	55.9%	28.8%	8.5%
	cum. %				62.7%	91.5%	100.0%
	Candidates		25.4%	44.1%	20.3%	7.6%	2.5%
	cum. %			69.5%	89.8%	97.4%	100.0%
Styria	Lists			10.5%	44.1%	25.5%	19.9%
	cum. %				54.6%	80.1%	100.0%
	No DEM						
Tyrol	Lists		11.6%	25.3%	28.9%	17.7%	16.6%
	cum. %			36.9%	65.8%	83.5%	100.0%
	Candidates		39.4%	37.9%	14.1%	6.1%	2.5%
	cum. %			77.3%	91.4%	97.5%	100.0%
Upper Austria	Lists		0.7%	13.2%	49.7%	29.5%	7.0%
	cum. %			13.9%	63.6%	93.1%	100.0%
	Candidates		27.2%	34.5%	28.1%	7.9%	2.3%
	cum. %			61.7%	89.8%	97.7%	100.0%
Vorarlberg	Lists	16.7%	35.4%	12.5%	12.5%	14.6%	8.3%
	cum. %		52.1%	64.6%	77.1%	91.7%	100.0%
	Candidates	37.5%	27.1%	15.6%	8.3%	5.2%	6.3%
	cum. %		64.6%	80.2%	88.5%	93.7%	100.0%

The proportion of female representatives is fairly high at the federal level. Currently 72 of the 183 members of the lower house (*Nationalrat*) are women (39.3%, up from 19.7% in 1990). Austria does not have mandatory gender quotas or provisions for ranking election proposals (lists). The parties have voluntarily committed themselves to increasing the share of female representatives (cf. Steininger 2000). Only the Greens call for obligatory parity in the list order. The ÖVP, SPÖ, and NEOS have voluntary quotas for federal election campaigns. The FPÖ has no such arrangements, Nor are there any provisions in general at the local level.

Unfortunately, there is a lack of detailed data about female representation at the local level in Austria. Schiestl (2010) found that Carinthia and Salzburg collected no data on the topic until 2009. Walenta (2020) recently was able to collect more precise data for most Länder through extensive research in the regional offices. The current figures for the overview in Table 9.5 were provided by the Austrian Association of Municipalities (*Gemeindebund*). By 2020, over 20% of local councilors were female, except in Vienna because of its dual function as the regional parliament. Only 180 or 8.6% of mayors are female (up from 45 in 1999). Because women

Table 9.4 Party politicization in recent local elections in Austria

Land	Year	Party	Votes	Seats	Mayors	Majority	Running	Represented
Burgenland	2017	SPÖ	45.4%	46.8%	48.0%	40.6%	100.0%	100.0%
Burgenland	2017	ÖVP	41.2%	43.1%	48.5%	36.5%	98.2%	98.2%
Burgenland	2017	FPÖ	6.0%	4.5%			55.9%	44.1%
Burgenland	2017	Other	6.0%	5.0%	3.5%	1.8%	30.6%	26.5%
Burgenland	2017	Grüne	1.5%	0.7%			15.3%	11.8%
Carinthia	2015	SPÖ	41.6%	39.4%	44.7%	19.1%	97.7%	97.7%
Carinthia	2015	ÖVP	23.4%	25.4%	25.8%	9.2%	84.0%	83.2%
Carinthia	2015	FPÖ	17.5%	18.3%	14.4%	4.6%	89.3%	87.8%
Carinthia	2015	Other	14.1%	14.7%	15.2%	4.6%	59.5%	53.4%
Carinthia	2015	Grüne	3.3%	2.2%			27.5%	22.9%
Lower Austria	2015	ÖVP	46.0%	52.6%	70.0%	62.5%	94.4%	94.4%
Lower Austria	2015	SPÖ	30.1%	28.8%	21.6%	16.0%	95.6%	95.1%
Lower Austria	2015	Other	11.5%	10.0%	8.2%	6.0%	37.5%	33.7%
Lower Austria	2015	FPÖ	7.7%	5.7%			58.9%	54.9%
Lower Austria	2015	Grüne	4.7%	2.8%	0.2%	0.2%	22.6%	20.9%
Salzburg	2019	ÖVP	47.5%	54.0%	80.7%	80.7%	97.5%	97.5%
Salzburg	2019	SPÖ	27.6%	26.2%	15.1%	16.0%	97.5%	97.5%
Salzburg	2019	FPÖ	10.1%	10.0%	0.8%		88.2%	86.1%
Salzburg	2019	Grüne	7.5%	4.0%			26.9%	24.9%
Salzburg	2019	Others	7.4%	5.8%	3.4%	3.4%	2.5%	2.5%
Styria	2020	ÖVP	47.2%	53.3%	69.7%	63.2%	100.0%	100.0%
Styria	2020	SPÖ	31.9%	30.6%	27.9%	21.4%	97.5%	95.8%
Styria	2020	FPÖ	8.2%	6.5%	0.3%		81.8%	61.4%
Styria	2020	Other	8.1%	6.3%	2.1%	2.1%	40.0%	30.2%
Styria	2020	Grüne	4.6%	3.4%			34.7%	30.2%
Tyrol	2016	Other*	67.9%	80.5%	88.4%	49.3%	95.7%	95.7%
Tyrol	2016	ÖVP	12.9%	9.2%	7.9%	6.9%	18.5%	18.1%
Tyrol	2016	SPÖ	8.7%	5.0%	2.5%	1.4%	19.9%	18.8%
Tyrol	2016	FPÖ	6.5%	3.3%	0.7%		22.5%	21.7%
Tyrol	2016	Grüne	4.0%	2.0%	0.4%		14.9%	14.1%
Upper Austria	2015	ÖVP	42.1%	49.1%	75.2%	53.2%	100.0%	100.0%
Upper Austria	2015	SPÖ	27.1%	24.4%	20.7%	4.6%	93.8%	93.4%
Upper Austria	2015	FPÖ	22.0%	20.3%	2.7%	0.7%	86.8%	86.8%
Upper Austria	2015	Grüne	5.7%	3.6%			27.4%	27.2%
Upper Austria	2015	Other	3.2%	2.6%	1.4%		19.4%	16.2%
Vorarlberg	2015	ÖVP	38.8%	31.5%	32.3%	20.8%	37.5%	37.5%
Vorarlberg	2015	Other	24.8%	45.1%	63.5%	44.8%	63.5%	63.5%
Vorarlberg	2015	FPÖ	14.5%	9.8%	2.1%	1.0%	33.3%	33.3%
Vorarlberg	2015	Grüne	11.8%	7.6%			22.9%	22.9%
Vorarlberg	2015	SPÖ	10.0%	6.1%	2.1%	1.0%	26.0%	25.0%
Vienna	2015	SPÖ	39.6%	44.0%				
Vienna	2015	FPÖ	30.8%	34.0%				
Vienna	2015	Grüne	11.8%	10.0%				
Vienna	2015	ÖVP	9.2%	7.0%				
Vienna	2015	Other	8.6%	5.0%				

* Majority of other lists are affiliated to the ÖVP but run with generic list names

Table 9.5 Female representation in recent local elections in Austria

Land	Female mayors	Female deputy mayors	Female councilors
Lower Austria (N = 573)	12.0%	17.9%	24.3%
Vorarlberg (N = 96)	9.4%	21.9%	20.4%
Styria (N = 287)	8.0%	14.8%	21.5%
Upper Austria (N = 438)	8.0%	21.3%	24.4%
Burgenland (N = 171)	7.0%	17.9%	24.1%
Salzburg (N = 119)	6.7%	21.0%	23.9%
Carinthia (N = 132)	6.1%	28.0%	18.4%
Tyrol (N = 279)	5.7%	10.2%	21.0%
Vienna (N = 1)	0.0%	50.0%	37.0%
Total	8.6%	18.1%	23.1%

Source: Gemeindebund

generally do more care work, it is harder for them to run for public office. A total of 70% of all mayors exercise their office alongside their main job, and half of incumbents claim that they spend more than 40 hours a week in office.[13] Nevertheless, about 15% of deputy mayors are female, which means that these women are represented *ex officio* in the local executive boards.

In general, there is no legal provision for the representation of minorities and foreign individuals at the local level. Only the regional law in Styria provides the option of communal migrant advisory boards (*MigrantInnenbeiräte*). In Graz, Leoben, and Kapfenberg, this nonbinding committee is elected alongside regular local elections. Ethnic minorities are not explicitly addressed at the local tier either. The large group of nearly 30% of migrants in Vienna is only eligible for district representative elections. Apart from them, the Carinthian Slovenes are the only political factor to be mentioned. Marginalized at the regional level until 2008 by an effective electoral threshold of about 10%, the *Enotna Lista* is traditionally present in more than 20 municipalities, especially in southern Carinthia (Stainer-Hämmerle 2013: 190).

Consensus on the status quo

Local elections in Austria are very diverse due to the federal state structure. Although most municipalities are small and share common demographics, there are wide horizontal differences between municipalities in terms of political competition at the local tier. All Länder commonly use open-list proportional representation systems and allow voting from the age of 16 at all levels. Six Länder hold direct mayoral elections; only Lower Austria and Styria abstain from direct elections, along with Vienna as a special case. Uncontested elections are almost exclusively held in the western Länder of Vorarlberg and Tyrol, which goes along with lower turnout rates despite participation in general being quite strong. The other Länder feature a more vibrant competition with more lists and candidates on the ballot. Nonetheless, over 70% of the municipalities are governed by an absolute (and mostly recurring) majority of one list, as is typical for small local governments. Karlhofer and Pallaver (2013a) analyze these particularities in detail for all Länder in their standard reference work on local elections. The Austrian political system is discussed extensively by Dachs (2006), the municipal level in particular by Steininger (2006), and direct democracy and reform proposals at the local level by Pleschberger (2015).

The former hegemonic parties SPÖ and ÖVP, who shaped the two-and-a-half party system (Blondel 1968; Sartori 1976; Müller 2006) along with the minor FPÖ, still essentially determine local politics through their chapters as small organizational units. In this, the democratization of local administration has always been a fundamental concern of the Social Democrats. The SPÖ thus defended its role as the second major party at the local tier, but the ÖVP is still the party with the most mayors in office. While other parties perform well in regional and federal elections, the vertical gap between the parties remains substantial. Although the Greens engaged in community politics via grassroots organizations early on, the party was never able to succeed at this tier because of its bottom-up democratic orientation and slack party discipline. The local level also differs essentially from national elections in the relative rigidity of voting behavior. Because the organizational penetration mentioned earlier is crucial, new parties like Team Stronach or NEOS have not been able to succeed at the local level.

A closer look at party finances shows how important this local level is for the national parties. The report of the Austrian Court of Audit (Rechnungshof Österreich 2020) lists the income of the parties from donations for the major election year 2015,[14] broken down into regional, district, and municipal organizations. Because there are no restrictions on campaign costs at the municipal level, this is used to circumvent the caps at the other levels. The ÖVP and the SPÖ generate 27% (€6.08 million) and 23% (€2.65 million) of their total income, respectively, through donations to local organizations (Huber 2020). This is even more important for the FPÖ with 30% (€0.88 million) of total income and the Greens with 38% (€1.03 million), although at significantly lower amounts.

The small-scale organization of the municipalities determines high electoral participation in Austria, as shown in this chapter and by Heinisch and Mühlböck (2016) in an in-depth analysis for the Land Salzburg. Therefore, turnout changes due to mergers can have profound effects. The highly controversial structural reform in Styria in 2015 in particular has led to well-documented changes in voter turnout (Teurezbacher 2019). Voters often rely on their personal relationships with local representatives, and the increase in population size as the result of a merger reduces potential interaction and, consequently, 'voters are less informed and engaged' (Schimpf et al. 2018: 468). However, mergers are not just implemented from the top down: three municipalities in Tyrol (Matrei am Brenner, Mühlbach, Pfons) recently merged after an initiative brought by the three mayors. The move found high agreement with the residents (95%, 77%, and 61%, respectively) and brought in €1.2 million in additional funds from the Tyrolean government. Apart from that, the lowering of the voting age to 16 had a significant impact on first-time voters at the national level. It is expected that this cohort will participate in elections more often than previous first-time voters (Aichholzer & Kritzinger 2020). Unfortunately, there are no electoral studies for the local level that are on par with the high-quality election surveys conducted by AUTNES (2020)[15] for national elections. Only occasionally are studies carried out on behalf of the Association of Municipalities.

Neither this association nor others are currently campaigning for changes or electoral reforms at the local tier. However, a change long called for by the opposition in Vorarlberg has just been implemented. The ÖVP has long rejected the introduction of a second ballot paper for mayoral elections, something that FPÖ, Greens, and SPÖ have demanded for years. In the 2020 elections, two different ballot papers will be used for the first time. The opposition expects that council elections will be decoupled in their favor, and it will finally be perceived more as an independent ballot with the possibility of splitting votes. While this was possible even before, some voters were unsure of that and tied their vote for the municipal council to the (more prominent) mayoral candidates.

The regulations on the eligibility of secondary residence holders and their registration in Lower Austria are being debated again and again in the media. There have been minor modifications to the municipalities' duty to control the lists of registered voters and to identify duplicate entries between them, but they cannot be implemented effectively. The predominant ÖVP benefits from this regulation, so no change is expected in the foreseeable future. Occasionally, *apparantement* in Tyrol is also criticized by opposition parties, but here too, no change is expected due to the hegemonic position of the ÖVP advocating for the status quo.

Notes

1 Burgenland, Carinthia, Upper Austria, Salzburg, Tyrol, and Vorarlberg.
2 https://gemeindebund.at/themen-zahlen-und-fakten-partnerschaften/
3 www.staedtebund.gv.at/
4 https://gemeindebund.at/unsere-buergermeister-innen/
5 The term lengths for local governments correspond to regional term lengths, except for Carinthia and Tyrol with six years for local and five years for regional terms.
6 One polling station per municipality is open for one day (always a Friday), nine days before the regular date.
7 Municipal Code of Tyrol, Section 126.
8 Since 1990, just 15 municipalities in Tyrol have called snap elections at the local level. Major cities with elections out of sync from the rest of the Land run elections for a full term.
9 Violation of the obligation to vote was not sanctioned
10 Where confusion might occur, the year of birth or occupation of the candidate is required.
11 For example, the farmers' association (*Bauernbund*) and the workers and employees' association (*ÖAAB*).
12 A manageable number of signatures is all that needs to be collected in the municipality, usually about 1% of the population, depending on which Land.
13 https://gemeindebund.at/buergermeister-und-buergermeisterinnen/
14 In 2015, six local elections and four regional elections were held.
15 www.autnes.at/en/

References

Aichholzer, J. & Kritzinger, S. (2020), Voting at 16 in practice: A review of the Austrian case. In: J. Eichhorn & J. Bergh (Eds.), *Lowering the voting age to 16: Learning from real experiences worldwide* (pp. 81–101). Basingstoke: Palgrave Macmillan.

AUTNES (2020), Austrian national election study, available at: www.autnes.at/en/ (accessed 3 February 2020).

Blais, A. (2006), What affects voter turnout? *Annual Review of Political Science*, 9(1), 111–125.

Blondel, J. (1968), Party systems and patterns of government in western democracies, *Canadian Journal of Political Science*, 1(2), 180–203.

Caciagli, M. (2013), Die Bürgermeisterdirektwahl im europäischen Vergleich. In: F. Karlhofer & G. Pallaver (Eds.), *Gemeindewahlen in Österreich im Bundesländervergleich* (pp. 231–244). Innsbruck, Wien, Bozen: Studienverlag.

Cancela, J. & Geys, B. (2016), Explaining voter turnout. A meta-analysis of national and subnational elections, *Electoral Studies*, 42, 264–275.

Dachs, H. (Ed.) (2006), *Politik in Österreich: Das Handbuch*, Wien: Manz.

Fallend, F., Ignits, G. & Swianiewicz, P. (2006), Divided loyalties? Mayors between party representation and local community interests. In: H. Bäck, H. Heinelt, & A. Magnier (Eds.), *The European mayor: Political leaders in the changing context of local democracy* (pp. 245–270). Wiesbaden: VS Verlag für Sozialwissenschaften.

Goldsmith, M. & Page, E. (2010), Conclusions. In: M. Goldsmith & E. Page (Eds.), *Changing Government Relations in Europe: From localism to intergovernmentalism* (pp. 247–260). London: Routledge.

Heinisch, R. & Mühlböck, A. (2016), Auf die Größe kommt es an! Neue empirische Evidenz zur Wahlbeteiligung in Gemeinden, *Zeitschrift für Vergleichende Politikwissenschaft*, 10(2), 165–190.

Hesse, J.J. & Sharpe, L.J. (1991), Local government in international perspective. Some comparative observations. In: J.J. Hesse & L.J. Sharpe (Eds.), *Local government and urban affairs in international perspective: Analyses of twenty western industrialised countries* (pp. 603–621). Baden-Baden: Nomos-Verlag.

Hooghe, L. & Marks, G. (2001), *Multi-level governance and European integration, governance in Europe*. Lanham: Rowman & Littlefield.

Huber, J. (2020), *NÖ: Wahl- und Geldschlacht*, available at: https://diesubstanz.at/laender/noe-wahl-und-geldschlacht/ (accessed 27 January 2020).

IDEA (2020), Voter turnout database, available at: www.idea.int/data-tools/data/voter-turnout (accessed 11 February 2020).

Jenny, M. (2007), Die Volatilität der österreichischen Wählerschaft im Bundesländervergleich, 1945–2006. In: F. Plasser, P.A. Ulram (Eds.), *Wechselwahlen: Analysen zur Nationalratswahl 2006* (pp. 213–230). Wien: Facultas.

Jenny, M. (2014), Austria, *European Journal of Political Research Political Data Yearbook*, 53(1), 27–38.

Karlhofer, F. (2013), Tirol. In: F. Karlhofer & F., G. Pallaver (Eds.), *Gemeindewahlen in Österreich im Bundesländervergleich* (pp. 129–146). Innsbruck, Wien, Bozen: Studienverlag.

Karlhofer, F. & Pallaver, G. (Eds.) (2013a), *Gemeindewahlen in Österreich im Bundesländervergleich*. Innsbruck, Wien, Bozen: Studienverlag.

Karlhofer, F. & Pallaver, G. (2013b), *Kommunalwahlen in den Bundesländern. Ein vergleichender Überblick*. In: F. Karlhofer & G. Pallaver (Eds.), *Gemeindewahlen in Österreich im Bundesländervergleich* (pp. 9–32). Innsbruck, Wien, Bozen: Studienverlag.

Ladner, A., Keuffer, N. & Baldersheim, H. (2016), Measuring local autonomy in 39 countries (1990–2014), *Regional & Federal Studies*, 26(3), 321–357.

Ladner, A., Keuffer, N., Baldersheim, H., Hlepas, N., Swianiewicz, P., Steyvers, K. & Navarro, C. (2019), *Patterns of local autonomy in Europe*. Cham: Springer International Publishing.

Lane, J.-E. & Ersson, S.O. (1999), *Politics and society in western Europe*. London: Sage Publications.

Mouritzen, P.E. & Svara, J.H. (2002), *Leadership at the apex: Politicians and administrators in Western local governments*, Pittsburgh: University of Pittsburgh Press.

Müller, W.C. (2006), Parteiensystem. In: H. Dachs (Ed.), *Politik in Österreich: Das Handbuch* (pp. 279–304). Wien: Manz.

Müller, W.C. & Steininger, B. (1994), Party organisation and party competitiveness. The case of the Austrian People's Party, 1945–1992, *European Journal of Political Research*, 26(1), 1–29.

Pleschberger, W. (2015), Kommunale direkte Demokratie in Österreich. Strukturelle und prozedurale Probleme und Reformvorschläge. In: T. Öhlinger & T.K. Poier (Eds.), *Direkte Demokratie und Parlamentarismus: Wie kommen wir zu den besten Entscheidungen? Studien zu Politik und Verwaltung* (pp. 359–396). Wien: Böhlau.

Rechnungshof Österreich (2020), Rechenschaftsberichte der Parteien, available at: www.rechnungshof.gv.at/rh/home/was-wir-tun/was-wir-tun_5/was-wir-tun_6/Kontrolle_der_Parteien.html (accessed 27 January 2020).

Reynolds, A., Reilly, B. & Ellis, A. (2008), *Electoral system design: The new international IDEA handbook*. Stockholm: International IDEA.

RIS (2020), Bundes-Verfassungsgesetz, available at: www.ris.bka.gv.at/GeltendeFassung.wxe?Abfrage=Bundesnormen&Gesetzesnummer=10000138 (accessed 19 January 2020).

Sartori, G. (1976), *Parties and party systems: A framework for analysis*. Cambridge: Cambridge University Press.

Schiestl, G. (2010), Frauen in der Kommunalpolitik. In: F. Karlhofer & F.G. Pallaver (Eds.), *Politik in Tirol: Jahrbuch 2010* (pp. 41–60). Innsbruck, Wien, Bozen: Studienverlag.

Schimpf, C.H., Heinisch, R., Lehner, T. & Mühlböck, A. (2018), How do municipal amalgamations affect turnout in local elections? Insights from the 2015 municipal reform in the Austrian state of Styria, *Local Government Studies*, 44(4), 465–491.

Stadlmair, J. (2018), Demokratische Mitbestimmung von Fremden aus politikwissenschaftlicher Perspektive. In: K. Weiser (Ed.), *Demokratische Zukunft der (Salzburger) Landesgesetzgebung: Festschrift 100 Jahre Erste Republik*. Wien: Jan Sramek Verlag KG. (pp. 121–155).

Stainer-Hämmerle, K. (2013), *Kärnten*. In: F. Karlhofer & G. Pallaver (Eds.), *Gemeindewahlen in Österreich im Bundesländervergleich* (pp. 177–204). Innsbruck, Wien, Bozen: Studienverlag.

Steininger, B. (2000), Representation of women in the Austrian political system 1945–1998, *Women & Politics*, 21(2), 81–106.

Steininger, B. (2006), *Gemeinden*. In: H. Dachs (Ed.), *Politik in Österreich: Das Handbuch* (pp. 990–1007). Wien: Manz.

Stelzer, M. (2011), The constitution of the Republic of Austria: A contextual analysis. In: *Constitutional systems of the world, Vol. 11*. Oxford: Hart.

Stockemer, D. (2017), What affects voter turnout? A review article/meta-analysis of aggregate research, *Government and Opposition*, 52(4), 698–722.

Teurezbacher, F. (2019), Politische Reformen als Auslöser großer Wählerwanderungen. Das Beispiel der Gemeindestrukturreform in der Steiermark 2013–2015, *Österreichische Zeitschrift für Politikwissenschaft*, 48(2), 23.

Vetter, A., Denters, B., Kersting, N. & Klimovský, D. (2016), Giving citizens more say in local government. Comparative analyses of change across Europe in time of crisis. In: S. Kuhlmann & G. Bouckaert (Eds.), *Local Public Sector Reforms in Times of Crisis: National trajectories and international comparisons* (pp. 273–286). London: Palgrave Macmillan.

Wagner, M., Johann, D. & Kritzinger, S. (2012), Voting at 16. Turnout and the quality of vote choice, *Electoral Studies*, 31(2), 372–383.

Walenta, C. (2020), *Does regional political representation affect the Provision of Childcare in Austria?* AuPSA Political Science Day, University of Vienna, 27 November 2020.

10

Belgium

Between national barometer and local atmosphere

Kristof Steyvers

Brief overview of the local government system: communalist, collective, and consensual

The Belgian state comprises three levels of territorially integrated, general-purpose government: the federal, the regional (i.e., regions and communities), and the local (De Becker 2013). The local government system essentially has two tiers, with municipalities ($N = 581$) as the first and provinces ($N = 10$) as the second.[1] This chapter focuses on municipalities (and the denominator *local* predominantly refers to the first tier only). Throughout most of the reference period, the number of municipalities has remained constant. Recently, however, 15 municipalities in the Region of Flanders have voluntary amalgamated into seven new ones (effective as of 2019). This process was legally, financially, and organizationally stimulated by the regional government (De Ceuninck et al. 2016). In 2020, the average number of inhabitants per municipality was 19,781. A bit less than 38% of all municipalities had fewer than 10,000 inhabitants. Ultimately, the range varies between 79 (*Herstappe*) and 529,274 (*Antwerpen*).

Intergovernmental relations can be situated in the Napoleonic (or Southern European) state tradition. An ethos of political communalism underpins a relatively fragmented municipal tier. This covers a fairly limited range of functions (combining self-government, co-governance, and the mere execution of centrally determined policy) with substantial central supervision mediated by direct access of (specific) local decision-makers to the center (through the prevalence of dual mandate-holders and/or party political networks). Belgium occupies an intermediate position in rankings of local autonomy; while the country scores above average on aspects such as institutional depth and financial and fiscal matters (self-reliance, transfer system, or borrowing), it scores below average on administrative supervision (De Rynck & Wayenberg 2010; Ladner et al. 2019).

Intragovernmental relations are often termed as collective (Heinelt et al. 2018). Members of the executive (aldermen and mayors) are drawn from and remain within the council. Though formally appointed, the mayor is thus indirectly elected. In principle, collegiate decision-making prevails with the mayor as the first among equals within the executive. In practice, portfolio allocation to aldermen within the confines of the local governmental agreement occurs. Equally, more presidential tendencies for the mayoralty can be discerned. The collective tradition is part of a wider consensual mode of local democracy (with proportional representation, multiparty systems, executive power-sharing, etc.).

Since 2002, local government has come largely within the constitutional orbit of the regional level. This stems from the federalization process in Belgium, where the regions have acquired the competence to set the constitutive framework for the municipalities and provinces in their area. This has been the basis for several reforms of the political and administrative organization of the local tiers. However, the preceding Belgian legislation continues to prevail as a reference point. Moreover, the constitutive competence followed the regionalization of more specific aspects of regulation. Last, some locally relevant domains (e.g., safety or social security) remain within the federal realm. Nevertheless, for most matters pertinent to municipalities, the constitutive reference point is the Flemish Region (300 municipalities), the Walloon Region (262 municipalities), or the Brussels Capital Region (19 municipalities) (Wayenberg et al. 2012).

The tiers of local government are complemented by an area-oriented layer of governance (i.e., functionally differentiated specific purpose). This refers to various forms of intermunicipal cooperation, informal deliberation, and coordination between local tier representatives or structures imposed by the regional or federal government in which either or both tiers partake. A recent inventory in the Flemish Region established about 2,200 of such entities (on average 68 per municipality).

Citizens attach relatively more importance to the local level, although the differences with its national (i.e., regional or federal) counterpart are not very pronounced (Lefevere 2013).

Local elections and their place in the multilevel system: in between or independent?

In Belgium, local elections take place every six years on the second Sunday of October (the latest were in 2018). They are organized by each Region (i.e., the Flemish, Walloon, and Brussels Capital Regions, framing these under slightly differing but largely similar electoral codes) in conjunction with their respective local authorities (assuming responsibility for the practical preparations and execution).[2]

The fixed term of office mentioned differs in length from the default of five years for the regional, federal, and European elections (the last were in 2019).[3] Whereas the chances that the latter three coincide are thus very high or given, this does not include the local level. Statistically speaking, this overall simultaneity is only likely to appear every 30 years. In practice, this has never occurred during the period covered in this chapter. This intermediate character substantially contributes to a national frame on the dynamics of local elections. These tend to be perceived as having a barometric function. They are interpreted as a popularity test of the sitting regional and/or federal governing majority (especially if these are mid-term) or as a forecast of the upcoming regional and/or federal elections. At the same time, they are often characterized by their own patterns and dynamics in an atmosphere of local storylines and place-bound actors (Steyvers & De Ceuninck 2013; Dandoy et al. 2020).

In line with the monist and parliamentary notions central to the consensual mode of democracy, only the members of the municipal council are directly elected.[4] Members of the executive are indirectly elected (aldermen) or (formally) appointed (mayor). This conception can also be found at the regional and federal levels. A direct election of the mayor has been debated in the past but never effectuated. (Reynaert & Steyvers 2007).

The mayor thus remains formally appointed by the regional government on the basis of nomination by and among the members of the council.[5] Informally, the designation of the mayoralty is part of the process of majority formation. It is usually assigned to the largest party (in terms of seats) in the majority (predominantly a coalition of parties) and the candidate receiving the most preference votes (usually the head of the list). This balance between formal and informal primarily pertains to the mayoralty in municipalities of the Flemish and the Brussels Capital Regions. In Wallonia, the informal rules have been formalized in a new regulatory framework where the person obtaining the most preference votes on the largest list in the majority is automatically designated as the mayor of the municipality by the regional government (Verstraete et al. 2018).

There are no legal provisions for recall referenda, neither for the council nor for the members of the executive.

Features of the local electoral system: compulsory voting on (semi-)open proportional lists

Electoral law makes a distinction between active (vote) and passive (candidate) rights according to nationality. To be able to vote as a Belgian, one has to have national citizenship and be a registered inhabitant of the designated electoral constituency (i.e., the municipality or province) before the closing of the list of voters (i.e., automatic registration). Moreover, one must have reached the age of 18 by the day of the local elections and not be in a situation of exclusion or suspension of the right to vote.[6] For Belgians to be able to run as a candidate, the same rules apply, supplemented by the exclusion of police officers for the locality where they exercise their profession and people who have incurred certain criminal convictions in their capacity as a public official.

Non-Belgian residents from within the EU can vote and stand as a candidate for the municipal (but not the provincial) elections. Apart from the conditions mentioned for Belgian citizens, all non-Belgians must make an appeal to their municipality to register as a voter through a written procedure (this administrative hurdle in fact somewhat limits the effective registration of those potentially eligible). In addition, non-Belgians from outside the EU must legally have been residing within the country for five years without interruption before being able to vote. Non-Belgians are excluded from active and passive voting rights for the regional and federal elections (Blaise et al. 2018).

Belgium maintains compulsory voting for all elections, including the local. More specifically, this implies the legal obligation of every called-upon voter to present himself or herself at the polling station, accept the ballot paper, enter the polling booth, and return the ballot to those administering the election. In principle, if one does not fulfill this obligation, it is considered a crime (and subject to a fine). In practice, very low priority is given to effectively prosecute those who do not turn out. Hence, a certain extent of absenteeism can be discerned. Moreover, deliberately voting blank or invalid is often seen as the legal equivalent of absenteeism in the Belgian context (Dandoy 2014).

The number of councilors to be elected is determined by law (the same rules apply in all three Regions) and depends on the number of inhabitants of the municipality. It varies between a minimum of seven (for municipalities with fewer than 1,000 inhabitants) and a maximum of 55 (for those with more than 300,000 inhabitants). In between, 23 additional categories exist (based on increasingly extensive ranges in the number of inhabitants). For each additional category with an increasing number of inhabitants, two seats are added (e.g., nine for municipalities with 1,000–2,000 inhabitants) up to the maximum. During the last local elections of 2018, a total of 13,450 municipal council seats had to be filled in Belgium.[7]

The electoral system for the local elections is largely uniform throughout the country, regardless of the size of the municipality. It can be summarized as a (semi-)open proportional list system (Steyvers & De Ceuninck 2013; Cole 2019). Lists must be submitted formally to the president of the main polling station of the municipality by their head or another designated candidate. This can be done on a particular day and location about one month before the date of the local elections. Lists come under the form of a nomination act and have to be supported by at least one of the resigning councilors (who can be from a different party than the one submitting a list) or a minimum number of voters (increasing with categories in the number of inhabitants of the municipality). Each list has a rank order of candidates (decided by those submitting it). The first and the last candidate on the list are often considered to, respectively, *pull* (i.e., heading those below) and *push* (i.e., supporting those above) it. In the 1990s, Belgium introduced a gender quota for the candidate lists (see later discussion).

In terms of districting, Belgium organizes local elections at large. Each list and all of its candidates are thereby eligible to run for the whole of the territory of the municipality. The number of candidates on each list can equal the number of council seats to be filled (or fewer if the list is incomplete).

The ballot structure offers several ways to vote. Voters can either opt for a list and/or one or more of the individuals thereon.[8] In the first instance, they implicitly accept the order of candidates on the list and the eventual devolution of a ratio of votes following the ranking as granted (see later discussion). In the second, voters explicitly express a preference for one or more candidates. They can cast multiple preference votes to the extent of the number of candidates on the list. As implied earlier, a combination of a list and (one or more) a preferential vote(s) is also possible. Determination between these options is only possible within one list, as *panachage* is not allowed. In Belgian local elections, voters tend to choose preference voting over list voting. Typically, about 75% of all votes that a list collects come through preferences for one or more of its candidates. This share increases for the traditional pillar parties with the strongest local anchorage (often through seasoned and popular mandate-holders) and is higher than that in national elections (where the balance is more equal). However, the mode of preferential voting is differentiated. To a certain extent, it is rather centralized as more than half of the voters who express a preference for one or more candidates include the front runner. To another extent, it is equally decentralized as many also incorporate other candidates or only vote for the latter (André et al. 2013).

With a proportional electoral formula, votes are transformed into seats through the *Imperiali* quota method (deviating from the *d'Hondt* method adopted in all other Belgian elections).[9] First, all votes that a list receives are aggregated. Second, this number is divided by a sequence of 1, 1.5, 2, 2.5, 3, 3.5, etc. This produces a set of electoral quotients for each list. Third, this set is ranked from the highest to the lowest to order the distribution of seats until the number to be elected has been reached.

After the number of seats is allotted to each list, these must be assigned to certain candidates. Here, a particular combination of list and preference votes is decisive in the Flemish and the Brussels Capital Regions. First, an eligibility quorum for each list is determined. To that end, all votes received by the list are multiplied by its number of seats and divided again by that number plus one. Those candidates reaching the eligibility quorum are elected. Because preference votes co-determine the total votes received by the list, and given the formulas mentioned, it is unlikely that all candidates will reach the eligibility number by those preference votes alone. Thus, a stock based on the list votes is created. To that end, all such votes for a particular list are multiplied by the number of seats it obtained and divided again by three.[10] Candidates may draw on that stock to attain the eligibility quorum in the order of the list and to the extent of the stock. This occurs in combination with their preference votes (hence, a candidate who obtains a lot of the latter leaves more of the stock for the next on the list). If the stock is exhausted but some seats still need to be filled, preference votes are determinative for the remainder. This procedure thus favors candidates with higher list positions (and thereby enhances the clout of the list's selectorate). In the Walloon Region, the procedure is largely similar but fully open. Since 2018, the devolution of stocked list votes has been abolished. Only preference votes are thus decisive in designating seats to candidates (Dodeigne et al. 2020).

The electoral outcomes: high turnout in a regionalized local party system

Given compulsory voting, the discussion of electoral turnout is particular in the case of Belgium. Figure 10.1 compares the mean percentage of turnout in the country for local and national elections since the beginning of the 1990s.[11] Despite the differences in electoral cycles, a few trends stand out (although all are relative due to the limited ranges of the evolutions to which these refer). First, turnout for local elections is systematically higher than for national elections (for the dates we can observe). For example, in the most recent national elections (2019), on average 88.4% of those registered turned out, while this was 90.4% for their most recent local counterparts (2018). Second, turnout in both elections follows a rather similar path over time, that is, one of decline. Whereas this started in the 1990s, Belgium witnessed a relative surge in electoral turnout at the beginning of the twenty-first century, followed by a corresponding drop in the most recent decade (note the lowest values in the national elections of 2010 and the local ones of 2012). In addition to absenteeism, it is also pertinent to consider (deliberately) blank or invalid votes in the context of Belgium (averaging around 5%) to obtain a comprehensive assessment of the share of the electorate forsaking an effective choice (Dandoy 2014).

Figure 10.2 disaggregates the turnout percentage for the most recent local elections by the number of eligible voters (natural logarithm) for all municipalities in Belgium. The figure demonstrates the inverse relationship between size and turnout: the more eligible voters, the lower the share participating (Pearson's correlation coefficient = −.367). Evidently, this relationship is not perfectly linear as highlighted by the variation of dots above and below the trend line.

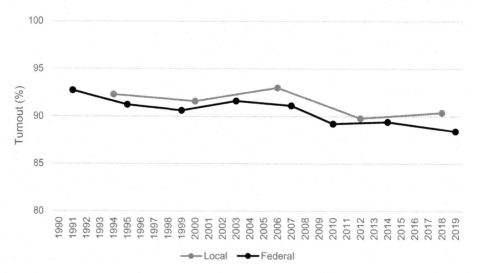

Figure 10.1 Voter turnout for local and national elections in Belgium, 1990–2020

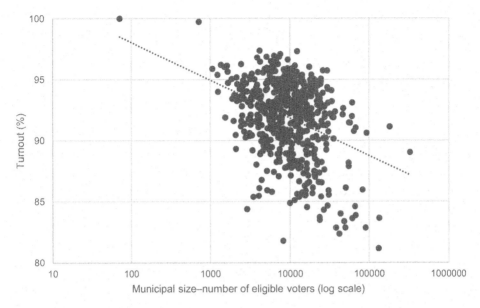

Figure 10.2 Voter turnout in the 2018 Belgian local elections by municipality size

Local elections in Belgium are relatively competitive (Steyvers & De Ceuninck 2013; Blaise et al. 2018). On the one hand, particularly since the 1990s, elections without contestation have become rather exceptional. Nowadays they are limited to a handful of cases. On the other hand, the number of lists wooing the voter has gradually increased. In many municipalities, the traditional pillar parties are currently complemented by newer parties, and the partisan offers have progressively come to resemble those at the national level (but see later discussion). The mean number of lists in recent local elections varied according to the region, from a bit fewer than four in Wallonia, to a bit more than five in Flanders, to a bit fewer than eight in Brussels. Nevertheless, local party system fragmentation remains less extensive than at the national level (following its tendencies, though with some delay).

Local elections are equally party politicized as demonstrated by the presence and success of national versus nonnational lists (Copus et al. 2012). To be precise, the party system is in fact completely regionalized: apart from the regionalist and radical right parties, each party family has a Dutch-speaking and a French-speaking branch. However, for the sake of cross-country comparison, we will speak of national parties. The distinction referred to is based on a procedure in electoral law by which a list submitted for the local elections can be officially acknowledged by a given parliamentary party by bearing its national name and/or number.

Local chapters of national political parties are now present almost everywhere and dominate the electoral offerings[12] (Steyvers & De Ceuninck 2013; Dandoy et al. 2013). While the traditional pillar parties (Christian-Democrats, Socialists, and Liberals) have the strongest local anchorage, their newer counterparts (Greens, regionalists, and radical right) are catching up. Consequently, in many places the partisan offerings increasingly mirror those at the national level (although some smaller parties like the radical left might prefer strategic instead of maximal presence). National lists also acquire the bulk of local votes in the Flemish (with a descending order of Christian-Democrats, regionalist, and Liberals as the ones with the largest shares) and the Walloon Regions (with a similar order of Socialists,

Liberals, and Christian-Democrats). However, differences with the national power relations between parties remain. In the long run, results evolve as in the national elections. Still, no unequivocal or increasing nationalization has occurred as the relative presence, vote shares, and vote switches within and/or between national lists in local elections stay territorially heterogeneous.

In addition, nonnational lists often complement the national parties (Dandoy et al. 2013; Steyvers & Heyerick 2017).[13] These lists are regularly designated as *local* as they lack a national name and/or number. Under the surface of this common denominator, we find a diversified set of phenomena. Classifications for the Flemish Region based on their decisional autonomy indicate that about 60% of them do have implicit links with national parties. As such, these lists combine the best of both worlds by drawing on a factual organization linkage with a national party while localizing their name. In many instances and contexts, this is a strategic choice to enhance their votes and improve their chances for office. Genuinely independent local lists thus operate in an electoral niche. Nonnational lists receive fewer votes in the Brussels and Flemish Regions than in the Walloon Region.

Finally, combinations between national and/or nonnational lists might exist in the form of preelectoral alliances. These are often established to maximize the potential of a seat bonus under the proportional electoral formula and to get into the local governing majority. Because of this diverging presence and success of (alliances of) national and nonnational lists, local party system nationalization varies highly across municipalities. By default, this system is mixed (with national and nonnational lists combined) to predominantly national, however.

Table 10.1 gives an overview of the participation and the performance of different families of lists in the most recent local elections in the three regions of Belgium. The designation of certain lists to (party) families is based on their ballot number.[14]

With local elections as a testing ground, Belgium introduced a gender quota on candidate lists in 1994 and gradually expanded the parameters toward parity overall and for the leading positions on the lists (Celis et al. 2013). The current legislation imposes two criteria. First, on each list (complete or not) the difference between the number of candidates of both genders cannot exceed one (i.e., a requirement of near parity). Second, the first two candidates on each list must differ in gender. Although the legal stipulations are formulated to be gender neutral, they clearly aim to enhance the number of female candidates (and thus also councilors and ultimately members of the executive). Still, even in the most recent local elections, only about 25% of all candidates heading a list were female. Hence, at the level of local councilors, there is no equal representation of men and women. Figure 10.3 indicates the share of female councilors in the three regions of Belgium since 1994.

Overall, the figure demonstrates an increasing share of female councilors over time in each region. This share has remained consistently higher in Brussels, where parity has nearly been met in the most recent local elections (with just under 49% female councilors). In Flanders and Wallonia, the percentage is relatively lower but has similarly increased to about 38%. In all regions, disaggregation of councilors by position indicates the share of females is lower among the members of the executive (i.e., aldermen and especially mayors, where it amounts to around 13% at best) than among those of the council. The percentage of female representatives is comparable at the national (i.e., regional or federal) level (where the same quota regulations apply). The gender quota is deemed to have accelerated the share of female candidates (Celis et al. 2013).

There is relatively little research on the incumbency effect in Belgian local elections. Some studies on mayors in Flanders at the beginning of the twenty-first century suggest that this varies over time. Whereas in one election it amounted to about 75%, in the subsequent election

Table 10.1 Participation and performance of families of lists in Belgian local elections by region, 2018

	% of municipalities where running	% of municipalities where represented	% of seats on local councils	% of (aggregate) votes in local elections	% of mayors affiliated with the party
Flanders					
Radical left	–	–	–	–	–
Greens	49.0	45.8	5.4	7.6	0.3
Socialists	51.0	43.1	7.1	9.3	4.3
Christian-Democrats	83.3	81.3	26.3	22.3	35.8
Liberals	51.3	46.8	10.7	10.6	12.7
Regionalists	88.3	85.9	19.9	20.5	17.1
Radical right	50.0	43.1	4.6	7.2	–
Nonnational	82.3	62.9	26.1	22.5	29.8
Wallonia					
Radical left	6.3	6.3	1.5	3.7	–
Greens	49.4	48.2	7.6	9.6	2.7
Socialists	38.3	37.5	16.8	21.1	22.5
Christian-Democrats	8.7	7.5	2.4	4.1	3.8
Liberals	28.9	28.1	8.6	10.5	10.3
Regionalists	–	–	–	–	–
Radical right	–	–	–	–	–
Nonnational	99.6	56.1	63.1	51.0	60.7
Brussels					
Radical left	36.8	36.8	5.2	6.8	–
Greens	100.0	100.0	23.0	20.3	15.8
Socialists	94.7	89.5	21.6	20.2	31.6
Christian-Democrats	94.7	84.2	9.2	9.6	15.8
Liberals	94.7	94.7	19.4	18.3	10.5
Regionalists	100.0	184.2	15.7	17.6	21.1
Radical right	26.3	–	–	0.7	–
Nonnational	89.5	3.2	5.9	6.5	5.2

it dropped to around 48%. This refers to the process in which the mayoralties are obtained. It is part of the majority formation where the mandate is usually assigned to the candidate with the most preference votes on the largest list included. Thus, it partly reflects the fluctuating fortunes of different lists in local elections. We do know that incumbent mayors tend to be vote champions, assuming a large share of preference votes on their own list (Reynaert et al. 2019).

Discussion: weathering second rounds and settling reforms

As in many countries, the scientific study of local elections and voting is still developing in Belgium. Most research has been concerned with aggregate election results, implicitly comparing them with their national counterparts and often from a second-order perspective. The latter stems from the tendency to formulate a national interpretation of the results galvanized by the participation of

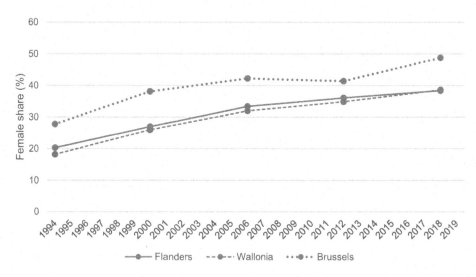

Figure 10.3 Women's representation among councilors in Belgium by region since 1994

national parties and politicians and from the simultaneity across municipalities and their intermediate timing vis-à-vis national elections. It is exacerbated by the media adopting a nationalized frame (focusing on larger cities and winners and losers among the national parties and figures).

Meanwhile, additional avenues have been explored for refining or challenging our view of each phase in the process. As it comes to the period before the local elections, some scholars have, for example, been concerned with candidate recruitment and selection (De Winter et al. 2013). They have found evidence for a predominantly local process (with local party officials and/or departing office holders drafting a list for the local members to approve), emphasizing local implantation (being known and active in associations and/or neighborhoods) and perceived competence (capability and availability). Thereby, the selectors attempt to produce a balanced ticket (with governmental experience and/or partisan anchorage particularly prone to be picked for the eligible positions).

The explanation of different sets of choices at the level of the individual voter through exit polls has exasperated the notion of local elections as a lower saliency derivative of national elections. Voters attach relatively more importance to the local level, and local motives (such as knowing a candidate, assessing the departing local governing majority, or position on a local theme or issue) dominate the vote choice. Contacts with local candidates and/or place-bound considerations may thus overwrite national party identification and/or ideological preferences for certain voters. However, more voters still display congruence between local and national voting (intentions) than splits (Marien et al. 2015).

Ultimately, majority formation is key as the proverbial second round of local elections in Belgium (given its local parliamentary investiture). Majorities range from a single list to a coalition thereof. Overall, the frequency of the former has diminished due to local party system fragmentation and an increasing number of lists with coalition potential (excluding the radical right). This holds particularly in Flanders and Brussels, whereas in Wallonia single-party majorities are still the rule (driven by the different mode of designation of the mayor and more consolidated competition, often through local alliances; see earlier discussion).

Thus, in most instances a bargaining process between two or more lists occurs. In many cases, this precedes the actual elections through (secret) prenegotiations, often leading to preagreements (in an estimated two-thirds of all municipalities). Thereby, potential partners explore the terrain and attempt to reduce uncertainty. Quite often, these preagreements need to be abandoned due to the actual election results. Still, most principal agreements are concluded on election night.

The choice of partners primarily appears to be a matter of calculation. Lists try to maximize their utility (in terms of seats or pivotal positions). Hence, coalitions that are minimal winning (without surplus partners) and minimal number of parties prevail (but a workable seat margin is preferred). This commonly leaves many options open. Then, an interplay of congruence in the electoral programs, personal relationships, and good experiences in the preceding majority emerges. Finally, a governmental agreement must be concluded and the composition of the executive determined. Regarding the latter, the iron law of proportionality applies (where the share of offices for a list corresponds with that of its seats brought into the majority). Although lists have portfolio preferences, the assignment of specific offices is usually based on the number of preferential votes, perceived competence, experience in political life, and a balance of territories and social groups in the municipality (Olislagers & Steyvers 2015).

Meanwhile, the regional winds of change are blowing into the local atmosphere. The current Flemish government has proposed a package to reform local representative democracy (Steyvers 2020). Aiming to amplify the voice of the citizen, it plans to abolish compulsory voting and the devolution of the list vote. The largest list would gain the right of initiative to form a majority, and the mayor will be automatically designated (i.e., candidate with most preference votes on the largest list in the majority). In addition, a constructive motion of distrust will allow the replacement of the sitting majority during the legislative term. Many measures seem inspired by the Walloon Region. The institutional climate thus becomes a bit more national again. If and how this weathers local elections and voting will only be clear in 2024.

Notes

1 The creation of a third tier is legally possible. Municipalities with more than 100,000 inhabitants can establish districts, referring to designated areas within the locality and disposing of a set of devolved competences. So far, only the city of Antwerp has brought this provision into practice.
2 The same division of labor holds for the regional elections. For their federal and European counterparts, the framing occurs at the federal level.
3 For the federal level, this term length was only introduced as a result of another round of state reforms in 2011 (hence, it was effective from 2014 onward). In the bicameral setting, this reform affected both the Chamber of Representatives and the Senate. The latter also ceased to be directly elected. Its members are now appointed or co-opted, and the institution is due to function as a meeting place for the different regions and communities of the country. Whereas the local and the regional levels have a fixed term of office, that at the federal level is more flexible as the Chamber can be dissolved and new elections called.
4 When applicable, the councils of the (submunicipal) districts are also directly elected. Moreover, in a few municipalities with language facilities, aldermen are equally directly elected.
5 A candidate needs the support of a majority of the council as a whole and those elected on his or her list.
6 This can be the case for people who are declared as (temporarily) incapacitated or have incurred certain criminal convictions.
7 This is 7,398 in the Flemish Region, 5,357 in the Walloon Region, and 695 in the Brussels Capital Region. It averages a bit more than 23 per municipality.
8 Voters can mark a circular void within a black frame next to the number and the name of the list or next to one or more specific candidates.

9 In comparison to the d'Hondt method, Imperiali is said to advantage lists with a larger number of votes.
10 The latter division reflects a gradual reduction in the effect of the devolution of the list vote coming about in various legislative steps beginning in the twenty-first century.
11 Calculated as the ratio of the number of deposed ballots to the number of registered voters (aggregated for the whole of the country and in percentage). Local refers to the election of municipal councils and national to that of the federal Chamber of Representatives (i.e., lower house).
12 In over 95% of all municipalities, at least one and on average about four.
13 They are present in just over 80% of all municipalities, with an average of one or two in the Flemish Region and almost anywhere in the Walloon Region. They comprise a little over 31% of the partisan offerings in the Flemish Region and 68% in the Walloon Region.
14 This refers to a certain list as submitted under the number of a given national party. It expresses the mutual acknowledgment between a list submitted for the local elections and its national mother party (even beyond strict nominal parameters). All other lists (including those national ones who opted out of the procedure, such as the radical left in Flanders) are treated as local. A more in-depth analysis should refine the partisan links of nonnational lists.

References

André, A., Pilet, J.-B., Depauw, S. & Van Aelst, P. (2013). De partij, de leider of een 'gewone' kandidaat? Het gebruik van de voorkeurstem bij de gemeenteraadsverkiezingen van 2012. In R. Dassonneville, M. Hooghe, S. Marien & J.-B. Pilet (Eds.), *De lokale kiezer. Het kiesgedrag bij de Belgische gemeenteraadsverkiezingen van oktober 2012* (pp. 117–140). ASP: Brussel.

Blaise, P., Demertizis, V., Faniel, J., Istasse, C. & Pitzeys, J. (2018). *La préparation des élections communales et provinciales du 14 octobre 2018.* Courrier Hebdomadaire du CRISP, 2381/2. Brussel: CRISP.

Celis, K., Erzeel, S. & Meier, P. (2013). Twintig jaar quota en wat nu? Een empirische reflectie op de tijdelijkheid van genderquota in de lokale politiek. In K. Deschouwer, T. Verthé & B. Rihoux (Eds.), *Op zoek naar kiezers. Lokale partijafdelingen en de gemeenteraadsverkiezingen van oktober 2012* (pp. 123–146). Brussel: ASP.

Cole, M. (2019). Local Electoral Systems. In R. Kerley, J. Liddle & P. Dunning (Eds.), *The Routledge Handbook of International Local Government* (pp. 13–24). London: Routledge.

Copus, C., Wingfield, M., Steyvers, K. & Reynaert, H. (2012). A Place to Party? Parties and Nonpartisanship in Local Government. In S. Clarke, P. John & K. Mossberger (Eds.), *The Oxford Handbook of Urban Politics* (pp. 210–230). Oxford: Oxford University Press.

Dandoy, R. (2014). The Impact of e-voting on Turnout: Insights from the Belgian Case. *Proceedings of the 2014 International Conference on eDemocracy & eGovernment (ICEDEG).* DOI: 10.1109/ICEDEG.2014.6819940.

Dandoy, R., Dodeigne, J., Matagne, G. & Reuchamps, M. (Eds.) (2013). *Les élections communales de 2012 en Wallonie.* Brugge: Vanden Broele.

Dandoy, R., Dodeigne, J., Steyvers, K. & Verthé, T. (Eds.) (2020). *Lokale kiezers hebben hun redenen. De gemeenteraadsverkiezingen van 2018 geanalyseerd.* Brugge: Vanden Broele.

De Becker, A. (2013). Local Government in Belgium. A 'Catch 22' between Autonomy and Hierarchy. In C. Panara, & M. Varney (Eds.), *Local Government in Europe. The 'fourth level' in the EU multi-layered system of governance* (pp. 26–51). London: Routledge.

De Ceuninck, K., Steyvers, K. & Valcke, T. (2016). As You Like It or Much Ado About Nothing? Structural Reform in Local Government in Belgium. In U. Sadioglu & K. Dede (Eds.), *Theoretical Foundations and Discussions on The Reformation Process in Local Governments* (pp. 237–264). Hershey: IGI Global.

De Rynck, F. & Wayenberg, E. (2010). Belgium. In E. Page & M. Goldsmith (Eds.), *Changing Government Relations in Europe: From Localism to Intergovernmentalism* (pp. 14–29). London: Sage.

De Winter, L., Erzeel, S., Vandeleene, A. & Wauters, B. (2013). Nationale bemoeienis of lokale autonomie? Het lijstvormingsproces bij de gemeenteraadsverkiezingen. In K. Deschouwer, T. Verthé & B. Rihoux (Eds.), *Op zoek naar kiezers. Lokale partijafdelingen en de gemeenteraadsverkiezingen van oktober 2012* (pp. 93–122). Brussel: ASP.

Dodeigne, J. Close, C., Jacquet, V. & Matagne, G. (Eds.) (2020). *Les élections locales du 14 octobre 2018 en Wallonie et à Bruxelles: une offre politique renouvelée?* Bruges: Vanden Broele.

Heinelt, H., Hlepas, N., Kuhlmann, S. & Swianiewicz, P. (2018). Local Government Systems: Grasping the Institutional Environment of Mayors. In H. Heinelt, A. Magnier, M. Cabria & H. Reynaert (Eds.), *Political Leaders and Changing Local Democracy. The European Mayor* (pp. 19–78). London: Palgrave Macmillan.

Ladner, A., Keuffer, N., Baldersheim, H., Hlepas, N., Swianiewicz, P., Steyvers, K. & Navarro, C. (2019). *Patterns of Local Autonomy in Europe.* London: Palgrave Macmillan.

Lefevere, J. (2013). Zijn lokale verkiezingen tweederangsverkiezingen? In R. Dassonneville, M. Hooghe, S. Marien & J.-B. Pilet (Eds.), *De lokale kiezer. Het kiesgedrag bij de Belgische gemeenteraadsverkiezingen van oktober 2012* (pp. 93–116). Brussel: ASP.

Marien, S., Dassonneville, R. & Hooghe, M. (2015). How Second Order Are Local Elections? Voting Motives and Party Preferences in Belgian Municipal Elections. *Local Government Studies, 41*(6), 898–916.

Olislagers, E. & Steyvers, K. (2015). Choosing Coalition Partners in Belgian Local Government. *Local Government Studies, 41*(2), 202–219.

Reynaert, H. & Steyvers, K. (2007). Towards a Direct Election of Mayors in Belgium: Giving up Representation or Giving in to Political Renewal? *Representation: The Journal of Representative Democracy, 43*(2), 121–134.

Reynaert, H., Steyvers, K. & Van de Voorde, N. (2019). Burgemeesters in Vlaanderen: lokale voorkeurstemmen en nationale mandaten. In: H. Reynaert (Ed.), *Verrekijkers voor lokale besturen. Een lange(re)termijnvisie?!* (pp. 133–160). Brugge: Vanden Broele.

Steyvers, K. (2020). De lokale vertegenwoordigende democratie hervormd: *multiple choice*? In H. Reynaert (Ed.), Wendbare lokale besturen in snel veranderende tijden (pp. 47–84). Brugge: Vanden Broele.

Steyvers, K. & De Ceuninck, K. (2013). De kracht van verandering of plus ça change? De gemeenteraadsverkiezingen van 2012 in het licht van de trends sinds de fusies van 1976. In H. Reynaert & K. Steyvers (Eds.), *De kracht van verankering? De verkiezingen van 14 oktober 2012* (pp. 15–40). Brugge: Vanden Broele.

Steyvers, K. & Heyerick, A. (2017). Fifty Shades of Rokkan? Reconceiving Local Party System Nationalisation in Belgium. *Croatian and Comparative Public Administration, 17*(4), 509–538.

Verstraete, D., Devillers, S., Dandoy, R., Dodeigne, J., Jacquet, V., Niessen, C. & Reuchamps, M. (2018). *Les rôles, fonctions et choix politiques des bourgmestres en Wallonie et à Bruxelles.* Courrier Hebdomadaire du CRISP, 2376. Brussel: CRISP.

Wayenberg, E., De Rynck, F., Steyvers, K. & Pilet, J.-B. (2012). Belgium: A Tale of Regional Divergence? In J. Loughlin, F. Hendriks & A. Lidström (Eds.), *The Oxford Handbook of Local and Regional Democracy in Europe* (pp. 72–95). Oxford: Oxford University Press.

11

Germany

A variety of local elections in a federal system

Angelika Vetter

The structure and functioning of local government in Germany

Germany has a long federal tradition. It formally comprises the federal level and the states (*Länder*). Constitutionally speaking, local government is not a third tier of government but part of the states' administrations (executive branches). However, Article 28(2) of the German Basic Law guarantees the protection of the institution of local authorities, the principle of 'universality of duties': local authorities can regulate and administer their own affairs in their own responsibilities, and they are entitled to defend themselves before the courts in cases of interference from their state governments or any other territorial corporation (Knemeyer 2001: 174). This guarantee applies to local governments across all states. Apart from that, each state has its own local government constitution (*Gemeindeordnung* or *GemO*) – enacted by the respective state governments – that defines the institutional framework of local government. Other state-specific laws such as local electoral laws complement these local constitutions.[1] Local government in Germany is attributed a high degree of autonomy (Ladner et al. 2019; Vetter 2007; Hesse 1991). Due to German cooperative federalism, local governments traditionally have a multipurpose profile. They fulfill not only self-governing functions (e.g., general administration of the municipality, housing construction and city planning, public transport, culture, recreation, and sports) but also functions delegated to them by the federal or respective state government. While they enjoy great discretion over self-governing functions, they have little to no discretion over mandatory or delegated responsibilities (water supply, wastewater disposal, waste disposal, issuing passports and identity cards, vehicle licensing, etc.). Germans show higher trust in local and regional authorities than in state or federal authorities. Similarly, they are more satisfied with local democracy than with democracy at higher levels of government (Vetter 2011: 6, 2019: 14).

Due to the federal structure, the institutional framework of local government varies from state to state. Germany has 16 states, three of which are city states: Berlin, Hamburg, and Bremen. As their administrations fulfill both state and local government functions, this chapter refers only to local governments and local elections in the remaining 13 states. In all of them, local government is a two-tier system consisting of districts (*Kreise*) and municipalities (*Kommunen*). Some of these municipalities – mainly large cities with more than 100,000 inhabitants – are independent (*kreisfreie Städte*), fulfilling the functions of both a district and a municipality. All other municipalities belong to a district. The 13 states differ with regard to the number and average size of their municipalities: while municipalities in densely populated North Rhine-Westphalia have about 45,000 inhabitants on average, municipalities in Rhineland-Palatinate have only 1,800 (see Table 11.1). After reunification, the total number of municipalities in Germany was about 16,000. Today, only about 10,800 remain, mainly as the consequence of amalgamations in the east German states, where the number of municipalities has been reduced by 68%. Similar amalgamations had already taken place in west Germany in the early 1970s, when the number of municipalities was reduced by more than 60%.

Until the 1990s, local government systems in Germany followed one of four models: the Magistrate form (*Magistratsverfassung*), the strong mayor form (*Bürgermeisterverfassung*), the North German council form (*Norddeutsche Ratsverfassung*), or the South German council form (*Süddeutsche Ratsverfassung*) (Gunlicks 1986: 73ff.; Knemeyer 1999). In all four models, the elected council was formally the highest decision-making body of the municipality. The systems

Table 11.1 Number and average size of municipalities across the German states, 1991 and 2020

	Number of municipalities (independent or part of a district)			Average number of inhabitants (in 1,000)		
	1991	2020	Change	1991	2020	Change
Schleswig-Holstein	1,131	1,106	−2%	2.3	2.6	12%
Hamburg	1	1	0%	1,659	1,841	11%
Lower Saxony	1,031	942	−9%	7.2	8.5	18%
Bremen	2	2	0%	341	341.5	0%
North Rhine-Westphalia	396	396	0%	44	45.3	3%
Hesse	426	422	−1%	13.6	14.8	9%
Rhineland-Palatinate	2,304	2,302	0%	1.6	1.8	8%
Baden-Wuerttemberg	1,111	1,101	−1%	8.9	10.1	13%
Bavaria	2,051	2,056	0%	5.6	6.4	13%
Saarland	52	52	0%	20.7	19.1	−8%
Berlin	1	1	0%	3,436	3,645	6%
Brandenburg	1,794	417	−77%	1.4	6	322%
Mecklenburg-Western Pomerania	1,124	726	−35%	1.7	2.2	31%
Saxony	1,626	419	−74%	2.9	9.7	235%
Saxony-Anhalt	1,367	218	−84%	2.1	10.1	386%
Thuringia	1,710	634	−63%	1.5	3.4	123%
Total East	7,621	2,414	−68%	1.9	5.2	171%
Total West	8,506	8,381	−1%	7.7	8.4	9%
Total	16,127	10,795	−33%	5.0	7.7	55%

Note: The table does not display the very limited number of areas not belonging to any municipality or district (gemeindefreie Gebiete; N = 210 in 2020, mainly located in Bavaria and Lower Saxony). These areas are either state or federal property or the property of the Bundesanstalt für Immobilienaufgaben. Most of these areas are uninhabited (forest and water areas, military training areas, etc.).

Sources: Number of municipalities and inhabitants 2020, www.destatis.de/DE/Themen/Laender-Regionen/Regionales/Gemeindeverzeichnis/Administrativ/Archiv/Verwaltungsgliederung/Verwalt1QAktuell.html (accessed August 2020); number of inhabitants 1991, www.statistik-bw.de/VGRdL/tbls/tab.jsp?rev=RV2014&tbl=tab20&lang=de-DE (accessed August 2020)

differed, however, in terms of the power of the local council vis-à-vis the local executive branch and the degree of party politicization. In the South German council form (Bavaria and Baden-Wuerttemberg), the council was weakest. The mayor was directly elected for eight years. He or she headed both the council and the administration, and consensual policymaking was dominant with a low degree of party politicization. In the strong mayor form (Rhineland-Palatinate, Saarland, and part of Schleswig-Holstein), the mayor was elected by council majority for a term of ten years. He or she not only chaired council committees and meetings and controlled the agenda but was also the chief administrative officer and the legal and ceremonial head of the town. In the Magistrat form (Hesse and parts of Schleswig-Holstein), the council was headed by a chairperson elected from the council members. The council elected the executive committee (*Magistrat*), consisting of the mayor and several deputies, with all members being equal and having one vote each. In the North German council form (North Rhine-Westphalia and Lower Saxony), the council was strongest vis-à-vis the executive branch. The mayor was elected by the council as the chairperson and the ceremonial head of town. However, the councilors also elected a chief administrative officer, leading to a kind of 'city manager form' of local government and administration. In the early 1990s, major institutional reforms that were described as the 'triumphal march of the South German municipal constitution' (Knemeyer 1999: 105; Wollmann 2003) led to a convergence of the local institutional systems: while citizens were given more means to participate in local politics, the strength of (national) parties in local politics weakened (Vetter 2009).

Today, local councils constitutionally are still the main body of the local political systems, but mayors are directly elected and citizens may initiate binding referendums in all states. Even small local lists may now obtain seats on the local councils, as thresholds have been abolished. And voters may change the parties' candidate lists by splitting and/or cumulating their multiple votes (exceptions: North-Rhine Westphalia and Saarland). These institutional features follow the model of local government that has predominated in Baden-Wuerttemberg and Bavaria since the 1950s. With the exception of these two forerunner states, all state governments also passed legislation in the 1990s that allows mayors to be recalled, with the vote being initiated either exclusively by the citizens or by the local councils or the citizens (Kuhlmann 2009: 240; Holtmann et al. 2017: 100–101). Due to these changes, today most local government systems follow the strong mayor model (Kuhlmann 2009; Egner 2017; Heinelt et al. 2018). Despite this trend of convergence, however, we still find differences in local policymaking due to path dependencies: there is higher politicization and a more competitive way of policymaking in North Rhine-Westphalia, Saarland, and Hesse, while local policymaking in Baden-Wuerttemberg and the east German states has always been characterized as more consensual (Holtkamp 2008: 121; Bogumil and Holtkamp 2013: 36ff.).

Horizontal and vertical characteristics of local elections in the German multilevel system

In every state, local elections for municipal and district councils are held on the same day, but election days (and years) differ from state to state. In general, the concurrence of local council and federal or state elections is avoided to guarantee the independence of local elections from political trends at higher levels of government. This is not the case for local and European elections, however: in 1979, two states (Saarland and Rhineland-Palatinate) started to hold local council elections on the day elections to the European Parliament were scheduled. Today, local council elections coincide with elections to the European Parliament in nine out of 16 states.

While federal elections are held every four years, the local council legislative term is five years in all states except Bavaria (six years). In Bavaria and Baden-Wuerttemberg, mayors have been elected directly since the 1950s. In the other 11 of the 13 states discussed here, the respective state governments introduced direct election of mayors during the 1990s, following a trend that had started in Hesse and was, in some states, partly a response to pressure from the opposition parties at the state levels (Vetter 2009). The direct election of mayors coincides with local council elections only in Bavaria. In all other states, mayoral and council elections are held separately, with the terms of office differing for councils and mayors (Bogumil and Holtkamp 2013: 32). North Rhine-Westphalia is currently changing back to concurrent elections of councils and mayors. Binding local referendums (direct democracy) have by now been institutionalized in all states, although the legal frameworks differ in terms of thresholds for signatures and quotas for the approval of the referendums. Referendums only rarely coincide with other local, state, European, or federal elections (Kost 2013; Mehr Demokratie e.V. 2018).

Whether local elections and their outcomes have a barometric function for the governments of the states or the federal government is questionable for two reasons. First, due to the differences between the local and the national party systems, it is unclear whether voters explicitly want to punish or reward the federal or state governments or whether they just prefer local lists to represent them in the local councils. Second, local elections are not held on the same day in all states (except for those states with concurrent local and European elections), and their outcomes do not affect the power relationship between governing and opposition parties either at the state or at the federal level. This is why their salience is low and nationwide attention to their outcomes from the media or the parties at higher system levels is limited.

Local electoral systems: trending toward more power to the citizens

Local electoral systems across the German states differ, and they underwent several changes in the 1990s (Meyer 2007; Table 12.2). The juridical regulations are specified either in the local constitution of each state or in additional state-specific local electoral laws. Voter registration is automatic for all elections in Germany. The active right to vote in federal elections is restricted to people with German citizenship, and the minimum voting age is 18. These regulations differ for local elections: citizens of Germany and other EU member states are entitled to vote if they have lived in the respective municipality for a certain time, which varies from state to state [e.g., three months in Baden-Wuerttemberg (§12(1) GemO BW) or 16 days in North Rhine-Westphalia (§7 KWG NRW)]. Voting age differs as well: since the 1990s, 11 out of 13 states have lowered the voting age in local elections from 18 to 16. The state legislators were more reluctant to change the minimum age for state elections. The proportion of 16- to 18-year-olds in the total population is about 3%. Empirical studies of federal elections have shown that turnout for the youngest age group is somewhat higher than for the age cohort 21–25, but nevertheless is well below the general average.[2] The same seems to hold for local elections (Leininger and Faas 2020: 155).

In all states, mayoral elections follow a two-round majority system (age and citizenship requirements for participation in mayoral elections are the same as for local council elections), while local councils are elected via systems of proportional representation with only minor exceptions, mainly in very small municipalities in Rhineland-Palatinate (Holtmann et al. 2017: 95; Meyer 2007: 432). Local elections are usually held at large. In those states where the local electoral laws allow voters to split and/or cumulate their multiple votes, parties offer open lists to the electorate.[3] The number of votes ranges from three (Lower Saxony and the five east

German states) to as many votes as there are seats on the council. Council sizes in the states differ according to the size of the municipalities. For example, the number of votes in Baden-Wuerttemberg is eight in municipalities with fewer than 1,000 inhabitants, and 60 in municipalities with more than 400,000 inhabitants. In Hesse, the number varies between 15 votes in municipalities with fewer than 3,000 inhabitants, and 105 votes in municipalities with more than 1 million inhabitants. North Rhine-Westphalia and Saarland are the only states where closed lists are still used, and voters may cast only one vote in the council elections. Local elections also differ with regard to the formula used to translate votes into seats: the d'Hondt method favoring bigger parties is used in Saxony and Saarland. The other states follow either the Hare/Niemeyer or the Sainte-Laguë/Schepers method. Finally, thresholds for local council elections, which used to vary between 3% and 5%, were abolished in all states where they existed (Table 11.2).

Turnout, party systems, and gender across states: variations in detail – similarities in trends

In Germany, voter registration is automatic for elections at all levels (local, state, federal, European). Therefore, the number of eligible voters and the number of registered voters are more or less the same, and turnout is measured as the percentage of eligible voters who actually cast their vote(s).[4] Turnout for local council elections in Germany has always been lower than turnout for national elections (Vetter 2019). Exceptions are rare cases of local elections that were held together with federal elections, as in North Rhine-Westphalia in 1994 and in Brandenburg in 1998. Comparing turnout figures across states and over time, the data indicate persistent differences in the levels of local turnout (Figure 11.1). In the 1950s, local turnout in Saarland, for example, was 87.6%, while in Baden-Wuerttemberg it was below 70% (18.4% difference; Vetter 2019). By the beginning of the new millennium (2002–2005), local turnout was 63.2% in Bavaria, but only 42.1% in Saxony-Anhalt (21.1% difference). This pattern suggests that the level of local council election turnout is affected by institutional, cultural, or political contexts that vary among states and that explain path dependency over time. Baden-Wuerttemberg, in general, shows the lowest local council turnout rates compared to other west German states. Turnout rates in Saarland, Bavaria, Hesse, and Rhineland-Palatinate have always been significantly higher. Voter participation in Lower Saxony, Schleswig-Holstein, and North Rhine-Westphalia tends to fall in between. Turnout in east Germany is generally lower than in west Germany, a fact that holds not only for local council elections but for federal and state elections as well.

Apart from these interstate differences, the level of turnout for local council elections in Germany has developed in remarkably similar ways over the last three decades. At the end of the 1980s, local council turnout averaged above 70%. The situation changed in the 1990s, when local turnout started to fall sharply in all states. By 2016, average participation in local elections in the west German states was 51.6%. In the east German states, turnout was even lower at 49.9% on average. To conclude, local election turnout has fallen by almost 20 percentage points since the beginning of the 1990s, and the decline in turnout was far more pronounced for local than for federal elections (1990–2013: −6.3 percentage points).

The declining trend seems to have come to a halt and even been reversed in those states where the latest local elections were held on the same day as the elections to the European Parliament on 26 May 2019: turnout for local council elections that day was, on average, about 10 percentage points higher than for the 2014 elections. This unexpected change is attributable to the high salience of EP elections in 2019. But turnout had already increased for the latest federal election in 2017 and the latest state elections. The rising trend is linked to increasing politicization due to issues such as climate change, immigration, the future of the European Union, and the rise of the

Table 11.2 Variations in the electoral systems in 13 German states

State	Legislative term (since year)	Voting systems (2019)[1]	Number of votes (since year)	Concurrent EU elections (since year)	Voting age (since year)	Seat allocation (since year)	Abolition of thresholds (year)
Baden-Wuerttemberg	5 (1979)	PR with open lists	Max. (1953)	Yes	16 (2014)	Sainte-Laguë (1946)	1953
Bavaria	6 (1960)	PR with open lists	Max. (1946)	(1994[2])	18	Sainte-Laguë (1949)	1956
Hesse	5 (2001)	PR with open lists	Max. (2001)	–	18	Hare/Niemeyer (2001)	1999
Lower Saxony	5 (1979)	PR with open lists	3 (1981)	–	16 (1996)	Hare/Niemeyer (1981)	1946
North Rhine-Westphalia	5 (1964)	PR with closed lists	1	Yes (2014[2])	16 (1999)	Sainte-Laguë (2009)	2004
Rhineland-Palatinate	5 (1964)	PR with open lists	Max. (1989)	Yes (1979)	18	Sainte-Laguë (2014)	1989
Saarland	5 (1974)	PR with closed lists	1	Yes (1979)	18	d'Hondt (1959)	2009
Schleswig-Holstein	5 (1998)	Personalized PR with closed lists	As many as there are direct mandates	–	16 (1998)	Sainte-Laguë (2013)	1994
Brandenburg	5 (1993)	PR with open lists	3 (1990)	Yes (2014)	16 (2014)	Hare/Niemeyer (1990)	1993
Mecklenburg-Western Pomerania	5 (1994)	PR with open lists	3 (1990)	Yes (1994)	16 (1999)	Hare/Niemeyer (1990)	2004
Saxony	5 (1990)	PR with open lists	3 (1990)	Yes (1994)	18	d'Hondt (1994)	1994
Saxony-Anhalt	5 (1994)	PR with open lists	3 (1990)	Yes (1994)	16 (1999)	Hare/Niemeyer (1990)	1994
Thuringia	5 (1994)	PR with open lists	3 (1990)	Yes (1994[2])	16 (2019)	Hare/Niemeyer (1990)	2009

[1] Abbreviations: PR, proportional representation; Max, as many votes as there are seats on the local council.
[2] Exceptions: Thuringia in 2004; Baden-Wuerttemberg in 1999; North Rhine-Westphalia in 2019.

Source: www.wahlrecht.de/kommunal/index.htm (accessed 13/3/2019) and Holtmann et al. (2017: 96f)

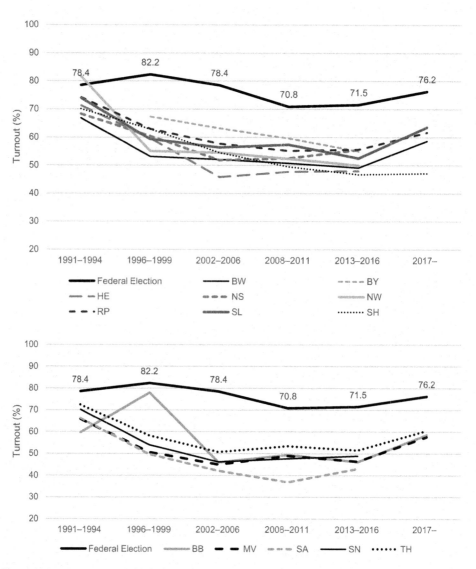

Figure 11.1 Voter turnout for federal and local elections in Germany, 1991–2019
Sources: Author's collection of aggregate data from the states' statistical offices

'new' right-wing party Alternative für Deutschland (AfD), which mobilized conservative, right-wing, and former nonvoters to cast their votes in these elections (Haußner and Leininger 2018).

Data for 11,323 municipalities across 12 states for the years between 1998 and 2002 show a significant and strong negative relationship between municipality size and local turnout (Pearson's $R = -0.56^{\star\star}$).[5] The strong negative effect holds for all states and was replicated using data from the most recent local council elections in Baden-Wuerttemberg (2019) and North-Rhine Westphalia (2014; see Figure 11.2).

Regarding the political context of local elections in Germany, the story is again one of differences. We find consensual patterns of local policymaking in states such as Baden-Wuerttemberg,

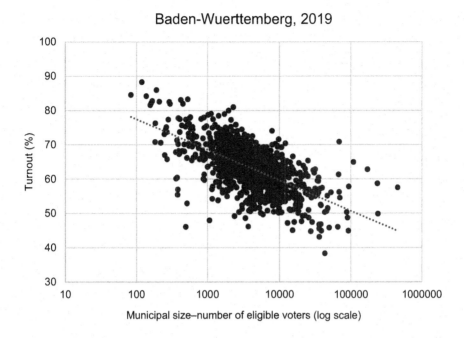

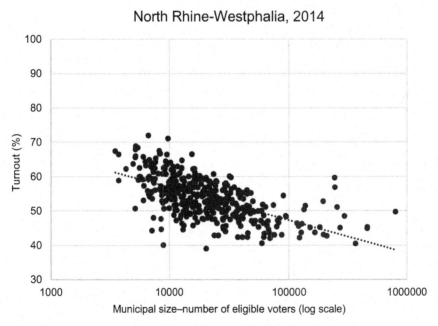

Figure 11.2 Voter turnout for local council elections in Baden-Wuerttemberg (2019) and North Rhine-Westphalia (2014) by number of eligible voters

Source: Author's calculations based on data collected from the statistical offices in North Rhine-Westphalia and Baden-Wuerttemberg

where the nationalization of the local party systems is low, municipalities tend to be small, mayors have a strong position vis-à-vis the councils, and electoral systems are more personalized. More competitive patterns of local policymaking still predominate in states such as North-Rhine Westphalia or Saarland, where the local party systems are characterized by a high degree of nationalization, municipalities tend to be large, electoral systems are less personalized, and mayors are less powerful vis-à-vis the councils. Since the institutional reforms in the early 1990s (see previous discussion), there has been a trend toward more consensual local policymaking, but competitive patterns in North Rhine-Westphalia and Saarland can still be observed due to path-dependencies and differences in the institutional design (Holtkamp 2008).

The fragmentation of the party systems in the German multilevel system has increased at all levels since 1990. At the federal level, the effective number of parliamentary parties rose from 2.6 in 1990 to 5.1 in 2017 due to losses by the two formerly largest parties, the Christian Democrats (CDU) and Social Democrats (SPD), a rising number of seats for smaller parties such as Bündnis 90/Die Grünen (Greens) and PDS/Die Linke (Left), and the emergence of the new right-wing party Alternative for Germany (AfD), which has held seats in the Bundestag since 2017. The trend at the local level is similar. First, local party systems traditionally differ across states with regard to their degree of nationalization (i.e., the presence of national parties at the local level). In North Rhine-Westphalia and Saarland, national political parties still win a high share of votes in local elections. These parties win far smaller percentages (of the vote) in other states, such as Baden-Wuerttemberg, Bavaria, Thuringia, and Saxony (Reiser et al. 2008; Holtkamp and Eimer 2006). Table 11.3 shows for two exemplary states (North Rhine Westphalia and Baden-Wuerttemberg) the aggregate shares of votes for national parties

Table 11.3 Shares of votes for national parties and 'other' parties/local lists in local elections in North Rhine-Westphalia and Baden-Wuerttemberg, 1994–2019

North Rhine-Westphalia	1994	1999	2004	2009	2014	
CDU (Christian Democrats)	40.3	50.3	43.3	38.7	37.5	–
SPD (Social Democrats)	42.3	33.9	31.7	29.4	31.4	–
Bündnis 90/Die Grünen (Greens)	10.2	7.3	10.3	12.0	11.7	–
FDP (Free Democrats – Liberals)	3.8	4.3	6.8	9.1	4.7	–
PDS/Die Linke (The Left)	–	0.8	1.4	4.3	4.7	–
AfD (Alternative for Germany)	–	–	–	–	2.6	–
Others	3.4	3.4	6.5	6.5	7.4	–
Baden-Wuerttemberg	1994	1999	2004	2009	2014	2019
CDU (Christian Democrats)	31.6	36.0	33.2	28.2	28.3	22.1
SPD (Social Democrats)	24.1	21.7	19.9	18.2	17.7	14.1
Bündnis 90/Die Grünen (Greens)	7.7	5.2	8.2	10.3	11.5	16.5
FDP (Liberals)	3.5	3.0	3.7	6.2	3.7	4.9
PDS/Die Linke (The Left)	–	–	–	–	1.7	2.2
AfD (Alternative for Germany)	–	–	–	–	1.5	3.0
Others	33.1	34.1	35.0	37.1	35.6	37.2

Notes: Numbers indicate the share of votes (percent) in local elections aggregated at the state level. For North Rhine-Westphalia, this includes council elections in districts and independent municipalities; for Baden-Wuerttemberg, it includes independent municipalities and municipalities that are part of a district. The category 'others' comprises local lists and independents, as well as small parties running in state and federal elections, lists from parties and local groups, or single candidates. The reporting of these groups/parties differs between the states' statistical offices.

Sources: Author's collection of data from the websites of the states' statistical offices.

that run in local elections and for other, mainly independent local lists, as well as for smaller parties running in federal elections (see also Goehlert et al. 2008; Morlok et al. 2012). Across all states, the degree of nationalization is lower in smaller municipalities than in larger ones (Kuhn and Vetter 2013). But recent studies show that other parties are becoming stronger even in medium-sized and larger cities. The trend of party system fragmentation therefore holds not only for the federal but also the local level, especially in larger cities (Bogumil 2010: 44f.).

There are no general gender quotas for local elections in Germany. Compared to the state and the federal levels, the number of female representatives is lowest on local councils (Eder et al. 2016). Across all states, the share of female councilors was far below 50% in 2019. The trend across all German states since 2008 shows a minimal increase of around 2 percentage points(Figure 11.3). Again, there is significant variation across the states: while the share of female councilors is around 30% in Hesse, North Rhine-Westphalia, and

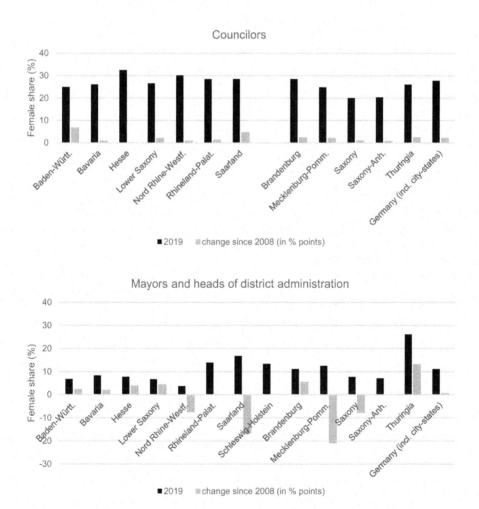

Figure 11.3 Women's representation among German councilors, mayors, and heads of district administrations by state (2019)

Source: Bundesministerium für Familie, Senioren, Frauen und Jugend (2020: 10, 16)

Rhineland-Palatinate, which is similar to the share of female MPs in the federal parliament 2019 (31.2%), it is only about 20% in Saxony and Saxony-Anhalt. The share of female candidates seems to be higher where the Greens, the Left, and the Social Democrats hold a significant number of seats on the local councils, as these parties introduced internal gender quotas in the 1980s and 1990s (Holtkamp and Schnittke 2010; Holtkamp et al. 2017). A similar pattern – although at an even lower level – can be observed for the share of female mayors and heads of administration in the districts and independent municipalities, varying between 4% in North Rhine-Westphalia and 26% in Thuringia (2019). Here too, the figures show only a minimal total increase of 0.6 percentage points since 2008.

Discussion

Federalism makes studying local elections in Germany a challenge. There is not only variation in local elections within states, with the size of the municipality being one of the most important variables affecting local elections, but also large variation across states in terms of local elections' institutional, political, and cultural contexts, which trace back for decades. As there is no central or federal office providing data on local elections, local electoral data have to be collected from each state's statistical office individually. This explains at least partly why local election studies in Germany are still rare. Studies using individual level data are even rarer and often refer to single municipalities (e.g., Gabriel et al. 1997; Schmitt-Beck et al. 2008). Despite these difficulties, it is the high number of cases embedded in different structural, institutional, and political contexts that makes studying local elections in Germany interesting.

The contexts of local elections have changed remarkably over the last few decades. We see a converging trend in the institutional frameworks of local politics and local elections across states, which can be summarized as a trend toward a more citizen-oriented way of local policymaking (introduction of directly elected mayors, binding local referendums, abolishment of thresholds for council elections, changes in the electoral systems with more open lists, and opportunities for splitting and cumulating votes; Vetter 2009).

Despite interstate differences and differences between municipalities of different size, local elections also share common characteristics: first, turnout levels remain lower for local than for federal or state elections. But we found a strong, declining trend across all states, which was more pronounced than turnout decline for federal elections. Whether the increasing turnout numbers observed during the latest elections will change this pattern remains to be seen. Some authors conclude that the institutional reforms from the 'decade of democratic innovations', such as the implementation of initiatives or referendums, were the main drivers behind this decline, thereby reducing the importance of local elections for political participation (Klein 2018). But referendums and initiatives are still only rarely used: around 300 initiatives and referendums were held across 11,460 municipalities and districts between 2013 and 2017 (Mehr Demokratie e.V. 2018: 19). And turnout also declined in states where institutional reforms were only marginal (e.g., Baden-Wuerttemberg). It is therefore plausible that the decline in turnout is not paralleled by a significant shift in local participation to other arenas of political activism, but instead has to be explained at least partly by factors such as the enlargement of the electorate due to the Maastricht treaty, which affects all states.

Second, we find similarities across states with regard to changes in the local party systems: fragmentation is rising at both the federal and state levels, but it is stronger at the local level especially in larger municipalities, where an increasing number of votes is cast for independent local lists or small parties challenging national parties in local elections.

Both trends might be indicators of a depoliticization and marginalization of local politics in the German multilevel system. Horizontally, at the local level the rising number of nonvoters might indicate an increasing detachment of citizens from local policymaking. And the fragmentation of the party systems might weaken the capacities of the local councils not only for forming coalitions for effective policymaking but also for controlling the now directly elected and often powerful mayors heading the local administrations. Vertically, fragmentation and the growing success of independent local lists might detach municipalities from policymaking at higher system levels. Local lists have no vertical party linkages across different system levels. They lack the vertically structured national parties' function of local interest representation at higher system levels, except for Bavaria where the *Freie Wähler* voting bloc has recently become a party and a coalition partner in the state government. Local (or municipal) interests in Germany are not represented in an additional chamber either at the state level or at the federal level (in contrast to the states' interests, which are represented in the German Bundesrat). The loss of the national parties' vertical linking potential might therefore result in the marginalization of local politics within the German multilevel governance system. Whether these trends will continue and what consequences they may have deserves attention during the coming years to identify the prospective role of German local democracy within an encompassing European multilevel governance system.

Notes

1 The local government constitutions in the west German states were adopted by the respective state governments after World War II and have since been amended several times. In the east German states, they were adopted in 1993 and 1994, followed by several amendments. The local constitutions and local electoral laws can be accessed via www.wahlrecht.de/gesetze.htm#bw-kw.
2 See www.bpb.de/nachschlagen/zahlen-und-fakten/bundestagswahlen/205686/wahlbeteiligung-nach-altersgruppen (accessed August 2020). Further comparative data regarding the openness of the local electoral markets, submunicipal and district voting, and whether and how municipalities are divided into electoral wards are currently not available.
3 There is no general information available on how intensively voters make use of ticket splitting and/or cumulating multiple votes in German local elections. Data from the local elections in Stuttgart, the state capital of Baden-Wuerttemberg, show that the number of voters changing ballots has fluctuated over the last 35 years by around 60%, not indicating any trend (Schwarz 2014: 204).
4 Data on local turnout refer to elections for the councils of districts and independent municipalities except for Baden-Wuerttemberg, where the data refer to council elections in independent municipalities and municipalities that are part of a district.
5 Aggregate turnout data at the municipal level across 12 German states had been collected for the research project 'Kommunale Wahlbeteiligung in den deutschen Bundesländern' (2006–2009) funded by the German Research Foundation DFG. Data for Schleswig-Holstein were not available. Municipal size was measured by the logged number of inhabitants in 2003.

References

Bogumil, J. (2010). Parteien in der Kommunalpolitik. Hoffnungsträger oder Auslaufmodell? In D. Gehne and T. Spier (Eds.), *Krise oder Wandel der Parteiendemokratie?* (pp. 37–48). Wiesbaden: VS Verlag.
Bogumil, J. and Holtkamp, L. (2013). *Kommunalpolitik und Kommunalverwaltung*. Bonn: Bundeszentrale für politische Bildung.
Bundesministerium für Familie, Senioren, Frauen und Jugend (Ed.) (2020). *4. Atlas zur Gleichstellung von Frauen und Männern in Deutschland/Tabellenanhang mit Länderdaten* (www.bmfsfj.de/bmfsfj/service/publikationen/4 − atlas-zur-gleichstellung-von-frauen-und-maennern-in-deutschland/160358; accessed November 2020).

Eder, C., Fortin-Rittberger, J. and Kroeber, C. (2016). The Higher the Fewer? Patterns of Female Representation Across Levels of Government in Germany. *Parliamentary Affairs*, 69(2), 366–386.

Egner, B. (2017). Directly Elected Mayors in Germany: Leadership and Institutional Context. In D. Sweeting (Ed.), *Directly Elected Mayors in Urban Governance. Impact and Practice* (pp. 159–178). Bristol: The Policy Press.

Gabriel, O.W., Brettschneider, F. and Vetter, A. (Eds.) (1997). *Politische Kultur und Wahlverhalten in einer Großstadt*. Opladen: Westdeutscher Verlag.

Goehlert, S., Holtmann, E., Krappidel, A. and Reiser, M. (2008). Independent Local Lists in East and West Germany. In M. Reiser and E. Holtmann (Eds.), *Farewell to the Party Model? Independent Local Lists in East and West European Countries* (pp. 127–148). Wiesbaden: VS Verlag für Sozialwissenschaften.

Gunlicks, A.B. (1986). *Local Government in the German Federal System*. Durham: Duke University Press.

Haußner, S. and Leininger, A. (2018). Die Erfolge der AfD und die Wahlbeteiligung: Gibt es einen Zusammenhang? *Zeitschrift für Parlamentsfragen*, 49(1), 69–90.

Heinelt, H., Hlepas, N., Kuhlmann, S. and Swianiewicz, P. (2018). Local Government Systems: Grasping the Institutional Environment of Mayors. In H. Heinelt, A. Magnier, M. Cabria and H. Reynaert (Eds.), *Political Leaders and Changing Local Democracy. The European Mayor* (pp. 19–78). Cham: Springer International Publishing.

Hesse, J.J. (1991). Local Government in a Federal State: The Case of West Germany. In J.J. Hesse (Ed.), *Local Government and Urban Affairs in International Perspective* (pp. 353–385). Baden-Baden: Nomos.

Holtkamp, L. (2008). *Kommunale Konkordanz- und Konkurrenzdemokratie. Parteien und Bürgermeister in der repräsentativen Demokratie*. Wiesbaden: VS Verlag für Sozialwissenschaften.

Holtkamp, L. and Eimer, T. (2006). Totgesagte leben länger . . . Kommunale Wählergemeinschaften in Westdeutschland. In U. Jun, H. Kreikenbom and V. Neu (Eds.), *Kleine Parteien im Aufwind* (pp. 249–276). Frankfurt am Main: Campus Verlag.

Holtkamp, L. and Schnittke, S. (2010). *Die Hälfte der Macht im Visier. Der Einfluss von Institutionen und Parteien auf die politische Repräsentation von Frauen*. Bielefeld: AJZ

Holtkamp, L., Wiechmann, W. and Buß, M. (2017). *Genderranking deutscher Großstädte 2017*. Heinrich Böll Stiftung (www.boell.de/sites/default/files/demokratiereform-03_genderranking_-_baf.pdf?dimension1=ds_genderranking17).

Holtmann, E., Rademacher, C. and Reiser, M. (2017). *Kommunalpolitik. Eine Einführung*. Wiesbaden: Springer VS.

Klein, M. (2018). Mehr Demokratie, weniger Beteiligung? Die Zerstörung der lokalen Beteiligungskultur in Hessen während des "Jahrzehnts der Demokratisierungsnovellen". *Zeitschrift für Parlamentsfragen*, 49(1), 148–171.

Knemeyer, F.L. (1999). Gemeindeverfassungen. In H. Wollmann and R. Roth (Eds.), *Kommunalpolitik. Politisches Handeln in den Gemeinden* (pp. 104–122). Opladen: Leske + Budrich.

Knemeyer, F.L. (2001). The Constitution of Local Government. In K. König and H. Siedentopf (Eds.), *Public Administration in Germany* (pp. 171–181). Baden-Baden: Nomos.

Kost, A. (2013). *Direkte Demokratie*. Wiesbaden: Springer VS.

Kuhlmann, S. (2009). Reforming Local Government in Germany: Institutional Changes and Performance Impacts. *Local Government Studies*, 18(2), 226–245.

Kuhn, S. and Vetter, A. (2013). Die Zukunft der nationalen Parteien vor Ort. In O. Niedermayer, B. Höhne and U. Jun (Eds.), *Abkehr von den Parteien? Parteiendemokratie und Bürgerprotest* (pp. 93–124). Wiesbaden: Springer VS.

Ladner, A., Keuffer, N., Baldersheim, H., Hlepas, N., Swianiewicz, P., Steyvers, K. and Navarro, C. (2019). *Patterns of Local Autonomy in Europe*. London: Palgrave Macmillan.

Leininger, A and Faas, T. (2020). Votes at 16 in Germany: Examining Subnational Variation. In J. Eichhorn and J. Bergh (Eds.), *Lowering the Voting Age to 16* (pp. 143–166). Cham: Springer International Publishing.

Mehr Demokratie e.V. (2018). Bürgerbegehrensbericht 2018 (www.mehr-demokratie.de/fileadmin/pdf/2018-12-04_BB-Bericht2018.pdf; accessed August 2020).

Meyer, H. (2007). Kommunalwahlrecht. In T. Mann and G. Püttner (Eds.), *Handbuch der kommunalen Wissenschaft und Praxis, Bd. 1: Grundlagen und Kommunalverfassung* (pp. 391–458). Berlin: Springer.

Morlok, M., Poguntke, T. and Walther, J. (Eds.) (2012). *Politik an den Parteien vorbei: Freie Wähler und Kommunale Wählergemeinschaften als Alternative*. Baden-Baden: Nomos.

Reiser, M., Rademacher, C. and Jaeck, T. (2008). Präsenz und Erfolg Kommunaler Wählergemeinschaften im Bundesländervergleich. In Vetter, A. (Ed.), *Erfolgsbedingungen lokaler Bürgerbeteiligung* (pp. 123–147). Wiesbaden: VS Verlag für Sozialwissenschaften.

Schmitt-Beck, R., Mackenrodt, C. and Faas, T. (2008). Hintergründe kommunaler Wahlbeteiligung: Eine Fallstudie zur Kommunalwahl 2004 in Duisburg. *Zeitschrift für Parlamentsfragen*, 39(3), 561–580.

Schwarz, T. (2014). Kumulieren und Panaschieren – Wie nutzten die Stuttgarter Wähler/-innen die Möglichkeiten des baden-württembergischen Stimmgebungsverfahrens bei der Gemeinderatswahl 2014? *Statistik und Informationsmanagement* 7/2014, 203–215.

Vetter, A. (2007). *Local Politics: A Resource for Democracy in Western Europe?* Lanham: Lexington.

Vetter, A. (2009). Citizens versus Parties: Explaining Change in German Local Government 1989–2008. *Local Government Studies*, 35(1), 125–142.

Vetter, A. (2011). Lokale Politik als Rettungsanker der Demokratie? *Aus Politik und Zeitgeschichte*, 7–8, 25–32.

Vetter, A. (2019). Lokale Wahlbeteiligung in der Bundesrepublik Deutschland und die Legitimation lokaler Demokratie. In A. Vetter and V. Haug (Eds.), *Kommunalwahlen, Beteiligung und die Legitimation lokaler Demokratie* (pp. 1–25). Wiesbaden: Kommunal- und Schulverlag.

Wollmann, H. (2003). German Local Government under the Double Impact of Democratic and Administrative Reforms. In N. Kersting and A. Vetter (Eds.), *Reforming Local Government in Europe. Closing the Gap between Democracy and Efficiency* (pp. 85–112). Opladen: Leske + Budrich.

12
Liechtenstein
Two leading parties in a direct democratic framework

Wilfried Marxer

Municipal council between national politics and local direct democracy

In Liechtenstein, there is only one local level in addition to the national level: the municipalities. They enjoy a relatively high degree of autonomy (The Congress 2015; Nell 1987); hence, the political system can basically be characterized as a decentralized unitary state (Waschkuhn 1994: 343). The Council of Europe's Congress of Local and Regional Authorities has stated that there is a strong culture of consultation and cooperation between the central and local governments, facilitated by their proximity due to the small size of the country (The Congress 2018). The Congress also highlights that the municipalities are in a favorable financial situation, as has been confirmed by scholars (Brunhart 2019). Therefore, discussions about merging municipalities are rare (Schiess Rütimann 2016: para. 9), as there is no financial or other urgent need, although there may be some rationale for creating larger municipalities (Derungs and Fetz 2018). Instead, cooperation between municipalities is practiced in various areas, such as the construction of sports facilities, water supply, waste management, etc., even cooperating with municipalities across the borders with Switzerland and Austria (Bussjäger 2019; Salomon 2012). The mayors of the municipalities meet regularly to discuss common issues and to promote coordination and cooperation (Meier 2018).

The 11 municipalities have existed in Liechtenstein for a very long time, with a tradition going back several centuries. The current number and names of communes have remained unchanged since 1842 (Frommelt 2019; Vogt 2019). They vary in size from approximately 500 to 6,000 inhabitants at present: six have more than 4,000 inhabitants and four have between 1,000 and 4,000. Local self-government is guaranteed by the constitution[1] and is further regulated by the Municipality Act. Article 110 of the Constitution states that the mayors and other governmental organs of the municipality, such as the council, must be freely elected and that the municipalities must manage the municipal assets autonomously. The municipality act[2] specifies that there are tasks and duties that are entirely the responsibility of the municipalities; other tasks can be transferred from the national to the local level, with the necessary funds being provided by the state (Schiess Rütimann 2015). On the local autonomy index, Liechtenstein ranks among the European countries with the highest scores and is listed in the group of 'empowered' countries regarding decentralization (Ladner et al. 2019: 236, 245; Heinelt et al. 2018: 34).

The mayors are full-time politicians, with the exception of the smallest municipality where the mayor is employed part-time. Council members are remunerated with an annual lump sum, as well as attendance fees for meetings or additional activities such as chairing municipal commissions. Although the mayor, who is directly elected by the people, plays a key role as head of the local administration, most decisions have to be taken by the municipal council (where the mayor also has a seat). In terms of the local administrative system, Liechtenstein can be classified as the continental European federal type, together with the other German-speaking countries, although it is not considered as a country case in the respective survey (see Heinelt et al. 2018: 58). With regard to the four ideal types of horizontal power relations distinguished by Mouritzen and Svara, the Liechtenstein municipalities can be considered the committee-leader form (see Heinelt et al. 2018: 27).

Finally, Liechtenstein has direct democratic instruments at both the national and local levels (Marxer 2018). For example, projects with a very high financial volume, or the municipal statutes, must be brought to a vote at the local level. A referendum can also be triggered by one-sixth of the local population voting against a decision of the local council. The small size of the municipalities and the various ways in which the population can express its will and intervene politically generate solid identification with the municipality and strong commitment, resulting in a high voter turnout. In the 2019 elections, this ranged from 71.4% to 92.9% in the various municipalities.

Parties and local elections reflect the national level

With regard to elections, there are some differences between the national and local levels. At the national level, parliament is elected by the people, while the government is proposed by parliament and appointed by the reigning Prince. At the local level, both the council and the mayors have been chosen by the local electorate since 1864.

Local elections are held every four years in March (Article 44 of the Municipality Act), the most recent being held on 24 March 2019. Regular elections at the national level are also held every four years in February or March (Article 47 of the Constitution), but independently from the local elections. The last parliamentary elections considered in this chapter were those held on 5 February 2017.[3] Should parliament be dissolved prematurely for any reason, a new four-year period will begin. In the period since 1990, local or national elections have taken place alternately every two years.[4] Referendums at the local or national level may also be combined with elections.

As the mayor and the council are elected separately by the electorate, it may happen that the mayor and the majority of the council members do not belong to the same party. In fact, in more than half of the terms of office since 1991, the mayors have been without a majority in their respective municipal councils.

As a rule, both the candidates for the municipal council and the candidates for mayor are proposed by political parties that are also active at national level. All mayors from 1991 to the present have belonged to one of the two dominant parties: the Progressive Citizens' Party (*Fortschrittliche Bürgerpartei*) and the Patriotic Union (*Vaterländische Union*).

Politics in Liechtenstein has largely been dominated by the two political parties just mentioned, both of which were founded in 1918 as the first parties in Liechtenstein. Their ideological profiles do not differ significantly, and both can be characterized as center-oriented, Christian-conservative parties or as catch-all parties (Marxer 2015). A threshold of 8% of all valid votes applies in elections to the national parliament, which is a major hurdle for new and small parties. The dominance of the two parties is even greater at the local level than at the national because, on the one hand, the mayors are directly elected by majority vote, and on the other hand the small number of seats on a municipal council implies a high effective threshold for achieving a mandate. Moreover, smaller parties usually have even greater recruitment problems than the larger, established parties. Until 1987, therefore, only the two large parties were represented on local councils and among the mayors.

Nevertheless, the fragmentation of the party system has developed continuously over the past decades. Currently, the Free List (*Freie Liste*), the Independents (*Die Unabhängigen*), and the Democrats (*Demokraten pro Liechtenstein*) are the three smaller parties. They are either moderate right-wing, populist parties (Independents and Democrats) or green (Free List), but their ideological spectrum is strongly center focused rather than being left-wing or right-wing extremist.

Due to the small size of the country and the even smaller size of the communities, personal characteristics of the candidates play an important role. This applies in particular to the direct election of mayors, which depends on personality and party affiliation, whereas the election of local council members is more strongly determined by long-standing party affiliations.

The municipality act does not provide for the recall of either the mayor or the council members, but the municipalities and their authorities are under the supervision of the central government. In the event of a serious violation, the government may intervene, resulting in forced administration,[5] but this has not yet happened. The government must also undertake an assessment if a complaint is made by the citizens.

Proportional and personalized electoral system

Only citizens of Liechtenstein whose ordinary residence has been in a Liechtenstein municipality for at least the previous month and who are above 18 are entitled to vote.[6] This is laid out in the people's rights act[7] and applies to both national and local elections (Ehrenzeller and Brägger 2012). Foreign nationals and Liechtenstein citizens living abroad are not entitled to vote. The right to vote includes the active and passive voting right (Article 1 of the People's Rights Act). There is an obligation to participate in elections, but because there is no punishment for abstaining, it is rather a general rule or a moral appeal (Article 3 of the People's Rights Act).

Mayoral and municipal council elections are held concurrently on the same day in all municipalities. Nominations for candidacy for both the mayor and the council must be made at the local electoral commission at least six weeks before the election and must be signed by a number of voters amounting to at least twice the number of councilors to be elected. Proposals for the council must have a specific name, usually the name of the party concerned, but it is not mandatory that a party organization be behind a nomination. The law does not use the term 'party', but instead speaks of electoral groups (*Wählergruppe*). Nominations for mayor are also usually made by the political parties. So far, only the years 1991, 2003, and 2019 have seen one nonpartisan candidacy for the mayor's office in a single municipality, that is, three out of a total of 152 candidacies – none of which was successful.

The proposals may not have more candidates on a list than there are members of the municipal council, but the lists need not be complete. According to the Municipality Act (Article 38(1)), there are either six or eight council members in municipalities with up to 1,500 inhabitants, eight or ten members in municipalities with up to 3,000 inhabitants, and ten or twelve members in municipalities with more than 3,000 inhabitants, plus the mayor. The exact number is determined locally by a direct vote on the municipal order.

On election day (in practice, most voters use postal voting before election day), official printed ballot papers must be used for the election of both the mayor and the council. In the mayoral election, votes are cast for a single candidate. In council elections, voters again use one of the official ballot papers, that is, a party (electoral group) list. The order or ranking on the list is decided by the party or group that nominates the candidates. As a rule, alphabetical order is chosen. Each ballot paper represents the number of municipal council seats in the municipality concerned (6–12 votes). Voters may remove candidates from the list and add candidates from other lists. The removal of candidates does not automatically reduce the number of votes attributed to that party, but it does reduce the number of votes for the eliminated candidate. The addition of candidates from other lists adds a candidate vote for that person and also assigns a vote to his or her party, while the party whose ballot paper the voter chose loses one vote. In the 2019 municipal elections, 60.3% of the ballot papers were modified (removal of candidates and/or support of candidates from other lists), while 39.7% remained unchanged.

After the ballot box closes on Sunday at noon on election day, the votes for the mayors are counted first. In the first round of this majority election, an absolute majority is required to be elected. If no candidate receives an absolute majority of valid votes, a second ballot is held within four weeks. In the respective municipalities, the ballot boxes of the council election remain closed. Candidates for mayor may withdraw their candidacy up until two weeks before the second round of voting. In the second round of voting, a relative majority applies. If two candidates have exactly the same number of voters behind them, the decision is made by the president of the election commission by lot (this has so far never happened).

As soon as the election of the mayor is completed and the election commission knows who has won, the ballots of the council election are counted. Each ballot paper represents as many votes as there are members of the council (i.e., six, eight, ten, or twelve). The removal and addition of candidates change the ranking of candidates on the party lists and also affect how many votes each party receives.

A system of open-list proportional representation is used for the allocation of seats to the local council. In a first step, the distribution of mandates is based on the method of Hagenbach-Bischoff: a quota is calculated by dividing the total number of votes of all parties by the number of mandates in the municipality plus one. If the elected mayor is a member of a party running for the council – which has always been the case – the divisor is increased by two. In the first round, the parties receive as many seats (basic mandates) as this quota included in their number of votes.

If not all seats are allocated in this basic mandate distribution, a remaining mandate distribution will take place. Until the elections of 2019, only the parties that achieved one or more basic mandates were considered for the distribution of the remaining seats.[8] In March 2020, however, parliament decided to skip this hurdle, meaning that all parties now are admitted to participate in the allocation of remaining mandates in future elections.[9] Until the 2015 elections, the second round was conducted according to the d'Hondt formula: the remaining votes of the parties were noted, then halved, divided by three, and so on. The remaining seats were allocated to electoral groups according to the highest numbers calculated under this method. Since the 2019 elections, the remaining seats have been distributed according to Hagenbach-Bischoff: each party's votes are divided by the number of their individual basic mandates plus one. The first remaining seat goes to the party with the highest number calculated. If a second or further remaining mandates are available for distribution, the same procedure is repeated.

Each party's seats are distributed to the candidates with the highest number of votes. Thus, the people decide not only on the number of seats allocated to the different parties but also who is the first, second, etc. candidate on each party's list. If a party wins more seats than candidates nominated, the remaining seats are distributed to other parties according to the usual procedure (Article 80(3) of the Municipality Act).

There are various reasons for exclusion in municipal elections. For example, municipal employees cannot be members of the municipal council, nor can members of the government or the various courts. Furthermore, close relatives cannot be members of the municipal council at the same time, including the mayor. If someone is closely related to a mayor, he or she must resign from the municipal council. If two close relatives are elected to the municipal council, the one who received more votes has priority (Article 47 Municipality Act).

Neither a gender nor any other quota is in place.[10] Also, there is no restriction on the number of terms of office for mayors or municipal council members. Mayors cannot be simple members of the local council at the same time, but local politicians can also be members of the national parliament. It occasionally happens that mayors run for parliament and are elected or, conversely, that members of the state parliament run for mayor and are elected.

Dominance of two parties – slow progress for women

On average, from 1991 to 2019, not even twice as many candidates were registered for municipal councils and mayoral offices as there were seats (see Table 12.1).[11]

Although the number of parties increased moderately during this period, the number of candidates declined (see Figure 12.1). The reason for this is that the two dominant parties increasingly share the practice of other groups of presenting incomplete lists. This tendency

Table 12.1 Mean number of local council and mayoral candidates in 11 municipalities in Liechtenstein, 1991–2019

	1991	1995	1999	2003	2007	2011	2015	2019	Total
Mean number of council candidates per seat	2.3	2.2	2.0	1.9	1.8	1.8	1.8	1.7	1.9
Mean number of mayoral candidates per seat	2.2	1.8	1.5	1.6	1.5	1.7	1.5	1.9	1.7

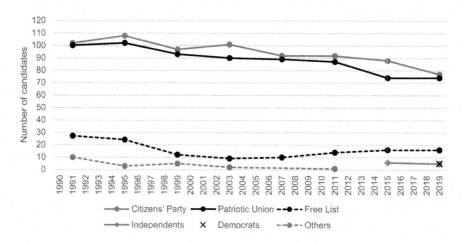

Figure 12.1 Number of candidates for local councils in Liechtenstein, 1991–2019
Source: Official election results announced by the government and author's calculations

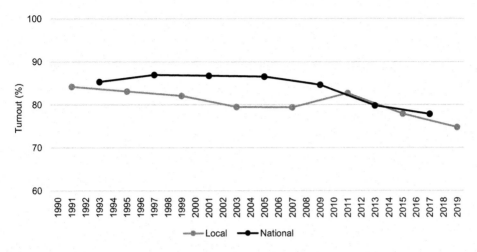

Figure 12.2 Voter turnout for local and national elections in Liechtenstein, 1990–2019
Source: Liechtenstein statistics and official election results announced by the government

Table 12.2 Participation and performance of parties in local elections in Liechtenstein, 2019

Party	% and number of municipalities where running		% and number of municipalities where represented		% of seats on local councils	% of votes in local elections	% of mayors affiliated with the party
Citizens' Party	100	11	100	11	46.2	42.9	63.6
Patriotic Union	100	11	100	11	44.2	41.6	36.4
Free List	82	9	64	7	7.7	10.4	–
Independents	36	4	9	1	1.0	2.9	–
Democrats	18	2	9	1	1.0	2.1	–

Source: Official election results announced by the government and calculations by the author

to not complete the lists is partly due to difficulties in recruiting candidates, but it also aims to avoid frustration with too many nonelected individuals (Marxer 2011).

There is a clear concentration of candidates in the age group between 35 and 55 years. Younger and older candidate numbers are below average and they also have a smaller chance of being elected (Marxer 2019: 8–9). The populations under the age of 30 and over 60 are clearly underrepresented on the lists, and even more so on the councils.

The two dominant parties – the Progressive Citizens' Party and the Patriotic Union – nominated candidates for local councils in all municipalities from 1991 to 2019 and also in the decades before. In the local elections of 2019, they won 46.2% and 44.2% of the council seats respectively, whereas the other parties together received fewer than 10% of the seats (see Table 12.2). The small parties were disadvantaged in the distribution of seats, in that together they received 15.4% of the votes, but only 9.7% of the seats.

Voter turnout in Liechtenstein is quite high at both the national and local levels, but it has been declining slowly since the 1990s (see Figure 12.2). In the last local elections of 2019, 74.8% of voters cast their vote. The increase in turnout for the 2011 municipal elections was due to the fact that, compared to 2007, more municipalities had two candidates for mayor instead of only one, making the elections more competitive and motivating for voters.

In the 2019 municipal elections, the details of voters were officially recorded for the first time. Women participated slightly more frequently than men. Voter turnout was lowest among 25- to 34-year-olds and highest in the oldest age range (see Table 12.3).

Voter turnout correlates with the size of the municipality (see Figure 12.3): local election figures for 1991–2019 show that voter turnout decreases moderately, the more people are eligible to vote in each municipality.

Voting rights for women were introduced at the national level in Liechtenstein in as late as 1984. Some municipalities introduced women's suffrage a few years before then, and some even later. The conservative attitude of many voters is reflected in the reduced chances of success for female candidates. This applies to both the local and national levels. It was not until 2019 that women won more than 40% of council seats at the local level, and for the first time two of the 11 mayors are women. In the parliamentary elections of 2013, and even more so in 2017, however, women suffered a setback. In 2017 the proportion of women in parliament collapsed to only 12% (see Figure 12.4).

Table 12.3 Voter turnout for local elections by gender and age for all municipalities in Liechtenstein, 2019

	Women	Men	18–24	25–34	35–49	50–64	65+	Total
Turnout (%)	75.9	73.5	63.6	55.7	73.4	82.3	85.3	74.8

Source: Municipalities' election commissions and government office

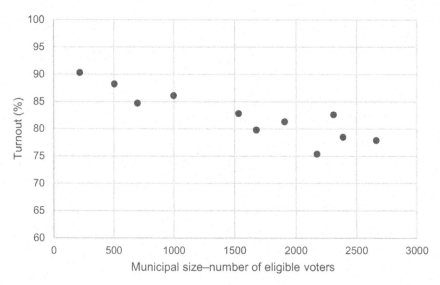

Figure 12.3 Average voter turnout for local elections in Liechtenstein by municipality size, 1991–2019

Source: Liechtenstein statistics, official election results published by the government, and calculations by the author

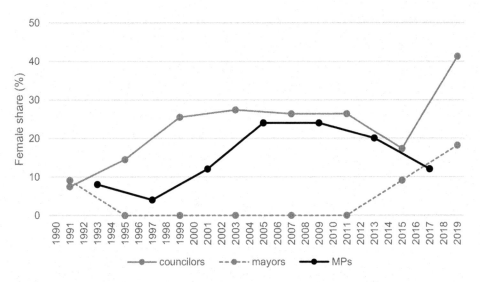

Figure 12.4 Women's representation among councilors, mayors, and MPs in Liechtenstein, 1991–2019

Source: Official election results announced by the government and calculations by the author

The Free List has the highest proportion of women among elected municipal councils, at 42.8% from 1991 to 2019, followed by the Progressive Citizens' Party (23.0%) and the Patriotic Union (21.9%). Other parties have not yet had successful female candidates.

There are no term limits, and the chances for mayors and council members to be reelected in the following elections are quite high, especially for mayors. Since 1991, only two incumbent mayors have not been reelected in subsequent elections, while in 61 elections mayors have successfully been reelected. In reality, between 1991 and 2019, the maximum number of terms of office of a mayor was six, while four mayors were elected five times (three of whom are still in office) and seven mayors were elected four times (one is still in office). None of them lost an election, but they all finally decided not to run again. In fact, it is very rare for an elected mayor to run for only one term or not to be reelected after the first term.

The position of council members is not as stable as that of mayors. From 1991 to 2019, out of 445 council members who ran for reelection, 369 were elected (82.9%), while 76 (17.1%) were not. Some were unsuccessful because their party lost seats, while others were overtaken by candidates from their own party.

Discussion

Academic research on local elections in Liechtenstein is rare. The focus is rather on the legal, historical, and economic aspects of municipalities in the national context. Past studies on political rights have tended to focus on the national level (Batliner 1993; Marxer 2000; Ehrenzeller and Brägger 2012; Wille 2015). More intensive studies on local elections have only recently been undertaken (Marxer 2011, 2019). Nevertheless, municipalities play an important role in Liechtenstein, not only for reasons of autonomy and the currently favorable financial situation but also as a political and cultural point of identification. The small size of the municipalities, the busy social life in rural communities, personal knowledge, and active participation of the population through electoral and direct democratic rights all contribute to increasing positive attitudes toward the municipalities. Voter turnout is therefore relatively high, reaching an average of around 75% for the last municipal elections.

Although personality plays an important role in the election of mayors and local councilors, many voters still identify strongly with one party or another. The parties are active at both the national and local levels. It is rare for political movements or parties to only run for office at the local level. Since the foundation of the first two parties in 1918, they have dominated the political scene. They organize themselves at the local level in the form of local party groups, which are embedded in the national party structure but act autonomously on local issues.

The difficulties in recruiting candidates even for the large parties are even worse for small parties and therefore limit their election outcomes in many municipalities. Thus, the two major parties collected almost 80% of the votes at the national level in 2017 and more than 90% at the local level in 2019.

The ideological differences between the two major parties are minimal, with both parties located in the political center. The smaller parties are moderate left or right, but the differences are not extreme. Liechtenstein's political culture is characterized by concordance and, thus, by the active involvement of the relevant actors in the political process. The direct election of the mayor and his or her responsibility for local government does indeed give the mayor special status in the community. However, important decisions must be supported by a majority of the local council, or they may end in a referendum. Moreover, because mayors often do not have a majority on the local council, there is an additional need for broad support of decisions.

In principle, the proportional representation system at the local and national levels is in line with the concordant political culture. On the other hand, the small number of seats on the councils creates an effective threshold to achieve a basic mandate in the first round of seat distribution, which discriminates against small parties. At the national level, a threshold of 8% of all votes nationwide is set, which of course also favors the larger parties. In March 2020, parliament decided to abolish the need for a basic mandate before the remaining seats are distributed at the local level, thereby lowering the hurdle for small parties if there are remaining seats to be distributed. This may increase party plurality in future elections.

Women are generally underrepresented in Liechtenstein politics, even though the local elections in 2019 brought significantly better results than in the past. However, a popular initiative to include the stronger promotion of women in politics in the constitution failed significantly in August 2020, with a rejection rate of 78.8%. Fears were too strong that free voting rights would be restricted and that a gender quota might be introduced.

Notes

1 Constitution of the Principality of Liechtenstein (*Verfassung des Fürstentums Liechtenstein vom 5. Oktober 1921*; LGBl. 1921.015).
2 Municipality Act (*Gemeindegesetz vom 20. März 1996*; LGBl. 1996.076).
3 Due to the closing of the data collection for the book, this publication does not consider the most recent ones of 2021.
4 Local elections took place in 1991, 1995, 1999, 2003, 2007, 2011, 2015, and 2019; national elections were held twice in 1993 and then in 1997, 2001, 2005, 2009, 2013, and 2017.
5 Public Administration Act (*Gesetz vom 21. Aptil 1922 über die allgemeine Landesverwaltungspflege;* LGBl. 1922.024).
6 For a review of the local electoral system and local elections, see Marxer (2020).
7 People's Rights Act (*Gesetz vom 17. Juli 1973 über die Ausübung der politischen Volksrechte in Landesangelegenheiten;* LGBl. 1973.050).

8 Depending on the number of seats on the municipal council and the party affiliation of the elected mayor, this informal but effective threshold for a council seat ranges from 7.1% (12 seats, dependent mayor) to 14.3% (6 seats, independent mayor).
9 Parliamentary resolution to delete Article 78.4 from the Municipality Act approved on 5 March 2020 (LGBl. 2020.163); see the government report on the issue (Regierung 2019).
10 The commission for equality between women and men published a paper about gender quotas, but it had no effect (Kommission 2012). In Autumn 2019, a committee launched a popular initiative for the introduction of a new article to the constitution in order to promote gender equality in politics [initiative 'HalbeHalbe' (half-half)]. The popular vote on 30 August 2020 resulted in a clear rejection of the new constitutional provision by 78.8%.
11 For information on the local electoral system and local elections, see Marxer (2020).

References

Batliner, M. (1993). *Die politischen Volksrechte im Fürstentum Liechtenstein*. Fribourg: Institut du Fédéralisme Fribourg Suisse (Diss. iur. Publikationen des Instituts für Föderalismus, 8).

Brunhart, A. (2019). Liechtensteins Gemeinde- und Landesfinanzen unter besonderer Berücksichtigung von Steuerwettbewerb und Gemeindeautonomie. In Liechtenstein-Institut (Ed.), *Gemeinden – Geschichte, Entwicklung, Bedeutung* (pp. 103–134). Bendern: Liechtenstein-Institut (Beiträge Liechtenstein-Institut, 45).

Bussjäger, P. (2019). Gemeindekooperationen in Liechtenstein und Vorarlberg. Rechtsgrundlagen und Vergleich. In Liechtenstein-Institut (Ed.), *Gemeinden – Geschichte, Entwicklung, Bedeutung* (pp. 135–148). Bendern: Liechtenstein-Institut (Beiträge Liechtenstein-Institut, 45).

Congress of Local and Regional Authorities (Ed.) (2015). *The Current Situation of Local and Regional Democracy in the Council of Europe Member States*. Strasbourg: CLRA.

Congress of Local and Regional Authorities (2018). *Local Democracy in Liechtenstein*. Monitoring report CG34(2018)15final. Strasbourg: CLRA.

Derungs, C. and Fetz, U. (2018). *Effizienzpotenziale der Liechtensteiner Gemeinden. Studie im Auftrag der Stiftung Zukunft.li. Hg. v. HTW Chur*. Chur.

Ehrenzeller, B. and Brägger, R. (2012). Politische Rechte. In A. Kley and K. Vallender (Eds.), *Grundrechtspraxis in Liechtenstein* (pp. 637–685). Schaan: Verlag der Liechtensteinischen Akademischen Gesellschaft (Liechtenstein Politische Schriften, 52).

Frommelt, F. (2019). Die vormoderne Gemeinde in Vaduz und Schellenberg. In Liechtenstein-Institut (Hg.): *Gemeinden – Geschichte, Entwicklung, Bedeutung* (pp. 11–46). Bendern: Liechtenstein-Institut (Beiträge Liechtenstein-Institut, 45).

Heinelt, H., Hlepas, N., Kuhlmann, S. and Swianiewicz, P. (2018). Local Government Systems: Grasping the Institutional Environment of Mayors. In H. Heinelt, A. Magnier, M. Cabria and H. Reynaert (Eds.), *Political Leaders and Changing Local Democracy: The European Mayor* (pp. 19–78). London: Palgrave Macmillan.

Kommission für die Gleichstellung von Frau und Mann (2012). *Einführung von Geschlechterquoten auf den Wahllisten auf Gemeinde- und Landesebene*. Bericht der Kommission für die Gleichstellung von Frau und Mann. Vaduz.

Ladner, A., Keuffer, N., Baldersheim, H., Hlepas, N., Swianiewicz, P., Steyvers, K. and Navarro, C. (2019). *Patterns of Local Autonomy in Europe*. London: Palgrave Macmillan.

Marxer, W. (2000). *Wahlverhalten und Wahlmotive im Fürstentum Liechtenstein*. Vaduz: Verlag der Liechtensteinischen Akademischen Gesellschaft.

Marxer, W. (2011). *Gemeinderatswahlen 2011: Probleme der Rekrutierung von Kandidatinnen und Kandidaten*. Bendern: Liechtenstein-Institut (Arbeitspapiere Liechtenstein-Institut, 31).

Marxer, W. (2015). Parteien im Wandel. In M. Frick, M. Ritter and A. Willi (Eds.), *Ein Bürger im Dienst für Staat und Wirtschaft* (pp. 241–270). Schaan: Verlag der Liechtensteinischen Akademischen Gesellschaft (Liechtenstein Politische Schriften, 56).

Marxer, W. (2018). *Direkte Demokratie in Liechtenstein. Entwicklung, Regelungen, Praxis*. Bendern: Verlag der Liechtensteinischen Akademischen Gesellschaft (Liechtenstein Politische Schriften, 60).

Marxer, W. (2019). *Gemeindewahlen seit 1975 und Vorschau auf 2019: Stand 18. März 2019*. Bendern: Liechtenstein-Institut.

Marxer, W. (2020). *Gemeindewahlen in Liechtenstein mit Fokus auf die Gemeindewahlen 2019*. Bendern: Liechtenstein-Institut (Beiträge Liechtenstein-Institut).

Meier, M. (2018). *60 Jahre liechtensteinische Vorsteherkonferenz*. Hg. v. Liechtensteinische Vorsteherkonferenz.

Nell, J. von (1987). *Die politischen Gemeinden im Fürstentum Liechtenstein*. Vaduz: Verlag der Liechtensteinischen Akademischen Gesellschaft (Liechtenstein Politische Schriften, 12).

Regierung (2019). Bericht und Antrag betreffend die Abänderung des Gemeindegesetzes. Vaduz.

Salomon, M. (2012). *Liechtenstein und die grenzüberschreitende Kooperation im Alpenrheintal*. Bendern: Liechtenstein-Institut (Arbeitspapiere Liechtenstein-Institut, 32).

Schiess Rütimann, P. (2015). *Die historische Entwicklung des liechtensteinischen Gemeinderechts*. Bendern: Liechtenstein-Institut (Arbeitspapiere Liechtenstein-Institut, 50).

Schiess Rütimann, P. (2016). Art. 110 LV. Stand: 14. Januar 2016. In Liechtenstein-Institut (Ed.), *Kommentar zur Liechtensteinischen Verfassung*. Online-Kommentar. Bendern: Liechtenstein-Institut www.verfassung.li.

Vogt, P. (2019). Kommunale Entwicklung von 1808 bis 1921. In Liechtenstein-Institut (Ed.), *Gemeinden – Geschichte, Entwicklung, Bedeutung* (pp. 47–60). Bendern: Liechtenstein-Institut (Beiträge Liechtenstein-Institut, 45).

Waschkuhn, A. (1994). *Politisches System Liechtensteins. Kontinuität und Wandel*. Vaduz: Verlag der Liechtensteinischen Akademischen Gesellschaft (Liechtenstein Politische Schriften, 18).

Wille, H. (2015). *Die liechtensteinische Staatsordnung. Verfassungsrechtliche Grundlagen und oberste Organe*. Schaan: Verlag der Liechtensteinischen Akademischen Gesellschaft (Liechtenstein Politische Schriften, 57).

13

Luxembourg

Toward a thinner relationship between local and national elections?

Dan Schmit, Raphaël Kies, and Patrick Dumont

Introduction to local elections in Luxembourg

As of 2018, Luxembourg is divided into 102 municipalities that constitute the only level of subnational politics. Half of Luxembourg municipalities have a population size under 3,000, with the capital city being the only municipality with more than 100,000 inhabitants in a country of 600,000 residents. Foreign residents constitute over 47% of this population, a share that varies across municipalities with a maximum of approximately 70% for Luxembourg City. The country's particular demographic situation has implications for democracy at the national and local levels, though arguably less so at the local level, as non-Luxembourgers have the right to vote in elections for local councils (see later discussion).

While these municipalities are technically under the supervision of the Ministry of the Interior, they usually have relatively extensive decisional autonomy (Kies and Nommesch 2015; Ladner et al. 2016). Some of the obligatory communal competences are enshrined in the Constitution (Dumont et al. 2011: 128). These co-exist with the more general principle of 'all what is of communal interest' in the Constitution and in the communal law, which can be understood as missions that communes only fulfill if their financial situation allows for it. Although the Ministry of Interior can question a municipality's decisions if there is a suspicion that the law is not being respected, but such cases remain extremely rare. The formal ministerial control over municipalities has steadily decreased in the last decades as part of a wider, ongoing effort to simplify public administration and reinforce local autonomy.[1]

Revenues from the municipal commercial tax (ICC) and the Communal Financial Endowment Fund (FCDF) form the main source of revenue for local governments. Since 2016, these two sources of income have been combined into a single fund, the *Fond de Dotation Globale Financière* (FDGF). These unrestricted incomes in fact constitute the guarantor of the municipal autonomy enshrined in the Constitution. In 2017, local government revenues amounted to €2.735 million or 4.9% of GDP.

The organization of local government has not changed substantially since the beginning of the twentieth century. The number of municipalities has been reduced from 130 to 102 through mergers, which have been encouraged and financially incentivized by successive cabinets. While the national government could theoretically impose such mergers on municipalities, negotiations on potential mergers are traditionally left to local authorities, who subsequently submit the merger proposal to citizens via referendum.[2] Following a positive referendum, a law recognizing the merger needs to be enacted at the national level in order for the merger to come into effect following the subsequent local elections.

Each municipality has a local council that fulfills the role of legislative body, voting on local regulations as well as the municipality's budget. Elections for local councils take place every six years. Following the elections, a majority of the new councilors presents a mayor from among their members to be nominated by the Grand Duke and a determined number of aldermen. Both the mayor and the aldermen are then sworn in by the Minister of Interior and will together constitute the executive branch of local government. Since 2011, these positions have been open to non-Luxembourgers, provided they meet the condition of residency set for active and passive electoral rights (see discussion to follow). This organization corresponds to a *collective form of* governance, where the decision center is one collegiate body, namely, the board of mayor and aldermen that is responsible for all executive functions (Mouritzen and Svara 2002; Heinelt and Hlepas 2006). The board of mayor and aldermen is not only the executive organ of local self-government but also the representative of the central government in the municipality, enforcing national laws and regulations in the territory of the municipality.[3]

Data on public opinion about local government are scarce, and it is therefore not easy to assess how the general public views local elections and the role of municipalities. The series of Eurobarometer surveys tapping the level of trust in regional or local public authorities, however, suggest that in Luxembourg local government is more trusted than the EU average and that this confidence has even progressed from 60% in 2008 to about 80% ten years later. On the other hand, the proportion of Luxembourgers who consider local government to be the level of authority that has the most impact on their life conditions is the lowest in the EU member states (EB 307: 2009). Nevertheless, voters tend to identify with the locality in which they live almost on a par with the national level and they recognize the importance of municipal elections (Legrand 2002).[4]

The sheer size of the country has long meant that state and municipality politics are intertwined, especially in terms of political personnel. Given the reinforcement of the local level through the merger of communes and the reforms envisaged to grant them further autonomy, it is important to study local elections in Luxembourg to provide for a greater understanding not only of that level of authority but also of its implications for broader party politics and democratic challenges in Luxembourg politics.

The organization of local elections

Local elections are organized every six years in October unless the election years for legislative and local elections coincide. In that case, a recent amendment of Luxembourg's electoral law stipulates that local elections should be moved forward to the beginning of June of the same year. This situation occurs every 30 years as the legislative cycle at the national level lasts five years.

Due to the absence of an electoral commission, the oversight of elections lies, in theory, with the executive branch of the national government. The election offices are, however, relatively autonomous. Their independence is reinforced through the tradition of favoring magistrates (mostly judges) as presidents of the election offices. In the case of Luxembourg City, for instance, the law says that the president of the District Court of Luxembourg should chair the central voting station. In most cases, the same officials would run the electoral offices for all elections held in Luxembourg (legislative, European, and local). The government runs a central office during elections, but this central office's role is limited to the centralization of election results in order to publish them on the official website.[5]

In large municipalities (see the following section), vacancies do not trigger by-elections; for these municipalities, the next candidate on a party list takes over a vacant mandate from a party colleague. In small municipalities, on the other hand, there would be a by-election to designate a new member to the local council. Such elections are, however, not compulsory as long as the number of councilors does not fall under the legal quorum of councilors necessary to make decisions.

The electoral law does not provide for the possibility of recall elections. The Grand Duke has the prerogative to dissolve a municipal council or to suspend or revoke individual members of the local executive when the management of the municipality is endangered, but this power is hardly ever used.

Two electoral systems

All Luxembourgian citizens aged 18 and over who possess their civil and political rights are automatically registered on the electoral roll; voting is compulsory for all except for those aged 75 years and over. Compulsory voting is widely respected, reasons for not voting must be provided, and punishment in terms of a fine is possible though not enforced.[6] EU residents who have been living in Luxembourg for at least six years have been allowed to vote or to be a candidate since 1999. In 2005, the residence condition was lowered to five years and voting rights were extended to non-EU nationals; the latter obtained the right to stand for election in 2011. Foreigners need to register on the electoral roll, and this process still constrains their participation to the local level. Since 1999, the share of eligible non-Luxembourgers who have registered for local elections has risen steadily. Together with a reform of citizenship legislation, this has contributed to a steady increase in the number of registered voters; however, the rate of non-Luxembourgers who registered in 2017 out of all those who satisfied the conditions to do so is still a mere 23% (CEFIS 2018). One of the reasons for the limited growth in non-Luxembourgers' registration may be partially linked to the result of a 2015 referendum on whether to grant foreigners voting rights for the national elections, which returned a resounding 'no' by the Luxembourg citizens-only voting population (78% voted no; see Dumont and Kies 2016: 182–183; Kies 2020).

For local elections, the entire municipality serves as a single, multimember electoral district whose magnitude corresponds to the size of the local council. The size of local councils varies across the 102 municipalities depending on population. For municipalities with up to 999 inhabitants, the local council has seven members (since 2017 there are only two communes of that size); those with between 1,000 and 2,999 inhabitants, which is by far the largest category (close to 50% in 2017) have nine councilors; larger communes with a population up to 5,999 have 11; and those with between 6,000 and 9,999 get 13. In 2017, there were still just a few communes with more than 10,000 inhabitants: the four below the 15,000 threshold have 15 councilors, the two above it have 17, and the three municipalities with over 20,000 inhabitants have 19 members. Luxembourg City is in a league of its own with a council made up of 27 members. Note that, despite having close to 115,000 inhabitants at the time of the 2017 election, there were only 34,399 registered voters for the election of the capital city's council as foreigners make up 70% of Luxembourg City's population. For municipalities that merge, the law, which defines the conditions of that merger, can also define a different council size for the newly created municipality for up to two election periods.

Two different electoral systems are being used, depending on the municipality's population. For municipalities with fewer than 3,000 inhabitants, the plurality bloc vote, a majoritarian electoral system, is being used. Each voter can express as many votes as there are seats to fill. Subsequently, the candidates receiving the most votes are elected to the local council. Officially, local elections in these small municipalities are nonpartisan; there are, however, a few instances where two sets of competing candidates stood for election. In such cases, they appear as individual candidates on the ballot, but they will, however, typically advertise their alliance in campaign materials. Due to the combined effects of the increase in the Grand Duchy's population size triggered by immigration and the merging of smaller communes, the median size of communes has doubled from 1991 to 2020 (from under 1,500 to 3,000). Given that both factors also have a direct effect on the number of communes over the 3,000-inhabitant threshold, the proportion of communes using the plurality system fell from 77% in 1993 to 55% in 2017, and it will go down further to 50% or less in the 2023 election (see later discussion).

About 80% of Luxembourg voters thus now live in municipalities with over 3,000 inhabitants, where a proportional open-list system is in use. Different candidate lists that can contain as many candidates as there are seats to be filled compete against each other. Voters can either express a list vote, which will be tallied as a single vote for each candidate, or they may express as many preferential votes as there are seats to fill. It is possible to cumulate votes, that is, to give up to two votes to a single candidate. Furthermore, *panachage* is possible, which means that a voter can spread his or her votes across different candidate lists. Seats are distributed proportionally to the candidate lists. The number of votes received by each candidate on the list are added, and the seat share is then distributed via the Hagenbach-Bischoff divisor, a variant of the d'Hondt method. The ranking of candidates is fully determined through the preferential votes expressed by the voters.

In 2017, 45% of the local elections organized were held under the PR system (representing 77% of the registered voters), but given that the threshold of 3,000 inhabitants did by then cut the 102 communes exactly in two halves, there would have been a perfect 50/50 balance (81% of registered voters would then have voted with PR) had a transition period not been awarded for recently merged communes.[7]

In order to register in municipalities with a plurality vote, a candidate simply needs to register with the president of the main voting station of the municipality. In municipalities with proportional voting, a current member of the local council or 50 registered voters must support a candidate list.

The mandate of local councilor (and by extension mayor or alderman) is compatible with that of member of parliament, but incompatible with the position of member of the national government. Furthermore, employees of the municipality or similar positions may not be a member of the local council in the municipality for which they work.

Election outcomes

As voting is compulsory in Luxembourg until the age of 75, voter turnout is naturally high for all types of elections, as shown by Table 13.1, with only a slightly higher level for the national elections. Participation appears to be declining for both levels. Unfortunately, we have no way of ascertaining whether this slight drop is due to higher levels of abstention by voters who do not respect compulsory voting or merely the result of an aging population, which would increase the share of voters no longer under such an obligation to cast a vote. More systematically, in 2017 turnout was 86.8% in PR communes and 92% in plurality ones. There is a clear and stable, general negative correlation between the number of registered voters and turnout

Table 13.1 Voter turnout (percent) for national and local elections in Luxembourg, 2004–2018

	2004	2005	2009	2011	2013	2017	2018
National	91.7		90.8		91.3		88.6
Local		91.1		89.7		88.0	

Table 13.2 Election results for the main parties in the 2017 local elections for 46 communes in Luxembourg (PR system only)

	% of municipalities where running	% of municipalities where represented	% of seats on local councils	% of (aggregate) votes in local elections	% of mayors affiliated with the party
CSV	100.0	100.0	35.3	30.4	47.8
LSAP	89.1	89.1	25.3	24.0	28.3
DP	93.5	93.5	18.2	18.2	13.0
Greens	73.9	73.9	12.2	16.3	2.2
ADR	21.7	8.7	0.7	2.6	0.0
The Left	17.4	10.9	1.3	4.1	0.0
Independents and nonnational (local) lists	17.4	17.4	5.7	2.0	8.7
Total			100.0	100.0	100.0

levels (around $r = -.55$), an association that appears, however, less marked within the plurality system communes than the PR ones.

Local elections are highly important for political parties and national politics in Luxembourg. First, a strong presence in some key municipalities can improve a party's influence nationally. For instance, the party that holds the position of mayor of Luxembourg City has an important bargaining position on several issues given the importance of the capital city in national matters. Second, the local level can be used as a testing ground for novel coalitions that can later be installed at the national level. The liberal/green coalition formed in Luxembourg City in 2005 and confirmed in 2011 was fully incongruent with the Christian-Social/Socialist national government in power from 2004 to 2013; its main actors (mayor and first alderman) were also the party leaders that managed to oust the Christian-Socials from national government for the first time since 1979 when they formed an alternative national coalition with the Socialists after the 2013 early elections. Third, local elections allow the building of electoral strongholds for parties; typically, parties tend to perform well in national elections in the municipalities where they have traditionally been strong in local elections. Finally, local elections have a strong influence on candidate selection as the largest parties generally select local incumbents for their parliamentary election lists: in the four most recent national elections, more than 60% of the candidates for the four largest parties held local office (see also Dumont et al. 2011: 133).

As previously highlighted, local elections are only officially partisan in municipalities with over 3,000 inhabitants. Table 13.2 presents the results for the 46 municipalities that ran the 2017 local elections under a PR system and provided 600 of the 1,120 seats to be filled on all of Luxembourg's local councils. In these elections, eight national parties managed to get local councilors elected. In addition to the six parties represented in parliament at the time of these elections, the Pirate Party (which entered national parliament in 2018) gained three seats and the Communist Party two seats.

The Christian-Social People's Party (*Chrëschtlech-Sozial Vollekspartei*; CSV) has been Luxembourg's largest party at the national level since 1945 and has held the prime minister position in all postwar government coalitions except for the periods 1974–1979 and since 2013. The party is generally strong across the entire territory and has historically always been well represented in all municipalities at local elections, but it had for a long time lagged behind the socialist party in the local elections organized under PR (as it usually does better in rural areas; most of Luxembourg's small communes are, however, dominated by the CSV). From a rare opposition position at the national level, it performed remarkably well in 2017. No fewer than 20 of its 23 national MPs were candidates in their municipalities, and the lists of the party were broadly rejuvenated, propelling the CSV to the first rank with a 10% gap over its main competitor. It won 35.3% of the 600 seats and won the mayorship in half of the PR communes, including Esch-sur-Alzette, a traditional stronghold of the LSAP and second largest city in the country.

The Luxembourgish Socialist Workers' Party (*Lëtzebuerger Sozialistesch Aarbechterpartei*; LSAP) has traditionally competed for the second position at the national level and has been the most frequent junior party to the CSV, but it ranked first until 2017 in the PR local elections. In 2005, it clearly outnumbered the CSV in its number of mayorships, with 17 out of the 37 communes voting with the PR system (including nine communes in which the LSAP had an absolute majority of seats), against 13 for its main competitor and only 7 for the liberals. In 2017, the LSAP lost more than 5% in terms of councilor seats compared with 2011 and 9% in comparison with 2005. It also lost in its traditional stronghold, the south of the country characterized by its industrial past, to the CSV.

The liberal Democratic Party (*Demokratesch Partei*; DP) has been the LSAP's historical competitor for second place in Luxembourg's national party system and the other usual junior party to the CSV. Contrary to the LSAP, which never gained the prime minister-ship, the DP has held the PM position on three occasions (1974, 2013, and since 2018), that is, each time the CSV was in opposition. While the party has traditionally been strong in the center of the country, including Luxembourg City whose mayors have come from the DP since 1969, it has a weaker position in the country's south. In 2017, the local elections returned stable results for the DP, even though it collapsed in the third city of the country (Differdange) and was ousted from its local government.

The Green Party (*déi Gréng*) has emerged as the fourth major party in Luxembourg since the 2004 legislative and 2005 local elections. The ecologist party has secured some level of support in almost all parts of the country and became part of the national government for the first time in 2013. Locally, it has managed to become a coalition party in a number of large municipalities in different constellations with the three other major parties, and it also held the mayoralty in a couple of the smaller PR communes and even, as early as in 1990 (and until 2013), in one of the plurality system communes. The 2017 local elections were, as in the case of the DP, rather stable in terms of their number of councilors. The Greens were, however, ousted from the Luxembourg City coalition after two terms in power, but it became the largest party in Differdange and thus for the first time held the position of mayor in one of the three largest municipalities of the Grand Duchy.

The sovereigntist Alternative Democratic Reform Party (*Alternativ Demokratesch Reformpartei*; ADR) was founded in the late 1980s as single-issue party promoting the rights of private sector pensioners. In the 2000s, it began shifting its discourse by increasingly adopting stances focused on national identity and immigration. In local politics, the party has never succeeded in gaining more than a handful of seats, and in 2017 it continued to remain in opposition in all PR communes.

The Left (*déi Lénk*) was created as a splinter party from the Communist Party in the late 1990s. Since 2009, the party has stabilized its position in national politics, with one or two representatives in parliament and, contrary to national politics, confirmed in 2017 that it ranks higher than the ADR in the local elections in the PR communes. This is due to its results in the south of the country (it was even a junior party in the Esch-sur-Alzette local government in the early 2000s), as well as in Luxembourg City.

Finally, let us note that, in some more rural municipalities where councils are elected under PR, a few independent candidate lists are often present. This frequently occurs when a municipality moves from plurality to PR voting and most national parties have not (yet) created a local branch, or when candidates of a national party are not numerous enough to form a full list on their own. As a result of the 2017 elections, no fewer than four mayors from independent lists were selected by local councils in municipalities with a PR system.

Turning to descriptive representation, Table 13.3 shows the share of female candidates and elected councilors for local elections from 1993 to 2017. The data are based on the National Council of Women's report on the 2017 local elections (CNFL 2018). Table 13.3 shows that both shares have increased over time; in 2017 over one-third of all candidates were female, while one-quarter of the elected councilors were female. This also shows that there is a substantial gap between those two shares, hinting at a disadvantage for female candidates to be elected. For PR municipalities, it should be noted that the statutes of three parties (CSV, Greens, and The Left[8]) have quotas for female candidates, which might partly explain this difference. Furthermore, a 2016 amendment to the public financing of parties' legislation has set reductions in endowments if party lists for the national elections do not include at least 40% female candidates (50% for European Parliament elections). Because parties often turn to local-level electoral performance when selecting candidates for higher level elections, this quota system may have created an incentive for parties to promote more women in the 2017 local elections.

Furthermore, Table 13.3 also shows that there is a clear difference between municipalities with proportional and plurality systems, with more female candidates and female councilors being elected under PR but a smaller gap between these shares within municipalities using a plurality system. Note that, over roughly the same period, the share of elected female members of parliament varied between 20% in 1994 and 27% in 2013 (it fell back to 25% in 2018 despite the quota system for candidates described previously). Furthermore, it is noteworthy that the

Table 13.3 Share (percent) of female candidates and councilors in Luxembourg, 1993–2017

Election	All municipalities		Proportional representation		Plurality vote	
	Candidates	Elected	Candidates	Elected	Candidates	Elected
1993	18.0	10.0	23.6	13.7	11.5	8.4
1999	24.6	15.0	30.1	17.4	16.2	13.6
2005	28.9	20.6	33.4	22.7	19.5	19.1
2011	32.1	21.5	36.3	23.8	20.1	19.3
2017	35.8	24.8	39.4	27.3	23.7	21.8

share of female mayors has remained relatively stable over the period between 1993 and 2017 at approximately 10% of all mayors in Luxembourg.

As noted earlier and elsewhere (Dumont et al. 2011), one of the main challenges in contemporary Luxembourg politics is the inclusion of foreigners in national and local democratic forums. Table 13.4 highlights additional reasons, aside from poor electoral participation and inefficient consultative bodies: a very low and barely progressing share of non-Luxembourgish candidates since they were allowed to stand in local elections, which matches the timid rise in non-Luxembourgish voter participation, as well as a microscopic share of the elected members of local councils (CEFIS 2018). The Luxembourgish language used in day-to-day politics, especially at the local level, remains one of the barriers to further inclusiveness (Dumont et al. 2011): in 2017, a Portuguese candidate won the largest amount of votes in the small commune of Bettendorf, but he decided not to become the very first nonnational mayor of the country, mentioning the potential problem of not mastering the Luxembourgish language as one motivation for his withdrawal (Dumont and Kies 2018: 193).

A new vertical relationship?

While from a horizontal power perspective Luxembourg is likely to remain a collective form of local governance, our analysis suggests that two opposing forces may transform the vertical dimension of power: one the one hand, the electoral dynamic that pushes for further political integration between the local and national powers and, on the other hand, new institutional reforms that could minimize this interaction.

As far as elections are concerned, the increasing use of a PR system – due to population growth and the recent series of municipality mergers – may reinforce the already strong integration between local and national politics, as parties are likely to be further incentivized to select their national candidates from among their successful members in large municipalities. As of December 2019, 39 of the 60 members of parliament were also members of a local council, and 15 of those were mayor of their municipality. This cumulation of local and national political offices, however, may decrease or even stop due to several institutional reforms presently under discussion. The first, which is part of communal law reform, is the reinforcement of local autonomy aimed at introducing less invasive and more efficient state surveillance. Ultimately, the objective of the new communal law is to roll back, without making it disappear, the 'controlling State' in favor of more of a 'partner State' and 'advising State'. The second is the reform of paid leave from work for local politicians. At present, it varies according to the size of the municipality, from 9 to 40 hours per week for mayors, 5–20 hours for aldermen, and 3–5 hours for the councilors. Following complaints from a large number of local politicians, particularly

Table 13.4 Share (percent) of non-Luxembourgish candidates and voters, 1999–2017

Election	Non-Luxembourgish candidates	Non-Luxembourgish councilors	Non-Luxembourgish voters (registered) out of full electorate
1999	4.3	0.8	6
2005	5.9	1.2	10
2011	7.1	1.5	12
2017	7.6	1.3	12

Source: We thank Nénad Dubajic and Sylvain Besch from CEFIS for providing these data

those from small or intermediary municipalities, the ministry of interior is discussing its extension. Third, and more importantly, the current coalition government has reopened the discussion over the *cumul des mandats*, which could introduce incompatibility between a local- and national-level MP mandate.

If these reforms are adopted, careers in local politics could become more attractive, professionalized, and incompatible with national politics. From a general perspective (John 2001; Heinelt and Hlepas 2006), this may imply that Luxembourg would increasingly evolve from a Southern European ('Napoleonic') local system – that is, a system with few functions and competencies, small local entities, multiple levels of government, low legal discretion, and high access of local politicians to the central level of government – to a Northern European local system, namely, a system characterized by the strong decentralization of functions, larger local entities, few levels of government, a high level of discretion, and low access of local politicians to the central state.

Arguably, this evolution is welcome in a local state like Luxembourg, where the need for representing local interests and culture at the national level appears to be less relevant and the relationship with the national level could be improved. However, the success of this major vertical transformation is not without challenges. It will ultimately depend on the involvement of competent politicians that privilege a local career over a national one. Even if the 'working' conditions are improved, the division of local and national politics is likely to further aggravate the existing shortage of competent political personnel overall. Salvation could come from the involvement of categories of the population that are mostly underrepresented in local politics, such as the younger generations and foreigners. This, however, can only occur if politics becomes more inclusive, modern, and participative. Despite scattered efforts to promote such changes, there is still a long way to go as demonstrated by the extremely low participation of foreigners in local politics.

Notes

1 This trend is illustrated by the abolition of district commissioners, who acted as a hierarchical intermediary between central government and municipal authorities, and by the intention to reform the 1988 law on local government with the aim of simplifying and accelerating administrative procedures, as well as reducing the oversight role of the national level of authority.
2 Some mergers have been abandoned (or at least postponed) because they failed to satisfy a majority of voters.
3 Note that, in contrast to the national level, where ministers cannot be members of parliament, the mayor and the aldermen remain members of the local council.
4 A vast majority would participate even if the vote were not compulsory (Legrand 2002).
5 https://elections.public.lu/fr/elections-communales/2017.html
6 A response from the Minister of Justice to a parliamentary question in 2012 indicated that the most recent judicial action for citizens failing to vote dated back to the early 1960s.
7 In the case of municipality mergers that would result in a population of over 3,000 inhabitants, the law defining the conditions of the merger can contain a transition period during which the plurality vote is still applied.
8 The Greens and The Left are committed to equal shares of both genders, while the CSV has formulated 40% as the goal.

References

CEFIS (2018). *Les élections communales d'octobre 2017*. www.cefis.lu/resources/RED22.pdf
CNFL (2018). *Observatoire de la participation des femmes aux élections politiques, Elections de 2017*. https://communes.cnfl.lu/files/81793.pdf

Dumont, P. and Kies, R. (2016). Luxembourg. *European Journal of Political Research Political Data Yearbook*, *56*(1), 175–182.

Dumont, P. and Kies, R. (2018). Luxembourg. *European Journal of Political Research Political Data Yearbook*, *57*(1), 188–194.

Dumont, P., Kies, R. and Poirier, P. (2011). Luxembourg: The Challenge of Inclusive Democracy in a 'Local State'. In J. Loughlin, F. Hendriks and A. Lidström (Eds.), *The Oxford Handbook of Local and Regional Democracy in Europe* (pp. 123–145). Oxford: Oxford University Press.

Heinelt, H. and Hlepas, N. (2006). Typologies of Local Government Systems. In H. Bäck, H. Heinet and A. Magnier (Eds.), *The European Mayor Political Leaders in the Changing Context of Local Democracy* (pp. 21–42). Wiesbaden: VS Verlag für Sozialwissenschaften.

John, P. (2001). *Local Governance in Western Europe*. London/Thousand Oaks: Sage.

Kies, R. (2020). Étendre le droit de vote des étrangers aux élections législatives: Pourquoi les Luxembourgeois n'en veulent pas? in N. Farhat and P. Poirier (Eds.), *Démocratie(s), parlementarisme(s) et légitimité(s)* (pp. 222–247). Bruxelles: Editions Bruylant.

Kies, R. and Nommesch, K. (2015). *Local Autonomy Index for the European Countries (1990–2014): Luxembourg (LUX)*. Brussels: European Commission. http://hdl.handle.net/10993/23830

Ladner, A., Keuffer, N. and Baldersheim, H. (2016). Measuring Local Autonomy in 39 Countries (1990–2014). *Regional and Federal Studies, 26*(3), 321–357.

Legrand, M. (2002). *Les Valeurs au Luxembourg*. Luxembourg: Saint-Paul.

Mouritzen, E. and Svara, J. (2002). *Leadership At The Apex: Politicians and Administrators in Western Local Governments*. Pittsburgh: University of Pittsburgh Press.

14

The Netherlands

Increasing responsibilities and nationalized elections

Henk van der Kolk

Dutch local government in context

Municipalities as a layer of government[1]

The Dutch governmental system in 2020 consists of a central government, 12 provinces,[2] and 355 municipalities.[3] Because of municipal amalgamations, the number of municipalities declined drastically from over 1,200 in the nineteenth century to 673 in 1990 and subsequently to the current 355 (CBS 2019a). Combined with the still increasing number of inhabitants in The Netherlands, amalgamations have led to a strong increase in the average size of municipalities. Between 1990 and 2020, the average size of Dutch municipalities doubled from about 22,000 to over 48,000.

Municipalities all have the same formal position within the system of decentralization. Differences in size, ranging from fewer than 1,000 (one of the smaller islands in the north) to over 870,000 inhabitants (Amsterdam), type (from mainly agricultural to strongly urban, for example), and social composition have a strong effect on the challenges municipalities face and, therefore, on the policies municipalities develop, but all municipalities are essentially treated and organized in the same way.

Municipalities first have a general and autonomous policy responsibility and are allowed to adopt new tasks. In addition, municipalities can be made responsible for specific tasks by the central government.[4] Generally, municipalities are responsible for urban planning and housing, traffic and roads, waste collection and maintenance of public spaces, education (mainly buildings, not the content of education or the payment of salaries for teachers), and social affairs. Since a series of decentralizations in 2015, municipalities have become increasingly responsible for youth care, employment, and care for vulnerable groups. This decentralization of responsibilities was not supported by an equally substantial transfer of budgetary support from the central government to the municipalities (Allers & Peters 2019). The system is typologized as 'Nordic', with a highly decentralized administrative structure and strong local government (Heinelt, Hlepas, Kuhlmann, & Swianiewicz 2018). But unlike other Nordic-type systems, the level of fiscal autonomy in The Netherlands is extremely low (Ladner et al. 2019).

The formal regulatory uniformity between municipalities, the increased responsibilities, and the lack of necessary funding have stimulated the smaller municipalities in particular to collaborate closely with each other or with some larger 'center municipalities', even to the point of outsourcing virtually all municipal services to another, larger municipality. This 'regionalization' of municipal policies reduces the opportunities for municipalities to autonomously determine municipal policies and also affects the democratic oversight of these policies (Boogers, Klok, Denters, & Sanders 2016).

Apart from a tax on building owners (about 6% of the total budget of municipalities) and fees for specific activities (for example, waste collection and issuing passports, which more or less cover the related costs of these activities), municipalities are financially fully dependent on the central government. Centrally levied taxes are distributed via a 'municipal fund', the distribution of which is based on a large set of formal criteria, including the number of inhabitants and the amount of land area in a municipality,[5] and via 'specified distributions', which are related to specific policy areas and cannot be used freely. Although municipalities are free, in principle, to make autonomous spending decisions, the large set of formal obligations that municipalities have makes decentralized choice and prioritization rather difficult.[6]

The organization of the local government

All municipalities are headed by a municipal council.[7] The number of seats on this council fully depends on the number of inhabitants in the municipality and ranges between nine and 45 (see Table 14.1). The meetings of the council are chaired by the mayor. A board made up of the mayor and aldermen is responsible for preparing policies and managing the functioning of the local administration.

Table 14.1 Municipal size, council seats, and aldermen in the Netherlands, 1990 and 2019

Size of the municipality (population)	# of councilors	Max # of aldermen	# of municipalities (1990)	# of councilors (1990)	# of municipalities (2019)	# of councilors (2019)
0–3,000	9	2	39	351	3	27
3,001–6,000	11	2	105	1155	3	33
6,001–10,000	13	3	141	1833	9	117
10,001–15,000	15	3	119	1785	31	465
15,001–20,000	17	3	85	1445	35	595
20,001–25,000	19	4	46	874	48	912
25,001–30,000	21	4	29	609	47	987
30,001–35,000	23	5	26	598	28	644
35,001–40,000	25	5	11	275	20	500
40,001–45,000	27	5	9	243	28	756
45,001–50,000	29	6	9	261	18	522
50,001–60,000	31	6	10	310	20	620
60,001–70,000	33	7	11	363	13	429
70,001–80,000	35	7	3	105	8	280
80,001–100,000	37	7	12	444	13	481
100,001–200,000	39	8	13	507	23	897
Over 200,000	45	9	4	180	8	360
Total			672	11338	355	8625

Aldermen are selected by majority vote by, but not necessarily from, the council (BZK 2017: 28). The maximum number of aldermen is determined by the size of the council (see Table 14.1).[8] If one or more aldermen are no longer supported by a majority in the council, they have to leave their post. Four out of 10 leave their post within four years for either personal or political reasons, most in their second year. The number of aldermen leaving their post for political reasons has not substantially increased in the past decades (Bouwmans 2019).

The mayor is not directly elected but is selected by a (operating confidentially) committee from the council after being vetted by the Commissioner of the King. The candidate is later formally appointed by the central government for a period of six years.[9] Because the mayor is appointed by the central government, s/he can also only be relieved from office by the Crown. The mayor may be dismissed at any time by Royal Decree on the recommendation of the minister of the interior. If there is a disturbed relationship between the mayor and the council, the council may, through the intervention of the Commissioner of the King, send a recommendation for dismissal.

Discussions about the introduction of a directly elected mayor led in 2018 to a change in the constitution. Until that year, the constitution ordained that mayors had to be appointed by the central government. Since 2018, the constitution has only included the rule that a majority in the national parliament will determine the rules used to appoint or elect mayors.[10] This, however, has not yet led to a change in the appointment procedure, because political parties are unable to agree on an alternative, favoring either the current procedure or directly (popular vote) or indirectly (by the council) elected mayors. Although the mayor can play a dominant role on both the board and the council and is most often linked to a political party, s/he is assumed to be politically neutral. Particularly in the larger municipalities, his or her role is largely confined to public order and security (including a relationship with the police force) and ceremonial functions. On the other hand, some of the mayors of the larger cities at times play a prominent role in discussions about more general policy issues, like the integration of immigrants and the powers of the local police force.

The main (and essentially only) change between 1990 and 2020 in the general institutional setup of municipalities is the formal separation of the position of the alderman from membership on the municipal council. Before 2002, aldermen were selected from and remained members of the council. As of 2002, aldermen may be selected from within or from outside the council, and after their appointment they are no longer members of the council. This change was part of a 'dualization' operation, which started with a Royal Commission, that recommended a stronger separation between council and aldermen in 2000, alongside a change in the role of the council to more representation and control/oversight and less governing. This process has been evaluated extensively (Berenschot 2004; De Groot 2009; Hanemaayer, Wever, Sinnema, & van den Berg 2008). The outcomes of these evaluations show that some changes were observed, but more in the attitudes and less in the behavior of councilors. It also seems that control/oversight indeed increased, but that the representative role of councilors was not substantially strengthened.

Public perceptions of local government: known less but liked more

Dutch citizens are somewhat less interested in local politics than they are in national politics. Surveys have shown that public knowledge about this tier of government is limited. The mayor is known by name by somewhat more than half of the population, but even aldermen are far less known, especially in the larger municipalities. On the other hand, the local council and especially the appointed mayor are trusted somewhat more than the national political actors.

The public perception of the municipal layer of government as compared to the other layers can therefore best be described as 'known less but liked more' (Jansen & Denters 2019; van der Meer & van der Kolk 2016).

Local elections and their place in a multilevel system

Local council elections are held every four years in most municipalities simultaneously. Only in the case of municipal amalgamations may elections in the newly formed municipality be held at another time. Unlike national elections, municipal elections do not take place when a coalition loses its majority. If a local coalition loses its majority on the council, a new coalition is formed, which has to get support from members of the current council. Of all of the aldermen that started in the last decades, 40% left their position before their formal term was over. Half lose their job for personal reasons, and the other half lose the support of a majority on the council. This does not always imply that the coalition is dissolved, because votes of no confidence can also be supported by the alderman's party. In those cases, the coalition may stay intact, but the alderman has to give up his or her position (Bouwmans 2019).

Sometimes local elections coincide with municipal referenda (van der Krieken, 2019: 88), but normally local elections are held independently of other elections. Only in 2018 did the municipal elections coincide with a national referendum (Jacobs et al. 2018).

Local council elections are organized formally by the mayor and aldermen, but effectively by the main electoral office, which consists of the mayor and a few members appointed by the board. The powers and responsibilities of the main electoral office range from registering lists and candidates to supervising the campaign and establishing the outcome of the election. The work of the municipal electoral offices is strongly supported by the national Electoral Council (*Kiesraad*) and the ministry of the interior, which offer all kinds of forms and booklets.

After local elections, new coalitions are formed, while the mayor remains in office. His or her appointment does not depend on the outcome of local elections. Because Dutch mayors are appointed and not elected and they position themselves mainly as politically neutral actors, their position does not fundamentally change because of elections (Magnier 2006; Schaap, Daemen, & Ringeling 2009).

Features of the electoral system

Voters

All municipalities use virtually the same electoral system to elect the municipal council, although there are some subtle differences between smaller and larger municipalities. Every municipality is a single electoral district in which political parties (or, more precisely, 'lists of candidates') compete for seats on the council. As long as a political party is registered as a formal association, it can register an official name up until six weeks before the elections.[11] This name can then be used on the ballot. However, registration of a party name is not necessary and, in some municipalities, lists without an official name are taking part in municipal elections.[12] Lists of candidates have to be supported by 10–20 signatures, depending on the number of seats on the council.

All Dutch and other EU citizens aged 18 or more are allowed to vote in municipal elections. Legal inhabitants over 18 from countries outside the EU who have lived in The Netherlands for more than five years are also allowed to vote. Restrictions on this general eligibility are negligible. Voters may vote for one person as presented on one of the lists of candidates. Voting for the list of candidates as such is not possible, while voting for more than one candidate on a list makes the ballot invalid.

Political parties and lists

After the election, the number of votes per list are counted first. Votes for individuals are assumed to be votes for the list. Seats are then distributed proportionally among lists. An 'electoral quotient' is calculated, which is the total number of valid votes divided by the total number of seats on the council. 'Full seats' are distributed to each of the lists using this quotient or, prior to 2017, to preelection coalitions (see later discussion). After that, the 'remaining seats' are distributed. The system is thus a straightforward list PR system (Reynolds, Reilly, & Ellis 2005).

The main difference and subtleties relate to the exact way in which the remaining seats are allocated. If a council consists of fewer than 19 seats (only 81 municipalities in 2018; see Table 14.1), the system of the largest remainders (Hare) is used. Larger municipalities use the system of d'Hondt.[13] Municipalities using the Hare system have a formal threshold, which is 75% of the electoral quotient.[14] This implies that in the smallest municipalities there is a formal threshold of over 8%.[15] This formal threshold is not used in the larger municipalities.

Another subtlety relates to the system of *apparentement*, which existed until 2018. Until that year, lists were allowed to form a preelection coalition. Seats were allocated to these preelection coalitions on the basis of their polled votes as if they were a single party. The system was mainly relevant in municipalities using d'Hondt because this system is based on the highest averages, which is advantageous for larger political parties and, thus, for preelection coalitions of parties. Because smaller municipalities use Hare, *apparentement* was less useful there unless the combined parties did not expect to pass the aforementioned 'threshold'. In 2017 the system was abolished, mainly because it did not serve its intended purpose of stimulating permanent collaboration between similar minded political parties.[16]

Individual candidates

When seats are allocated to individual candidates, the list order prevails unless a candidate receives more than 50% (in smaller municipalities) or more than 25% (in the other municipalities) of the electoral quotient.[17] This relatively low individual threshold, introduced in 1998, enables lower placed candidates to receive an individual mandate.[18] Because of this rather low *individual* threshold, the Dutch electoral system sometimes looks like an open-list system, in which candidates with a relatively strong (ethnic or localized) support group can upset the established list order. In comparative terms, party leaders in Dutch municipalities present party ballots, while voters may 'disturb' the list. Voters cast a single vote below the party level, and votes are pooled across the whole party (Carey & Shugart 1995). And because the opportunity for voters to disturb the list is limited, this system is often called only 'semi-open'. In the municipal elections of 2014, 8,550 candidates were elected, 767 of whom broke the list order at the expense of a senior candidate or about 9% of the (elected) candidates (Parliamentary Paper 31142, no. 46). In 2018, that percentage had risen to nearly 10% (de Jong 2018).

Candidates can only assume their position if they are over 18 and are not part of any executive board at the national, provincial, or local level. So, they cannot be minister or alderman. They also cannot be a civil servant working for the local government.[19] This implies that members of parliament or employees of the provincial states can be and sometimes are also council members. Most political parties, however, do not encourage this type of *cumul des mandats*, and these combinations in The Netherlands are more the exceptions than the rule (Van de Voorde 2017).

The outcome of Dutch local elections

Turnout

Compulsory turnout (not compulsory voting, which never existed in The Netherlands; it was enough to show up at the polling station, you were not obliged to actually vote) was abolished in 1970. Since then, turnout for elections has declined substantially. Turnout for elections for the municipal councils in the beginning of the twenty-first century is around 55% (see Figure 14.1). It is thus substantially lower than turnout for national elections, which is closer to 80%. While turnout for local elections shows a gradual decline since 1990, there has been no such a decline in that period at the national level.

There is a strong relationship between the size of a municipality and turnout: turnout in larger municipalities is substantially lower (Gerritsen & Ter Weel 2014). This relationship is presented for 2018 in Figure 14.2.

It has been argued that one factor in the decreasing levels of turnout for local elections (as compared to national elections) since the 1980s is the continuing amalgamation of municipalities and their increasing average size. Extensive analyses have shown that amalgamations indeed have had such a negative impact (Gerritsen & Ter Weel 2014).

The lower turnout for municipal elections is also caused by an additional number of 'people dropping out': national nonvoters are also local nonvoters, and in addition some people who vote at the national level do not vote locally. Factors explaining turnout are pretty well-known (Smets & van Ham 2013). It seems that the same factors just have a stronger effect on municipal elections: younger people, people with lower levels of education, and those not interested in politics vote even less in local elections (Steenvoorden & van der Waal 2016).

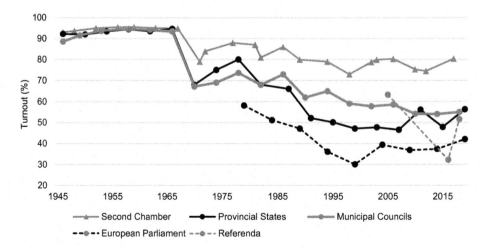

Figure 14.1 Voter turnout for Dutch elections and referenda, 1945–2020

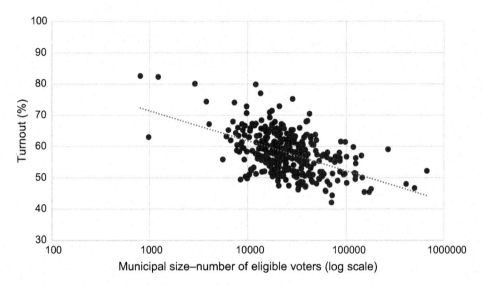

Figure 14.2 Voter turnout in the 2018 Dutch local elections by municipality size

Politicization and nationalization of municipal elections

In the media, local elections are often interpreted as polls for national elections or as 'second-order elections' (Reif & Schmitt 1980). The political (mis)fortunes of national political parties indeed have mirror images in many municipalities. Even the gains and losses of nonnational parties and lists seem to follow a national trend, partly determined by a general dissatisfaction or indifference with regard to the national political parties (Van der Kolk 1997). The CDA, the third largest party nationally in 2017, was able to take part in almost all municipalities. The VVD, the biggest party in 2017, was able to successfully compete in 310 (out of 335) municipalities under its own name and in a few more in combination with other (local or national) political parties (Jansen & Boogers 2019). In all municipalities, at least one local branch of a national political party participated in the local elections of 2018 (see Table 14.2).

Dutch municipal elections, however, are not just second-order elections. First, some strong national parties are insufficiently organized to compete in all municipalities. The populist radical right PVV, the second largest party, for example, in 2018 participated in only 30 municipalities, because the party lacks a formal organization with local branches. Second, other nationally organized political parties are simply too small to compete successfully, especially in the smaller municipalities. In 2017, none of the political parties competing in the national elections won more than 22% of the votes. And right after these elections, 13 political parties were represented in parliament. The chances of winning a seat on councils with 23 or 25 seats are therefore pretty slim. In quite a few municipalities, political parties on the left (PvdA, GreenLeft, and sometimes D66) create combined lists, sometimes labeled with the combined national party names (GroenLinks/PvdA) and sometimes with local names (e.g., Platform Progressief Wierden). Smaller orthodox protestant parties act in a similar way.

A third indication that municipal elections are not simple reflections of national trends is the strong position of local lists in municipal elections. In recent decades, local lists have gained a stronger foothold on municipal councils (van Ostaaijen 2019). In the 1960s and

Table 14.2 Party politicization in Dutch local elections, 2018[1,2]

	% of municipalities where running	% of municipalities where represented	% of seats on local councils	% of (aggregate) votes in local elections	% of mayors affiliated with the party (appointed)[4]
VVD	94.0	93.4	14.2	13.5	28.8
PVV	9.0	9.0	0.9	1.4	0.0
CDA	99.1	99.1	16.2	13.4	29.4
D66	77.3	76.7	7.5	9.2	6.6
GroenLinks	54.3	53.4	6.6	8.9	3.4
SP	32.8	32.8	3.6	4.4	0.0
PvdA[3]	76.1	80.3	6.9	7.5	18.4
ChristenUnie	38.8	38.8	3.8	3.8	2.8
PvdD	4.5	4.5	0.4	1.2	0.0
50Plus	6.0	5.7	0.4	0.8	0.0
SGP	17.6	17.6	2.2	1.9	2.8
DENK	4.2	4.2	0.3	1.0	0.0
FvD	0.3	0.9	0.0	0.3	0.0
Local lists[3]	97.3	97.6	32.7	28.7	
Total			95.6	96.0	
None					4.1

[1] All 'combinations' of national parties or combinations of national and local parties were left out. This is thus an underestimation of the extent to which national political parties are represented at the local level.
[2] Only parties represented in the national parliament and the pure local lists are reported; combined lists are ignored.
[3] This rather weird difference between participation and receiving seats occurs due to a party participating on a combined list but receiving a seat under its original name.
[4] 18/2/2020, based on 320 positions (not the temporary ones).

1970s, local lists were mainly a phenomenon of the south. Because the Catholic party KVP (later part of the Christian Democratic CDA) was dominant in the southern region, and local divisions thus became part of internal party conflicts, the KVP decided to accept the existence of local lists (Boogers, Lucardie, & Voerman, 2007: 4). However, when the dominance of the KVP declined and other nationally organized political parties started competing in the south, these local lists disappeared. Around 1990, they gradually reemerged all over the country as an alternative to national political parties. The exact level of support for these lists, however, is difficult to pin down, because some national parties form (sometimes permanent) coalitions with local lists and compete under their combined name. Also, sometimes combinations of national party branches adopt local names (see Figure 14.3). It is therefore not easy to assess exactly how 'politicized' or 'nationalized' municipal elections in the Netherlands are.

Characteristics of representatives

The percentage of female councilors is still relatively low. In 1990, it was 20% and it gradually increased to slightly over 30% in 2018 (VNG 2018). This only gradual increase and strong

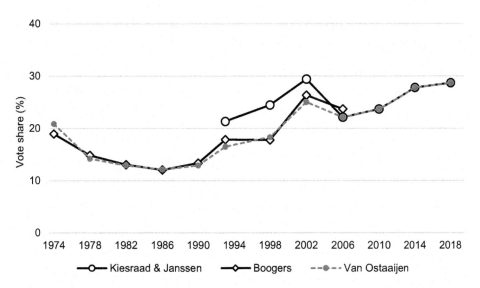

Figure 14.3 Percentages of votes for local lists not formally connected to national lists from three somewhat different sources, 1970–2020

Source: This figure is based on data from Boogers, Lucardie, & Voerman (2007), Jansen and Boogers (2019), and van Ostaaijen (2019)

differences between municipalities (probably partly stimulated by some activities in the context of 100 years of female suffrage in The Netherlands) has led to some attention to this topic in recent years.[20] Because women are somewhat better represented in relatively larger political parties, and because some smaller left-wing parties are only represented in larger municipalities, the number of female councilors is somewhat greater in the larger municipalities, but the relationship between municipal size and the percentage of female councilors is not very strong.

Partly because of the low number of female councilors, and partly because some voters like descriptive representation, women in particular tend to vote for women on the party lists (Jansen & Boogers 2019: 15–16). According to Van Holsteyn and Andeweg (2012: 2), this type of intraparty preference voting also seems to be a form of expressive rather than instrumental electoral behavior: female candidates, and to a lesser extent ethnic candidates, receive more preference votes, but such votes are cast predominantly for the highest placed female (or ethnic) candidate on the list – candidates who would be elected on the basis of their position on the party list anyway.

Compared to the national level, however, it seems that in local elections not only 'voting for the first woman on the list' but also 'voting for a person I know personally' is an important reason to cast a preferential vote (Jansen & Boogers 2019).

Representation of persons of foreign origin at the local level is increasing, but it is still much lower than the percentage of these people in the population warrants. Of all people living in The Netherlands, 78% have a Dutch background (both parents were born in The Netherlands) and 22% have a migration background (10% Western, 12% non-Western). According to a survey in 2016, 87% of council members have a Dutch background and only 6% a migration background (7% unknown) (BZK 2017: 23). According to the same definition,

12% of the members of the Second Chamber have a migration background (3% Western, 9% non-Western).[21]

After both the election of 2014 and that of 2018, about half the number of council positions were filled with new councilors (BZK 2017, 2019). Because part of the turnover is due to changes in support for political parties (political volatility, the rest is councilors voluntarily stepping down or a consequence of internal party politics), and because electoral volatility has increased in the last few decades, the turnover percentage probably used to be smaller. Turnover is relatively lower in small municipalities (BZK 2019: 40). By implication, there is only a limited amount of continuity, especially in the larger municipalities, which makes the building up of expertise rather difficult in the municipalities facing the biggest challenges.

Studying local democracy in The Netherlands

Because of national laws, all municipalities basically have the same institutional structure and regulatory autonomy. And because that regulatory autonomy is strongly limited, local policies across municipalities have a lot in common. Because many national political parties see councils and provincial states as a way to recruit new representatives, a means to attract additional voters, and a way to give their members a meaningful way to stay involved in party political affairs, they aim to have local branches in as many municipalities as possible. That aim is mainly hindered by the large and increasing number of effective political parties in The Netherlands. Many voters like the idea of voting for the same party nationally and locally, and at least some people have difficulty understanding the differences between the local, provincial, and national systems of governance. Nevertheless, support for local lists is increasing and is now around 30% of the local popular vote. Therefore, not only the national institutional system but also the national party system is reflected at the local level, and journalists often treat local elections as an indication of trends associated with national elections.

These similarities, however, should not obscure important differences between municipalities. Two of the small islands in the north of the country have fewer than 1,000 inhabitants, while Amsterdam has over 800,000. The richest inhabitants live in the municipalities in the west of the country, and the mean income in these municipalities is more than twice as high as income in the poorest municipalities (see CBS 2019b). Thus, the composition of municipalities differs significantly. Several other indications show that municipalities differ in many ways, and because of that policies can be different.

In recent years, there has been a trend toward decentralization in order to facilitate a better connection between local preferences and local policies and, thus, greater differences between municipalities. However, this decentralization was not accompanied by an equal decentralization of money. Because Dutch municipalities cannot easily levy local taxes, this means that the increased burden of decentralization is not always evaluated positively. In addition, some dislike the idea that citizens in municipalities are treated differently because of local policy differences.

In the past decades, the existing heterogeneity and the expected further increase in heterogeneity because of decentralization have stimulated much research about the causes and consequences of the found differences. Municipalities in the Netherlands have been and continue to be studied extensively by various organizations, and data about municipalities are widely shared. Local electoral behavior is studied in a way similar to the national electoral behavior, and data are publicly available via the national data archive (Jansen & Denters 2019; van der Meer & van der Kolk 2016). All local election results since 1931 are available electronically and can be connected to various types of municipal data. There is a long tradition of studying local political parties, especially local lists (van Ostaaijen 2019). Also, the sometimes difficult recruitment of new candidates for local lists has been monitored (Voerman & Boogers 2014). Several other monitoring studies, including the composition of local councils and their activities, are systematically summarized in a biannual publication of the Ministry of the Interior (BZK 2017, 2019). Recently, efforts have been made by researchers from various universities to more systematically study all people holding elected office. Finally, local taxes and local public expenditures are monitored as well by the Centre for Research on Local Government Economics.[22] Data on this topic can also be found on the website of Statistics Netherlands.

This research allows a better understanding of the functioning of Dutch democracy with its 'nationalized' elections and its relatively dependent municipalities with limited fiscal autonomy and increasing responsibilities for social policies.

Notes

1 A rich source (in Dutch only) summarizing the outcome of many other studies covering various aspects of local government is BZK (2019).
2 The number of provinces has been stable at 11 since the nineteenth century. Only in 1986 was a 12th province instituted consisting of large areas of new claimed lands ('polders') in the center of the country.
3 In addition to the three layers mentioned in the main text, there is a set of 21 specialized water boards that are responsible for water quantity and quality, sometimes but not always covering the same areas as the provinces. The Caribbean islands Bonaire, Sint Eustatius, and Saba have been public bodies since 2010 but are not part of any province. Until 2014, the two largest municipalities (Amsterdam and Rotterdam) also had formal 'stadsdelen' with democratic council elections. These institutional elements of Dutch decentralized democracy will be ignored for the remainder of this chapter.
4 Both the idea of 'municipal autonomy' and the idea that specific tasks can be assigned by the central government can be found in the Dutch constitution (Article 124).
5 Check the 'Toelichting op de berekening van de uitkering uit het gemeentefonds 2019' [Explanation of the calculation of the transfers from the 2019 municipal fund] (in Dutch). Available at: https://kennisopenbaarbestuur.nl/media/256201/toelichting-op-de-berekening-van-de-uitkering-gemeentefonds-2019.pdf.
6 The documents and descriptions related to the Local Autonomy Index paint a rather positive picture of the level of local autonomy in The Netherlands. The large number of responsibilities (especially after the recent decentralizations) and the relatively small budgets to fulfill the associated tasks, combined with extremely limited opportunities to levy local taxes, make this a combination of autonomy and austerity (Ladner, Keuffer, & Baldersheim 2016).
7 Article 125 of the Dutch constitution.
8 Article 36 Gemeentewet (Municipal law).
9 Article 61.1 Gemeentewet (Municipal law).
10 Wet van 26 november 2018, houdende verandering in de Grondwet, strekkende tot de deconstitutionalisering van de benoeming van de commissaris van de Koning en de burgemeester, 21/12/2018 Ministerie van Binnenlandse Zaken en Koninkrijksrelaties, Staatsblad 2018, 493, Wet 26/11/2018, Stb. 2018, 493. https://zoek.officielebekendmakingen.nl/stb-2018-493
11 Chapter G, Kieswet (Electoral law).
12 In 2018, 28 'blank lists' participated in local elections, 9 of which won at least one seat. One such list (that because of an administrative mistake was unable to deliver a party name) even won four seats in a municipality facing amalgamation (calculations are based on data from www.verkiezingsuitslagen.nl).
13 Article P 7 Kieswet (Electoral law).
14 Article P 8 Kieswet (Electoral law).
15 Because councils have an uneven number of seats, it is possible that a list receiving 50% plus 1 of the votes will not receive more than half the number of seats. To account for this eventuality, another correction may take place after the initial distribution of all seats that also gives the party with more than 50% of the votes more than 50% of the seats (Article P 9 Kieswet, Electoral law).
16 The proposal 'Wijziging van de Kieswet in verband met het afschaffen van de mogelijkheid voor politieke groeperingen om lijstencombinaties te vormen' ['Amendment to the Electoral Act to Abolish the Ability for Political Groups to Form List Combinations (apparentement)'] (34377).

17 Article P 15 Kieswet (Electoral law).
18 This individual threshold was lowered from 50% to 25% in 1998. The reason for not using the same threshold for smaller municipalities was that the minister proposing the change thought that an individual threshold of 25% implied receiving only 20–140 votes. This was thought to be too simple. The minister did not discuss the number of votes it takes in these small municipalities to receive a high position on the party list. Later attempts to reduce the individual threshold even further failed in 2006.
19 Articles 13 and 15 Gemeentewet (Municipal law).
20 For an example, see Mügge, Runderkamp, and Kranendonk in their essay 'Op weg naar een betere m/v-balans in politiek en bestuur' (UvA 2019) ('Toward a better gender balance in politics and governance'). They also discuss the relationship between the size of municipalities and the number of female councilors.
21 Check the web page www.parlement.com/id/vk6gbgxlvuxs/afkomst_tweede_kamerleden
22 See www.coelo.nl. The Centre for Research on Local Government Economics (COELO) conducts research on economic and financial aspects of local government.

References

Allers, M., & Peters, K. (2019). Decentralisatiebeleid van de overheid niet in uitgaven terug te zien. *Economische en Statistische Berichten*, *104*(4776), 376–378.

Berenschot, B. (2004). *Evaluatie van de Wet dualisering gemeentebestuur: eindrapport*. Berenschot: Utrecht.

Boogers, M., Klok, P. J., Denters, B., & Sanders, M. (2016). *Effecten van regionaal bestuur voor gemeenten; Bestuursstructuur, samenwerkingsrelaties, democratische kwaliteit en bestuurlijke effectiviteit*. Enschede: University of Twente.

Boogers, M., Lucardie, P., & Voerman, G. (2007). *Lokale politieke groeperingen; Belangenbehartiging, protest en lokalisme*. Groningen/Tilburg: Rijksuniversiteit Groningen/Universiteit van Tilburg.

Bouwmans, H. (2019). *Valkuilen voor wethouders; Lessen uit valpartijen van wethouders in de periode 2002–2018*. Den Haag: Boom bestuurskunde.

BZK. (2017). *Staat van het bestuur 2016*. Den Haag: Ministerie van Binnenlandse Zaken en Koninkrijksrelaties. Retrieved from www.rijksoverheid.nl/documenten/rapporten/2017/02/09/staat-van-het-bestuur-2016

BZK. (2019). *Staat van het bestuur 2018*. Den Haag: Ministerie van Binnenlandse Zaken en Koninkrijksrelaties. Retrieved from https://kennisopenbaarbestuur.nl/media/256047/staat-van-het-bestuur-2018.pdf

Carey, J. M., & Shugart, M. S. (1995). Incentives to cultivate a personal vote: A rank ordering of electoral formulas. *Electoral Studies*, *14*(4), 417–439.

CBS. (2019a). *Gemeentelijke indeling ongewijzigd in 2020*. Den Haag: CBS [Press release].

CBS. (2019b). *Welvaart in Nederland (Welfare in The Netherlands)*. Den Haag: CBS.

De Groot, M. (2009). *Democratic effects of institutional reform in local government; The Case of the Dutch Local Government Act 2002* (PhD). Enschede: University of Twente.

Gerritsen, S., & Ter Weel, B. (2014). *Beantwoording vragen opkomstpercentage en herindelingen*. The Hague: CPB Netherlands Bureau for Economic Policy Analysis.

Hanemaayer, D., Wever, Y., Sinnema, M., & van den Berg, Y. (2008). *Staat van het Dualisme; Eindrapport*. MBZK: Den Haag.

Heinelt, H., Hlepas, N., Kuhlmann, S., & Swianiewicz, P. (2018). Local government systems: Grasping the institutional environment of mayors. In H. Heinelt, A. Magnier, M. Cabria, & H. Reynaert (Eds.), *Political leaders and changing local democracy: The European mayor* (pp. 19–78). London: Palgrave Macmillan.

Jacobs, K., van Klingeren, M., van der Kolk, H., van der Krieken, K., Rooduijn, M., & Wagenaar, C. (2018). *Het Wiv-referendum: Nationaal Referendum Onderzoek 2018*. Nijmegen: SKON/BZK.

Jansen, G., & Boogers, M. (2019). Opkomst en stemgedrag. In G. Jansen & B. Denters (Eds.), *Democratie dichterbij: Lokaal Kiezersonderzoek 2018* (pp. 7–17). Enschede: SKON.

Jansen, G., & Denters, S. A. H. (2019). *Democratie dichterbij: Lokaal Kiezersonderzoek 2018*. Enschede: SKON.

Jong, R. de. (2018). *Het gebruik van voorkeurstemmen bij verkiezingen*. Retrieved from http://stukroodvlees.nl/10096-2/

Ladner, A., Keuffer, N., & Baldersheim, H. (2016). *Self-rule index for local authorities (Release 1.0)*. Brussels: Publications Office of the European Union

Ladner, A., Keuffer, N., Baldersheim, H., Hlepas, N., Swianiewicz, P., Steyvers, K., & Navarro, C. (2019). *Patterns of local autonomy in Europe*. London: Palgrave Macmillan.

Magnier, A. (2006). Strong mayors? On direct election and political entrepreneurship. In H. Bäck, H. Heinelt, & A. Magnier (Eds.), *The European mayor: Political leaders in the changing context of local democracy* (pp. 353–376). Wiesbaden: VS Verlag für Sozialwissenschaften.

Reif, K.-H., & Schmitt, H. (1980). Nine second-order national elections: A conceptual framework for the analysis of European election results. *European Journal of Political Research*, 8(1), 3–44.

Reynolds, A., Reilly, B., & Ellis, A. (2005). *The new international IDEA handbook of Electoral system design*. Stockholm: International Institute for Democracy and Electoral Assistance (IDEA).

Schaap, L., Daemen, H., & Ringeling, A. (2009). Mayors in seven European countries: Part II – performance and analysis. *Local Government Studies*, 35(2), 235–249.

Smets, K., & van Ham, C. (2013). The embarrassment of riches? A meta-analysis of individual-level research on voter turnout. *Electoral Studies*, 32(2), 344–359.

Steenvoorden, E., & van der Waal, J. (2016). Stemgedrag bij gemeenteraadsverkiezingen. In T. v. d. Meer & H. Kolk van der (Eds.), *Democratie dichterbij: lokaal kiezersonderzoek 2016* (pp. 57–63). Amsterdam: Stichting Kiezersonderzoek Nederland/Ministerie van Binnenlandse Zaken en Koninkrijksrelaties.

Van de Voorde, N. (2017). Verticale politieke cumul in de Lage Landen: evolutie en verklaringen. *Res Publica*, 59(3), 281–307.

Van der Kolk, H. (1997). *Electorale controle; lokale verkiezingen en responsiviteit van politici* ((dissertatie) ed.). Enschede: Twente University Press.

van der Krieken, K. (2019). *Winst of verlies: Het lokale referendum in Nederland 1906–2018*. Tilburg: Ridderprint bv.

van der Meer, T., & van der Kolk, H. (2016). *Democratie dichterbij: lokaal kiezersonderzoek 2016*. Amsterdam/Twente: SKON.

Van Holsteyn, J. J., & Andeweg, R. B. (2012). Tweede orde personalisering: Voorkeurstemmen in Nederland. *Res Publica*, 54(2), 163–191.

van Ostaaijen, J. (2019). *Lokale partijen in Nederland: Een overzicht van kennis over lokale partijen 2002–2019*. Tilburg: Tilburg University.

VNG. (2018). *Raadsleden 2018*. Retrieved from https://vng.nl/sites/default/files/2020-01/rapport_raadsleden_2018_na_verkiezingen.pdf

Voerman, G., & Boogers, M. (2014). *Rekrutering van kandidaten voor de gemeenteraads-verkiezingen in 2006, 2010 en 2014: kandidaatstellingsproblemen vergeleken en verklaard*. Groningen/Enschede: Universiteit van Groningen/Universiteit van Twente.

15

Switzerland

Low turnout but no second-order elections

Andreas Ladner

The Swiss system of local government: small but autonomous municipalities

Swiss municipalities form the lowest level of the Swiss three-tier state organization. The two tiers above the municipalities are the cantonal government and the federal or national government. On 1 January 2020, the 26 cantons (intermediate tier) counted 2,202 municipalities. Despite an increasing number of amalgamations since the 1990s, the country still has a large number of municipalities, and most of them are very small. About 50% of the municipalities have fewer than 1,500 inhabitants. Over the last 30 years, about 820 or almost 27% of the municipalities disappeared, and more amalgamations are going to take place. Nevertheless, Switzerland is very unlikely to join countries like Denmark or important parts of Germany, where large-scale territorial reforms completely changed the system of local government. Amalgamations of municipalities are in the realm of the cantons and they usually need the consent of the citizens of the municipalities concerned, which makes nationwide top-down amalgamation processes almost impossible.

Only since 1999 are the Swiss municipalities explicitly mentioned in the Federal Constitution. Article 50 stipulates, on the one hand, that local autonomy is an important principle to uphold and that the Confederation has to take into account the consequences of its activities for the communes; on the other hand, it is left to the cantons to decide upon the regulatory framework for the municipalities. As a result, there are 26 different cantonal legislations assigning their municipalities different degrees of autonomy and, in some cases, also different functions and competences when it comes to specific tasks. This makes it impossible to describe the Swiss system of local government in a few sentences.[1] There are always exceptions, and a brief description has to concentrate on general trends and the most common arrangements, which gives more weight to the more numerous German-speaking municipalities of small and medium size.

The national constitution, as well as many cantonal constitutions, upholds the principle of subsidiarity, assigning competences and responsibilities to the lowest level possible, and it claims that the principle of fiscal equivalence shall be applied. The idea of fiscal equivalence is particularly interesting as it matches their competences and discretion with the high degree of financial and fiscal autonomy they enjoy. The collective body that benefits from a public service bears the costs thereof, and the collective body that bears the costs of a public service may decide on the nature of that service [FC Article 43a (2) and (3)]. Formulated for the relation between the federal state and cantons, this principle is also applied to intergovernmental relations between the cantons and their municipalities. In the field of their own competences, where the municipality takes the benefit of a service or where it has decisional power, it also has to find the necessary financial resources, which are not provided through transfers from higher levels. Their resources stem from income taxes and fees from their own citizens. Roughly one-third of income taxes are paid directly to the municipalities. The municipalities have quite some discretion to influence the amount of tax income by setting the tax rate. This leads to large differences between the municipalities (and the cantons, where the same principles are applied) with respect to the tax burden and public expenditures. When it comes to voting (elections or decisions on local projects), however, the citizens are well aware that this can have an impact on the amount of tax they will have to pay (Ladner 2011a; Steiner & Kaiser 2013).

From a comparative perspective, Swiss municipalities enjoy a high degree of autonomy. According to Ladner et al. (2019), they are even more autonomous than the municipalities of the Nordic countries. This might come as a little bit of a surprise because they are rather small and, not atypically for a three-tier federal system, the intermediate tier, the cantons, also has a large amount of competences with respect to public tasks and services. The high degree of autonomy is due to their already mentioned fiscal and financial autonomy, their constitutional right of existence, their autonomy in organizing their political systems and their administration (organizational autonomy), their constitutional guarantee of existence, and the lack of political supervision.

Despite the large variation in population, which falls between a few hundred and a few hundred thousand inhabitants, all municipalities are formally equal, meaning that the system of municipalities is considered symmetric. In practice, however, this is only partly true. Larger municipalities not only provide more tasks and services but they also may have farther reaching decisional competences, and, of course, they are much more influential when it comes to decisions on the cantonal and national levels.

The most decisive element of Swiss local government is the question of whether the municipalities have an assembly system or a local parliament (Ladner 2005, 2016). In the former case, which applies to about 80% of the municipalities, the citizens who are entitled to vote gather between two and four times a year to decide on important issues, usually after an open debate, by a show of hands. In the latter, citizens elect their representatives, who form a local council or parliament that interacts with the local government. In the French-speaking part of the country, local parliaments are much more widespread, and in some cantons (Genève, Neuchâtel) all municipalities have a local parliament, whereas in the German-speaking part, most municipalities have a local assembly and only the largest municipalities have a local parliament.

Elections on the local level: no second-order elections

In all Swiss municipalities, citizens elect their executive and their mayor, which form the local government directly. In about 20% of the municipalities, citizens also elect a local council, which is a sort of local parliament. When we talk about local elections in this chapter, we are referring to the elections for the local collective executive, which are the only comparable elections for the vast majority of municipalities.

The government of the municipality consists of people from the municipality, some of whom are members of different parties while others are without any party affiliation. Most fulfill their mandate on a voluntary or part-time basis and are only modestly remunerated (*Milizsystem*). The mode of government follows the consensus model, where the members of the government make the important decisions together (collegial system). The mayor is always directly elected. The mayor leads the government and sometimes the administration, and she or he represents the municipality.

Given the importance of municipalities for the provision of public services, their far-reaching autonomy, and the fact that the activities of local government have quite an important impact on the amount of tax citizens have to pay, it is not astonishing that local politics matters. Local elections are not seen as second-order elections (Ladner 2011b: 1), nor are they commonly used to sanction parties in power on the national level. Local elections are considered to be important elections in their own right. This is also reflected in the fact that citizens believe that the local level of government has a greater impact on their everyday lives than decisions made on the national level (see Ladner & Bühlmann 2007: 52).

Elected authorities (mayors, members of the executive, and members of the local parliament) usually remain in office for a period of four years, as is the case for members of the national parliament or the national government. In some cantons, the electoral cycle is shorter and in others it amounts to five years, quite often following cantonal practices that deviate from the most common pattern.

Across Switzerland, local elections do not take place on the same day as national or cantonal elections. Every canton has its own weekend(s) for local elections and sometimes times the election days even vary within a canton. In general, all authorities (mayors, executives, local council) are elected on the same weekend, but there are also exceptions (see Ladner 2011b: 6). Local elections are organized by the cantons or, more precisely, by the municipalities and their administration. There is no national electoral commission that organizes and supervises local elections. An electoral commission can exist on the cantonal level, but often it is left to the municipalities to administer their elections. In most cantons, all municipalities organize their elections on the same weekend. In some cantons, however, the municipalities are entirely free to choose the weekend, sometimes during a specific period of the year. In the canton of Bern, for example, local elections do not even take place in the same year.

The direct election of the mayor has a long tradition. It was gradually introduced in the course of the institutional reforms called for by democratic and liberal forces in the 1830s (Steiner 2012). The canton of Fribourg, where the local executive decides who is going to be mayor, and Neuchâtel, where the local parliament elects the executive and the mayor, are nowadays rather exotic exceptions.

The majority of the Swiss municipalities do not have a political recall mechanism to force the local government to resign during its term of office. Specific opportunities to force a member of the local government to resign exist in cases of misconduct and legal problems. The citizens, however, do have the opportunity to intervene in governmental affairs by means of direct democracy. In general, important expenses of local government and changes in the municipal code need the consent of the citizens (referendum), and citizens have the opportunity to change parts of the municipal code or the corresponding regulations by means of an initiative.

Electoral system: a variety of electoral provisions

Swiss municipalities take advantage of their organizational autonomy when it comes to the organization of their political and electoral systems. Elections usually are ballot votes (postal voting). Traditional polling stations still exist, but – especially in larger municipalities and in cities – citizens prefer postal voting. In about 15% of the municipalities, the elections take place in the local assembly, a gathering of all citizens with political rights. Here, because meeting attendance is more demanding than ballot voting, turnout rates are much lower (see also Ladner 2011b: 8).

All Swiss citizens over the age of 18 (an exception here is the canton of Glarus, where the voting age has been lowered to 16) are entitled to vote on local matters. In some cantons and municipalities, non-Swiss residents have active or even passive electoral rights. These rights mainly depend on their length of residence in the country and not on whether they are citizens of an EU or another country. Compulsory voting, nowadays, is only applied in one canton (Schaffhausen).[2] For local elections, non-Swiss residents have political rights, particularly in the French-speaking part of the country (except Wallis), and in the German-speaking part there are a few cantons (Basel-Stadt, Appenzell-Ausserrhoden, Graubünden) where the municipalities are free to grant such political rights to non-Swiss residents.[3]

The size of the local executive varies, and so does the size of the council (local parliament). The number of seats for local executives ranges between 3 and 30 seats, with 5 or 7 being the most popular size. The local councils (local parliaments) have between 9 and 125 seats (the City of Zurich). In general, the number of seats for the executive and the parliament (if there is one) is subject to cantonal or local legislation. The cantonal legislation sets the framework (at least three, between 3 and 7, any odd number, etc., in the case of the executives), and the municipalities use the discretion given according to their needs and preferences. In most of the municipalities there are no specific criteria for setting the number of seats in relation to the number of inhabitants; only a very few cantonal laws provide such regulations (like, for example, Fribourg). Taken all together, the slightly over 2,200 municipalities at the beginning of 2020 had about 13,000 members of local executives and about 17,400 members of local parliaments.

Local election procedures are, in general, set by cantonal legislation prescribing the electoral system and the way in which elections are to be carried out. For the local executive, about 75% of the municipalities use a majority system (see Ladner 2011b: 9), in which the voters cast as many votes as there are seats (two-round bloc vote). In the first round, the candidates need an absolute majority of the votes cast to win their seat. If not all candidates reach an absolute majority – which is not the rule but not uncommon either, because there is usually a larger number of candidates running for office – a second round with a relative majority is needed. The second round usually takes place two or more weeks later. In the rest of the municipalities, one of the various forms of the list proportional representation system is used [free list or open-list PR, see Reynolds et al. (2008: 88)].

The mayor is elected in a separate election usually taking place the same day. He or she commonly also has to be elected as a member of the executive, and a two-round vote with an absolute majority in the first round and a relative majority in the second is applied.

When it comes to the system to choose, some of the cantons are more directive than others, opting for PR or majority voting, whereas others leave it to the municipalities to choose the system they prefer. Quite often, the cantonal electoral system serves as a reference. Studies show that PR voting fosters turnout and goes hand in hand with a more developed system of local political parties (Ladner & Milner 1999).

For the local council, PR voting (usually open list with different methods to allocate seats) is much more common, especially in the larger municipalities where different local parties participate in the elections. Most frequently, it is the method of Hagenbach-Bischoff, which is also applied on national level, and voters have the opportunity to select candidates from other parties (*panaschieren*, cross-voting) and to give two votes to some of the candidates (*kumulieren*, accumulate).

There is hardly any clear pattern as far as the use of the different electoral systems is concerned. Occasionally, PR systems have been introduced in areas with strong party cleavages (Ticino, Valais) or with important minorities (Bern), and if it is left to the municipalities, it is mainly the larger ones that opt for PR. The integration of the important parties into governmental responsibilities (*Konkordanz*), however, also successfully takes place on a more or less voluntary basis under majority voting. Majority voting brings the personal characteristics of the candidate to the forefront, whereas party affiliation seems to play a more important role in PR elections.

Given the small size of most of the municipalities, electoral districts are not common. There is only one exception, the city of Zurich, and quotas or minimal thresholds of votes to get elected are hardly used on the local level, either. A higher number of parties is not seen as an important problem, and a low number of seats for the local executive restricts the chance to win a seat to larger parties only.

Because of the high and time-consuming demands, the decreasing prestige, and the limited number of suitable persons in the small municipalities, many of them struggle to find a sufficient number of qualified candidates for the numerous political mandates. This is increasingly seen as a problem and as an important challenge for the prevailing practice to put politics in the hands of benevolent, part-time politicians (*Milizsystem*). The local political system can be seen as quite open, both for potentially interested office holders and for the citizens who are entitled to vote. As soon as they are registered in a municipality, they are also invited to participate politically.

The *cumul des mandats* is generally seen as a welcome opportunity to defend the municipality's interests at higher levels, more often the cantonal level in the case of smaller municipalities, and sometimes also the national level in the case of cities. In the canton of Bern, for example, more than 60 out of the 160 members of the cantonal parliament also actually have an important political mandate in their municipality. If the mayor or other members of the local government are full-time politicians with a 100% mandate, municipal regulations might explicitly exclude an additional mandate.

The electoral outcomes

Electoral turnout in Switzerland is comparatively low. This can be explained by the limited importance of party majorities in the Swiss consensus system, which unites the representatives of the most important parties in government. Elections do not lead to completely different policies; at the very best they strengthen political tendencies. The opportunities to influence the most important decisions by the means of direct democracy additionally lower the importance of elections.

In the last elections for which we have comparable data, the average turnout[4] in the municipalities analyzed was 49.8% for local elections[5] and 48.7% for national elections. The cantonal level lagged behind with 44%. These figures stem from municipalities with ballot voting for local elections. In municipalities with assembly voting for local elections, turnout would be considerably lower (it drops from over 50% to about 25% in comparable municipalities) and is hardly comparable with turnout for cantonal or national elections, which almost nowhere takes place in an assembly.

In the 1990s turnout for the local elections used to be considerably higher than the turnout for the cantonal and national elections.[6] Table 15.1 shows quite a significant drop between 1988

Table 15.1 Electoral turnout (percent) at all three levels in Switzerland

	1988	1998	2009	2017
Local elections	63.1	55.0	48.2	49.8
Cantonal elections	52.8	46.8	43.7	44.0
National elections	50.4	45.4	47.2	48.7
N Local elections	1,848	1,456	997	1,262
N Cantonal elections	1,827	1,473	1,003	1,287
N National elections	1,833	1,458	997	1,291

Notes: Mean values across all municipalities participating in the respective surveys; includes municipalities with ballot voting only.

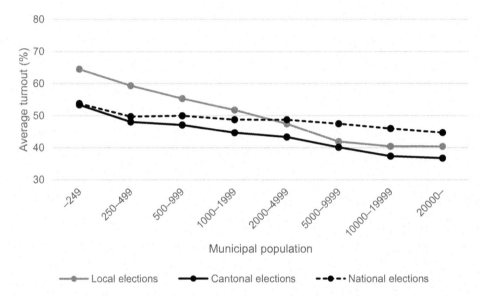

Figure 15.1 Average voter turnout at all three levels in 2017 by municipality size N local elections = 1,279, N cantonal elections = 1,302, N national elections = 1,303; municipalities with ballot voting only.

and 2009 for local and cantonal turnout. Turnout on the national level has not changed that much. Thus, in terms of turnout, national elections have become relatively more important. Turnout for cantonal elections is clearly the lowest, which is to some extent astonishing given the importance of the cantonal level when it comes to public tasks and expenditures (see Ladner 2019). The gain in importance of national elections compared to the lower level elections is due to increased polarization of the national party system and the success of the right-wing Swiss People's Party. On the local level, particularly in smaller municipalities, political parties have lost their importance, they find it difficult to mobilize their supporters, and voting is considered a citizen's duty to a lesser extent.

Turnout – in an aggregate perspective – is clearly linked to the size of the municipality. The correlations between the number of inhabitants and turnout on all three levels are negative and highly significant.[7] As can be seen in Figure 15.1, the decrease is strongest for local level turnout. In small municipalities, turnout for local level elections is still considerably higher than for elections at the other two levels. This might be a little surprising, because for many of these local elections there are hardly more candidates than there are seats (only in about half of the municipalities are there more candidates participating in the elections for the local executive than there are seats contested), and everybody running for office gets elected. Media coverage, a greater offer, parties, and more candidates do not seem to be sufficient to guarantee higher turnout in larger municipalities. It is likely that social control and a lack of anonymity makes it more difficult to abstain from voting in smaller municipalities, and one might even believe that it is also a way to express one's consent and gratitude toward the people taking care of this kind of public responsibility for some years.

Local elections, if they do not take place in the larger municipalities with more than 10,000 inhabitants, are thus not very competitive. About 40% of the respondents in an earlier survey of local secretaries do not consider the elections competitive at all ($N = 1,388$). In addition to the elections with a limited number of candidates, incumbents usually are reelected, and most of the time the results are already clear in advance and hardly very astonishing. This goes hand in hand with complaints that it is very difficult to find enough good candidates for the different mandates. Analyses show that PR elections are more competitive than majority elections (Ladner 2011b: 25).

Table 15.2 Aggregate electoral results of the most important parties in the most recent local elections (prior to 2017) in Switzerland

	% of municipalities where represented	% of seats on local councils	% of mayors affiliated with the party
Liberal Party (FDP)	42.9	17.0	20.4
Christian Democrats (CVP)	31.2	12.5	12.2
Swiss People's Party (SVP)	33.5	11.6	10.6
Social Democrats (SPS)	25.3	7.4	3.8
Conservative Democratic Party (BDP)	4.4	0.5	1.4
Christian Social Party (CSP)	2.6	0.5	0.9
Evangelical People's Party (EVP)	2.8	1.2	0.4
Green Party (GPS)	2.4	0.6	0.3
Green Liberal Party (GLP)	2.1	1.0	0.2
Lega dei Ticinesi	1.7	0.4	0.1
Federal Democratic Union (EDU)	1.0	0.2	0.1
Other parties	6.0	2.4	1.5
Local parties/groups	9.7	4.9	6.0
No party affiliation	53.5	39.7	42.0
Total		100.0	100.0
Number of seats		9,702	1,626
Number of municipalities	1,868		1,626

Source: Local secretary survey (2017) and Steiner et al. (2021)

When it comes to party politics, local politics is dominated by the four big traditional parties. However, the largest 'party' consists of those without any party affiliation (see Table 15.2).[8] This is especially true for smaller municipalities, where local politics is no longer dominated by party representatives. There are thus two forms of local politics: a version without parties in the smaller municipalities and a partisan version in the larger municipalities. In the latter case, we occasionally also find representatives of smaller parties or municipality-specific groups of citizens.[9] The biggest cities are dominated by left and green parties, whereas in the middle-sized municipalities center and right-wing parties are stronger. Across all municipalities and not including those with no party affiliation, the Liberal Party (FDP) is the strongest party with 17% of the seats, followed by the Christian Democrats with 12.5%, the Swiss People's Party with 11.6%, and the Social Democrats with 7.4%.

Female representation in local government is rather low (see Table 15.3). At the end of the 1980s, fewer than 10% of the members of local government were female, and almost two-thirds of the executives had no female representation. Thirty years later, this has clearly improved and about every fourth seat is held by a woman. There are only about 15% of the municipalities without women in their government. The increased rates, however, were much higher in the 1990s than in more recent times, and it does not, at the moment, look like women were catching up in the very near future. Interesting to note is the fact that women are much better represented on the national level, where they won more than 40% of the seats on the national council in 2019, compared to 14.5% in 1987. Parties seem to be quite successful at promoting female candidates for the more prestigious higher level elections, whereas in the municipalities, where the access is generally easier, it is still more difficult to persuade women to run for office.

Discussion

Local elections in Switzerland are in no way second-order elections. In smaller municipalities, turnout rates are higher for local elections than for national elections, and the electoral results differ quite often from the results on the national level. To some extent, this can be explained

Table 15.3 Representation of women in Swiss local government and percentage of executives without women

	1988	1994	1998	2005	2009	2017
Number of seats	14,582	12,206	14,435	12,744	8,057	10,338
Women	1,066	1,684	2,717	2,764	1,883	2,525
Percentage of women (%)	7.3	13.8	18.8	21.7	23.4	24.4
Without women (%)[1]	62.3	38.9	26.0	19.7	16.4	15.6
Number of municipalities Covered (N)	2,421	2,029	2,427	2,175	1,372	1,775
National Council (200 seats)	1987 1991	1995	1999	2005	2009 2013	2017
Percentage of women	14.5 17.5	21.5	23.5	26.0	29.0 32.0	42.0

Source: Local secretary surveys
[1] Percentage of executives.

by the fact that local politicians are closer to the citizens and their election is part of local self-government, which is an important issue for Swiss citizens. Furthermore, the allocation of competences and fiscal autonomy can lead to politically inconsistent party preferences, depending on the level at which decisions have to be taken. On the local level, citizens might favor a more restrictive financial policy because they have to pay for it with their own tax money, whereas for national policies their financial commitment is lower as the circle of contributors is much larger, and they might even benefit from transfers.

There is also impressive diversity when we compare turnout figures between different cantons and areas. Here, there are historical and cultural reasons and different configurations of the electoral and political systems that explain the differences. In some cantons, local politics are still highly politicized, opposing the Liberal party and the Christian Democrats, the two historical opponents of the 'Kulturkampf'; in others, direct democracy lessens the importance of elections, and finally in some cantons PR voting fosters additional turnout.

In an international comparative perspective, however, turnout figures for local elections are rather low, especially in light of the municipalities' high degree of autonomy and their importance for the citizens. In Switzerland, turnout figures at all political levels are relatively low. This has to be seen in relation to the Swiss consensus democracy and the means of direct democracy, which are also widespread in Swiss municipalities. All of the important parties have governmental responsibilities, and elections do not lead to a shift of the majority from one party to another. This lowers the importance of elections, as does the fact that the citizens decide on all important issues, projects, and expenditures by means of direct democracy and the competences of local governments are thus limited.

Given the small size of most of the municipalities, there is another important development to be addressed. In the smaller municipalities in particular, political parties are lacking members and support and are no longer present all over the country. A significant portion of the members of local government and quite a few mayors are nowadays without party affiliation. Elections are thus more about people and less about parties, and local decisions seem to have become more pragmatic or technical and less ideological. This can be seen either positively or negatively; politicians, however, are more individualized and cannot rely on the support of a group of people sharing the same ideas and objectives.

Municipalities have, apart from the very large ones and the cities, difficulty finding the personnel for all the different jobs and offices. This holds true not only for the local council but also for the local executives and the mayors. This difficulty endangers the Swiss militia system, that is, the idea that political affairs should not be in the hands of professional politicians but rather in the hands of 'ordinary' people doing it on a voluntary and part-time basis. Although this problem is addressed frequently, a solution is not easy to find.

The increasing complexity of local policies has made political mandates more time-consuming and challenging. This has led to a debate about possible reforms and attempts to separate political or strategic activities from operational and administrative activities. Up to now, models in which the local executive takes the form of a board of directors and a city manager serves as the CEO of the municipality are rare exceptions, but there is a tendency for the administrative side to become more influential, and the political side finds it increasingly difficult to steer the affairs of the municipality. At the end of the day, this could lead to a shift of power from the elected to the nonelected arena of local government. The increasing number of amalgamations has not changed this, because most of the amalgamated municipalities did not reach a critical size to become a more viable polity. Amalgamations in Switzerland are usually driven by output arguments and hardly ever by democracy arguments.

Notes

1 For more about the Swiss municipalities and the cantonal differences, see also Ladner (1991) and more generally Ladner (2011a.)
2 The 26 Swiss cantons and their abbreviations are: Zürich (ZH), Graubünden (GR), Bern (BE), Basel-Stadt (BS), Waadt (VD), Neuenburg (NE), Aargau (AG), Schwyz (SZ), Zug (TG), St. Gallen (SG), Genf (GE), Schaffhausen (SH), Luzern (LU), Jura (JU), Tessin (TI), Appenzell A.Rh. (AR), Wallis (VS), Nidwalden (IR), Freiburg (FR), Glarus (GL), Basel-Landschaft (BL), Obwalden (OW), Solothurn (SO), Uri (UR), Thurgau (TG), Appenzell I.Rh. (AI).
3 See www.bfs.admin.ch/bfs/de/home/statistiken/bevoelkerung/migration-integration/integrationindikatoren/schluesselindikatoren/politik/gemeinde-kantone-recht.html (accessed 16/1/2020).
4 Because local elections do not take place on the same day, the electorate changes and we are not able to compare the percentages of people participating altogether. By taking the means of the turnout rates at all three levels across the municipalities under scrutiny, the many smaller municipalities, where turnout is higher, have more weight and the overall value is slightly higher.
5 On the local level, the data stem from elections for the local executive, because only 20% of the municipalities have a local parliament. These are, however, the more important elections and are comparable with the elections for the cantonal and national parliaments.
6 Because we are confronted with survey data, the results have to be analyzed with some precautions. For an analysis of trends, the municipalities we look at might change. For more reliable data here, we would need to look at municipalities that participated in all surveys, which considerably lowers the number of municipalities to consider and gives the larger municipalities more weight.
7 The correlation coefficients between size (log) and turnout are as follows: local elections $-.419$ (sig. .000, $N = 1{,}279$), cantonal elections $-.273$ (sig. .000, $N = 1{,}302$), and national elections $-.134$ (sig. .000, $N = 1{,}303$).
8 Because political parties are no longer present in the smaller municipalities with their own local party organizations, the number of nonaffiliated members of the local executives has increased considerably. They do not have any party ties and are not considered to be representatives of a particular party.
9 A distinction has to be made between representatives of smaller parties that are also organized on the national level, or take party in national politics, and local groups and parties that only care about questions related to their municipality.

References

Parteien und lokale Politik. Eine empirische Untersuchung in den Gemeinden der Schweiz. Zürich: Seismo.
Ladner, A. (2005). Laymen and Executives in Swiss Local Government. In R. Berg & N. Rao (Eds.), *Transforming Political Leadership in Local Government* (pp. 101–115). London: Palgrave Macmillan.
Ladner, A. (2011a). Switzerland: Subsidiarity, Power Sharing and Direct Democracy. In J. Loughlin, F. Hendriks & A. Lidström (Eds.), *The Oxford Handbook of Local and Regional Democracy in Europe* (pp. 196–220). Oxford: Oxford University Press.
Ladner, A. (2011b). *Wahlen in den Schweizer Gemeinden. Durchführung, Verlauf, Beteiligung und Ergebnisse 1988–2009*. Lausanne: Cahier de l'IDHEAP Nr. 263.
Ladner, A. (2016). *Gemeindeversammlung und Gemeindeparlament. Überlegungen und empirische Befunde zur Ausgestaltung der Legislativfunktion in den Schweizer Gemeinden*. Lausanne: Cahier de l'IDHEAP Nr. 292.
Ladner, A. (2019). The Organization and Provision of Public Services. In A. Ladner, N. Soguel, Y. Emery, S. Weerts & S. Nahrath (Eds.), *Swiss Public Administration. Making the State Work Successfully* (pp. 21–42). London: Palgrave Macmillan.
Ladner, A. & Bühlmann, M. (2007). *Demokratie in den Gemeinden. Der Einfluss der Gemeindegrösse und anderer Faktoren auf die Qualität der Demokratie in den Gemeinden*. Zürich/Chur: Rüegger.
Ladner, A, Keuffer, N., Baldersheim, H., Hlepas, N., Swianiewicz, P., Steyvers, K. & Navarro, C. (2019). *Patterns of Local Autonomy in Europe*. London: Palgrave Macmillan.
Ladner, A. & Milner, H. (1999). Do Voters Turn Out More Under Proportional than Majoritarian Systems? The Evidence from Swiss Communal Elections. *Electoral Studies*, 18, 235–250.
Reynolds, A, Reilly, B. & Ellis, A. (2008). *Electoral System Design: The New International IDEA Handbook*. Stockholm: International Institute for Democracy and Electoral Assistance.

Steiner, P. (2012). Gemeindepräsident. In *Historisches Lexikon der Schweiz*. https://hls-dhs-dss.ch/de/articles/027477/2012-06-12/ (download: 16.1.2020).

Steiner, R. & Kaiser, C. (2013). Die Gemeindeverwaltungen. In A. Ladner, J.-L. Chappelet, Y. Emery, P. Knoepfel, L. Mader, N. Soguel & F. Varone (Eds.), *Handbuch der öffentlichen Verwaltung in der Schweiz* (pp. 149–166). Zürich: NZZ libro.

Steiner, R., Ladner, A., Kaiser, C., Haus, A., Amsellem, A. & Keuffer, N. (2021). *Zustand und Entwicklung der Schweizer Gemeinden. Ergebnisse des nationalen Gemeindemonitorings 2017*. Glaris: Somedia Buchverlag.

Part 5
The Southern European States

16

Andorra

Local elections in quasi-federal institutions

Lluís Medir, Pere Vilanova, and Esther Pano

The State of Andorra as a relatively unknown European state

Andorra is indeed a small country in terms of territory and population (77,543 inhabitants in 468 km²). It is totally surrounded by the Pyrenees, and it is a unique case in Europe. Its main political characteristics go back to at least the thirteenth century [the first legal document, the *Pareatges* (1278), is considered to be quite similar to the Magna Carta in England]. Before that time, the valleys of Andorra formed the last frontier of the *Marca Hispanica*: the territories set up by Charlemagne in order to prohibit the Moors from invading the Frankish kingdom. The current 'balance of power' between the Bishop of Urgell (in the southern part of the Pyrenees) and the *Compte de Foix* (in the northern part) makes it a case of an independent state with strong ties – constitutionally granted today – to two different states (France and Spain in this case, through the Bishop of Urgell). French King Henry IV took Andorra under his authority and thus incorporated it to the French Crown in 1572, where it remained until the French revolution, when the French republicans renounced France's sovereignty over it. However, since 1806, when Napoleon I reestablished France's co-sovereignty, the system grounded on the double co-sovereignty (a condominium under joint sovereignty) of Andorra has remained untouched (Mickoleit 2010).

The previously mentioned balance of power between the two neighbors may help to understand why Andorra has been able to avoid being involved in any war (including both world wars) and has remained territorially and socially stable for almost eight centuries. It retains Catalan as the official language, and most of the traditions and consuetudinary norms have been alive since feudal times. The local traditions well rooted in Andorran society revolve around the solid nature of the parishes, which very soon took the institutional and administrative name of *comuns*. Traditionally there were six parishes, but in 1978, due to the growth of the population of Andorra La Vella, this main parish was split into *Andorra la Vella* (the capital of the country) and *Les Escaldes-Engordany*. The existing seven local units are, in political terms, the soul of Andorra, because no operational central state apparatus existed until 1993.

The political evolution of the surrounding neighbors, together with the reinforcement of the European Union, forced the Andorran state to evolve into an EU-standard democratic state, without becoming member (Bartomeu 2010). Therefore, in March 1993 Andorra adopted a liberal Constitution establishing it as a parliamentary democracy that still retains its chiefs of state in the form of a co-principality. As a result of history, the two princes (also known as the *coprínceps*) are the President of France and the Bishop of *La Seu d'Urgell* in Catalonia, Spain, establishing a unique 'joint sovereignty' (López Burniol 1999). It operates with a single national parliament, which elects the prime minister (*Cap de Govern del Principat d'Andorra*), an independent judiciary, and a constitutional court.

The Principality of Andorra is territorially organized into two levels of government: *comuns* (traditionally known as *parròquies*) and the central state. The *comuns* are public corporations with legal status and can issue local regulations; they operate under the principle of self-government, recognized and guaranteed by the constitution.[1] Their seven names are explicitly mentioned in the constitution.

In fact, the constitutional nature of Andorra's local governments places them similar to Swiss cantons: conforming institutions with a large set of competencies, their own budget, and strong political influence in the national arena. Indeed, local governments participate by different means in the shaping of national policy through different constitutional forms and institutions (Bartomeu 2010). Their interests are expressed, managed, and protected by the commons (*comuns*) under the principle of self-government. While the total population of Andorra in 2019 was 77,543, the local electoral census was 27,823, only about 35% of the people living in the territory. The average population of the seven municipalities is 11,077 residents, ranging from 4,325 (Canilllo) to 22,440 (Andorra la Vella, the capital).

Article 80 of the Constitution of Andorra, developed by the *Llei Qualificada de delimitació de competències dels Comuns*,[2] states that the local units have administrative and financial autonomy in the following matters: population census; electoral roll and participation in the management of the electoral procedure; popular consultations; commerce, industry, and professional activities; delimitation of the communal territory; property of their own and of the communal public domain; natural resources; cadastral register; local planning; public thoroughfares; culture, sports, and social activities; and communal public services. Their large competencies are grounded on constitutionally granted fiscal autonomy,[3] which includes the use and exploitation of natural resources, traditional tributes, and the taxes for communal services, administrative licenses, the establishment of commercial, industrial, and professional activities, and real estate property. Local units spend about 23% of total public expenditures, which would be a significant contribution except when one considers that there is no regional or meso level.

Finally, in order to better frame the particular institutional position of local governments in Andorra, it is important to emphasize that the Constitutional Court shall settle the conflicts arising from the interpretation or exercise of jurisdiction between the general organs of the state and the *comuns*. Indeed, the *comuns* have legislative initiative and are entitled to lodge appeals of unconstitutionality in front of the Constitutional Court under the terms provided for in the constitution.

In conclusion, if local governments in Andorra were to be placed in existing categories of local government systems, they would probably belong to the Franco group (Hesse & Sharpe 1991) under the strong mayor form (Mouritzen & Svara 2002). Concerning the LAI Index, municipal units in Andorra would probably fit into medium values on the index.

The two-tier system of the Principality of Andorra

Two elections happen in Andorra: the national ones (to elect the *consell general*[4]) and the local ones to elect the seven city councils. They have never overlapped on the same day, but the last three local and national elections were held the same year. The duration of the mandate of the councilors and the mayors lasts for four years, and elections are held automatically every four years in mid-December. There is no anticipated dissolution of the local governments' assembly; therefore, the local electoral cycle is fixed. This is not the case for the national elections: the *cap de govern*, after consulting the government and under his or her own responsibility, may request the *coprínceps* to the dissolve the *consell general* prematurely and call for new elections.[5]

Until 1993, Andorra ran local elections without constitutional provisions, maintaining an ancient system where local candidates were elected using a two-round, plurality-at-large voting system with open lists. Voters could vote for as many candidates as there were open seats. All of the candidates who received more than 50% of the votes were chosen. Those who received fewer than 50%, if there were still seats to be allocated, could try again in a second round without needing an absolute majority. Until 1993, political parties were not legalized, and all lists were officially labeled as independent.

Currently, even if mayors (*cònsol major*) are indirectly elected by the members of the city council [those members also elect the vice mayor (*cònsol menor*)], they represent strong political power. Up to the present, the person in the first position of the winning list has always been selected mayor by the city council and has never been removed from office by a motion of no confidence. Besides their local competences, mayors can easily endorse or support candidates for the national elections. The *comuns* –municipalities – and their political environment are crucial for national elections, because they elect 50% of the seats in the national parliament. This produces strong bargaining power inside each *comú* for managing and forming both the national and local lists, because there is legal incompatibility between both types of lists. In addition, 14 seats (out of 28) of the national parliament are elected by a proportional national list (Hare), and 14 seats are elected by the *parròquies* [two seats for each of the seven elected by a first past the post (FPTP) system].

Moreover, since 2011, national and local elections have been held the same year, and this has generated an increase in the bargaining dynamics at the local level (and given the small size of the political constituencies, it happens at almost a personal level, mostly focusing on territorial identities and personal ties). The incompatibility of candidates running for both elections (national and local) forces a distribution of people among political lists during the same year, which takes place at the local circumscription. In very small constituencies, the confection of lists for running at one or another level becomes a constant trade-off.

A majoritarian system with a proportional facade

There is no specific mandate for the design of the local electoral system in the Constitution of Andorra. It simply states that the councilors (*els comuns*) should be elected democratically. Therefore, the decision about the specific design of the electoral system belonged to the legislative branch, with no limits other than the democratic nature of the election. However, the electoral system is described by a special law, which was adopted with a reinforced majority (*Llei Qualificada*).

In September 1993, the national parliament (*consell general*) approved a general electoral code as a fundamental part of the newborn democratic state, called *Llei qualificada del règim electoral i del referendum*. This law has been amended several times, and the current text dates from December 2014 and is titled *Text refós de la Llei qualificada del règim electoral i del referendum*. None of the changes made since 1993 included major changes concerning local elections.[6]

The current local electoral system in Andorra is a mixed electoral system, or more precisely a majority bonus system (MBS), in one round, which combines a subsidiary distribution of seats by proportional representation (PR) with a strong majoritarian attribution system. Clearly, it resembles the French local election system for municipalities over 1,000 inhabitants with a large bonus for the winner, but with a single round and a different subsequent proportional distribution.

The eligibility rules have been the same for local and national elections since 1993: all (and only) nationals over the age of 18 are entitled to vote. Because Andorra is not an EU member state, only citizens of Andorra are entitled to vote. This includes those living permanently abroad, as they can always vote for the local government where they were born or were registered for the first time. The right to stand for the local council elections is granted to all adult voters, with the exception of members of the judiciary branch and the electoral commission.[7] Moreover, as mentioned previously, the electoral code excludes the *cumul des mandats*.

The number of municipal councilors to be elected within each *parròquia* (municipality) ranges from a minimum of ten to a maximum of 16; this a number is completely independent from the population of the local government. The specific size of the assembly within this range is determined by each local government, after a positive vote with a reinforced majority of two-thirds of the city council.

The electoral system is the same for each of the seven *parròquies*. The nomination rules establish that the electoral list should be presented with the popular support of at least 0.5% of people on the local census, implying a minimum of ten signatures of ordinary registered voters of the *parròquia* (*presentadors*). As in most of the proportional systems, the party list should include the total number of councilors to be elected, plus two substitutes. The lists of candidates are closed and blocked, so the order of candidates is fixed when the list is registered, and voters are unable to transform or alter the ballot in any way. Voters may only vote for the whole list, without any influence on the party-supplied order in which party candidates are elected. Moreover, *apparentement* is not permitted, and electors have a single vote.

The elections are held on Sunday, but early voting is possible.[8] The electoral lists are contested in a single round by a proportional representation system with a strong majority bonus. The list that comes in first in the voting will automatically receive half of all seats, and the rest of the seats will be distributed proportionally among the rest of the electoral lists, as in France, without any threshold and using the Hare quota with largest remainders method. The use of a set bonus (direct attribution of half of all seats) for the list receiving the most votes, regardless the percentage of the vote obtained, reinforces the effect pursued by majority bonus systems (MBS): to build a majority or, in more general terms, to maximize bargaining power in the elected assembly (Bedock & Sauger 2014). This construction of large majorities in the local assemblies significantly facilitates the election of mayors (*cònsol major*), who are indirectly elected by a simple majority of the councilors (*comuns*) of the city council.

The *cònsol major* has a limitation on his or her mandate, as he or she can only stay in office for two consecutive and complete terms (8 years in a row). The *cònsol major* is dependent on the majority of the council and can be removed by a vote of no confidence if an alternative candidate reaches an absolute majority of the votes in the local assembly. This possibility has never happened up to the present. The aim of all mixed electoral systems is to combine the positive attributes of both majority and proportional electoral systems (Reynolds et al. 2008), and therefore they pursue a double goal: to represent a large spectrum of parties and to ensure a stable governing majority (Bedock & Sauger 2014). However, these 'majority-assuring' systems have often been depicted as the prerogative of countries with weak democracies (Shugart & Wattenberg 2001). In any case, in the Andorran electoral system, the stability-seeking aim of a strong majoritarian design clearly prevails in the electoral outcomes.

A stable system evolving toward increased openness?

As mentioned before, the electoral system – both the local and the national – used since 1993 has resulted in stable and solid political institutions with narrow eligibility rules (only Andorrans can vote). However, in the framework of the majoritarian effects on the electoral system and the strong incentives toward stability, the turnout for local elections shows a clear pattern of reduction and an even sharper decline compared to national turnout. In small constituencies with majoritarian configurations, like the ones described here, a combination of several factors may account for the observed decline.

First, a fundamental change in the law governing the acquisition of Andorran citizenship resulted in a large increase in the electoral census. In 1993, the first Law on Nationality was approved, and very strict criteria that a person must meet to obtain Andorran citizenship were defined.[9] From 1996 to 2004, the number of Andorran citizens increased modestly, but after it was amended in 2004, the gain was considerable, reaching more than 1,000 new citizens per year in the mid-2000s. The electoral census in 1995 was 10,411 citizens, and it almost tripled to 27,823 in 2019 (Figure 16.1). This fact may help to explain a decrease in participation in local elections from 77% to 56% in 2019, because we have evidence that the incorporation of newcomers into the electoral census does not seem to engage them straightforwardly in local politics (Magre et al. 2016).

Moreover, the decrease in turnout for national elections, with the same increase in the electoral census, is not so evident. Actually, the turnout for the parliamentary elections remains slightly more stable than the local turnout. The average turnout for parliamentary elections is 75.84% and for local elections it is 69.71% (Figure 16.2). In fact, the participation gap between 2015 and 2019, years in which both elections were held (first the parliamentary ones and afterward the local ones), is 4.83% and 11.79%, respectively, in favor of the parliamentary elections.

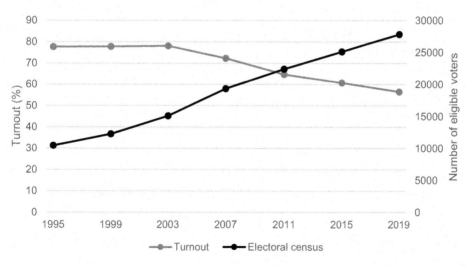

Figure 16.1 Size of the electorate and voter turnout for local elections in Andorra, 1995–2019
Source: Electoral Commission

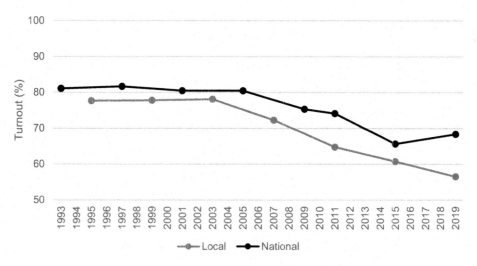

Figure 16.2 Voter turnout for local and national elections in Andorra, 1993–2019
Source: Electoral Commission

Second, in most majority bonus systems, the allocation of the bonus is decisive for the outcome of the election. Thus, this type of system follows a strong majoritarian logic, making it possible to produce a majority. In this framework, if parties and voters correctly anticipate this mechanical effect, the equilibrium of the game is a two-party competition, with the bonus serving as the real prize of the race. This leads to an analysis of the electoral offerings.

In Andorra, parties have only been allowed since 1993, so at the local level, the first multiparty free elections were held in 1995. Since then, the number of electoral candidatures has tended to increase slightly. In 1995, a total of 15 lists were presented in the seven parishes, whereas this number increased to 21 in the last elections in 2019. Moreover, the number of candidatures presented under a preelectoral coalition agreement[10] evolved from five in 1999 (no data for 1995) to 11 in 2019, showing not only the mechanical effect of the electoral bonus going to the biggest list but also an increase in the plurality and heterogeneity of local lists. It seems that the bonus of the electoral system no longer produces incentives for a two-party system, and the number of parties running in the elections has not ceased to increase at the local level, even if the average bonus attributed to the winning list is around 21% over the years (see Figure 16.3).

In addition, the presence of the national parties in local elections has also decreased since 1995. In small constituencies, like the *comuns*, personal relationships and the importance of local matters explain the low institutionalization of national parties. In the last elections, almost 60% of the council seats and mayors were associated with local lists and local independent parties (see Table 16.1). The local elites have strong incentives to adapt their political platform far away from the national parties. Moreover, the fact that the law does not control or limit the creation and cease of political parties, encourages the local elites to frequently change labels and names of parties, creating personal platforms (Serra 2015).

In this vein, it is also typical to find noncompetitive constituencies varying from election to election (for all data, see Table 16.2). The most extreme case being the appearance of only one list of candidates (it has happened five times since 1995); there are also cases of lists taking far

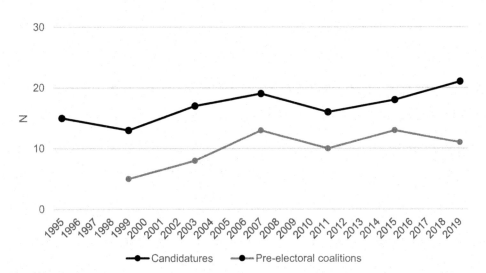

Figure 16.3 Voter turnout and the number of candidatures and preelectoral coalitions in Andorra

Source: Electoral Commission and authors' calculations

Table 16.1 Political parties in the 2019 local elections in Andorra

	% of municipalities where running	% of municipalities where represented	% of seats on local councils	% of (aggregate) votes in local elections	% of mayors affiliated with the party
Demòcrates per Andorra (conservative, center-right)	28.6	28.6	13.8	12.6	14.3
Partit Socialdemòcrata	42.9	42.9	17.5	36.9	14.3
Terceravia (liberals)	71.4	14.2	11.2	13.4	14.3
Independents and nonnational (local) lists	100.0	100.0	57.5	37.1	57.1

Source: Electoral Commission and authors' calculations

more than 60% of the votes, despite the presence of other lists. In fact, the average percentage of votes obtained by the first parties in each of the parishes is around 59% since the first election in 1995, and the average percentage of seats obtained by the winner of each election is almost 80% of the seats on the city council.

These data apparently show a very stable picture, but the changing nature of lists (more and more local) and their increase in absolute numbers, the strong personalization of local lists, and the growing number of preelectoral alliances configure a more complicated scenario where some degree of openness seems to be disclosed. Moreover, the presence of women at the local

Table 16.2 Electoral trends in Andorra

Averages per parish (N = 7)	Elections							
	1995	1999	2003	2007	2011	2015	2019	Total mean
Number of lists	2.14	1.9	2.4	2.7	2.3	2.6	3.0	2.4
Preelectoral coalitions	–	0.7	1.1	1.9	1.4	1.9	1.6	1.4
% of votes for winner	59.8	63.8	50.2	57.9	64.3	59.9	55.9	58.8
% of seats winner	78.6	84.1	76.9	77.4	82.0	80.4	80.0	79.9
Bonus (%)	18.8	20.3	26.7	19.6	17.7	20.5	24.1	21.1

Source: Electoral Commission and authors' calculations

Table 16.3 Percentage of female councilors and mayors in Andorra

Election year	1995	1999	2003	2007	2011	2015	2019
Councilors	15	18.3	25.6	34.9	34.9	37.5	41.3
Mayors	27.6	42.9	0.0	14.3	42.9	27.6	57.1

Source: Electoral Commission and authors' calculations

level is also an indicator of the evolution of the political system. Without a system of gender quotas at any level, in 2019 four *cònsol major* (57.5%) and 33 councilors (41.25%) elected were women, evenly distributed among parties and lists. Table 16.3 shows a clear tendency toward an increase in female representation at the local level, with a similar picture for national elections.

Conclusions

The Andorran municipalities are far more than strictly local institutions. Their existence and importance are deeply grounded in history and tradition, and the new constitution recognizes this particular situation. In a two-tier political system, the parishes appear to be the crucial political actor because there is no second legislative chamber, but half of the national MPs are elected on a local basis with a strong majoritarian system. Indeed, national and local elections are increasingly related, as the last three elections have overlapped in the same year (2011, 2015, and 2019). Historical trends show similar patterns of declining turnout and also increasing numbers of lists running for elections. Nevertheless, no relevant debates on reform of the local electoral system have appeared.

Furthermore, the electoral system of the local governmental units in Andorra results in very stable institutions in their ordinary functioning. The mixed system in place forces strong majorities on the city councils that easily elect the mayors, who hold them for the fixed term of four years. The majority bonus assigned to the winner of the election contributes to induce an FPTP effect and generates elections with a low degree of competition, because the average number of lists running for election in each local unit is rather low, and the final results for the winner facilitate its permanence and continuity. However, local elites show an increasing pattern of change and replacement due to the expansion of the number of lists running for elections.

These changes in the electoral offering at the local level seem to indicate that the system is evolving toward more complexity. In a framework of decreasing participation and political disaffection, we have shown an increase in the average number of lists running for election during the last campaigns accompanied by more coalitions of a preelectoral nature. Indeed, there seems to be an increasing 'localization' of the electoral offerings, because more independent platforms and fewer national parties are present. Still, the powerful position of local elites probably explains the apparent changes in the electoral offerings, but not the politics inside every local unit.

Notes

1 However, Andorra ratified the European Charter of Local Self-Government quite recently, on 27/10/2010, which took effect on 01/07/2011.
2 A *Llei Qualificada* is a special law that requires a large majority to be passed in a single vote on the whole text in the national parliament (absolute majority of the MPs elected on the local government's basis on the national level and absolute majority of the elected MPs at the national level). The *Llei Qualificada de delimitació de competències dels Comuns* gives the precise general constitutional provisions.
3 Besides their own tributes and taxes, a qualified law determines the capital transfers of the general budget to the commons, in order to guarantee the exercise of their capacities. This law determines an equal budget for each of the parishes, plus a variable amount according to their population, extension of their territory, and other related indicators.
4 The *consell general* expresses a mixed and apportioned representation of the national population and of the seven parishes, represents the Andorran people, exercises legislative powers, approves the budget of the State, and prompts and controls the political actions of the government. It is elected by a mixed system of double lists (the parish list and the national list), which are independent, and voters cast two separate ballots.
5 This has happened only once since 1993. In 2011, only after two years of the legislature, the head of government called for new elections because of the political instability derived from the first tie that ever happened (14 seats for the government and 14 seats for the opposition in the parliament).
6 It has been amended five times.
7 Without being a cause of ineligibility, it is also important to note the strict incompatibility clause of Article 17 of the electoral code, which states that the exercise of the civil service by officials and by those who have employment in direct relationship with the administration is incompatible with the performance of any elective post in the administration to which they are attached.
8 As a matter of curiosity, there are only seven polling stations, one for each *parròquia*, and free food and beverages are offered by the council to all citizens casting in-person votes on election day. It is customary to eat only once the ballot is cast and not before.
9 Andorran citizenship is based primarily on the principle of *jus sanguinis*, although since 1994 the access to citizenship has been expanded 'under time of residence' (what does it mean: you can gain citizenship if you are a resident long enough?) and also marriage, so the electoral body has been growing accordingly.
10 We understand preelectoral coalitions to be those lists explicitly stating on the ballot that they are composed of, at least, two different parties.

References

Bartomeu, I. (2010). *Introducció al Sistema Constitucional del Principat d'Andorra*. Andorrana, SA: Fundacio Julià reig i Premsa.

Bedock, C., & Sauger, N. (2014). Electoral systems with a majority bonus as unconventional mixed systems. *Representation, 50*(1), 99–112.

Hesse, J.J., & Sharpe, L.J. (1991). Local government in international perspective: Some comparative observations. In: J.J. Hesse (Ed.) *Local government and urban affairs in international perspective* (pp. 603–621). Baden-Baden: Nomos Verlagsgesellschaft.

López Burniol, J.J. (1999). Dret constitucional. Tradició i Constitució a Andorra. *Anuari de la Societat Catalana d'Estudis Jurídics*, 95–105.

Mickoleit, A. (2010). Andorra. In: D. Nohlen & P. Stöver (Eds.) *Elections in Europe: A data handbook* (pp. 149–168). Baden-Baden: Nomos Verlagsgesellschaft.

Mouritzen, P.E., & Svara, J. (2002). *Leadership in the apex. Politicians and administrators in Western local governments*. Pittsburgh, PA: University of Pittsburgh Press.

Reynolds, A., Reilly, B., & Ellis, A. (2008). *Electoral system design: The new international IDEA handbook*. Stockholm: International Institute for Democracy and Electoral Assistance.

Serra, J. (2015). *Volatilidad y legitimidad del sistema de partidos del Principado de Andorra; dos dimensiones de la institucionalización de su sistema de partidos*. Ponencia Congreso AECPA. Available: https://aecpa.es/files/view/pdf/congress-papers/12-0/1041/.

Shugart, M., & Wattenberg, M.P. (Eds.). (2001). *Mixed-member electoral systems: The best of both worlds?* Oxford: Oxford University Press.

Magre, J., Vallbé, J.-J., & Tomàs, M. (2016). Moving to suburbia? Effects of residential mobility on community engagement. *Urban Studies*, *53*(1), 17–39.

17

Cyprus

National parties' dominance and the decline of electoral participation

Andreas Kirlappos

Brief overview of the local government system

The Republic of Cyprus is divided into six districts for administrative reasons, while its local government system consists of of two distinct types of single-tier local authorities, that is, municipalities (39) and communities (491),[1] governed by separate laws. At present, nine municipalities and 135 communities have been displaced to the southern, government-controlled area of the island due to the illegal occupation of 37% of Cyprus by Turkish troops. Municipalities are typically located in urban, suburban, and tourist areas demonstrating, on average, relatively small populations, that is, 19,950 inhabitants, while communities constitute the local structure in rural areas (National School of Government International 2014). This chapter is focused on the municipalities, and the term *local* predominantly refers to the first tier only.

Intergovernmental relations in Cyprus can be situated in the Southern European state tradition (Hendriks et al. 2011). A fully fledged local government system was instituted in Cyprus prior to the island's independence, particularly during the Ottoman (1571–1878) and the British colonial periods (1878–1960). These two eras initiated restrictions on the local government system that are still in existence, manifested in the form of limited responsibilities, functions, and sources of revenues, defining the nature of intergovernmental relations. Local democracy was also restricted, as local elections were postponed numerous times during British rule. In fact, persons were appointed to be in charge of local government, instead of locally elected officials (Tornaritis 1972).

The independence of Cyprus (1960) did not meaningfully change the condition of the Cypriot local government. The implementation of constitutional provisions related to local government was central to the outburst of violence in 1963. There was a specific provision –Article 173 – for separate municipalities between the Greek Cypriots and the Turkish Cypriots in the main cities of the island for a four-year trial period. According to Markides (2009), increased political importance was attributed to this issue, with the Greek Cypriots and the Turkish Cypriots adopting opposing positions. As a result, efforts to solve problematic aspects of the constitution, including the issue of the separate municipalities, failed, resulting in the outburst of violence. Local elections were again postponed because of the following events, that is, the Greek military coup d'état and the Turkish invasion in 1974, with the Council of Ministers therefore appointing persons in charge of local government actors.

This situation changed with the introduction of more modern legislative texts: the 1985 Municipalities Law and the 1999 Communities Law, along with their successive amendments. Nevertheless, these were primarily based on previous British and Ottoman colonial laws, reproducing the dominance of central structures over local actors. Thus, the former exerted firm administrative control, while the latter had limited local responsibilities, functions, and financial means (Kirlappos 2020). Despite minimal improvement, Cypriot local government is among the least autonomous in Europe. According to the Local Autonomy Index data, Cyprus is ranked 34th among 39 European countries on the scale of overall local autonomy for the period 2010–2014 (Ladner et al. 2019: 240–242). The country has scored above average on specific financial and fiscal matters (self-reliance) and below average on others (financial transfer system) (Ladner et al. 2019: 146–147). Cyprus has also scored below average on indices such as institutional depth (Ladner et al. 2019: 87).

The current legal framework defines the responsibilities of Cypriot municipalities by enumerating them. Municipalities have responsibilities for waste disposal, water supply, and public health, along with social services and building permits. Larger urban municipalities function as town planning authorities and therefore have supplementary responsibilities for planning permission.

The horizontal power relations in Cypriot municipalities are dominated by the strong institutional and executive position of the mayor vis-à-vis the council, classified as local presidentialism (Heinelt & Hlepas 2006). Mayors continued to be appointed by the national government for a long time, but since 1985 they have been directly elected. As a result, executive power is concentrated in the hands of directly elected mayors, thus favoring individual political leadership and raising questions of political accountability (Ladner et al. 2019: 158). Cypriot mayors preside over council meetings and can cast the tie-breaking vote. They head the municipal administration, whose services they guide and direct. This position can be vacated if a mayor fails to perform his or her prescribed duties for a period longer than three consecutive months.

Deputy mayors constitute the additional executive position within the context of the horizontal power relations in Cyprus. Each municipal council elects one deputy mayor right after the municipal elections. However, deputy mayors do not have a strong role. Their main responsibilities include presiding over council meetings or over the meetings of the municipal management committee in the absence of the mayor.

The accession of the island to the European Union (2004) and the memorandum of understanding agreement (2013) triggered several local government reform processes that were never completed, mainly due to strong opposition to the proposed changes (Kirlappos 2018). A new reformist attempt was initiated in December 2019 with the government presenting its local government reform plan in the form of several bills, which were submitted to the parliament on March 2020. However, the outbreak of COVID-19 and the subsequent lockdowns have temporary prevented the completion of the process.

Citizens attach importance to the local level and access municipalities because they attempt to resolve local problems related to municipal responsibilities. In addition, according to empirical data derived from two field studies (Kirlappos 2013, 2019), citizens see the municipalities as a way to access the wider political and administrative system. In particular, they tend to communicate with municipalities about issues that are not specifically assigned to the local level, indicating that divisions with the central level are not clearly understood.

Local elections and their place in the multilevel system

In Cyprus, local elections take place every five years (the latest was in 2016), and they do not coincide with other types of elections. Prior to the end of the current term, the interior ministry issues an official decree proclaiming the date of the local elections. The central elections service, which is part of the interior ministry, organizes all of the electoral processes in Cyprus. In this context, the minister appoints high-ranking civil servants as election commissioners to conduct the elections.

In 1991, Cypriots voted in local elections for just the second time since the establishment of their republic. Yet, these elections did not include the displaced municipalities,[2] whose mayors continued to be appointed by the Council of Ministers. In 1996, this practice stopped and local elections since have included both the displaced and the nondisplaced municipalities. Initially, mayors were elected separately from the council. Since 1996, mayors have been elected directly based on a simple majority (first past the post), meaning that whoever secures the higher number of votes is elected for a five-year term. Mayors are usually supported by a preelectoral coalition that also forms an alliance in the council, consolidating the procedural ties between mayoral and council elections.

Direct mayor elections have, in fact, influenced local politics in Cyprus by extending the influence of political parties over local society and politics. Existing research indicates that the introduction of direct elections substantially increased the number of political positions, because only a mere 36 Cypriot officials – the president and the members of the parliament – were elected prior to that (Faustmann 2010: 276). This development further enhanced clientelist practices at the local level. Recent research verifies the strong connection between mayors and national political parties and the holding of central party positions by mayors (Kirlappos 2017, 2020). Councilors, on the other hand, are elected for a five-year term based on a proportional electoral system.

Local elections in Cyprus typically act as the intermediate level of an extensive process, during which three successive electoral procedures occur, including the parliamentary, the local (municipalities and communities), and the presidential elections. All three elections are synchronized with the same five-year term of office. Up until a few years ago, local elections served as the testing ground for the presidential elections that followed, giving parties the opportunity to test their proposed alliances and candidates. This was the norm for the period 1985–2006. On the basis of the electoral results of the parliamentary elections, the parties formed alliances that were tested in subsequent local elections that occurred six months later. The long electoral cycle peaked with the presidential elections that took place 13 months after the local elections. Success in larger cities and the overall number of mayors elected by each coalition were interpreted by the parties as popular confirmation of their proposed alliances. This usually influenced whether the parties would continue to maintain their suggested alliances or simply formulate new ones. Therefore, when people voted in the local elections in Cyprus, they voted for matters that were not solely related to local issues.

Clear indications of party dealignment have been noted in Cyprus, indicating a historic decrease in the public's trust in political, social, and representative institutions (Katsourides 2013). Since 2011, and as a response to the global financial crisis and the consequent decreases in voter turnout (Christophorou 2012), parties have been trying to form ad hoc local coalitions to elect widely accepted candidates. In this context, local elections have gradually started to be more focused on local politics and challenges.

There are no legal provisions for recall referenda, neither for the mayor and council nor for the members of the executive.

Features of the electoral system

There are several differences in the eligibility rules for the local government elections and the national (parliamentary) elections. In particular, to be able to vote in either the parliamentary or the municipal elections, one must have Cypriot citizenship, be 18 years old or over, and be enrolled in separate electoral catalogues. Those who are not enrolled in the catalogues are not entitled to vote. As a result, voter turnout is based on the percentage of enrolled voters effectively turning out. For the 2016 local elections, a mere 12% of the eligible population was registered in the electoral catalogues (Stock watch 2016).

It should be noted that a deliberate act of the voter is required, as the registration process is not an automatic one. This practice is an inheritance from the British period, because they established separate electoral catalogues for the Greek Cypriot and the Turkish Cypriot communities of the island so as to prevent them from voting for each other and thus cooperating (Tornaritis 1972).

To be able to be elected in either the parliamentary or the municipal elections, the same rules are applied, although there are different age limits, that is, 25 for parliamentary elections and 21 for municipal elections. The latter applies to both the council and mayoral elections.

Voting is compulsory for all types of elections. Despite this, those who do not turn out for the elections suffer no consequences whatsoever, as these provisions have been inactive for years. European citizens have to enroll themselves in special electoral catalogues by filling in a specific application for registration. The overall number of European citizens who were registered and had the right to vote during the 2016 local elections was 16,740 (Cyprus News Agency 2016). The same eligibility rules that apply to Cypriots apply to European citizens as well.

A candidate can register to participate in the local elections by a relatively simple process, provided that the eligibility rules described earlier have been fulfilled. Two citizens of that specific municipality who have been enrolled in the electoral catalogue must first propose the candidate. They must submit specific and separate documents proposing the candidate to the district election commissioners. The candidate must submit an affidavit and pay a specific amount to secure his or her candidacy (€100 for councilor and €1,000 for mayor). During this process, the district election commissioners have the responsibility to examine any complaints against specific candidates based on the eligibility criteria and exclude them, if necessary, from the process.

There are exclusions and strong incompatibilities regarding the candidacy and effective taking up of a mandate. In this context, a person cannot be a candidate for the local elections if (s)he is mentally incapacitated, bankrupt, or has become subject to certain criminal convictions. On the other hand, members of the parliament, ministers, judges, civil and municipal servants, police and military officers, and teachers are eligible to be candidates in the local elections even though, if elected, they must first resign their current position. This practice constitutes an additional inheritance from the British period because it established strong incompatibilities (Tornaritis 1972), probably to prevent the election of educated people. These strong incompatibilities were preserved by the legal texts that currently regulate local government in Cyprus.

The number of councilors to be elected was determined by the 1985 Municipalities Law, and the same provisions apply to all municipalities in Cyprus. This law defines the number of the councilors on the basis of the number of registered voters in each municipality. This varies between a minimum of eight for municipalities with fewer than 6,000 inhabitants and a maximum of 26 for municipalities with more than 26,000 inhabitants. In between, eight additional categories exist that are based on progressively increasing ranges in the number of inhabitants. For each added category with an increasing number of inhabitants, two seats are added (e.g., ten for municipalities with 6,000–8,500 inhabitants) up to the maximum. During the most recent local elections of 2016, a total of 478 municipal council seats had to be filled in Cyprus for all 39 municipalities.

The current electoral system is not divided into subsystems, and the same rules apply equally to all municipalities, regardless of size. As mentioned, a plurality system is utilized for the mayoral elections (Reynolds et al. 2005) characterized by the first past the post rationale. Councilors are elected on an open-list proportional electoral system. Voters have the right to vote for up to seven candidates from the list, depending on the number of councilors to be elected in each municipality. However, they may only choose persons from the same party or coalition list, which prevents them from choosing candidates from different coalitions (Institute of Local Self-government 2017).

With a proportional electoral formula, votes are converted into seats via the Hare quota. This method focuses on the largest remainder and establishes different electoral quotas per distribution. In the first distribution, the total number of votes is divided by the number of council seats, thus forming the electoral quorum. Seats are distributed among lists by dividing the total number of votes received by each list by the electoral quorum (Council of Europe 2014). This process is repeated in a second distribution, where the electoral quorum changes because the remaining votes are divided by the number of remaining seats on the municipal council. These are distributed among the parties or coalitions that won at least one seat based on the first distribution. A third distribution follows in the case of remaining seats, where the parties that have the largest remainders from the previous rounds secure these seats.

Local elections are organized in Cyprus on an at-large basis. Candidates are therefore eligible for the entire territory of the municipality, rather than just a part or district of that municipality. The number of candidates on each list may consequently be equal to that of the council seats to be elected, or fewer in the case where the list is only partly composed.

Depending on the electoral process, the ballot structure offers two ways to vote. Because there is only one seat per electoral district, only one candidate can be elected to the position of the mayor for a given municipality. Therefore, voters utilize a separate ballot to cast their vote for the mayoral election. The candidates may be supported by a party or a coalition, or they may even be independent. The person who secures the greater number of votes is elected mayor.

Due to the entirely open-list proportional electoral system, preference votes are extremely important in the process of seat distribution. In practice, the order decided by voters is more important than the order of candidates decided by the party. In this context, voters first select the list of a party or coalition or even a single independent candidate. Then, depending on the number of councilors that should be elected in each municipality, they select their preferences within the list. Specifically, for municipalities that have up to 16 councilors, voters can mark four preference votes (Council of Europe 2014). For municipalities that have a greater number of councilors to be elected, for example, 20, 22, and 26, voters may cast five, six, and seven preference votes, respectively. To avoid confusion, instructions are given by the central elections service prior to and during the elections. Voters also have the ability to vote for a particular list without indicating any personal preferences.

For the first distribution, candidates who have secured more crosses of preference take the seats. The same method is followed in the second and third distributions based on the new electoral quotas.

The electoral outcomes

Given compulsory voting, examination and analysis of electoral turnout is significant in the case of Cyprus. Figure 17.1 presents the mean percentage on the island for local and national elections since the beginning of the 1990s.[3] Some trends are obvious, despite the differences in electoral cycles. Turnout for national elections seems to be higher than for local elections. In fact,

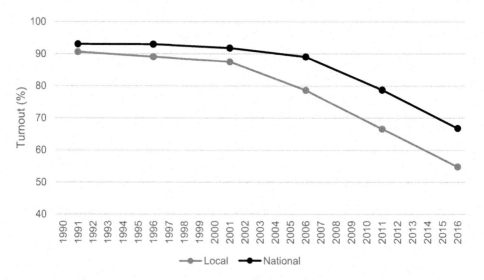

Figure 17.1 Voter turnout for local and national elections in Cyprus, 1991–2016
Source: Electoral Service (2019) and Union of Cyprus Municipalities (2019)
Note: Data for the 2016 elections are from 36 municipalities, as local elections did not occur in three municipalities).

the observed difference during the period under examination seems to be progressively in favor of the national elections, ranging from 2.3% in 1991 to 11.9% in 2016. There is also a similar trend in terms of electoral participation both for local and national elections. In particular, voter turnout has gradually decreased for both elections since 1991. However, the total decline for the local elections is far greater (−35.9%) than the that for national elections (−26.3%).

Figure 17.2 exhibits the turnout percentage of enrolled voters for all municipalities in Cyprus based on the results of the most recent local elections (2016). As explained earlier, only enrolled voters have the right to vote, and therefore voter turnout is based on the percentage of enrolled voters effectively turning out. Turnout percentage varies depending on the size of the municipality. Despite the moderate correlation, Figure 17.2 demonstrates the inverse relationship between the size of the municipality and the enrolled voters and turnout: the larger the population of a municipality, the lower the share of eligible voters voting in the elections (Pearson's correlation coefficient = −.499).

Local elections in Cyprus are quite competitive, and uncontested elections have become exceptional, especially since the 1990s. Nonetheless, in 2016, local elections did not occur for three municipalities. When elections are uncontested, they mostly take place in smaller and/or displaced municipalities.

The number of lists offered to the voters has gradually expanded. This can be explained by the increase in the number of parties represented in the parliament, that is, from six in 2006 to eight in 2016, offering more party-supported lists at the local level. On the other hand, the overall increase in the number of independent candidates running for local elections since 2011 also seems to have increased the number of lists offered to the voters. The mean number of lists in the 2016 local elections was 6.3. Yet, differentiations were noticed that could be attributed to factors such as size, as larger municipalities had a mean number of 7, and whether a municipality was displaced (4.5).

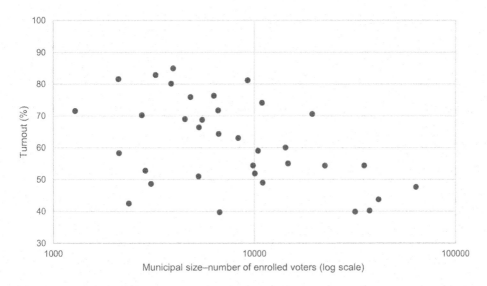

Figure 17.2 Voter turnout for local elections by number of enrolled voters in Cyprus, 2016.

Source: Electoral service (2019) and Union of Cyprus Municipalities (2019)

Note: Data for the 2016 elections are from 36 municipalities, as local elections did not occur in three municipalities).

Table 17.1 presents the participation and performance of families of lists in the 2016 local elections. It should be noted that the fifth column – percent of mayors affiliated with the party – illustrates data based on the preelectoral alliances that the parties formed for the mayoral elections of 2016. Party politicization is quite high in Cyprus, and local elections have been dominated by the national parties due to the small size of the island, which enables them to effectively access the local level. In fact, the national party system is organized in a hierarchical manner, including district and local representations of the parties. National lists tend to dominate over nonnational lists, indicating the success of the national party system in terms of the electoral outcomes. This can be associated with restrictions, imposed by law, on the access to public funding, which is limited only to parties that are represented in the national parliament. Regarding new parties, as soon as they manage to gain representation in the parliament, they become publicly funded, allowing them to organize their structures and increase their resources. Access to public funding usually gives new parties increased chances to base themselves at the local level.

Barometer features were observed in 2011 in local elections in Cyprus. These elections were dominated by national issues and considerations – mainly the deteriorating economic conditions – which were based on factors deriving from the main political arena (Reif & Schmitt 1980). These had enabled the opposition parties to be successful both in terms of the votes they received and the number of elected mayors in the larger cities of the island. Nevertheless, as is illustrated further by Figure 17.1, this development went hand in hand with decreased interest demonstrated by the voters.

While nonnational lists have been met with marginal success during the last local elections, this should be examined with caution. In the vast majority, these coalitions were formed by central party dissidents and others who did not manage to secure support for their candidacy

Table 17.1 Participation and performance of families of lists in local elections in Cyprus, 2016

	% of municipalities where running	% of municipalities where represented	% of seats on local councils	% of (aggregate) votes in local elections [1]	% of mayors affiliated with the
Movement of Ecologists-Citizens' Cooperation (GREENS)	20.5	10.0	0.4	1.2	20.5
Progressive Party of Working People (AKEL)	92.0	89.7	26.8	24.8	41.0
Movement for Social Democracy (EDEK)	71.8	61.5	7.7	6.7	33.3
Democratic Party (DHKO)	89.8	87.2	15.5	14.5	41.0
Democratic Rally (DHSY)	89.8	87.2	35.1	33.4	48.7
Citizens' Alliance (SIMMAXIA POLITON)	35.9	13.0	1.0	1.9	33.3
Solidarity Movement (ALLILEGI)	43.5	23.0	2.5	2.7	33.3
National Popular Front (ELAM)	43.5	18.0	1.5	1.9	0.0
Independents and nonnational (local) lists	56.4	51.3	9.6	7.2	5.2

[1] The data for the 2016 elections are from 36 municipalities, as local elections did not occur in three municipalities.
Source: Electoral service (2019) and Union of Cyprus Municipalities (2019)

from one of the national parties. On a comparative level, local lists had a greater presence in small, displaced municipalities. However, these lists demonstrated a single-minded focus on the wish to return to the occupied areas of Cyprus.

Independent candidates for the mayoral elections present similar characteristics as the vast majority have strong connections with the national party system.

A small increase in female representation can be observed at the local level in Cyprus, as shown in Figure 17.3.

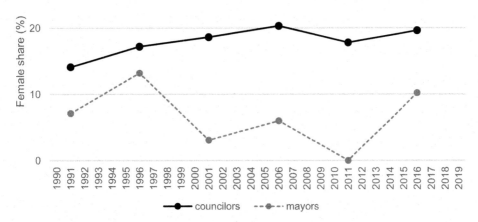

Figure 17.3 Women's representation among elected councilors and mayors in Cyprus, 1991–2016

Source: Electoral service (2019) and Union of Cyprus Municipalities (2019)

Note: Data for the 2016 elections are from 36 municipalities, as local elections did not occur in three municipalities).

This increase, however, is greater for elected councilors than for elected mayors. Despite percentage fluctuations, the share of female councilors elected in 2016 was 5.5% greater than that in 1991. At the same time, this rise in the number of female councilors is consistent with a far greater growth in the number of female parliamentarians. The latter was a mere 5.3% of the total number of the members of the parliament in 1991. Based on the results of the latest (2016) national elections, this percentage has increased to 17.8%. On the other hand, little progress was made in female representation as elected mayors. While there has been a small increase since 1991, that is, 3%, in the number of female mayors, important percentage fluctuations can be seen. To make matters worse, in 2011 there were no female mayors at all. Therefore, women have been clearly and constantly underrepresented at the mayoral level in Cyprus, proving that the strong executive mayor model is almost entirely associated with men. This can be attributed both to selection bias within parties causing a lack of female candidates and to the fact that voters are not as inclined to vote for female candidates.

Legal quotas have not been introduced yet for national and local elections in Cyprus, in spite of the ongoing discussion about institutionalizing them on party lists. Also, some parties have adopted voluntary quotas internally, increasing the representation of women in party organs (Charalambous & Christophorou 2015; Katsourides 2015). Substantial differences in female representation at the local level can be traced between parties on the basis of the results of the 2011 and 2016 local elections. In particular, the two largest parties demonstrated greater female representation (21–23%) than the rest (5–16%).

There has been no research focusing exclusively on local elections in Cyprus, let alone on the incumbency effect and on its impact on local elections. Some characteristics of local elections, such as the central position of political parties, were included in research focusing on wider issues, such as party change and development (Christophorou 2006).

Up to 38.5% of incumbent mayors were reelected, based on the results of the latest local elections of 2016. The incumbency ratio was higher in 2006 (46.2%) and 1991 (48.7%), indicating that previous trends favored the reelection of incumbent mayors who served for a number of consecutive terms. During the period under examination, 1991–2016, 10% of the incumbent mayors were long term (reelected for more than three consecutive terms). Finally, up to 43.5% of incumbent councilors were reelected, based on the results of the latest local elections of 2016.

Discussion

The local government system in Cyprus demonstrates specific burdens, most of which were initiated several decades prior to the island's independence. In this context, local elections were postponed for long periods during both the immediate preindependence and the immediate postindependence eras due to a number of external and internal factors. Furthermore, local elections were eventually introduced 25 years after Cyprus gained its independence, with the first municipal elections taking place in 1985. Direct mayoral elections have affected local politics in Cyprus by expanding the impact of political parties over local society and politics. This has been accomplished through a substantial increase in the number of political positions, which further increased clientelist practices at the local level. In general, local elections have been seen as second-order elections, and for decades they served as the testing ground for the presidential elections. Success in larger cities and the overall number of mayors elected by each coalition was perceived by the parties as popular confirmation of their proposed alliances in relation to the presidential elections. Additionally, since 2011, local elections have become more focused on local politics due to the global economic crisis and the decreasing voter turnout.

Debates about changes and municipal electoral reforms have been rare in Cyprus, despite several failed attempts to reform the local government system during the last decade. In fact, the COVID-19 pandemic and the subsequent lockdowns have temporary prevented the completion of the ongoing process. This was re-enacted with the incorporation of a specific provision into Cyprus's Recovery Plan in June 2021, focusing on local government reform. The new reformist attempt aims to decrease the number of municipalities and to give them greater responsibilities and increased financial support. However, smaller municipalities, which are expected to be merged into larger entities, strongly object. Finally, there is no survey of local elections in Cyprus, and regular public opinion polls provide survey data on local voting. In terms of vertical integration, local elections present interesting features when compared to those at the national level. Voter turnout, which is based on the percentage of enrolled voters effectively turning out, has been decreasing both for the national parliamentary and for the local elections. Nonetheless, there is an evident dissimilarity, as the total decline in voter turnout is far greater for local elections than for national elections.

At the same time, the number of lists offered to voters in both the national and the local elections gradually increased during the period under examination. Other dynamics include high party politicization that goes hand in hand with the continuous dominance of national parties. This is associated with specific factors such as the small size of Cyprus, which enables national parties to effectively access the local level, and restrictions imposed on public funding by law. These factors also include the continuous supremacy of national lists over nonnational lists. Other similar patterns and dynamics between local and national elections include constant female underrepresentation. On the basis of the findings, and despite marginal progress, this tendency is much greater in terms of the elected mayors than in terms of elected councilors. This verifies that the strong executive mayor model is almost exclusively associated with men in Cyprus.

In terms of horizontal variation, Cypriot municipalities have demonstrated increased homogeneity. Key factors that explain the observed homogeneity are related to the strong institutional and executive position of the mayor vis-à-vis the council and the deputy mayor, which is common to all municipalities, thus favoring individual political leadership.

Notes

1 Communities exhibit changes in their overall number due to the existence of several very small units in terms of population.
2 These preserve their legal identity even though their voters, along with their councils and mayors, are temporarily displaced to the free part of Cyprus. When municipal elections are held, the displaced residents vote both for their occupied municipality of origin and for their new municipality of residence.
3 Calculated as the ratio of the number of deposed ballots to the number of registered voters (aggregated for the whole of the country and in percentage). 'Local' refers to the election of mayors and 'national' to that of the house of representatives, the unicameral parliament.

References

Charalambous, G. & Christophorou, C. (2015). The Cypriot communists between protest and the establishment: A second look at AKEL's linkages with society. In G. Charalambous & C. Christophorou (Eds.), *Party-society relations in the republic of Cyprus: Political and societal strategies* (pp. 17–46). Routledge: London.

Christophorou, C. (2006). Party change and development in Cyprus (1995–2005). *South European Society and Politics*, 11(3), 513–542.

Christophorou, C. (2012). Disengaging citizens: Parliamentary elections in the republic of Cyprus. *South European Society and Politics*, 17(2), 295–307.

Council of Europe, European Commission for Democracy through Law (Venice commission) (2014). *Comparative table on proportional electoral systems: the allocation of seats inside the lists (open/closed lists)* no. 764/2014. Viewed on 13 January 2020. www.venice.coe.int/webforms/documents/default.aspx?pdffile=CDL(2014)058-bil.

Cyprus News Agency (2016). Συνολικά 16,740 Ευρωπαίοι έχουν δικαίωμα ψήφου στις δημοτικές εκλογές [*A total of 16,740 Europeans have the right to vote in the municipal elections*]. Viewed on 10 July 2020. www.cna.org.cy/webnews.aspx?a=b4eedfcc77c94a4daaa9905b3c0e5004.

Faustmann, H. (2010). Rusfeti and political patronage in the Republic of Cyprus. *Cyprus Review*, 22(2), 269–289.

Heinelt, H. & Hlepas, N. (2006). Typologies of local government systems. In H. Bäck, H. Heinelt & A. Magnier (Eds.), *The European mayor: Political leaders in the changing context of local democracy* (pp. 21–42). Verlag für Sozialwissenschaften: Wiesbaden.

Hendriks, F., Lidström, A. & Loughlin, J. (2011). Introduction: Subnational democracy in Europe: Changing backgrounds and theoretical models. In J. Loughlin, F. Hendriks & A. Lidström (Eds.), *The Oxford handbook of local and regional democracy in Europe* (pp. 1–23). Oxford University Press: Oxford.

Institute of Local Self-government (2017). Εκλογικά συστήματα της τοπικής αυτοδιοίκησης και τοπικά δημοψηφίσματα: Διεθνής εμπειρικά και Ελλάδα [*Electoral systems of local self-government and local referendums: International experience and Greece*]. Viewed on 15 January 2020. www.ita.org.gr/el/images/meletes_ita/meleth_EKLOGIKA.pdf.

Katsourides, Y. (2013). *Political parties and trade unions in Cyprus*. Hellenic Observatory Papers on Greece and Southeast Europe, no.74. Viewed on 20 June 2020. http://eprints.lse.ac.uk/52625/1/GreeSE%20No74.pdf.

Katsourides, Y. (2015). DISY's linkages with society: Diverse and diversified. In G. Charalambous & C. Christophorou (Eds.), *Party-society relations in the republic of Cyprus: Political and societal strategies* (pp. 47–68). Routledge: London.

Kirlappos, A. (2013). *The Europeanization of Cypriot local government: Round 1*. Structured Questionnaires.

Kirlappos, A. (2017). Local government in the republic of Cyprus: Path dependent Europeanization. *Cyprus Review*, 29(1), 89–109.

Kirlappos, A. (2018). Reforming local government in the republic of Cyprus: Resistance and differentiations. *Cyprus Review*, 30(2), pp. 101–122.

Kirlappos, A. (2019). *The Europeanization of Cypriot local government: Round 2*. Structured Questionnaires.

Kirlappos, A. (2020). Limits of Europeanization at the municipal level: Evidence from the republic of Cyprus. *Local Government Studies*. DOI: 10.1080/03003930.2020.1753707.

Ladner, A., Keuffer, N., Baldersheim, H., Hlepas, N., Swianiewicz, P., Steyvers, K., & Navarro, C. (2019). *Patterns of local autonomy in Europe*. Palgrave: London.

Markides, D. (2009). *Κύπρος: 1957–1963 [Cyprus: 1957–1963]*. Mesogeios: Athens.

National School of Government International (2014). *Local government reform in Cyprus: Final options report*. Viewed on 18 January 2020. www.crcs.gov.cy/crcs/crcs.nsf/All/A9A11EF491A77B8FC2257E34002FD5B5/$file/Local%20Government_Final%20Report.pdf.

Reif, K., & Schmitt, H. (1980). Nine second-order national elections – A conceptual framework for the analysis of European election results. *European Journal of Political Research*, 8(1), 3–44.

Reynolds, A., Reilly, B., & Ellis, A. (2005). *Electoral system design: The new international IDEA handbook*. IDEA: Stockholm.

Stock watch (2016). *Γυρίζουν πλάτη για δημοτικές [Citizens are turning their back on municipal elections]*. Viewed on 11 July 2020. www.stockwatch.com.cy/el/article/genika/gyrizoyn-plati-gia-dimotikes.

Tornaritis, C. (1972). *Η τοπική αυτοδιοίκησης εν Κύπρω [Local self-government in Cyprus]*. Nicosia.

18

France

Competition only in large cities

Bernard Dolez and Annie Laurent

Brief overview of the local government system

France has three tiers of local government: municipalities or *communes* (*N* = 34,970 as of January 1, 2019[1]), which are the successors of the *Ancien Régime*'s parishes; *départements* (*N* = 101), which are roughly equivalent to counties and were created during the French Revolution, and *regions* (*N* = 18), created in 1972 and later transformed into fully functioning regional government entities whose officials have been elected by direct universal suffrage since 1986.

France is home to roughly 40% of the municipalities in the EU, which shows how heavily fragmented the municipal government system is. Seventy-two percent of French municipalities have fewer than 1,000 inhabitants, and one-fourth have fewer than 200 inhabitants. The national government has never succeeded in redrawing the map of French municipalities, and so, since 1999, it has relied on intermunicipal cooperation. Today, every French municipality belongs to one of the 1,259 groups of municipalities known as Public Intermunicipal Cooperative Federations (*Établissements Publics de Coopération Intercommunale* or EPCI). This fourth tier of local government is tasked with, among other things, land-use planning, economic development, and (often) managing a certain number of local public services.

Regardless of their size, all French municipalities are governed under the same conditions, which are set out in national legislation and are endowed with identical powers and responsibilities. Nevertheless, two major exceptions to this principle exist: the first is the City of Paris, which is both a city and a *département* but which has only had a mayor since 1977 – the result of the central government's long-standing mistrust in matters regarding France's capital. For the same reason, general police powers in Paris belong to the Prefect of Police, who is appointed by the executive. The second exception concerns France's three largest cities – Paris, Lyon, and Marseille – which have a specific organizational structure and are divided into districts (*arrondissements*) or sectors (*secteurs*). However, district councils and their mayors have only limited authority.

Historically, France has been an exceedingly centralized country marked by Jacobinism. Yet, since the passage of the Decentralization Act of 1982, municipalities have gained in autonomy. According to the Local Autonomy Index (LAI) database, France now ranks in the top third of countries, despite the fact that the French local government system is organized by national law

(Ladner et al. 2019). French local governments and groups of local governments, respectively, spent €100 billion and €36 billion in 2019 (€136 billion in all) – 6% of France's GDP.

The present territorial layout of France remains shaped by the heritage of Napoleonic rule. As in many other countries in Southern Europe, the national government uniformly exercises its power across the territory of France and remains responsible for social and educational policy. In Heinelt and Hlepas' synthetic index, France is at the bottom of the ranking alongside Spain, Portugal, and Greece, with the opposite end of the scale occupied by Northern European countries (Denmark, Sweden) and Central European countries such as Hungary (Heinelt et al. 2006).

In contrast, French mayors are the very archetype of the strong mayor form (Mouritzen & Svara 2002). In terms of horizontal power relations, the law provides that municipalities are legally governed by two bodies: a deliberative body (the municipal council) and an executive authority (the mayor). The mayor and deputy mayor(s) are elected by the municipal council (by absolute majority vote in the first two rounds and by a plurality of votes cast in the third round). Yet in reality, there is a severe imbalance in the relationship between the municipal council and the mayor. Mayors preside over the municipal council, setting its agenda. They direct municipal government activities and have specific powers. They cannot be dismissed by the municipal council. Above all, the winning electoral list can, under the rules in place, rely on a comfortable majority (see the following point), and the municipal council always chooses the list's leader as mayor. This mechanism has been adopted universally, and municipal elections – in practice – primarily serve to 'elect' the future mayor of the municipality, who shows great care in selecting his or her list mates ahead of time. Mayors' relationships with their majorities on the municipal council work the reverse of the system described in the law: while from a legislative standpoint, the municipal council technically elects the mayor, the political reality is that the mayor is responsible for the composition of the majority on the municipal council, if not the council as a whole. In practice, mayors are therefore certain to benefit from the majority's support throughout their term unless dissent or division arises within the municipal government's majority. The mayor's dominion over the majority in the municipal council is bolstered even further by the fact that the mayor has resources that fellow members of the majority and opponents lack. Mayors have a seat on the intermunicipal council, where they sometimes serve as president (and often as vice president). In medium and large cities, they are often the only professional politicians, a situation made possible by the compensation they receive as mayor and as member of the intermunicipal council and, in some cases, from another – regional or departmental – elected office they hold (Douillet & Lefebvre 2017: 101–145). Nowhere else in Europe do mayors wield such great power. They are 'political mayors' who embody the municipality itself, particularly in its relations with the national government and with subnational governments, that is, the region and the *département* (Heinelt et al. 2006).

In addition to being strongly associated with their municipalities, the small size of most French municipalities means that mayors are close to their communities. These two factors likely explain why mayors are the only category of elected officials viewed favorably by French voters in a climate in which cynicism toward elected officials has undoubtedly never been greater. An Institut français d'opinion publique (Ifop) survey published in August 2019 found that 83% of French respondents had a 'positive opinion' of mayors, compared to a mere 38% for elected officials in general.[2]

Surveys unanimously show that, more than any other tier of government, the French identify with their nation and their municipality. Municipalities are therefore the local level of government to which the French show the greatest attachment – likely as a result of their longer existence. This attachment to municipalities and their mayors – veritable 'pillars of the

Republic'³ – today stands as the greatest obstacle to undertaking a territorial reform to reduce the number of French communes.

Local elections and their place in the multilevel system

Since 2000, representatives in the lower house of parliament and the President serve five-year terms, municipal council members are elected to six-year terms. Regional council and departmental council members are elected to identical six-year terms. Municipal elections are sometimes combined with other local elections (departmental councils in 2001 and 2008, when half of the members of each departmental council came up for election every three years), but more often than not they are held separately (1995, 2014, and 2020).

Municipal elections – as with all elections in France – are organized by the Ministry of the Interior and are traditionally held on a Sunday, usually in March. At times, however, they coincide with presidential or legislative elections, and in that case they are postponed for a number of months (from March to June 1995) and sometimes even an entire year (from March 2007 to March 2008) to avoid interference with the presidential and legislative elections, stemming, in particular, from the fact that mayors publicly endorse presidential candidates.

The place of municipal elections in the national electoral cycle is therefore subject to variation. Since the beginning of the 1990s, only once (in 1995) have they been held in the same year as the presidential election. In every other case, they have been kept distant from presidential races, once being postponed to the following year (2008), other times to two or three years later (2014 and 2020), and still another time to four years later in the run-up to the next presidential election (2001). Opposing parties then work to transform these local elections into a sort of 'national political test', calling on voters to sanction the party in power, which favors the nationalization of the ballot. Candidates with close ties to the majority, on the other hand, will insist on the local nature of the election in an attempt to deter voters from casting a sanction vote.

However, municipal elections have a national dimension in their own right. Their results have a decisive impact on the composition of the Senate, the upper house of the French Parliament, which is elected through indirect universal suffrage by an electoral college – 95% of which is made up of delegates from municipal councils (Grangé 1988; Dolez 2011).

The law does not provide for any sort of recall elections. However, if the municipal council fails several times to elect a mayor and his or her deputy mayors, or if serious dissent prevents it from conducting business and jeopardizes the city or town's governance, the municipal council may be dissolved at the prefect's request by a decree passed in the Council of Ministers, resulting in new elections. However, this procedure is rare and has been seen almost exclusively in small municipalities.

Features of the electoral system

In France, the right to vote is open to French nationals who are over 18 years of age and who possess civil and political rights. While voter registration is mandatory (and now automatic for young people), voting in France is considered to be a right – and as such is not mandatory.

Since the adoption of the Maastricht Treaty, citizens from other EU countries living in France have been eligible to vote in municipal elections (and European elections), provided they have registered to join a so-called 'supplementary' electoral roll. Even still, in 2014, only 23% of them (278,000 of 1.2 million) had registered, although this number is constantly on the rise. At the time, they represented 0.6% of an electorate made up of 44 million voters. EU citizens are also eligible to run for office, but they cannot serve as mayor or deputy mayor. In 2014, they also accounted for 0.6% of municipal elected officials.

Non-EU nationals, on the other hand, do not have the right to vote. While François Mitterrand in 1981 – and, more recently, Lionel Jospin and François Hollande – showed support for the idea, he stopped short of enacting such a measure primarily because of legal and political difficulties associated with the process of amending the constitution.

The number of members on the municipal council is set out in national law. It varies in accordance with the population of the municipality: seven municipal council seats for municipalities with under 100 inhabitants, 69 for those with over 300,000 inhabitants, and for France's three largest cities (Paris, Lyon, and Marseille) between 73 and 163 municipal council members. A simple ratio between the number of municipal council members and the number of inhabitants in the municipality shows that holding an elected office does not have the same social significance in a small town as it does in a large city. In a town of 200 inhabitants and 132 voters, for example, each member of the municipal council would represent 12 voters, or roughly four or five households. Willing candidates are often hard to come by (and in some cases elections are uncontested; see discussion to follow). In a city of 200,000 inhabitants, each municipal council member represents thousands of residents, making him or her a person of note.

Two electoral systems exist. The first applies to small municipalities and the second to larger ones. The dividing line used to be 3,500 inhabitants, but in the run-up to the 2014 elections it was lowered to 1,000 inhabitants to allow equal numbers of men and women to be represented in municipalities with populations exceeding this threshold.

In towns with populations under 1,000 – 72% of the total share of municipalities in 2014 but only 13% of the national population – municipal council members are elected under a two-round bloc vote system with *panachage* (TR-BV). For many years, there was no requirement to declare one's candidacy for an election, and 'write-in' lists were common practice. Voters could fill in a blank ballot with as many names as the number of available seats. In 2014, declaration was made mandatory, although lists can still be incomplete. Municipalities form a single, unified electoral district. Votes are tallied on a candidate-by-candidate basis. To win in the first round, a candidate must receive an absolute majority of the votes cast from over 25% of the number of registered voters. Elections are generally won in the first round in over 80% of these municipalities.[4] When this is not the case, a second round is organized in which candidates are elected by a plurality of the votes cast.

In municipalities with over 1,000 inhabitants (only 28% of the total share of municipalities but 87% of the population), municipal council members are elected under a majority bonus system in two rounds (MBS), with a 50% majoritarian bonus going to the largest party. Voters cast a single vote for one of the lists of candidates running. Except in Paris, Lyon, and Marseille, each municipality forms a single, unified electoral district. Lists are closed and must have as many candidates as there are unfilled seats (plus no more than two additional candidates), and the list must alternate successively between women and men (a so-called 'zip-list'). A second round of voting is held one week later if no list receives an absolute majority of the votes cast. Only lists that earn over 10% of the vote continue to the second round. They can also merge with any other list that receives at least 5% of the votes cast. This electoral formula combines 'two formulas within one district' and can therefore be described as a 'hybrid system' (Massicotte & Blais 1999: 352): (1) whichever list carries over 50% of the vote in the first round (or emerges ahead of the other lists in the second round) receives half of the available seats; (2) in both the first and second rounds, the remaining seats are distributed by PR among every list that received at least 5% of the votes cast (including the list that won the overall election) using a highest average formula (d'Hondt method). Tangibly, this means that the winning party is certain to have at least a two-thirds majority on the municipal council.

In Paris, Lyon, and Marseille, the same voting system (MBS) applies at an electoral district level. The 1982 PLM Act provides for a system in which voting takes place at a sector level. Sectors each feature one or more districts (*arrondissements*). Paris is divided into 17 sectors [district magnitude (M) from three to 18], Lyon into nine sectors (M from four to 12), and Marseille into eight sectors (M from eight to 16). In these three cities, the overall popular vote and voting results in districts or sectors do not systematically coincide, as the 1983 elections in Marseille or the 2001 elections in Paris and Lyon attest: in each of these three cases, the party with the most overall votes earned fewer seats than its main competitor, which succeeded in putting its mayoral candidate in office.

In the 2014 elections, a second round was necessary in fewer than one in five municipalities with over 1,000 inhabitants. Yet, once again, the size of the municipality itself is an important variable. In small towns, there is rarely a second round. It is only the norm in municipalities with over 9,000 inhabitants (567 out of 1,052).

The right to simultaneously hold multiple elected offices and functions has progressively been restricted by three successive laws (1985, 2000, and 2014). Municipal elected officials are barred from holding more than one other elected office (1985). Additional limitations are placed on mayors, who since 2000 have been prohibited from serving as president of another local executive authority (i.e., the departmental or regional council), and since 2014 they can no longer simultaneously hold office in parliament.

However, the rules on holding multiple elected offices do not apply to offices and functions held with EPCIs. Indeed, under the law, elected officials serving on these intermunicipal bodies are already municipal elected officials. In municipalities with more than 1,000 inhabitants, future members of EPCI councils are simultaneously elected during municipal elections using a technique known as *fléchage* (marking), in which the candidates running for municipal office who will also serve on the EPCI's council are clearly identified on ballots. In small towns, the municipality is represented on the EPCI council by local elected officials who are chosen by order of rank: mayors automatically have a seat.

When mayors were officially prohibited from simultaneously serving as senators or representatives in 2017, most mayors from large cities chose to relinquish their seat in parliament and continue at the helm of their municipality – an implicit reminder that, in the hierarchy of elected offices, the mayor stands at the pinnacle. Mayors of towns with fewer than 10,000 inhabitants, on the other hand, have frequently prioritized their parliamentary seats.

The electoral outcomes

Elections that mobilize (fewer and fewer) voters

Voter turnout for municipal elections is systematically lower than for presidential elections. For many years, it was lower even than the turnout numbers for legislative elections, which now is no longer the case since the advent of the five-year presidential term and the 'inversion' of the electoral calendar in 2002. Turnout is also far higher than for elections of departmental and regional council members or European members of parliament, which only mobilize around half of registered voters. As such, apart from presidential elections, municipal elections draw the greatest number of voters of all elections.

However, evolutions in voter turnout for municipal elections have undergone a more general shift. The 1960s and 1970s saw high participation, with record turnout in 1977 (78.4%).

However, overall voter turnout has been on the wane for elections in general since the early 1980s, with only 63.5% of registered voters casting a vote in the 2014 municipal elections (Figure 18.1).

Large cities vs. small towns

In any given electoral race, voter turnout is contingent on the size of the municipality. In 2014, turnout in towns with fewer than 1,000 inhabitants (TR-BV) stood at 75.3%, compared to 61.2% in municipalities with more than 1,000 inhabitants (MBS).

In municipalities with more than 1,000 inhabitants, turnout steadily falls as the number of registered voters grows. In competitive elections (with more than one list in the running), average turnout in 2014 stood at 76.6% in municipalities with fewer than 1,000 registered voters, 69.7% in small cities (1,000–10,000 registered voters), 57% in medium-sized cities (10,000–100,000 registered voters), and only 52.8% in large cities (over 100,000 registered voters). The correlation between voter turnout and the logarithm of the number of registered voters therefore stood at −0.72 at the 1% significant level (Figure 18.2).

In some cases, no candidate or list runs for an election. In 2014, this happened in 63 municipalities with fewer than 1,000 inhabitants and one municipality with more than 1,000 inhabitants. In these cases, the municipality is governed by a three-person delegation appointed by the prefect, pending a new election. In addition to these exceptional cases, municipal elections are often uncompetitive. In 45% of French municipalities, there was no competition in the 2014 municipal race. In half of all municipalities with under 1,000 inhabitants (TR-BV), the number of candidates was equal to (or less than) the number of available seats (Table 18.1, column 1). Likewise, approximately one-third of municipalities with more than 1,000 inhabitants (MBS) had only a single list in the running. However, this number obscures significant disparities, as smaller municipalities are far more likely to fall into this category than larger ones. In nearly

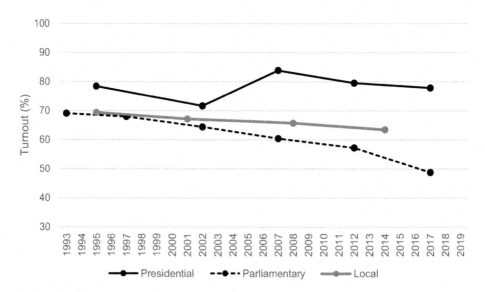

Figure 18.1 Voter turnout for local and national elections in France since 1990

Source: Ministry of the Interior; chart produced by the authors

France

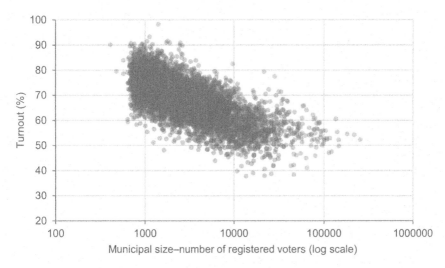

Figure 18.2 Voter turnout in the 2017 French local elections according to the number of registered voters (competitive elections in municipalities with more than 1,000 inhabitants; Pearson's r= -0.72)

Source: Ministry of the Interior; chart produced by the authors

half of all municipalities with between 1,000 and 1,500 inhabitants, only a single list was running. In contrast, multiple lists ran in every single city with over 20,000 inhabitants (Table 18.1, column 1).

Logically, the overall average for competitiveness in elections is low. Municipalities with fewer than 1,000 inhabitants averaged 1.3 candidates per available seat. In municipalities with more than 1,000 inhabitants, an average of 2.1 lists ran for election (Table 18.1, column 2). Yet, once more, the level of competitiveness in a given election is highly correlated with the size of the municipality. Whereas municipalities with fewer than 3,500 inhabitants average two lists, cities with over 20,000 boast an average of greater than four lists (Table 18.1).

On the scale of France's 35,000 municipalities, elections are hardly politicized at all when viewed from the perspective of political party labels. Over 40% of mayors do not fit into the existing national political framework ('Miscellaneous' = 22.8% and 'Unclassified' = 20.6%, according to the classification used by the Ministry of the Interior) (Table 18.2).[5]

In addition, although a majority of mayors can ostensibly be placed onto a left-right spectrum, only 15% of these can be clearly tied to a political party. It bears emphasizing that it is strictly impossible to quantitatively compare the scores achieved by lists (see the French data file) and the party affiliation of mayors (Table 18.2), in light of the different naming conventions used by the Ministry of the Interior. For instance, if the Union of the Left (the result of a coalition between several parties) wins an election, the mayor in reality might be socialist, communist, or miscellaneous left.

The level of politicization of elections also varies with the size of the municipality. In 2008 and 2014, two radically different situations were clearly distinguishable.

In the country's largest cities, municipal elections are clearly in line with second-order elections (Reif & Schmitt 1980; Parodi 1983; Gaxie & Lehingue 2014; Foucault 2015). In both 2008 and 2014, the incumbent mayor clearly belonged to one of the two major political families that regularly have succeeded each other in power, the right and the left, systematically

Table 18.1 Competitiveness in the 2014 French municipal elections according to the electoral system and the number of inhabitants

	Uncompetitive elections (# of candidates less than or equal to # of available seats)	# of candidates/# of seats
Fewer than 100 inhabitants	55%	1.2
100–499 inhabitants	51%	1.3
500–1,000 inhabitants	45%	1.4
Total fewer than 1,000 inhabitants	50%	1.3
	Uncompetitive elections (a single list in the running)	# of lists in the running (average)
1,000–1,499 inhabitants	48%	1.6
1,500–2,499 inhabitants	29%	1.8
2,500–3,499 inhabitants	28%	2.0
3,500–4,999 inhabitants	18%	2.3
5,000–9,999 inhabitants	6%	2.7
10,000–19,999 inhabitants	2%	3.6
20,000–29,999 inhabitants		4.2
30,000–39,999 inhabitants		4.9
40,000–49,999 inhabitants		5.2
50,000–59,999 inhabitants		5.6
60,000–79,999 inhabitants		5.8
80,000–99,999 inhabitants		6.7
100,000–149,999 inhabitants		7.4
150,000–199,999 inhabitants		6.5
200,000–249,999 inhabitants		8.3
250,000–299,999 inhabitants		9.7
300,000 or more inhabitants		9.0
Total more than 1,000 inhabitants	31%	2.1

Note: Table produced by the authors.
Source: Ministry of the Interior

competing against one another (Foucault & Gougou 2014). Local alliances were a mere reflection of the coalitions organized at the national level around the center-left Socialist Party (PS) and the center-right *Les Républicains* (LR), even whenever candidates did not publicly exhibit a specific political party label. The electoral campaign was dominated by national issues: candidates from the majority party were made to shoulder the blame for the governing party's politics, while candidates from the opposition party called upon voters to show their discontent with the government. An Ipsos poll revealed that 34% of French voters had sought to express their opposition to François Hollande and his government, while only 11% had sought to show their support.[6]

Table 18.2 The level of politicization of French mayors in 2014

	% of mayors affiliated with a party or classified according to political leanings Total France
Extreme left	0.0
Parti communiste français	1.0
Parti de Gauche	0.1
Parti Socialiste	5.5
Radicaux de Gauche	0.6
Miscellaneous left	13.5
Europe-Ecologie-Les Verts	0.2
Miscellaneous green parties	0.1
Miscellaneous	22.8
Regionalists	0.2
Modem	0.5
Union des Démocrates et Indépendants	1.8
Miscellaneous right	27.5
Union pour un Mouvement Populaire	5.6
Front National	0.0
Extreme right	0.0
Unclassified	20.6
Total	100.0

Source: Ministry of the Interior

The outcome in each city was used to tally individual victories and losses on a national scale, resulting in a 'national' assessment of the election results as a whole. The shifts that occurred were almost universally in a single direction – in favor of the opposition. In 2008, one year after Nicolas Sarkozy's election, the left enjoyed a massive surge in the municipal elections (Martin 2008; Dolez & Laurent 2008). By contrast, in 2014 – two years after François Hollande's victory – the municipal elections resulted in a dramatic shift to the right. When the votes were counted, the right found itself in charge of 158 of France's 242 cities with over 30,000 inhabitants – 53 more than in 2008 (Martin 2014).

In contrast, there is little competition for elections in the smallest municipalities (fewer than 5,000 inhabitants). Even when several lists are in the running, the distinct identification of which political party they belong to is often no small feat. Yet, even when they are clearly identifiable, national issues find themselves eclipsed by local ones (Barone & Toupel 2008; Ripoll & Rivière 2010; Vignon 2014). Evaluation of the underlying political significance of such elections is a complex task.

Small cities (with between 5,000 and 30,000 inhabitants) occupy a sort of 'in between'. Multiple lists are always in the running, and the party to which lists belong is often clearly identifiable. Yet aggregation of the results of these elections in an attempt to analyze their significance on a national scale is a treacherous – and artificial – exercise at best; each city has its own specific political landscape, and results are first and foremost a reflection of the local political offering and the local issues at stake.

Consequently, it is simple to understand how the electoral outcome, that is, 'Who won? Who lost?' as it is used by stakeholders and political commentators on election night, depends on the conditions in which it is produced and the population threshold used (Lehingue 2001). In 2001, an assessment of the election results among cities with over 30,000 inhabitants showed a strong shift to the right (Jaffré 2001; Martin 2001a, 2001b). But when this assessment was broadened to cities with over 3,500 inhabitants, the results showed that a sort of status quo had remained in place (Le Gall 2001).

Ultimately, if every one of France's 35,000 municipalities is taken into account, municipal elections are characterized by more stability than any other type of election, with mayors often remaining in power for several consecutive terms, even in large cities (Rouban 2014). Electoral results are also more varied there than in any other type of election (Dolez & Laurent 2001). Incumbent mayors running for reelection also benefit from a significant 'incumbent bonus', which is greatest at the end of their first term and progressively decreases until they ultimately are in a position to succumb to declining popularity by the end of their third term (Martin 1996). In 2014, 60% of incumbent mayors were reelected, 27% did not run for reelection, and 13% were defeated at the polls (Foucault 2019).

A distorted reflection of French society

The French Constitution of 1958 was amended in 1999 to allow legislation to be passed to encourage women's representation (Haut conseil à l'égalité entre les femmes et les hommes 2015).

For legislative elections, which use a two-round electoral system, the law simply incentivizes parties via financial penalties for those without an equal share of men and women running for office.

For municipal elections, a gender quota was introduced just ahead of the 2001 vote for all municipalities using the list system (municipalities with more than 3,500 inhabitants). Initially, each list was required to include three women and three men per block of six candidates. In 2008, the law was changed to require lists to alternate successively between women and men. The population threshold between the subsystems was lowered from 3,500 to 1,000 inhabitants prior to the 2014 municipal elections to expand the gender quota to smaller towns.

The introduction of a gender quota immediately resulted in almost identical numbers of men and women on the municipal councils targeted by the statute. Overall, the share of women in power in French municipalities has nearly doubled in 20 years, growing from 21.7% in 1995 to 40.3% in 2014 (Table 18.3). Yet, although the share of women serving as mayor also doubled over the same period, only one in six mayors was female.

Table 18.3 Share of women elected as municipal councilors and mayors in France, 1995–2014

Election year	% of female municipal councilors	Included BV with panachage*(no legal penalty)	Included CLPR with bonus**(legal penalty)	% of female mayors
1995	21.7			7.5
2001	31.7	30.0	47.5	10.9
2008	34.9	32.1	48.5	13.9
2014	40.3	34.9	48.3	16.0

Source: High Gender Equality Council

Notes: Table produced by the authors. *2001 and 2008: <3,500 inhabitants; 2014: <1,000 inhabitants. **2001 and 2008: >3,500 inhabitants; 2014: >1,000 inhabitants.

More generally, it should come as little surprise that municipal elected officials – let alone mayors – are a poor representation of the French population as a whole. Christian Le Bart points out that 23% of mayors come from an executive or senior management background or an intellectual profession, compared to 7% for the population at large; conversely, a mere 2.7% of the mayors elected in 2014 were from a blue-collar background, despite representing 15% of the French workforce.[7]

Likewise, French people of immigrant origin are underrepresented: 6.7% of municipal elected officials (compared to 3.2% in 2001) according to a High Integration Council (*Haut Conseil à l'Intégration, HCI*) study conducted in the wake of the 2008 municipal elections. However, they represent a mere 5.2% of deputy mayors and only 0.4% of mayors (Amadieu 2009).

Conclusion

The mayor plays a central role in French politics and government, although a dual paradox is worth noting. French mayors are 'political mayors' who embody their municipalities, yet they are at the helm of a government entity that has traditionally been vested with only very limited powers. They are also elected in municipal races in which there is often little competition, except in the country's largest cities.

Municipal council members are elected under a bloc vote system in two rounds, with *panachage* in small municipalities. In municipalities with over 1,000 inhabitants, they are elected under a closed-list PR system in two rounds, with a 50% majoritarian bonus for the largest party.

Although it was fiercely contested at the time of its inception, this electoral system now has widespread support. Regional councils, long elected by PR, today are elected using an electoral system similar to the one in place for municipal elections (only the majority bonus is different: 25% rather than 50%).

While EPCIs are steadily supplanting cities and towns in terms of their relative importance, the debate has shifted toward whether members of intermunicipal councils should be elected separately. This possibility was brought up in the late 2000s and early 2010s, but today it has fallen flat, as it is widely understood that such a reform would spell the beginning of the end for municipalities. For the time being, the idea of such a reform has fallen by the wayside, with the desire being to allow municipalities to retain their central role in local politics and preserve – but for how long, ultimately? – the 'French model' of local government in which mayors play a central role.

On a more general note, it bears mentioning that French political scientists have long demonstrated a certain lack of interest in municipal elections. Beyond analyses of local election results (Dolez & Laurent 2002), academic studies on local elections have now broadened in scope, with work on the political trajectory of cities (Nadeau et al. 2018), the social determinants of political behavior in municipal elections, particularly in terms of voter turnout (Braconnier & Dormagen 2014), and strategic voting (Dolez et al. 2017).

But more than anything, French political scientists give pride of place to sociological approaches – and primarily qualitative ones – to political phenomena. This explains the fact that much research is based on case studies and aims to analyze local list-building and voter-mobilization processes, electoral campaigns, the range of actions available to parties and candidates (Gaxie & Lehingue 1984; Lagroye et al. 2005; Levêque & Taiclet 2018), or even the sociology of local elected officials and the exercise of the profession of mayor (Le Bart 2002; Douillet & Lefebvre 2017; Foucault 2020).

Notes

1 This number includes only municipalities in metropolitan France and overseas *départements*, not those in French overseas territories. In addition, the rules described in this text do not apply to municipalities in New Caledonia and French Polynesia, which have a special system of their own.
2 Ifop, *Les Français et leurs élus*, 12 August 2019. www.ifop.com/publication/les-francais-et-leurs-elus/ (accessed 6 January 2020).
3 An expression often used and reused by Emmanuel Macron from his televised 2020 New Year's speech delivered on 31 December 2019.
4 www.courrierdesmaires.fr/33027/3645-dabstention-au-1er-tour-des-municipales-chiffre-definitif/ (accessed 6 January 2020).
5 The 'Miscellaneous' category consists of mayors deemed by the Ministry of the Interior to be politically 'unclassifiable'. The 'Unclassified' category is composed of mayors to whom the Ministry of the Interior has not assigned a political party label, primarily those from municipalities with under 1,000 inhabitants.
6 www.courrierdesmaires.fr/33027/3645-dabstention-au-1er-tour-des-municipales-chiffre-definitif/ (accessed 6 January 2020).
7 Le Bart, C. (2017). 'Le regard du sociologue sur le maire', *La Gazette des communes*, available at www.lagazettedescommunes.com/535186/le-regard-du-sociologue-sur-le-maire/ (accessed 6 January 2020).

References

Amadieu, J.-F. (2009). *Les élus issus de l'immigration dans les conseils municipaux (2001–2008)*. Haut conseil à l'intégration, Rapport remis au premier ministre: La Documentation française.
Barone, S. & Troupel, A. (2008). Les usages d'un mode de scrutin particulier. Les élections municipales dans les très petites communes. *Pôle Sud*, 29(2), 95–109.
Braconnier, C. & Dormagen, J.-Y. (2014). Une démocratie de l'abstention. Retour sur le non-vote et ses conséquences politiques lors des scrutins municipaux et européens de 2014. *Hérodote*, 3(154), 42–58.
Dolez, B. (2011). Notables enrôlés. Le vote (obligatoire) des électeurs sénatoriaux. In A. Amjahad, M. Hastings, & J.-M. De Waele (Eds), *Le vote obligatoire* (pp. 89–106). Paris: Economica, Collection Politiques Comparées.
Dolez, B. & Laurent, A. (2001). La nationalisation des comportements électoraux. In P. Perrineau & D. Reynié (Eds.), *Dictionnaire du vote* (pp. 682–683). Paris: Presses universitaires de France.
Dolez, B. & Laurent, A. (Eds.) (2002). *Le vote des villes. Les élections municipales des 11 et 18 mars 2001*. Paris: Presses de Sciences Po, Collection Chroniques Electorales.
Dolez, B. & Laurent, A. (2008). Les élections municipales de mars 2008: des élections intermédiaires d'un nouveau genre. *Regards sur l'actualité*, 342, 68–77.
Dolez, B., Laurent, A. & Blais, A. (2017). Strategic Voting in the Second Round of a Two-Round System: The 2014 French Municipal Elections. *French Politics*, 15(1), 27–42.
Douillet, A.-C. & Lefebvre, R. (2017). *Sociologie politique du pouvoir local*. Paris: Armand Colin, Collection U Sociologie.
Foucault, M. (2015). Les élections municipales de mars 2014: un vote sanction dans la logique des élections intermédiaires. *Revue politique et parlementaire*, 1075, 109–127.
Foucault, M. (2019). Des maires plus combatifs à quatre mois des élections municipales. In *Troisième enquête de l'Observatoire de la démocratie de proximité AMF-Cevipof/Sciences Po*. Paris: Sciences Po.
Foucault, M. (2020). *Maires au bord de la crise de nerfs*. La Tour d'Aigues: Editions de l'Aube.
Foucault, M. & Gougou, F. (2014). *Bilan des élections municipales françaises de 2014 dans les villes de plus de 9 000 habitants*. Hal-01064761. Paris: CEVIPOF.
Gaxie, D. & Lehingue, P. (Eds.). (1984). *Enjeux municipaux: la constitution des enjeux politiques dans une élection municipale*. Paris: Presses universitaires de France.
Gaxie, D. & Lehingue, P. (2014). Remarques sur le modèle des élections intermédiaires. In Y. Déloye, A. Dézé, & S. Maurer (Eds.), *Institutions, élections, opinion. Mélanges en l'honneur de Jean-Luc Parodi* (pp. 159–176). Paris: Presses de Sciences Po, Collection Académique.
Grangé, J. (1988). Le système d'élection des sénateurs et ses effets. *Pouvoirs*, 44, 35–57.

Haut conseil à l'égalité entre les femmes et les hommes (2015). *Parité en politique: entre progrès et stagnations. Evaluation de la mise en œuvre des lois dites de parité dans le cadre des élections de 2014: municipales et communautaires, européennes, sénatoriales*. Paris: Rapport n°2015-02-26-PAR-015.

Heinelt, H. & Hlepas, N. (2006). Typologies of Local Government Systems. In H. Bäck, H. Heinelt, & A. Magnier (Eds.), *The European Mayor. Political Leaders in the Changing Context of Local Democracy* (pp. 21–42). Weisbaden: Verlag für Sozialwissenschaften.

Jaffré, J. (2001). Les municipales et les cantonales de mars 2001, un retournement électoral bien réel. *Pouvoirs, 100*, 163–172.

Ladner, A., Keuffer, N., Baldersheim, H., Hlepas, N., Swianiewicz, P., Steyvers, K. & Navarro, C. (2019). *Patterns of Local Autonomy in Europe*. London: Palgrave Macmillan.

Lagroye, J., Lehingue, P. & Sawicki, F. (Eds.). (2005). *Mobilisations électorales. Le cas des élections municipales de 2001*. Paris: Presses universitaires de France – CURAPP.

Le Bart, C. (2002). *Les maires. Sociologie d'un rôle*. Villeneuve d'Ascq: Presses universitaires du Septentrion.

Le Gall, G. (2001). L'étrange consultation électorale de 2001 ou l'invention d'une défaite. *Revue politique et parlementaire, 103* (1011), 2–32.

Lehingue, P. (2001). Faire parler d'une seule voix? Les scrutins municipaux des 11–18 mars 2001. *Regards sur l'Actualité, 270*, 13–18.

Levêque, S. & Taiclet, A.-F. (2018). *A la conquête des villes. Sociologie politique des élections municipales de 2014 en France*. Villeneuve d'Ascq: Presses universitaires du Septentrion.

Martin, P. (1996). Existe-t-il en France un cycle électoral municipal? *Revue française de science politique, 46*(6), 961–995.

Martin, P. (2001a). *Les Élections municipales en France depuis 1945*. Paris: La Documentation française.

Martin, P. (2001b). Chronique des élections françaises (I): Les municipales et cantonales des 11 et 18 mars 2001. *Commentaire, 94*(2), 361–372.

Martin, P. (2008). Les élections de mars 2008. *Commentaire, 122*(2), 471–484.

Martin, P. (2014). La gauche, la droite et les élections municipales. *Commentaire, 146*(2), 357–364.

Massicotte, L. & Blais, A. (1999). Mixed Electoral Systems. A Conceptual and Empirical Survey. *Electoral Studies, 18*(3), 341–366.

Mouritzen, P.-E. & Svara, J. (2002). *Leadership at the Apex: Politicians and Administrators in Western Local Governments*. Pittsburgh: University of Pittsburgh Press.

Nadeau, R., Foucault, M., Jérôme, B. & Jérôme-Speziari, V. (2018). *Villes de gauche, villes de droite*. Paris: Presses de Sciences Po.

Parodi, J.-L. (1983). Dans la logique des élections intermédiaires. *Revue politique et parlementaire, 903*, 42–70.

Reif, K. & Schmitt, H. (1980). Nine Second Order National Elections – A Conceptual Framework for the Analysis of European Election Results. *European Journal of Political Research, 8*(1), 3–44.

Ripoll, F., & Rivière, J. (2010). Il y a campagne et campagne. Approche statistique des élections municipales de 2008 dans des communes périurbaines. In S. Barone & A. Troupel (Eds.), *Battre la campagne. Élections et pouvoir municipal en milieu rural* (pp. 47–74). Paris: L'Harmattan.

Rouban, L. (2014). Le nouveau pouvoir urbain en 2014: les maires des villes de plus de 30.000 habitants. *Élections 2014, Les enjeux. Note n°11*. Paris: CEVIPOF.

Vignon, S. (2014). Les élections municipales au village: un scrutin consensuel? Quelques éléments à partir du département de la Somme. *Métropolitiques*, 24 mars.

19

Greece

Mayors in the foreground, parties behind the scenes

Nikos Hlepas and Theodore Chadjipadelis

From a fragmented single tier to a solid multilevel system of local government

Apart from the national level, the Greek state consists of one level of territorially integrated, general-purpose, subnational state administration and two levels of self-government: the supra-regional (seven decentralized administrations: territorial state administration), the regional (13 regions: supralocal self-government), and the local (332 municipalities) administrations. Apart from the aforementioned seven general-purpose administrations, decentralized state administration includes a plethora of single-purpose territorial authorities and quangos directly subordinated to their respective line ministries. Since 2010, regions have been territorial self-governments, focusing on regional development, provincial roads, public works, and emergency management. On their part, municipalities are responsible for basic local infrastructure (including water supply and sewage treatment, school buildings and kindergartens, childcare facilities and elderly homes, roads, and local public transport) and permitting and examining buildings and small businesses.

This chapter focuses on municipalities. Since 1990, their number has changed several times. At the beginning of the reference period, there were no fewer than 361 (mostly urban) municipalities and 5,560 (mostly rural) communities, while the average population of local authorities was 1,733 inhabitants and the average area was 22.9 km². There was only one tier of local government. By 1995, the second tier of local self-government (at the level of the former prefectures) was inaugurated, and a small reduction in communities through voluntary amalgamations to 5,388 was achieved, while the number of municipalities increased to 437. In 1998, the first wave of mandatory and comprehensive (with the exception of the metropolitan areas of Athens and Thessaloniki) amalgamations further reduced the number of communities to 133, while the number of municipalities reached 900. The average population of local authorities had increased to 9,931 inhabitants, while the average area reached 127.7 km². In 2010, there was a second wave of obligatory and comprehensive amalgamations, this time also including the two major metropolitan areas of the country. All communities were abolished, and the local level was reorganized into 325 municipalities with an average population of 34,215 and an average area of 406 km². Following this reform ('Kallikratis-Project'; Hlepas & Getimis 2011: 529), the average size of the Greek municipality became one of the largest in Europe.[1] Finally, in 2019, following local demands and/or political expedience, five local authorities were split into 12 new municipalities, thus slightly increasing the total number nationwide into 332.

Intergovernmental relations can be situated in the Napoleonic (or Southern European) state tradition. Despite successive waves of amalgamations, political communalism remains strong and party networks are often used to facilitate access to decision-makers at higher levels of governance in exchange for loyalty and support. Municipalities lack taxation, planning, and regulatory powers. Implementation of centrally determined policies constitutes a large share of municipal tasks, and state funding covers 70% of municipal resources while less than 30% derives from local taxation and fees (Stolzenberg et al. 2016: 47). According to Ladner et al. (2019: 241), Greece is ranked quite low regarding local autonomy. The country scores above average on indices such as legal autonomy and noninterference (administrative supervision and financial transfer system), but it scores below average on policy scope, policy discretion, organizational autonomy, and access (corporatized influence of local governments on political decisions at higher levels of government; Ladner et al. 2019: 230).

The intragovernmental system of horizontal power relations is marked by the strong position of the mayor and is labeled as a strong mayor type of local political leadership (Heinelt et al. 2018: 40). The mayor enjoys a strong democratic legitimacy as she/he is directly elected by the absolute majority of votes, if necessary, in a second (runoff) round. She/he is also in charge of the administration; furthermore, she/he appoints the CEO and selects councilors to be vice mayors, defining their portfolio through ad hoc decisions.

As far as the citizens are concerned and their views on local governance, they feel closer to their municipality than to higher tiers of governance. According to the citizens, based on a series of surveys, mayors and local authorities are taking care of everyday life issues and are the ones most interested in citizen well-being (Chadjipadelis 2002).

Elections are about the mayor but also a barometer for national politics

In Greece, municipal and regional elections take place every four years on the second Sunday of October (and only on Sunday). The last elections were held, however, in May 2019 (the first round) simultaneously with the European elections, due to a previous change in the term of office that had prolonged the traditional 4-year term to a 5-year one. This change in the term length was implemented in May 2014, when local elections were held simultaneously with the European elections for the first time. The next local and regional elections will be held in October 2023.

Similar to elections on other tiers (regional, national, European), local elections are organized by the Ministry of Interior, together with the civil justice system and the municipalities. The Ministry of Interior assists candidates and municipalities; moreover, it coordinates the assortment and classification of election results. Civil courts of the first instance are responsible for checking the legitimacy of and proclaiming the candidatures. Municipalities are responsible for organizing and supplying the voting stations. The Audit Committees for Campaign Expenses and Infringements (one in each one of the seven territorial state administrations) are responsible for transparency and fairness during the campaign. The President of the Supreme Civil Court (*Areopag*) is the chairman of the central election committee, which also comprises two more judges from the Areopag and two senior civil servants. In each polling station, a local election committee is formed consisting of citizens who are randomly selected by lot and a representative of the courts (usually a lawyer or a court clerk). It is responsible for the smooth running of the voting procedure as well as for vote counting. Civil courts proclaim the winners who are elected as mayors or councilors as well as the substitutes for the latter. Any voter or candidate can lodge an objection in the administrative court. Election litigation unsurprisingly occurs primarily whenever there is an electoral victory by a small margin.

The fixed term for municipal office does not differ in length from the corresponding four-year term of the parliament, but early parliamentary elections are the rule, not the exception, in Greece. The simultaneity of local and regional elections is provided by law, but the simultaneity of local and parliamentary elections never occurred during the reference period. The central government and the national parliament (the only bodies that can initiate early parliamentary elections) tend to avoid simultaneity of local or regional and national elections. As they usually have a more or less intermediate position in the national electoral cycle, local elections (and even more the politicized regional elections) tend to be perceived as having a barometric function for the popularity of the central government. The best example was the last premature election of 7 July 2019, which was called by the incumbent government right after its defeat in the European election of 26 May 2019 and the disastrous results in both rounds (26 May and 2 June) of local and regional elections.

The direct election of mayors was introduced as early as 1864. Throughout the reference period, mayors were directly elected, and this system has never been seriously questioned, possibly because periods of indirect election during the twentieth century (1925–1927, 1951–1954, and 1959–1963 in municipalities and 1911–1963 in rural communities) are not remembered positively and certainly because mayors dominate the influential national association of municipalities (KEDE).

Municipal law used to endow directly elected mayors with a strong majority on the council because the list led by the mayor would receive no fewer than 60% of the seats. Following the introduction of a proportional election system for municipal (and regional) councils in 2018 (see later discussion), Greek mayors no longer are able to rely on the support of a legally predetermined council majority and are often obliged to seek consensus with opposition lists, mostly on a case-by-case basis. On the other hand, several opposition councilors have abandoned their lists in exchange for political posts and influence, causing a new phenomenon of 'disintegration' that affected opposition lists. Because several mayors nevertheless have complained about the 'blackmailing practices' in decision-making and party elites are afraid of losing control over local politics, the current government has announced its willingness to initiate appropriate legal amendments to restore 'governability' at the local level. To this end, mayors obtained additional responsibilities and the power to nominate some members of council committees. The proportional election system for councils, however, has not yet been amended. In 85 out of 332 municipalities, a governing coalition has been formed and/or some councilors moved to the mayor's bloc.

There are no legal provisions for recall referenda, neither for the council nor for the members of the executive.

Features of the local electoral system: the winner no longer takes it all

Electoral law makes a distinction between active (vote) and passive (candidate) rights along with age and nationality. To be able to vote as a Greek citizen, one has to be a registered 'local citizen' ('*demotis*') of the municipality before the closing of the list of voters (i.e., automatic registration). Greek citizens can vote in elections at the age of 17. Citizens are prevented from voting or being elected if they are in a situation of exclusion or suspension of these rights.[2] Candidates for the post of councilor must have reached the age of 18 by the day of the elections, while candidates for the post of mayor must have reached the age of 21. MPs are allowed to submit their candidature for local elective offices, but they are obliged to resign from their parliamentary office if they are elected as mayor.

The law rules out the candidature of judges, army and police officers, priests, CEOs and employees of the respective municipality and its public law entities, and CEOs of municipal enterprises. Apart from the priests, persons belonging to the aforementioned categories are accepted as candidates if they resign from their post. Not having served in the respective municipality within 24 months before filing their candidature is an additional precondition for judges and army and police officers. Employees of the state and state-controlled enterprises who have acted in their capacity as directors or directors-general within the borders of the respective municipality within the last 18 months before the election date cannot be elected as mayors or councilors, even if they resign before they submit their candidature. Former mayors or councilors who were suspended from office because they were irrevocably convicted for serious crimes are legally prevented from standing for election anywhere in the country.

Non-Greek residents from within the EU may vote and run as a candidate for the municipal (but not for the regional) elections. Apart from the conditions mentioned for Greek citizens, all non-Greek EU citizens must appeal to their municipality to register as a voter through a written procedure. In 2010, non-Greeks from outside the EU who legally resided within the country were able to vote for the first and the last time, because the supreme administrative court (Council of State) ruled in 2013 that voting by non-EU aliens would violate the constitution.

Greece maintains compulsory voting for all elections, including the local ones. Citizens who reside abroad, are farther than 200 km away from their polling station on election day, or are older than 70 are exempted from this obligation. For all other citizens, abstention from voting is formally a crime (and subject to a fine); after all, citizens are offered the opportunity to cast a blank ballot if they cannot find candidates they can trust. Authorities would, nevertheless, practically refrain from prosecuting those who do not turn out.

The number of councilors to be elected is determined by law and it depends on the number of inhabitants of the municipality (Table 19.1). It varies between a minimum of 13 (for municipalities with fewer than 2,000 inhabitants) and a maximum of 49 (for those with more than 150,000), with six additional categories in between (based on increasingly greater ranges in the number of inhabitants). The law provides that municipalities that include six or more former municipalities that have been merged will have the number of councilors stipulated for the next higher population category. During the last local elections of 2019, a total of 9,470 municipal councilors and 332 mayors were elected. Double mandate holding at the municipal and regional levels is not allowed, and the constitution (Article 56) rules out the candidatures of mayors and regional governors for the parliament. Municipal (or regional) councilors can be elected as MPs and vice versa, but this is a rather exceptional phenomenon. Therefore, *cumul des mandats* is not an issue within the Greek context.

The main features of the electoral system for municipalities are uniform throughout the country. There is a formal prohibition on lists being under the label of a national party, and in each municipality, local lists must be formed with their own names and logos. Party affiliations and endorsements are nevertheless quite common, and they are widely known and debated in local societies. Each list includes a mayoral candidate at its head, while the names of the candidate councilors follow in alphabetical order. A valid list should include, apart from the mayoral candidate, a total number of candidate councilors that is equal, at least, to the total number of council seats; single candidatures of mayors or councilors not belonging to any list are not allowed. Each gender must be represented by 40%, at least, of the total number of candidate

Table 19.1 Number of council seats by population in Greek municipalities

Population	Council seats
500–2,000	13
2,001–5,000	17
5,001–10,000	21
10,001–30,000	27
30,001–60,000	33
60,001–100,000	41
100,001–150,000	45
150,000+	49

councilors on each list (the gender quota had been 33% since 2002 and was increased in 2018). Candidate registration for municipal elections is done at the level of the local civil court, and the procedure is quite simple, easily accessible, and affordable for minor lists and newcomers. Political parties are legally prevented from candidacy, but their resources and their support can be very important for candidates, especially in large cities.

In terms of districting, local elections are organized at large in the municipalities that were not affected by the last wave of amalgamations in 2010. Each list and all of its candidates are thereby eligible to run in the whole of the territory of each of these 80 municipalities. Districting is different, however, in the 252 municipalities that were affected by the aforementioned amalgamations. In these municipalities, the territories of each of the former municipalities and communities that were merged in 2010 are now used as constituencies for the election of councilors. According to the electoral formula, the number of seats for every electoral list is proportional to the total number of votes in the municipality. The number of seats assigned to each constituency is proportional to its population. Therefore, the number of seats across the municipalities in each constituency varies from one to 49.

The ballot structure offers some different ways to vote. Voters can cast a valid ballot without giving a preference vote to any candidate councilor on this list. Alternatively, they have the opportunity for additional preferential voting for candidate councilors by marking their names on the ballot. Depending on the population of their constituency, voters may check one, up to two, or up to three names of candidate councilors. Voters of merged municipalities have the option to check the name of one councilor candidate from a different constituency in addition to candidates from their own constituency. In any case, each ballot cast is counted as a vote for the mayor at the top of the list, and voters are not supposed to mark his or her name on the ballot; they can only check the names of councilor candidates on the same list. Greek voters cannot split votes between lists (*panachage*).

The electoral system before 2019 included a two-round majority system for the election of the mayor and a mixed proportional system for the election of councilors (which resembled a majority bonus system). The seats were allocated using an electoral formula that ensured the majority of the winning list. If, in the first round, the winning list reached 50–60% of the votes, then it would receive 60% of the council seats, while the rest of the seats would be proportionally distributed among the remaining lists. If the winning list received more than 60% of the votes, then all seats would be distributed proportionally. If the winning list received fewer than 50% of the votes in the first round, then 50% of the seats would be proportionally distributed among all lists. The remaining half of the seats would be distributed to the two strongest lists that had taken part in the second round, but in any case, the winning list would not receive fewer than 60% of the council seats. The only crucial change in the electoral system before 2018 was a temporary modification implemented in the 2006 municipal election: the threshold for victory in the first round was set to 42%. Before the following election, however, the law was switched back to the traditional threshold of 50%. The recent reform of 2018 changed the electoral system for the council to a fully proportional system without a legal threshold for the allocation of seats. Seats are allocated according to the number of votes in the whole municipality. These seats are captured by the candidates who receive the largest numbers of preference votes on the respective list. The number of available preference votes for candidates varies from one to three according to the number of councilors. On average, the voter expresses his or her preference for 0.7, 1.4, or 2.1 candidates accordingly.

The electoral outcomes

The turnout for local elections presents a downward trend from 1990 to 2019. From 1990 to 2006, participation in local elections seemed to be stable at around 70%, while for the elections of 2010 through 2019 (during the economic crisis), the turnout rate decreased. However, we should bear in mind that around 20% of registered voters reside abroad, and there is an additional 10% of citizens registered in a different municipality than the one in which they reside (*heterodemotes*). Because postal and proxy voting are not allowed, turnout among registered voters who have a real opportunity to vote is much higher (possibly around 30% higher than the registered turnout: nearly 90% before the crisis), but it is nearly impossible to reach an accurate calculation.

If we compare the turnout for local and national elections, there seems to be a statistically insignificant difference (Figure 19.1). The pattern of electoral participation in national and local elections appears to be similar. As per the turnout percentages, we observe that there is a decreasing rate from the national elections of May 2012 onward, possibly due to the emerging changes in the political landscape of Greece within the framework of the unprecedented economic crisis (Teperoglou & Tsatsanis 2014; Verney 2014; Hlepas 2020: 9, 14). The general

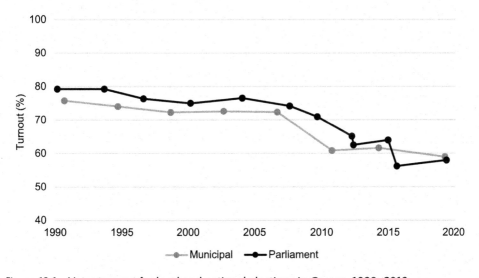

Figure 19.1 Voter turnout for local and national elections in Greece, 1990–2019

trend seems to be that the national elections that follow the local ones attract more interest but with no important statistically significant difference.

In the most recent municipal election of May 2019, turnout reached 59% in the first round, including the 4.8% invalid or blank votes out of the total votes cast. Unsurprisingly, turnout fell to 44.8% in the second round, including the 4.4% invalid or blank votes. If we compare the general turnout percentage to the turnout for clusters of municipalities on the basis of their population, there is no significant correlation between size and turnout rate (Table 19.2). However, if we look at the standard deviation and the coefficient of variation, it seems that in the smaller municipalities there is a higher deviation in the turnout rate, while in larger municipalities the turnout is more stable within the cluster. A possible explanation is that the party effect is stronger in larger municipalities than in smaller ones, where we experience a personalized vote. Another possible explanation is that, in Greece, local citizens of smaller municipalities who do not reside in their place of origin are going to their electoral constituency to vote, and their percentage reaches an average of ca. 40% in these municipalities.

Regarding electoral competition, on the basis of data for the most recent elections, the average number of lists participating in each municipality is about five, while only in four island municipalities – with small populations– was there just one list participating in the elections (Sikinos, Leipsi, Agathonisi, and Ag. Efstratios).

As mentioned, national parties are not allowed to participate in municipal and regional elections. This dates back to the early 1950s, following the civil war (1946–1949), to prevent the transfer of nationwide cleavages to the local level. Another reason was the prevailing, in those years, perception of local self-government as a predominantly 'administrative' institution where party politicization should be avoided. Today, the political affiliation and leanings of each candidate are widely known in local communities, but the lack of official party lists facilitates the formation of local catch-all alliances. In many cases, there are also explicit endorsements of the local candidates by the parties. Nevertheless, a candidate list must have a discrete name and logo in each municipality. An exceptional case is the Communist Party of Greece (KKE), which endorses lists that share a common communist orientation and use similar names all over Greece.

The political affiliation is not considered a significant criterion for voting for a candidate, except in municipalities that are located in urban city centers. In the elections of May 2019, only 51 out of a total number of 332 directly elected mayors had the official endorsement of one or more political parties. The elected mayors with official party support are generally located in

Table 19.2 Turnout and council size in Greece, 2019

	Turnout %		
# of councilors	Average	SD	CV
13	54	16	0.29
17	55	12	0.21
21	55	8	0.15
27	58	8	0.14
33	59	7	0.11
41	57	6	0.11
45	56	5	0.09
49	55	6	0.11

Notes: SD – standard deviation, CV – coefficient of variation.

the municipalities of metropolitan and other urban areas. While this kind of endorsement used to be perceived by many candidates as a major asset, the denigration of political parties during the crisis was a powerful incentive for local politicians to distance themselves from national politics, and especially from the governing parties. Therefore, while official party endorsement had been registered for 150 out of 325 elected mayors at the beginning of the crisis (2010 municipal elections), this number dropped to only 45 mayors in 2014. In that year, the governing PASOK party refrained from offering official endorsements even though many candidates were well-known party members or incumbents elected with official PASOK support in 2010 (Tsirbas 2015: 138). In 2019, the governing SYRIZA party hesitated before offering official support, while many candidates eagerly denied party endorsements. The real picture, however, seems to be reflected in the simultaneous politicized regional election held in the same year where the largest opposition party, *Nea Demokratia* (ND), received 46.2% of the votes cast. The ruling SYRIZA came second (12.3%), while the new socialist party KINAL came third (10.2%) and lists jointly endorsed by SYRIZA/KINAL received 9.1% (Chadjipadelis 2019). On the basis of the results of the explicitly politicized election for the national association of municipalities, where the newly elected mayors cast their votes, we can estimate their party affiliations (Table 19.3). Due to the electoral procedure (representatives to the national association are elected by each regional union of municipalities by PR), however, the ND-affiliated share is overestimated. Nevertheless, this does not alter the fact that municipal elections remain elections 'on their own terms' (Tsirbas 2015: 134, 152), where local networks dominate the political arenas and the liberal-conservatives (and, to a smaller extent this time, the socialists) manage to perform particularly well.

Election results confirm personalized voting in municipal elections, because there is an obvious deviation from the results in the European elections taking part on the same day (Table 19.3) and also from the results in the national elections that occurred shortly afterward (7 July), when the conservative-liberal ND received 39.9% of votes, while the leftist SYRIZA came second with 31.5% and the socialist KINAL reached third place with 8.1%. Prime Minister Tsipras had called these snap elections after the heavy defeat of his party in three different polls (European, regional, and municipal). Local and regional elections were not simply an instant barometric measurement, showing a bearable decline in popularity; moreover, they proved to be an important test of political legitimacy that the government did not pass just four months before the expiration of its ordinary term of office (September 2019). The simultaneity of three different polls did not blur, as some anticipated, the political message of the election results; moreover, it frustrated any attempt to downplay the defeat using arguments based on the alleged 'second-order character' of European and/or subnational elections (Reif 1997; Schakel & Jeffery 2013). Just one month later, the incumbent SYRIZA party performed markedly better in the parliamentary elections, demonstrating the dynamics of its polarizing campaign at the national level while at the same time confirming its persistent weakness, especially in terms of political personnel, in the subnational political arena.

Concerning female representation, despite a gender quota for candidate councilors, women are still extremely underrepresented on municipal councils and very few manage to be elected as mayors. In the local elections of May 2019, 184 lists (out of 1,628) were led by female candidates, from which only 19 were elected. Female councilors do not surpass 20% of the total number, while differences in female representation between urban and rural areas is still striking.

Councilors and mayors with a minority background are usually elected in the subregion of Thrace where a Muslim minority (comprising Turks, Pomaks, and Roma) lives, who enjoy special status according to the Treaty of Lausanne (1923) that provided for the reciprocal protection of this Muslim minority in Thrace (Greece) and of the corresponding Greek Orthodox

Table 19.3 Party performance in four different Greek polls, 2019

	European elections	Regional elections	Parliamentary elections	Municipal elections
	(26/5/2019) %	(26/5/2019) %	(7/7/2019) %	% mayors support
Turnout	58.8	58.4	57.9	
Blank or invalid	4.5	6.8	2.1	
SYRIZA (left)	23.7	12.3	31.5	9.0
ND (liberal-conservative)	33.1	46.2	39.9	63.9
KINAL (Socialist)	7.7	10.2	8.1	17.8
KKE (Communist)	5.4	6.9	5.3	2.0
EL-LY (right wing)	4.2		3.7	
MERA25 (leftist)	3.0		3.4	
LS-XA (far right)	4.9	3.6	2.9	
Independents	5.7	8.5	0.3	7.3
Other left parties	4.5	3.2	2.9	
Other right parties	4.8		0.7	
Other center parties	3.0		1.3	
KINAL and SYRIZA		9.1		
Total (valid)	100	100	100	100

Christian minority in Istanbul (Turkey). Citizens of EU countries who reside in Greece are also sometimes included on candidate lists, but their overall presence is barely noticeable.

The total number of candidates for municipal councils in May 2019 was 70,940 participating on 1,628 lists. The average number of candidate lists per municipality was about five (4.9), and the average number of candidates per list was 40. A comparison of the results in the local elections of 2019 shows that 39.5% of incumbent mayors were reelected. This was the same as in 2014 (40%) but lower than in precrisis times when the reelection rate reached 59% in 2010 and 56% in 2006 (Tsirbas 2015: 141). In 2019, based on their gender, there were 128 males and only three females who were reelected mayor. It is also significant that only 16 out of the 131 who were reelected were incumbent mayors in urban centers. Regarding the number of previous terms, roughly half (49.1% or 163 out of 332) of the elected mayors had already served as mayor for 1–6 terms (Table 19.4), while 40.8% of the candidates who had previously served at some time were elected this time (163 out of 400).

Discussion: back to the winner takes all system?

A peculiarity of the Greek local government system is the position of submunicipal units. In Greece, 252 municipalities (out of 332) are subdivided into communities where thousands of submunicipal councils are elected. Former communities or municipalities nowadays constitute a separate intramunicipal level. The same holds for 36 territorial subdivisions of eight large cities (Hlepas 2018: 134). Candidates for the community council are separate from the municipal lists. This may cause several problems if we consider that the majority on the community council may be different (and this is often the case) from the majority on the municipal council. Community councils are short of resources and formal powers (mainly advisory and a few

Table 19.4 Incumbency of Greek mayors

# of terms (before 2019)	Candidates	Elected	Percent
0	1,234	169	13.7
1	196	86	43.9
2	90	33	36.7
3	64	21	32.8
4	24	10	41.7
5	16	8	50.0
6	9	5	55.6
7	1	0	0
Total	1,634	332	20.3

co-decision powers, e.g., for local shops and small businesses), but they can mobilize opposition and become important veto players, blocking the generation and implementation of municipal decisions, especially on planning and investing.

Although there are several surveys, mainly conducted during the electoral period, on electoral outcomes, voting criteria, and issues, there is no national election survey on the local level. We intend to organize such an initiative based on the current Hellenic national election survey that we run (in the framework of the comparative study of electoral systems and the comparative candidate survey). Nevertheless, several academic studies show that party affiliation plays a less important role than the characteristics of the candidates and local issues (Chadjipadelis 2019).

The introduction of the proportional system for the election of municipal councils in 2018 had been fiercely criticized both by the ND opposition and by the national association of municipalities. Opponents rejected arguments about the putative democratization effect and highlighted the risk of nongovernability; moreover, criticisms referred to the iron law of proportionality that would oblige mayors to allocate posts to small lists that were rejected by voters, frustrating both transparency and accountability. Soon after coming to power, the ND government initiated a debate about reforming the electoral law to ensure that the elected mayor holds the majority on the local council. Also, there is a question about the electoral system for the election of mayor returning to the 42% rule (that is, changing the threshold from 50% + 1 to 42% + 1 votes) in a two-round majority system or changing the two-round majority to AV (alternative voting). Finally, there is also an open question about the appropriate electoral procedure for community councils.

A concrete initiative for amending the law is expected to unfold in Autumn 2020. The anticipated comeback of the old electoral system would consolidate well-known path dependencies and peculiarities. The unchallenged position of the directly elected mayor at the municipal level would be restored and opposition would be considerably weakened. Another important particularity of the Greek system, the ban on official party candidatures, will be maintained because local catch-all lists seem to facilitate strategies of both the mayors and the national parties.

Party resources are nevertheless important in local political arenas, mainly in larger municipalities. But the campaign and mobilization patterns deviate from those of national elections. In municipal elections, local issues are at the epicenter of the debate, while candidate mayors tend to foster local catch-all alliances, surpassing party affiliations and ideological cleavages. Personalization of voting and politics is far more explicit in municipalities, not only due to scale and tradition but also due to the institutional framework. The lack of official politicization, which is an important homogenizing mechanism, is also an important factor enhancing discontinuities and increasing deviations across the different local political arenas. In a country already characterized by geographic fragmentation, the variety of local contexts, debates, and personalities can therefore strongly differentiate patterns and dynamics of elections and voting.

Notes

1 This was a major reform predominantly aimed at increasing efficiency and decentralizing responsibilities; see Hlepas and Getimis 2011.
2 This can be the case for people who are declared to be (temporarily) incapacitated or have incurred certain criminal convictions.

References

Chadjipadelis, T. (2002). *Local government in the twenty-first century, contemporary problems and perspectives. Report for the national association of local authorities*. Athens: KEDE (in Greek).

Chadjipadelis, T. (2019). *What was the case? The analysis of the 2019 elections in Greece*. Politeia conference 'Europe at the crossroads: Leadership, challenges, and state of play'. Athens: Greece.

Heinelt, H., Hlepas, N., Kuhlmann, S. & Swianiewicz, P. (2018). Local government systems: Grasping the institutional environment of mayors. In H. Heinelt, A. Magnier, M. Cabria & H. Reynaert (Eds.), *Political leaders and changing local democracy. The European mayor* (pp. 19–78). London: Palgrave Macmillan.

Hlepas, N. (2018). Between identity politics and the politics of scale: Sub-municipal governance in Greece. In N. Hlepas, N. Kersting, S. Kuhlmann, P. Swianiewicz & F. Teles (Eds.), *Sub-municipal governance in Europe. Decentralization beyond the municipal tier* (pp. 119–143). London: Palgrave Macmillan.

Hlepas, N. (2020). Checking the mechanics of Europeanization in a centralist state: The case of Greece. *Regional & Federal Studies, 30*(2), 243–261.

Hlepas, N. & Getimis, P. (2011). Impacts of local government reforms in Greece: An interim assessment. *Local Government Studies, 37*(5), 517–532.

Ladner, A., Keuffer, N., Baldersheim, H., Hlepas, N., Swianiewicz, P., Steyvers, K. & Navarro, C. (2019). *Patterns of local autonomy in Europe*. London: Palgrave Macmillan.

Reif, K. (1997). Reflections: European elections as member states second-order elections revisited. *European Journal of Political Research, 31*(1), 115–124.

Schakel, A. & Jeffery, C. (2013). Are regional elections really second-order elections? *Regional Studies, 47*(3), 323–341.

Stolzenberg, P., Terizakis, G., Hlepas, N. & Getimis, P. (2016). *Cities in Times of Crisis: Fiscal Consolidation in Germany and Greece*. Baden-Baden: Nomos.

Teperoglou, E. & Tsatsanis, E. (2014). Dealignment, de-legitimation and the implosion of the two-party system in Greece: The earthquake election of 6 May 2012. *Journal of Elections, Public Opinion and Parties, 24*(2), 222–242.

Tsirbas, Y. (2015). The 2014 local elections in Greece: Looking for patterns in a changing political system. *South European Society and Politics, 20*(1), 133–155.

Verney, S. (2014). Broken and can't be fixed: The impact of the economic crisis on the Greek party system. *The International Spectator, 49*(1), 18–35.

20
Italy
Hard-to-decipher local elections and voting

Silvia Bolgherini and Selena Grimaldi

A changing local government system

The Italian local government landscape in 2020 includes 7,904 municipalities (*comuni*), 102 provinces and metropolitan cities as a second-tier level, and 20 regions —five that have been granted special status (SSRs)[1] and 15 ordinary status regions (OSRs). The term 'local level' usually means municipalities and second-tier authorities.

Italian municipalities count an average population of around 7,600 inhabitants. Those with more than 100,000 inhabitants number fewer than 50, while those with fewer than 5,000 inhabitants represent 69.5% of the total. The number of municipalities has been slightly but steadily decreasing since the mid-2010s, with several amalgamations occurring in the last years (Bolgherini, Casula, & Marotta 2018).

Local governments in Italy play a significant role in intergovernmental relations and public service delivery. Except for the capital (Rome), all municipalities are subject to the same legislation and ruled by the same principles without differentiation in terms of competencies and power. Municipalities are endowed with local public service provision competences and local policymaking power concerning a series of basic municipal tasks (e.g., waste and water management, urban planning, municipal police, land register, registry office), which they have to manage either alone or in cooperation with others (Vandelli 2012).

Since the 1990s, Italian local government has experienced a series of reforms that applied three different 'R-approaches' (Bolgherini & Lippi 2016): a reallocation of administrative and organizational powers (decentralization) from 1990 to 2000; a reshaping of the institutional setting (devolution) from 2001 to 2009; and a rescaling (recentralization) in times of economic crisis since 2008. In a country that traditionally reports a low level of trust in governmental authorities,[2] municipalities instead rally a certain level of support, being trusted around 10% more than other government levels, especially the state (Demos & Pi 2019).

Indeed, according to the LAI index (Ladner et al. 2019: 242) Italy increased its local autonomy level from 56.1 in the early 1990s to 62.4 and 64.7 in the early and late 2000s, respectively, and to 66.4 in the early 2010s. Nonetheless, if we consider the OECD tax autonomy indicator, local tax revenues decreased from over 5% of total Italian tax revenue in the pre-crisis years, to under 4% at the peak of the crisis, to finally recover in more recent years (5.9% in 2014). As a percentage of GDP, local tax revenues rose from 1.6% at the peak of the crisis to 2.6% in 2014 (OECD 2017).

This rise in financial autonomy led Ladner et al. (2019: 268) to consider Italy among the medium-level political discretion/high-level financial autonomy countries (type II), thus stressing the decreasing impact of political discretion (although mainly related to service delivery), one of the most striking features that has always caused Italy to be considered among the Southern European (Page & Goldsmith 1987; Goldsmith & Page 2010) or the Continental Europe Napoleonic (CEN) model countries (Kuhlmann & Wollmann 2014; Loughlin, Hendriks, & Lidström 2011). Its unitary arrangement (originally grounded in the French system) favored many small-sized municipalities with limited legal power, but entitled to numerous administrative tasks, significant political relevance, and access to the national political system, along with a traditional Weberian bureaucracy aspiring to, and controlled by, the state bureaucracy.

Significant changes since the 1990s stepwise have added innovative elements to the Italian Southern CEN variant: directly legitimated local politics (direct election of mayors); a pervasive new public management approach at the local level (much more than at the central one); stronger fiscal autonomy; intense outsourcing and privatization (public-private partnerships and involvement of NGOs in management and delivery of some public services); and increasing up- and trans-scaling trends in many policy areas (Brunazzo 2010; Lippi 2011; Baldini & Baldi 2014; Bolgherini, Casula, & Marotta 2018). Almost all of these provisions only indirectly involved municipalities, thus formally leaving the primary legislative framework unaltered and acting through a series of oblique changes that nonetheless substantially affected their daily functioning (Bolgherini & Lippi 2021). What indeed did impact the municipal system was the direct election of the mayor beginning in 1993, which defined his/her pivotal role toward the council and the electorate and which will be addressed in detail in the following section.

The mayor at the center

Municipal elections in Italy are held each year for a (different) group of municipalities. No simultaneity has been foreseen for such elections since the beginning of the republican era in 1946. A 1991 national law establishes that municipal elections are to be held on a Sunday between 15 April and 15 June and, when possible, coupled with other elections (usually European and regional), although no mandatory rule applies. As a consequence, each year, several hundred or thousands of municipalities of all sizes go to the polls, usually on the same day in all OSRs and on different dates according to their own calendar in the SSRs.[3] Runoffs take place two weeks later. In the last three years (2017–2019), around 71% of all Italian municipalities and 63.6% of those in the OSRs[4] voted.

The mayor and the council are elected for five-year terms. Special status regions (except Sardinia) organize local elections through their own electoral offices. The other 15 regions rely on the State Directorate General for electoral services managed by the Ministry of Interior, supported on the ground by the prefectures and the municipalities.

The direct election of mayors (and presidents of provincial councils, followed later by that for regional governors) was introduced in 1993 in a period of a generalized trend toward mayoral empowerment in Europe (Bäck, Heinelt, & Magnier 2006). The main goals of this reform were as follows: to increase local government stability by reinforcing the head of the executive; to slow down political demobilization by allowing a more involved role for citizens; to reduce party fragmentation with a majority-assuring electoral system; and to increase the mayoral decision-making room to maneuver (Baldini 2011; Bolgherini & Lippi 2016).

Since this reform, the Italian municipal government displays a co-existence between a directly elected mayor and the parliamentary principle linking the executive to his/her majority on the council. This principle is the so-called *simul stabunt simul cadent*, which states that if the mayor resigns (or ceases to serve or receives a motion of distrust), his/her municipal cabinet also resigns and the municipal council is dissolved (and the other way around in case of the resignation of the majority of the councilors). The law provided mayor-empowering competencies that were hitherto unknown in Italian local government. Differently from the past – when the council chose the municipal cabinet members (*giunta*) and the mayor – the directly elected mayor appoints and revokes his/her own local ministers who are directly responsible to him/her and tightly linked by a (often personal) trust relation (Bolgherini & Lippi 2016: 269). The *giunta* is, thus, despite its collegial nature guided by the mayor's monocratic leadership, as in municipal presidentialism (Kuhlmann & Wollmann 2014) or in the strong political mayor form of local government (Heinelt & Hlepas 2006).

Local recalls are not allowed. The removal of mayors before the end of their term is possible with new elections to the municipal council, following its automatic dissolution. The underlying principle is again the previously described *simul stabunt simul cadent*. This has brought the increased governmental stability that was desired, as the mayor's resignation happens quite rarely (yearly around 0.5% of all municipalities, i.e., one-fifth of those dissolved early).

A convoluted electoral system

In Italy, the eligibility rules, substantially unchanged since 1975, establish that all citizens aged 18 are entitled to vote in local elections. The same applies for the lower chamber (*Camera dei deputati*) elections, whereas for the senate electors must be 25 (Article 58 Cost.). Contrary to parliamentary elections, subnational elections do not allow citizens who reside abroad to vote. The right to stand for local council elections and the mayor's office is granted to all citizens aged 18, comprising those residing in another Italian municipality. Since the ratification of the Maastricht Treaty, EU citizens of other countries who are living in Italy may vote in local elections, and they can stand for the office of councilor (but not mayor) in the municipality in which they legally reside. Compulsory voting existed until 1993, although it was never really enforced.

The local electoral system changed in 1993 with the introduction of the direct election of the mayor (Baldini & Legnante 2000; Caciagli & Di Virgilio 2005). This reform represented the first large-scale experience with a majoritarian model in Italy, a country with strongly rooted proportional political culture and habits. Since then, except for some minor changes, the essential features of the municipal electoral system have remained stable, that is, the combination of a plurality representation in small municipalities (those below 15,000 inhabitants, which is around 92% of all Italian *comuni*) and a majoritarian TRS representation in large municipalities (over 15,000 inhabitants) for mayoral elections and an open-list proportional system (OLPR) with a majority bonus for council elections (basic features are reported in Table 20.1). In a nutshell, the municipal electoral system is a majority-assuring system, that is, a system with a majority bonus for the party or list backing the mayor to facilitate the formation of stable majorities on the council.

In small municipalities, each mayoral candidate must be associated with a single list only, forcing political parties to coalesce in a cartel list or form a civic list. The elected mayor is the mayoral candidate who receives the most votes (a runoff is held in case of a tie). In large municipalities, each mayoral candidate may instead be associated with one or more lists of candidates for councilor. If no mayoral candidate achieves 50% of the vote, a runoff between the two candidates who received the most votes occurs in a fortnight. In the second round, electors can vote only for the mayoral candidate, but lists initially supporting other candidates may back one of the final two competitors. Second rounds are quite common in larger municipalities. However, because these municipalities are not so numerous, overall runoff figures remain limited: in the 5,000 municipalities voting in 2017–2019,[5] a second round took place in only 6% of elections.

The size of a municipal council in Italy depends on the size of the population; however, since the onset of the economic crisis in 2008, council sizes have been repeatedly reduced. The smallest councils (in municipalities with a population under 3,000 inhabitants) are currently composed of 10 councilors, while the largest ones (over 1 million inhabitants) have 48. In the municipalities voting in 2017-2019 years 2017–2019, the council sizes ranged between 10 and 40 seats (municipalities with over 500,000 inhabitants),[6] for a total of 59,093 elected councilors and 5,000 mayors.

There is no districting in council elections. Each candidate for the council is eligible across the whole territory of the municipality. The number of candidates on each list cannot exceed the number of council seats to be filled and cannot be fewer than three-fourths of the seats in small municipalities or fewer than two-thirds in large ones.

The ballot structure offers several ways to cast a valid vote. In small municipalities (under 15,000 inhabitants), voters may vote for a mayoral candidate only, which automatically implies a vote for his/her supporting list. As for list preferences, in those municipalities with fewer than 5,000 inhabitants, voters may cast only one preference vote, while in those over 5,000 inhabitants, two preference votes within the same list are allowed (double preference is valid only if candidates of different gender are selected; otherwise, the second preference is invalid).

In large municipalities (over 15,000 inhabitants), voters may (1) cast a vote for a list only, thus implying a vote for the mayoral candidate supported by that list; (2) cast a vote for a mayoral candidate only, which is valid only for the election of the mayor (*partial or personalized vote*); (3) cast a vote for a mayoral candidate and a vote for a list supporting him/her;[7] or (4) cast a vote for a mayoral candidate and a vote for a list not supporting him/her (*split vote*).[8] Voters may cast up to two preference votes under these rules. This preference system has increasingly been employed in recent years, albeit unevenly (used more in the south than in the rest of the country) (Rombi 2017).

In small municipalities, a plurality system elects the candidate who receives the most votes for mayor. The list supporting the winning mayor receives a 'majority bonus' of two-thirds of the seats regardless of the share of votes received by the mayoral candidate, while the remaining one-third of the seats are allocated proportionally among the other lists using the d'Hondt method. In the case of a single competing list (and a unique mayoral candidate), all candidates for councilor are elected. In the years 2017–2019, this occurred in around 15% of the municipalities and always the tiniest ones due to a scarcity of available candidates. In large municipalities, seats are allocated using the d'Hondt method, only among those lists passing the legal threshold of 3%. The list(s) supporting the winning mayoral candidate – not necessarily linked by a formal preelectoral alliance – receives a 'majority bonus' of at least 60% of the seats if (1) the mayor has been elected in the first round, his/her list(s) received 40% of the votes, and no other list(s) exceeded 50% of valid votes; or (2) the mayor is elected in the second round and no other list(s) exceeded 50% of valid votes in the first round. These extra seats are allocated among the lists supporting the winning mayoral candidate by the d'Hondt method. The remaining 40% of the seats are allocated proportionally (d'Hondt formula) among the lists supporting the losing mayoral candidates. All losing mayoral candidates supported by a list or lists that have obtained at least one seat are elected councilors.

To summarize: first, the mayor is elected; second, seats are allocated among the winning (and then the losing) lists; third, the seats to be allocated to losing mayoral candidates are subtracted;

finally, individual councilors are elected according to the preference votes they obtained. This system is usually classified as a mixed system, namely, a 'majority bonus system'.

The entry rules are easy: candidacies (the list(s) of councilors supporting a mayoral candidate and the mayoral candidate) are presented to the administrative office of the municipality, along with a number of citizens' signatures (fixed by law and related to the size of the municipality).

As far as incompatibilities with other political offices are concerned, mayors and municipal executive members (*assessori*) cannot be regional councilors in the same region; councilors cannot be councilors in other municipalities; in large municipalities, a councilor cannot be a municipal executive member; and mayors cannot be MPs, MEPs, or national ministers.

Local lists in small municipalities vs. nationwide parties in larger units

Turnout for Italian local elections displays a decreasing trend: in the last 20 years[9] it sank from around 82% to 68%. When comparing these data with those for national and regional elections (Table 20.2), local electoral participation was equal to that at the national level only at the beginning of the millennium. By the middle of the first decade, the gap with the legislative vote

Table 20.1 Main features of the municipal electoral system in Italy

	Population size	Electoral system and rules (after 1993)
Election of the mayor	All	Direct
	<15,000 inhabitants	Plurality (for each mayoral candidate, only one list associated)
	>15,000 inhabitants	TRS with majority bonus
Election of the council	All	OLPR, d'Hondt, majority bonus
Majority bonus	<15,000 inhabitants	Two-thirds of the council seats for the list supporting the winning mayoral candidate
	>15,000 inhabitants	60% of the seats may be allocated to the list(s) supporting the winning mayoral candidate under specific conditions (see text)
# of candidates for councilor	<15,000 inhabitants	For each list, no fewer than three-fourths of the total the council seats and no more than the total seats
	>15,000 inhabitants	For each list, no fewer than two-thirds of the total the council seats and no more than the total seats
Threshold	<15,000 inhabitants	None
	>15,000 inhabitants	3%
Preferences	<15,000 inhabitants	1
	>15,000 inhabitants	Two within the same list for candidates of different gender

Source: Authors' compilation

Table 20.2 Turnout for local, regional, and legislative elections in Italy per year

Election year	Average turnout (%) in OSRs	# voting OSR municipalities	# of total municipalities	% voting municipalities out of total	Turnout for legislative election (lower chamber)	Turnout for regional election (# of voting OSRs)
2001	81.8	1,149	8,101	14.2	81.4	73² (15)
2002	76.7	733	8,101	9.1		
2003	77.0	638	8,101	7.9		
2004	79.3	4,321	8,101	53.3		
2005	76.1	367	8,101	4.6		71.4 (14)
2006	74.3	1,163	8,101	14.4	83.6	
2007	73.2	774	8,101	9.6		
2008	79.0	425	8,101	5.3	80.6	
2009	76.9	4,087	8,101	50.5		
2010	72.2	462	8,100	5.7		64.2 (13)
2011	72.4	1,179	8,094	14.6		
2012	67.9	777	8,092	9.6		
2013	67.4	530	8,090	6.6	75.2	
2014	71.3	3,900	8,057	48.4		
2015	64.2	516	8,046	6.4		53.9 (7)
2016	66.3	1,172	7,998	14.7		
2017	60.0	785	7,978	9.8		
2018	61.0	590	7,954	7.4	72.9	
2019	68.0	3,654	7,914	46.2		

Source: Authors' compilation of official data from the Italian Ministry of Interior.
[1] Several different dates in each year.
[2] Percentage refers to the regional election in 2000.

(in decline, in its turn) was several points lower. Conversely, local turnout has always exceeded that for regional elections.

Generally speaking, in cases of simultaneity with other elections, local turnout tends to increase. Just to give an example, in 2019, those municipalities involved in a double election (local and European) scored a turnout of around 70%, while those voting in 2018 only in the municipal elections turned out at around 60% (CISE 2018, 2019). Nonetheless, this cannot be taken as a systematic finding because the municipal electoral calendar is, as explained previously, extremely scattered, so that electoral simultaneity, if any, is occasional and always limited to the voting municipalities in that year.

Higher turnout rates are usually associated with a smaller jurisdiction size as far as local elections are concerned (Frandsen 2002). Italy is no exception: medium- to large-sized municipalities (those over 15,000 inhabitants) do confirm the assumption that the larger the size, the lower the turnout rate in local elections (Emanuele 2011), with even larger gaps in the most recent cycles (CISE 2016, 2017, 2018, 2019). Longitudinal data covering the last two decades (2001–2019) show that smaller municipalities (under 15,000 and up to 20,000) had an average turnout of 73.5%, which is 1–2% higher than larger ones. Interestingly, tiny municipalities with fewer than 1,000 inhabitants ($N = 1,950$, 24.6% of the total) do have as low (around 71%) of a turnout as the larger towns with over 100,000 inhabitants. Finally, the few large cities (in Italy, those with over half a million inhabitants) are those with the lowest turnout rates, in line with turnout in other European countries. This sort of inverted-U-shape trend in turnout may possibly be explained by the presence of two latent size thresholds – an 'isolation threshold' for tiny municipalities and a 'dispersion threshold' for the bigger ones (Bolgherini 2021). Up to the isolation threshold, voters perceive the municipal stakes in small-sized units as too unimportant to mobilize for, while over the dispersion threshold, it is the low political efficacy perception, more usual in larger units, that affects turnout negatively.

Competitiveness also depends on size: it is limited in smaller municipalities, while extremely high in larger ones.[10] This divide is quite impressive in the 2017–2019 period: in municipalities under 30,000 inhabitants, the average number of competing lists reached only 2.8 (from 3.8 in 2017 to 2.5 in 2019) in smaller municipalities (96.5% of the total). In municipalities with over 30,000 inhabitants (3.5% of the total), competitiveness was very high, with an average number of competing lists ranging between 18.1 in 2017 and 15.1 in 2019 (16.7 on average).[11] Mayoral candidatures also confirm this: in smaller municipalities, the average number of mayoral candidates was 2.4, while in larger municipalities it more than doubled (6.1 on average) (Figure 20.1).

Uncontested mayoral elections occurred in small municipalities only. Nonetheless, a clear trend is difficult to assess. If uncontested elections were in fact marginal in both 2017 and 2018 – occurring in around 4.5% of the municipalities – they skyrocketed in 2019 (19.2% of all voting municipalities). Consequently, by taking into account this 3-year period, uncontested mayoral elections have occurred quite often, on average in 15.2% of the municipalities. This is possibly due to the high number of micro municipalities that held elections in 2019.

When it comes to assessing the capacity of nationwide parties to dominate local elections to the detriment of independent or local lists, once again in Italy the picture varies, depending on the size of the municipality. While independent local lists clearly take the lion's share in smaller municipalities (under 30,000 inhabitants), they do also run in larger municipalities (over 30,000 inhabitants); major nationwide parties are present in over 85% of larger municipalities.

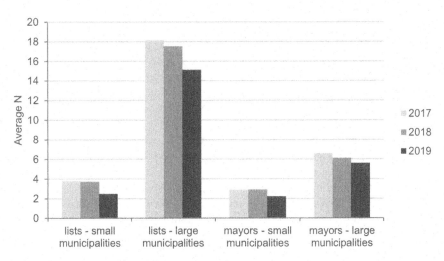

Figure 20.1 Average number of competing lists and mayoral candidates in smaller (SM) and larger (LM) municipalities in Italy, 2017–2019

Source: Authors' compilation

In contrast, their presence is much more limited in smaller municipalities. As shown by data in Table 20.3 (second column), the presence of nationwide parties in local elections dropped from 2017 to 2019, the years with the highest and the lowest share, respectively, of larger municipalities at the polls.

If we compare the second and third columns of Table 20.3, the evidence shows that well-established parties have a more successful seat-winning strategy. Both the center-left Democratic Party (PD) and the right-wing League led by Matteo Salvini only run in those municipalities with at least one 'sure' seat (e.g., in 2018 the League ran in 15.8% of the municipalities and won at least one seat in 14.8%). On the other hand, the Five Stars Movement (M5S) was able to win at least one seat in fewer than half of the municipalities in which the party ran.

Municipal vote performances of the main nationwide parties show some weakness in M5S at the local level, most likely due to its still sparse organization on the ground. In the 2017–2019 period, M5S received, in fact, only 10.4% of the votes in the municipalities where it ran, whereas in the 2018 parliamentary elections it was the most popular party, receiving 32.7% of the votes. Taking into account all of the valid votes per year, M5S' share of the municipal vote decreased from 6.8% in 2017 to 4.1% in 2019 (fourth column in parentheses). The Democratic Party's votes in the municipal elections (except for 2019) were below its national level results in 2018, and by taking into account all of the valid votes per year, it slid from 10.5% in 2017 to 8.9% in 2019. Conversely, the League showed a remarkable capacity to handle local elections. Despite both 2017 and 2018 when the League won a lower share compared to the 2018 parliamentary elections (17.4%), it outperformed in the 2019 municipal elections (with a peak of 22% of the votes). By considering all of the valid votes per year, the League increased from 5.4% in 2017 to 10.2% in 2019.

Turning to relevant, but minor, nationwide parties, Berlusconi's center-right Go Italy (FI) lost at the national level in 2018, being surpassed by the League in the center-right alliance. This situation was anticipated at the municipal level the previous year when FI received only 7.9% of the votes where it ran, a result that decreased in the following years. Conversely, in the same year, the radical right-wing Brothers of Italy (FdI) anticipated its parliamentary election performance at the local level and increased it in the following local elections in both 2018 and 2019. Finally, center parties seem to perform better than radical left parties at the local level. The former won 7.3% of the votes compared to 4.2% for the left-wing parties, differing from their respective national performances (well below 3% and around 4%, respectively).

Given the remarkable number of non-national lists (around 90% of the total; Table 20.3, last column) and their electoral success (Vampa 2016), one could be induced to conclude that local elections in Italy are not particularly politicized. This is not entirely true. In small municipalities, national parties are often present, although they cannot be officially counted as such, that is, when they decide to run with different names or when they form cartel party lists, and often recall the name of the municipality. Hence, it is difficult to assess their true electoral strength. And this is even truer in the smaller municipalities: the electoral system forces mayoral candidates in small units to be supported by one list only, which is often formed by several entities of differing local and national nature (see the preceding section).

Therefore, if we look at national parties' performance in smaller and larger municipalities separately, it turns out that the League is the only nationwide party, which is present as such in around 10.5% of smaller municipalities in the 3-year period analyzed. This party is also present in larger municipalities (around 84%), confirming its current national reach, rather than its original regional(ist) north-centered focus of the past (Passarelli & Tuorto 2018), and the success of its double strategy of remaining locally rooted while displaying an appealing national leadership. Both PD and M5S show the greatest presence in larger municipalities (over 90%), but from

Italy

2017 (775 municipalities)	% of municipalities where running	% of municipalities where represented	% of seats on local councils [2]	% of (aggregate) votes in local elections [2]	% of mayors affiliated with the party [3]
PD (Democratic Party)	16.8	15.4	22.8 (5.1)	16.8 (10.5)	5.2
M5S (Five Stars Movement)	23.1	10.3	16.3 (2.3)	10.2 (6.8)	1.3
LN (League)	16.1	13.0	22.6 (3.9)	11.3 (5.4)	3.6
FI (Go Italy)	12.5	9.4	13.3 (1.9)	7.9 (3.9)	0.9
FDI (Brothers of Italy)	9.6	4.0	9.4 (0.7)	7.2 (1.7)	0.1
Radical left[4]	4.9	0.8	9.0 (0.1)	3.3 (0.8)	0.0
Center parties[4]	10.3	5.4	10.8 (0.9)	5.9 (2.6)	0.0
Independents and non-national (local) lists	100.0	99.7	83.3 (83.0)	64.9 (64.9)	87.6
2018 (581 municipalities)					
PD	12.2	10.7	21.1 (3.5)	16.1 (8.2)	3.3
M5S	19.5	8.4	15.0 (1.8)	11.6 (6.6)	1.0
LN	15.8	14.8	24.6 (5.1)	15.0 (7.8)	5.5
FI	11.7	9.1	10.2 (1.5)	7.3 (3.6)	0.7
FDI	10.7	5.2	9.1 (0.8)	4.9 (2.2)	0.3
Radical left[4]	5.7	1.2	7.6 (0.1)	3.1 (0.9)	0.0
Center parties[4]	8.3	2.8	10.9 (0.4)	3.4 (1.3)	0.2
Independents and non-national (local) lists	99.8	99.5	84.6 (83.9)	66.4 (66.4)	87.1
2019 (3,644 municipalities)					
PD	5.4	5.1	33.7 (2.7)	24.1 (8.9)	2.7
M5S	7.9	4.0	10.4 (0.6)	10.1 (4.1)	0.1
LN	12.1	11.4	33.3 (4.9)	22.1 (10.2)	4.4
FI	4.4	2.7	10.2 (0.5)	6.4 (2.2)	0.1
FDI	4.2	2.0	9.1 (0.3)	5.2 (1.6)	0.1
Radical left[4]	2.0	0.4	8.3 (0.0)	3.6 (0.5)	0.0
Center parties[4]	1.5	0.7	15.7 (0.2)	4.7 (0.5)	0.1
Independents and non-national (local) lists	99.6	99.4	87.5 (87.0)	66.5 (66.2)	90.2

Source: Authors' compilation

[1] The total number of national lists in 2017 was 903 (602 in 2018, 1,889 in 2019), with 723 (487 in 2018, 1,364 in 2019) referring to the parties reported in the table. A total of 180 national lists (115 in 2018, 525 in 2019) are not reported here as they represented coalitions (mostly center-right or center-left), and thus data are not attributable to a single national party list.
[2] Percentages refer to the share of seats/votes won in the municipalities where the party ran (in parentheses the share of seats/votes out of the total seats/valid votes per year).
[3] In 2017, 0.8% of elected mayors were part of a center-right cartel and 0.4% were part of a center-left cartel. Those percentages were 1.4% and 0.0% in 2018, and 2.2% and 0.2% in 2019, respectively.
[4] Radical left includes all extreme left-wing parties and cartels; Center parties includes all Catholic and explicitly center-oriented small parties and cartels.

2017 to 2019, their presence dropped in smaller jurisdictions. In particular, PD – one of the most territorially rooted national parties – seems to have lost part of its political capital, even in that area (central Italy) in which it had its stronghold. Following the decreasing popularity of its former Secretary General and former Prime Minister, Matteo Renzi, this party also lost a potentially strong leadership (Ignazi 2018).

As for female representation, no longitudinal studies are available for local elections. As a consequence, it is quite difficult to fully assess the success of the provisions introduced to fill the gender gap in local institutions. A gender quota was introduced in 2012 for those municipalities over 5,000 inhabitants, stating that no gender should be represented by more than two-thirds of each electoral list,[12] along with the already-mentioned gender-balanced double preference. Albeit partial, available analyses show that these provisions have had an impact on reducing the gender gap: in fact, from 2012 to 2016, female councilors have increased from 19.2% to 34.5% mainly in smaller municipalities (under 15,000 inhabitants) (CNR-IRPPS 2018). As for female mayors, data are available only for the most recent elections. In all Italian municipalities voting between 2014 and 2019, 1,131 female mayors were elected, that is, 14.5% of all mayors. The peak was in 2019, with 17% of the mayors being women.[13] If we consider voting municipalities in OSRs only during the investigated period (2017–2019), an increasing trend emerges with 11.9% female mayors in 2017, 13.3% in 2018, and 16.7% in 2019. Most female mayors serve in small municipalities of under 15,000 inhabitants (91.6%) with only a limited number serving in large municipalities (8.4%). This may signal the parties' hesitancy to nominate women in large municipalities (with some notable exceptions like Rome and Turin), where there is 'more at stake'. Finally, the most female mayors are elected in the northwest of the country and the lowest share is elected in the south. This confirms a traditional political divide in which women are more active and better represented (socially and politically) in the north compared to the south, for both cultural and economic reasons. Positive changes nonetheless have also occurred in institutions where no gender quota were implemented, such as the national parliament: the share of women elected increased by around 20% from 2001 to 2013 in both chambers, with a peak of female MPs in 2018 (36.1% female representatives and 35.1% female senators).

The representation of minorities and persons of foreign origin at the local level is also rising, but it is still insignificant in its overall figures.

Hard-to-decipher local voting: three reasons

As the evidence presented thus far has shown, the Italian form of local government is a particularly complex one. There are three main factors.

First, a convoluted electoral system – which is differentiated in several ways according to the municipalities' population clusters – which is a majority-assuring, mixed system revolving around the mayor. Since direct election was introduced in 1993, the mayor plays a pivotal role in local politics and in the life of local communities. The perceived efficacy of this system and the appreciated higher accountability of the mayor and his/her staff, as well as the reputation of the local level of government to be more efficient and responsive than others, render this reform one of the most successful in Italian local government institutional history. And in fact, unlike the national level where the debate about electoral reform has never really exited the agenda since the 1990s – the 1993 reform has never been contested.

Second, the absence of an official nationwide municipal election day leads to limited horizontal simultaneity. This has two possible implications. On the one hand, the overall impact of every single municipal round is difficult to assess. It is instead more proficuous to take into account, as has been done in this chapter, some consecutive years together in order to be able to observe some trends and gain some insights on the local-national voting congruence (Bolgherini, Grimaldi, & Paparo 2021). On the other hand, the fact that there is no proper municipal electoral cycle, despite the limitation just described, makes each municipal round – when larger municipalities of over 15,000 inhabitants, particularly the provincial capitals or the biggest cities like Rome, Milan, or Turin, are involved – a sort of barometer election (Massetti 2018) for the national or regional elections and political equilibria. This leads to a growing salience for local level electoral results, also in terms of the electoral strategies of the nationwide parties.

The third feature of Italian local voting is the remarkably high number (around 90% of the total) of local or independent lists, especially in the small-sized municipalities that make up a large percentage of all Italian municipalities. In the smallest units, candidates are hard to find, and they often stems directly from civil society. National parties' labels are not necessarily considered a plus for candidates (quite the opposite). Indeed, in larger municipalities, the nationwide parties' role grows proportionally to municipal size, although under 15,000 inhabitants it is still hard to discern when local lists are indirect party lists or effective civic ones.

A clear assessment of the role of national lists compared to local ones is one of the difficulties scholars face when retrieving data at the municipal level, which are (too) often un-systematic and rarely available. Despite this, studies on the local level in Italy are increasing both in number and in the accuracy of analysis, and are thus starting to fill in some data and information gaps, for example, on female representation (Carbone & Farina 2020), mayoral personalization (Freschi & Mete 2020), and municipal primaries (Sandri & Venturino 2016).

Notes

1. The five SSRs are Aosta Valley, Trentino-South Tyrol, Friuli-Venezia Giulia, Sicily, and Sardinia.
2. Eurobarometer survey data place Italy among the 'tend-not-to-trust' countries with an average percentage of 68%: https://ec.europa.eu/commfrontoffice/publicopinion/index.cfm, *Interactive barometer – Trust in institutions – Regional or local public authorities*, accessed on 5 May 2020.
3. Differently from the OSRs, SSRs and autonomous provinces (Trient and Bozen) are entitled, by their relevant statutes, to establish their own electoral calendar for both regional and local elections. A scientific debate addressing the limited horizontal simultaneity in municipal elections and supporting the idea of an election year (Astrid 2006) flourished around the mid-2000s, although without success.
4. In this chapter, we rely on a data set that comprises OSRs only. Data on SSRs are archived differently and, in some cases, difficult to retrieve.
5. To be precise, during our time frame, 5,032 elections were held, but 32 of them have been annulled because they did not comply with the *double quorum* requirement – that is, in municipalities of up to 15,000 inhabitants, if only one list is running, the election is valid only if (1) the number of voters is not less than 50% of those entitled to vote, and (2) the list received a valid number of votes that is not less than 50% of the registered voters.
6. To be precise, among those municipalities voting during the time span considered, the council size ranged from 10 to 40 seats (municipalities with over 500,000 inhabitants) in 2017, from 10 to 32 seats (municipalities with over 100,000 inhabitants or those that are provincial capital municipalities) in 2018, and from 10 to 36 seats (municipalities with over 250,000 inhabitants) in 2019.
7. Options (1) and (3) are equivalent in their output (a vote counted for both the mayor and the list), whereas (1) has been explicitly noted to be the most likely to avoid invalidation of the ballot paper in the case of double-crossing.
8. The Italian split vote (*voto disgiunto*) in the municipal (and regional) elections is not equivalent to the *panachage* employed in other countries. It allows voters to cast a vote for a mayoral candidate and a vote for a list supporting another mayoral candidate.
9. Electoral data presented in this section on turnout refer to the last two decades (2001–2019) of municipal elections held in the OSRs, for they show the most similar patterns and timing. Data referring to the last elections (2017–2019) cover 5,032 municipalities in the OSRs.

10 For this discussion, the cutoff between small and large municipalities differs from the usual one (15,000 inhabitants), because the latter impedes a clear categorization in the allocation of seats and, thus, in the competitiveness discussion. Hence, in this section, small municipalities are considered to be those with under 30,000 inhabitants and a number of seats up to 16.
11 Yet, these numbers are still lower than for national parliamentary elections, where a higher number of competing lists is usually present (i.e., 28 in 2018 and 47 in 2013).
12 In 2014, a gender quota – stating that no gender may be represented by less than 40% of the candidates – was also introduced for municipal executives (*giunte*) in all municipalities with over 3,000 inhabitants
13 Data are taken from the ANCI website, www.comuniverso.it, *Le donne sindaco*, accessed on 5 May 2020.

References

Astrid Association (2006). *L'accorpamento delle consultazioni elettorali: verso l'election year*. Roma: Astrid.
Bäck, H., Heinelt, H. & Magnier, A. (Eds.). (2006). *The European Mayor*. Wiesbaden: Springer.
Baldini, G. (2011). The different trajectories of Italian electoral reforms. *West European Politics*, *34*(3), 644–663.
Baldini, G. & Baldi, B. (2014). Decentralization in Italy and the troubles of federalization. *Regional & Federal Studies*, *24*(1), 87–108.
Baldini, G. & Legnante, G. (2000). *Città al voto. I sindaci e le elezioni comunali*. Bologna: Il Mulino.
Bolgherini, S., Casula, M. & Marotta, M. (2018). Pursuing defragmentation at the municipal level: signs of a changing pattern? *Modern Italy*, *23*(1), 85–102.
Bolgherini, S., Grimaldi, S. & Paparo, A. (2021). Assessing multi-level congruence in voting in comparative perspective. Introducing the municipal level. *Local Government Studies*, *47*(2), 54–78.
Bolgherini, S. & Lippi, A. (2016), Italy. Remapping local government from re-allocation and re-shaping to re-scaling. In U. Sadioglu & K. Dede (Eds.), *Theoretical Foundations and Discussions on the Reformation Process in Local Governments* (pp. 265–287). Hershey: IGI.
Bolgherini, S. & Lippi, A. (2021). Oblique-change Matters. 'Bradyseismic' institutional change in local government. *Italian Political Science Review*, *51*(1), 117–135.
Bolgherini, S. (2021). Fusioni di comuni e affluenza alle urne: la (contro)tendenza in Italia [Municipal amalgamations and turnout: the (counter)trend in Italy]. In M.Degni (Ed.), La risposta dei comuni alla crisi pandemica (pp. 114-133). Rome: Castelvecchi.
Brunazzo, M. (2010). Italian regionalism: A semi federation is taking shape – or is it? In H. Baldersheim & L. Rose (Eds.), *Territorial Choice: The Politics of Boundaries and Borders* (pp. 180–197). London: Palgrave Macmillan.
Caciagli, M. & Di Virgilio, A. (2005). *Eleggere il sindaco. La nuova democrazia locale in Italia e in Europa*. Torino: UTET.
Carbone, D. & Farina, F. (2020). Women in the local political system in Italy. A longitudinal perspective. *Contemporary Italian Politics*, *12*(3), 314–328.
CISE Dossier (2016) (2017) (2018) (2019) available on cise.luiss.it/cise/.
CNR-IRPPS (2018). *Rapporto finale in materia di cariche elettive e di governo*. Roma: CNR.
Demos & Pi (2019). *Rapporto gli italiani e lo Stato* (demos.it/a01676.php).
Emanuele, V. (2011). Riscoprire il territorio: dimensione demografica dei comuni e comportamento elettorale in Italia. *Meridiana*, *70*, 115–148.
Frandsen, A. (2002). Size and electoral participation in local elections. *Environment & Planning C*, *20*, 853–869.
Freschi, A. C. & Mete, V. (2020). The electoral personalization of Italian mayors. A study of 25 years of direct election. *Italian Political Science Review*, *50*(1), 271–290.
Goldsmith, M. & Page, E. (Eds.). (2010). *Changing Government Relations in Europe: From Localism to Intergovernmentalism*. Abingdon: Taylor & Francis.
Heinelt, H. & Hlepas, N. (2006). Typologies of local government systems. In H. Bäck, H. Heinelt & A. Magnier (Eds.). *The European Mayor* (pp. 21–42). Wiesbaden: VS Verlag.

Ignazi, P. (2018). *I partiti in Italia dal 1945 al 2018*. Bologna: Il Mulino.

Kuhlmann, S. & Wollmann, H. (2014). *Introduction to Comparative Public Administration*. Cheltenham: Elgar Press.

Ladner, A., Keuffer, N., Baldersheim, H., Hlepas, N., Swianiewicz, P., Steyvers, K. & Navarro, C. (2019). *Patterns of Local Autonomy in Europe*. London: Palgrave Macmillan.

Lippi, A. (2011). Evaluating the "quasi federalist" programme of decentralisation in Italy since the 1990s: A side-effect approach. *Local Government Studies, 37*(5), 495–516.

Loughlin, J., Hendriks, F. & Lidström, A. (2011) (Eds.). *The Oxford Handbook of Local and Regional Democracy in Europe*. Oxford: Oxford University Press.

Massetti, E. (2018). Regional elections in Italy (2012–15): Low turnout, tri-polar competition and democratic party's (multi-level) dominance. *Regional & Federal Studies, 28*(3), 325–351.

OECD (2017). Fiscal decentralisation database. www.oecd.org/ctp/federalism/fiscal-decentralisation-database.htm.

Page, E. & Goldsmith, M. (1987). *Central and Local Government Relations*. London: Sage.

Passarelli, G. & Tuorto, D. (2018). *La Lega di Salvini. Estrema destra di governo*. Bologna: Il Mulino.

Rombi, S. (2017). L'uso del voto di preferenza alle elezioni comunali del 2017. In A. Paparo (Ed.), *La rinascita del centrodestra? Le elezioni comunali 2017* (pp. 83–87). Roma: CISE.

Sandri, G. & Venturino, F. (2016). Primaries at the municipal level: How, how many and why. *Contemporary Italian Politics, 8*(1), 62–82.

Vampa, D. (2016). Declining partisan representation at the sub-national level: Assessing and explaining the strengthening of local lists in Italian municipalities (1995–2014). *Local Government Studies, 42*(4), 579–597.

Vandelli, L. (2012). Local government in Italy. In A.-M. Moreno (Ed.), *Local Government in the Member States of the European Union: A Comparative Legal Perspective* (pp. 327–350). Madrid: INAP.

21
Portugal
Elections and voting in a dual-tier, local government system

António F. Tavares and Pedro J. Camões

Brief overview of the local government system

In Portugal, the local government system can be characterized as a dual-tier system that includes both a municipal and a submunicipal level. This system is protected under Article 236 of the Portuguese Constitution, which establishes two categories of local government: municipalities (*municípios*) and parishes (*freguesias*). Both types of local government operate with elected executives and deliberative decision-making bodies and possess financial and administrative autonomy.[1] The literature is consensual in placing Portugal in the group of countries following a strong mayor tradition (Heinelt & Hlepas 2006; Magre & Bertrana 2007), where the mayor represents the interests of the community. While not included in the original Page and Goldsmith (1987) typology, Portugal is often referred to as a variant of the southern model (John 2001). Despite being described as possessing high political discretion and medium financial autonomy (Ladner et al. 2019), municipalities and parishes are only responsible for about 9.6% of all public expenditures, which places Portugal as one of the most centralized countries in the European Union (DGO 2018). The unique nature of the Portuguese system requires a brief description of both levels and their implications for local elections.

Municipalities

All 308 municipal governments in Portugal[2] follow a strong mayor type executive imposed by constitutional rule; the figure of a city manager is completely absent from the Portuguese setting. Portugal uses a joint system for the election of the mayor and the local executive, which is considered to be an exception in the European context (Magre & Bertrana 2007). Mayors are always the head of the party or the independent movement list receiving the most votes in the municipal executive election, and the members of the municipal executive are also directly elected from party lists and chosen using the proportional formula (Pires de Almeida 2008b). The mayor has exclusive competences assigned by law and is able to allocate portfolios among the elected members of the executive, thereby securing a strong influence over executive decision-making (Mendes & Camões 2008). The executive body also has a specific set of competences assigned by law beyond those allocated to the mayor. As more evidence of this strong mayor status, Portuguese mayors can only be removed through a judiciary process and not through a political process (recall election or vote of no confidence by the council). As a result of this strong executive authority, municipal executive elections can be described as first-order elections at the local level (Tavares et al. 2020). As the head of their list, mayoral candidates enjoy most of the attention during the electoral campaigns and are largely the reason why voters go to the polls. Most Portuguese mayors are 'locally born and bred and therefore have extensive knowledge of their communities, as well as many formal and informal contacts with their citizens' (Elcock 2008: 808). One of the unique traits of the executive branch of local government is the formation of minority executives, a product of multiparty elections and proportional representation. On rare occasions, the winning list (and the mayor in office) may not have the majority of the members on the cabinet executive. Under these circumstances, the mayor uses portfolio allocation to build quasi-formal coalitions that secure a majority. As the mayor is always the head of the list receiving the most votes, postelectoral coalitions are only set up to achieve governability. In some instances, political instability in the running of daily affairs may occur, with implications for the types of policies proposed and adopted by the local executive.

Municipal councils are also elected through a system of proportional representation. As oversight bodies, city councils are responsible for budget approval, setting up land use plans, selling municipal bonds, setting municipal tax rates, and approving local ordinances and regulations. The separation between the executive and the council is clear (Magre & Bertrana 2007), but, with the exception of Lisbon, the overwhelming majority of municipal councils have limited resources and councilors have little to no administrative support and are generally incapable of effectively fulfilling their oversight function.

Parishes

Article 238 of the Portuguese Constitution recognizes parishes as the smallest unit of local government. Parishes are submunicipal units of self-government composed of an elected assembly (deliberative body) and an executive body, and each parish is contained within the boundaries of the municipality (Tavares & Teles 2017). The chief of the executive (*presidente de junta*) is directly elected, but, contrary to the municipal level, the members of the executive require approval by the parish assembly. Each municipality is divided into several parishes, each resembling a form of neighborhood government similar to what one can find in Germany, Greece, Norway, Poland, and Spain (Komninos-Hlepas et al. 2018).

The origins of the *freguesias* can be traced back to the Catholic parishes starting in the fifth century. The *paróquia* was the name given to the congregation of the followers of the Catholic Church, still known today as the *paroquianos*. After the Liberal Revolution of 1820, many religious institutions were secularized, with a more evident separation between church and state, and the parishes assumed different names, depending on their nature. In 1830, parishes were incorporated into the administrative system as civil parishes (*paróquias civis*) as opposed to religious parishes (*paróquias eclesiásticas*) (Tavares & Teles 2017). After 1878, the Catholic parishes remained *paróquias*, but their political equivalent became the *freguesia* (Pereira 1985). As submunicipal government units, parishes have evolved since the 1830s to become a full-fledged lower tier of local government.

The number of parishes per municipality varies significantly, ranging from one (in five municipalities), where the boundary of the *freguesia* coincides with the boundary of the municipality, up to 61 (in the municipality of Barcelos), where each parish is essentially equivalent to a neighborhood government. The total number of parishes peaked at 4,259 in 2012, but it was reduced to 3,092 following a territorial reform triggered by the Memorandum of

Understanding signed by the IMF/EU/ECB and the Portuguese government in 2013 as part of a financial bailout agreement.

The responsibilities of parishes are assigned by law and include the management of rural and urban infrastructure, preschool and elementary school buildings, cemeteries, public kennels, and vacant lands. Parishes also have powers assigned by national legislation to engage in emergency management, planning, and community development. In some cases, municipal governments delegate tasks to parishes, including the funding and managing of physical infrastructure. While municipal spending represents 8.7% of all public spending, the financial autonomy of the parishes is merely statutory, with the 3,092 parishes accounting for just 0.86% of total public spending (DGO 2018). In substantive terms, they manage very small budgets and are largely dependent on central government transfers. For an in-depth discussion of the Portuguese *freguesias* as a submunicipal unit of local government, please refer to Tavares and Teles (2017).

Local elections and their place in a multilevel system

The decade following the Democratic Revolution of 1974 was characterized by the pursuit of political decentralization through direct elections and universal suffrage of local elected officials. Elections are organized by the National Electoral Commission (*Comissão Nacional de Eleições*), and, since 1985, local officials serve four-year terms. Elections to both tiers of local government take place concurrently and separately from all other elections (national parliament or European Parliament).

Despite financial limitations and the lack of technical and human capacity, the first two decades after the Revolution witnessed significant investments in key areas, such as water supply and basic sanitation. Municipalities received support from the central government through financial assistance and technical training. Historically, local political autonomy had always been curtailed, either through restricted suffrage or by the direct appointment of local political officials by the central government. As a result, local populations were ill prepared to exercise local democracy, thus justifying the rhetorical argument often used by the central government to limit political and administrative decentralization in the post-Revolution era.

In the aftermath of the Revolution, most of Portuguese society suffered from insufficient politicization (Opello 1981). With the exceptions of municipalities in urban areas and the Alentejo region due to the strong presence of radical left-wing parties, the overwhelming majority of citizens remained largely depoliticized and rural municipalities (and all parishes) were administrative arms of the state. On the one hand, the financial dependence that characterized this group of municipalities prevented the choice of political priorities by the local executives (Mozzicafreddo et al. 1988). On the other hand, municipalities had been systematically depoliticized throughout the previous century, so it is not surprising that local elected officials considered themselves more administrators than politicians (Opello 1981). As a result of this scenario, local referenda on substantive issues are still extremely rare, with only a handful having been conducted over the past 40 years. In addition, recall elections to remove the mayor or executive by popular vote are not allowed by law in the Portuguese electoral system.

Studies in political science and sociology have focused on mayors' party affiliations, career paths, and social backgrounds. Pires de Almeida (2008a) summarizes this research stating that Portuguese mayors' careers have been driven primarily by their party affiliations and vertical mobility, both upward and downward. The author mentions upward mobility for those cases in which the mayor has moved to become a member of the national parliament, European Parliament, or minister. Lisbon has been particularly visible as a springboard, with one former mayor becoming president of the Republic and two former mayors becoming prime ministers.

The current prime minister, António Costa, was the mayor of Lisbon between 2007 and 2013, whereas the current president of the Republic, Marcelo Rebelo de Sousa, ran and lost in 1989. In other cases, former ministers and members of the Portuguese parliament went on to run successful bids for mayor.

Parties have played a crucial role in selecting their representatives running local campaigns. Over the years, the choice of local officials largely reflects the centralized decision-making processes of national political parties (Pires de Almeida 2008a). This tendency toward centralization started to change in August 2001, when the Portuguese parliament approved Organic Law n°1/2001 (*Lei Eleitoral dos Órgãos das Autarquias Locais*) allowing 'groups of citizens' to present lists in local elections (Pires de Almeida 2008a). As a result, Portuguese local elections now follow a hybrid system, allowing both partisan and nonpartisan lists.

Thus, national political parties may lose the monopoly on candidates for municipal elections in two ways (Tavares et al. 2020). In some cases, the incumbent mayor affiliated with a national political party seeks reelection as the party's candidate, but the national party structure supports another candidate. In response, the incumbent decides to run against all of the other parties, including her/his own former party, as the head of an independent list. In other cases, independent candidates are not affiliated with a political party but have prior experience in civil society organizations. They wish to extend their contribution to civic life by becoming a mayor. This may be motivated by general dissatisfaction with party politics or simply for personal reasons.

Features of the electoral system

In local elections, active and passive electoral capacity is assigned to all Portuguese residents and to European Union citizens and nationals from countries with which Portugal has a reciprocity treaty who have been residing in Portugal for two or four years (active and passive electoral capacity, respectively) if from a Portuguese-speaking country and for three or five years if from a non-Portuguese-speaking country. The minimum voting age is 18. These rules are not as strict as those that apply to parliamentary elections, in which only Portuguese citizens are allowed to vote. The number of non-Portuguese eligible voters in the 2017 local election was estimated to be around 80,000 (Comissão Nacional de Eleições, 2017).

Municipalities

Portuguese law establishes a mixed composition of the city council, combining the heads of the parish executives and members elected at large. Parish (or district) representatives can never outnumber the number of councilors elected at large. The size of the latter is equal to the number of the former plus one. As a result, the municipal council size varies with the level of territorial division of the municipality into parishes. Figure 21.1 displays the relationship between the number of municipal councilors and municipal population size. Most municipalities have small councils. The lowest number is 16 members, in the case of six municipalities with under 10,000 residents and only one parish government (one parish representative plus 15 councilors directly elected at large, corresponding to three times the number of members of the municipal executive). The largest municipal council is located in the city of Barcelos with 123 members (61 parish representatives and 62 members directly elected at large). The average size of municipal councils is 31. Municipalities above 50,000 tend to be much more diverse in terms of council size, largely due to the wide variation in the number of parishes in larger municipalities.

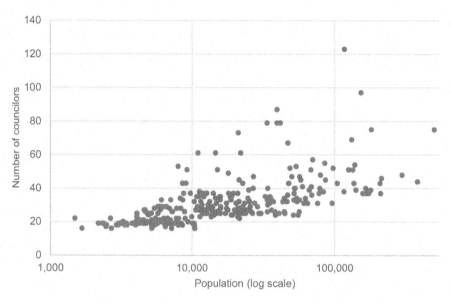

Figure 21.1 Number of councilors in Portugal municipalities by municipal population size
Source: National Electoral Commission

Table 21.1 includes information about the relationship between municipal population size and the number of members of the executive cabinet. The overwhelming majority of Portuguese municipalities have fewer than 50,000 inhabitants and, as a result, smaller executive cabinets. Slightly over 40% of the population live in cities with over 100,000 residents and about 50% reside in municipalities with between 10,000 and 100,000 inhabitants. Only 7.2% of the Portuguese live in localities of under 10,000 residents. The last column in Table 21.1 shows the direct proportional relationship between the size of the municipal population and the number of constituents per cabinet executive member. In larger municipalities, this is ten times higher than in smaller ones (1 representative per 14,802 versus 1 per 1,418).

All local elections follow a proportional representation system with closed lists, no formal threshold, and a single categorical ballot. The seat allocation method is the d'Hondt system. This system of proportional representation promotes the inclusion of different political and social groups on the municipal council. Classical political science suggests that proportional representation can undermine governability by preventing the formation of a stable majority, which can lead to political uncertainty in managing local government affairs (Hermens 1941). The theoretical argument holds that majority executives ensure the governability of the municipality by allowing the formation of homogeneous executives (single party or coalition). Several attempts to change the local electoral system in Portugal have been grounded on this rhetorical argument. However, the way the problem is framed fails to recognize either the results or the practical implications of the Portuguese electoral system. A study by Lima (2004) reached important conclusions about the conditions of governability in Portuguese municipalities. First, the proportional representation system based on the d'Hondt method generates levels of political representation (number of mandates) for competing parties that promote the formation of stable majorities. Second, as the size of the district decreases, proportionality goes down (Rae 1971; see also Lijphart 1990). Given the small size of most Portuguese districts, the

Table 21.1 Municipal council and municipal executive size in Portugal

Municipal population	Number of municipalities (2017)	Total number of elected executive members	Total number of registered voters (2017)	Proportion of the electorate	Registered voters per member of the executive cabinet
Lisboa (16 executive members)	1	16	493,415	5.3	30,838
Porto (12 executive members)	1	12	214,270	2.3	17,856
Over 100,000 (10 executive members)	22	220	3,256,497	34.7	14,802
50,000 to 100,000 (8 executive members)	26	208	1,627,772	17.3	7,826
10,000 to 50,000 (6 executive members)	139	834	3,129,735	33.3	3,753
Under 10,000 (4 executive members)	119	476	674,991	7.2	1,418
Total	308	1,766	9,396,680	100	

Source: National Electoral Commission

conversion of votes into mandates favors the larger national parties to the detriment of smaller ones, leading to a scenario in which there are two dominant parties in local elections. Third, prior attempts to reform the system have been driven by the goal of strengthening power not solving the 'governability crisis' (Lima 2004: 243). Recent empirical analyses support these findings, suggesting that the percentage of natural and artificial majorities has varied between 88% and 91%, respectively, between 2001 and 2009 (Freire et al. 2012). The authors argue that these percentages reflect a highly disproportional system favoring political stability and advantaging the largest political parties with more professional organization (Socialists and Social Democrats). The 2017 election confirms this tendency toward political stability in the executive: 274 municipal governments were majority executives (89% of the total) and only 34 were minority executives (11%).

Parishes

Parishes have democratically elected leaders, including both an executive and a legislative body. The parish council (*Assembleia de Freguesia*) is the deliberative body elected by the registered voters residing in the territory of the *freguesia*. Parish council size is determined according to the rules given in Table 21.2.

Contrary to municipal elections, there is only one type of election at the parish level: the head of the parish executive is the first candidate on the list receiving the most votes in the election for the parish council. The parish executive (*junta de freguesia*) is composed of the president and a variable number of cabinet members determined by law, two of whom serve as secretary and treasurer. The size of each parish executive also varies according to the number of registered voters (Tavares & Teles 2017). The rules are also presented in Table 21.2.

The electoral outcomes

In general, turnout is lower at the local level compared to parliamentary elections and the patterns are consistent over time (see Table 21.3). First, turnout has been declining since the early 1990s for both types of elections, with a slight increase at the local level in the last election cycle. Second, voter turnout decreased in parallel and in similar magnitude with the previous parliamentary election. Last, there was a significant drop in turnout at the local level in 2013, following the top-down territorial reform that resulted in the amalgamation of over 1,000 parish governments.

All local elections are concurrent. Contests for the municipal executive, municipal council, and parish council take place on the same day, so turnout tends to be similar for all contests. Figure 21.2 depicts voter turnout for local and parliamentary elections in municipalities of different size. The relationship is positive for parliamentary elections, suggesting that turnout increases with the size of the municipality. In contrast, the association is negative for local elections, indicating that smaller municipalities have higher turnout rates than larger ones. The explanation for this apparent paradox is that parliamentary elections tend to focus on national level issues, thus attracting higher electoral participation in larger cities, whereas local elections are primarily concerned with local problems, which are more relevant for smaller jurisdictions (Freire et al. 2012).

The negative relationship between size and turnout in local elections was shown first in an empirical analysis conducted by Freire et al. (2012) for the Portuguese context. Later, Tavares and Carr (2013) also found strong support for this claim, showing that this negative effect is mitigated in municipalities with higher population density. Tavares and Raudla (2018) analyzed the association between voter turnout and parish population size and reached a similar conclusion.

Table 21.2 Parish council and parish executive size in Portugal

Registered voters	Parish council	Registered voters	Parish executive
Under 150	Plenary		
Under 1,000	7		
Between 1,000 and 5,000	9	**Under 5,000**	3
Between 5,000 and 20,000	13	**Between 5,000 and 20,000**	5
Between 20,000 and 30,000	19	**More than 20,000**	7
For each additional 10,000	+1		

Source: National Electoral Commission

Portugal

Table 21.3 Voter turnout (percent) for local and national elections in Portugal since 1990

Local elections		Parliamentary elections	
Election date	Voter turnout (%)	Election date	Voter turnout (%)
17/12/1989		6/10/1991	68.5
12/12/1993	63.4	1/10/1995	67.1
14/12/1997	60.1	10/10/1999	61.8
16/12/2001	60.1	17/02/2002	62.3
9/10/2005	61.0	20/02/2005	65.0
11/10/2009	59.0	27/09/2009	60.6
29/09/2013	52.6	5/6/2011	58.9
1/10/2017	55.0	4/10/2015	57.0
		6/10/2019	51.4

Source: National Electoral Commission and Marktest

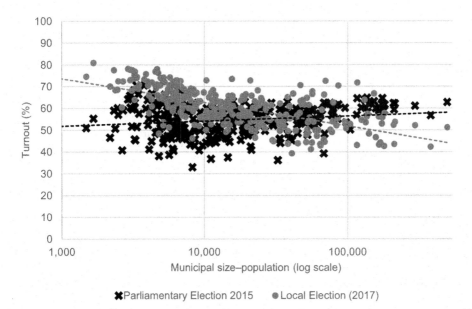

✖ Parliamentary Election 2015   ● Local Election (2017)

Figure 21.2 Voter turnout for local and parliamentary elections in Portugal municipalities of different size

Source: National Electoral Commission

These results in the Portuguese context support an abundant number of empirical studies in the literature showing that voter turnout increases in smaller, local electoral arenas due to the close proximity between voters, issues, and local officials (Cancela & Geys 2016).

The initial effect of the institutional change allowing nonpartisan candidates was small due to campaign finance rules. Elections in Portugal are financed primarily through public funds apportioned to political parties that elect councilors. This represents a substantial barrier to the entry of new candidates (Jalali 2015). Despite these institutional obstacles, the number of independent lists has been growing steadily over the last five election cycles (Freire & Lisi 2015). Their popularity and success are demonstrated by the number of independent candidates elected: 3 mayors in 2001, 7 in 2005 and in 2009, 13 in 2013, and 17 in 2017; 31 municipal councilors in 2001, 45 in 2005, 67 in 2009, 112 in 2013, and 130 in 2017. A total of 396 independent candidates were elected to the 308 municipal assemblies, representing 6.5% of the total number of votes. At the parish level, 3,355 candidates were elected, corresponding to 9.8% (about 500,000 votes) (Comissão Nacional de Eleições, 2017). Moreover, the growth in the number and diversity of candidates resulted in an increase in voter turnout. Tavares et al. (2020) report that an increase of 10% in the ratio of independent lists to the total number of lists has increased turnout for mayoral elections by 0.38% and for parish council elections by 0.33%.

Law no. 46/2005 determines that mayors and parish heads may only be elected for three consecutive terms. Before the law came into effect in 2013, many mayors and parish heads had been serving for many terms, with a few of them having served up to ten consecutive terms. Empirical studies of the impact of this reform upon the regeneration of local political elites, the reduction in the impact of political machines, and the level of electoral competition are still lacking, but there is some evidence that municipalities in which mayors were serving more consecutive terms displayed lower levels of transparency (Tavares & da Cruz 2017). More generally, the introduction of term limits represented an important step toward curbing local political monopolies and improving voter participation (Veiga & Veiga 2018).

Table 21.4 reports the share of all seats in local executive elections that were received by national parties and independent lists in the last election (2017). Three national political parties – Socialists, Social Democrats, and Communists – ran candidates in almost all municipal elections. Christian Democrats compete in about three-fourths of municipalities, either alone or in coalitions with the Social Democrats. Only two parties – Socialists and Social

Table 21.4 Share of all seats on municipal executives received by the main (parliamentary) parties in the last local elections in Portugal, 2017

Parties	(1) % of municipalities where running	(2) % of municipalities where represented	(3) % of seats in the executive branch	(4) % of (aggregate) votes in local elections	(5) % of mayors affiliated with the party
PS (Socialist Party)	97.1	93.8	46.7	39.1	51.9
PSD (Social Democratic Party)	64.6	56.8	24.6	17.5	25.6
PCP (Portuguese Communist Party)	98.4	23.7	8.2	9.5	7.8
CDS-PP (Christian Democrats)	47.7	7.8	2.4	4.0	1.9
BE (Left Bloc)	40.3	3.6	0.6	3.3	0.0
Coalition of PSD and CDS-PP	32.8	27.6	10.7	13.0	6.2
Independent lists	27.0	17.2	6.3	6.8	6.5

Source: National Electoral Commission
Note: Percentages in columns (3) and (4) do not add up 100% due to the exclusion of smaller parties.

Table 21.5 Share of women elected councilors, members of the executive, and mayors in Portugal, 1989–2017

Election year	1989	1993	1997	2001	2005	2009	2013	2017
Councilors	NA	NA	NA	17.3%	21.3%	30.0%	31.7%	34.6%
Executive members	NA	NA	NA	13.6%	18.5%	25.3%	26.6%	29.2%
Mayors	2.0%	1.6%	3.9%	5.2%	6.2%	7.5%	7.5%	10.4%

Source: DGAI
Note: NA = not available.

Democrats – have widespread representation at the local level (at least one seat on the municipal executive). Historically, the two parties have dominated both national elections and the majority of local contests. The Communist Party holds the majority on about two dozen municipal executives at the local level situated in the Alentejo region, often regarded as their stronghold. It is also worth noting the rise in the number of independent candidates (competing in 27% of municipalities) and the proportion of votes received by independent candidates (close to 7%), making them the fourth largest 'party' at the local level.

Table 21.5 displays the share of female councilors, members of the executive, and mayors elected in municipal elections in the period between 1989 and 2017. The proportion of women in municipal assemblies and municipal executives has been growing over time, reaching about one-third of all seats in 2017. This progress was largely due to gender parity laws approved in 2006 and 2017, establishing 33% and 40% mandatory gender quotas, respectively, but they did not translate into the election of a larger proportion of female mayors. Currently, only 32 women are serving as mayors, corresponding to about 10% of the total.

Discussion

Despite the traces of democratic deficit still present, the political culture of Portuguese citizens has evolved toward strengthening political participation, mechanisms for civic representation, and the active exercise of citizenship (Barreto 2000). Local elections have enhanced the opportunities for participation in local public life, and democratic processes have improved significantly. The high number of local elected members per capita – mayors, members of the executive, city councilors, and parish representatives – is one of the most remarkable traits of local democracy in Portugal, and it is no coincidence that the municipalities with the highest number of parish governments are also those with the highest rates of electoral participation and civic activity (Tavares & Carr 2013).

In practice, some obstacles to effective political participation remain. The local electoral system is one of the most disproportional in Europe (Freire 2011), which helps to secure governability at the local level but poses a barrier to the entry of new candidates and parties, with adverse effects on pluralism. Closed lists and campaign financing rules favoring the status quo intensify this further (Jalali 2015).

Despite these aspects, the last decade witnessed significant progress in promoting local democracy and reducing the elitism that has characterized the exercise of local decision-making in the past. The hybrid system mixing partisan and nonpartisan candidates and the introduction of term limits improved turnout rates and contributed to a much-needed generational renewal of local elected officials.

Notes

1 In the case of the parishes, financial autonomy is merely statutory. In substantive terms, they manage very small budgets and are largely dependent on central government transfers.
2 There are 278 municipal governments in continental Portugal and 11 and 19 in the Madeira and Azores archipelagos, respectively.

References

Barreto, A. (2000). *A Situação Social em Portugal, 1960–1999*. Lisboa: Imprensa de Ciências Sociais.
Cancela, J., & Geys, B. (2016). Explaining Voter Turnout: A Meta-Analysis of National and Subnational Elections. *Electoral Studies*, 42, 264–275.
Comissão Nacional de Eleições (2017). Eleições Autárquicas de 2017. Lisboa: Secretaria Geral do Ministério da Administração Interna.
DGO (2018). Conta Geral do Estado. Lisboa: Ministério das Finanças.
Elcock, H. (2008). Elected Mayors: Lesson Drawing from Four Countries. *Public Administration*, 86 (3), 795–811.
Freire, A. (2011). *Eleições e Sistemas Eleitorais no Século XX Português: Uma Perspectiva Histórica e Comparativa*. Lisboa: Colibri.
Freire, A., & Lisi, M. (2015). Reformas Eleitorais Autárquicas (Passadas e Futuras). In: L. de Sousa, A. F. Tavares, N. F. da Cruz, & S. Jorge (Eds). *A Reforma do Poder Local em Debate* (pp. 109–120). Lisboa: Imprensa de Ciências Sociais.
Freire, A., Martins, R., & Meirinho, M. (2012). Electoral Rules, Political Competition and Citizens' Participation in the Portuguese Local Elections, 1979–2009. *Portuguese Journal of Political Science*, 11 (2), 189–208.
Heinelt, H., & Hlepas, N.-K. (2006). Typologies of Local Government Systems. In: H. Bäck, H. Heinelt, & A. Magnier (Eds). *The European Mayor. Political Leaders in the Changing Context of Local Democracy*. Wiesbaden: VS Verlag für Sozialwissenschaften.
Hermens, F. A. (1941). *Democracy or Anarchy? A Study of Proportional Representation*. Notre Dame, IN: University of Notre Dame Press.
Jalali, C. (2015). A Reforma do Sistema Político Local. In: L. de Sousa, A. F. Tavares, N. F. da Cruz, & S. Jorge (Eds). *A Reforma do Poder Local em Debate* (pp. 103–108). Lisboa: Imprensa de Ciências Sociais.
John, P. (2001). *Local Governance in Western Europe*. London, Thousand Oaks, New Delhi: Sage.
Komninos-Hlepas, N., Kerstig, N., Kuhlmann, S., Swianiewicz, P., & Teles, F. (Eds). (2018). *Sub-Municipal Governance in Europe: Decentralization Beyond the Municipal Tier*. Basingstoke, UK: Palgrave Macmillan.
Ladner, A., Keuffer, N., Baldersheim, H., Hlepas, N., Swianiewicz, P., Steyvers, K., & Navarro, C. (2019) *Patterns of Local Autonomy in Europe*. Cham: Palgrave Macmillan.
Lijphart, A. (1990). The Political Consequences of Electoral Laws, 1945–85. *American Political Science Review*, 84 (2), 481–496.
Lima, J. M. M. V. (2004). *Executivos Municipais e Governabilidade: Efeitos do Sistema de Eleitoral na Criação de Condições de Governabilidade nos Executivos Municipais*. Lisboa: Universidade Lusófona de Humanidades e Tecnologias.
Magre, J., & Bertrana, X. (2007). Exploring the Limits of Institutional Change: The Direct Election of Mayors in Western Europe. *Local Government Studies*, 33 (2), 181–194.
Mendes, S., & Camões, P. J. (2008). Party Politics and Local Government Coalition Formation in Portugal. In: D. Giannetti & K. Benoit (Eds). *Intra-party Politics and Coalition Governments in Parliamentary Democracies*. London: Routledge.
Mozzicafreddo, J., Guerra, I., Fernandes, M. A., & Quintela, J. (1988). O Grau Zero do Poder Local. *Sociologia, Problemas e Práticas*, 4, 45–59.
Opello Jr., W. (1981). Local Government and Political Culture in a Portuguese Rural County. *Comparative Politics*, 13 (3), 271–289.
Page, E., & Goldsmith, M. (1987). *Central and Local Government Relation*. Beverly Hills: Sage.

Pereira, A. (1985). *Conhecer as Autarquias Locais*. Porto: Porto Editora.

Pires de Almeida, M. A. (2008a). Party Politics in Portugal: Municipalities and Central Government. *European Societies*, 10 (3), 357–378.

Pires de Almeida, M. A. (2008b). Independents and Citizen's Groups in Portuguese Municipalities. In: M. Reiser & E. Holtmann (Eds). *Farewell to the Party Model? Independent Local Lists in East and West European Countries* (pp. 233–251). Wiesbaden: VS Verlag für Sozialwissenschaften.

Rae, D.W. (1971). *The Political Consequences of Electoral Laws. Revised edition*. New Heaven: Yale University Press.

Tavares, A. F., & Carr, J. B. (2013). So Close, Yet So Far Away? The Effects of City Size, Density, and Growth on Local Civic Participation. *Journal of Urban Affairs*, 35 (3), 283–302.

Tavares, A. F., & da Cruz, N. F. (2017). Explaining the Transparency of Local Government Websites Through a Political Market Framework. *Government Information Quarterly*, 101249.

Tavares, A. F., & Raudla, R. (2018). Size, Density, and Small Scale Elections: A Multi-Level Analysis of Voter Turnout in Sub-Municipal Governments. *Electoral Studies*, 56, 1–13.

Tavares, A. F., Raudla, R., & Silva, T. (2020). Best of Both Worlds? Independent Lists and Voter Turnout in Local Elections. *Journal of Urban Affairs*, 42 (7), 955–974.

Tavares, A. F., & Teles, F. (2017). Deeply Rooted but Still Striving for a Role: The Portuguese Freguesias under Reform. In: N. Komninos-Hlepas, N. Kersting, S. Kuhlmann, P. Swianiewicz, & F. Teles (Eds). *Sub-Municipal Governance in Europe: Decentralization Beyond the Municipal Tier*. Basingstoke, UK: Palgrave Macmillan.

Veiga, F. J., & Veiga, L. G. (2018). Term Limits and Voter Turnout. *Electoral Studies*, 53, 20–28.

22
Spain
One main system to govern them all? Stable institutions in heterogeneous contexts

Carmen Navarro, Lluís Medir, and Jaume Magre

Introduction

The Spanish decentralization model is often classified as a quasi-federal system (Gunther & Montero 2009) in which autonomous communities – governmental units between the central state and local governments – enjoy a high degree of power and resources. Autonomous communities emerged in the Constitution of 1978 to address regional diversity and had not existed during the previous authoritarian period. Local governments complete the multilevel government framework and consist of both municipalities and a provincial meso level.

Municipalities and provinces have existed for almost 200 years, deployed in figures and geographical boundaries similar to those that exist currently. The territorial limits of the 50 provinces were set up in the mid-nineteenth century, and the current figure of 8,124 municipalities does not differ greatly from the around 9,000 that existed at the beginning of the twentieth century. The average size of 5,751 inhabitants per municipality hides great diversity: many municipalities are small (35% have fewer than 250 inhabitants), but there are numerous big cities as well (62 with more than 100,000 inhabitants in which more than one-third of the country's population resides) (Table 22.1). The high level of fragmentation of the Spanish local map makes the role played by provincial governments particularly relevant in assisting small municipalities that depend on them to deliver services. But municipalities are the backbone of the local political system. They are multipurpose governments that deliver services such as garbage collection, transport, and local police, and they are responsible for urban planning, promoting their economies, and trying to meet other citizens' demands thanks to the authority they are granted to complement the action of other levels of government. Unlike legislative representatives in provincial institutions, municipal councilors are directly elected.

Spanish municipalities do not rank high in overall level of autonomy, in a comparative perspective. The Local Autonomy Index ranked them, in 2014, 26th out of 39 countries (Ladner et al. 2019), finding that they had relatively high levels of financial autonomy and noninterference from other levels of government, but medium levels of organizational autonomy and low levels of policy discretion.

Table 22.1 Municipalities and population in Spain, 2018

Population	Municipalities	% municipalities	Aggregate population	% of population
0–100	1,360	16.74	78,080	0.17
101–250	1,476	18.17	244,003	0.52
251–1,000	2,159	26.58	1,137,762	2.44
1,001–2,000	877	10.80	1,245,796	2.67
2,001–5,000	953	11.73	3,005,045	6.43
5,001–10,000	543	6.68	3,804,913	8.14
10,001–20,000	351	4.32	4,946,227	10.59
20,001–50,000	260	3.20	7,688,220	16.45
50,001–100,000	82	1.01	5,884,410	12.59
More than 100,000	63	0.78	18,688,524	40.00
Total	8.124	100.00	46,722,980	100.00

Source: The authors' elaboration from INE information, 2018

Although their share in total government expenditure only amounts to 11% (Eurostat 2020), local governments in Spain have played a key role in the modernization of the country and the consolidation of democracy (Magre et al. 2019). They were the spaces, at the beginning of the democratic transition, where citizens became familiar with a new culture of freedom, elections, and participation in public affairs, and they collaborated decisively in establishing the bases – in services and infrastructure – for economic activity. In the 1980s, local governments implemented policies that provided cities and towns with basic infrastructures, and later, thanks to a long period of economic prosperity around the turn of the twenty-first century, they developed additional services, such as care for the elderly and infants, complementary education policies, and social actions (Navarro & Velasco 2016).

Despite the fragmentation, financial constraints, and medium levels of autonomy, municipal governments have acquired remarkable popularity. When Spaniards are asked about public services in surveys, they tend to express more positive views of local administrations than of regional and national governments. In general, local administrations are considered to be the fastest, the best in terms of treatment of citizens, and the first to provide information (CIS 2007–2013).

The local political system fits into the strong mayor form of local government (Heinelt et al. 2018). Mayors are indirectly elected by councilors, but they have traditionally been remarkably strong figures in local governance, and they work in institutional settings where the executive board is quite influential as well; at the same time, among European countries under the strong mayor model, municipal CEOs are the weakest, and Spanish local councilors are also perceived as relatively weak (Navarro et al. 2018).

Homogeneous and simultaneous elections for all municipalities

The regulation of the local electoral system is largely set forth in Spanish electoral law (Ley 5/1985 *Ley Orgánica del Régimen Electoral General*, LOREG), with some particularities included in the local government law (Ley 7/1985 *Ley Reguladora de las Bases del Régimen Local*, LRBRL). This legislation requires that municipal elections be held on the same day in all of Spain, every four years, across the 8,124 units. Currently, municipal elections are held concurrently with 12 out of 17 regional elections, although that number will tend to decrease in the future. At the beginning of the decentralization process, only four regions (Spain's historic units – Catalonia, Basque Country, Galicia, and Andalucia) were granted autonomy with respect to calling for elections. But when the Statutes of Autonomy (the regional 'constitutional' charters regulating each autonomous community's self-government) went through a wave of reforms beginning in 1996, most of those charters were amended to include the right to call for elections. Valencia and Madrid regions have already made use of their right to dissolve their autonomous communities' parliaments and to call for regional elections. Others will probably follow in the near future.

The call for local elections is automatic because there is a legal mandate that sets a preestablished date (the fourth Sunday in May every four years), except in very exceptional circumstances. Thus, municipal assemblies' configurations arising from the electoral results are maintained throughout the term, for all municipalities.

Provincial elections follow a different path, as provincial assemblies' members are indirectly elected. On the basis of municipal electoral results, candidates are allocated on provincial councils according to the d'Hondt rule of proportional representation. Candidates are municipal councilors proposed by political parties and by other local groups represented in municipal assemblies. The number of members on each provincial council is determined by the population of the province. For example, Seville's has 31 seats and Barcelona has 51. In total, there are 1,040 provincial councilors in Spain as a whole.

There are no legal requirements limiting the concurrence of municipal elections with national and European elections, but it has occurred only three times with the European elections (1987, 1999, and 2019) and never with the national elections. Indeed, a single entity organizes and monitors all elections, the *Junta Electoral Central*, which functions in a decentralized way throughout all of Spain. In sum, Spanish municipalities are subject to very similar contextual conditions.

Mayors play a crucial role in legitimizing the political system in a country with more than 8,000 municipalities. The law does not provide for local recall referenda, but mayors can be recalled from their positions by municipal councils when motions of no confidence are presented and supported by an absolute majority of councilors. In such cases, any councilor (and not, as distinct from the process for appointing mayors after elections, only the first person on the parties' lists) can become mayor. In fact, however, mayors are only recalled very infrequently. The strong mayor model emphasizes the principle of political leadership, personified by the mayor, because the elected mayor controls the majority of the municipality and is, both de jure and de facto, fully in charge of all executive functions (Magre & Pano 2018). Mayors are responsible for executing council decisions and for managing and overseeing the organization of local government operations and staff.

In addition, the entire Spanish intergovernmental system is strongly marked by the political relations among levels of government through political parties (Agranoff 2010). *Cumul des mandats* is allowed, which results in mayors sometimes also being provincial and/or regional MPs. When they also hold such elected positions in higher level assemblies, mayors become particularly powerful political actors.

In this dense multilevel framework, a vast majority of mayors are against mergers and amalgamations, while supporting intermunicipal cooperation as a preferred way to overcome municipal fragmentation and to increase mayors' bargaining power without dissolving local institutions (Medir et al. 2018).

A preeminent proportional system with two minor variations

Local (municipal) elections are regulated by a national law that contains all of the elements of the electoral system and applies to all municipalities in the country. They have, in essence, remained unchanged to the present day. Elections are simultaneous in all municipalities, each municipality, regardless of population size, is a single electoral district, and voters elect a number of councilors that varies with population size (ranging from three in the smallest municipalities to 57 in the largest city, Madrid). Three different electoral systems apply to municipal elections: the first applies to municipalities with over 250 inhabitants, the second to almost all municipalities with populations under 250 inhabitants, and the third, residual one applies only to some municipalities with fewer than 100 inhabitants.

Municipalities with more than 250 inhabitants (about 65% of the total) are subject to what electoral law calls 'common regime', characterized by its similarity to the electoral system applied to the lower chamber of parliament in national elections. Lists are closed and blocked, and the distribution of councilors is determined using the d'Hondt system with a 5% legal threshold (higher than for general elections where the legal threshold is set at 3%). In this proportional system, candidates are grouped in lists (party lists or citizens groups' lists) that are closed and blocked (without the possibility of altering the order of candidates on each list). This system, which encompasses the great majority of the population of Spain, is quite restricted in terms of openness to civil society, as the legal requirements for forming an electoral list – without the umbrella of an established political party – are quite difficult to satisfy.

For municipalities with fewer than 250 inhabitants, electoral law provides two additional electoral system options: an open-list option and a directly elected assembly, very limited in scope. The former applies to all municipalities with fewer than 250 inhabitants (almost 35% of the total) except for those in which the residual system of open council is still in place. It implies the election of the councilors by an open list and preference vote. Each party or group of citizens submits a list of three candidates for municipalities with under 100 inhabitants or of five candidates for those with between 100 and 250 inhabitants. Electors select two (smallest municipalities) or four candidates (the rest) from an open list, and the councils comprise the candidates who received the most votes. Once the council is elected, the 'common regime' rules for electing the mayor apply (the councilor who receives an absolute majority of the councilors' votes is elected mayor). The second option is for those municipalities with fewer than 100 inhabitants that choose it. Under this 'open-council' (*concejo abierto*) system, the mayor is directly elected and electors are members of an assembly that acts as a plenary board. This system used to be more common, but it was restricted by the electoral law reform in 2011 due the management complexity of such an open governance system. Many municipalities that followed the open-council system changed to the open-list system, and currently the open-council system is very uncommon. Although there is no national register of municipalities operating under open-council rules, the data that do exist suggest that those municipalities are in the minority. For instance, in Catalonia, only 6 of the 38 municipalities with fewer than 100 inhabitants function under the open-council system (Medina 2020: 142).

The eligibility rules are quite open for local elections, and they are the same for all three variations: all Spaniards over the age of 18 and registered, non-Spanish EU citizens of the same age residing in Spain who meet the requirements to vote and have expressed their willingness to exercise the right to vote in Spain may cast their votes in local elections. Foreigners residing in Spain whose (non-EU) countries of origin allow Spaniards to vote in their local elections may also vote.[1] These legal provisions add, approximately, 500,000 people to the census of local elections (EU citizens and non-EU citizens combined) and to the voter rolls for national elections. The same eligibility criteria apply for candidates in local elections. However, the electoral system facilitates the presentation of candidatures by the preexisting and registered political parties, while purely independent and local lists need to present a concrete number of signatures, which is determined by population size.

In all of the common regime and the open-list systems, the mayor is elected in the first council session, which is required by law to take place 20 days after the election in all municipalities. In the common regime system, mayors are elected from among the council members heading electoral lists following the LOREG provision. In these systems, an absolute majority of councilors' votes is required to become mayor. However, if a majority is not reached in the first vote, the councilor heading the electoral list with the most popular votes automatically becomes the mayor. The great a larger quest for political stability, an electoral reform in 1999 included the option for mayors without clear governing majorities on their councils to approve annual budgets by means of the rejection of a no confidence motion: if a no confidence vote is rejected by the council (i.e., if it does not gain an absolute majority), the annual budget is approved.

A divided nationalized system

The average participation in the 11 municipal elections that have been held since 1979 stands at 65.8%; in other words, almost two-thirds of the electorate votes in the municipal elections. As Figure 22.1 shows, this percentage has somehow been iterative over the past few years. Indeed, the results of the municipal elections confirm that participation rates are always lower than for general elections: the moments of greatest mobilization have been expressed in the national arena, but this trend is also perceived in local elections. Hence, local turnout shows links to elements exogenous to the local electoral process, particularly to national politics.

It is also clear from Figure 22.1 that the patterns in the evolution of voter turnout in both types of elections are consistently similar, but always with a lower rate for municipal elections.

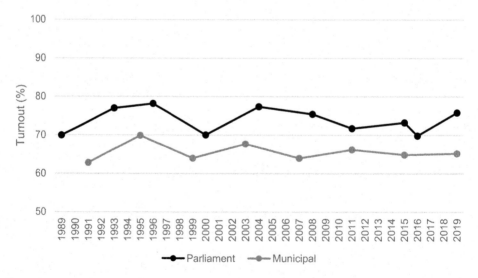

Figure 22.1 Voter turnout for local and national elections in Spain, 1989–2019
Source: The authors' elaboration from official data

In this vein, the higher turnouts at the local level are those linked to the most participatory national elections. The higher rates at the local level appear, with a weaker echo, for local elections following the most participatory national elections. Figure 22.1 shows how the two lines diverged only recently, when Spaniards went to the polls in large numbers for the April 2019 general elections, while their turnout for the May local elections remained stable. This broader gap could be the effect of the territorial and left-right polarization in general elections, which boosted participation (Simón 2020).

However, this pattern does not work in the same way in all municipalities. On the contrary, the structural pattern of turnout observed for every election is that of an inverse relationship between population size and voter turnout: small municipalities generally vote far more than urban municipalities with larger populations (Figure 22.2). In other words, the existence of more participative local elections shown in figure 22.1 is due to the greater 'sensitivity' to the cyclical phenomena coming from larger urban electorates, while rural ones are more stable and less dependent on the national context.

Large urban agglomerations and medium-large municipalities are, in Spain, far more dependent on mass media to analyze local (and nonlocal) politics than small and rural localities, where citizens engage in more personal and direct relations with political networks and local elected politicians. This informational and relational gap fosters greater influence of the conjuncture factors on the behavior of the former and greater stability in the latter. A complementary explanation for this turnout gap is the different level of politicization and, therefore, the different ideological content attributed to the same political conflicts (Kelleher & Lowery 2004). In any case, in 80% of all municipalities, citizens tend to participate significantly more in local elections (Magre and Delgado 2020).

Concerning the level of nationalization of local elections, the dominance of candidacies associated with national parties is absolutely clear. National parties perform as the main drivers of the nationalization of local politics, as is shown in Table 22.2 and as Eisenstadt and Rokkan (1973) remind us. The widespread presence of national parties at the local level means that, in more

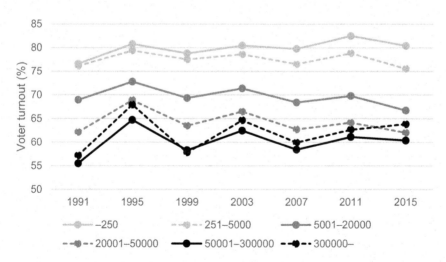

Figure 22.2 Average voter turnout for local elections in Spain by population tranches, 1990–2015

Source: The authors' elaboration from official data

Table 22.2 Councilors from national parties in Spanish local elections, 1991–2019 (percent of municipalities)

	1991	1995	1999	2003	2007	2011	2015
PP (Partido Popular)	53.3	58.6	57.7	55.7	54.2	55.7	52.0
PSOE (Partido Socialista Obrero Español)	61.5	58.4	58.3	59.8	60.4	58.0	53.5
IU (Izquierda Unida)/ Podemos	18.5	17.9	13.8	13.8	14.0	13.8	14.6
Ciudadanos					0.1	0.1	8.0
Others	51.0	44.8	46.3	46.8	49.6	47.7	46.1

Source: The authors' elaboration from official data

than 60% of municipalities, at least one candidate from a national party wins a seat on the council. But, in the case of the historical communities, both Catalonia and the Basque Country, and to a much lesser extent Galicia, have a different party system from the rest of the Spanish regions, and the same pattern is replicated in all elections, at the local, regional and national levels.

In this competitive structure, some space does remain for independent lists as well. Although they are a minority phenomenon, independent lists also have their place in Spain's municipal elections. Over the last 30 years, an average of around 1,200 independent candidates' lists have achieved representation on municipal councils (Figure 22.3). This figure reached a maximum of 1,283 independent lists in 1995, dropped to 1,086 in 1999, and increased again in 2007 (Martínez Fernández 2020).

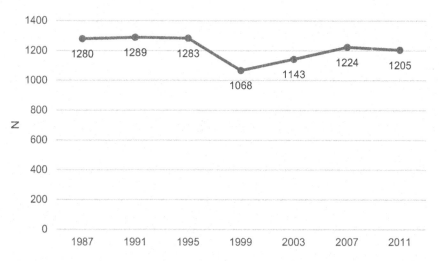

Figure 22.3 Total number of independent lists with representation on councils in Spain, by election year

Source: The authors' elaboration from Martínez Fernández (2020)

The territorial dominance of national parties has, logically, a direct impact on electoral outcomes. The concentration index – the sum of the votes received by the most important parties at the national level, PSOE and PP – in local elections shows that the percentage of votes for these parties in all elections represents at least two-thirds of the ballots cast. The only exception was in 2015, when two new, nationwide parties appeared in the national arena, Ciudadanos and Podemos, which strongly affected the two-party system that had operated in Spain since 1980. In 2015, the results for PP and PSOE fell abruptly, especially in larger municipalities. In line with the previous explanation, larger cities in Spain show a greater tendency toward political change than small municipalities, which tend to be far more stable. Therefore, changes in the party system are primarily expressed in more populous cities, rather than in less populated cities. This resistance to change in smaller municipalities is fundamentally explained, together with the idiosyncratic nature of the smaller municipalities, by the strict criteria of the electoral code for building candidatures out of political parties and by the difficulties new parties face in reaching a territorial presence that is strong enough to fulfill the legal requirements for presenting candidatures in most localities.

The general description outlined previously requires more nuance if the historical regions of Spain (Basque Country, Catalonia, and Galicia) are considered. Those historical regions have a particular party system, in which nationalist and/or regionalist parties are much stronger on a local basis. Table 22.3 presents the share of votes for each national party and the aggregate percentages of major nationalist and regionalist parties, solely in the four historical regions.

Therefore, the first main pattern of local electoral behavior in Spain is that it is partially subordinate to a general framework dominated by national elections (*Congreso de los Diputados*). The general elections create a powerful political frame that affects citizens' perceptions and strategies, mainly of the national parties when they compete in the local arena. However, this nationalization is complicated by contextual factors such as local government size.

Concerning the institutional effects of the local electoral system, the main distinctive feature is that the system allows for the regular election of almost 70,000 councilors and more than 8,000 mayors; Spain has more local elected officials than many European countries. Moreover, almost 70% of those elected officials belong to the main nationwide parties. That is to say, seven out of ten councilors are either from the Partido Popular (PP) or the Partido Socialista (PSOE). This is a strong indicator of the degree of nationalization of the local elections. However, although in the last two elections the two main national parties received two-thirds of the votes cast (Table 22.4), that figure was lower than in previous elections due to the emergence of two

Table 22.3 Percent of votes for national political parties in local elections in historical regions of Spain, 1991–2019 (Catalunya, Galicia, Euskadi)

	1991	1995	1999	2003	2007	2011	2015
PP	16.2	22.4	22.2	21.3	20.3	22.8	15.5
PSOE/PSC	33.2	28.6	30.7	30.6	30.5	24.4	19.3
IU/IC/Podemos	6.0	8.8	6.3	7.6	6.8	5.9	9.6
Nationalists[1]	31.2	31.7	33.9	33.7	32.7	33.6	35.6
Others	13.4	8.4	6.8	6.9	9.7	13.3	20.0

[1] Catalunya, Convergència Democràtica; Junts per Catalunya, Esquerra Republicana de Catalunya; Galicia, Bloque Nacionalista Galego; Euskadi, Partido Nacionalista Vasco.
Source: The authors' elaboration from official data

Table 22.4 Percent of councilors by political party in Spain, 1991–2019

	1991	1995	1999	2003	2007	2011	2015	2019
PP	29.1	37.6	37.8	36.0	35.3	38.8	33.7	30.4
PSOE	38.1	32.2	33.6	35.4	36.3	31.9	30.9	33.4
Others	32.8	30.2	28.6	28.5	28.4	29.2	35.4	36.2

Source: The authors' elaboration from official data

new statewide parties (Podemos and Ciudadanos). Therefore, in the local arena, the decline of the national bipartisan system is more complicated and less evident.

This basic description of the electoral outcomes of the Spanish local electoral system can be complemented by two additional factors. First, the important number of municipalities that are governed by a single-party executive with the support of an absolute majority of the councilors: in the 2019 elections, this was the case for 6,568 municipalities (or 80.8%) in Spain (Magre & Delgado 2020). Second, the data on the reelection of incumbent mayors show that 70% of mayors elected in 2019 had already served one or more terms in office. Only in the most populated cities, those with over 100,000 inhabitants, was the percentage of change of incumbent mayors lower: 'only' 40% of incumbents were reelected. The combination of these two aspects of the electoral outcomes clearly indicates a stable system at the local level.

Finally, concerning the presence of women as local candidates and on councils, it should be noted that, in 2007, a national law established gender quotas.[2] This law requires a balanced mix of candidates, establishing an obligation for political parties to ensure that every list for every election includes at least 40% women. The law incorporates effective sanctions and is structured to ensure that women are not systematically allocated unwinnable places at the bottom of the lists, as the 40% quota applies not only to the list as a whole but also to each group of five candidates. This explains the steady increase in the number of women elected as local councilors, who in 2019 represented 35.6%. However, the effect on mayoral elections has been much more limited: only around 20% of mayors are women, without showing a clear pattern of increase since the law was passed.

Conclusions

With the arrival of the new democracy in 1978, policymakers' concerns regarding municipal matters were to prevent the local arena from becoming a focus of political destabilization, as it had been during the second Republic, and also to avoid *caciquismo* (political strongmen at the apex of local governments). Therefore, despite the strict proportionality of the electoral system and the parliamentary logic of local councils for decision-making and for the election of mayors, the design and functioning of the electoral system have tended to produce very stable institutions.

The electoral code has been changed several times to adjust it to specific circumstances (i.e., extending the right to vote to non-Spanish EU citizens residing in Spain). But none of the adjustments has imposed a major revision of the local electoral provisions. Over the years, initiatives for reforming those provisions' main structure have been rare and limited to a timid proposal by the Socialist Party to introduce the system of directly elected mayors and another by the Popular Party to include a majority bonus for the list receiving the most popular votes. Neither proposal has reached the phase of parliamentary debate. The model that emerged in the late 1970s has enjoyed remarkable stability for over four decades. Its resemblance to the national system, together with the strong presence of national parties at the local level, has produced a very stable general electoral picture.

The main outcomes of the local electoral system are steady and continuous institutions: the configuration of a strong mayor model, regardless of the indirect and proportional electoral system; the opportunity to hold regional and other local mandates along with the mayoralty; the relatively high threshold for obtaining representation; the practical nonexistence of successful motions of no confidence; the fact that mayors are frequently reelected (which produces a combination of the coexistence of new elites with some degree of seniority at the apex of the local institutions); and the high degree of nationalization of the party system and the vast territorial presence of national parties.

Indeed, the national two-party system holds together much better at the local level. The new nationwide parties (Podemos, Ciudadanos, Vox) lack the presence and party structure at the municipal level that the two older parties have, which results in difficulties with presenting lists and candidatures that are sufficiently competitive, particularly in medium and small municipalities. As the years progress, the new nationwide parties may succeed in settling in at the local level. They have done so at the regional level, where some of them are part of governmental coalitions. But to spread throughout more than 8,000 municipalities is a much more challenging task.

Finally, municipal size is a variable that must be taken into account to complete one's understanding of the whole system. The overall picture of municipal elections and their outcomes is mainly driven by the existence of more than 6,000 municipalities with fewer than 10,000 inhabitants. However, for larger cities, most of the stable elements of the overall system do not hold in the same proportion. In fact, the Spanish local electoral system should probably be analyzed using two different frameworks: larger cities are more dependent on the national cycle, are more reflective of the national mood in terms of political parties and national discourse, and are characterized by lower voter turnout. The smallest local authorities, for their part, have turnout rates that are permanently higher regardless of the main electoral cycle; in those authorities, national parties are better able to resist the competition of newcomers, and communitarian ties are dominant. One main system does not govern them all.

Notes

1 Currently: Bolivia, Cape Verde, Chile, Colombia, South Korea, Ecuador, Iceland, Norway, New Zealand, Paraguay, Peru, and Trinidad and Tobago.
2 Ley Orgánica 3/2007, de 22 de marzo, para la igualdad efectiva de mujeres y hombres.

References

Agranoff, R. (2010). *Local governments and their intergovernmental networks in federalizing Spain*. Montreal: McGill-Queen's Press.
Centro de Investigaciones Sociológicas. (2007–2013). *Calidad de los Servicios públicos* Estudios: 2706, 2762, 2813, 2840, 2908, 2950, 2986. www.cis.es.
Eisenstadt, S. & Rokkan, S. (1973). *Building states and nations*. London: Sage Publications.
Eurostat (2020). Government finance statistics: Revenue and expenditure by subsector of general government. https://ec.europa.eu/eurostat/statistics-explained/index.php?title=Archive:Government_finance_statistics_-_revenue_and_expenditure_by_subsector_of_general_government&direction=next&oldid=464300#Share_of_subsectors_in_general_government_total_revenue_and_total_expenditure.
Gunther, R. & J. R Montero (2009) *The politics of Spain*. Cambridge: Cambridge University Press.
Heinelt, H., Magnier, A., Cabria, M. & Reynaert, H. (2018). Political leaders and changing local democracy. In: *The European mayor*. Basingstoke: Palgrave Macmillan.

Kelleher, C. & Lowery, D. (2004). Political participation and metropolitan institutional contexts. *Urban Affairs Review*, *39*(6), 720–757.

Ladner, A., Keuffer, N., Baldersheim, H., Hlepas, N., Swianiewicz, P., Steyvers, K. & Navarro, C. (2019). *Patterns of local autonomy in Europe*. Basingstoke: Palgrave Macmillan.

Magre, J. & Delgado, I. (2020). Las elecciones municipales de 2019 en España. In: T. Font & A. Galan (Eds). *Anuario de Gobierno Local 2019*. Barcelona: Institut de Dret Públic, Fundación Democracia y Gobierno Local.

Magre, J., Navarro, C. & Zafra, M. (2019). El gobierno local en España. In: J. Montabes & A. Martínez (Eds). *Gobierno y política en España* (pp. 713–740). Tirant lo Blanch.

Magre, J. & Pano, E. (2018). The architecture of the local political community: France, Italy, Portugal and Spain. In: R. Kerley, J. Liddle, & P.T. Dunning (Eds). *The Routledge handbook of international local government* (pp. 418–432). London: Routledge.

Martínez Fernández, J.B. (2020) Los partidos de ámbito local en España, entre la vieja política y el nuevo municipalismo (1987–2011). Doctoral Thesis, University of Murcia.

Medina, L. (Ed). (2020) *Anuari Polític de Catalunya 2019*. Barcelona: Institut de Ciencies Polítiques i Socials. www.icps.cat/archivos/APC/anuari-2019.pdf?noga=1 last accessed 12.12.2020.

Medir, L., Magre, J. & Tomàs, M. (2018). Mayors' perceptions on local government reforms and decentralization in Spain. *Revista Española de Ciencia Política*, *46*, 129–115.

Navarro, C., Karlsson, D., Magre, J. & Reinholde, I. (2018). Mayors in the town hall: Patterns of relations and conflict among municipal actors. In: H. Heinelt, A. Magnier, M. Cabria, & H. Reynaert (Eds). *Political leaders and changing local democracy* (pp. 359–385). Basingstoke: Palgrave Macmillan.

Navarro, C. & Velasco, F. (2016). "In wealth and in poverty?" The changing role of Spanish municipalities in implementing childcare policies. *International Review of Administrative Sciences*, *82*(2), 315–334.

Simón, P. (2020). The multiple Spanish elections of April and May 2019: The impact of territorial and left-right polarisation. *South European Society and Politics*, 1–34.

Part 6
New democracies
The Central and Eastern European States

23
Czech Republic
Local elections in a fragmented municipal system

Petr Voda

The local government system

Governance in the Czech Republic is carried out on three levels: the state, the regions, and the municipalities. The regional level was reorganized in 2000 when regions were changed from purely administrative units to self-governing ones and their number was increased from eight to 14. The self-governance of municipalities was introduced in 1990. A massive wave of municipal splits followed this change, and the number of municipalities increased from 4,100 in 1990 to 6,258 in 2019 (CZSO 2020). Some municipalities, so-called statutory cities, may establish submunicipal units – city districts or city parts – which serve as quasi-municipalities with a limited range of independent and transferred responsibilities (Lysek 2016). However, this currently applies to only eight cities nationwide, forming 140 submunicipal units.

The number of municipalities, in combination with the population of the Czech Republic of approximately 10 million inhabitants, indicates the highly fragmented nature of the Czech local system of government, comparable within the EU with only France and Slovakia (Ladner et al. 2019). However, municipal sizes range from a dozen people to more than 1 million, with an average size of about 1,700 inhabitants (86% municipalities are smaller than the average), making municipality size an even more important explanatory variable in the Czech context than in systems where all municipalities have relatively similarly sized populations.

Given the fact that the Czech Republic is a new democracy, it does not fit very well into the South vs. North typology of intergovernmental relations. Baldersheim et al. (1996) claim that the Czech system has more in common with Northern than Southern Europe. The municipal tier is very fragmented territorially. The Czech Republic occupies an intermediate position in rankings of local autonomy, whereas the extent of autonomy on different dimensions varies significantly. While the country scores high on organizational autonomy, legal protection, institutional depth, policy autonomy, and some features of financial and fiscal matters, local autonomy is rather low for policy scope and administrative supervision (Ladner et al. 2019). As Ladner et al. (2019) point out, in the Czech Republic local government has few functions but much freedom of decision-making concerning these functions. According to the law, municipalities have their own independent competences and competences transferred by the state. For its own competences, municipalities may impose decrees, dispose with municipal ownership, prepare and carry out a municipal budget, create and dissolve municipal organizations (e.g., municipal police, waste management, culture, sport, technical support), appoint members to the supervisory boards of organizations at least partially owned by the municipality, deal with several legal and financial issues, and make decisions about the functions of councilors and aldermen, the names of streets, and cooperation with other municipalities. Moreover, some municipalities (centers of microregions) have further competences delegated from state.

Intragovernmental relations can be described as collective (Heinelt et al. 2018). Similar to other countries, the collective tradition is part of a wider consensual mode of local democracy, including proportional representation and multiparty systems. Members of the executive (aldermen, the mayor, and vice mayors) are elected by the council from among themselves, and they can be removed from office by a council vote on individual aldermen or the board of councilors as a whole. The number of aldermen must be an odd number between five and 11, but cannot exceed one-third the total number of councilors. Those elected to executive positions remain on the council. Aldermen are elected only in municipalities with more than 15 councilors. The mayor is indirectly elected at the first session of a new council after the election. If a new mayor is not elected, the former mayor remains in the position until a new mayor is elected, even if he or she is not part of the council – but this is a very rare event (Kopecký & Zach 2019). Formally, according to law, the mayor is only the first among equals. In terms of horizontal power relations, the position of mayor indicates a monistic system (Wollmann 2004) or the collective form (Mouritzen & Svara 2002). In practice, portfolio allocation to aldermen within the confines of the local governmental agreement occurs and it is thus part of coalition deals, especially in cities. Equally, more presidential tendencies for the mayoralty can be discerned. At some point in national politics, it was part of coalition agreement of the Nečas government (2010–2013) to introduce the direct election of mayors into the political system. However, this intention was not carried out, probably because the change required a qualified majority in parliament (Vláda 2011).

Unfortunately, there are no data indicating the relative importance of institutions on different levels, but we have several indices produced by evaluations of some aspects of local politics. First, public opinion agencies ask about the importance of elections; the results show that local elections are seen as just as important as presidential and parliamentary contests, with about 85% of citizens stating that these elections are very or rather important (STEM 2014). The least important are senate and European elections, with only about 50% of citizens stating that they are important. Second, data about relations to different geographical levels – including municipalities – show that citizens feel themselves most closely attached to local units (CVVM 2015).

The electoral cycle and local referenda

Local elections in the Czech Republic are held every four years on a Friday and Saturday in the autumn. Voters may cast their ballots on one of these days and they may do so only in person. The rules for announcing elections do not allow elections exactly every four years; therefore, each new term begins one week earlier than the previous one. Thus, the first local elections after 1989 took place on 24 November, while the most recent fell on 5 and 6 October 2018. Local elections, as all others in the Czech Republic, are organized by the Ministry of the Interior in collaboration with the Czech Statistical Office, and the same electoral code applies throughout the country.

The fixed term of office is four years and is thus the same as that for regional elected officeholders and members of the lower chamber of parliament (Chamber of Deputies). These elections are always organized on different dates. The length of mandate differs from that of the president (five years), senators (six years – with one-third of seats up for election every two years), and the European Parliament (five years). Elections for president and the EP occur at different times of the year, but since 1998 one of two rounds of senate elections has coincided with the local elections.

The temporal and systemic aspects of local elections strongly undermine their possible signaling function for other levels of governance. From 1998 to 2010, local elections were held just a few months after the parliamentary elections. Moreover, parliamentary parties participate in only a minority of municipalities (see discussion to follow), and different numbers of votes in different municipalities make the assessment of national performance in these elections a difficult task.

Although there is an ongoing debate about introducing direct elections for mayors (Jüptner 2009, 2012), currently only the members of the municipal council are directly elected. The mayor and aldermen are elected indirectly. The same concept is applied at the regional level. The mayor takes the position when he or she is elected, without any formal appointment. Similar to other countries with indirectly elected mayors, the designation of the mayoralty is part of the process of majority formation. It is usually assigned to the largest party (in terms of seats) in the majority (most often a coalition of parties) and to the candidate who is the front runner. Although legally the position of mayor is not strong, the mayor can be a key person in some aspects of local governance, for example, in investment projects or in promoting the municipal development agenda (Čopík et al. 2019). However, in smaller municipalities in particular, the choice of mayor depends on the willingness of candidates to take the position, because in numerous municipalities it is not a full-time position and therefore not accompanied by a full-time salary (Ryšavý & Bernard 2013).

In the Czech Republic, mechanisms of direct democracy are present on the local level. A law on local referendums was introduced in 1992, and the first referendum was held in 2000 (Smith 2011). There are three circumstances in which a referendum can be held. First, if there is a plan to divide the municipality, a referendum is obligatory. In the case of part of a municipality seceding, only the inhabitants of the affected area may take part. Second, a referendum may be organized in the case of municipalities merging and the case of the creation or dissolution of a city part. However, if the referendum is not held, then the councils of the affected municipalities decide. Third, a council can decide to hold a local referendum on any issue relating to municipal self-governance, except for local fees and budget, local internal institutions (including the mayor – thus, recall referenda are not allowed), local directives, and personal appointments to executive offices, and the referendum question cannot conflict with other laws and must allow only a yes or no answer.

A referendum can be initiated by the council or by citizens of the municipality through a preparation committee. For the latter option, the referendum proposal must be supported by a list of signatures of inhabitants. The required minimum number of signatures varies from 30% of registered inhabitants in municipalities with fewer than 3,000 inhabitants to 6% in cities with more than 200,000 inhabitants. Since 2006, when referenda were first officially monitored, almost 300 referenda have been organized (Ministry of the Interior 2020). Local referenda are also the subject of numerous studies (e.g., Nový 2016; Jüptner et al. 2014)

The local electoral system

According to electoral law, almost the same conditions exist for active (vote) and passive (candidate) rights. However, these rights, and especially access to them, differ between citizens of the Czech Republic, the EU, and other foreign countries. The criteria to vote for Czech citizens include being of age 18 or above, maintaining permanent residency in the municipality, not being imprisoned for a crime, and not being on a foreign mission as a soldier. For EU citizens, the same rules apply, but registration to vote is not automatic and has to be done at the municipal office. Citizens of non-EU countries are not allowed to vote or to stand as candidates.

For candidacy, the conditions are almost the same. However, the function of councilor is incompatible with employment by the same municipality if the employee's duties include carrying out state administrative tasks related to the municipality or if the employee is appointed by the mayor. There is no limitation regarding other levels of politics, and local councilors, aldermen, and mayors are often represented at the regional and national levels. Hájek (2017) found that more than half of MPs during the electoral term of 2010–2013 were simultaneously local councilors, and one-quarter held positions as aldermen or mayor.

The number of councilors to be elected is determined by law and by a decision made by the municipal council. The law sets the boundaries for the minimum and maximum number of councilors for each municipality, and the municipal council may then itself decide the number for the next term from within this interval. Usually the number is odd; fewer than 1% of municipalities have an even number of councilors. The minimum number of seats is five and the maximum is 65, but theoretically it can be 75. During the last local elections of 2018, a total of 59,331 municipal councilors and 2,561 councilors of submunicipal units within statutory cities were elected.

The system for local elections is uniform throughout the country, regardless of the size of the municipality. The system is proportional, and formally it is an open-list system. However, the system does not actually function as such, because it is not possible for the voters to affect the order of candidates within the parties. Lists have to be submitted formally to the municipal office with extended authority by the front-running candidate or another designated candidate at least 66 days before the election. If the list is submitted by a party or political organization registered with the Ministry of the Interior, there is no need to demonstrate support for the list. If the candidacy is submitted by an independent candidate, the law sets a minimum requirement for the percentage of local voter signatures needed, decreasing with the number of inhabitants of the municipality. The percentage decreases from 5% in municipalities with fewer than 500 inhabitants to 0.5% in municipalities with over 15,000 inhabitants. For a group of candidates, the signatures of 7% of voters are needed regardless of the size of the municipality. Each list has a rank order of candidates (decided by those submitting it for election).

The council can decide whether the municipality will be divided into electoral districts. However, the minimum number of electoral districts in differently sized municipalities is set by law, and it ranges from five to nine depending on the size of the municipality. If the municipality is divided into districts, a party must submit a different list for each district. In practice, districts are created only as an exception. This possibility was used regularly in Prague, but it was seen as an attempt to increase the natural threshold (Charvát 2011). In municipalities where at least eight councilors are elected, the number of candidates on each list can be any number equal to the number of council seats to be filled or fewer. In municipalities where seven or fewer councilors are elected, the list can be longer by one-third (e.g., eight candidates in a municipality with six mandates).

The ballot structure offers three ways to cast a valid vote. First, a voter can vote across the board for one party, making a cross in the field next to the party name (big cross option). In this case, the party receives the number of votes equal to the number of mandates (or the number of candidates written on the list, if the list is not full). Second, a voter can choose individual candidates from different parties, marking a maximum number of candidates equal to the number of mandates (personal vote option). Third, a voter can combine the first two ways of voting, but this is not valid if the voter chooses individual candidates from the party chosen with the big cross option. Therefore, although the system seems to allow personalized voting, it does not allow voters to give preferential votes to candidates from the selected party. The misleading character of this system has been discussed in the literature (Lebeda 2009).

The reporting of electoral results does not reveal how the lists were filled; thus, we have no exact numbers regarding the popularity of different ways of voting. Balík et al. (2015) estimate that the proportion of voters voting for individual candidates is only about 10% of all votes cast, and the proportion decreases from small to large municipalities. The pattern according to size was also found by Voda et al. (2018) in data based on exit polls. However, their results suggest that up to 50% of voters in cities with around 20,000 inhabitants cast personal votes, whereas in Brno, with about 350,000 inhabitants, only about 30% did so. This suggests that voting for individual candidates is rather rare, because the physical size of the paper ballot and the need to mark a large number of votes takes time and is risky, because it can easily lead to mistakes, making the ballot invalid. According to Voda et al. (2018), it seems that personal voting is mostly used to split one's vote among ideologically similar parties.

With the use of a proportional electoral formula, votes are transformed into seats distributed among the parties winning at least 5% of valid votes through the *d'Hondt* method, which is also used in other elections in the Czech Republic. After the number of seats won are allotted to each list, they are then designated to certain candidates. In this step, personal votes can be decisive. For this purpose, the candidate must obtain 10% more than the average number of votes for candidates on the list. Therefore, all of the votes for individual candidates are summed and divided by the number of candidates. This number is divided by 100 and multiplied by 110. Candidates with higher numbers of votes move to the top of the list. Particularly in municipalities with a high number of seats, changes in position are not very likely. For example, in the three biggest cities, only five of 165 councilors won seats while occupying seemingly ineligible places on their lists. The procedure thus favors candidates with higher list positions.

The results of the elections

Figure 23.1 compares percentages in turnout for local and national elections since 1990. As in other countries of the former Communist bloc, that year has particular meaning for the revitalization of democratic institutions. Therefore, electoral turnout was very high in 1990 for both parliamentary and local elections, although it was about 20% lower in the case of local elections compared to national. Turnout dropped through the 1990s for both national and local elections. However, the decrease for local elections has been faster, resulting in a difference between turnout for local and parliamentary elections of almost 30%. Second, turnout for both levels of elections follows a rather similar path over time. Since the beginning of the 2000s, the turnout for local elections has stabilized at 45–50% and around 60% for elections to the Chamber of Deputies. In 2000, regional elections were introduced. This turnout is usually about 10% lower than that for local elections.

Table 23.1 disaggregates the turnout percentages for the most recent local elections by municipality size. Table 23.1 shows the steep decrease from the smallest municipalities, where turnout is about 65% on average, to relatively large cities (37%) with 50,000–150,000 inhabitants, most of which are regional centers. The turnout is over 40% in the four largest cities – Prague, Brno, Ostrava, and Plzeň.

Given the large number of municipalities and the varying degrees of electoral competition in them, it is almost impossible to describe the level of competitiveness in general. On the one hand, there are municipalities in which the number of candidates is equal to the number of

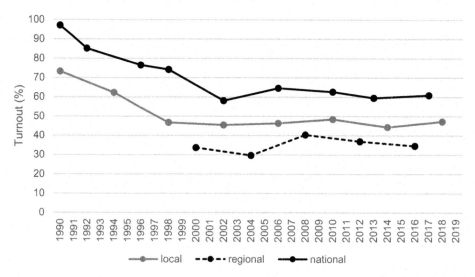

Figure 23.1 Voter turnout for national, regional, and local elections in the Czech Republic, 1990–2018

available seats, and in each election, there are several municipalities in which elections are not held due to the low number of candidates. In the last elections, there were 1,616 municipalities (25% of the total number) where voters could only vote for one list. Although there is no real competition in such municipalities, elections are still held there. On the other hand, in numerous municipalities the number of candidates exceeds the number of mandates by many multiples. From the perspective of participation, even a low number of candidates in small municipalities implies significant involvement by citizens in local democracy (Voda et al. 2017). However, local politics do not reflect the national party landscape, especially in small municipalities.

As Table 23.2 illustrates, parties with their roots in the period before 1989 (actually even before 1939) have been able to run in a relatively high portion of municipalities. The Christian Democratic Party (KDU-ČSL) has its own list in almost 17% of municipalities, and in an additional 4% it runs candidates as members of coalitions. The electoral system forces parties, if they do not have a sufficient number of candidates, to form coalitions, because presenting a full list has clear advantages over putting forward an incomplete one. Taking into account the small size of municipalities and the rather personalized character of local politics in the Czech Republic, the preelectoral coalitions are almost a natural kind of electoral strategy. Similarly, the Communist Party runs both individually and in coalition in 17.5% of municipalities, and the Social Democratic Party does so in almost 15%. Among the parties established after 1989, only Občanská demokratická strana (ODS) and Starostové a nezávislí (STAN) are able to run candidates in at least 10% of local elections. However, STAN is rather special because it is based on cooperation between independent mayors and local lists.

In contrast, relatively new parties – which have been labeled entrepreneur parties (Hloušek et al. 2020) – run in a smaller fraction of municipalities, which probably reflects their lack of members and poor presence on the local level (in the case of SPD, this is in combination with their position to the far right on the political spectrum), which also prevents them from forming coalitions. Therefore, ANO, despite being the strongest party on the national level, submits

Table 23.1 Turnout in 2018 Czech local elections by size of municipality

Size category (# of inhabitants)	Turnout in 2018 elections (%)
<500	63.2
501–3,000	55.7
3,001–10,000	47.5
10,001–50,000	40.0
50,001–150,000	37.4
>150,000	43.3
Total	47.3

Table 23.2 Participation and performance of families of lists in local elections in the Czech Republic, 2018

	% of municipalities where running	% of municipalities where represented	% of votes in local elections	% of seats on local councils	% of mayors affiliated with the party
ANO	5.5	5.4	14.8	2.3	1.1
ČSSD	12.8	10.4	5.6	3.3	2.4
KDU-ČSL	19.9	18.5	6.0	6.4	4.0
KSČM	15.9	12.5	5.1	2.5	0.9
Pirates	1.3	1.1	7.7	0.3	0.0
ODS	11.9	11.3	13.2	4.0	2.5
SPD	2.7	1.5	3.3	0.2	
STAN	13.4	12.8	10.0	6.4	2.9
TOP 09	4.1	3.3	7.4	1.1	0.2
Independent	89.9	89.3	19.1	69.2	78.5
Others	12.3	9.4	17.5	5.4	7.5

Note: 'Others' includes nonparliamentary subjects registered as parties or movements. The sum of votes and seats is over 100% because the gains of coalitions are counted for each party in the coalition. Abbreviations: KSČM, Communist Party of Bohemia and Moravia; KDU-ČSL, Christian Democratic Union-Czechoslovak Peoples Party; ČSSD, Czech Social Democratic Party; ODS, Civic Democratic Party; ANO 2011, Yes Movement; STAN, Mayors and Independents; SPD, Freedom and Direct Democracy; Pirates, Czech Pirate Party. TOP 09 is a name, not an abbreviation.

lists in only 7.5% of municipalities and SPD does so in fewer than 5%. Given the statistics about the representation of parliamentary political parties, it is obvious that independent and local lists play a key role in local politics in the Czech Republic, as they run in almost all municipalities and occupy 70% of the seats on local councils.

The mean number of lists, including lists of independent candidates, in the most recent local elections reached four. This number is not exceeded in almost 4,500 municipalities, which means that in most municipalities the electoral competition, and consequently local councils, does not experience a high level of fragmentation. As is shown by the low penetration of national political parties in local politics, local governments are, in general, not very politicized.

Table 23.2 also includes the proportion of votes. This information does not represent the overall support for the party nationwide, due to the nature of the electoral system. Each voter casts a number of votes equal to the number of mandates; thus, every person in Prague counts 65 times, whereas every person in a small village counts only five times. This mechanism leads

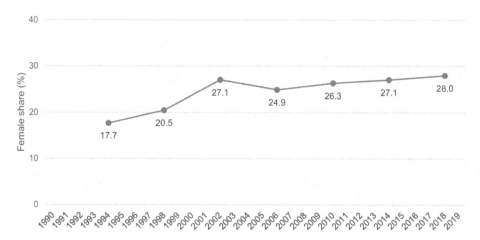

Figure 23.2 Women's representation among councilors in the Czech Republic, 1990–2018

to a high share of votes for parties like ANO, ODS, and the Pirate Party, which are successful in big cities, even though these parties win a much lower proportion of mandates overall than KDU-ČSL. The latter wins a lower total number of votes, but it is hard to estimate whether this means the party was supported by a smaller number of voters.

Parliamentary parties are not the most important actors. The vast majority of mayors were elected to local councils on independent lists (65%) or as individual independent candidates (15%). Only 15% of municipalities have a who was mayor elected on the list of a parliamentary party. This is relatively tricky to parse because of the partisans on independent lists. For example, there was no mayor elected from among the candidates on the lists of SPD, but there are two mayors affiliated with this party who were elected on independent lists. At the same time, not all mayors elected on party lists are members of their nominating parties, because parties can nominate candidates without party affiliation.

The legal framework does not contain any sort of gender quota for any type of election. Some parties have their own internal rules, but these are not applied on the local level. The Social Democratic Party, until 2018, had a rule that at least 40% of candidates had to be of a different gender than the rest of the list, but for local elections this rule was understood to be only a recommendation. Despite these conditions, female representation has seen a rising trend over the past 30 years. Figure 23.2 indicates the share of female councilors in the Czech Republic since 1994. The increase was especially significant between the 1994 and the 2002 elections, when the representation of women increased by 10%. After a drop in 2006, the proportion has again been slowly but steadily rising, and in the last elections female representation reached nearly 30%. Compared to other levels of governance, the representation of women is highest on the local level. After the 2018 elections, female councilors became mayors in one-fourth of all municipalities. The percentage of female mayors is, thus, just about 2% lower than the proportion of female councilors. This means that the glass ceiling (the notion that the higher up the political ladder, the more infrequent female representation becomes) is not as thick in the Czech local elections.

Discussion

As in many countries, the scientific study of local elections and voting is still developing in the Czech Republic, and especially rare are studies dealing with municipalities. Given the tremendous number of municipalities and lack of systematically collected data, it is common for existing studies to focus only on selected municipalities. Selection is usually conducted regionally (e.g., Balík 2008a; Kopřiva 2010) or functionally (Balík 2008b; Čmejrek et al. 2009; Maškarinec et al. 2018). Studies covering the whole set of municipalities nationwide are often concerned with candidacy (Ryšavý & Bernard 2013; Voda et al. 2017), especially the phenomenon of independent lists. Several studies have also analyzed the representation stemming from elections (Ryšavý & Šaradín 2010; Voda & Svačinová 2020). These aspects of local elections are relatively well covered by data, and these data can be processed with relatively little effort. Furthermore, various aspects specific to local elections are addressed in the current literature – from the phenomenon of new elections (Jaroš & Balík 2018) to an analysis of preferential voting (Bernard 2012; Smolkova & Balík 2018). Also well covered are issues connected to electoral law generally (Lebeda 2009; Trávníček 2014), as well as the debate about introducing direct elections for mayors (Blechová 2016; Copus et al. 2016; Jüptner 2009, 2012; Šaradín 2010).

However, although our knowledge about local elections is increasing, there are still many blank spots left on the map. Almost nothing is known about the nomination processes within both parliamentary and local parties. We have only little knowledge about how local party systems are emerging and about their relation to the national party system and local issues. These issues were partially addressed in a book by Hudák et al. (2003), who analyzed in detail the party systems of 15 municipalities across the country, and by Bubeníček and Kubálek (2010), who focused on longitudinal evolution in just one municipality.

It remains unknown when or why a candidate decides to run as a representative of a party registered with the ministry or as an independent candidate. When it comes to voting, we have only very sparse information based on individual data coming from a few exit polls (Kopřiva 2010; Voda et al. 2018), which may not be generalizable. However, these data inform us about the strong relation between voting in local and parliamentary elections if parliamentary parties are present in the competition. However, even when voters support the same party on both levels, they are probably still able to recognize the local level of elections as distinct, and they emphasize the importance of local issues and, especially in smaller municipalities, the importance of the personalities of candidates.

When we move to the consequences of local elections for local politics, we again do not know much about how mayors are selected from among councilors and how coalitions are formed. However, extant research has captured the nature of local coalitions quite well. This particular aspect of local politics has, so far, been analyzed in large municipalities (Balík et al. 2003; Charvátová 2020) as well as in small ones (Ryšavý 2006; Jüptner 2004). It is not unusual to find a board of councilors made up of all parties who are able to cooperate, even though such cooperation at the national level is impossible (Balík et al. 2003; Ryšavý 2006). Moreover, Škvrňák (2020) found that the social capital of councilors as measured by membership in football clubs helps them to form coalitions. Analyses of mayors usually rely on data from the European mayor project (Heinelt et al. 2018), which collected information from municipalities with more than 10,000 inhabitants, thus leaving out the majority of Czech municipalities. More systematic research in this area is limited by the fact that there are no official lists of mayors, and it is a difficult task to collect the names manually.

As indicated previously, research on local elections in the Czech Republic is still an emerging field, but some important case studies and studies answering specific detailed questions have already been conducted. However, the specifics of this fragmented system, the specific nature of electoral competition caused by the strong role of independent and local lists, the quality of electoral data, and the increasing amount of information related to municipalities all make the Czech Republic a very promising case for numerous future analyses.

References

Baldersheim, H., Illner, M., Offerdal, A., Rose, L. & Swianiewicz, P. (1996). *Local democracy and the processes of transformation in East-central Europe*. Boulder: Westview Press.

Balík, S. (2008a). Radniční koalice po komunálních volbách 2006 ve čtyřech okresech České republiky. *Středoevropské politické studie*, 10(1), 17–33.

Balík, S. (2008b). *Česká komunální politika v obcích s rozšířenou působností. Koalice, voličské vzorce a politické strany na místní úrovni v letech 1994–2006*. Brno: Centrum pro studium demokracie a kultury.

Balík, S., Gongala, P. & Gregor, K. (2015). *Dvacet let komunálních voleb v ČR*. Brno: Centrum pro studium demokracie a kultury.

Balík, S., Krutílek, O., Rojčík, O. & Vilímek, P. (2003). *Komunální volby v České republice v roce 2002*. Brno: Mezinárodní politologický ústav.

Bernard, J. (2012). Individuální charakteristiky kandidátů ve volbách do zastupitelstev obcí a jejich vliv na volební výsledky. *Sociologický časopis*, 48(4), 613–640.

Blechová, V. (2016). Přímá volba starostů v ČR: Analýza situace v malých obcích. *Contemporary European Studies*, 11(2): 5–18.

Bubeníček, V. & Kubálek, M. (2010). Konfliktní linie v malých obcích. *Acta Politologica*, 2(3), 30–45.

Charvát, J. (2011). Malapportionment, hodnota hlasu a volby do Zastupitelstva hlavního města Prahy 2010. *Politologický časopis-Czech Journal of Political Science*, 18(4), 335–353.

Charvátová, L. (2020). Local coalitions in the Czech republic: Crucial cohesion factor. *Politologický časopis-Czech Journal of Political Science*, 27(1), 45–64.

Čmejrek, J., Čopík, J., Kopřiva, R., Bubeníček, V., Kociánová, J. & Wagnerová, J. (2009). *Participace občanů na veřejném životě venkovských obcí ČR*. Praha: Kernberg.

Čopík, J, Kopřiva, R. & Čmejrek, J. (2019). Mayors as a variable in typologies of local governments: A case study of the Czech Republic. *Local Government Studies*, 1–19.

Copus, C., Iglesias, A., Hacek, M., Illner, M. & Lidström, A. (2016). Have mayors will travel: Trends and developments in the direct election of the mayor: A five-nation study. In S. Kuhlmann & G. Bouckaert (Eds.), *Local public sector reforms in times of crisis* (pp. 301–315). London: Palgrave Macmillan.

CVVM (2015). *Naše společnost 2015 – říjen* [dataset] [online]. Ver. 1.0. Praha: Český sociálněvědní datový archiv, 2015 [cited 20 June 2020]. DOI 10.14473/V1510.

CZSO (2020). Vývoj počtu obcí v České republice podle krajů (stav k 1.1.) [dataset] [online]. www.czso.cz/documents/10180/46173161/32018117_0201.xlsx/c97714a6-25bf-42d0-bdb1-00e0d1aca072?version=1.0 [cited 20 June 2020].

Hájek, L. (2017). The effect of multiple-office holding on the parliamentary activity of MPs in the Czech Republic. *The Journal of Legislative Studies*, 23(4), 484–507.

Heinelt, H., Hlepas, N., Kuhlmann, S. & Swianiewicz, P. (2018). Local government systems: grasping the institutional environment of mayors. In H. Heinelt, A. Magnier, M. Cabria & H. Reynaert (Eds.), *Political leaders and changing local democracy. The European mayor* (pp. 19–78). London: Palgrave Macmillan.

Hloušek, V., Kopeček, L. & Vodová, P. (2020). *The rise of entrepreneurial parties in European politics*. Cham: Palgrave Macmillan.

Hudák, J., Jüptner, P. & Svoboda, J. (2003). *Komunální politické systémy*. Praha: Univerzita Karlova, Filosofická fakulta.

Jaroš, B. & Balík, S. (2018). Nové komunální volby v ČR 2002–2017: blokující menšiny? *Acta Politologica*, 10(1), 139–152.

Jüptner, P. (2004). Komunální koalice a politické modely. *Politologická revue*, 10(2), 81–100.

Jüptner, P. (2009). Ministerská diskuse k případnému zavedení přímé volby starostů: velmi nízká priorita? *Acta Politologica*, 1(3), 305–331.

Jüptner, P. (2012). Přímá volba starostů v evropské komparaci a české diskusi. *Acta Politologica*, 4(3), 232–245.

Jüptner, P., Valušová, P. & Kruntorádová, I. (2014). Participation and elements of direct democracy in the Czech Republic: Part I. *Public Policy and Administration*, 13(4), 644–658.

Kopecký, M. & Zach, D. (2019). Kojčice u Pelhřimova mají starostu, který není členem zastupitelstva. Zcela podle pravidel. *iRozhlas.cz*. www.irozhlas.cz/zpravy-domov/kojcice-starost-zastupitelstvo-komunalni-volby_1910261603_vtk [cited 20 June 2020].

Kopřiva, R. (2010). Stabilita volební podpory politických stran v komunálních volbách. *Acta Politologica*, 2(3), 3–16.

Ladner, A., Keuffer, N., Baldersheim, H., Hlepas, N., Swianiewicz, P., Steyvers, K. & Navarro, C. (2019). *Patterns of local autonomy in Europe*. London: Palgrave Macmillan.

Lebeda, T. (2009). Komunální volby klamou. Krátké zastavení nad problematickými aspekty volebního systému pro obecní zastupitelstva. *Acta Politologica*, 1(3), 332–343.

Lysek, J. (2016): Tackling bureaucracy growth in time of crisis: The case of Czech statutory cities. *Lex Localis*, 14(4), 783–806.

Maškarinec, P., Klimovský, D. & Danišová, S. (2018). Politická reprezentace žen na pozicích starostek v Česku a na Slovensku v letech 2006–2014: Srovnávací analýza faktorů úspěšnosti. *Sociologický časopis*, 54(4), 529–560.

Ministry of Interior. (2020): Místní referendum. www.mvcr.cz/clanek/obcanske-aktivity-118893.aspx [cited 20 June 2020].

Mouritzen, P.E. & Svara, J.H. (2002). *Leadership at the apex: Politicians and administrators in Western local governments*. Pittsburgh: University of Pittsburgh Press.

Nový, M. (2016). Explaining turnout in local referenda in the Czech Republic: Does a NIMBY question enhance citizen engagement? *East European Politics*, 32(4), 487–504.

Ryšavý, D. (2006). Komunální je komunální a velká je velká! K hypotéze politizace lokálních politických elit. *Sociologický časopis*, 42(5), 953–970.

Ryšavý, D. & Bernard, J. (2013). Size and local democracy: The case of Czech municipal representatives. *Local Government Studies*, 39(6), 833–852.

Ryšavý, D. & Šaradín, P. (2010). Straníci, bezpartijní a nezávislí zastupitelé na českých radnicích. *Sociologický časopis*, 46(5), 719–743.

Šaradín, P. (2010). Direct elections of mayors in the Czech Republic? Data from research and political support. *Contemporary European Studies*, 2, 77–85.

Škvrňák, M. (2020). You'll never rule alone: how football clubs and party membership affect coalition formation. *Local Government Studies*, 1–19.

Smith, M.L. (2011). The uneasy balance between participation and representation: Local direct democracy in the Czech Republic. In T. Schiller (Eds.), *Local direct democracy in Europe* (pp. 33–53). Wiesbaden: VS Verlag für Sozialwissenschaften.7.

Smolkova, A. & Balík, S. (2018). Personalizace na komunální úrovni: existuje a lze ji v českém prostředí zkoumat? *Středoevropské politické studie*, 20(2), 204–221.

STEM. (2014). Tisková Informace Z Výzkumu Stem Trendy 2/2014. www.stem.cz/dulezitost-voleb/ [cited 20 June 2020].

Trávníček, M. (2014). Současná podoba a perspektivy volebního systému pro komunální volby v České republice. *Acta Politologica*, 6(2), 212–237.

Vláda. (2011). Vláda přerušila diskusi k přímé volbě starostů. www.vlada.cz/scripts/detail.php?id=84564&tmplid=50 [cited 20 June 2020].

Voda, P., Spáč, P. & Pink, M. (2018). *Exit Poll: závěrečná zpráva*. Brno: Masaryk University.

Voda, P. & Svačinová, P. (2020). To be central or peripheral? What matters for political representation in amalgamated municipalities? *Urban Affairs Review*, 56(4), 1206–1236.

Voda, P., Svačinová, P., Smolková, A. & Balík, S. (2017). Local and more local: Impact of size and organization type of settlement units on candidacy. *Political Geography*, 59, 24–35.

Wollmann, H. (2004). Local government reforms in Great Britain, Sweden, Germany and France: Between multi-function and single-purpose organisations. *Local Government Studies*, 30(4), 639–665.

24

Estonia

The consolidation of partisan politics in a small country with small municipalities

Tõnis Saarts, Georg Sootla, and Kersten Kattai

A brief overview of the local government system

The current local government system in Estonia was reestablished in 1989 after its abolition in 1940. It was then reconfigured in the 1990s, introducing the single-tier system of local governance. Within this system, municipalities are the only local government units, and there is no meso-level local self-government. However, municipal-level governments are supplemented by voluntary submunicipal tier institutions (rural municipality districts and urban districts) and voluntary organizations for intermunicipal cooperation at the regional level.

At the beginning of the 1990s, there were 254 municipalities in Estonia. The number of municipalities was gradually reduced by voluntary amalgamations, and by 2014 only 213 municipalities were left. The radical administrative-territorial reform that was launched in 2015–2017 reduced the number of territorial units by almost threefold, so that currently there are 79 (15 urban and 64 rural) municipalities in Estonia.

The municipalities are responsible for providing social services and benefits, health care, primary and secondary education, organizing water supply and sewage, waste management, spatial planning, public transportation, and services within each municipality, like the construction and maintenance of public infrastructure (roads or city streets), libraries, museums, and sports facilities (LGO 2020).

The reform of 1989 initially introduced a two-tier local government system (municipal and county level). After the restoration of independence in 1991, a new constitution was adopted in 1992, which outlined the detailed and extensive guarantees of local autonomy. Before the first democratic local elections in 1993, the Local Government Organisation Act (LGO) and the Municipal Council Election Act (MCEA) were adopted. The LGO established a single-tier local government system for Estonia; county-level governments were reorganized to central government field agencies. It was a farsighted strategic move aimed, first, to weaken the power base of the former Soviet-era regional elites who had become too powerful at the county level of self-government. Second, it aimed to prevent possible separatist tendencies in the regions mostly populated by Russian speakers in Northeastern Estonia (see Sootla & Kattai 2011; Saarts 2020).

The extensive autonomy that was granted by the Constitution and the LGO also meant that the municipalities were expected to provide a broad scope of public services in their territory. However, those responsibilities were supported by neither tax reforms (which provided only a minor local tax base) nor land reform, which restrained the transfer of land into municipal ownership. It was envisaged that intermunicipal cooperation and further amalgamation of the territorial units would address the problems appearing in the fiscal and administrative capacities of smaller municipalities, but the reform did not succeed as intended (Sootla & Kattai 2011).

This paradoxical situation is reflected in the data of the Local Autonomy Index (Ladner et al. 2019: 232, 237) in which the various components of the index, such as political discretion and policy scope are above the European average, but fiscal autonomy is noticeably underdeveloped. Also, there are very few channels for local governments to influence decision-making processes at the central level. Overall, Estonia ranks 17th on the European Local Autonomy Index, which is slightly above the European average and can still be considered an achievement.

The extensive administrative-territorial reforms introduced in 2017 addressed only a few of the previously mentioned contradictions plaguing effective local governance in Estonia (Valner 2018). On the one hand, the major goal of the reform was to enhance the administrative capacity of municipalities by territorial amalgamation, but on the other hand, the reform neither introduced any avenue or new model for financing local governments nor increased the level of vertical decentralization. Furthermore, the county-level governments were abolished as administrative units in 2018, and their former functions were transferred to the central government agencies, ministries, or local governments.

According to the typology introduced by Heinelt et al. (2018), the power relations found in Estonian municipalities are closest to the executive mayor type, although mayors are not directly elected. However, due to extensive party politicization, mayors have become indispensable and powerful political figures at the local level, while serving as the head of both the majority coalition and the collegial local government 'cabinet'. Mayors are also the head of local administration with the capacity to appoint all administrative staff, including heads of public offices (i.e., directors of schools and other organizations). The extensive authority to run the local administration is delegated to the mayor by the council. Hence, the mayor is highly dependent on the political support he/she can mobilize from the council.

The organization of local elections and their place in a multilevel system

Because there are no meso-level local governments or directly elected mayors in Estonia, there is only one type of local election, in which Estonian voters elect councilors of municipalities.

Prior to 2005, local elections were held every three years, but since 2005, they have been held every four years. The change was made in order to accommodate the standard policymaking cycle at the local level (which is usually four years). Since this alteration, local government (LG) elections have become classical mid-term elections, placed almost midway in the national electoral cycle, so that they occur approximately two years after the most recent parliamentary elections and two years before the next ones.

Although there is no directly elected president in Estonia, presidential elections usually take place in a special electoral college, composed of the members of parliament and representatives of municipalities. Before the administrative-territorial reform in 2017 (which radically reduced the number of municipalities) the proportions between the two groups of representatives were as follows: one-third were MPs and two-thirds were representatives of local governments. Now the proportion is roughly 50/50, and the local representatives have largely lost the leverage they enjoyed previously. According to the constitution, a candidate for the presidency has to secure two-thirds of the votes in the national parliament, and if the parliament fails to elect the president after three ballots, the electoral college is authorized to do so. It provides relatively strong (but temporary) bargaining power for local elites in national politics: anyone who does not enjoy sufficient support among the local or rural elites could not be elected president.

The mayor is appointed by the council, in which a ruling coalition is formed by political parties (or/and nonparty lists) represented on the council. The mayor has the power to appoint members of the cabinet. This position is usually given to the biggest party in the coalition, although this is not always the rule as some smaller parties in the coalition can occupy the mayor position. A mayor may be recalled from office by a motion of no confidence initiated by the council; a simple majority of the councilors has to support the motion. It is relatively common in Estonian municipalities for coalitions to change, and thus the mayors are also replaced.

There are no binding local referendums in Estonia. Municipalities can organize nonbinding public consultations (or polls), and so the council is free to adopt or ignore the results of the consultative referendum. Nonetheless, many local consultative referendums were organized in conjunction with the latest administrative-territorial reform in 2017, in which case, there were public enquiries to support the amalgamation of the respective territorial units. On some occasions, local authorities reject the results of the advisory referendums due to low turnout at the polls, but more often they accept the outcome. The law does not give room to either recall referendums or elections concerning the councilors or mayors already in office.

The responsibility for organizing and supervising the local elections is borne by the local electoral committees, which are placed under tutelage of the National Electoral Committee (ENEC). They are also charged with registering candidates, confirming election results in municipalities, etc. A local electoral committee is appointed by the local council and chaired by the municipal secretary (equivalent to legal chancellor), who also appoints members of the committee. The National Electoral Committee ensures compliance with the laws and procedures and announces the results of elections.

There is a widespread practice of e-voting in Estonia, whereby in the 2017 elections, 31.7% of votes were cast electronically. Electronic voting was introduced for the local elections of 2005, and thus Estonia became the first country in the world to hold nationwide elections using the method. The voting system builds on the Estonian ID card, which is compulsory for all citizens. It allows voters to cast their ballots from any internet-connected computer, anywhere in the world. The internet voting is allowed only during an early voting period in which the voter may change his/her electronic vote an unlimited number of times up to the day before election day (but not on election day itself). Regardless of some criticism and controversies, most experts consider the system to be secure and transparent (E-Estonia 2020).

Features of the electoral system

Local elections in Estonia are based on universal suffrage of all permanent residents. This means that, in addition to Estonian citizens, noncitizens without EU citizenship (6.6% of the population), EU citizens, and other foreign nationals (mostly Russian citizens) with long-term residence permits are eligible to vote (see also Statistikablogi 2016). Although for parliamentary elections the minimum voting age is 18, it was lowered to 16 for the 2017 local elections after a heated public debate. For national parliamentary elections, only Estonian citizens are eligible to vote, which makes the electorate for both types of elections distinct (for instance, the number of eligible voters for the local elections in 2017 was 24% larger than for the national elections). The right to stand as a candidate in local elections is reserved for Estonians (86.6% of the population) or EU citizens (below 1%), who are at least 18 years old. Thus, noncitizens and Russian citizens only enjoy passive but not active voting rights. Voting in Estonia is voluntary and is based on residential registration on the Estonian population register. As a rule, the personal official invitation letter or voter's card is sent to eligible voters.

The municipal council size in Estonia depends on the size of the respective municipality. The Municipal Council Election Act (MCEA) only stipulates a possible range to be considered, but every municipality has the authority to determine the actual size of the council before an election. For instance, a community with fewer than 2,000 inhabitants should have at least 13 seats (voters/seat ratio = 154) and a community with over 10,000 residents should have at least 21 seats (ratio = 476). Overall, 1,729 councilors were elected in 2017 into 79 municipal councils (22 councilors per council on average).

Electoral districts were introduced only in the capital city Tallinn. In Tallinn, which has historically or geographically demarcated areas, in every district, the neighborhood councils are appointed by the city council. The Tallinn districts are all multimember districts. Although electoral districts may be established by the councils in cities with over 50,000 residents, even Tartu, the second largest city in Estonia, has not introduced them. Districts may also be applied after a merger of municipalities (for two subsequent elections). The municipalities that have established the inner districts (neighborhood councils) may also use the district structure. After the amalgamation reforms, only eight municipalities (10%) took the opportunity to establish districts. As a result of political bargaining over the electoral rules in Tallinn, there are huge disparities in district size: the larger districts, in which the proportion of Russian speakers is also higher, are underrepresented on the city council, whereas many smaller districts have more seats than their size would otherwise accommodate.

National parties, nonparty lists, and individual candidates are eligible to run in elections. The registration rules for candidates are relatively simple, and every candidate has to submit a standard application to the electoral committee. The registration of the candidates and procedures should be finalized 40 days before the elections. Only active members of the Defense Forces and persons convicted of crimes and/or serving a sentence cannot stand as candidates.

The list proportional representation electoral system is used for local elections in Estonia. It is an open-list system (OLPR) with a 5% electoral threshold in which individual candidates are competing along with party lists. A similar system is also used for national elections; thus, there are relatively few discrepancies between the electoral systems used for both elections. The mechanics of the electoral system and seat distribution works as follows: the quotum is calculated in which the number of voters in an electoral district (municipality) is divided by the number of seats available; the candidates who receive more votes than the simple quotum or equal to it, obtain a personal mandate. After the distribution of personal mandates, the remaining mandates are divided according to the d'Hondt formula; only the electoral lists (either party or nonpartisan lists) that have surpassed the 5% threshold are eligible to win seats on the council. For the distribution of electoral list mandates, each candidate is reranked according to the number of votes received, and those topping the list have a better chance to obtain a seat. Seat distribution in a municipality with districts follows the same principles just outlined, but the seats are distributed within each district separately; however, the list must obtain at least 5% of votes across the districts. Only in the capital city Tallinn is even a more sophisticated compensatory mechanism (d'Hondt formula) used for achieving a greater proportionality between the lists, in which all of the mandates that were not divided at the district level (because they did not reach the quotum) are divided between the lists at the municipality level. As was mentioned, only one-tenth of Estonian municipalities used the district arrangement for the local elections in 2017.

Each voter has one vote, and he/she has to select a candidate on an electoral list. Voters write the number of their preferred candidate on the ballot. The sequence of the electoral lists, put on the walls of a ballot box, is determined by sheer luck at a draw by the electoral committee. Parties or nonparty lists determine the specific ranking of candidates within the lists according to their internal rules, in which the candidates are usually rank ordered and not placed alphabetically.

One of the central issues with local elections in Estonia has been the legal status of the nonparty lists (local electoral unions) and the question of *cumul des mandats* (where a member of the national parliament can simultaneously serve as a member of a municipal council). There was an attempt to ban nonparty lists in local elections at the beginning of the 2000s, but this was overruled by the Supreme Court and vetoed by the president. Thus, electoral unions were allowed to participate in both the 2002 and 2005 elections, and finally the partisan elites gave up. Although *cumul des mandats* was abolished by parliament in 2002, it was reintroduced before the 2017 elections in conjunction with the administrative-territorial reform that occurred the same year. Despite widespread public criticism, quite a few MPs still decided to run in local elections and were elected to local councils. Nonetheless, it is important to note that *cumul des mandats* does not apply to the executive positions in the local administration: the members of parliament are not allowed to serve as mayors or members of municipal governments.

The electoral outcomes and partisan politics at the local level

Electoral turnout in Estonia has been moderate compared to other advanced democracies. It has been steadily around 15–25% lower than for parliamentary elections (see Table 24.1). This disparity is due to the fact that local elections are often considered second-order elections. Nonetheless, the number of eligible voters for local elections is larger than for national elections (see preceding information). This is mainly because noncitizens, foreign nationals, and young voters aged 16 and 17 can vote in local elections, but they are excluded from voting in national elections. In the 2017 local elections, although the absolute number of voters was 4% larger than for the national elections, voter turnout for the local elections was more than 10% lower.

There is a clear trend that voter turnout is significantly higher in smaller communities than in larger ones. In the years 2002–2013, the average correlation between the size of a municipality

Table 24.1 Voter turnout (percent) for local and national elections in Estonia

Year	Local elections	Year	National elections	Year	European elections
1993	52.6	1992	**67.8**		
1996	52.5	1995	**68.9**		
1999	49.8	1999	**57.4**		
2002	52.5	2003	**58.2**		
2005	47.4	2007	**61.9**	2004	26.8
2009	60.6	2011	**63.5**	2009	43.9
2013	58.0	2015	**64.2**	2014	36.5
2017	53.3	2019	**63.7**	2019	37.6

Source: LED (2020) and the Estonian National Electoral Committee (2020)

and voter turnout was −0.3. Even after the amalgamation reform in 2017, it remained at −0.4, although the overall median size of municipalities has increased. It could also be a temporary effect, in which the smaller communities were very eager to elect their representatives to new and enlarged councils.

Curiously, the introduction of e-voting has not significantly affected voter turnout. In the first election, the sociodemographic profile of the e-voters was somewhat distinct, due to the digital divide. However, in the subsequent elections, the characteristics of first-time e-voters gradually became more similar to those of the traditional paper ballot voters. (Vassil et al. 2016)

There are three indicators one could use for measuring competitiveness in local elections in Estonia: the number of candidates per seat, the number of electoral lists, and the proportion of votes that the winning list receives. It is important to note that if we talk about 'electoral lists' in the following paragraphs, we mean either partisan or nonparty lists.

First, the number of candidates per seat is gradually increasing; in the 2002 elections it was 4.6 per seat, but in the 2017 elections it was 6.8. This is mostly due to the amalgamation reform, which reduced the total number of available seats on the municipal councils in 2017, which subsequently made the elections more competitive.

Second, prior to the recent amalgamation reform, the mean number of electoral lists presented in the local municipality council elections used to be around three, but after the reforms it has increased to 4.3 (LED 2020).

The competitiveness of elections has been dependent on the size of a municipality. This was more evident before the amalgamation reforms: although there were fewer small municipalities in which there was only one electoral list present (usually in the municipalities with under 1,000 inhabitants), only two electoral lists were competing in half of the communities under 2,000 inhabitants. Competitiveness usually increases considerably if the number of inhabitants exceeds 3,500. Hence, there is a high correlation between the size of a municipality and the number of lists (in the 2017 elections it was 0.5) (LED 2020).

Third, the actual political pluralism found on a council is mirrored by the division of seats between the electoral lists. Data from the 2013 and 2017 elections show that, in a majority of municipalities with a population under 5,000, one list usually wins more than 50% of the votes (see Table 24.2), whereas in larger communities, the emergence of a dominant electoral list is a relatively rare phenomenon. Before the amalgamation reform, electoral competitiveness usually increased considerably if the number of inhabitants exceeded 3,500 (Sootla et al. 2015). The low level of electoral competitiveness in smaller communities was one of the reasons for the reform. However, evidence shows that the amalgamation reform only slightly increased the role of coalition governments in smaller communities but made them even less common in medium-sized communities (between 5,001 and 11,000 residents; see Table 24.2). The correlation between the size of a municipality and the share of votes obtained by the winners is still high: −0.3, as compared to −0.4 in 2013.

Given the fact that individual candidates run against party lists and have to surpass the 5% threshold alone, they are rarely successful in local elections. For example, in the 2017 elections, individual candidates received 0.4% of the votes nationwide and only two seats in some very tiny municipalities.

The share of female candidates has steadily increased since the 1990s (see Table 24.3). However, female representation on the municipal councils is not much changed: it remains about 28%, as it was in 1999. Nonetheless, the proportion of female candidates in recent parliamentary elections was lower (32.1%) than in local elections (38.6%), and the number of female MPs is currently 29%, reaching the same level as women on the local councils only after the 2019 elections. Currently, there are virtually no discussions on gender quotas in Estonia. However,

Table 24.2 Size of local government and the proportion of votes received by the election winners in Estonia

Percentage of votes the winners of the elections receive/ size of municipality	2013			2017		
	Up to 49.9% of votes	50–69.9% of votes	More than 70% of votes	Up to 49.9% of votes	50–69.9% of votes	More than 70% of votes
Up to 5,000 inhabitants	37.8	42.4	19.8	46.7	20.0	33.3
5,001–11,000 inhabitants	76.9	15.4	7.7	61.1	36.1	2.8
Over 11,000 inhabitants	70.6	17.6	11.8	75.0	21.4	3.6
Average	61.8	25.1	13.1	60.9	25.8	13.2

Source: LED (2020)

Table 24.3 Female representation in local elections in Estonia

Year	% of female candidates	% of female elected candidates
1993	28.3	23.9
1996	33.0	26.6
1999	35.6	28.3
2002	37.7	28.4
2005	39.3	29.6
2009	38.7	29.6
2013	40.0	31.1
2017	38.6	28.6

Source: Estonian National Electoral Committee (2020)

some parties (e.g., Social Democrats) have initiated 'zipper system lists', whereby female and male candidates are alternated on the lists for elections (but they have done it entirely on their own initiative).

As mentioned earlier, there is a large Russophone minority residing in Estonia. Unfortunately, no reliable data are available on minority representation and candidacy at the local level. Several ethnic Russian parties and nonparty lists were running in both the local and national elections in the 1990s, and they performed relatively well. Nonetheless, since the 2000s, the Estonian Centre Party (KE) has attracted the majority of the Russian votes and has gradually pushed the ethnic Russian parties to the margins of electoral competition.[1] Nowadays, even at the local level, there are almost no nonparty lists that claim to represent the interests of the Russian speakers exclusively.

The Estonian party system could be classified as a moderate multiparty system with a balance among parties, in which 5–6 parties usually win seats in the national parliament (Saarts 2015). The local and national level party systems are not very different, because the parties active at the national level often constitute the backbone of local party competition (see Table 24.4). This has been possible mostly because major Estonian parties have quite extensive party organizations geographically, and they usually have local party branches even in small municipalities (Saarts 2015). Nonetheless, there are some discrepancies between party performance at the national

Table 24.4 The role of parties in national and local elections in Estonia (percent of all votes)

	National elections				Local elections			
	2019	2015	2011	2007	2017	2013	2009	2005
RE (Reform Party)	28.9	27.7	28.6	27.8	19.5	13.7	16.7	16.9
KE (Centre Party)	23.1	24.8	23.3	26.1	27.3	31.9	31.5	25.5
SDE (Social Democratic Party)	9.8	15.2	17.1	10.6	10.4	12.5	7.5	6.4
IRL (Pro Patria and Res Publica Union)/ Isamaa (Pro Patria)	11.4	13.7	20.5	17.9	8.0	17.2	13.9	17.0
ERL (Peoples' Union)	–	–	2.1	7.1	–	–	1.9	12.5
EKRE (Estonian Conservative Peoples' Party	17.8	8.1	–	–	6.7	1.3	–	–
The Greens	1.8	0.9	3.8	7.1	0.8	–	1.1	–
Other national parties	7.2	9.6	4.6	3.4	0.5		0.1	1.3
Local electoral alliances	None	None	None	None	26.8	23.4	27.3	20.3

Source: Estonian National Electoral Committee (2020)

and local levels: for example, the Centre Party (KE) habitually performs better at the local level than its major rival, the Reform Party (RE), because the former enjoys large support among the Russian-speaking minority residing mostly in large cities such as Tallinn and the towns of Northeastern Estonia (in which they make up a majority of the population). The new populist radical right party, EKRE, is on the rise, and it seems that the party can efficiently compete with the older parties at both the national and local levels.

Local politics need not necessarily be linked only to partisan politics; in many countries, nonparty lists are also playing quite a significant role (Kjaer & Elklit 2010; Gendźwiłł & Żółtak 2014). Earlier studies have indicated that political competition at the local level has been relatively well structured in Estonia compared with other countries in Central and Eastern Europe (e.g., Slovakia, Hungary) – mostly because of the high level of party politicization (Sootla & Küngas 2007). National parties have received 70–75% of votes in local elections in 2005–2017, while the nonparty lists have steadily won one-quarter of votes. Nonetheless, the situation was different in the 1990s, when the nonparty lists (also known as local electoral unions) usually won more than 50% of votes (Toomla 2009). The failed legislative initiative, described earlier, before the 2002 elections to ban the local electoral unions somewhat demotivated local elites from joining the nonparty lists and enabled the parties to improve their electoral position vis-à-vis electoral unions.

However, after a temporal setback in the 2002 and 2005 elections, nonparty lists still remain dominant in smaller municipalities. Before the amalgamation reform of 2017, the local electoral unions emerged as winners of elections in 50% of the communities that had fewer than 3,500 inhabitants, and the situation did not change much with the latest reform. Thus, in two-thirds of the smaller municipalities, those with fewer than 11,000 inhabitants, nonparty lists performed better than the parties and won elections in 2017 (LED 2020). Consequently, the amalgamation reforms did not alter the proportion of votes received by the parties and nonparty unions nationwide (see Table 24.4), contrary to what has been seen in some other countries (see Kjaer & Elklit 2010 on Denmark).

The relatively stable support for the local electoral unions in Estonia is underpinned by antipartisan attitudes that are relatively widespread in society and are particularly manifested in local elections. Regardless of the flexible registration procedures, electoral unions often act as relatively stable political associations operating for several elections; thus, it is mostly incorrect to depict them as fluid and random political actors. Members of parties sometimes hide their true political affiliation when joining nonparty lists because they anticipate that the antipartisan attitudes of their potential voters could affect their chances of winning.

The concentration of votes in the hands of a few top candidates is often evident in Estonian municipalities, which demonstrates a high level of personalization of local politics. Therefore, the incumbency ratio is relatively high in Estonia. Analysis of the top three candidates in elections reveals that more than 70% of them had previously won a seat on the council and about 50% of them had been elected for more than two consecutive terms (see Table 24.5). Thus, one can argue that only one-quarter of the top elites on a council are replaced after every election. The evidence (Table 24.5) shows that even the recent amalgamation reform did not efficiently disrupt the strong incumbency effect. Nonetheless, the size of the municipality matters here again, as limited elite replacement is a bigger concern for smaller municipalities than for larger ones (Sootla, Kattai & Viks 2015).

Discussion and conclusion

There are several key differences between local and national elections in Estonia. First, local elections are predominately focused on local issues (except in larger cities and Tallinn), and even if local politics is highly politicized (dominated by national parties), it does not mean that the confrontations between the parties at the local level are played out in ideological terms; rather, the personalities and local elite networks matter more than the ideological party labels. Second, the electorate is slightly different for both elections. Concerning local elections, both Estonian citizens, noncitizens, and Russian citizens have the right to vote, and this assures the Russian speakers of more representation in local elections than is the case for the national elections, and somehow increases the legitimacy of the political system as a whole in the eyes of the ethnic minority.

We may point out four important implications of local elections for national politics. First, the voting rights of the Russian speakers, on the one hand, have made the ethnic cleavage

Table 24.5 Incumbency ratio (percent) on the councils among the top three candidates in the Estonian elections

	Top three candidates 2005			Top three candidates 2009			Top three candidates 2013			Top three candidates 2017		
	1	2	3	1	2	3	1	2	3	1	2	3
Had a seat on the council in 2002	77.5	73.5	64.3	61.9	54.9	50	51.6	43.7	35.8	35.9	40.6	32.8
Had a seat on the council in 2005				78.8	75.0	65.9	63.7	57.9	46.5	45.3	48.4	48.4
Had a seat on the council in 2009							78.3	71.6	67.0	65.6	65.6	62.5
Had a seat on the council in 2013										79.7	71.9	75.0

very pronounced in electoral competition even at the local level, but on the other hand, the extended voting rights have provided some additional career opportunities for the Russian-speaking local political elites. It is also worth mentioning that the possible secessionist tendencies in Northeastern Estonia in 1993 convinced the national elites that there is no need for a strong meso tier of local government in Estonia – a decision that later had a profound impact on the local government system as a whole. Second, in most cases, the national parliament has failed to elect a president, and therefore elections have happened in the electoral college. This has provided remarkable leverage to local elites in national level politics, and their political opinions cannot be just ignored. Third, although there have been so many political struggles over questions of the legitimacy of nonparty lists, one-quarter of voters still continue to vote for them, which provides an important medium for citizens to express their antiparty sentiments. Fourth, local elections have facilitated the consolidation and stabilization of the national party system, such that parties lacking strong organization to compete in local elections rarely manage to survive in national politics either. Thus, local elections have served as an additional mechanism for institutionalizing party competition in Estonia.

Discussions on electoral reforms in Estonia have been almost nonexistent. Only recently has there been a debate about how to reform the electoral college for presidential elections. The recent administrative reform drastically reduced the number of municipalities; however, at the same time, the laws regulating presidential elections remained unchanged. This means that the number of local government representatives in the electoral college was reduced accordingly, and now they make up only 50% of the members (previously they controlled two-thirds of the seats).

At the end of the 2000s, there was an initiative to introduce concurrent elections in which European elections and local elections would be organized on the same day, but the plan was quickly watered down and discussions closed.

Estonia is very proud of its e-voting system. Although some (populist) political parties have been critical toward it, there has been no major initiative to reform it in a substantial way.

Nevertheless, even if substantial electoral reform were to happen in the future, it would not be enough to address major institutional inconsistencies existing in the current local government system in Estonia, whereby substantial political and legal autonomy co-exist with very limited fiscal autonomy.

Note

1 The Estonian Centre Party has attracted the Russian voters mainly by raising specific issues such as educational policy (defending the policy in which Russian schools are allowed to retain the Russian language as the language of instruction) and citizenship policy (liberalizing the requirements for naturalization). Those policies belong to the domain of national politics, but they are still important for the Russian speakers because the other Estonian parties do not pay much attention to their specific needs and interests.

References

E-Estonia (2020). I-voting. Accessible: https://e-estonia.com/solutions/e-governance/i-voting/ (Accessed on August 25, 2020).

Gendźwiłł, A. & Żółtak, T. (2014). Why Do Non-Partisans Challenge Parties in Local Politics? The (Extreme) Case of Poland. *Europe-Asia Studies*, 66 (7), 1122–1145.

Heinelt, H., Hlepas, N., Kuhlmann, S., & Swianiewicz P. (2018) Local Government Systems: Grasping the Institutional Environment of Mayors. In H. Heinelt, A. Magnier, M. Cabria, H. Reynaert (Eds.),

Political Leaders and Changing Local Democracy. Governance and Public Management (pp. 19–78). Cham: Palgrave Macmillan.

Kjaer, U. & Elklit, J. (2010). Party Politicisation of Local Councils: Cultural or Institutional Explanations for Trends in Denmark, 1966–2005. *European Journal of Political Research*, 49 (3), 337–358.

Ladner, A., Keuffer, N., Baldersheim, H., Hlepas, N., Swianiewicz, P., Steyvers, K. & Navarro, C. (2019). *Patterns of Local Autonomy in Europe*. Cham: Palgrave Macmillan.

LED (2020). *Local Elections Analytical Database (1993–2017)*. Developed by K. Kattai, G. Sootla [not published, in authors' possession].

LGO (2020). Local Government Organisation Act. Accessible: www.riigiteataja.ee/en/eli/ee/509012014 003/consolide/current (Accessed on January 25, 2020).

Saarts, T. (2015). Persistence and Decline of Political Parties: The Case of Estonia. *East European Politics*, 31 (2), 208–228.

Saarts, T. (2020). Introducing Regional Self-Governments in Central and Eastern Europe: Paths to Success and Failure. *Regional & Federal Studies*, 30 (5), 625–649.

Sootla, G. & Kattai, K. (2011). Estonia: Challenges and Lessons of the Development of Local Autonomy. In J. Loughlin, F. Hendriks, & A. Lidström (Eds.), *The Oxford Handbook of Local and Regional Democracy in Europe* (pp. 576–595). Oxford; New York: Oxford University Press.

Sootla, G., Kattai, K. & Viks, A. (2015). Size of Municipalities and Democracy: An Institutional Approach. Paper presented at 23rd NISPAcee Annual Conference, May 21–May 23, 2015, Tbilisi, Georgia.

Sootla, G. & Küngas, K. (2007). Effects of Institutionalisation of Local Policymaking. The Study of Central-Eastern European Experience. In J. Franzke, M. Boogers, J. M. Ruano, & L. Schaap (Eds). *Tension Between Local Governance and Local democracy* (pp. 52–64). The Hague: Reed Elsevier.

Statistikablogi (2016). Noppeid ajaloost: kodakondsus ja sünnikoht. Accessible: https://blog.stat.ee/tag/kodakondsus/ (Accessed on January 22, 2020).

Toomla, R. (2009). Valimisliitudest mitme kandi pealt. *Kesknädal*, September 30. Accessible: http://vana.kesknadal.ee/g2/uudised?id=13320.

Valner, S. (Ed.). (2018). *Administrative Reform 2017 in Estonia. Collection of Articles. Decisions. Background. Implementation*. Tallinn, Estonia: Ministry of Finance. Accessible: https://haldusreform.fin.ee/static/sites/3/2019/01/lg_reform_eng_finale_screen.pdf (Accessed on January 22, 2020).

Vassil, K., Solvak, M., Vinkel, P., Trechsel, A. H., & Alvarez, R. M. (2016). The Diffusion of Internet Voting. Usage Patterns of Internet Voting in Estonia Between 2005 and 2015. *Government Information Quarterly*, 33 (3), 453–459.

25
Hungary
The expansion and the limits of national politics at the local level

Gábor Dobos

The Hungarian local government system

After the fall of the Communist regime, a highly autonomous, decentralized local government system was introduced to Hungary in 1990 (Act LXV of 1990). A total of 3,092 local governments (*helyi önkormányzatok*) were established on the lower tier following the 'one settlement, one local government' principle, while 19 counties and the capital Budapest formed the middle tier of the subnational system. Budapest is composed of 23 districts, which function as fully autonomous local governments. In the Hungarian system, county centres are ranked in the middle level as they can provide services that would normally be the competences of county governments. Thus, they are called 'cities with county rights' (*megyei jogú városok*). In addition, cities with more than 50,000 inhabitants can apply for county rights. At present, there are 23 cities with county rights in Hungary. Currently, there are 3,177 local governments in Hungary. Most of them are small communities: 91% have fewer than 5,000 inhabitants (the average population size is 3,076 inhabitants).

Although local autonomy was an emphasized value in the constitutional and legal framework of the system and in the early years decentralization was considered a great success (Soós & Kálmán 2002: 21), it did not result in truly autonomous and effective functioning. Based on the Local Autonomy Index (LAI; see Ladner et al. 2019), in 1990 the Hungarian system was fairly autonomous, with local government having abundant discretion to provide services[1] with moderate room to maneuver regarding policy scope and fiscal autonomy. Following the Orbán cabinet's reform (Act CLXXXIX of 2011), between 2011 and 2014 the situation significantly changed. The reform decreased local governments' formal and effective autonomy in numerous policy areas (health care, education, and social assistance), their fiscal capacity (with activity-based financing and more rigorous conditions of issuing bonds and taking out credit), and their decision-making freedom (through effective legal control by the central government). Thus, while in most other countries the level of local autonomy has been gradually growing over the past 20–25 years, Hungary has followed a completely different path: after 2011, Hungarian local autonomy decreased to below the European average, demonstrating the most dramatic decline among the 39 countries covered by the LAI project.

According to the Heinelt and Hlepas typology (2006: 34), Hungary is a Central-East European type country with a strong mayor form of local government. Based on the typology, Hungarian local governments are relatively strong actors in vertical (local-central) relations, with a wide spectrum of local competencies and financial discretion.[2] However, local governments' financial autonomy has been gradually shrinking since 1990, and due to the 2011 reform, local communities have suffered a dramatic loss of their competencies in the public services (Pálné Kovács et al. 2017: 797–800).

Considering horizontal relations, Hungarian directly elected mayors are dominant actors at the local level, who can effectively direct the decision-making of the local council and control executive functions (Várnagy & Dobos 2011: 145). After 2011, the Fidesz reform further strengthened mayors as they gained more control over decision-making and implementation (Dobos 2016: 84–85).

In sum, in its vertical relations, the Hungarian local government system has significantly diverted from the Central-East European group, as the model of decentralized territorial governance has been replaced by a centralized (deconcentrated) 'local state' model (Pálné Kovács 2016: 599), while in horizontal relations mayors have become even more dominant actors in local governments.

Local elections in the Hungarian political system

In Hungary, the National Election Office organizes the elections of the national parliament, the European Parliament, and the local communities in addition to regional (county-level) elections and the local and national elections of minorities. Simultaneously with county and minority council elections, local elections are held in October in election years.[3] From 1990 to 2014, local representatives and mayors were elected for four-year terms; thus, local and regional electoral cycles coincided with parliamentary elections. Since 2014, mayors and local council members have been elected for a term of five years.

In the first local elections in 1990, only smaller municipalities (with 10,000 or fewer inhabitants) elected their mayors directly, while in the larger communities direct election of mayors was not introduced until 1994. Direct election increases the legitimacy of mayors and strengthens their position within local (horizontal) power relations (Várnagy 2012: 40). As the local politics of larger cities is dominated by nationwide political parties, directly elected mayors have gained a more significant position in the overall political system.

As a general rule, local communities govern the municipalities through an elected mayor and local councilors, and, in addition, local referendums may have a complementary role in deciding local matters (Act CCXXXVIII of 2013). With a few exceptions (budget, local taxes, the staffing and structure of the mayor's office, and the dissolution of the council), a local referendum may be held on any subject that falls within the competence of the council. A local referendum may be initiated by at least one-quarter of the local councilors, by the committees of the council, or by the local community. The exact number of voters required to initiate a local referendum is specified in the local governments' decrees, but the minimum is between 10% and 25% of voters.

The electoral system

In Hungary, every adult citizen of a Member State of the European Union with residence in the country is eligible to vote and to be voted for in the elections of local representatives and mayors. In contrast to parliamentary elections, Hungarian residency (i.e., locality) is a key element of the eligibility to vote in local elections; in parliamentary elections, only Hungarian citizens are eligible to vote (if they do not have a residence in another country), and this eligibility also covers Hungarians without a residence in Hungary (typically members of the Hungarian diaspora in neighboring countries).

Similar to several European countries, Hungarian local governments are divided into two subsystems on the basis of the population size of the municipalities. The first subsystem consists of settlements with 10,000 or fewer inhabitants (3,006 municipalities in 2019), while larger local governments are in the second subsystem (169 municipalities). In this differentiation, the districts of Budapest are regarded as local governments with more than 10,000 inhabitants. All municipalities in the second subsystem have the same electoral formula in the local elections. However, there is a difference based on their relation to the middle tier: the voters of 'regular' municipalities (over 10,000 inhabitants) vote for the county government candidates, while cities with county rights have no middle-tier (county) elections (because they have the status of middle-tier unit) and voters in districts of the capital do not directly elect the assembly of Budapest. The Capital City Assembly (*Fővárosi Közgyűlés*) consists of district mayors; additional compensatory seats are allocated on the basis of the surplus votes of the losing organizations in the districts' mayoral elections.

In 1990, the idea behind the division of the electoral system into two subsystems was that local politics in smaller communities should be about local issues, while in larger cities it should mirror the divisions of national politics. This separation works through the electoral formulas: the plurality bloc vote formula (BV) favors the selection of individual representatives, while the mixed-member proportional formula (MMP)[4] with single-member districts and compensatory lists allows organizations, especially national parties, to compete on the local level (Kákai 2004: 122). This differentiation between subsystems is clearly reflected in the party politicization of the local level.

Based on Hungarian electoral law (Act L of 2010), it is relatively easy to run for local councilor positions: in the BV subsystem candidates need signatures from 1% of the voters in the municipality to have their name put on the ballot paper, while in the MMP subsystem a person has to be proposed by at least 1% of the voters in the given single-member district (SMD) in order to become a candidate in that district. To set up a party list (to compete for compensatory mandates), nominating organizations have to put forward candidates in more than half of the SMDs of the local government. To be a mayoral candidate, at least 3% of voters' signatures have to be collected in the first subsystem's municipalities, 300 signatures in settlements of 10,000–100,000 inhabitants, and 500 signatures in settlements with more than 100,000 inhabitants.

In smaller municipalities using the BV system, voters may cast as many votes as the number of seats on the local council, with the restriction that they can cast only one vote per candidate (i.e., cumulative voting is not allowed), and candidates with a simple majority of the votes win mandates. In the other subsystem, there are two tiers. There is a first-past-the-post (FPTP) tier, where the candidate with a simple majority of votes gains a seat in a single-member district, and the proportional (PR) tier. Thus, the MMP subsystem incorporates both territorial representation (via the single-member districts) and partisan representation (via the proportional tier). In the PR tier, seats are distributed among closed compensatory lists (i.e., voters have no influence on the order of candidates) that often consist of candidates who also run for seats in the FPTP tier. The seats are assigned within the lists on the basis of the order of candidates. Voters do not vote directly for these lists; instead, surplus votes from the FPTP tier are transferred to the PR tier. Surplus votes are votes that are cast for an SMD candidate who does not win a mandate, and they count as votes for the party list of the candidate's nominating organization. The compensatory seats are distributed among the lists on the basis of the aggregate surplus votes from single-member districts using the Sainte-Laguë method. To curb the fragmentation of the local party system this method causes, the system uses a 5% threshold in the allocation of seats (i.e., only organizations that have at least 5% of the aggregate surplus votes can gain a mandate in the proportional tier). In the mayoral elections of both subsystems, a simple majority of the votes is necessary for gaining a position (FPTP system). The institutional setting, namely, that the mayoral election is not connected to the election of the council members, often results in a divided local government in which the mayor faces an opposition council.

The size of local councils is determined by the law that regulates the number of mandates in the BV subsystem and in the two tiers of the MMP subsystem on the basis of the population of municipalities. In the smallest municipalities (under 100 inhabitants), the council consists of only two representatives, while the maximum number of mandates in the BV subsystem is eight. The smallest communities in the second subsystem (with 10,000–25,000 inhabitants) have eight SMD mandates, and three seats are allocated from compensatory lists. Theoretically, there is no maximum obtainable mandate in this subsystem; in the 2019 local elections, the maximum number of councilors was 32 (23 from SMDs and nine from compensatory lists). The ratio of mandates allocated to the FPTP and PR tiers is approximately 60 to 40.

In Hungary currently, elected local officials cannot have dual mandates (*cumul des mandats* is forbidden). While between 1994 and 2014, mayors could serve as MPs, since 2014 local councilors and mayors have not been allowed to be members of parliament, heads of central public administration offices, government officials, or public servants.

Local elections 1990–2019

The Hungarian local and regional elections are often regarded as second-order elections, in which national politics dominates the local level (see Dobos & Várnagy 2017; Wiener 2010). Before 2019, local elections were held six months after the national elections, voters considered them as the next round of the parliamentary elections (Bőhm 2006: 14), and voter turnout was significantly lower for local elections (Table 25.1). Although local and regional electoral cycles have been pushed up by one year (as local electoral terms were changed from four to five years), this does not show in the turnout rate for the 2019 local elections. Voters generally show limited interest in voting in local elections. Although citizens in larger local governments are slightly

Table 25.1 Voter turnout (percent) for local and national elections in Hungary since 1990

Local elections		Parliamentary elections[1]	
Election date	Voter turnout (%)	Election date	Voter turnout (%)
30 September 1990	40.2	**25 March 1990**	65.1
11 December 1994	43.4	**8 May 1994**	68.9
18 October 1998	45.7	**10 May 1998**	56.3
20 October 2002	51.1	**7 April 2002**	70.5
1 October 2006	53.1	**9 April 2006**	67.8
3 October 2010	46.6	**11 April 2010**	64.4
12 October 2014	44.3	**6 April 2014**	61.7
13 October 2019	48.6	**8 April 2018**	70.2

[1] 1990–2010: first round data.
Source: National Election Office

more active than voters in small communities, the difference is not significant (in 2019, the turnout was 46.8% in the BV subsystem and 51.2% in the MMP subsystem).

The lower interest in local politics is reflected not only in the relatively low turnout but also in the competitiveness of the elections: in 2019, there were more than 900 municipalities (almost 30% of local governments in Hungary) with only one candidate running for the mayoral position. In the 2019 council elections, there were about 2.4 times as many candidates as councilor positions in the BV subsystem and 2.6 times as many in the MMP subsystem. These relatively low ratios can be explained by the low level of political interest in the smaller communities, the dominance of national party politics, and the competition of two blocs in the cities.

To understand recent local party politics in Hungary, national politics needs to be considered. Before 2006, the political system could be characterized as a 'two-bloc' system with the right-wing conservative Fidesz on one side and the left-wing Hungarian Socialist Party and its coalition partner, the Alliance of Free Democrats, on the other. After the political (2006) and economic (2008) crises, the left-wing bloc collapsed and disintegrated into several parties, and new parties emerged.[5] Fidesz won the 2010 national elections and gained a two-thirds majority in parliament, allowing for restructuring of the constitutional framework; subsequently, it implemented a series of comprehensive reforms in every segment of the political system (see Körösényi et al. 2020). Since 2010, the story of the opposition has been about forging unity and forming a viable alliance against the governing party. The first relative success of this venture (after three lost general elections and two local electoral defeats) were the local elections in 2019 (Table 25.2). The joint opposition (*ellenzéki összefogás*) consisted of ten national parties with different ideological backgrounds. Their aim was to agree on a joint candidate in every place for the 2019 elections, for example, they even held primaries in a capital district and for the mayoral

Table 25.2 Electoral results by electoral subsystems in Hungary, 2019

	Share of aggregate votes in local elections		Share of seats on local councils		Share of mayors affiliated with the party	
	BV	MMP	BV	MMP	BV	MMP
Fidesz and its allies[1]	13.7	40.1	7.5	45.2	17.0	51.5
Joint opposition[2]	1.2	23.8	0.3	18.5	0.3	13.6
Other national parties[3]	0.4	1.6	0.2	0.8	0.1	0.0
Fidesz, its allies, and locals	0.5	4.0	0.2	3.0	0.1	1.8
Joint opposition and locals	0.0	10.9	0.0	7.6	0.0	3.6
Other national parties and locals	0.0	0.0	0.0	0.0	0.0	0.0
Local and independent lists	84.0	19.6	91.8	24.9	82.4	29.6

[1] Fidesz's allies are the Christian Democratic People's Party and the Hungarian Entrepreneurs' Party. In addition, there are seemingly civil organizations that can be considered either as Fidesz's civil wing (National Forum Association) or as local branches of Fidesz (e.g., Balázs Bús for Óbuda Association). In cases where these organizations set candidates or lists, they run jointly with Fidesz.

[2] Ten national parties are members of the joint opposition (Democratic Coalition, Dialogue for Hungary, Everyone's Hungary Movement, Hungarian Liberal Party, Hungarian Socialist Party, Hungarian Solidarity Movement, Hungarian Two-Tailed Dog Party, Jobbik, Momentum, and Politics Can Be Different) in addition to these parties' local electoral movements (e.g., Viva Szombathely Association). Because the joint opposition ran in more than 80 different constellations of these parties in 2019, it is impossible to include all of the results in the table separately.

[3] Other national parties are organizations that do not fit the Fidesz-joint opposition dichotomy (Hungarian Justice and Life Party, Hungarian Workers' Party, Independent Smallholders Party, and the Our Homeland Movement) and national organizations of the Roma minority (e.g., National Alliance of Roma Youth). I define nonlocal (national) parties as organizations that had candidates in more than one municipality.

position of Budapest. Although there were a few cases in which members of the joint opposition ran against each other, they achieved unity in almost every city and capital district. When an opposition party was absent from a local alliance, it usually did not run a candidate. The 2019 electoral results show that Fidesz is still the dominant national party in local politics, although the joint opposition managed to gain positions in some of the more significant urban areas.

Hungarian local politics is clearly shaped by the local electoral system, as electoral rules have a statistically significant effect on local party politicization (Soós 2015: 142). In the past 30 years, about 80% of mayors have been independent candidates in the BV subsystem, while only 8% in the MMP subsystem (Pálné Kovács 2012: 185). However, the increasing dominance of national parties is traceable in every subsystem. As Bőhm (2006: 14–15) argues, national politics suppresses local politics by controlling local issues, attempting to solve all of the problems from 'above', and enforcing its own interests. Local politics mirrors national politics, especially in larger communities, as the policy of a local government is determined by the party position of the municipality in relation to party positions at the national level (Pálné Kovács 2008).[6]

General features of Hungarian local politics are also reflected in the 2019 electoral results. The electoral system clearly has an effect on the nationalization of local party systems, because there is a significant difference between the electoral results of the two subsystems. In the smaller communities (municipalities of the BV subsystem), most local councilors and mayors are independent and local candidates. They are either local individuals (typically members of the local economic and cultural elite) or members of local (nonnational) parties. Approximately 80% of these parties are locally rooted civil organizations with the aim of helping their local communities (Soós 2008: 74). While more than 90% of councilors are independent and members of local organizations, candidates of national parties are rarely successful in smaller communities (only 8.2% of local councilors are affiliated with any national party). Based on the 2019 results, even in this subsystem the mayoral position is somewhat more exposed to national politics. Considering that this is one of the most important positions in Hungarian local politics, it could be argued that the share of mayors affiliated with a party is an indicator of party politicization in smaller communities: national parties are present in approximately 20% of municipalities with 10,000 or fewer inhabitants.

The politics of larger local governments (municipalities of the MMP subsystem) shows a very different picture. Here, locals and independents are not as relevant. National parties receive four-fifths of the votes and three-fourths of the council seats, while only 25% of local councilor positions and 30% of mayoral positions are held by locals or independents. These ratios are not negligible, although in several municipalities independent candidates are informally supported by national parties (especially in the case of mayoral positions, e.g., Békéscsaba or Pécs in 2019). Another indicator of party politicization is the emergence of national-local alliances: about 10% of councilors were elected as joint candidates of a local civil organization and a national party – this phenomenon is almost entirely missing from the local governments of the BV subsystem.

In sum, the nature of Hungarian local politics is different in the small communities and in larger towns and cities: small municipalities are ruled by locally rooted independents and members of civil organizations, while national politics is more successful in the MMP subsystem. The phenomenon that the results of the parliamentary and local elections tend to move together in the larger local communities implies that local politics is subordinate to national party politics in these municipalities.

In Hungary, female representation shows slow but gradual growth on the local level (Table 25.3). The percentage of female councilors is somewhat higher than in other Central-East European countries but is still behind Western Europe (see Sundström & Stockemer 2015),

Table 25.3 Share (percent) of women among elected councilors, mayors, and members of parliament in Hungary, 1990–2019

Election year	1990	1994	1998	2002	2006	2010	2014	2019[1]
Councilors	N/A	19.9	22.7	26.5	28.4	29.2	30.1	32.7
Mayors	10.5	10.4	12.7	14.9	15.9	18.0	20.2	21.7
Members of parliament	7.3	11.1	8.3	9.1	10.6	9.1	10.1	11.2

[1] 2018 election data are used for members of parliament.
Source: National Election Office and Vajda (2019)

while in national politics, Hungary is far behind the region's other countries in terms of female representation (Montgomery & Ilonszki 2016: 701). In 2019, every third elected councilor and every fifth mayor was a woman. However, there is a major difference between the two local subsystems: while 34.2% of councilors and 22.3% of mayors are women in smaller local governments, their share is only 23.4% and 9.5%, respectively, in municipalities with more than 10,000 inhabitants. As these larger settlements are clearly more important for national politics, it may be argued that the more national politics is involved in local politics, the less markedly women are represented. This gender bias cannot be traced in the voters' behavior; rather, it is the product of the candidate selection processes of parties (Tóth & Ilonszki 2015). The same argument can be made about women's parliamentary representation, as there has been a large gap between local and national female representation data every election year since 1990. While the number of women in local politics has been steadily and significantly increasing over the past three decades, on the national level it has been stagnant. Although several studies show that there is a general career path from the local to the national level (e.g., Kjaer 2006; Borchert & Stolz 2011), based on women's counterselection, it seems that this career progression path is seriously flawed for women in Hungary.

Based on the limited data on incumbency in local politics, it seems that the mayoral position is fairly stable. In every election between 1994 and 2002, approximately two-thirds of mayors were reelected, and 30% of mayors held their position continuously for the first 16 years after the transition (Fekete 2006: 176). This reelection rate does not seem to depend on settlement size. In cities with county rights, 83% of mayors have been reelected every time since 2006, and in one case, the mayor of a city has held his position since 1994 (Petrovszki 2019: 43).

Discussion

The Hungarian local level of government is characterized by two simultaneous processes: national parties are gaining weight in a system that is gradually losing its significance in the political structure.

Hungarian local politics has always been two-faced. Although to some extent the impact of national party politics can be felt even in smaller communities, these municipalities are ruled primarily by local and independent political actors. At the same time, national parties are the dominant actors in the politically more significant urban areas, holding most of the mayoral and councilor positions. Since the mid-1990s, party dominance has increased in municipalities with more than 5,000 inhabitants (Tóth 2013: 126).

The electoral system amplifies differences between the two worlds of Hungarian local politics: the bloc vote method used by the small communities is favorable for independent candidates, while the application of the MMP formula in municipalities with more than 10,000 inhabitants results in candidates with ties to political organizations. What national politics concentrates on is even reflected in the 2010 local electoral reform. The reform primarily affected elections in the larger local governments and shifted the system into a more majoritarian direction.[7]

The history of local elections of the MMP subsystem has met the expectations of the legislators of the democratic transition: indeed, the local politics of municipalities with more than 10,000 inhabitants mirrors national politics. These elections can be considered as the next round of the parliamentary elections. Electoral results are determined primarily by the national political situation, and the changes in national politics (for example, the concentration of the party system in the 2000s or the recent attempts by the opposition parties to jointly face Fidesz) are followed by the shift in local politics.

Notes

1 The local governments have mandatory tasks (providing basic health care and social assistance services, maintaining municipal roads, etc.). In addition, they may provide any voluntary services that are not under the jurisdiction of other state organs.
2 In practice, Hungary fits into the Central-East European group only to a certain extent, as even in the early 1990s local governments were underfinanced relative to their tasks, and the central government had effective control over local budgets (see Vigvári 2010). As a result of this narrow financial elbow room, in the first 20 years, local governments accumulated huge debts. The Orbán cabinet consolidated the local level's finances in 2012–214 and unconditionally assumed not only local competencies but also the municipal debt of over €4 billion.
3 Although minorities can elect representatives of local minority governments, this study does not consider minority elections as local elections, because only about 45% of municipalities have minority governments and most minorities had elections in only a few municipalities in 2019. Furthermore, the processes of election, nomination, and voting are different from those in local elections.
Local minority governments have a supplementary role to local governments: they fulfill tasks and competences handed over by local councils, maintain minority institutions and preserve the traditions of the local minority, initiate minority-related policies, etc.
4 The subsystem fits into the MMP category in the typology of Reynolds et al. (2005), although it can be described as a mixed-member majoritarian (MMM) system with partial compensation according to Shugart and Wattenberg (2001).
5 One of the new parties was the radical-right Jobbik. As Jobbik won 12% of mandates in 2010, Fidesz had opposition on both ends of the political spectrum in parliament. Since 2010, the main question for the opposition parties was whether the left-wing and right-wing parties should (or could) form a common front against Fidesz.
6 An example of national politics forcing its own agenda on local governments may be the issue of migrants, which is a key element of Fidesz's political strategy. Right before the 2019 local elections, the prime minister sent a letter to every citizen claiming, '[this Sunday] we decide whether our cities and villages will have pro- or anti-migration leaders' (source: https://24.hu/kozelet/2019/10/07/orban-viktor-level-onkormanyzati-valasztas/).
7 The process of nomination was changed slightly, and they introduced the 5% threshold in the MMP subsystem, but the main point concerned the number of mandates (see Dobos 2016: 79–81). The number of seats was decreased by an average of 25% in the majority tiers (BV subsystem and SMDs of the MMP subsystem), while the number of mandates allocated with proportional formulas (compensatory mandates in MMP subsystem, county or capital government mandates) was halved.

References

Bőhm, A. (2006). Az önkormányzati választások a parlamenti választások tükrében [Local elections in the mirror of parliamentary elections]. In A. Bőhm (Ed.) *A helyi hatalom és az önkormányzati választások Magyarországon 1990–2002* (pp. 11–18). Budapest: MTA Politikai Tudományok Intézete.
Borchert, J. & Stolz, K. (2011). Introduction: Political careers in multi-level systems. *Regional & Federal Studies*, 21(2), 107–115.

Dobos, G. (2016). Changing local relations: Effects of the 2010–2014 political and administrative reforms in Hungary. In M.W. Sienkiewicz & K. Kuc-Czajkowska (Eds.) *Local Government in Selected Central and Eastern European Countries: Experiences, Reforms, and Determinants of Development* (pp. 73–90). Lublin: Maria Curie-Skłodowska University Press.

Dobos, G. & Várnagy, R. (2017). Hungary: Are neglected regional elections second-order elections? In A.H. Schakel (Ed.) *Regional and National Elections in Eastern Europe: Territoriality of the Vote in Ten Countries* (pp. 105–128). London: Palgrave Macmillan.

Fekete, A. (2006). A polgármesteri tisztség stabilitása' [Stability of the mayoral position]. In A. Bőhm (Ed.) *A helyi hatalom és az önkormányzati választások Magyarországon 1990–2002* (pp. 175–190). Budapest: MTA Politikai Tudományok Intézete.

Heinelt, H. & Hlepas, N.K. (2006). Typologies of local government systems. In H. Bäck, H. Heinelt & A. Magnier (Eds.) *The European Mayor: Political Leaders in the Changing Context of Local Democracy* (pp. 21–33). Wiesbaden: VS Verlag Für Sozialwissenschaften.

Kákai, L. (2004). *Önkormányzunk értetek, de nélkületek! [We govern for you but without you!]* Budapest: Századvég.

Kjaer, U. (2006) The mayor's political career. In H. Bäck, H. Heinelt & A. Magnier (Eds.) *The European Mayor: Political Leaders in the Changing Context of Local Democracy* (pp. 75–98). Wiesbaden: VS Verlag Für Sozialwissenschaften.

Körösényi, A., Illés, G. & Gyulai, A. (2020). *The Orbán Regime: Plebiscitary Leader Democracy in the Making*. London: Routledge.

Ladner, A., Keuffer, N., Baldersheim, H., Hlepas, N., Swianiewicz, P., Steyvers, K. & Navarro, C. (2019). *Patterns of Local Autonomy in Europe*. London: Palgrave Macmillan.

Montgomery, K.A. & Ilonszki, G. (2016). Stuck in the basement: A pathway case analysis of female recruitment in Hungary's 2010 national assembly elections. *Politics & Gender*, 12(4), 700–726.

Pálné Kovács, I. (2008). *Helyi kormányzás Magyarországon [Local governance in Hungary]* Pécs: Dialóg Campus.

Pálné Kovács, I. (2012). Roots and consequences of local governance reforms in Hungary, *Revue d'études comparatives Est-Ouest*, 43(3), 173–197.

Pálné Kovács, I. (2016). Modellváltás a magyar önkormányzati rendszerben [Model change in the Hungarian local governments system]. In A. Jakab & G. Gajduschek (Eds.) *A magyar jogrendszer állapota* (pp. 583–599). Budapest: MTA Társadalomtudományi Kutatóközpont.

Pálné Kovács, I., Bodor, Á., Finta, I., Grünhut, Z., Zongor, G. & Kacziba, P. (2017). Farewell to decentralisation: The Hungarian story and its general implications. *Croatian and Comparative Public Administration*, 16(4), 789–816.

Petrovszki, L. (2019). Polgármesterek inkumbencia előnye a megyei jogú városokban Magyarországon [Incumbency advantage of mayors in cities with county rights in Hungary]. *Metszetek*, 8(4), 40–51.

Reynolds, A., Reilly, B. & Ellis, A. (2005). *Electoral System Design: The New International IDEA Handbook*. Stockholm: International IDEA.

Shugart, M. & Wattenberg, M.P. (2001). *Mixed-Member Electoral Systems: The Best of Both Worlds?* Oxford: Oxford University Press.

Soós, G. (2008). Local and national parties in Hungary. In M. Reiser & E. Holtmann (Eds.) *Farewell to the Party Model? Independent Local Lists in East and West European Countries* (pp. 63–84). Wiesbaden: VS Verlag für Sozialwissenschaften.

Soós, G. (2015). *Local Government Institutionalization in Hungary*. Frankfurt am Main: Peter Lang.

Soós, G. & Kálmán, J. (2002). Report on the state of local democracy in Hungary. In G. Soós, G. Tóka & G. Wright (Eds.) *The State of Local Democracy in Central Europe* (pp. 15–106). Budapest: Open Society Institute.

Sundström, A. & Stockemer, D. (2015). What determines women's political representation at the local level? A fine-grained analysis of the European regions. *International Journal of Comparative Sociology*, 56(3–4), 254–274.

Tóth, A. (2013). Országos pártok – helyi önkormányzatok [National parties – local governments]. *Politikatudományi Szemle*, 22(3), 117–137.

Tóth, A., & Ilonszki, G. (2015). Pártok vagy választók? A női jelöltek esélye az egyéni választókerületekben, 1998–2010. [Parties or Voters? The Opportunity Structures of Female Candidates in Single Member Districts 1998-2010]. *Politikatudományi Szemle*, 24(3), 27–51.

Vajda, A. (2019). Lehetséges-e a nők képviselete nők nélkül? A női ügyek megjelenése a magyar Országgyűlésben (1998–2014). [Is it possible to represent women without women? The appearance of women's issues in the Hungarian national assembly (1998–2014)]. Unpublished dissertation, Corvinus University of Budapest. Available at: http://phd.lib.uni-corvinus.hu/1062/1/Vajda%20Adrienn.pdf (Accessed: 29 August 2020).

Várnagy, R. (2012). *Polgármesterek a magyar Országgyűlésben* [Mayors in the Hungarian National Assembly] Budapest: Ad Librum.

Várnagy, R. & Dobos, G. (2011). Ki az úr a háznál? Döntéshozatal a magyar önkormányzati rendszerben [Who is in charge? Decision-making in the Hungarian local government system]. *Pro Publico Bono*, Special Issue no. 1, 130–146.

Vigvári, A. (2010). Is the conflict container full? Problems of fiscal sustainability at the local government level in Hungary. *Acta Oeconomica*, 60(1), 49–77.

Wiener, G. (2010). Pártok az önkormányzati választásokon 1990–2006 [Parties in the local elections 1990–2006]. In L. Kákai (Ed.) *20 évesek az önkormányzatok: Születésnap vagy halotti tor?* (pp. 117–148). Pécs: Publikon.

26
Latvia
Electoral drama in local governments

Iveta Reinholde and Malvīne Stučka

A reformed local government system

After the restoration of independence in 1990, Latvia invested enormous effort in establishing a modern and democratic system of governance, in which local governments would have their own unique role. The government had already drafted laws expressing idealistic visions of municipal operations in the early 1990s. The first law on local self-government was approved in April 1991, while the law regulating districts on the regional level (*rajons*) was approved a year later – in February 1992 (Vanags & Vilka 2005:114). Both were transitional laws moving toward fully democratic municipalities. Established in 1993, the Ministry of State Reform designed a new law 'On local self-governments' (1994), taking the Danish experience as a role model. However, municipal governments spent the whole first part of the 1990s searching for the best models of municipal function by learning about service delivery and a community-focused approach.

In 2009, Latvia finally completed part of a major 11-year administrative territorial reform by amalgamating the existing 556 municipalities into 119. The average number of inhabitants per rural municipality reached 19,100 instead of the previous 4,300. Since 2009, Latvia has only had municipalities at the local level, as the regional-level districts were abolished. Out of 119 municipalities, 110 are rural municipalities (*novads*) and nine are 'republic' cities (*republikas pilsēta*), representing municipalities in the urban area. A 'republic' city, as described in the law 'On administrative territories' (2008), performs commercial activities, has a public transport network and community facilities, has social and culture-related infrastructure, and has at least 25,000 permanent residents. Thus, Latvia is represented by two tiers of government – the central public administration and municipalities at the local level.

In order to foster economic development and manage EU funding, five planning regions were created in 2006 as cooperative structures to coordinate joint actions of the central level and municipalities. However, these planning regions cannot be considered 'regions' in the meaning of the Framework Reference for Regional Democracy as they are not recognized as self-governing (Saeima 2002).

In 2019, the government launched another round of administrative territorial reforms, aiming to cut the number of municipalities by a factor of three. The debate on the role of a regional level of governance is still open, as no political consensus has been reached regarding a functional municipal division.

A recent law, 'On administrative territories and populated areas' (approved by the Latvian parliament, the Saeima on 10 June 2020), aims to have the municipal elections in 2021 in 42 newly formed municipalities instead of the current 119. The reform initiative was criticized by the municipalities because of insufficient communication among the levels of governance and political ignorance expressed by local communities toward possible mergers. As a result, more and more municipalities decided to submit claims to the Constitutional Court during the summer of 2020. Meanwhile, before the approval of the law, the Congress of Regional and Local Governments of the Council of Europe discerned a lack of adequate, timely, and appropriate consultation of local communities regarding the design of the territorial reform during a fact-finding mission in December 2019. The Congress suggested the suspension of the reform in order to carry out a renewed, proper consultation (Council of Europe 2020).

The Latvian municipalities are focused on public service delivery, while the national level sets the policy design frame. The institutional settings of municipalities, taxation, power, and sources of revenue are homogeneous across the country. There are no 'genuine' local taxes in Latvia, as all taxes are collected centrally and afterward distributed proportionally to municipalities on the basis of a set criteria derived from service delivery data, except for the real estate tax, which is designed centrally and collected locally. The local tax revenue (i.e., real estate tax) in 2017 was around 6% of GDP, which reflects the constrained fiscal autonomy of Latvian municipalities (Cadoret & Cools 2018). Thus, the financial self-reliance of Latvian municipalities is exceptionally low, and municipalities keep a small share of their income, while the functions to be performed are numerous.

According to the Local Autonomy index, Latvian municipalities are measured to be close to the European average as Latvia scored 19.7 in 1995 and 20.3 in 2014. Latvia is somewhere in the second half of all countries in terms of its overall score (ranked 26th out of the 39 cases) (Ladner et al. 2015). The index remains generally stable with organizational autonomy, as administrative supervision and legal protection have been steady since 1994, aiming only to ensure legal compliance, while fiscal autonomy has been restricted. Latvian municipalities are responsible for basic infrastructure and communal services (e.g., water and sewage management, waste management, maintenance of infrastructure), child care, schools, social care, and culture. Local spatial planning and support for development initiatives are also part of the tasks performed by municipalities. Latvia, like the United Kingdom and Hungary, belongs to that group of countries in which municipalities are characterized by high spending responsibilities and low local autonomy (Heinelt et al. 2018). While Latvian municipalities are autonomous regarding their organizational structures, low local tax autonomy and limited financial self-reliance reflects a tendency toward recentralization.

In the design of the system of municipalities, horizontal power relations were instituted as well. Latvia belongs to the group of countries with a committee leader form of government (Mouritzen & Svara 2002), and there are no directly elected mayors in Latvian municipalities. All members of the local council are elected by the residents, and then the newly elected councilors select the chairperson of the council [who becomes the mayor (*domes priekšsēdētājs*)], vice chairs, and chairs of committees. Thus, the chairperson of the council is a political leader who shares power with strong committee leaders or the executive director (i.e., an administrative leader), thus establishing a division of powers between the elected local councils (local legislative power) and the administration of the municipalities (executive power of the municipality) (Navarro et al. 2018).

In general, citizens are relatively satisfied with the performance of municipalities: in 2018, 51% of respondents trusted the municipalities in Latvia, which is a high percentage in comparison with the level of trust in the Parliament (*Saeima*) – 21% (European Commission 2019:6). Stable trust tendencies can also be seen toward municipalities since 2013, when approximately 58% of residents were satisfied with the performance of municipalities (Leta 2019). The lowest level of satisfaction was identified during the economic recession of 2009, when approximately 52% of respondents were dissatisfied with the performance of municipalities. In 2010, dissatisfaction was around 48% and it reached the same level of dissatisfaction as in 2001 (Ibid.).

The local election cycle

All elections in Latvia – local, national, and European Parliament elections – are organized by a single central government body, the Central Election Commission, which was reinstituted in 1992 after the long period of Soviet occupation.

The City Council and Municipality Council (hereinafter, council) is elected for a period of four years in equal, direct, and proportional elections. The elections of the council usually take place on the first Saturday of June. National elections are also held every four years. However, local and national elections are not simultaneous, as the current election follows the cycles started separately at the beginning of the 1990s. Thus, the next local level elections will take place in 2021, while the national elections will be in 2022 and the European Parliament elections in 2024. Simultaneous elections for the local level and European Parliament occurred only in 2009. Local elections are one year ahead of the national elections and are perceived as a kind of public opinion poll before the national elections to test general political trends in the region and the public's acceptance of political party manifestos.

As parliament is elected by open-list proportional representation from five multimember constituencies [Vidzeme, Latgale, Zemgale, Kurzeme, and Rīga (in which overseas votes are counted)], the successes and failures of the political parties in municipalities of a particular region are capable of signaling voter preferences and mood. However, voter turnout has always been higher for the national elections than for local ones, as the latter serve as a piloting platform for campaign ideas that are later displayed in the national preelection campaign.

With respect to local autonomy, it is assumed that regular local elections are organized every four years. However, the law 'On local government' describes certain conditions for the recall of a local council, as well as the chair of the council. The *Saeima* (parliament) and the court have the power to recall a council while the local community does not, not even via a referendum. However, while rare, some recall cases have occurred. New elections, followed by a dissolution of the council by the *Saeima*, were held in the Renda municipality in 2003 and in the Ķekava municipality in 2008. In 2010, new council elections took place in the Roja and Mērsrags municipalities, as the previously larger municipality was split into two smaller ones (Balode 2018). Finally, the Rīga city council was dissolved in February 2020 as the council failed to organize three sequential council meetings with the necessary number of councilors participating. The parliament justified this dissolution on the basis of illegal actions in implementing autonomous municipal functions, as the Rīga city council failed to manage residential waste, which is quite remarkable for a capital.

The issue of local referenda for recalling the council is on the political agenda. The draft law on local referenda was submitted to the parliament in 2013. However, after two readings in the parliament, it was impeded as the ministry overseeing municipalities was questioning the rationality of such a law (Ņikona 2019). Multiple arguments followed against the draft law, for example, the creation of additional budgetary costs.

The recall of local authorities is possible under specific conditions aimed to safeguard local autonomy. Usually, parliament dissolves the council if it acted illegally or ignored or broke national laws, or if the council has inner political tensions leading to the failure to elect the chair of the council, the vice chair, and permanent committees within two months after the elections. Political tensions between elected political parties are the most common reason for the lack of a quorum in the council meetings, resulting in a recall. However, Latvian laws do not foresee an option to recall the chairperson of the council (i.e., the mayor) or an individual councilor. Politically diverse opinions among the councilors may result in the change of the council chairperson, as he/she is elected from among the councilors. Often, relocation of the chairperson is part of the political consensus seeking process in the local councils where no elected political parties have been capable of winning the majority of seats.

The dissolution procedure requires the ministry overseeing municipalities (i.e., the Ministry of Regional Development and Environmental Protection) to submit a draft law to the parliament. Afterward, the parliament – either by rejecting or by accepting such law – sets the new date for extraordinary elections. Yet, if fewer than 15 months are left before the regular elections, the extraordinary elections are not organized. Thus, Latvia follows the traditions of a parliamentary republic, where councils are safeguarded from the citizens' changing mood in immediate recall.

The local election system

The Latvian electoral system is based on proportional representation, as the *Saeima* and local councils are elected in equal, general, and direct elections by secret ballot.

Any Latvian citizen who is at least 18 years old is eligible to vote in both local and national elections. In addition, EU citizens on the voters' registry are eligible for participation in the local elections. The residence requirement for enrolment on the voters' registry at least 90 days before the election or property ownership is a condition applied for the local elections only. These conditions highlight the links between the person and a local territory, as expressed in the European Charter of Local Self-Government. Permanent municipal residents are the main electorate for the local elections, while national elections accept votes from Latvian citizens working and traveling abroad.

From time to time, there are debates about the rights of Latvian noncitizens to vote in the local elections. Data reflect that 11.4% (242,560) of the population are noncitizens representing many ethnic groups mainly using the Russian language as their primary language of communication (Balode 2017). However, ethnically, the Russian-speaking minority is not homogeneous, as it consists of such ethnic groups as Russians, Belarusians, Ukrainians, Roma, and Jews who are both citizens and noncitizens. Noncitizens permanently residing in Latvia can apply for Latvian citizenship by a naturalization procedure. Because citizens and permanent noncitizens have equal social and economic rights, the motivation for noncitizens to change their political status is rather low (Balode 2017).

The voters' registry (or electoral roll, electoral register) is a system containing the data of citizens who are entitled to vote. In Latvia, the voters' registry is used only for elections of the European Parliament and local (municipal) elections. Based on the data included in the registry, the voters' lists are produced and handed to the polling stations. Usually, the Office of Citizenship and Migration Affairs (a central government body) creates a list of voters for each local authority for an early check and update at least 120 days before local elections. However, it is possible for voters to change their polling station (i.e., to vote either in their place of residence or where they own real estate) up until the 25th day before elections.

There are only three conditions for ineligibility to vote: (1) the person has been declared incapable by a national court, (2) the person has been sentenced and is serving time in prison, or (3) the person has been denied the right to vote in another EU member state (Saeima 1994).

The local councilors are elected on the basis of an open-list proportional representation (OLPR) system according to the IDEA typology. Citizens vote for a political party or an association of two or more political parties. In smaller municipalities with fewer than 5,000 residents, citizens may form voters' unions (nonparty or independent electoral associations), which consist of a list of nonpartisan candidates. Whatever the list is (partisan or nonpartisan), voters have the opportunity to either cross out (i.e., to place a minus sign '−') or emphasize (i.e., to place a plus sign '+') candidates on the list, expressing their popularity rating for each candidate and, thus, changing the order of candidates on the list. For example, a voter may cross out or emphasize all candidates, or a voter may choose to cross out or emphasize only one candidate as there are no limits on the number of minus or plus symbols on the list. In addition, it is possible to vote for the list without giving any preferential votes. This feature is also common for the national elections. However, Latvian voters are not allowed to split their vote between more than one list, as the principle – 'one vote, one list' – prevails. For example, 80.5% (578,697) of all valid lists were modified in the 2017 local elections by adding a plus sign or minus sign.

Each municipality is a separate electoral district, whatever the size of the municipality. Thus, the administrative territory of a local government forms a separate constituency. The threshold of 5% is set for both local and national elections, ensuring that any list (single party or coalition) receiving fewer than 5% of the total number of votes in the local elections is excluded from the distribution of seats in the municipality. To distribute seats among the lists, the Sainte-Laguë method is applied. Within the list, the candidates are ranked according to the number of votes they receive. The formula is as follows. The number of votes cast for the candidate is equal to the number of votes collected for the whole list where the candidate was included. From the total number of votes on the list, ballots on which the candidate was crossed out are deducted and ballots with a '+' are added. In case in which candidates on the same list are equally popular among the electorate, the sequence of candidates on the list plays a role. (Saeima 1994) Political parties usually place their most popular candidates in the top positions of the list to increase their election prospects.

For both political parties and voters' unions, equal entry rules are set for preparing and submitting a list of candidates. Therefore, the number of candidates on the list may exceed the number of seats on the council in question by three. Voters' unions are expected to submit their list of candidates along with the signatures of at least 20 residents. Candidates can stand for elections only on a single list. If the electoral commission identifies that a candidate is running for more than one list, the candidate is disqualified from all lists.

The municipal electoral commission checks all candidate lists along with all of the supporting documents submitted by the political parties and voters' unions within one day and can only make two decisions – to accept it or to reject it. Electoral commissions (each municipality has its own) only accept lists of candidates that have paid a deposit to the special account in the State Treasury. The sums vary between €120 and €210, depending on the number of residents in the relevant municipality (Saeima 1994). For national elections, the deposit applied to a list is €1,400 regardless of the size of the political party (Saeima 1995). Comparing national and local elections, the local ones are more open to motivating citizens to participate and to stand for elections. The local election rules apply for all municipalities.

The security deposit for submitting a list of candidates applies to only a single administrative territory. If the political party would like to submit candidate lists in several municipalities, the security deposit shall be paid for each of them. The party receives the deposit back if it wins at least one seat, while the deposits of those who lost are incorporated in the municipal budget. Thus, participation in the local elections also requires financial commitment from the participants.

There are some legal restrictions on candidates standing for election. As a rule, a candidate is rejected if he/she is serving a sentence in prison or is banned by the court from standing in elections. Latvia also excludes candidates who have been either a member of an illegal organization or an agent of the Soviet secret and intelligence services during the occupation period (Saeima 1994). Latvia has set the ineligibility rule to prevent persons who supported the Latvian occupation from coming to power, considering the political consequences of the Soviet occupation.

Finally, the president, the members of parliament, members of the government, prosecutors, judges, the state auditor, members of the Board of the State Audit Office, and soldiers may stand for local elections, but, if they are elected, they are required to resign their current administrative or political position as dual mandates are not possible. This also explains why top level administrators are rare on the lists as candidates.

The results of the local elections

Since the beginning of the 1990s, the ratio between councilors and inhabitants has increased due to limits on the number of councilors and natural population decline. The first sharp decrease in the number of elected councilors was in 1994 – on average three times fewer councilors were elected after 1994. After 1994, the number of councilors was directly linked to the number of residents, whatever administrative border changes may occur (see Table 26.1). Currently, there are 1,614 councilors in 119 municipalities; it is expected that the mergers of 2021 will result in another round of reductions and approximately 50% fewer councilors will be elected. Thus, the smallest municipality currently has nine councilors, while the largest, Riga city, has 60 councilors. It is expected that after the reform of 2021, the number of councilors will be linked to the number of residents in all municipalities, eliminating the special status for republic cities and the Riga city council.

Finally, even though Latvian municipalities are ruled by a committee, the chairperson is still an influential official as he/she should organize the effective and reasonable operation of the municipality. Thus, the top position on the list is occupied by a person who is popular and well recognized in the municipality and who, after the elections, will most probably take the seat of chairperson.

Table 26.1 Number of councilors in municipalities in Latvia

Number of residents in municipality	Between 2013 and 2021		After 2021	
	Local council (novads)	Republic city	Number of residents in municipality	
Up to 5,000	9			
5,001–20,000	15			
20,001–50,000	17		Up to 30,000	15
More than 50,000	19	15	30,001–60,000	19
Up to 50,000		13	More than 60,000	23
		60 (only Riga city council)		

Source: Saeima (1994, 2020)

Voting is not mandatory in local or parliament elections, affecting the turnout for elections. Even though the trust in municipalities (49%) is higher than in the national parliament (19%) (European Commission 2019), citizens are still less active in local elections (see Figure 26.1).

The data reflect a decrease in participation over time for both local and national elections. The local elections have faced both ups and downs. The slight increase in the participation rate in 2001 may potentially be explained by the rise of preelection campaigns and the first steps of political parties to market their political platform. On the contrary, the turnout in 2005 reflected a political slowdown and relaxation after Latvia entered the EU in 2004. Another potential explanation for the downturn in turnout could be related to the fact that municipalities are getting bigger in size, however, in Latvia, the size of the municipality does not affect the turnout rate for the local elections.

The local elections of 2013 had the lowest turnout rate so far. There are several explanations. First, these were the first elections after the economic downturn of 2008–2009, coinciding with a generally pessimistic mood about the ability of municipalities to provide help. Another relevant factor is related to campaign limits: a new law was approved forbidding electoral advertisements on TV at least 30 days prior to the elections. Finally, the low turnout may be related to decreasing political competition at the local level. All factors together might have led to low turnout.

In a survey by the opinion research center SKDS in 2017, profiles of the 'average voter' and 'average nonvoter' were developed. The 'average voter' is a person with a university education, working in the public sector with average or high income, and at least 45 years old. The 'average nonvoter' is stereotypically a person with basic education, mostly unemployed, low income, and 18–44 years old (SKDS 2017). The place of residence also differs – the typical 'voter' most probably lives in Riga or another relatively large city, whereas the typical 'nonvoter' probably lives in a rural region (Ibid.). These sociological findings relate to the turnout data showing that rural areas are less active than cities. At the same time, larger municipalities (by population size) are

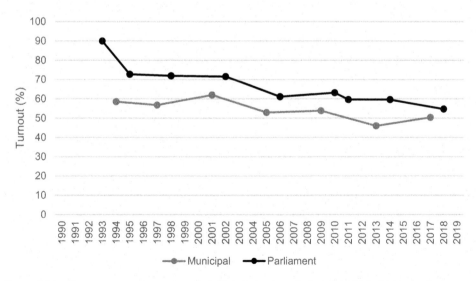

Figure 26.1 Voter turnout for national and local elections in Latvia, 1993–2018
Source: Central Election Commission.

also facing decreasing turnout. Data in Figure 26.2 highlight a positive correlation – the larger the municipality, the more active the electorate. As this trend is observed in rural municipalities, one would expect that election turnout might increase as a result of amalgamation into larger municipal entities. However, the size of the municipality matters, as the positive correlation is related to the small municipalities with around 60% election turnout. In this context, Latvia is not unique, as Koch and Rochat (2017) have argued that in larger municipalities the turnout is significantly lower than in smaller municipalities.

The size of municipalities in terms of population affects the turnout for local elections. Data reflect that small communities are the most active, while community interest is a bit lower in larger cities (van Houwelingen 2017). The heightened activity of small communities is most likely explained by higher interpersonal relationships among community members and easier access to councilors for resolving community-related issues.

The number of lists and candidates also decreased after the administrative territorial reform of 2009. For example, the average number of submitted candidate lists participating in the last local elections (2017) was ten for the republic cities, including Riga. On the other hand, the average number of political parties meeting the 5% threshold was only four. In the last elections of 2017, 8,945 candidates ran for the 1,614 seats on 119 councils. There were thus approximately 5.5 persons competing for each council seat. For comparison, in the municipal elections of 2013, competition was similar with around 5.3 candidates per seat (LPS 2017:6). There is a trend that higher competition for seats is observed in municipalities with higher economic capacity (see Figure 26.3).

In five municipalities – Varakļāni, Vaiņode, Pārgauja, Lubāna, and Rundāle – the submission of lists was extended for another ten days in 2017, as only one list was submitted, limiting political competition and voters' choices. The extra time nudged local political activists to form voters' unions in four of these municipalities, while in the remaining municipality, the election was recognized as legitimate as the single submitted list contained the necessary minimum

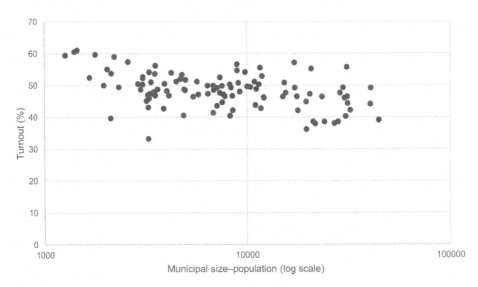

Figure 26.2 Voter turnout in the 2017 Latvian local elections by municipality size
Source: Central Election Commission.

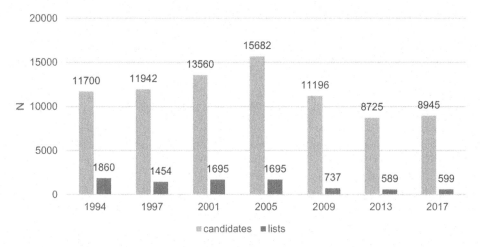

Figure 26.3 Competitiveness in the 2017 Latvian local elections (lists and candidates)
Source: Central Election Commission and Central Statistical Bureau of Latvia

number of candidates. In general, there are extremely rare cases of uncontested local election results being brought to court. Historically, the courts canceled the election results of two municipalities back in 2001.

In the last election (2017), out of all of the political parties and party associations competing for seats on the municipal level, the political party Visu Latvijai/Tēvzemei un Brīvībai [All for Latvia! – Fatherland and Freedom (LNNK)] won the most seats – 166 – followed by the coalition of two political parties – Zaļo un Zemnieku Savienība (ZZS) (the Greens and Farmers' Union) – with 157 seats. The political party Zemnieku Savienība (Farmer's Union) itself was able to collect 145 seats (LPS 2017:9). There is another relevant trend – the partisan lists with independent candidates are more attractive to voters.

However, national political parties usually compete for seats in cities, while rural municipalities are facing the competition of local political parties and voters' associations. Voters' associations can submit lists of candidates for local elections only in small municipalities with a population of fewer than 5,000 residents (Saeima 1994). From 1994 to 2005, most councilors were elected from lists submitted by voters' associations capable of attracting the locally recognized political activists and local leaders. Voters' unions are not permanent and, in most cases, they have a life cycle of only one term; the municipal territorial amalgamation of 2009 has substantially weakened their position.

There were 103 voters' unions lists with 1,045 candidates (11.6% of all candidates) submitted in the 2017 local elections. Thus, voters' unions become less active once the number of inhabitants of a municipality increases. After the amalgamation of 2020 aimed at substantially increasing the number of inhabitants per municipality, only the political parties will compete for seats on councils. There were several arguments to exclude voters' unions from political competition, among which the most significant was related to the nontransparent finances of such unions. The political parties dominating national politics intend to increase their political influence at the local level, while voters' unions having local leaders on their lists are serious competitors for the seats in the municipalities (Kupčs 2020). In Latvia, voters' unions having no partisan affiliation are perceived as representatives of 'fair' politics, while political parties are commonly labeled with social biases of corruption and unfair politics (Dubois & Leprince 2017).

After the 2017 elections, 24% of the approved elected council chairs were women, while 34% of councilor seats were filled by women (see Table 26.2). In the 2018 national elections, women made up 31% of the members elected to parliament. Typically, the elected chairwomen govern small, rural municipalities with more female councilors, while towns and cities tend to have more male councilors (LPS 2017:9).

Ethnically, most candidates are Latvians – 6,929 or 77.5% (67.6% in the 2013 elections) – while 1,520 candidates (17.0%) did not state their nationality. Other ethnic groups represented in the local elections of 2017 were Russians (331 candidates, 3.7%), Poles (43 candidates, 0.5%), Lithuanians (42, 0.5%), Belarusians (30, 0.3%), Ukrainians (28, 0.3%), and Estonians (4, 0.1%) (LPS 2017). Out of 119 municipalities, 30 elected a new council chairperson with no previous experience as a top local politician in the respective position (LPS 2017). However, most of these 'freshmen' have professional experience related to local government issues – they were councilors or worked in municipal executive agencies and are familiar with the operational mode of municipalities. At the same time, one-third of the council chairpersons in nine republic cities have been in office for more than 15 years (Balode 2017).

A calculation highlights that there are 321 councilors (approximately 20% of the total number) who were reelected in each of the last four local elections (Kažoka et al. 2017). This highlights that being a councilor is recognized as an activity worthy of investing one's personal time and resources.

Despite the huge diversity in remuneration, local councilors receive nonmaterial benefits for their efforts: being a local councilor provides social prestige and recognition as well as access to administrative resources. Remuneration for local councilors may range from €3.59 per month (in smaller municipalities) up to €749 per month (in cities) (Reinholde & Stučka2019a). The difference in salary between ordinary elected councilors and the chairperson might be a factor of €420 (Reinholde and Stučka 2019a).

Discussion

Since it regained its independence in 1991, Latvia has faced intense political, administrative, economic, and territorial reforms. Serious governance reforms pushed forward by its accession to the EU were required for the transition to a full democracy and market economy. The Latvian municipal system is representative of the Central and Eastern European model. It is

Table 26.2 Female representation in local and national office in Latvia

Local election	% of seats won by women	National elections	% of seats won by women
		1993	14
		1995	8
		1998	17
2001	41	2002	18
2005	42	2006	19
2009	35	2010	19
2013	31	2011	21
2017	34	2014	19
		2018	31

Source: Central Election Commission and Central Statistical Bureau of Latvia

characterized as a breakout form from the Soviet legacy of strong centralization that was established during the occupation by the USSR (1940–1990). Thus, after regaining independence, municipalities were ensured high decentralization and a wide scope of functions.

After almost 30 years of independence, Latvian municipalities face an influx of new local politicians. These new politicians have obtained their professional experience in a democratic regime, replacing the 'old' generation of politicians who obtained their experience with the previous regime. In the 1990s and early 2000s, it was common for officials to have gained their professional experience in Soviet times. Therefore, local politics was characterized by enduring local leaders and low interest from national political parties to stand for election in the smaller municipalities. The smaller municipalities and the seclusion of local communities explains why national political parties avoid campaigning in small rural municipalities. It is worth noting that small municipalities (by population) are also usually weaker in economic terms.

In fact, local and national elections are built around the same principles, as both are based on proportional representation. Within this party list system of preferential voting, electors can express their support for or rejection of specific candidates while still voting for the party itself. In addition, both elections have a threshold line set at 5% for a political party to be elected. The similarity makes it is easier for the voter as he/she is already familiar with the primary electoral procedure. In general, local elections prove to be reliable over the years, even though the debate on the direct election of city mayors comes up from time to time. The public debate about having such mayors is still open. This might increase the political interest and motivation of local leaders to stand for elections. It should positively affect competition in municipalities and, therefore, provide higher potential for economic development (Reinholde & Stučka 2019b).

The future restrictions to limit voters' unions in the local elections will certainly strengthen the system of political partisanship and push parties to search for regional affiliations. Meanwhile, as the next local elections of 2021 are expected to be a race among only political parties, some municipalities may still face the risk that no list is submitted for the elections. Because political parties have the lowest trust rates in Latvia, this aspect may have negative consequences – there might be exceptionally low voter turnout. Just for illustration – in Autumn 2019, only 6% of Latvian citizens expressed trust in political parties (European Commission 2019:7).

Regarding municipalities – they are getting larger in terms of population and economic strength, while the divide between urban and rural municipalities remains present. Political competition is higher in economically active areas. Latvian cities and municipalities around the Riga area accumulating the largest proportion of wealth always were an object of special interest from parties, as councilors receive better pay and municipal development might indirectly have a positive effect on their political reputation.

In conclusion, the next local elections in 2021 will highlight several concerns related to the image and functioning of political parties. If low trust leads to a low participation rate, the issue of voters' unions as an alternative political entity at the local level will be on the governmental agenda again. The fact remains that the local elections held a year ahead of the national elections will test the general political situation in the Latvian regions, provide a litmus test for the approval of political proposals in an area, and increase the nationalization of local politics.

References

Balode, L. (2017). Nepilsoņi un pašvaldību vēlēšanas. Vai vajadzētu piešķirt balsstiesības? Available at: https://lvportals.lv/viedokli/286702-nepilsoni-un-pasvaldibu-velesanas-vai-vajadzetu-pieskirt-balsstiesibas-2017.

Balode, L. (2018). Kādos gadījumos un kā var atlaist pašvaldības domi. *Latvijas Vēstnesis*, 2018.gada 18.decembris. Available at: https://lvportals.lv/norises/300948-kados-gadijumos-un-ka-var-atlaist-pasvaldibas-domi-2018.

Cadoret, X., & Cools, M. (2018). Local and regional democracy in Latvia. Available at: https://rm.coe.int/local-and-regional-democracy-in-latvia-monitoring-committee-rapporteur/168079c2e8.

Council of Europe (2020). Congress Chamber President calls for suspension of territorial reform in Latvia to allow for proper consultation. Available at: www.coe.int/en/web/congress/-/congress-chamber-president-calls-for-suspension-of-territorial-reform-in-latvia-to-allow-for-proper-consultation.

Dubois, E., & Leprince, M. (2017). Do closeness and stake increase voter turnout? Evidence from election results in small French towns in Brittany. *Regional Studies*, 51(4): 575–585.

European Commission (2019). Standard Eurobarometer 91. National Report – Latvia. 2019.

Heinelt, H. Magnier, A. Cabria, M., & Reynaert, H. (eds.), *Political Leaders and Changing Local Democracy. The European Mayor* (pp. 19–78). London: Palgrave Macmillan.

Kažoka, I., Stafecka, L. (2017). Varas līdzsvars un kontrole Latvijas pašvaldībās. Available at:https://www.lps.lv/uploads/docs_module/2017_7_p5.pdf

Koch, P., & Rochat, P.E. (2017). The effects of local government consolidation on turnout: Evidence from a quasi-experiment in Switzerland. *Swiss Political Science Review*, 23: 215–230.

Kupčs, E. (2020). Ar liegumu pašvaldību vēlēšanās startēt vēlētāju apvienībām Saeima nostiprina partiju monopolu. Available at: www.lsm.lv/raksts/zinas/latvija/ar-liegumu-pasvaldibu-velesanas-startet-veletaju-apvienibam-saeima-nostiprina-partiju-monopolu.a358618/.

Ladner, A., Keuffer, N., & Baldersheim, H. (2015). Self-rule Index for Local Authorities (Release 1.0). Final report. Tender No 2014CE16BAT031. Available at: https://ec.europa.eu/regional_policy/sources/docgener/studies/pdf/self_rule_index_en.pdf.

Leta (2019). Aptauja: Vairums Latvijas iedzīvotāju ir apmierināti ar savas pašvaldības darbu. Available at: www.aprinkis.lv/index.php/sabiedriba/pasvaldibas/7885-aptauja-vairums-latvijas-iedzivotaju-ir-apmierinati-ar-savas-pasvaldibas-darbu.

LPS (2017). Pašvaldības deputāta rokasgrāmata. *Logs*. Jūlijs/augusts 2017, Nr.6 (246). Available at: www.lps.lv/uploads/magazine_module/Rokasgramata_2017_KMEkXeEpkx.pdf.

Mouritzen, P. E., & Svara, J. H. (2002). *Leadership at the Apex: Politicians and Administrators in Western Local Governments*. Pittsburgh: University of Pittsburgh Press.

Navarro, C., Karlsson, D., Magre, J., & Reinholde, I. (2018). Mayors in the Town Hall: Patters of Relations and Conflict Among Municipal Actors. In: Heinelt, H., Magnier, A., Cabria, M., & Reynaert, H (eds.), *Political Leaders and Changing Local Democracy. The European Mayors*. Basingstoke: Palgrave Macmillan.

Ņikona, L. (2019). Pašvaldību referendumu likums – darba kārtībā kopš 6. Saeimas. *Latvijas Vēstnesis*. 2019.gada 6.septembrī. Available at: https://lvportals.lv/norises/307867-pasvaldibu-referendumu-likums-darba-kartiba-kops-6-saeimas-2019.

Reinholde, I., & Stučka, M. (2019a). La rémunération du travail politique en Lettonie. Entre cadre national et adaptations locales. In: Le Saout, R. (ed.), *La rémunération du travail politique en Europe*. Boulogne-Billancourt: Berger-Levrault.

Reinholde, I., & Stučka, M. (2019b). Urban Governance in Latvia: Feeling Urban and Thinking Rural. In: Armondi, S., & De Gregorio Hurtado, S. (eds.), *Foregrounding Urban Agendas: The New Urban Issue in European Experiences of Policy Making* (The Urban Books Series). Springer, Switzerland.

Saeima (1994). Republikas pilsētas domes un novada domes vēlēšanu likums. Available at: https://likumi.lv/doc.php?id=57839.

Saeima (1995). Saeimas vēlēšanu likums. Adopted on 25.05.1995. Available at: https://likumi.lv/doc.php?id=35261.

Saeima (2002). Regional Development Law. Adopted on 21.03.2002. Available at: https://likumi.lv/doc.php?id=61002.

Saeima (2020). Law on Administrative Territories and Populated Areas. Adopted on 10.06.2020. Available at: https://likumi.lv/ta/id/315654-administrativo-teritoriju-un-apdzivoto-vietu-likums.

SKDS (2017). Vēlētāju attieksmju pētījums 2017. *Pēcvēlēšanu aptauja*. 2017.gada jūlijs. Available at: www.cvk.lv/upload_file/Atskaite_CVK_072017.pdf.

Van Houwelingen, P. (2017). Political Participation and Municipal Population Size: A Meta-Study. *Local Government Studies*, 43(3).

Vanags, E., & Vilka, I. (2005). *Pašvaldību darbība un attīstība*. Valoda: LU Akadēmiskais apgāds.

27
Lithuania
Between a volatile electorate and the revival of nonpartisanship

Aistė Lazauskienė and Jurga Bučaitė-Vilkė

A brief overview of the local government system: towards a strong mayor system

In 1940, when Lithuania was occupied and incorporated into the Soviet Union, the constitutional institutions of local self-government were abolished, leaving municipalities without any autonomy. Institutions of local governance became part of the centralized, hierarchical governance system. Independence from the Soviet Union was declared on 11 March 1990, and on 24 March, the first democratic local election was held. The administrative-territorial division remained the same as it had been under Soviet rule, and the system of local self-government institutions functioned until 1995. In July 1994, the Law on the Territorial Administrative Units of the Republic of Lithuania and their Boundaries replaced the former system with a new administrative structure for the state territory and a one-tier system of self-government (Šaparnienė & Lazauskienė 2012).

Lithuania is a unitary state divided into 60 municipalities. The Constitution of Lithuania guarantees municipalities the right of self-governance. In terms of both territory and the number of inhabitants, municipalities in Lithuania are very large in comparison to other European countries. The average municipality population is approximately 45,000. The smallest municipality is Neringa, with 2,500 inhabitants, and the largest is the capital city of Vilnius with a total of 540,000 inhabitants. Regardless of size, every municipality must perform the same functions and services.

The Local Autonomy Index data demonstrate that the overall ranking for Lithuanian municipalities increased considerably from 1990 to 2014 (Ladner et al. 2019). However, a few factors – for example, financial autonomy, which includes fiscal autonomy, financial self-reliance, and central control within administrative supervision – remain at lower levels (Burbulytė-Tsiskarishvili et al. 2018). According to the constitution (1999), local governments are autonomous, but the parliament is entitled to dictate a variety of state-delegated functions as regulated by legislation.

We look to the literature to classify the Lithuanian self-government system by comparison with the variety of European self-governance models. Favoring a multidimensional approach, the Local Autonomy Index (LAI) discusses the changes in Eastern European countries

(Ladner et al. 2019). In reference to the relationship between central-local tiers, Lithuania is part of the group of countries (together with Latvia, Estonia, Romania, Slovenia, Czech Republic, The Netherlands) with relatively low financial self-reliance, but high political discretion (Ladner et al. 2019, 271). From the political transformation perspective, Lithuania is part of a cluster of countries (together with Serbia and Georgia) with a very high level of territorial consolidation (Swianiewicz 2014). Another characteristic of Lithuania's system is the strong mayor model (Heinelt et al. 2018), which came into being in 2015.

The horizontal power relations within Lithuanian municipalities have changed several times. From 1990 to 1995, the institutional structure was dominated by a diarchy. In essence, the council was headed by a council chairman elected from among the council members. The mayor (or the administrator, in the case of district councils) equally held the administrative position 'together with' an executive authority power. Starting in 1995, the mayor was given executive powers and was also the chairman (head) of the municipal council and the head of the collegial executive institution (board). Several legislative amendments were passed in 1997–1999, which consolidated the mayor's role even more. (Astrauskas 2004). A change occurred in 2003 when the Constitutional Court of the Republic of Lithuania concluded that one element of the model was contrary to the constitution (the mayor cannot be the executive authority as well as the head of the council). The change in the municipal institution model in 2003, when executive functions were transferred to the municipality's administrative director, caused a kind of disarray and complicated the work of local administrations, especially in municipalities where the mayor and the administrative director, appointed by a council majority, represented different parties (Mačiulytė & Ragauskas 2007).

The current system was implemented in 2015, when direct mayoral elections were also introduced. After the Seimas passed amendments to the laws on municipal council elections and local self-government on 26 June 2014, the decision was made to hold direct mayoral elections in Lithuania. Following the law, the mayor's authority was not greatly expanded, and perhaps it was not the kind of power that the voters expected a directly elected politician to have (Lazauskienė & Bučaite-Vilkė 2018). The mayor appoints and removes heads of the municipality's public institutions. The current model of horizontal relations between the mayor and the administrative director is based more on power disproportion and antagonism than on symbiosis. The competencies of the mayor include the representative functions, in contrast to the administrative director, who holds a wide-ranging executive role in municipal administration.

The higher level of trust in local mayors, who were positively affected by the introduction of direct mayoral elections in 2015, is also observable (Lazauskienė 2016; Lazauskienė & Bučaite-Vilkė 2018). Consistent public opinion survey data indicate that the recent changes in and political debates on municipal autonomy and electoral systems do not affect citizens' trust in the local decision-making arena, as the level of trust in the local authority system remains relatively low.

Organization of local elections in the one-tier system

The National Electoral Commission (*Vyriausioji rinkimų komisija*) organizes all popular elections, including local ones. As the National Electoral Commission was not established until 1992, the first local elections held in March 1990 were organized by local authorities. The 1990 elections are not considered in this chapter as data are unavailable(un).

One of the fundamental shifts in the local electoral system occurred when the Law on the Election of Municipal Councils was passed in 1994, which replaced the majoritarian rule used initially with a proportional system. The new legislation tried to provide the conditions for parties to become stronger, as it was argued that the proportional system is more favorable to political parties; additionally, preconditions for the creation of party coalitions were also introduced.

Municipal council elections have been held nine times since the declaration of independence in 1990. The duration of each term has fluctuated: it has been five, two, three, and, since 2003, four years long (see also Table 27.2). In two instances, when the duration of the term was changed, that is, in 1996 and 2002, the constitution had to be amended, which is a rather complicated procedure (Astrauskas 2013). The electoral cycles of the parliamentary and local elections are not synchronized. In the last four cycles (2007, 2011, 2015, 2019), local elections took place almost a year and a half before the parliamentary elections (2008, 2012, 2016, 2020). These elections can hardly be considered 'opinion polls' for the main parliamentary elections. Local elections are usually held in February or March, while parliamentary elections are held in October. Councilors are elected the same day as mayors. Presidential elections are held every five years, the same year as European Parliament elections (e.g., 2009, 2014, 2019).

Since 2015, mayors have been elected directly in a two-round majority system. If none of the candidates receives more than 50% of the votes, a second round with two main competitors is organized two weeks after the first. The direct election of mayors was the subject of a lively debate in the Lithuanian Parliament for almost 20 years (Mažylis & Leščiauskaitė 2015). So far, only two direct elections have been held (2015 and 2019), so it is difficult to determine trends, as it is still a novel feature. However, public opinion polls demonstrate that the population has positively accepted mayoral elections, especially given the corresponding increase in the political stability of the mayoral position. Before direct mayoral elections were introduced, it was common for the mayor's position to be rather unstable, particularly when the ruling coalition was composed of more than two parties.

There are no legal provisions for recall referenda. In practice, it is very complicated to recall a directly elected mayor. The process to initiate the removal of a directly elected mayor is very complicated and requires a ruling by the Chief Administrative Court.

Local electoral system: benefiting or losing from the proportional list system

The right to elect municipal councilors is enjoyed by permanent residents of each respective municipality who are 18 years of age on election day. Persons who have been found legally incapable by the court cannot participate in municipal council elections. A permanent resident of a particular municipality is any citizen of Lithuania who declared his/her home address within the territory of that municipality more than 90 days before polling day. Also, a permanent resident is a citizen of another member state of the EU or any other person who has the right to permanently reside in Lithuania, holds the document confirming this right, and declares his/her home address within the territory of that municipality more than 90 days before polling day. Non-EU nationals obtain the right to reside permanently in Lithuania if they have legally resided in Lithuania for the previous five years and hold a temporary residence permit. This term can be shorter if the individual passes an examination in the state language.

This is different from the national elections, where only people with Lithuanian citizenship are eligible to vote. Voting is not compulsory in Lithuania. In 2019, 54,054 noncitizens were included on the list of voters and 16,610 of them voted, thus comprising approximately 0.7% of all voters. People from approximately 50 ethnicities ran for election (several Germans, Latvians, Greeks, and French; see Table 27.1).

The council size (this includes the mayor, who also becomes a member of the municipal council) depends on the size of the municipality and varies between 15 (up to 5,000 inhabitants)

Table 27.1 Representation of Lithuanians and national minorities on the local level

Lithuanians	Not specified	Poles	Russians	Ukrainians	Belarusians	Other
67.3	27.0	3.8	1.4	0.2	0.2	0.2

Source: Central Electoral Commission (2015)

and 51 (more than 500,000 inhabitants). A total of 1,442 municipal councilors and 60 mayors were elected in 2019. The Central Electoral Commission announces the number of municipal councilors to be elected at least 110 days before an election. The electoral system for the local elections is uniform across the country, regardless of the size of the municipality.

The electoral system at the local level is an open-list proportional system. From 1995 until 2011, only parties and political organizations nominated candidates in elections. The list format was modified before the election in 2000: the closed-list system was changed to an open one, allowing the voters to choose not only the party lists but also specific candidates on those lists. In the 2000 election, a maximum of three candidates could be chosen, while from 2003 onward, up to five candidates may be chosen. Neither *panachage* nor cumulative voting is allowed. Preference votes modify the original list order quite significantly.[1]

It is also possible to vote only for the party without indicating a preference for specific individuals. According to the Central Electoral Commission, 55.5% of valid ballots had preference votes and the rest had only party votes in 2019. In six municipalities, the percentage of ballots with preference votes exceeded 70%. Interestingly, this phenomenon occurred only in very small municipalities. Each list and all of its candidates is eligible for the whole territory of the municipality. Each municipality forms a multimember district for municipal council elections.

Council seats are allocated to the political parties in proportion to the share of the vote each party receives. There is a specific legal threshold: parties receiving less than 4% of the vote and party coalitions receiving less than 6% of the vote are not eligible to receive any seats unless the remaining eligible parties have received less than 60% of the vote (in practice, this condition is rarely fulfilled). Mayors are elected directly in a two-round majority system. The second round is organized two weeks after the first. Usually, around 30% of mayors are elected in the first round.

Since 2011, persons without any political party affiliation have been able to nominate themselves as candidates. Since 2015, a list of candidates for the municipal council must be nominated by a party or the electoral committee (*visuomeninis rinkimų komitetas*),[2] and candidates for the municipal council and mayor must be supported in a relevant municipality by no fewer than 20% of the voters of that municipality, which accounts for one mandate of the municipal council.

A party or electoral committee nominates candidates by presenting a general list of candidates for the municipal council in which the candidates are entered in an order established by the party. In total, the number of candidates on the list submitted by the party cannot make up fewer than half or more than twice the number of councilors to be elected in that municipality.

Another recent change in the election system is related to the principle of the incompatibility of duties, that is, persons who can run for election but cannot get a mandate when elected. Since 2003, individuals who head municipal budgetary institutions or municipality-controlled companies or who work in the municipal administration have had to decide before the day of the first meeting of the newly elected council whether they will become a municipal council member and leave their current duties or continue working in their current office and cede the mandate to another nominee from their political party.[3] In practice, parties generally do not have enough candidates to fill the lists.

The outcomes of low turnout on electoral system

In general, electoral participation in Lithuania has been relatively low, regardless of the type of election. The average voter turnout for the eight local elections held between 1995 and 2019 was 45%, while the average turnout for national elections was 55%. Thus, the local-national turnout gap is rather significant. The highest turnout for a national election was 75.3% in 1992, while the highest local turnout was only 53.8% in 2002. Extremely low turnout was observed in the local election in 1997 (35.6%). Even the introduction of direct mayoral elections in 2015 did not increase electoral participation as much as election analysts predicted (table 27.2). In the first round of the mayoral elections, the turnout rate was just 47.2 %. Additionally, it must be noted that the number of eligible voters decreased from 2,698,391 in 2002 to 2,458,013 in 2019 due to intense emigration.

Ongoing political initiatives focused on territorial consolidation have resulted in higher internal variations in municipal population size. Consequently, the questions about the relationship between the size of municipalities and voter turnout have emerged in public discourse. The Central Electoral Commission data demonstrate that the average turnout for local elections is relatively higher in larger urban municipalities than in smaller rural municipalities (Central Electoral Commission 2019; Bučaite-Vilkė & Lazauskiene 2019), which partly contradicts dominant theoretical arguments about higher participatory democratic engagement in small jurisdictions. One of the explanations for this difference is related to higher social and economic capital and higher political activism in urban municipalities than in rural municipalities.

In principle, all council seats are contested. In total, 14 political parties, 14 coalitions of parties, and 90 electoral committees contested local elections in 2019. In 2019, there were 13,662 candidates for 1,442 available seats, which equals an average of nine candidates per seat. Table 27.3 demonstrates that the number of candidates gradually increased until 2015.[4] There were 410 candidates for mayoral offices (the average was 6.8 for one seat) in 2019 (Table 27.3).

The national party system in Lithuania is organized around two quite stable opposite poles: the Homeland Union-Lithuanian Christian Democrats (a right-wing party) and the Social Democratic Party of Lithuania (descending from reformed communists, formed after merging

Table 27.2 Voter turnout (percent) for local and national elections in Lithuania

Local elections		Parliamentary elections	
Election date	Voter turnout (%)	Election date	Voter turnout (%)
1995	44.9	**1992**	75.3
1997	35.6	**1996**	52.9
2000	49.6	**2000**	58.6
2002	53.8	**2004**	46.1
2007	41.3	**2008**	48.6
2011	44.1	**2012**	52.9
2015	47.2	**2016**	50.6
2019	47.8	**2020**	

Source: Central Electoral Commission (2020)

Table 27.3 Number of candidates in local elections in Lithuania, 1995–2019

Election	Candidates (joint list of council and mayoral candidates)	Seats (mandates) including mayor	Average number of candidates/seat
1995	7,245	1,488	4.9
1997	6,276	1,488	4.2
2000	9,881	1,562	6.3
2002	10,316	1,560	6.6
2007	13,146	1,550	8.5
2011	16,404	1,526	10.7
2015[1]	15,127 (including 433 mayoral candidates)	1,524	9.9
2019	13,663 (including 410 mayoral candidates)	1,502	9.1

1 The first direct mayoral election was introduced in 2015, prompting the separation of lists for council and mayoral candidates.
Source: Central Electoral Commission and Seimas report

with a smaller social democratic party). However, since the 2000 elections, fragmentation has increased significantly: in the period 2004–2011, the number of parliamentary parties fluctuated between seven and nine, and the number of parties forming the government never dropped below four (Jastramskis 2012). In the 2016 parliamentary election, the winner was the Farmers and Greens Union party. The main appeal of this political party probably lies in its centrist stance and the catch-all nature of the party, giving it an advantage during runoffs against competitors – both on the right and on the left (Jastramskis & Ramonaitė 2017).

Local party systems in Lithuania are also fragmented and additionally quite unstable. Usually, the governing majority on the municipal council is formed by five or more parties. The average number of parties that have at least one seat on the municipal councils in Lithuania is 6.7 (Jastramskis 2012). Considering that all parties usually have the potential to participate in the governing municipal coalition, it can be stated that the common format of municipal party systems resembles the situation at the national level (Jastramskis 2012).

Table 27.4 includes the political parties that were running in more than 10% of municipalities in 2019.[5] Additionally, they all have representatives in the Seimas [except the Lithuanian Freedom Union (Liberals)]. The most significant shares of councilors represent the four most stable parties with traditionally well-developed local structures: Lithuanian Social Democratic party, Homeland Union-Lithuanian Christian Democrats (conservatives), Farmers and Greens Union, and the liberal movement. A new party called the Social Democratic Labour Party also won several seats. Electoral volatility in Lithuania is extremely high, even compared to other post-Communist countries; party mergers and splits are a common phenomenon, and new political powers achieve success in elections quite steadily (Jastramskis 2010).

In total, 78.3% of mayors and 66.9% of councilors elected in 2019 ran as party candidates (Table 27.4). Since the first local elections, nationwide parties have been deeply embedded in local electoral processes. One of the reasons for this is that the evolution of the electoral rules over time has favored political parties more than independent lists. Until the 2011 local elections, only political parties were allowed to run for election. One of the fundamental changes in the municipal election system was to permit independent candidates to run for election in 2011 and for electoral committees in 2015. These amendments were made following the ruling of the constitutional court, which acknowledged that the law according to the Constitution of

Table 27.4 Share of all seats on local councils received by the main parties in the latest local elections in Lithuania, 2019

	% of municipalities where running	% of municipalities where represented	% of seats on local councils	% of (aggregate) votes in local elections	% of mayors affiliated with the party
Lithuanian Social Democratic Party	100.0	91.0	18.0	13.8	25.0
Homeland Union-Lithuanian Christian Democrats (conservatives)	95.0	90.0	18.2	16.7	18.3
Liberal Movement	80.0	78.3	8.3	6.1	10.0
Farmers and Greens Union	93.3	90.0	15.0	11.6	10.0
Green Party	10.0	6.7	0.3	0.7	0.0
Social Democratic Labour Party	46.6	23.3	1.7	1.7	0.0
Order and Justice Party	56.6	26.7	3.4	3.1	8.3
Lithuanian Center Party	35.0	5.0	0.6	1.3	0.0
The Electoral Action of Poles in Lithuania and Russian Alliance	28.2	10.0	3.9	5.3	3.3
Labour Party	23.3	48.3	4.2	5.3	1.7
The Lithuanian Freedom Union (liberals)	78.3	15.0	2.1	1.3	1.7
Independent electoral committees	78.3	75.0	21.2	27.8	21.7

Source: Central Electoral Commission (2020)

the Republic of Lithuania does not decree that people must be elected to municipal councils through party lists.

In the municipal election of 2015, 54 electoral committees were registered, and several of them received much support. In 2019, 87 electoral committees were running for election in 47 out of 60 municipalities (78.3%), while in 2015, the electoral committees appeared in only 29 local jurisdictions (48.3%). Seven electoral committees were running for election in the capital city; in other municipalities, the total number of committees varied between one and five.

The number of 'independent' councilors is increasing. In 2011, independent candidates won 67 seats (4.4%), excluding mayoral seats while in 2015 they won 115 seats (8.1%) and in 2019 they won 305 seats (21.2%). To summarize, independent candidates took fourth place after the three main Lithuanian parties in terms of the number of mandates received in 2015, and they took first place in 2019. Most independent committees are headed by former party members or local businessmen.

The results of the 2015 and 2019 local elections (as well as of the previous elections) demonstrate that independent electoral committees are more successful in larger cities. In 2015, for the first time, five nonpartisan mayors were elected (8.3%). The successful participation of nonpartisan mayors was a new phenomenon in Lithuania. In 2019, 13 (21.7%) mayors were elected without running for one of the nationwide political parties. Unlike the independent mayors elected in 2015, several 'nonpartisan' mayors elected in 2019 had close ties to parties or had previously belonged to parties that had lost popularity.

The number of female council members has increased since 2000. They constituted 18% of all council members in 2000, and with each election the rate has increased, reaching 29.4% in 2019. This is similar to national tendencies, as only 7% of the members of parliament were women in 1992, and this grew to 21% in 2016.

No gender quotas exist in Lithuanian elections. However, some parties, such as the Lithuanian Social Democratic party, try to apply gender quotas when ordering their party lists. The number of male candidates was 8.7% higher than that of female candidates in recent local elections. Only four mayoral positions out of the 60 municipalities (6.6%) were occupied by women in 2015, and almost the same situation was observed following the 2019 elections, when only five women were elected (8.3%) (Table 27.5). It is more complicated to count how many female mayors were indirectly elected to office prior to 2015 because some of them did not serve the entire term of office (Lazauskienė 2016).

Two main national minorities are represented on local councils: Poles and Russians.[6] The Polish minority is represented in the municipalities of the city of Vilnius, the district of Vilnius, Šalčininkai, and Švenčionys, while Russians win seats on the Klaipėda city and Vilnius city councils. There are no special electoral provisions for minority candidates.

Little research has been done on the incumbency effect in local elections. The percentage of reelected councilors is relatively high and stable: 2007, 52.4%; 2011, 56.9%; 2015, 56.5%. In several municipalities, as many as seven out of ten councilors are reelected candidates.

In Lithuania, 72% of mayors were reelected in the 2011 local elections, and 58.3% were reelected in 2015 when direct mayoral elections were implemented for the first time (Kukovič & Lazauskienė 2018). In the most recent 2019 elections, 63.3% of the mayors were reelected. Ten out of 60 mayors were elected for more than three terms, and two have been in office since 2000.

Table 27.5 Share of women among Seimas members and councilors in Lithuania

Election	Women elected to the Seimas		Election	Women elected to local councils	
1992	10	7%	1997	318	22%
1996	24	17%	2000	275	18%
2000	15	11%	2002	321	21%
2004	31	22%	2007	344	22%
2008	25	18%	2011	342	22%
2012	33	24%	2015	363	25%
2016	30	21%	2019	424	29%

Source: Central Electoral Commission

Discussion: the revival of independent electoral committees

Since Lithuania declared independence from the Soviet Union in 1990, there has been a constant search for an optimal local electoral system for the country. Several significant changes in the rules have been implemented in recent decades, for example, the introduction of preference voting and direct mayoral elections. On the national level, the crucial turning point was when the right to nominate candidates for elected offices was extended to independent electoral committees and residents themselves. This change occurred only after the issue was considered by the constitutional court (Astrauskas 2013). As a result, residents have been eligible for nomination as candidates on nonpartisan lists since 2011, and the number of nonpartisan councilors has gradually increased (while the number of nonpartisan members of parliament is still minimal).

The main change in the local arena is related to the increasing power of independent electoral committees, which has had an impact on the local political landscape. While the voters positively accepted direct mayoral elections, such elections were criticized by politicians as increasing political personalization and reinforcing the power monopoly of some hegemonic local leaders. The main political parties are losing their electoral support; in contrast, nonpartisans are winning more seats every year. It seems that voters regard electoral committees as a fresh alternative to the political establishment, especially in large urban municipalities.

In the assessment of the local electoral system, discussions often arise regarding the fact that the list proportional election system does not allow for territorial units to be properly represented within the municipalities. A constantly recurring idea in the popular debate posits that Lithuania could adopt a mixed system, similar to the one used since 1992 in parliamentary elections, in which half of the council would be elected on the basis of the proportional rule and the other half would be elected on the basis of the majoritarian system in single-member constituencies. Several parties have supported such a change, arguing for the importance of aligning the local electoral system with that of the national legislature. The main counterarguments have included electoral engineering problems such as disproportionality, thresholds, and majority runoffs (Jastramskis 2019).

Another subject of discussion concerns the principle of the incompatibility of duties. In the election of 2011, almost 30% of elected council members gave up their mandates because they already held another public office. Since the election of 2015, a provision has come into effect stating that if the nominee list has candidates who hold an office that is incompatible with the office of municipal council member, the election deposit for every such candidate is equal to the average wage for two months. This legal amendment, which reduced the likelihood that 'undecided' candidates would be nominated, should be evaluated positively. After the 2015 election, the number of those who gave up their mandates diminished significantly; however, in individual municipalities, this number still amounted to approximately 12–15% (Morkūnaitė-Lazauskienė 2017).

As discussed in this chapter, the Lithuanian local electoral system is experiencing a turn toward a less partisan local politics. The recent reform of direct mayoral elections and the success of independent electoral committees have increased the localization of municipal politics and political leadership. Knowledge of local candidates and increasing concerns about local issues are changing the electoral landscape in terms of trust in elected officials, voter turnout, and voting motives.

Notes

1 There were cases in which some candidates moved up on their lists by several or even several dozen positions. For instance, one representative of the Conservative Party in Kaunas moved from 74th (last place on the list) to 10th and entered the council.

2 The law allows the establishment of electoral committees for participating in a particular election as long as the Central Electoral Commission registered the committee at least three months before the election.
3 This change had significant influence on the composition of district (rural) municipal councils: the school principals, hospital directors, and heads of municipal enterprises, who had previously dominated the municipal councils, lost the ability to become councilors. The local elite, who had previously been elected to councils, frequently conceded their place to business representatives. Nevertheless, political parties continued to strive to create attractive candidate lists, adding foremen (elders), school principals, and other individuals who were popular in the city, as well as local MPs, who did not even think about working on the municipal council and gave up their mandate immediately after the election. In the election of 2011, almost 30% of the elected council members gave up their mandates.
4 The number of candidates is higher because new regulations appeared for independent candidates (for the first time, independent candidates were running for election); in 2015, public electoral committees started to run for election.
5 Small nonparliamentary parties, such as the Union of Lithuanian Nationalists and Republicans, Lithuanian Russian Union, and Lithuanian Christian Democrat Party, that also ran for election are not presented.
6 The Electoral Action of Poles in Lithuania-Christian Families Alliance (EAPL-CFA) is the only political party representing Poles, while the Russian minority is represented by the Lithuanian Russian Union. In most cases, the political parties run for election together as a coalition.

References

Astrauskas, A. (2004). Optimalaus Lietuvos savivaldybių institucinės struktūros modelio paieška. *Viešoji politika ir administravimas*, 8, 9–24.

Astrauskas, A. (2013). Vietos savivaldos raida Lietuvoje nuo 1990 metų iki dabar. *Viešoji politika ir administravimas*, 12(2), 260–271.

Bučaitė-Vilkė, J., & Lazauskiene, A. (2019). Territorial policy agenda revised: Public perceptions on local non-electoral participation capacities in lithuania. *Hrvatska i komparativna javna uprava: časopis za teoriju i praksu javne uprave*, 19(2), 207–236.

Burbulytė-Tsiskarishvili, G., Dvorak, J., & Žernytė, A. (2018). Savivaldybių funkcijų ir galių kaita Lietuvoje 1994–2016 metais. *Viešoji politika ir administravimas*, 17(3), 399–420.

Central Electoral Commission Lithuania. (2019). Database. https://www.vrk.lt/en/rinkimai

Heinelt, H., Hlepas, N., Kuhlmann, S., & Swianiewicz, P. (2018). Local government systems: Grasping the institutional environment of mayors. In H. Heinelt et al. (eds.) *Political leaders and changing local democracy* (pp. 19–78). Cham: Palgrave Macmillan.

Jastramskis, M. (2010). Partinių sistemų stabilumo samprata ir matavimas: Lietuvos situacija 1990–2010 metais. *Parlamento studijos*, 9, 144–169.

Jastramskis, M. (2012). Election forecasting in Lithuania: The case of municipal elections, *International Journal of Forecasting*, 28(4), 822–829.

Jastramskis, M. (2019). Effects of the mixed parallel electoral system in lithuania: The worst of all worlds? *Parliamentary Affairs*, 72(3), 561–587.

Jastramskis, M., & Ramonaitė, A. (2017). Lithuania. *European Journal of Political Research Political Data Yearbook*, 56, 176–184.

Kukovič, S., & Lazauskienė, A. (2018). Pre-mayoral career and incumbency of local leaders in post-communist countries: Evidence from lithuania and slovenia. *Political Preferences*, 18, 5–22.

Ladner, A., Keuffer, N., Baldersheim, H., Hlepas, N., Swianiewicz, P., Steyvers, K., & Navarro, C. (2019). *Patterns of local autonomy in Europe*. Cham: Palgrave Macmillan.

Lazauskienė, A. (2016). Lietuvos merų politinės karjeros bruožai. *Kultūra ir visuomenė: socialinių tyrimų žurnalas. Culture and Society: Journal of Social Research*, 7(1), 113–134.

Lazauskienė, A., & Bučaitė-Vilkė, J. (2018). Vietos politinės lyderystės paieškos: kokio mero nori Lietuvos gyventojai. *Filosofija. Sociologija*, 29(4), 276–284.

Mačiulytė, J., & Ragauskas, P. (2007). *Lietuvos savivalda: savarankiškos visuomenės link?* Vilnius: Versus Aureus.

Mažylis, L., & Leščiauskaitė, V. (2015). Tiesioginiai merų rinkimai Lietuvoje: Užtrukę debatai ir šviežia patirtis. *Politikos mokslų almanachas, 17*, 33–56.

Morkūnaitė-Lazauskienė, A. (2017). Samorząd lokalny w II Republice Litewskiej: oczekiwania i perspektywy. In M. Drzonek, M. Musiał-Karg, & A. Wołek (eds.) *Ćwierć wieku polityki lokalnej w Europie Środkowo-wschodniej* (pp. 29–48). Kraków: Akademia Ignatianum.

Šaparnienė, D., & Lazauskienė, A. (2012). Local government in lithuania. In A.M. Moreno (ed.) *Local government in the member states of the European union: A comparative legal perspective* (pp. 389–410). Madrid: National Institute of Public Administration.

Swianiewicz, P. (2014). An empirical typology of local government systems in Eastern Europe. *Local Government Studies, 40*(2), 292–311.

28
Poland
A hyperlocalized system?

Adam Gendźwiłł

Three decades of local democracy: a brief overview of the local government system

Local government in Poland was reestablished in 1990 as a part of the process of democratic transition.[1] Municipalities (*gminy*), which also functioned as the administrative units of the lowest tier during the Communist period, were granted considerable autonomy and popularly elected democratic institutions – municipal councils. Along with the transfer of basic responsibilities to the local level, a significant part of state-owned land, infrastructure, and public utilities were transferred by the state to these newly established municipal governments; subsequently, these resources additionally strengthened the autonomy of the local tier.

Extensive local government reform, designed and implemented by a team of 'Solidarity' experts led by Jerzy Regulski, was considered to be a remedy for the economic crisis and a means of securing access to power for the former democratic opposition (Regulski 1993). Local elections, which took place in May 1990, were organized shortly after the first free presidential elections (won by Lech Wałęsa) and preceded the first fully democratic parliamentary elections (conducted in 1991). The 1990 local elections brought a significant change among the local elites – Bartkowski (1996) estimates that 75% of the new municipal councilors were elected for the first time.

Since 1998, Poland has had three tiers of subnational government, with 16 regions, 315 counties, and 2,477 municipalities, of which 66 are cities with county status (which are unitary authorities combining the powers of the municipal and county tiers of government). The basic three-tier territorial structure is supplemented by the voluntary submunicipal tier (both in rural and in urban municipalities) and voluntary institutions of intermunicipal cooperation.

The territorial division at the municipal level is relatively stable and has been since the territorial reforms held in the 1970s during Communist rule. After the transition, only a dozen municipal splits occurred, the majority of them occurring in the early 1990s, with one voluntary merger in 2014. In 2020, the average population size of a Polish municipality was 15,490 inhabitants, with the smallest numbering 1,279 inhabitants. Despite the debates about the detrimental consequences of depopulation and problems with maintaining adequate levels of public services in sparsely populated areas, there are no discussions about systematic amalgamation reform in Poland.

The system of local government in Poland is among the most autonomous in Eastern Europe, yet its revenues still mainly rely on transfers from the central budget. According to the Local Autonomy Index data, Poland is ranked sixth among 39 European countries on the scale of overall local autonomy, which includes the organizational, legal, and financial dimensions of autonomy, as well as the scope of responsibilities (Ladner et al. 2019: 240). Polish municipalities are responsible for basic local infrastructure (including water supply and sewage treatment, roads, and local public transport), child care and elementary education, social care, and spatial planning. Poland also has a relatively strong level of attachment to local communities and a long-standing tradition of self-rule at the local level, yet this developed differently during the period of the country's partition in the eighteenth and nineteenth centuries and was also interrupted by decades of Communist rule.

Public opinion surveys demonstrate that Polish municipalities are perceived by citizens as much more important political arenas than the upper tiers of subnational government introduced in 1998: counties (*powiaty*) and regions (*województwa*). In a 2018 CBOS (*Centrum Badania Opinii Społecznej*) survey, 86% of Poles declared interest in national politics, 79% in local (municipal) politics, 65% in county politics, and only 40% in regional politics. Simultaneously, subnational elections (local, county, and regional held together) are considered to be equally or even more important than the parliamentary and presidential elections. In 2018, 47% of Poles surveyed assessed the subnational elections as being 'very important', while for the parliamentary and presidential elections these shares were 41% and 40%, respectively; the European elections were assessed as being very important by only 25% of citizens (Gendźwiłł & Żerkowska-Balas 2017). These findings, along with the patterns of electoral participation at different tiers, undermine the usual assumption that local elections are 'less-at-stake' contests (Reif & Schmitt 1980).

Horizontal power relations in Polish municipalities changed in 2002 along with the introduction of direct mayoral elections. The former *collective executive model* (with a municipal executive elected by the council and accountable to the councilors) was replaced by the *strong mayor model*, a local variant of presidentialism (Heinelt & Hlepas 2006). Since 2002, directly elected mayors have been responsible for executive power at the local level, and they are both political leaders and heads of local administration (Gendźwiłł & Swianiewicz 2017).

Local elections and their place in the multilevel system

While in 1990's local elections Poles elected only local councilors, currently, the election of municipal councils is accompanied by the direct mayoral elections (since 2002) and the elections of assemblies of the upper-tier units (since 1998). All subnational elections are horizontally simultaneous, that is, they take place on the same day. They were organized every four years until 2018; since the 2018 elections, the term of office has been extended to five years. The elections are organized by the National Electoral Commission (*Państwowa Komisja Wyborcza*), which is supported by the state and municipal administrations. It is the same body that is responsible for the other popular elections in Poland. The new, five-year term of office of subnational governments will 'asynchronize' the electoral cycles between the parliamentary and local elections – in the last four cycles (2006, 2010, 2014, 2018) local elections took place almost a year before the parliamentary election (2007, 2011, 2015, 2019).

Since 1998, when the three-tier system of subnational government was introduced, municipal elections have been coupled with the elections to county councils (*rada powiatu*; in 66 larger cities, the functions of county councils are performed by the city council), as well as regional assemblies (*sejmik wojewódzki*). The elections at the upper tiers are dominated by the nationwide political parties to a larger extent.

Since 2002, mayors[2] have been elected directly in all municipalities in a majority two-round system (TRS). If none of the candidates receives more than 50% of the votes, the second round is organized two weeks after the first between the two leading competitors. If the election is unopposed, the sole candidate is still required to receive more than 50% of the popular vote; otherwise, the mayor is elected by the council. Although the mayoral elections are formally separate from the election of councilors, the candidate for mayor must be endorsed by the electoral committee or a party that has registered its candidates in at least half of the electoral districts in the municipality. Nevertheless, this regulation does not necessarily secure political support for the executive on the council. It is still possible that local power can be divided between the mayor and an unfriendly majority on the council – usually with negative consequences for the conduct of local politics (Kuć-Czajkowska & Sidor 2017).

Generally, there is strong popular support for the direct election of mayors in Poland. It is argued that mayors, popularly recognized, are held accountable for their decisions by the local electorate. The introduction of the direct vote stabilized local political systems, personalized local elections, and challenged the nationwide political parties by securing the position of strong independent candidates and their local lists. It also strengthened the incumbency advantage (Gendźwiłł & Swianiewicz 2017). Critics point out that mayors overly dominate local politics due to effective political patronage and clientelism (Bartnicki 2017). In many municipalities, they benefit from the incumbency advantage and, being practically unchallenged, inherit the office almost automatically. These arguments supported the legislation that passed in 2018 and limited the number of terms of office that a mayor can serve (two consecutive terms, i.e., 10 years).

Mayors can be removed only by a recall election (a special type of local referendum initiated either by the council or by 10% of eligible voters). The recall election is valid if the turnout exceeds three-fifths of the turnout for the previous regular election in which a mayor was elected. Once the referendum is valid, a mayor is recalled by a majority of votes. This is rare but far from 'exotic' – during the 2010–2014 term, almost 4.5% of mayors in Poland were threatened by recall procedures, and 16 out of 111 (i.e., 14%) recall elections were binding and resulted in the recall of a mayor.

It is also worth noting that, since 1990, the local government in the capital city of Warsaw has had a more complicated structure than other local governments. Moreover, the provisions of the local electoral system differ slightly in Warsaw, even if the local elections there are held along with elections in other jurisdictions. Until 2002, the capital city was considered a mandatory union of city districts, with each electing its own council. However, since 2002, the city of Warsaw has been considered a single municipality with its districts being mandatory submunicipal units (currently, there are 18 districts with delegated responsibilities for schools, parks, culture, social housing, and small investments). District councils in Warsaw are popularly elected along with the council of Warsaw. Executives in the districts of Warsaw are collegial and elected by the district councils.

Features of the electoral system: the mix of two worlds

The local electoral system that is used to elect local councils in Poland has been changing over the last decades; this is also due to the instrumental usage of the electoral rules by legislators (Ptak 2010). However, its essential feature – the combination of majoritarian representation in smaller municipalities and proportional representation with a list system in the larger municipalities – has remained stable.

The size of municipal councils in Poland depends on the population size and is determined by the degressive rule described in the Electoral Code. Currently, the smallest councils (in municipalities with a population of under 20,000) are composed of 15 councilors, while the largest – the council of Warsaw – numbers 60 councilors. Since 2002, the size of municipal councils has been substantially reduced – the number of local councilors decreased by 40% from 52,379 in 1998 to 39,579 in 2002. The electoral code offers a special provision for amalgamated municipalities, which can have enlarged councils in the first term after the merger.

The main parameters of the local electoral system in Poland are presented in Table 28.1. Currently, the threshold between the majoritarian and proportional rules is set at 20,000 inhabitants, which divides the country's population almost equally: ca. 56% of the population elect their local councilors under the open-list proportional system (OLPR), while the others living in smaller jurisdictions use the first-past-the-post (FPTP) system. Formerly, the population threshold was set at 40,000 (in 1990 and 1994). In an exceptional case in 2014, the threshold did not directly refer to size but to legal status: OLPR was used only in the 65 largest cities.

Between 1998 and 2010, Poland also used the bloc vote system (BV, sometimes described as *plurality at large*) in small districts. Larger districts were used mainly to encompass larger submunicipal communities (e.g., larger villages within a wider rural municipality), yet it was criticized due to its vulnerability to paradoxes stemming from split-ticket voting and confusion among voters entitled to cast more than one vote on one of the ballot cards.

The usage of FPTP in local elections proliferated over time despite the criticism this system has received. FPTP assures clear personal accountability of the councilors and guarantees simple electoral choices, yet it has proven to cause greater disproportionality and additional bias toward the local lists, mainly the 'mayoral local parties' (Gendźwiłł & Żółtak 2017).

Table 28.1 Main parameters of the local electoral system in Poland, 1990–2018

Election year	Population threshold between subsystems	Properties of the majoritarian subsystem	Properties of the OLPR subsystem
1990	40,000	FPTP	OLPR, modified Sainte-Laguë, magnitude 5–10
1994	40,000	FPTP	OLPR, modified Sainte-Laguë, magnitude 5–10
1998	20,000	FPTP + BV, magnitude 2–5	OLPR, d'Hondt, threshold 5% in larger cities, magnitude 5–10
2002	20,000	FPTP + BV, magnitude 2–5	OLPR, d'Hondt, threshold 5% in larger cities, magnitude 5–8
2006	20,000	FPTP + BV, magnitude 2–5	OLPR, d'Hondt, threshold 5% in larger cities, magnitude 5–8, *apparentement*
2010	20,000	FPTP + BV, magnitude 2–5	OLPR, d'Hondt, threshold 5% in larger cities, magnitude 5–8
2014	legal (city with county status)	FPTP	OLPR, d'Hondt, threshold 5%, magnitude 5–10
2018	20,000	FPTP	OLPR, d'Hondt, threshold 5%, magnitude 5–8

The OLPR system, used in larger municipalities, in its current version is similar to the system used for national elections (for the *Sejm*), yet it uses smaller electoral districts (with possible magnitudes from five to eight; empirically, the average was 5.7 in 2018). This feature, along with the 5% legal threshold at the municipal level and the d'Hondt rule, results in an effective threshold that is high and, in turn, results in a high disproportionality of electoral results. As Table 28.1 demonstrates, the initial version of the OLPR system was more permissive; thus, it was also more proportional than the current version.

In the 2006 local elections, Poland experimented with the *apparentement* rule – the seats were first assigned to the alliances of lists, then subsequently (using the Sainte-Laguë method) to the particular lists within each alliance, and finally to the candidates according to the ranking of preference votes. This institution was introduced instrumentally by the governing parties shortly before the subnational elections and was heavily criticized for exacerbating voter confusion and anomalies (Ptak 2010; Raciborski & Ochremiak 2006).

In 2011 a 35% candidate gender quota was introduced for all lists in the elections at all levels. However, no additional rules geared toward improving female representation (e.g., the 'zipper rule') were established (Gwiazda 2015). While parties and other electoral committees are responsible for the ballot order of candidates, the voters are obliged to cast one preferential vote (personal choice is mandatory; it is impossible to vote for the whole list). Significant ballot position effects are observed in local elections, particularly the effect for those listed first, yet ca. 25–30% of seats on the councils are still assigned due to the concentration of preference votes modifying the original order (Gendźwiłł & Marcinkiewicz 2019). Under the OLPR system, the minimum required length of the list (equal to district magnitude) results in a more difficult electoral choice, with numerous excessive candidates.

It is worth noting that, since 1990, all municipalities, even the smallest and most territorially homogeneous, have been mandatorily divided into electoral districts. Thus, the political representation on the councils is, to a large extent, territorialized in both the FPTP and OLPR systems. None of the elected councilors is able to receive the support of voters representing all parts of the municipality, although formally he/she is obliged to represent the municipality as a whole.

The eligibility rules have not substantially changed since 1990: all citizens over the age of 18 are entitled to vote. Subnational elections, contrary to the presidential and parliamentary elections, do not allow citizens residing abroad to vote. In 2004, Poland adopted a law enfranchising EU citizens of other countries living in Poland (but only in local council elections), yet this regulation is of marginal significance (in the 2018 elections, only 1,800 foreign voters were registered). The right to stand in the local council elections is granted to all adult voters; the candidate for mayor should be at least 25 years old on the election day. Polish law excludes *cumul des mandats*.

The electoral outcomes: 'splendid isolation' from national politics

Electoral turnout in Poland is relatively low, even in comparison with other post-Communist countries. However, the difference between participation rates for local elections and parliamentary elections (*local-national turnout gap*) is very small (Gendźwiłł 2017). The average voter turnout for eight local elections held between 1990 and 2018 was equal to 45% (systematically increasing since 2002), while the average voter turnout for parliamentary elections during the corresponding period (the partly free parliamentary elections of 1989 are excluded) was 48% (see Table 28.2).

Electoral participation in both types of elections differs significantly between different size municipalities. The usual pattern in the previous electoral cycles was that voter turnout for local elections was negatively correlated with population size, while voter turnout for parliamentary

Table 28.2 Voter turnout (percent) for local and national elections in Poland since 1990

Local elections		Parliamentary elections	
Election date	Voter turnout (%)	Election date	Voter turnout (%)
27.05.1990	42.3	27.10.1991	43.2
19.06.1994	33.8	19.09.1993	52.1
11.10.1998	45.4	21.09.1997	47.9
27.10.2002	44.1	23.09.2001	46.2
12.11.2006	46.0	25.09.2005	40.6
21.11.2010	47.3	21.10.2007	53.9
16.11.2014	47.4	04.08.2011	48.9
21.10.2018	55.0	03.08.2015	50.9

Source: National Electoral Commission

elections was positively correlated with population size. With the exception of the 1994 local elections (with a very low overall voter turnout), the majority of small municipalities noted systematically higher participation rates for local than for parliamentary elections. In the recent 2018 local elections, one could observe the mobilization of the electorate, particularly in the large cities (with a population of over 100,000); thus, the usual pattern was less pronounced (Figure 28.1). More detailed analyses of the survey data demonstrate that the effect of jurisdiction size on electoral participation is persistent, even when the individual voters' traits are controlled (Gendźwiłł 2017).

Competitiveness is the other feature of local elections that is dependent on jurisdiction size – limited in the smaller municipalities for both council and mayoral elections. Unopposed mayoral elections occur quite frequently; in 2018, single candidates competed for the office of mayor in 13% of municipalities. In the case of the council elections, when there is only one candidate in a single-member district, he/she receives the seat without an election. In 2018, such a situation occurred in more than 3,000 electoral districts, that is, for 7.7% of all seats on the local councils. This is practically impossible under the OLPR rule, which secures the minimum length of each list as equal to district magnitude.

The indicators demonstrate a decreasing supply of candidates and more consolidated competition in mayoral elections. While in 2002 the average number of candidates per mayoral seat was 4.2, it dropped to 2.8 in 2018. While in 2002 a second round was needed in almost every second municipality, in 2018 it was held only in 26% of municipalities.

In local elections in Poland, one may observe a strong incumbency advantage. In 2018, in 85% of municipalities incumbent mayors stood for reelection; 79% of them succeeded (in either the first or the second round), which gave an overall incumbency ratio of 67%. A similar level had been observed in the previous mayoral elections, except for the first direct mayoral election in 2002, when approximately half of the former mayors were replaced (Gendźwiłł & Swianiewicz 2017). Kukołowicz and Górecki (2018) found that the incumbency advantage in Polish mayoral elections can be only partly ascribed to economic voting effects.

Local elections in Poland are dominated by the local independent lists and candidates who are not affiliated with nationwide parties (Dudzińska 2008). From the beginning, local elections were dominated by local lists and independent candidates. The candidates affiliated with the Solidarity movement created local civic committees (*Komitety Obywatelskie*), which played an important role in the first term of office, but they failed to institutionalize as a statewide party

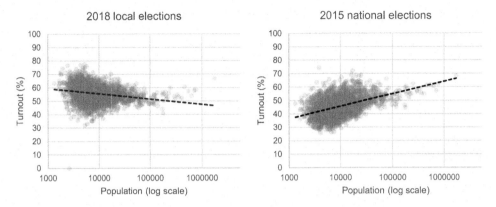

Figure 28.1 Voter turnout for local and parliamentary elections in Poland, by municipality size

or join the developing structures of new parties (Słodkowska 2014). In the early 1990s, only the post-Communist successor parties had local branches, but their candidates were usually defeated by those supported by the former democratic opposition. This separation of national politics, dominated by parties and local politics as well as by local lists and independents, has remained an important distinctive feature of local governments in Poland. Many prominent local politicians fuel antiparty resentment and juxtapose the 'local interest', which they claim to serve, and 'partisan interest', which they claim will be served by the party candidates (Gendźwiłł 2012).

Subsequently, party politicization, that is, the domination of local politics by nationwide parties, described by Rokkan as the last construction stage of popular democracy, is very limited in Poland. Since the first local elections, the presence of nationwide parties has been weak, even if the evolution of the electoral rules over time has favored political parties more than the independent lists. The strongest local independent committees are established by the mayors and their main opponents to serve as political support on the councils. Therefore, local party systems in Polish municipalities usually display very low levels of nationalization – particularly in smaller municipalities.

In many cases, independent candidates and local lists are loosely related to the local structures of nationwide parties. Sometimes the label 'independent' is considered to be part of a campaign strategy, advantageous for candidates in the context of strong antiparty resentment among the electorate (Gendźwiłł 2012). Nevertheless, even if the party endorsements for independent candidates and lists are taken into account, parliamentary parties receive only a small share of the total number of seats on the councils (27.1% in 2018), mainly in larger cities. Simultaneously, only 34.2% of mayors elected in 2018 either ranas party candidates or were formally supported by one of the main (parliamentary) parties (Table 28.3). The most significant shares of councilors represent four of the most stable parties with sufficiently developed local structures: PiS, PO, SLD, and PSL. Recently created parties (Ruch Palikota, Nowoczesna, Kukiz'15), which had been successful in parliamentary elections, were not able to secure their presence in local councils. It is worth mentioning that none of these parties emerged from local independent lists; thus local politics does not perform the function of 'incubator' for new political initiatives (Kjaer 2012).

The results of the 2018 local elections (as well as the previous ones) demonstrate that the parties are more successful in the larger cities, where the OLPR system is used to elect councils and where political parties have established local branches. However, this group also includes

Table 28.3 Share of all seats on local councils received by the main (parliamentary) parties in the last local elections in Poland, 2018

Parties	% of municipalities where running	% of municipalities where represented	% of seats on local councils	% of (aggregate) votes in local elections	% of mayors affiliated with the party[1]
PiS (Prawo i Sprawiedliwość)	67.4	51.8	14.7	21.4	9.5/13.5
PO + Modern (Platforma Obywatelska + Nowoczesna)[2]	12.2	8.6	2.8	14.7	1.3/5.7
PSL (Polskie Stronnictwo Ludowe)	43.8	32.7	8.1	3.9	7.0/12.7
SLD (Sojusz Lewicy Demokratycznej)	15.8	6.4	0.8	1.2	0.2/1.7
Kukiz'15	9.9	2.4	0.2	0.2	0.2/0.2
German Minority	1.5	1.3	0.5	0.2	0.5/0.5
Independents and nonnational (local) lists	99.0	97.9	72.9	58.4	81.2/65.8

[1] The first figure corresponds to the mayors officially endorsed by party committees, and the second figure corresponds to mayors who are members of a given party or have been officially supported by a given party.
[2] Coalition with PO in the dominant position. In the 2015 parliamentary elections, PO and Modern ran separately.

Table 28.4 Share of women among elected councilors (1990–2018) and mayors (1994–2018) in Poland

Election year	1990	1994	1998	2002	2006	2010	2014	2018
Councilors	10.9	13.2	16.0	18.1	21.5	25.4	27.3	30.3
Mayors	n/a	5.9[1]	5.7[1]	6.6	8.3	9.4	10.8	12.3

[1] Mayors were elected by the councils.
Source: National Electoral Commission

councilors who represent nationwide parties and who are in the minority, despite increasing party system polarization at the national level. The weakness or absence of party cues in many local electoral arenas presumably increases the impact of local concerns on the local vote.

One can observe a gradual, yet slow, increase in female representation among elected officials at the local level (Table 28.4). However, a large gap still exists between the legislative and executive at the local level. Only 12.3% of directly elected mayors are women. The share of female councilors elected in 2018's local elections amounted to 30.3%, which is higher than at the county level (23.9%), the regional level (28.8%), or in the lower chamber of the national parliament (27% in 2015). The electoral system, particularly the use of gender quotas, cannot serve as the main explanation for differences in female representation. In Polish local governments, the share of female councilors is slightly higher in the smaller municipalities, which use the FPTP system (usually considered disadvantageous for female representation), than in the larger municipalities, which use the OLPR system (since 2014 has had a 35% gender quota). The shares of women elected were 27.3% in OLPR vs 31.0% in FPTP in the 2018 local elections. It is likely that this difference is related to the higher competitiveness of elections in larger municipalities, the higher supply of candidates, and patterns of ballot ranking.

Discussion

The local electoral system in Poland has been evolving since the reestablishment of local government in Poland, yet it is still a combination of a majoritarian and proportional logic of representation. The latter has been even more pronounced since the introduction of direct two-round mayoral elections (in 2002) and the proliferation of the FPTP system (since 2014). The OLPR system used in larger municipalities closely resembles the system used for parliamentary elections, yet with smaller district magnitudes it displays fewer features of proportionality. One of the distinct characteristics of the local electoral system in Poland is that it encompasses the territorial divisions within municipalities. Thus, it produces incentives to cultivate the 'local vote' even in the smallest municipalities.

Local electoral politics in Poland is strongly personalized, not only by formal rules but also by contextual factors, such as the long-lasting dominance of local independent lists (usually organized around local leaders) and the weakness (underinstitutionalization) of nationwide political parties. The poor presence of parliamentary parties at the local level and the separation of local and national politics might be perceived as a 'backstop' against the consolidation of the PiS (Law and Justice) party. The prominence of directly elected mayors and the two-round system incentivize strategic cooperation between the opposition parties and independents. It is emblematic that, despite its electoral successes in different arenas, after the 2018 elections the largest cities with PiS-affiliated mayors were Chełm and Zamość (both with a population just over 60,000). At the same time, the mayor of Warsaw, Rafał Trzaskowski, emerged as one of the main leaders of the opposition and challenged the incumbent president Andrzej Duda in the 2020 presidential election (Duda won in the second round by a narrow margin).

The aggregate data demonstrate the divergent patterns of electoral mobilization in national (parliamentary) and subnational (local) elections, as well as distinct patterns of vote choice. However, voting behavior in Polish local elections has not been systematically studied with the use of individual-level data. As there is no local election survey in Poland, the main source of the survey data covering the basic issues related to local voting is regular public opinion polls conducted by CBOS, a public opinion research organization that also publishes basic descriptive reports on this topic.[3]

Notes

1 This work was supported by the Bekker Program of the Polish National Agency for Academic Exchange.
2 The traditional nomenclature differentiates between a mayor of rural municipalities (*wójt*), small and medium urban municipalities (*burmistrz*), and larger urban municipalities (*prezydent miasta*).
3 The list of the reports can be accessed online: www.cbos.pl/EN/publications/reports.php Some of the reports are available in English.

References

Bartkowski, J. (1996). *Lokalne elity władzy w Polsce w latach 1966–1995*. Warszawa: Interart.
Bartnicki, S. (2017). Wybrane determinanty poparcia kandydatów podczas wyborów gminnego organu wykonawczego. *Studia Wyborcze, 23*, 107–129.

Dudzińska, A. (2008). Non-party lists in local election in Poland. In: M. Reiser & E. Holtmann (Eds.), *Farewell to the Party Model?* (pp. 105–126). Baden-Baden: VS Verlag für Sozialwissenschaften.

Gendźwiłł, A. (2012). Independent mayors and local lists in large Polish cities: towards a non-partisan model of local government? *Local Government Studies*, *38*(4), 501–518.

Gendźwiłł, A. (2017). Różne wybory, różne elektoraty? Specyfika uczestnictwa w wyborach lokalnych. *Studia Socjologiczne*, 1(224), 81–102.

Gendźwiłł, A., & Marcinkiewicz, K. (2019) Interventionism of voters: district size, level of government, and the use of preference votes. *Acta Politica*, 54(1), 1–21.

Gendźwiłł, A., & Swianiewicz, P. (2017). Breeding grounds for local independents, bonus for incumbents: directly elected mayors in Poland. In: D. Sweeting (Ed.), *Directly Elected Mayors in Urban Governance: Impact and Practice* (pp. 179–200). Bristol: Policy Press.

Gendźwiłł, A., & Żerkowska-Balas, M. (2017) *Polacy o samorządach. Opinia publiczna u progu samorządowej kampanii wyborczej*. Warszawa: Fundacja im. Stefana Batorego.

Gendźwiłł, A., & Żółtak, T. (2017). How single-member districts are reinforcing local independents and strengthening mayors: on the electoral reform in Polish local government. *Local Government Studies*, *43*(1), 110–131.

Gwiazda, A. (2015). Women's representation and gender quotas: the case of the Polish parliament. *Democratization*, *22*(4), 679–697.

Heinelt, H., & Hlepas, N. K. (2006). Typologies of local government systems. In: H. Bäck, H. Heinelt, & A. Magnier (Eds.), *The European Mayor Political Leaders in the Changing Context of Local Democracy* (pp. 21–42). Baden-Baden: VS Verlag für Sozialwissenschaften.

Kjaer, U. (2012). Local politics: incubator or respirator for political parties? In: J. Blom-Hansen, C. Green-Pedersen, & S-E. Skaaning (Eds.), *Democracy, Elections, and Political Parties. Essays in Honour of Jørgen Elklit* (pp. 201–209). Aarhus: Aarhus University Press.

Kuć-Czajkowska, K., & Sidor, M. (2017). *Koabitacja na poziomie gminnym w Polsce*. Warszawa: Wyd. Naukowe Scholar.

Kukołowicz, P., & Górecki, M. A. (2018). When incumbents can only gain: economic voting in local government elections in Poland. *West European Politics*, *41*(3), 640–659.

Ladner, A., Keuffer, N., Baldersheim, H., Hlepas, N., Swianiewicz, P., Steyvers, K., & Navarro, C. (2019). *Patterns of Local Autonomy in Europe*. Cham: Palgrave Macmillan.

Ptak, A. (2010). Ewolucja systemu wyborczego do organów samorządu terytorialnego w Polsce. In: A Stelmach (Ed.), *Prawo wyborcze i wybory. Doświadczenia dwudziestu lat procesów demokratyzacyjnych w Polsce* (pp. 143–152). Poznań: Wydawnictwo Naukowe WNPiD UAM.

Raciborski, J., & Ochremiak, J. (2006). O blokowaniu list w wyborach samorządowych 2006 roku io racjonalności partii politycznych. *Decyzje*, *6*, 59–80.

Regulski, J. (1993). Rebuilding local government in Poland. In: R.J. Bennett (Ed.), *Local government in the new Europe* (pp. 197–207). Chichester: John Wiley & Sons.

Reif, K., & Schmitt, H. (1980). Nine second-order national elections – a conceptual framework for the analysis of European Election results. *European Journal of Political Research*, *8*(1), 3–44.

Słodkowska, I. (2014). *Komitety obywatelskie 1989–1992: rdzeń polskiej transformacji*. Warszawa: Instytut Studiów Politycznych PAN.

29
Slovakia
A gradual weakening of political parties in a stable local electoral system

Daniel Klimovský

The local government system and its recent development

The roots of the modern democratic local government system in Slovakia can be traced back to the first Czechoslovak Republic, which existed from 1918 to 1938 (Bakoš, Soukopová & Selešovský 2015). Before 1990, the federal parts of Czechoslovakia used identical systems of local administration; however, since then they have decided to use different local government systems (Klimovský, Pinterič & Jüptner 2019). Local governments legally obtained self-government status in 1990. However, in the 1990s they experienced difficulty developing due to the dominance of national politics, economic problems linked to the transition, and their own financial dependence on the state. In addition, the fragmented structure of local governments became even more pronounced: the total number of local governments increased from 2,669 units in 1989 to 2,891 units in 2002, when the fragmentation wave was stopped (Klimovský 2016).

Important systemic changes were implemented in the early 2000s as new regional governments with directly elected bodies were established; the state transferred a significant number of tasks to both regional and local governments, and conditions for the division of local governments were tightened. Consequently, fiscal decentralization was implemented, and the relevant stakeholders recognized this as an essential systemic change (Klimovský 2016). Due to strong resistance from local governments, only a very limited discussion of amalgamation reform developed in the mid-2000s. Nowadays, local governments in Slovakia are responsible for spatial planning, the construction and maintenance of local infrastructure, social care, child care, elementary education, and local development, including socioeconomic and cultural development.

Slovakia has two levels of subnational government comprising eight regional governments (from a legal point of view, two different names are used: *vyššie územné celky* and *samosprávne kraje*) and 2,890 municipalities (*obce*). While a clear majority (2,750) of all municipalities are of a rural nature, there are 141 towns (*mestá*) in Slovakia. In terms of competences and tasks, they are equal to any other municipality. Furthermore, not all towns have a real urban character. In several cases, being a town is a kind of honorary status that was acquired in the past; indeed, the population in the smallest towns is fewer than 2,000 inhabitants (Klimovský 2016). The largest cities (Bratislava and Košice) use two-tier local governments, that is, local governments at the levels of city and city district. The local elections in the city districts follow the same rules as local elections at the city level. Although more than two-thirds of all municipalities in Slovakia are very small, having a population size of under 1,000 inhabitants, the sizes vary significantly. While the largest city is Bratislava (about 432,000 permanent inhabitants), only 12 people have their permanent residence in the rural municipality of Príkra. The average size of municipalities in Slovakia is 1,870 inhabitants. If one used the median instead (642 inhabitants), the municipal structure of Slovakia would look even more fragmented (Klobučník & Bačík 2016).

From the perspective of multilevel governance, Slovakia uses the multipurpose model (Type I) in which local and regional governments are responsible for delivering a wide range of local services (Hooghe & Marks 2001). According to the typology of Swianiewicz (2014), Slovakia could be seen as a champion of decentralization. Taking into account the Local Autonomy Index developed by Ladner et al. (2019), Slovakia's total score for the period 2010–2014 is 60.9, making it an example of Type III local autonomy (i.e., a medium level of political discretion accompanied by a medium level of financial autonomy). From the perspective of horizontal power relations, the local governments in Slovakia have a strong mayoral model (Heinelt et al. 2018) that can be understood as a local variant of presidentialism (Heinelt & Hlepas 2006). Taking into account their position and tasks, mayors have executive powers and are political leaders, as well as the heads of the local administration. In addition, despite single-winner plurality voting, they dominate local politics thanks to their power over local councils. Deputy mayors also act in the local government system, but their tasks are determined by the mayors themselves, and they usually only play a minor role in terms of political and administrative importance.

The simple rules of local elections

The first local elections took place on 23 and 24 November 1990, shortly after the legal reestablishment of democratic local government, and in many cases previous local political elites defended their mandates in these elections. For the renewed local government system, it was typical that the legal removal of the 'old principles' was a much easier task than the proper implementation of democratic institutions; indeed, the replacement of the 'old-timers' with new local politicians was slower than in some other post-Communist European countries (Illner 1999).

Local elections are organized by the State Commission for Elections and the Control of Financing of Political Parties (*Štátna komisia pre voľby a kontrolu financovania politických strán*). This independent authority manages and coordinates the activities of other involved authorities, and it is responsible for the verification of the results of all popular elections in Slovakia. Local elections are organized on the same day in all municipalities.

All collective representative bodies in Slovakia have the same four-year term of office, and the national elections and local elections used to be organized in the same years. However, this changed in 2012 due to national elections being held early. A measure of synchronization of local elections with regional elections is due to be implemented in 2022. This change required a constitutional amendment to be approved by the parliament in February 2017, with the term of office of regional governments being extended to a one-off period of five years after the elections in November 2017. The main reason for such a measure is the effort to significantly increase voter turnout for the regional elections. Surprisingly, there was an underdeveloped debate on the risks of such synchronization (e.g., both elections might get mixed up with each other and voters might become confused).

Mayors are directly elected in all municipalities regardless of size using a first-past-the-post system. A majority two-round system was never a serious topic of official political discourse, but some political parties have tried to advocate for this idea, particularly with regard to the election of mayors of the largest cities. Mayoral elections are formally separated from the elections of local councilors, but they are held on the same day. Interestingly, one person can simultaneously run for both mayor and councilor. Due to the fact that mayoral elections attract more media interest, mayoral candidates usually enjoy more visibility; indeed, for some of them it is a campaign strategy to at least secure a seat on the local council. There is no specific mechanism for the distribution of seats on local councils in order to set up majority support for mayors in Slovakia, but a system of mutual checks and balances forces elected mayors and local councilors to collaborate. A binding recall referendum is possible in local politics in Slovakia. It can be called by the local council itself if the mayor has been unable to work for more than six months. A recall referendum must be announced by a local council if there is a supporting petition of at least 30% of eligible voters; the law does not specify the need for a stated reason for such a petition.

In local council elections, a multiple nontransferable vote, also known as a 'bloc vote' or 'plurality-at-large voting', has been used since 1990. Each voter has a number of votes corresponding to the number of councilors in the relevant constituency. The candidates are ordered alphabetically by surname. Those candidates who receive the highest numbers of all valid votes obtain seats on the local councils.

Cumul des mandats is a phenomenon that is permitted in the multilevel political system of Slovakia. It is possible to combine legislative functions as well as executive and legislative ones. To have a mayoral mandate and that of an MP is quite common in Slovakia (e.g., 14 mayors were also MPs in 2015, and 13 mayors successfully ran for seats in the national parliament in 2020); however, this has been highly criticized, and there have been discussions about forbidding such an accumulation of political positions (Swianiewicz 2005: 110). Incumbency advantage is another feature of local elections in Slovakia, because the incumbents are often unchallenged. In discussing the phenomenon of incumbency, Sloboda (2014) analyzed the results of mayoral elections in Slovak towns and cities in 2006 and 2010 and concluded that the incumbency rate was approximately 85%. A deeper look at these candidates showed that about 61% were successful in the 2006 elections and 72% were successful in the 2010 elections.

An interesting possibility linked to the mergers of municipalities was approved by the parliament on 1 February 2018. Due to the fact that in a few municipalities nobody had run for mayor or local councilor, the local governments became practically dysfunctional, and the previous governments were meant to continue performing all tasks even though they had not been reelected. According to the new rules, if there are no candidates in a regular term of local elections, new elections are announced. If again nobody runs for mayor or local councilor, the government can merge this municipality with a neighboring one if the council of the neighboring municipality gives its formal approval.

Features of the electoral system

Any inhabitant with permanent residency in the municipality (regardless of citizenship) can apply for candidacy. The rule is that one person may run for mayor and/or local councilor in one electoral constituency. If a person runs for mayor and for local councilor within the same local election and wins both, that person then becomes mayor.

There are two ways to be a candidate: (1) as a candidate of political party or (2) as an independent (i.e., nonparty) candidate. Each political party registered by the Ministry of

Interior of the Slovak Republic in the Register of Political Parties and Political Movements can nominate as many candidates as the number of seats in the constituency allows; obviously, it can nominate fewer candidates as well (Klimovský 2016). Unlike political parties, independent candidates must show their support from eligible voters through petitions with voters' signatures. While only ten supporting signatures are required in municipalities of up to 50 inhabitants, 600 supporting signatures are required in cities with populations over 100,000.

Local councils can determine their own number of seats, and they are responsible for the definition of electoral constituency boundaries within some legal limits. While in mayoral elections each municipality is equal to one electoral constituency, the situation is different in the case of council elections. A basic rule is that each constituency should comprise about 1,000 voters. However, due to the fact that there are many micro municipalities in Slovakia, it is not uncommon for a constituency to be equal to the municipality as a whole. Single-member constituencies are not rare either, but usually multiple-member constituencies predominate in the municipalities and towns of Slovakia. On the other hand, there is a legal maximum of 12 local councilors that can be elected in one constituency. While larger constituencies are very common for small municipalities, in larger towns and cities, smaller constituencies comprising only a few mandates are used. District magnitude offers a possible explanation for this behavior. Because voters expect their councilors to maintain strong links with them and act as their 'delegates', it is no surprise that smaller constituencies are preferred in densely populated areas. Despite the discretion of local authorities to set the borders of constituencies, gerrymandering is not a common phenomenon at the local level. The constituencies usually respect traditional settlement structures.

The local electoral system has not significantly changed since its introduction in 1990. However, there have been a few adjustments. They have been particularly linked to the high level of municipal fragmentation. The collapse of the Communist Party regime brought about political euphoria at the end of 1989; it is thus no surprise that the number of seats on local councils was legally changed from nine to 60 councilors in 1990, with 38,490 local councilors being elected in total. The fragmentation wave of the early 1990s and the existence of micro municipalities required an amendment of the electoral law in 1992. According to this amendment, the minimum number of local councilors dropped to five councilors in those municipalities with a population of under 40 inhabitants. Although the logic of this legal effort was clear, the set minimum number of local councilors remained too high. The next significant amendment on this matter was approved in 2001: while the minimum number of local councilors dropped to three, the maximum number dropped to 45. Thanks to this amendment, the total number of local councilors decreased to 21,644 in 2002. In the following local elections, the total number of local councilors stabilized at the level of about 21,000 (20,789 local councilors were elected in Slovakia in 2018).

Basic eligibility rules were defined in 1990 and have not substantially changed. All municipal inhabitants who are 18 years or older are entitled to vote. Thanks to membership in the EU, citizens of other EU countries who are permanent residents of Slovak municipalities also have the right to vote in local elections. Voters can only vote in the municipality in which they have their permanent residence. It is not possible to vote from abroad nor in any other municipality in Slovakia. In addition, no early voting is allowed. While the right to stand for the local council elections is granted to all eligible adult voters, a candidate for mayor must be at least 25 years old during the election. Such an age requirement in the case of mayoral elections is rather common in the Central European region, and one can also find it in the history of local elections in Slovakia (Klimovský, Pinterič & Jüptner 2019).

No gender quota has been introduced in Slovakia since 1990. Interestingly, strong resistance to gender quotas has been visible in rural local political environments, which are considered more conservative in terms of various social issues, as well as in urban ones (Krivý 2013). A very interesting story is linked to the idea of introducing a minimum educational requirement for mayors. A few municipalities have experienced illiterate mayors in the past decade, especially those with large Roma communities. In 2014, this led to a decision by the parliament to introduce a minimum educational requirement for those running for mayor. The completion of secondary level education was approved as a minimum requirement. However, the constitution guarantees equal access to elected public functions, and therefore this amendment was recognized as unconstitutional, meaning that it could not become law. The parliament did not want to give up, and a new, neutral legal provision (in Section 13 of the Local Government Act) was approved: 'The mayor shall improve their knowledge [of what is] necessary to perform the function of mayor.' Obviously, this is a vague and tricky legal provision that has the nature of a political statement given that no sanction mechanism is connected with this 'requirement', and there is neither a legal definition of 'knowledge improvement' nor any further specification of the desired knowledge.

The gradual retreat of party candidates

Local elections had high turnout in the 1990s; the highest voter participation was achieved in 1990, when almost two-thirds of all eligible voters took part. However, voter turnout dropped to under 50% for the local elections in 2002, and since then has never achieved the participation of the majority of voters. The first four local elections (1990–2002) were organized as two-day elections, whereas all subsequent local elections were organized as one-day affairs. The local–national turnout gap is quite large in Slovakia, and parliamentary elections always attract higher voter participation in comparison with local elections (see Table 29.1). Even worse electoral participation is typical for other subnational elections, that is, regional elections. Since 2001 when the first regional elections were held, the average voter turnout for these elections has never achieved 30%.

Table 29.1 Voter turnout (percent) for local and national elections in Slovakia since 1990

Local elections		Parliamentary elections	
Election date	Voter turnout (%)	Election date	Voter turnout (%)
23–24 November 1990	63.8	**8–9 June 1990**[1]	95.4
		5–6 June 1992[1]	84.2
18–19 November 1994	52.4	**30 September–1 October 1994**	75.7
18–19 December 1998	54.0	**25–26 September 1998**[2]	84.2
6–7 December 2002	49.5	**20–21 September 2002**	70.1
2 December 2006	47.7	**17 June 2006**	54.7
27 November 2010	49.7	**12 June 2010**	58.8
		10 March 2012	59.1
15 November 2014	48.3	**5 March 2016**	59.8
10 November 2018	48.7	**29 February 2020**	65.8

[1] Elections to the National Parliament were synchronized with elections to the Federal Parliament of Czechoslovakia.
[2] National elections were synchronized with a national referendum on nonprivatization of strategic public enterprises.
Source: Official website of the Statistical Office of the Slovak Republic, sub-website 'Elections and Referendums'

Electoral participation partially depends on the population size of the municipalities. Although there is no clear negative correlation between voter turnout and population size, voter turnout for the local elections organized in the largest cities and district capitals is usually below the average.

Local elections are organized even when the total number of candidates is lower than or equal to the number of seats on the local councils, and uncompetitive mayoral elections are also not uncommon. In the latest local elections, which took place in 2018, uncompetitive mayoral elections occurred in 762 municipalities (or 26% of the total). This situation is common in small rural municipalities, and the uncontested candidates for mayor are usually the incumbents. Several local elections in 2018 were uncontested due to either an excessively low number of candidates for councilor or a lack of candidates for mayoral or council positions (see Table 29.2). This usually happens in very small municipalities with either an elderly population or a high level of debt.

Local politics in Slovakia was particularly influenced by national political parties in the 1990s. While independent candidates in some other Central European countries used to obtain high shares of all seats on local councils, independent candidates were significantly less successful in Slovakia. According to Klimovský (2016), the results of three recent mayoral elections showed a kind of 'escape-from-party-domination' trend, because independent candidates succeeded in more than one-third of all mayoral elections (see Table 29.3). In addition, it must be stressed that independent candidates were also successful in the largest cities and district capitals (e.g., Bratislava, Košice, Trenčín, and Trnava), which are traditionally considered the most important local battlefields, even for national political parties. More precisely, although independent candidates were common after 1990, especially in small municipalities, the share of independent mayors and independent councilors has also dramatically increased in larger towns and cities.

A few additional points must be stressed within this context. First, being 'independent' became a kind of label, and two different approaches can be seen. The first group of independent candidates consists of those who were not supported by any political party from the very beginning. The second group consists of those who declared themselves independent on local lists, but who enjoyed more or less open support during the electoral campaign from one or more political parties. This group also includes those who decided to run for mayor or councilor as independent candidates exclusively within local elections (i.e., it is their local campaign strategy) even though they have clear connections to a political party. Second, only a few national political parties have nationwide structures with sufficient numbers of their own

Table 29.2 Numbers of cases with missing candidates in two recent local elections in Slovakia, 2014 and 2018

Reasons for uncompetitive local elections	Number of municipalities	
	2014	2018
Number of candidates was lower than number of seats on the local council	14	23
Nobody ran for local councilor	3	5
Nobody ran for mayor	6	11

Table 29.3 Share of independent candidates among elected councilors and mayors in Slovakia, 1990–2018

Year of local elections	1990	1994	1998	2002	2006	2010	2014	2018
Councilors	15.9	7.8	8.9	13.5	17.1	22.7	28.9	35.4
Mayors	25.9	28.8	28.3	32.7	30.8	33.7	38.0	42.4

Source: Official website of the Statistical Office of the Slovak Republic, subwebsite 'Elections and Referendums'

members making up potential local cadres that are ready to compete in subnational elections. From this point of view, Slovakia is a country where political parties play only a minor role in the everyday practice of local councilors (Egner, Sweeting & Klok 2013). Therefore, declared affiliation with a party might be an inaccurate indication from an analytical point of view, especially in rural areas where many candidates use party nominations in order to avoid having to collect supporting signatures (Maškarinec & Klimovský 2016).

The most successful party nominees in the 2018 local elections were from the most stable (traditional) parties with their own, well-developed local structures, especially Smer-SD, KDH, and SNS. Some parties (e.g., SaS and ĽSNS) have never established strong local structures, and others (e.g., OĽaNO and Sme Rodina) have never even had that ambition. Za ľudí was established just recently and became a member of the ruling coalition in 2020. A comparison of the electoral results of the relevant political parties (see Table 29.4) indicates that the existence of well-developed local structures is likely to be a much more important determinant of success in local elections than the number of seats held by the party in the national parliament.

There are no special provisions for ethnic or national minorities in local elections. However, political parties focusing on the Hungarian minority (especially SMK-MKP and Most-Híd) have enjoyed stable, long-lasting support, especially in regions where the Hungarian minority lives, and subnational electoral results confirm this. The Roma minority is also strong in terms of the total number of its members, but its political representation is very fragmented. This is visible in the case of parliamentary elections in particular, because political parties have their own candidates in these elections, and no ethnically Roma party has attracted any broad support from voters belonging to that ethnic group as yet. Local elections lead to different results; for instance, more than 40 Roma mayors and more than 500 Roma councilors were elected in the latest elections.

In the 1990s, women were significantly more successful in local elections in small municipalities (Filadelfiová, Radičová & Puliš 2000: 54–56). However, according to Bútorová and Filadelfiová (2011), one can see a clear, long-lasting trend of an overall increase in women's representation in local politics. Although a critical mass has not yet been achieved (see Table 29.5), there has been continuously higher representation of women among mayors since 1994 (Maškarinec & Klimovský 2017). Women were rather successful in the 2018 local elections and gained 740 mayoral positions and 5,404 seats on local councils. In other words, one out of four mayors is now female and approximately the same ratio between men and women exists on local councils.

Discussion: the stability of the system and the gradual weakening of political parties

Partly spontaneous and partly coordinated democratization led to the establishment of several 'traditional' political parties in Slovakia in the 1990s and early 2000s. These parties sought,

Table 29.4 Comparison of national and subnational electoral results of selected political parties in Slovakia

Political parties and their coalitions (political parties with poorly developed subnational structures are in italics)	% of votes in the parliamentary election in 2016: proportional electoral system (results of the ruling coalition are in italics)	% of seats on regional councils in 2017: number of seats won/ total number of regional councilors elected (416 seats)	% of seats on local councils in 2018: number of seats won/ total number of local councilors elected	% of mayors affiliated with the party in 2018: directly elected	% of votes in the parliamentary election in 2020: proportional electoral system (results of the ruling coalition are in italics)
Parliamentary parties					
Smer-SD	28.3	13.9	17.8	20.4	18.3
SNS	8.6	2.2	8.1	5.5	3.2
Most-Híd	6.5	1.9	4.4	4.4	2.1
OĽaNO	11.0	–	0.4	0.0	25.0
Sme Rodina	6.6	–	0.6	0.4	8.2
SaS	12.1	–	0.5	0.2	6.2
Za ľudí	–	–	–	–	5.8
ĽSNS	8.0	0.5	0.2	–	8.0
Ruling coalition's candidates (i.e., Smer-SD + SNS + Most-Híd or Smer-SD + SNS or Smer-SD + Most-Híd)	–	3.8	2.7	7.8	–
Candidates of coalitions consisting of the parliamentary opposition parties (OĽaNO, Sme Rodina, SaS)	–	16.3 (total result of different coalitions that included OĽaNO, SaS, KDH and some other parties)	3.7	0.5	–
The most important nonparliamentary parties and independent candidates					
KDH	4.9	–	11.4	5.4	4.7
SMK-MKP	4.0	7.2	6.0	4.0	3.9
Independent candidates (only in the subnational elections)	–	38.7	35.4	42.4	–

Source: Official website of the Statistical Office of the Slovak Republic, sub-website 'Elections and Referendums'

Table 29.5 Share of women among elected councilors and mayors in Slovakia, 1990–2018

Year of local elections	1990	1994	1998	2002	2006	2010	2014	2018
Councilors	n/a	n/a	n/a	n/a	n/a	n/a	26.4	26.0
Mayors	n/a	15.2	17.5	18.6	20.7	21.2	23	25.3

Source: Official website of the Statistical Office of the Slovak Republic, subwebsite 'Elections and Referendums'

among other things, to establish their own organizational units at the local level. Several other parties that were established later did not follow this organizational logic (Marušiak 2017). Instead of the development of strong local roots, some of them were established as entrepreneurial parties and they invested in modern technologies that allowed them to predict voter preferences and tailor their electoral strategies to the expectations and desires of their target groups (Žúborová 2015). It seems that these developments also significantly influenced the electoral behavior of the voters. While in the local elections they still preferred parties with clear organizational links to their communities, in national elections they tended to be subject to modern as well as unconventional strategies.

From the horizontal point of view, the high level of fragmentation used to play a significant role, and a few clear differences were visible when, for instance, comparing local electoral results from urban centers (large cities) with those from rural municipalities. The rural political environment was more favorable for independent candidates and female candidates and was much less competitive (Klimovský & Žúborová 2011). The last of these features has remained due to the low interest of parliamentary parties in local politics, especially in rural municipalities, and the phenomenon of incumbency (Sloboda 2014). However, a gradual increase in women's representation (Maškarinec, Klimovský & Bláha 2019) and the significantly increasing success of independent candidates (Maškarinec & Klimovský 2016) have become new local political trends.

The local electoral system in Slovakia can be described as rather stable because it has not significantly changed since its introduction in 1990. The most important legal amendments reduced the size of local councils and changed the conditions to begin mayoral recall referenda, as well as the conditions of voters' support for independent candidates (Klimovský 2016). Some of the recently approved legal adjustments have responded to publicized cases and were not of a systemic nature, for example, the minimum education requirement for mayoral candidates. At the same time, the introduction of the opportunity to merge those municipalities in which the local governments are dysfunctional and nobody seems interested in local politics seems to be a better choice than maintaining the undesired status quo.

References

Bakoš, E., Soukopová, J. & Selešovský, J. (2015). The Historical Roots of Local Self-Government in Czech and Slovak Republics. *Lex Localis – Journal of Local Self-Government, 13*(1), 1–19.

Bútorová, Z. & Filadelfiová, J. (2011). Parlamentné voľby 2010 v rodovej perspektíve. In Z. Bútorová et al. (Eds.), *Slovenské voľby'10: Šanca na zmenu* (pp. 181–207). Bratislava: Inštitút pre verejné otázky.

Egner, B., Sweeting, D. & Klok, P.-J. (2013). Local Councillors in Comparative Perspective: Drawing Conclusions. In B. Egner, D. Sweeting & P.J. Klok (Eds.), *Local Councillors in Europe* (pp. 255–262). Wiesbaden: Springer VS.

Filadelfiová, J., Radičová, I. & Puliš, P. (2000). *Ženy v politike*. 1st ed. Bratislava: S.P.A.C.E./MPSVaR SR.

Heinelt, H. & Hlepas, N. (2006). Typologies of Local Government Systems. In H. Bäck, H. Heinelt & A. Magnier (Eds.) *The European Mayor: Political Leaders in the Changing Context of Local Democracy* (pp. 21–42). Baden-Baden: VS Verlag für Sozialwissenschaften.

Heinelt, H., Hlepas, N., Kuhlmann, S. & Swianiewicz, P. (2018). Local Government Systems: Grasping the Institutional Environment of Mayors. In H. Heinelt, A. Magnier, M. Cabria & H. Reynaert (Eds.), *Political Leaders and Changing Local Democracy: The European Mayor* (pp. 19–78). London: Palgrave Macmillan.

Hooghe, L. & Marks, G. (2001). *Multi-Level Governance and European Integration*. Lanham: Rowman & Littlefield.

Illner, M. (1999). Territorial Decentralization: An Obstacle to Democratic Reform in Central and Eastern Europe? In J. D. Kimball (Ed.), *The Transfer of Power: Decentralization in Central and Eastern Europe* (pp. 7–42) Budapest: OSI/LGI.

Klimovský, D. (2016). Experience with Managerial and Political Reform Measures at the Local Level in Slovakia: Intended and Unintended Outcomes. In U. Sadioglu & K. Dede (Eds.), *Comparative Studies and Regionally-Focused Cases Examining Local Governments* (pp. 135–160). Hershey: IGI Global.

Klimovský, D., Pinterič, U. & Jüptner, P. (2019). Path Dependence and Local (Self-) Government Systems: A Comparison of Three CEE Countries. *Politics in Central Europe*, 15(2), 193–218.

Klimovský, D. & Žúborová, V. (2011). Komunálne voľby 2010. In M. Bútora, M. Kollár & G. Mesežnikov (Eds.), *Slovensko 2010: Správa o stave spoločnosti a demokracie a o trendoch na rok 2011* (pp. 131–150). Bratislava: Inštitút pre verejné otázky.

Klobučník, M. & Bačík, V. (2016). Local Self-Government Structure in the EU Member States in 2011. *Journal of Maps*, 12(4), 671–675.

Krivý, V. (Ed.). (2013). *Ako sa mení slovenská spoločnosť*. Bratislava: Sociologický ústav SAV.

Ladner, A., Keuffer, N., Baldersheim, H., Hlepas, N., Swianiewicz, P., Steyvers, K. & Navarro, C. (2019). *Patterns of Local Autonomy in Europe*. London: Palgrave Macmillan.

Marušiak, J. (2017). Political Entrepreneurs as a Challenge for the Party System in Slovakia. *Czech Journal of Political Science*, 24(2), 179–200.

Maškarinec, P. & Klimovský, D. (2017). Determinants of Women's Descriptive Representation in the 2014 Czech and Slovak Local Elections. *Lex Localis – Journal of Local Self-Government*, 15(3), 387–410.

Maškarinec, P. & Klimovský, D. (2016). Independent Candidates in the Local Elections of 2014 in the Czech Republic and Slovakia: Analysis of Determinants of Their Successfulness. *Lex Localis – Journal of Local Self-Government*, 14(4), 853–871.

Maškarinec, P., Klimovský, D. & Bláha, P. (2019). *Where Have All the Women Gone? Women's Political Representation in Local Councils of Czech and Slovak Towns, 1994–2014*. Praha: Dokořán.

Sloboda, M. (2014). Women's Participation and Incumbency Advantage in Slovak Cities: The Case Study of Mayoral Elections in Slovakia. *Socialiniai tyrimai/Social Research*, 36(3), 101–112.

Swianiewicz, P. (2014). An Empirical Typology of Local Government Systems in Eastern Europe. *Local Government Studies*, 40(2), 292–311.

Swianiewicz, P. (2005). Cities in Transition: From Statism to Democracy. In M. Haus, H. Heinelt & M. Stewart (Eds.), *Urban Governance and Democracy: Leadership and Community Involvement* (pp. 102–128). London/New York: Routledge.

Žúborová, V. (2015). Newcomers in Politics? The Success of New Political Parties in the Slovak and Czech Republic after 2010? *Baltic Journal of Law & Politics*, 8(2), 91–111.

30

Ukraine

The first experiences with voting in the amalgamated territorial communities

Valentyna Romanova

The local government system at a turning point

Ukraine is a unitary state in Eastern Europe; it gained independence from Soviet rule in 1991.[1] In 1997, the parliament (*Verkhovna Rada*) ratified the European Charter on Local Self-Government and approved the domestic law on local governance. Ukraine inherited three main tiers of administrative and territorial divisions from the Soviet era: regional, subregional, and local (see Table 30.1). The local tier changed in the years between 2015 and 2020, when 10,961 urban and rural communities – cities and towns, as well as villages and settlements – merged into 1,470 amalgamated territorial communities (ATCs). Before 2020, amalgamation had been voluntary. On 12 June 2020, the government completed amalgamation by using administrative stimuli. A typical ATC consists of 4.6 cities and towns and/or villages and settlements, with 11,326 residents on average. On 17 July 2020, the parliament decreased the number of subregions (*rayons*) from 490 to 136. Since 1991, the number of regions had remained the same: 24 *oblasts*, the Autonomous Republic of Crimea, and two cities – Kyiv (the capital) and Sevastopol. In March 2014, Russia illegally annexed Crimea, including Sevastopol.

In the period 1991–2014, local self-government followed the Napoleonic state tradition. Local governments' own revenues were limited (Swianiewicz 2014), and they were therefore largely dependent on financial transfers from the central budget (Ladner et al. 2016: 334, 335). According to the comparative study of Ladner and colleagues (2015), Ukraine had the second lowest local autonomy scores among European countries: 16.1, 17.1, and 16.6 in 2000, 2010, and 2014, respectively. With the exception of cities of oblast significance, most localities did not have sufficient capacity to take partial responsibility for running public transport services, maintaining school buildings, and financing public health centers.

The amalgamation of localities into ATCs brings Ukraine closer to the North and Middle European group (Heinelt and Hlepas 2006: 24–26). First, the amalgamation reform has already reduced the extent of fragmentation on the local scale: it has allowed the merging of 10,961 communities into 1,470 ATCs. Second, the reform has introduced direct interbudgetary relations between ATCs and the central budget, allocated more tax shares to ATCs, including a 60% share of personal income taxes (Levitas and Djikic 2017), and, thus, made ATCs better able

Table 30.1 The tiers of administrative and territorial divisions in Ukraine

Three tiers of administrative and territorial divisions	Number of units inherited from the Soviet era	Number of units after finalizing local amalgamation in 2020
Local	10,961 territorial communities: cities, towns, villages, and settlements	1,470 amalgamated territorial communities (ATCs), including 31 ATCs in the non-government-controlled territories of Ukraine
Subregional	490 subregions	136 subregions
Regional	27 regions	27 regions

Source: Author's compilation

to take responsibility for public service provision (managing primary and secondary education, providing administrative services, etc.) and local development.

The local amalgamation reform affects vertical power relations. Prior to its implementation, the centrally appointed regional executives administered the central budget's transfers to municipalities – the majority of which were conditional (Ladner et al. 2014: 334) – and took responsibility for the delivery of public services locally. The amalgamation reform reduces the power of regional authorities over municipalities and strengthens interbudgetary relations between the central and local budgets.

Since 1991, local self-government in Ukraine fits the strong mayor type, in particular, the executive mayor type. Voters directly elect mayors and local councils. A local council establishes its executive committee, and a mayor is in charge of suggesting the list of candidacies for the respective executive committee. The councilors cannot suggest any alternatives; however, they can decline the mayor's list of candidates, and this legal mechanism helps to balance power relations between a mayor and a majority of councilors on a local council. The mayor chairs the executive committee and can veto its decisions, as well as the decisions of the respective local council. A mayor cannot dismiss a local council, but a local council can dismiss a mayor (by a minimum two-thirds vote in the respective local council). When localities amalgamate with others into an ATC, voters elect one local council and one mayor in the respective ATC. In 2016–2019, when the process of local amalgamation was voluntary, those voters who resided in an ATC but outside the administrative center of the respective ATC directly elected their representatives (*starostas*) (according to FPTP), who joined the ATC's executive committee chaired by the ATC's mayor. However, the direct election of *starostas* proved to be a temporary arrangement: at the 2020 local elections, there were no direct elections of *starostas*; instead, each newly elected local council appointed *starostas* at the suggestion of its mayor. The functions of the appointed *starostas* stay the same, and they would join the ATC's executive committee to carry out its duties.

Executive committees are accountable to local councils with respect to matters of local governance. In addition, (sub)regional executives, appointed by the president, have the right to supervise executive committees, when it comes to fulfilling the duties that the state delegates. Sometimes, this leads to conflicts, like during the anti-COVID-19 quarantine in Spring-Summer 2020, when a few city mayors and local councils opposed the quarantine-related decisions taken by the government.

There is no legal way for central authorities to dismiss a mayor. Only the parliament can announce early mayoral elections after a mayor's dismissal by the respective local council. Also, the parliament can call for early local elections in a locality if the respective local council breaks the law; however, local councils are careful enough to avoid such situations. After the military conflict in Donbas (including the Donetsk and Luhansk *oblast*s) was fueled in 2014, the central authorities terminated the powers of some local councils in the government-controlled territories of the Donetsk and Luhansk *oblast*s and established military-civil administrations by the president's decree.

Ukraine's local elections in brief

The parliament announces local elections, with the exception of announcing the first local elections in the newly established ATCs: the latter is the function of the Central Electoral Commission. When it comes to the administration of any local electoral contests in Ukraine, it is the exclusive responsibility of the Central Electoral Commission. Ukraine held direct elections of local councils and mayors in 1994, 1998, 2002, 2006, 2010, and 2015. Local elections are nationwide and are always held simultaneously with regional and subregional council elections. In 1994, presidential and local elections were held together. In 1998, 2002, and 2006, there were simultaneous local and parliamentary elections.

The constitution (Article 38) and the 1997 law on local self-government (Article 7) allow local referenda with respect to matters that are the prerogative of local self-government. However, the procedures of local referenda have to be guided by a separate law. In July 1991, prior to Ukraine's independence from Soviet rule, the parliament of Soviet Ukraine introduced a law on all-Ukrainian and local referenda, which provided some guidelines for holding local referenda (Congress of Local and Regional Authorities 2013). In 1991–2012, there were 178 registered initiatives to hold local referenda throughout Ukraine.[2] However, in 2012, the national parliament approved the law on all-Ukrainian referenda that replaced the 1991 law on all-Ukrainian and local referenda. Because the 2012 law allows only all-Ukrainian referenda, local referenda lost their legal framework. For example, the so-called local referenda with separatist agendas, organized during the military conflict in Donbas, had no legal background.

Frequent revisions of the electoral rules[3]

Every citizen who is at least 18 years old is eligible to vote in national and local elections, except for those whom the court has recognized as incapacitated. Ukrainians abroad have no right to vote in local elections, but can vote in presidential electoral contests. Ukrainians living abroad do have the right to vote in parliamentary elections, unless the latter requires voting for the national party lists according to PR (only those who reside in Ukraine can vote for candidates in majoritarian constituencies according to FPTP).

Citizens eligible to vote can stand for local elections. Noncitizens are not allowed to vote in elections or on referenda in Ukraine. Voting is not compulsory, and therefore there is no penalty for absenteeism. Since 2002, it has been impossible to simultaneously serve as a local and a (sub) regional councilor (the 2002 law on the status of local councilors, Article 7.3).

Most often, there is divergence between the electoral rules for parliamentary and for local contests, with one major exception. During the Orange Revolution of 2004, policymakers negotiated the electoral rules that allowed the election of parliament and local councils in cities and towns according to CLPR with a 3% threshold. Local councils in villages and settlements are elected according to FPTP. The respective territorial electoral committees established single-seat constituencies whose numbers corresponded to the numbers of seats on the local councils.

Electoral rules for local elections change often in Ukraine. In the 1994 local elections, voters elected local councils according to FPTP in single-member electoral districts, and, in order to be elected, a candidate had to receive more votes than his/her competitors and turnout had to be more than 10%. Also, voters directly elected the heads of local councils, using separate lists of candidates. In order to become the head of a local council, one had to receive more votes than other candidates and, at the same time, obtain the electoral support of no fewer than 25% of the voters. Often, it was difficult to pass this threshold, so the elections of the heads of local councils were often held several times. Prior to the 1998 local elections, parliament removed the so-called turnout threshold for local elections, which was too demanding, and abolished the direct election of the heads of local councils. The 2010 electoral law introduced a brand new system: the voters who resided in villages and settlements were to elect local councils according to FPTP, while local councils in towns and cities were elected according to the parallel system with a 50/50 split (50% of councillors were elected according to FPTP in single-member electoral districts, while another 50% were elected according to CLPR in multimember electoral districts, with a 3% threshold). The whole city or town was considered as one multimember district. There was no connection between the two components of the electoral rules.

The 2015 electoral law, introduced prior to the 2015 local elections (IFES 2015), prescribed the exact number of councilors, depending on the number of voters in localities and decreasing the maximum number from 150 to 120 (see Table 30.2). Previous electoral laws provided guidelines on the minimum and maximum numbers of councilors and allowed local councils to choose the exact number prior to the coming local election.

Local councils in villages and settlements were elected according to FPTP, while local elections in cities and towns were held according to CLPR with a 5% threshold. In rural areas, candidates could stand for elections to local councils as either independents or party members, while local electoral contests in urban areas allowed only competition between party lists. Thus, candidates for local councils in urban areas could be nominated by their local party branch, while candidates for local councils in rural areas could be self-nominated and did not necessarily require a party affiliation.

Table 30.2 Number of councilors on local councils elected in the 2015 Ukrainian local elections

Number of voters	Number of councilors
1,000	12
1,000–3,000	14
3,000–5,000	22
5,000–20,000	26
20,000–50,000	34
50,000–100,000	36
100,000–250,000	42
250,000–500,000	54
500,000 to 1 million voters	64
1–2 million voters	84
>2 million voters	120

Source: 2015 Law 'On local elections' [the official website of the parliament of Ukraine: https://zakon.rada.gov.ua/laws/show/595-19 (accessed on 16 December 2020)]

In each urban area, multimember constituencies were divided into nomination districts whose number corresponded to the number of seats on the respective council. At a polling station in a city or a town, a voter received an electoral bulletin with a list of parties standing for local elections, supplemented with a list of up to two candidates written next to the name of each party: (1) the party leader of the electoral list and (2) the candidate standing in the respective electoral district (a party could nominate one candidate in each nomination district; however, parties were not obliged to do so in each electoral district). The leader of the local party's list was not assigned to any nomination district, and he/she was elected in any case when the party received at least one seat. Voters could tick one box, and by doing so they cast their vote for respective party, the leader of the electoral list, and the candidate standing in the particular electoral district at the same time. No preferential voting was allowed.

The method of calculating the election quota was as follows. The total number of valid votes cast for the local lists of parties that passed the electoral threshold was divided by the number of local council mandates in each multimember constituency. Each party received a number of seats in accordance with its electoral quota. The remaining seats were allocated according to the method of the largest remainder, in particular, the Hare quota: the party that had the largest remainder was the first one to receive an additional seat, the party with the second largest was the second one to receive an additional seat, etc.; this rule was applied until all seats were allocated. The candidates who were at the top of the list – party leaders – were the luckiest: they were the first ones to receive their mandates in the respective local councils. Then, the electoral commission allocated seats to party candidates from each party in nomination districts in accordance with the percentage of votes that were cast for the local branch of the respective party in territorial election districts.

The 2015 law also introduced a new system for electing mayors. In previous elections, mayors were elected according to FPTP, with each local unit (a city or town, a village or settlement) as one electoral district. In the 2015 local elections, voters in small towns with a population of fewer than 90,000 voters elected mayors according to FPTP; candidates could be either nominated by parties or self-nominated (no special support for self-nominated candidates was required). In larger cities with a population of 90,000 or more, mayors were elected according to a two-round system (TRS), and candidates could only be nominated by parties.

Finally, the 2015 law introduced a 30% quota for women on parties' electoral lists. However, the Central Electoral Commission disregarded that requirement when registering and approving parties to stand for the 2015 electoral contests.

Electoral outcomes in the amalgamated and nonamalgamated territorial communities

Prior to the local amalgamation reform (2015–2020), there was not much at stake in local elections, apart from the local elections in 187 cities of oblast significance, which were the only localities that enjoyed a direct interbudgetary relationship with the central budget prior to local amalgamation. This was the major reason that parties often neglected local elections and prioritized national electoral contests. Also, domestic parties suffer from low party institutionalization: parties are institutionally too weak to contest local elections throughout the country. Instead, self-nominated independents actively contest local elections in Ukraine.

Unlike parties, voters used to pay a lot of attention to local elections. In 1994, turnout was 75.6%; it declined for the subsequent elections, but stayed relatively high (70.8% in 1998, 69.3% in 2002, and 67.6% in 2006; OPORA 2015). A major drop in turnout occurred in 2010 (48.7%), when Ukraine held nonsimultaneous local electoral contests for the first time.

The local elections held on 25 October 2015 were nonsimultaneous with national elections. They were held in those ATCs that had merged by that time (159 units), as well as in the remaining local communities (10,562 units). On the one hand, there was more at stake in local elections in ATCs than in the rest of the localities. On the other hand, the 2015 local elections were held at the very beginning of the amalgamation reform: the parliament approved the 2015 law on local amalgamation in February 2015 and introduced fiscal decentralization, which was beneficial for ATCs, in the 2014 amendments to the Budget Code and the Tax Code. Moreover, the 2015 local elections were held soon after the statewide political regime shifted as a result of the Euromaidan Revolution (massive public protests against the government's decision not to sign the Association Agreement with the EU at the Eastern Partnership Summit in November 2013 and the subsequent public protests against the political leadership of the country) and after Ukraine's territorial integrity was violated in Crimea and Donbas. It is no wonder that a national agenda dominated during the 2015 electoral campaign.

In most of the country, the local elections respected international democratic standards (the Congress of Local and Regional Authorities 2016). Due to the military conflict in Donbas and Russia's illegal annexation of Crimea, it was impossible to hold local elections there. Thus, no local elections were held in (1) Crimea, (2) the non-government-controlled territories of the Donetsk and Luhansk *oblasts*, and (3) 91 localities in Donetsk *oblast* and 31 localities in Luhansk *oblast* in the government-controlled Donbas. Also, there were serious violations of the electoral law in localities situated close to the front line (i.e., local elections in the cities of Mariupil and Krasnoarmiysk had to be rescheduled for 29 November 2015).

The 2015 local elections were competitive: 140 parties ran, including ones that contested elections only in a few localities. In Ukraine, all parties are formally statewide. They must maintain a statewide program of social development (the 2001 law on political parties, Article 2); in order to be officially registered, parties should provide evidence of their public support in at least two-thirds of *rayons* in at least two-thirds of *oblasts* of Ukraine (Article 10). In practice, parties may choose not to participate in local elections all over the country; in cases where they do so, they tend to gain significantly more votes in some parts of the country and suffer severe electoral losses in the rest of Ukraine. This reflects both regionalized public preferences (with respect to such salient issues as foreign policy priorities, attitudes toward the Euromaidan Revolution, the conflict in Donbas, etc.) and parties' electoral strategy of campaigning predominantly in their core constituencies.

Turnout for the 2015 local elections (46.6%) witnessed a decrease of approximately 6% compared to the 2014 parliamentary elections (52.4%) and a drop of 2% compared to the 2010 local elections (48.7%). Western Ukraine traditionally demonstrated the highest turnout (over 50%). The lowest turnout was in Donetsk *oblast* (31.6%). In cities, where there was a second round of mayoral elections on 15 November 2015, turnout was 34.1%. In an interview with this author on 20 September 2020, Yevhenii Radchenko, deputy head of the Central Electoral Commission (2018–2019), stated that turnout did not differ much in the 159 ATCs. Also, the majority of the 1.4 million internally displaced persons, who had to leave the non-government-controlled territories of Donbas or Crimea, did not manage to vote, because it proved too difficult for them to obtain permanent residency elsewhere in Ukraine (most often they were only temporarily registered).

Self-nominated independents scored best in both ATCs and the rest of the localities (see Tables 30.3–30.6). The electoral outcomes in 159 ATCs demonstrate slightly lower numbers of independents among the elected councilors and mayors (64.7% and 72.8%, respectively) in comparison with their electoral results in nonamalgamated communities (66.9% and 80.9%, respectively). In both types of localities, the party in office Petro Poroshenko Bloc 'Solidarity'

Table 30.3 Results of the 2015 Ukrainian local elections in nonamalgamated communities

Party nomination/self-nominated independents	Number of elected councilors	% of elected councilors
Self-nominated independents	72,939	66.95
Petro Poroshenko Bloc 'Solidarnist' (*Bloc Petra Poroshenko 'Solidarnist'*)	7,451	6.84
Fatherland (*Batkivshchyna*)	6,489	5.96
Opposition Bloc (*Opozytsiinyi Bloc*)	3,397	3.12
Our Land (*Nash Krai*)	2,809	2.58
Agrarian Party (*Ahrarna Partiya*)	2,477	2.27
Radical Party of Oleh Lyashko (*Radykalna Partiya Oleha Lyashka*)	2,121	1.95
Ukrainian Association of Patriots 'UKROP' (*Ukrainske Obyednannia Patriotiv 'UKROP'*)	1,886	1.73
Renaissance (*Vidrodzhennia*)	1,447	1.33
'Freedom' (*'Svoboda'*)	1,441	1.32
Self-Reliance (*Samopomich*)	852	0.78

Source: Official website of the Central Electoral Commission: www.cvk.gov.ua/pls/vm2015/pvm002pt001f01=100pt00_t001f01=100.html (accessed on 16 December 2020).

Note: The list in this table includes the ten parties with the highest vote shares.

Table 30.4 Results of the 2015 Ukrainian mayoral elections in nonamalgamated communities

Party nomination/self-nominated independents	Number of elected mayors	% of elected mayors
Self-nominated independents	5,176	80.94
Petro Poroshenko Bloc 'Solidarnist' (*Bloc Petra Poroshenko 'Solidarnist'*)	372	5.82
Fatherland (*Batkivshchyna*)	258	4.03
Agrarian Party (*Ahrarna Partiya*)	106	1.66
Our Land (*Nash Krai*)	82	1.28
Opposition Bloc (*Opozytsiinyi Bloc*)	45	0.70
'Freedom' (*'Svoboda'*)	41	0.64
Renaissance (*Vidrodzhennia*)	40	0.63
Ukrainian Association of Patriots 'UKROP' (*Ukrainske Obyednannia Patriotiv 'UKROP'*)	28	0.44
Radical Party of Oleh Lyashko (*Radykalna Partiya Oleha Lyashka*)	26	0.41
'Volition' (*'Volya'*)	22	0.34

Source: Official website of the Central Electoral Commission: www.cvk.gov.ua/pls/vm2015/pvm003pt001f01=100pt00_t001f01=100.html (accessed on 16 December 2020)

Note: The list in this table includes the ten parties with the highest vote shares.

Table 30.5 Results of the 2015 local elections in 159 ATCs in Ukraine

Party nomination/self-nominated independents	Number of elected councilors	% of elected councilors
Self-nominated independents	2,222	64.65
Petro Poroshenko Bloc 'Solidarnist' (*Bloc Petra Poroshenko 'Solidarnist'*)	278	8.09
Fatherland (*Batkivshchyna*)	166	4.83
Agrarian Party (*Ahrarna Partiya*)	137	3.99
'For Concrete Actions' ('*Za Konkretni Spravy*')	85	2.47
Opposition Bloc (*Opozytsiinyi Bloc*)	74	2.15
Our Land (*Nash Krai*)	71	2.07
'Freedom' ('*Svoboda*')	69	2.01
Radical Party of Oleh Lyashko (*Radykalna Partiya Oleha Lyashka*)	65	1.89
'Civil Position' ('*Hromadianska Pozytsiya*')	48	1.40
Ukrainian Association of Patriots 'UKROP' (*Ukrainske Obyednannia Patriotiv 'UKROP'*)	41	1.19

Note: The list in this table includes the ten parties with the highest vote shares.
Source: Official website of the Central Electoral Commission: www.cvk.gov.ua/pls/vm2015/pvm002pt001f01 = 101pt00_t001f01 = 100.html (accessed on 16 December 2020)

Table 30.6 Results of the 2015 mayoral elections in 159 ATCs in Ukraine

Party nomination/self-nominated independents	Number of elected mayors	% of elected mayors
Self-nominated independents	115	72.78
Petro Poroshenko Bloc 'Solidarnist' (*Bloc Petra Poroshenko 'Solidarnist'*)	17	10.76
Agrarian Party (*Ahrarna Partiya*)	4	2.53
Fatherland (*Batkivshchyna*)	4	2.53
Our Land (*Nash Krai*)	4	2.53
Opposition Bloc (*Opozytsiinyi Bloc*)	4	2.53
'For Concrete Actions' ('*Za Konkretni Spravy*')	3	1.90
'Volition' ('*Volya*')	2	1.27
'Freedom' ('*Svoboda*')	2	1.27
'Civil Position' ('*Hromadianska Pozytsiya*')	1	0.63
The People's Movement of Ukraine ('*Narodnyi Rukh Ukrainy*')	1	0.63

Note: The list in this table includes the ten parties with the highest vote shares.
Source: Official website of the Central Electoral Commission: www.cvk.gov.ua/pls/vm2015/pvm003pt001f01 = 101pt00_t001f01 = 100.html (accessed on 16 December 2020).

Table 30.7 Official results of the 2020 local elections in Ukraine

Party nomination/self-nominated independents	Number of elected councillors	% of elected councillors
Self-nominated independents	6,547	15.41
'Servant of the People' ('*Sluha Narodu*')	6,411	15.09
Fatherland (*Batkivshchyna*)	4,478	10.54
'The Opposition Platform For Life' ('*Opozytsiina Platforma "Za Zhyttya"*')	4,218	9.93
'For the Future' ('*Za Maibutnye*')	4,078	9.60
'European Solidarity' ('*Yevropeiska Solidarnist*')	3,910	9.20
Our Land (*Nash Krai*)	1,892	4.45
'Freedom' ('*Svoboda*')	890	2.09
'The Ukrainian Strategy of Hroysman' ('*Ukrainska Stratehiya Hroysmana*')	679	1.60
Radical Party of Oleh Lyashko (*Radykalna Partiya Oleha Lyashka*)	584	1.37
'Proposition' ('*Propozytsiya*')	574	1.35

Note: The list in this table includes the ten parties with the highest vote shares.
Source: Official website of the Central Electoral Commission: www.cvk.gov.ua/pls/vm2020/pvm002pt001f01 = 695pt00_t001f01 = 695.html (accessed on 17 November 2021).

(PPB, *Bloc Petra Poroshenko 'Solidarnist'*) demonstrated the highest electoral results among political parties. It gained 8.1% of seats on local councils in ATCs and 6.8% of seats on other local councils. A total of 10.8% of the mayors elected in ATCs and 5.8% of mayors elected elsewhere were nominated by the PPB. Another parliamentary party, which was the PPB's partner in the parliamentary coalition – Fatherland (*Batkivshchyna*) – was the second most successful. It won 4.8% of seats on ATCs' local councils and 6% of seats on local councils in other localities. It also managed to secure 4% of mayoral positions in those localities that stayed away from local amalgamation. However, in the mayoral elections in ATCs, Fatherland achieved the same electoral result as the Agrarian Party (*Ahrarna Partiya*) and Our Land (*Nash Krai*) (nonparliamentary parties) and the Opposition Bloc (*Opozytsiinyi Bloc*) (the parliamentary party in opposition): 2.5%.

The outcomes of the 2015 local elections resembled, but did not replicate, those of the 2014 parliamentary elections.[4] Parties from the parliamentary coalition continued to gain most of their electoral support in the west and the center; the Opposition Bloc won mainly in the south and the east. However, the differences between the electoral outcomes of the two electoral contests were striking. Most parliamentary parties did not manage to contest local elections throughout Ukraine. Only the PPB and Fatherland nominated candidates to all city councils. The People's Front (*Narodnyi Front*) decided not to contest the 2015 local elections due to its weak party institutionalization on the local scale. The Opposition Bloc lost a considerable share of its electoral support because (1) no local elections were held in its electoral strongholds in Donbas and Crimea and (2) a number of incumbent mayors, who ended up winning mayoral elections in the east and the south, decided to decline their previous affiliation with the Opposition Bloc and to contest the elections as representatives of nonparliamentary parties [like Renaissance

(*Vidrodzhennia*) in the city of Kharkiv in the east of Ukraine and Trust in Actions (*Doviryai Dilam*) in the city of Odesa in the south of the country]. There were numerous cases in which nonparliamentary parties successfully contested local elections in only one or several localities, that is, the Vinnytsya European Strategy (*Vinnytska Yevropeiska Stratehiya*), associated with then prime minister Volodymyr Hroysman, gained the majority of votes on the Vinnytsya City Council (20 out of 54 seats); Trust in Actions, led by the mayor of the city of Odesa, obtained the majority of votes on the Odesa City Council (27 out of 64 mandates); and the Ukrainian Association of Patriots 'UKROP' (*Ukrainske Obyednannia Patriotiv 'UKROP'*) gained 21 out of 64 seats on Dnipro City Council – the second largest electoral score after the Opposition Bloc.

As a result of the 2015 local elections, fewer females than males won seats on local councils in cities or towns (29% or 2,394 women), villages (56% or 42,830 women), and settlements (46% or 2,965 women). A total of 2,256 women (29.3%) won mayoral positions. Although the number of women on local councils in Ukraine looks modest, it is higher than the number elected to parliament in 2014 (11.8% or 53 women among 450 MPs). The majority of newly elected councilors in cities and towns had completed higher education, while only 38% of councilors in villages and settlements graduated from university. Approximately 70% of local councilors had a permanent job when they stood for the 2015 elections, 7–9% of local councilors were pensioners, and the rest claimed to be officially unemployed while campaigning. The overwhelming majority of mayors and councilors who were elected in the 2015 local elections were ethnic Ukrainians. There were some rare exceptions, like ethnic Hungarians in Transcarpathia, where the Party of the Hungarians in Ukraine and the Democratic Party of Hungarians in Ukraine secured three and one mayoral seat, respectively.

Thus, the case of the 2015 local elections demonstrates that nonsimultaneity does not help to increase turnout. There was more at stake in local elections in ATCs than elsewhere, and there was a slightly higher level of party politicization there. The electoral outcomes of the 2015 local elections partially resembled the electoral results of the 2014 parliamentary electoral contests. There was an impressive share of self-nominated independents among the elected councilors and mayors. Two parliamentary parties – the PPB and Fatherland – successfully contested local elections throughout the country, and their major competitor was not only their parliamentary opponent (the Opposition Bloc) but mainly nonparliamentary parties, especially in ATCs.

The 2020 local elections held exclusively in ATCs

There was more at stake in the local elections held on 25 October 2020 compared with the previous local electoral contests, because they were held exclusively in ATCs. Prior to the 2020 local elections, no nonamalgamated territorial communities were left in Ukraine. Also, the 2020 local elections were important because the presidential and parliamentary elections[5] held in 2019 shifted the political landscape at the statewide level but did not change the balance of power on local councils. In 2019, Volodymyr Zelenskiy became president of Ukraine, and his brand-new party, 'Servant of the People' (*'Sluha Narodu'*), established a one-party majority in the parliament. Most parliamentary parties, with the exception of Fatherland, were newly established.[6]

In advance of the 2020 local elections, the parliament introduced new electoral rules that provided institutional stimuli for parties to actively contest local contests. The Electoral Code, approved on 19 December 2019, introduced OLPR with a 5% threshold for electing local councils in rural and urban localities with more than 10,000 voters,[7] as well as the single nontransferable vote for local elections in rural and urban localities with fewer than

Table 30.8 Official results of the 2020 mayoral elections in Ukraine

Party nomination/self-nominated independents	Number of elected mayors	% of elected mayors
Self-nominated independents	662	47.38
'Servant of the People' (*'Sluha Narodu'*)	225	16.35
'For the Future' (*'Za Maibutnye'*)	92	6.69
Fatherland (*Batkivshchyna*)	52	3.78
'The Opposition Platform For Life' (*'Opozytsiina Platforma "Za Zhyttya"'*)	52	3.78
Our Land (*Nash Krai*)	44	3.20
'European Solidarity' (*'Yevropeiska Solidarnist'*)	41	2.98
'The Ukrainian Strategy of Hroysman' (*'Ukrainska Stratehiya Hroysmana'*)	27	1.96
'Trust' (*'Dovira'*)	23	1.67
'Native Home' (*'Ridnyi Dim'*)	19	1.38
'Freedom' (*'Svoboda'*)	18	1.31

Note: The list in this table includes the ten parties with the highest vote shares.
Source: Official website of the Central Electoral Commission: www.cvk.gov.ua/pls/vm2020/pvm003pt001f01=695pt00_t001f01=695.html (accessed on 17 November 2021).

10,000 voters.[8] In localities with fewer than 75,000 voters, mayors are elected according to FPTP, while in urban localities with over 75,000 voters, mayors are elected under the TRS.

Turnout for the local electoral contests held on 25 October 2020 was only 36.9%. It was nearly 10% lower than in 2015 (46.6%) and proved to be the lowest level of participation in local elections since Ukraine's independence. However, the extent of party politicization greatly increased compared to the 2015 local elections: 194 parties contested the 2020 electoral contests. Moreover, only 15.4% of the elected councilors and 47.4% of the elected mayors were self-nominated independents. The preliminary electoral outcomes demonstrate that the party in office ('Servant of the People') gains the highest number of seats on local councils (15%) and the greatest number of elected mayors (16.4%) among political parties (see Tables 30.7 and 30.8 for more details). However, it does not win any mayoral positions in those cities that represent the administrative centers of *oblasts*. The parliamentary parties win approximately half of the seats on the newly elected local councils.

The newly elected bodies of local self-government are expected to take better care of public service provision and local development. The central government claims that it might amend the geographical boundaries of those ATCs in which local councils and mayors demonstrate poor results. The author of this chapter doubts this would happen, but believes that voters would assess the performance of local governance when they cast their votes in the next local elections.

Notes

1 I am grateful to Yevhenii Radchenko, deputy head of the Central Electoral Commission (2018–2019), for discussion of the interplay between local elections, the amalgamation reform, and parties' electoral strategies in the 2015 local elections. Also, I am thankful to Andriy Gorbal and Serhij Vasylchenko

from the Ukrainian Centre for Social Data (https://socialdata.org.ua/en/) for their timely consultation regarding Ukraine's electoral data.
2 According to a domestic study based on the analysis of primary sources (Agency for Legal Initiatives 2016: 8), in 1991–2012 there were 122 cases in which the majority of voters who cast their votes on legal local referenda approved the suggested initiatives and the respective referenda's decisions were implemented. The same study indicates that five local referenda tried to violate the constitution.
3 See the 1994 Law 'On elections of deputies and heads of councils in settlements, villages, districts, towns, districts in towns, regions' https://zakon.rada.gov.ua/laws/show/3996-12?lang=en; the 1998 Law 'On elections of deputies of local councils and heads of settlements, villages, towns' https://zakon.rada.gov.ua/laws/show/14/98-%D0%B2%D1%80?lang=uk; the 2004 Law 'On elections of deputies of Verkhovna Rada of the Autonomous Republic of Crimea, local councils, and heads of settlements, villages, towns' https://zakon.rada.gov.ua/laws/show/1667-15; the 2010 Law 'On elections of deputies of Verkhovna Rada of the Autonomous Republic of Crimea, local councils, and heads of settlements, villages, towns' https://zakon.rada.gov.ua/laws/show/2487-17; the 2015 Law 'On local elections' https://zakon.rada.gov.ua/laws/show/595-19; and the Electoral Code of Ukraine: https://zakon.rada.gov.ua/laws/show/396-20#Text.
4 The early parliamentary elections, held on 26 October 2014, followed the parallel system with a 50/50 split, when 50% of MPs were elected according to FPTP, while the other 50% were elected according to CLPR with a 5% threshold. The electoral results according to CLPR were as follows: the People's Front (*Narodnyi Front*), chaired by the prime minister, 22.14%; the Petro Poroshenko Bloc 'Solidarnist' (*Bloc Petra Poroshenko 'Solidarnist'*), established by the president, 21.82%; Self-Reliance (*Samopomich*), 10.97%; the Opposition Bloc (*Opozytsiinyi Bloc*), 9.43%; the Radical Party of Oleh Lyashko (*Radykalna Partiya Oleha Lyashka*), 7.44%; and Fatherland (*Batkivshchyna*), 5.68%. The parliamentary coalition consisted of five parties, while the Opposition Bloc opposed it.
5 The early parliamentary elections, held on 21 July 2019, followed the same electoral rules as the 2014 parliamentary contests. In 2019, the electoral results according to CLPR were as follows: 'Servant of the People' ('*Sluha Narodu*'), 43.16%; 'The Opposition Platform For Life' ('*Opozytsiina Platforma "Za Zhyttya"* '), 13.05%; Fatherland, 8.18%; 'European Solidarity' ('*Yevropeiska Solidarnist*'), 8.10%; and 'Voice' ('*Holos*'), 5.82%.

In the newly elected parliament, there were five fractions ('Servant of the People', 248 MPs; 'The Opposition Platform For Life', 44 MPs; Fatherland, 24 MPs; 'European Solidarity', 27 MPs; 'Voice', 19 MPs) and two deputy groups ('For the Future', 24 MPs; 'Trust', 20 MPs).
6 'Servant of the People' and 'Voice' were newly established parties in the 2019 parliamentary elections. The Petro Poroshenko Bloc 'Solidarity' changed its name to 'European Solidarity' ('*Yevropeiska Solidarnist*'). 'The Opposition Platform For Life' ('Opozytsiina Platforma "Za Zhyttya"') was established on the basis of the Opposition Bloc in 2018.
7 The territory of multiple-mandate electoral districts is identical to the territory of the local unit or locality where the respective local council is elected. In an electoral bulletin, voters see the lists of parties, with lists of 5–12 party candidates in each party list (Article 219.5). A voter can tick the box once; by doing so, s/he votes for the preferred party. Also, a voter is able, but not obliged, to put down the number associated with the preferred candidate on the respective party list on the electoral bulletin. Voters' preferences can affect the arrangement of candidates on the party lists only if the latter receive electoral support greater than 25% of the electoral quota. The electoral quota is calculated in the following way: the total number of votes cast in the election is divided by the total number of seats on the local council. In order to calculate the number of territorial districts, one should divide the number of councilors by ten.
8 Each voter is expected to cast one vote for the preferred candidate in a multiple-mandate electoral district. The number of territorial districts is calculated by dividing the number of local councilors by three. In each district, no fewer than two and no more than four seats may be filled. In order to identify the exact number of mandates in multiple-mandate electoral districts, the respective territorial electoral commission divides the number of registered voters by the number of councilors on the respective local council.

References

Agency for Legal Initiatives (2016). *Local Referenda in Ukraine as a Component of Local Democracy (Shadow Report)*. Kyiv. https://parlament.org.ua/2016/10/06/dosvid-zastosuvannya-mistsevogo-referendumu-v-ukrayini-yak-skladovoyi-mistsevoyi-demokratiyi-shadow-report/ (accessed on 16 December 2020).

Congress of Local and Regional Authorities (2013). *Local and Regional Democracy in Ukraine*. Monitoring Committee, 25th Session. Strasbourg, 29–31 October. https://rm.coe.int/local-and-regional-democracy-in-ukraine-recommendation-mr-marc-cools-b/168071a834 (accessed on 16 December 2020).

Congress of Local and Regional Authorities (2016). *Observation of Local Elections in Ukraine (25 October 2015)*. Monitoring Committee, 30th Session. Strasbourg, 22–24 March. https://rm.coe.int/1680719c74 (accessed on 16 December 2020).

Heinelt, H. & Hlepas, N.-K. (2006). Typologies of Local Government Systems. In: H. Bäck, H. Heinelt & A. Magnier (Eds.), *The European Mayor. VS Verlag für Sozialwissenschaften* (pp. 21–42). Wiesbaden: VS Verlag für Sozialwissenschaften.

IFES (2015). *Report on Local Elections in Ukraine 2015*. Kyiv, 9 December. https://rm.coe.int/168062e26e (accessed on 16 December 2020).

Ladner, A., Keuffer, N. & Baldersheim, H. (2015). *Self-rule Index for Local Authorities* (Final Report). Brussels: The European Commission. http://local-autonomy.andreasladner.ch/Documents/LAI_FINAL%20REPORT.pdf (accessed on 16 November 2021).

Ladner, A., Keuffer, N. & Baldersheim, H. (2016). Measuring Local Autonomy in 39 Countries (1990–2014). *Regional & Federal Studies*, 26(3), 321–357.

Levitas, T. & Djikic, J. (2017). *Caught Mid-Stream: 'Decentralization', Local Government Finance Reform, and the Restructuring of Ukraine's Public Sector 2014 to 2016*. Kyiv: SIDA-SKL. http://sklinternational.org.ua/wp-content/uploads/2017/10/UkraineCaughtMidStream-ENG-FINAL-06.10.2017.pdf (accessed on 16 November 2021).

OPORA (2015). *Local Elections: Preliminary Observation Summary From OPORA*, 26 October. https://www.oporaua.org/report/vybory/mistsevi-vybory/mistsevi-vybory-2015/9865-miscevi-vybory-promizhni-pidsumky-sposterezhennja-opory (accessed on 16 November 2021).

Swianiewicz, P. (2014). An Empirical Typology of Local Government Systems in Eastern Europe. *Local Government Studies*, 40(2), 292–311.

Part 7
New democracies
The Southeastern European States

31
Albania
The path to decentralized democratic governance

Naz Feka, Iain Frank Wilson, and Alba Dakoli Wilson

Transition toward a more decentralized system

Albania's system of local government has undergone several rapid structural changes since the fall of Communism. Prior to 1991, the concept of local governance was absent from the extremely centralized and authoritarian state, with every aspect of the lives of citizens subject to decision making at the central level. Local authorities were present but were organs of central government. With the fall of Communism, a transition began toward the introduction of democratic governance. Albania adopted a set of reforms that, among others, started the process of decentralization, introducing a subnational first-tier level of government in the form of 44 urban municipalities (*bashki*) and 313 rural communes (*komune*), as well as 36 second-tier districts. This reform was followed by a law in 1992 that established 12 prefectures (each comprising 2–4 districts), with the prefects answerable to the Council of Ministers (CoM). In its early phase of transition, the country was concerned mainly with reform of the political system at the central level, with the process of decentralization mainly concerned with the form of administration and not with finance and policies. However, following the adoption of its first democratic constitution in 1998, the country adopted a new law in 2000 entitled 'On Organisation and Functioning of Local Government in Albania'. This new law removed the districts and rearranged the two layers of local government: the first comprising 65 municipalities and 309 communes, and the second comprising 12 counties (*qark*).

Even though at the beginning of the new millennium local government decentralization in Albania was based upon the principle of symmetric decentralization, in practice it was widely seen as asymmetric due to deep inequalities between the communes and municipalities (Kapidani 2015: 30). In 2015, the local government system changed again. The communes (now 308 following an earlier merger of two communes) and 65 municipalities were consolidated into 61 municipalities, with the consequent redrawing of the administrative boundaries, while a new law defined the competences and functions of local government units (LGUs). Since then, local government in Albania has comprised two layers: 61 municipalities distributed among 12 counties.

The Territorial-Administration Reform (TAR) of 2015 was conceived in such a way as to create a more balanced distribution of local authorities. While the former administrative boundaries of the LGUs set a clear distinction between urban areas and rural areas, almost all of the 61 municipalities that were created comprise a mix of these two types of area. The average population size of the 61 municipalities is 47,000 inhabitants, ranging from just over 3,000 in Pustec to 550,000 in Tirana,[1] and from 3,600 in Libohovë (the second smallest municipality) to 175,000 in Durres (the second largest).[2] Meanwhile, Tirana County, a second-tier government comprising five municipalities, is home to 31% of the total population of Albania. In contrast, Gjirokaster County, which comprises seven municipalities, is home to just 2% of the population of the country.

The country's overall score on the comparative Local Autonomy Index (Ladner et al. (2019), with primary data research on Albania undertaken by the Foundation for Local Autonomy and Governance) ranks around the center, with, for example, the indices political discretion at 53.1 and financial autonomy at 46.9 (on a scale from 0 to 100). Since 1992, the overall direction of change in the subnational institutional structures has been progressive, with the focus of development (reforms) upon further decentralization.

In the municipalities, the municipal council is the representative body, while the mayor is the executive body. In the counties, the representative body is the regional council, and the executive functions are performed by the head and the board of that council. The representative and executive municipal bodies are elected as provided for in the Electoral Code of the Republic of Albania, while the representative body of the county comprises representatives of the elected bodies of the constituent municipalities, as provided for in the Constitution and in Chapter XIII of Law 139/2015 'On Local Self-Governance'. The regional council's head and board are elected by the regional council. The bodies of the LGUs exercise their powers by issuing decisions, ordinances, and orders.

The municipal council is the local decision-making body and approves all decisions on behalf of the municipality. Mayors exercise their powers in performing their municipal functions, except those that are the sole competence of the council. The mayor implements municipal council acts, makes arrangements for council meetings, and reports to the council on the economic and financial situation of the municipality, including its administrative units, at least every six months (or when requested by the council) and on issues related to municipal functions. The mayor also holds membership on the regional council and appoints and dismisses vice mayors, administrative unit administrators, members of the cabinet and of bodies governing municipal-owned companies, directors of enterprises and institutions, and staff not subject to the Law on Civil Servants. The mayor ensures the rights and fulfillment of all obligations of the municipality, represents it, ensures the qualification and training of personnel of the administration and educational, social, cultural, and sports institutions, exercises (only once) the right to return decisions found to violate the interests of the community to the council for reconsideration, approves the organizational structure, the salaries of each civil service position, and the basic statutes of the municipal administration, municipal budgetary units, and its institutions, and ensures the gathering, processing, and publication of local statistics classified by gender.

In terms of power relations within the municipal leadership, the mayor and the council are strongly interdependent and rely heavily on each other. The council is the deliberative body and includes councilors directly elected for a four-year term under a proportional system (within the municipal administrative-geographical area). The mayor is elected directly under a majoritarian first past the post (FPTP) system and does not fall under the authority or the competence of the municipal council [only the Council of Ministers (CoM) can remove the mayor].[3] Thus, Albania has a strong mayoral system, especially as a mayor can appeal a decision to fire him/her, while a CoM decision must be validated by the Constitutional Court, which normally bases such a decision on a court order issued against the mayor.

Local elections in a multilevel democracy

Since 1992, eight rounds of local elections have been held in Albania. The Central Election Commission (CEC) is responsible for organizing the country's local and national elections. The Albanian constitution stipulates that local elections, in which citizens vote for municipal councilors as well as the mayor, be held every four years. For the second tier of local government – the county – the structures and institutions function through elected municipal officials who, in turn, nominate the county council members. Members of Parliament (MPs) are also elected for a four-year term, though usually offset from the local elections by two years.

In the event of an abrupt interruption to the mayoral mandate, partial elections are held to elect a new mayor, who will complete the four-year term. In Albania, since the establishment of the local government system in 1992, mayors and municipal councilors are all elected by a direct vote. Because of the political culture in Albania, the mayors are almost always candidates put forward and sponsored by a party. They tend to be relatively powerful figures who have the backing of the party headquarters and often its leader, a feature that has developed to such an extent over the last decade that it is now commonplace for a mayoral candidate, unless he or she is independent, to have to win the backing or endorsement of the party leader to be able to stand in the local elections (Krasniqi 2017: 93–94). Meanwhile, there is an influence of central politics upon local government councils, such as Tirana Municipal Council, whose members include several high-ranking central government officials.

The law does not allow for local recall referenda. According to the Law on Local Self-Governance, the municipal council and the mayor are both subject to a central government decision (through the CoM) for their dismissal. The municipal council cannot take a vote of no confidence but can only propose the dismissal of the mayor to the CoM, and in only one situation: 'failure to appear in office for an uninterrupted three-month period' (Article 62 of Law 139/2015 'On Local Self-Governance'). Meanwhile, there have been a few cases where the CoM has dismissed elected mayors, in one case on the grounds of 'gross misconduct' (where the mayor resigned following accusations of indecent behavior) and in others (three recent cases) where they supported a court decision that found the mayor had broken the law.

Local electoral system

Article 45 of the Albanian Constitution and Article 44 of the Electoral Code stipulate that every Albanian citizen who has reached 18 years of age on the date of the election is eligible to vote, though voting is not compulsory. The eligibility rules are the same for both national and local elections. The Electoral Code specifies in Article 46 that voter lists are compiled from the Civil

Table 31.1 Number of municipal councilors according to population size in Albania

Population	No. of councilors
< 20,001	15
20,001–50,000	21
50,001–100,000	31
100,001–200,000	41
200,001–400,000	51
> 400,000	61

Register and contain the names of all of the voters who have a residence in the polling unit of the LGU. Noncitizens are not eligible to vote in local elections, irrespective of their length of residency. The voters can only vote in person; there are no provisions for voting abroad, by mail, by mobile ballot box,[4] or by proxy. Albanians residing abroad have the right to vote but must return to the country to do so. Special voting centers can be organized in hospitals, prisons, and pretrial detention centers for voters who are residents of the respective municipality.

The size of the municipal council varies both within and among municipalities according to their population size on 1 January of the election year. According to the Albanian law, there are six categories of municipalities, and these determine the number of councilors (see Table 31.1).

In the most recent local elections (30 June 2019), the total number of council seats allocated among all 61 municipalities was 1,619 (706 were won by women, or 44%). Along with the 61 mayors (8 women, or 13%), the total number of directly elected councilors and mayors was 1,680.[5]

Albania's local electoral system is uniform across municipalities in that the same rules apply for all 61 municipalities, irrespective of differences in population, territory size, or any other parameter. Likewise, the electoral system is uniform among all 12 counties.

Prior to the 2009 elections, Albania had been using the mixed member proportional (MMP) system for parliamentary elections (Reynolds et al. 2005). Since 2009, however, the country has utilized the regional PR system (with the 12 counties, or regions, serving as electoral districts) in parliamentary elections. The election formula at the local level comprises a closed-list PR system for local municipal councilors and a majority (FPTP) system for mayors. In the local elections, a municipality (as an administrative-geographical territory) serves as a single electoral district for electing the mayor, while the municipality serves as a multiple-member electoral district for electing city councilors.

Table 31.2 Voter turnout for local and national elections in Albania since 1992 and 1991, respectively

Local elections		Parliamentary (national) elections	
Year	Turnout (%)	Year	Turnout (%)
–	–	1991	98.9
1992	70.7	1992	91.5
1996	58.5	1996	89.1
2000	50.7	1997	72.6
2003	45.7	2001	55.0
2007	46.3	2005	48.7
2011	49.1	2009	50.8
2015	47.8	2013	53.3
2019	23.0	2017	46.8

Source: www.cec.org.al; www.idea.int/data-tools/country-view/47/40. The CEC does not hold data prior to the 2000 elections; only those for more recent elections are available on the CEC website, and data are incomplete until the 2015 and 2019 elections. Some data on the local elections can be found on the following websites: www.idea.int/data-tools/country-view/47/40, www.electionguide.org/countries/id/3/, http://illyriapress.com/historik-i-zgjedhjeve-vendore-ne-shqiperi-pas-vitit-1990/. www.electionguide.org/countries/id/3/; *Historik i zgjedhjeve vendore në Shqipëri pas vitit 1990*: http://illyriapress.com/historik-i-zgjedhjeve-vendore-ne-shqiperi-pas-vitit-1990/ (1992 elections). For data on participation in the local elections of 1996, 2000, 2003, and 2007, see The Institute of Political Studies (2018): https://isp.com.al/index.php/2019/07/08/pjesemarrja-ne-zgjedhje-1992-2019-kontraste-dhe-faktore-ndikues/.

The methodology and the formula applied for the allocation of seats are the same for both local and national elections. Seats are distributed to winning coalitions and parties by using d'Hondt's formula, and within winning coalitions by using the Saint-Laguë formula (Dyrmishi 2010). Lists are closed, with candidates elected in sequence from the party list.

Albania applies a closed-list variant of the PR system for electing municipal councilors, with voters expressing their preference only for a party or a coalition. In contrast, when the mayor is elected, voters express their preference from an open list of candidates. *Apparentement*, cumulative voting, *panachage*, and ordering are not applicable in Albania. Since 2015, the law has required that women make up 50% of candidates on the lists for municipal council. If the list put forward by a party does not fulfill this criterion, the CEC rejects the list outright.

Any eligible voter who is a resident of a municipality and a holder of Albanian citizenship can stand in an election. Political parties, coalitions, and groups of voters must first register their candidates with the CEC as electoral subjects by submitting supporting signatures numbering no fewer than 1% of voters from the respective municipality, unless they have represented a constituency in parliament or been in municipal government for at least six months. The entry rules are relatively flexible, though the matter is shrouded in so much ambiguity that the process of registration is seen as an area needing improvement (OSCE–ODIHR Election Observation Mission Final Report, 30 June 2019). Meanwhile, the process of registration for independent candidates contains further provisions (Chamber of Local Authorities and Council of Europe Final Report, 21 June 2015).[6]

The Albanian legislation has legal restrictions in place that prohibit *cumul des mandats* (dual mandates). For example, mayors are restricted from running as MPs, and the latter are restricted from running for any other official position. The same applies to certain categories for which the constitution prohibits the right to stand.[7] Furthermore, the 2015 Law on Decriminalisation restricts those who have contravened the law from holding office.[8]

Table 31.3 Number of inhabitants in municipalities (2011 census) and voter turnout (percent) in large and small municipalities for the elections of 2011 and 2015 in Albania in decreasing order of voter turnout in 2011

Large municipalities	Population size (2011 census)	Turnout 2011	Turnout 2015	Small municipalities	Population size (2011 census)	Turnout 2011	Turnout 2015
Tirana	557,422	47[1]	50	**Prrenjas**	24,906	65	57
Elbasan	141,714	47	47	**Devoll (Bilisht)**	26,716	63	58
Korçë	75,994	45	42	**Kruja**	59,814	62	59
Durrës	175,110	42	43	**Skrapar (Çorovodë)**	12,403	61	56
Vlorë	104,827	41	35	**Ura Vajgurore**	27,295	53	54
Shkodër	135,612	39	45	**Kuçove**	31,262	40	45

Source: INSTAT; www.instat.gov.al; Albanian Association of Municipalities, Interactive Map of the Republic of Albania, https://aam.org.al/harta/; Dossier of Albanian Municipalities, https://portavendore.al. Voter turnout figures for all municipalities, excluding Tirana, were obtained from CEC www.cec.org.al.
[1] No data are available for Tirana in 2011 on the CEC website; see instead http://top-channel.tv/2011/05/08/votimet-kqz-pjesemarrja-ne-rang-vendi-50–9-perqind/.

Electoral outcomes

Table 31.2 reports voter turnout for local and national elections, with the highest levels of participation in the first elections (local, 1992; national, 1991), with a decreasing overall trend ever since. The turnout for the local elections since the new millennium ranges from 46% to 51%, with recent participation of 23%,[9] and less than 50% for the national elections, a worrying sign for Albania's relatively young democracy. The electoral concerns and other factors related to the level of citizen confidence in the political parties, the issue of mass emigration, and difficulties deriving from nontransparent mechanisms have had a direct impact by gradually decreasing voter participation on election day (Krasniqi 2012).

The local elections of 2019 are not included for comparative analysis as they were boycotted in all municipalities by the opposition parties following accusations that the government had failed to ensure that free and fair elections would be held. The opposition parties walked out of parliament four months before the local elections were due to be held and refused to participate in the poll. The opposition parties that did not endorse the boycott had little political influence and no representation in parliament, though some had seats on local councils across the country.

Table 31.3 reports the voter turnout[10] for the large and small municipalities (urban centers) in the elections of 2011 and 2015.

In general, local elections in Albania are competitive, though in a rather volatile and polarized political climate, they are heavily influenced by the central political actors. Nevertheless, apart from the June 2019 local elections, there have been no cases of uncontested seats. The opposition vowed to take the case of the recently boycotted local elections to court, but a quorum has not been reached in the Constitutional Court since 2017, and the opposition's room for maneuver is limited (the Court regained functionality December 2020). Meanwhile, as a result of the boycott of those elections, in which only 23% of the electorate voted, 60 of the 61 municipalities are governed by a mayor representing the ruling (nationally) Socialist Party (SP, *Partia Socialiste*).

In most mayoral elections there are two or three candidates, with the SP and Democratic Party (DP, *Partia Demokratike*) always, until June 2019, putting forward a candidate in all municipalities. The Socialist Movement for Integration (SMI, the third largest party) would often provide the third such candidate in many municipalities, with very few municipalities having a candidate from another party, coalition, or independent. Nevertheless, in the 2015 elections, there were 158 candidates for the position of mayor in the 61 municipalities. They were nominated by 12 subjects (party, coalition, or independent). Nearly all (60) of the municipalities were won by one of the two main parties. Meanwhile, in the same elections, 61 subjects nominated candidates for 1,595 councilor positions across all 61 municipalities.

The history of the political party system in Albania begins in 1920 and goes through various developments, including the takeover of the country by the Communists in 1944. The one-party system that was installed shortly afterward stayed in place for more than 45 years before it was succeeded by the introduction of a pluralist democracy in 1991. A new Albanian constitution was ratified in November 1998, establishing a democratic system of government based upon the rule of law and guaranteeing the protection of fundamental human rights. In Albania, ethnic and religious issues, though present, do not dominate the multiparty system. National parties are spread across the country and compete for votes in every electoral zone.

A large number of political parties were formed in 1991. However, despite the diversity, the electoral thresholds (3% for parties and 5% for coalitions) created a multiparty system that has been dominated by two parties – the center-right DP and center-left SP – whose influence has brought about every major reform of the country's political system. The system favors coalitions headed by either of these parties (Berhani 2012). Nevertheless, a number of parties that have

Table 31.4 Votes won by the various party groups in the municipal council and mayoral elections in Albania of 2011 and 2015

	2011		2015	
	Municipal council (%)	Mayor (no.)	Municipal council (%)	Mayor (no.)
SP-headed coalition	42.75	145	63.48	45
DP-headed coalition	51.77	218	32.47	15
Parties outside of a coalition	4.82	0	3.58	1
Independent	0.66	10	0.47	0
Total	100.00	373	100.00	61
SP share	27.55		25.78	
DP share	21.06		20.33	
SMI share	7.49		16.64	

Source: CEC

no seats in Parliament have won seats on local councils. The position of the two main parties was further cemented in 2008 with changes made to the electoral system for national elections. Despite favoring a regional PR system, these changes, in the view of the smaller parties, strengthened the positions of the DP and SP (Dyrmishi 2010; Krasniqi 2012).

In the 2017 national elections, SMI earned more than 14% of the vote, although, along with the DP, it boycotted the 2019 local elections. The party system in Albania approximates to two plus one, often favoring a coalition government, though the main power within such a coalition still rests with one of the two main parties. The local party system mirrors that of the national system, though with a larger share of other, smaller parties on the local councils.

Table 31.4 reports the share of the vote among the three largest parties compared with the other parties in the local elections of 2011 and 2015. In 2011, the coalition headed by the SP (comprising 23 parties) and the one headed by the DP (22 parties) won, between them, 94.5% of the total votes cast, with 4.8% taken by the other parties (9) that competed on their own, and 0.7% by independent candidates.[11] This dominance was strengthened slightly further in 2015, when the two largest parties won 96% of the vote between them. Meanwhile, in 2011, of the 373 LGUs, only ten were won by independent candidates, while the coalition headed by the DP won 218 mayoral seats and the one headed by the SP won 145. In 2015, the coalition headed by the SP won 45 mayor seats, the one headed by the DP won 15, and the Greek minority won 1.[12]

Mayors almost always come from the two (and in a few cases, three) main parties, receiving powerful support from the national party. Nevertheless, although the mayoral system is very strong, it does not always lead to a smooth running of municipal affairs as the municipal council may comprise a majority of members of opposition parties. The most common challenge materializes during the voting on the budget, where the version proposed by the mayor must be approved by council.

It is clear from Table 31.4 that there are few independent candidates elected as mayor or to the local council, with no successful candidates in the last two election cycles of 2015 and 2019. The legal framework that covers elections has often been criticized for not offering equal access to elections for independent candidates and nonparliamentary parties. As mentioned previously, independent candidates and political parties that are not part of a coalition, parliament, or a municipal council are required to collect a considerable number of supporting signatures (at least 10,000 votes for a party and 15,000 for a coalition, for parliament, or 1% of the number of voters in the municipal election zone) in order to enter the election. Independent candidates are exempt from the use of public funds and are often, if not always, ignored by the media, which tend to focus on the main parties and their candidates during election campaigns (Institute for Democracy and Mediation 2014). For example, in the local elections of 2011, independent candidates won 18 out of the 6,152 seats allocated for all 373 LGUs, while in 2015, only three independent candidates won seats (CEC) out of 1,595 elected councilors among all 61 municipalities.

Women's representation in Albania's democratic institutions increased considerably following the application of a gender quota in the 2013 national and 2015 local elections.[13] Women's participation in national elections is regulated through the constitution and the Law on Gender Equality (2008) and, with regard to local political participation and decision making, through the 2015 Law on Local Self-Governance, which specifically deals with this issue in many of its articles. In 2008, changes to the Electoral Code included the adoption of a quota of at least 30% participation of women in parliamentary and local elections, while subsequent changes to the code in 2015 specified a 50% quota for local councilors.[14] According to the code, political parties are required to adhere to these quotas before they submit their lists to the election authorities. Furthermore, the Law on Local Self-Governance of 2015 states clearly that local decision-making structures must adhere to the Law on Gender Equality.[15]

Women's participation in and election to local government increased considerably following the application of quotas. In 2011, women comprised 12% of elected councilors, while in 2015 the proportion had increased to 35%. Meanwhile, the percentage of female mayors increased from 1.3% in 2011 to 14% in 2015,[16] with a similar proportion in the 2019 local elections.

The rights to vote and to be elected are protected in the constitution for every Albanian citizen, without prejudice. The country recognizes several minorities whose population, according to the census data of 2011, does not exceed 2% of the total population. Among these groups, more than 90% are members of the Greek minority. Given Albania's regional proportional system, the territorial distribution of the Greek minority means that they always have national and local representation. The system facilitates the representation of other minorities on the country's local councils through various ethnic parties though, because of the small number of these minorities, election to parliament is effectively impossible.

Last, one provision in Albanian law in force since 2015 prohibits municipal mayors from being elected more than three times in a row, while for councilors there is no term limit.

Electoral processes in Albania: some of the main issues and characteristics

In the post-1991 history of elections in Albania, there have been four different electoral systems applied: majoritarian, mixed majoritarian with two rounds, plurality majoritarian (simple majority), and a regional proportional system, the one that is currently in place.

A striking feature of these elections is that, apart from the one in 1992, either every election has been disputed by the losing party or its coalition or the process has been marred by irregularities. Another important feature is that the administration of elections continues to be political, that is, in the hands of the (main) political parties. The influence of party politics is so strong that the dynamics of local elections and voting have been strongly affected by the national political agenda of the two main parties and, to a much lesser extent, the SMI. For example, it is common in local elections for a party chairman to participate in the electoral campaign by supporting a local candidate, with more similarities than differences between the party manifestos for the local and national elections.

Another very important issue is the one of participation. For every election, a list of registered voters is compiled on the basis of the National Civil Registry. However, the numbers do not reflect the country's number of residents, given that, since 1991, a large number of people have emigrated. Whereas the National Institute of Statistics (INSTAT) reports that the resident population of Albania on 1 January 2019 was 2,862,487, the number of registered voters for the 2019 June elections was, according to the CEC, 3,536,016.

Meanwhile, according to the Institute for Political Studies in Tirana, it is estimated that the voter turnout for elections in Albania has ranged from 67% to 70% (apart from the local elections of 2019).

Various studies have attempted to explain the electoral systems applied in Albania, particularly after so many experiments with different systems – the most in Europe within such a short period, demonstrating the impact of the country's political culture. Nevertheless, the various systems and their administration have, since 1991, continuously produced dissatisfaction, not least with the voters but also with the parties, as well as external observers, including the Organization for Security and Cooperation in Europe (OSCE) Office for Democratic Institutions and Human Rights (ODIHR), the Council of Europe (e.g., Chamber of Local Authorities and Council of Europe 2015), and the various embassies and missions present in Tirana. Albania has amended its constitution several times since 1998 with regard to the electoral system, including returning the length of the local mandate back from three years to four years, specifying a new system and a new formula for the composition of the electoral administration, and limiting immunity for MPs. Despite these changes, the election system is still not regarded as efficient by either domestic or international observers. It has become customary after every election for a set of recommendations to be issued by OSCE in order for the country to hold its next elections in a way that adheres to best international practices. According to many observers, local elections in Albania are seen as national elections, in that the whole central political apparatus is engaged in the process (Krasniqi 2020). Thus, local elections often are held in a volatile political climate, heavily influenced by the relationship among the two or three main parties at the national level, and have very little to do with the daily concerns of citizens at the local level.

The most recent local elections, with the boycott and the management of the electoral process by government, produced local governments comprising a majority of mayors and councilors from the center-left of the political spectrum, with no sharing of power and only one-quarter of the electorate voting.

At the time of writing, the government and the opposition are in negotiations over electoral reform. Both are under pressure from the EC to conclude the much-needed reforms and to pave the way for inclusive national elections in 2021. In June 2020, the government and the opposition finally reached an agreement on Electoral Reform, requiring an amendment to the constitution. Parliament (dominated by the ruling Socialist Party with more than two-thirds of the seats following the opposition walkout in February 2019) proceeded with the changes, even though the extraparliamentary opposition protested that the majority had reneged on the deal reached in June. Parliament made further changes in October 2020, again with objections voiced by the opposition. Nevertheless, the changes were incorporated and the next scheduled parliamentary elections are due to go ahead on 25 April 2021. On 02.11.2021, the Constitutional Court reached a decision on the matter of local elections in 2019. It ruled against the claim made by the Albanian Association of Municipalities (acting on behalf of the opposition) which regarded local elections as unlawful and unconstitutional. It has yet to publish its final decision.

The main changes made to the electoral system, affecting both national and local elections, include the following:

- Open lists of candidates (two-thirds of the list) enabling a vote to be made for a candidate and for a party (until now there were closed lists where the voter could only vote for a party).
- Voting threshold reduced from 3% to 1% (nationally).
- Financing of independent candidates and of newly formed parties that have not yet participated in elections increased from 5% to 10%.
- Elections to be held only between 5 April and 15 May or between 15 October and 15 November.
- Structural changes made to the composition and administration of the Central Election Commission.
- Albanian diaspora entitled to vote from their country of residence (though it has been left to the CEC to find and develop appropriate ways of enabling this right).
- Coalitions to participate in a single list under one logo. This was interpreted by the opposition as an attempt by the ruling Socialist Party to prevent the possibility of the opposition winning the election by joining forces together against the Socialist Party.

However, one of the main (regular) recommendations made by OSCE-ODIHR, on the need to depoliticize the administration of elections, remains to be passed (again), and therefore, the administration of the elections remains in the hands of the (main) political forces.

Notes

1. Local Finances Platform. For profiles of the municipalities in Albania, see http://financatvendore.al/analiza/profilet. See also Gjergj Erebara (2019). *Sa banorë dhe sa votues ka Shqipëria?* (How many inhabitants and voters does Albania have?) www.reporter.al/sa-banore-dhe-sa-votues-ka-shqiperia/
2. In Albania, there is a large difference between the number of people registered on the Civil Registry and the number that are resident. According to the 2011 census, Albania had a resident population of 2.8 million, in contrast to the registered population of just over 4.5 million. Thus, Tirana Municipality, for example, according to INSTAT data for 2019 (published also by the Ministry of Finance for the purpose of budget allocation,) has 557,421 residents, as opposed to the Civil Registry of 757,361 inhabitants. Discrepancies are evident in all 61 municipalities.
3. Law 139/2015, On Local Self-Governance, Article 62.
4. OSCE 2019. ODIHR Needs Assessment Mission Report for Local Elections of 30 June. 19–21 March 2019.
5. http://cec.org.al/wp-content/uploads/2019/07/ZGJEDHJE-VENDORE-2019-TABELA-PERMBLEDHESE.pdf
6. *Observation of Local Elections in Albania*, https://rm.coe.int/1680718db0
7. President, high state officials, judges, prosecutors, military, national security and police staff, diplomats, and members of election commissions.
8. Including citizens convicted of certain crimes or who have been deported, even in the absence of a final court decision, from an EU member state, Australia, Canada, or the United States, as well as those under an international warrant.
9. In 2019, the local elections were boycotted by the opposition.
10. CEC uses data based on the Civil Registry and not the number of residents determined by census. The data used are probably overestimates, as many individuals recorded on the register reside abroad. For example, the 2011 census reported the population size of Tirana as 557,422, while the Civil Registry reports it as 734,573, and the voter turnout for Tirana (47%) was based upon the latter. Nevertheless, as the statistic is based upon the same source, any proportional changes taking place should reflect the real trend.

11 http://cec.org.al/Portals/0/Documents/CEC%202013/Legjislacioni_2011/Vendime_2011/VENDIM%201229/Lidhja%202.pdf, accessed 07 May 2020.
12 Following the Territorial-Administration Reform of 2015, the number of LGUs decreased from 373 to 61.
13 *Standards of representation in political parties in Albania* (Institute of Political Studies 2018), http://isp.com.al/wp-content/uploads/2018/07/STANDARDS-OF-REPRESENTATION-IN-POLITICAL-PARTIES.pdf
14 The quota system is only applied to the proportional representation system for electing MPs and local councilors and not to the majoritarian FPTP for electing the mayors of municipalities.
15 According to Articles 59 and 64, the mayor appoints the vice mayor(s) and heads of the administrative units (mostly former communes), adhering to the Law on Gender Equality (*Gender equality and discrimination in appointed local government bodies*; UN Women 2019).
16 *Standards of representation in political parties* in Albania (Institute of Political Studies 2018), http://isp.com.al/wp-content/uploads/2018/07/STANDARDS-OF-REPRESENTATION-IN-POLITICAL-PARTIES.pdf

References

Berhani I, 2012. The influence of electoral systems on the elections in Albania. *European Scientific Journal*, Vol. 8 (24).

Chamber of Local Authorities, and Council of Europe, 2015. Observation of Local Elections in Albania, Final Report. 21 June 2015. https://rm.coe.int/1680718db0.

Dyrmishi A, 2010. *Përzgjedhja dhe Efektet e Sistemeve Elektorale në Shqipëri* (*Selection and Effects of Electoral Systems in Albania*). Tiranë: Qendra për Studimin e Demokracisë dhe Qeverisjes (CSDG). www.csdgalbania.org.

Institute for Democracy and Mediation, 2014. *Indeksi i Integritetit të Zgjedhjeve – Zgjedhjet Vendore në Shqipëri* (*Index of Elections Integrity – Local Elections in Albania*). Tirana, Albania. https://idmalbania.org.

Institute of Political Studies, 2018. *Standards of Representation in Political Parties in Albania*. Tirana. http://isp.com.al/wp-content/uploads/2018/07/STANDARDS-OF-REPRESENTATION-IN-POLITICAL-PARTIES.pdf.

Kapidani M, 2015. Fiscal decentralization in Albania: Effects of territorial and administrative reform. *Scientific Bulletin; Economic Sciences*, Vol. 14 (3). https://ideas.repec.org/a/pts/journl/y2015i3p29-36.html.

Krasniqi A, 2012. *The Electoral Systems and Election Administration in Albania*. ACFR & FEF. www.researchgate.net/publication/266143978_THE_ELECTORAL_SYSTEMS_AND_ELECTIONS_ADMINISTRATION_IN_ALBANIA.

Krasniqi A, 2017. Partitë politike në Shqipëri (Political Parties in Albania). In: Wilhelm Hofmeister and Karsten Grabow (eds.), *Partite politike – funksioni dhe organizimi në shoqëritë demokratike* (*Political Parties – Functioning and Organization of Democratic Associations*). Konrad Adenauer Stiftung, Chapter on Albania by Afrim Krasniqi. http://isp.com.al/wp-content/uploads/2018/02/LIBRI-MBI-PARTITE-POLITIKE.pdf.

Krasniqi A, 2020. Interview with lead author on 29 June 2020, in Tirana, Albania.

Ladner A, Keuffer N, Baldersheim H, Hlepas N, Swianiewicz P, Steyvers K, and Navarro C, 2019. *Patterns of Local Autonomy in Europe*, pp. 229–230. Switzerland: Palgrave Macmillan.

OSCE, 2019. ODIHR Needs Assessment Mission Report for Local Elections of 30 June. 19–21 March 2019.

Reynolds A, Reilly B, and Ellis A, 2005. *Electoral System Design: The New International IDEA Handbook*. Stockholm: International Institute for Democracy and Electoral Assistance (IDEA).

UN Women, 2019. *Barazia gjinore dhe diskriminimi në organet e emëruara të pushtetit vendor* (*Gender Equality and Discrimination in Appointed Local Government Bodies*). Commissioner for Protection from Discrimination. https://portavendore.al/wp-content/uploads/2019/06/Barazia-gjinore-dhe-diskriminimi-ne-organet-e-meruara-te-pushtetit-vendor.pdf.

32
Bosnia and Herzegovina
Local elections within a weak and contested state

Kiran Auerbach

Decentralization as an instrument of postconflict state-building and democratization

Bosnia and Herzegovina (BiH) has a highly decentralized structure that consists of a patchwork of subnational governments operating under the umbrella of a weak central state.[1] Established in December 1995 as part of the Dayton Peace Agreement, BiH's asymmetric federal structure reflects ethnic power-sharing arrangements to accommodate its three warring factions: Bosniaks, Croats, and Serbs. Dayton concentrated constitutional powers in Bosnia's two ethnofederal regions (formally called 'entities') rather than at the central level.[2] These entities, the Federation of BiH (FBiH) and Republika Srpska (RS), establish laws that regulate their respective municipal governments. In addition, Dayton established a small, multiethnic territory called Brčko District that is not part of either entity. Figure 32.1 presents an overview of Bosnia's different levels of governance.

FBiH is mainly populated by Bosniaks and Croats. To accommodate these two ethnic groups, FBiH is further divided into ten cantons (eight of which have a clear ethnic majority). The cantons have their own governments with executive, legislative, and judicial authority. There are 79 municipalities below the cantonal level. The Republika Srpska, on the other hand, is more ethnically homogeneous as Serbs account for over 80% of the population in this entity. The RS is administratively centralized, with 63 municipalities directly below the entity level.

The territorialization of ethnic identity in BiH extends to the local level. Ethnic power-sharing arrangements and demographic shifts that are legacies of the 1992–1995 Bosnian War have led most municipalities toward a clear ethnic majority. Before war broke out in 1992, BiH had 109 municipalities (Gavrić et al. 2013: 58), whereas today there are 143 (including Brčko District as a unit of local government). The increase has resulted in several small, ethnically homogeneous municipalities that were created from districts within a former municipality in which a minority group was dominant.

Ten municipalities are designated as cities: four municipal units in the Federation (Bihać, Tuzla, Zenica, and Široki Brijeg) and six in the RS (Prijedor, Bijeljina, Banja Luka, Doboj, Zvornik, and Trebinje). Two additional cities, Sarajevo (FBiH) and East Sarajevo (RS),

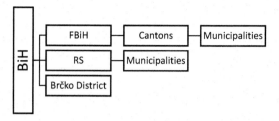

Figure 32.1 Decentralization in Bosnia and Herzegovina

encompass four and six municipalities, respectively, and have their own metropolitan governments consisting of a city council and city mayor. City council members in these two cities are selected from municipal councils; the city council then selects the city mayor.

BiH fits within the strong mayor form of local government systems (Heinelt & Hlepas 2006). In both the RS and FBiH, mayors are considered the chief executive of municipalities. Their main tasks include the proposal of an annual budget and various policy initiatives, while the council serves as a legislature that must approve most decisions by a two-thirds majority. Disagreements between the mayor and the president of the municipal council, therefore, often hold up decision-making processes.

Municipalities are subdivided into districts called *mjesne zajednice*. A remnant of the former Yugoslavian regime, these submunicipal districts serve as electoral precincts for all types of elections and venues in which to address neighborhood concerns. In particular, the 1974 Yugoslav Constitution introduced district councils for citizens to participate in local self-management (Leonardson & Mirčev 1979). These consultative bodies continue to function as local deliberative institutions.

BiH became a member of the Council of Europe in 2002, which put pressure on Bosnian authorities to align legislation on decentralization with the European Charter of Local Self-Government (Bojičić-Dželilović 2011). Pushed by international actors in the mid-2000s, the RS and FBiH entities adopted local self-governance laws in 2004 and 2006, respectively, which strengthened the autonomy of municipal governments across BiH. These laws delegated specific developmental competencies, such as infrastructure, spatial planning, local economic policies, and public financing through taxes and other income-generating activities, to municipalities. In 2016, the Republika Srpska adopted a new law on local self-governance.[3] The Federation of BiH has not updated its local self-government law since 2006.

Most Bosnian citizens view local governments as the most important level of governance for their daily lives. Survey data consistently show that citizens express greater trust in and satisfaction with local governments compared to higher levels of governance.[4] Despite efforts to strengthen local self-governance and delegate additional competencies to municipalities, however, Bosnian municipalities struggle financially to carry out their responsibilities. With limited sources of local revenue, municipalities are dependent on transfers and grants from the entities and cantons to finance their activities. For example, compared to the EU average of 10.9%, local revenue accounted for only 4.6% of BiH's GDP in 2018 (6.2% in the RS and 4.1% in FBiH) and has actually declined since 2006 (NALAS 2018, 2019). Shared taxes (including VAT and personal income tax) and general grants account for 50% of local government revenue in FBiH and 57% in the RS, while their own sources of revenue lag behind at 36% in FBiH and 37% in the RS (NALAS 2019).[5]

The evolution of local elections: a mix of international and domestic reforms

The first two democratic local elections took place in 1997 and 2000 and were under the purview of the Organization for Security and Cooperation in Europe (OSCE). Annex 3 of the Dayton Peace Agreement delegated electoral oversight to the OSCE, which was tasked to set up a Provisional Election Commission (General Framework Agreement for Peace in BiH 1995). Domestic authorities did not adopt a national election law until 2001. As a result, the OSCE regulated and implemented BiH's electoral system until the 2002 general elections and 2004 local elections (see Bose 2002; Belloni 2008; Bieber 2006). The 2001 Electoral Law of BiH set up the Central Election Commission to oversee and monitor elections at all levels of government and to collect electoral data.[6] This body also verifies candidate lists for political parties and reviews whether political parties comply with campaign finance regulations.

Local elections in Bosnia and Herzegovina consist of elections for mayors, municipal councils, and city councils. They take place simultaneously every four years throughout the entire territory of BiH on the first Sunday in October. Local elections are held two years apart from general elections, which refer to parliamentary and presidential elections at the central, entity, and cantonal levels. Elections are organized by the Central Election Commission, municipal election commissions, and polling station committees. Municipalities bear the costs of local elections.

Mayors and municipal councilors are elected to four-year terms, and there are no term limits. Until 2004, municipal council members elected mayors, which meant that the mayor usually came from the party that obtained the most seats on the council. The RS and FBiH parliaments reformed their laws and citizens began to elect mayors directly in 2004.[7] The direct election of mayors was lauded by the international community as a way to increase the accountability of mayors to citizens (Council of Europe 2004; OSCE/ODIHR Election Observation Mission 2005). The new system also led to a greater division of power between mayors and municipal councils. The reform improved the visibility of mayors as the chief executive of the municipality and strengthened their relationship with citizens. However, political parties continue to nominate mayoral candidates for local elections, and most mayors run for office under a party label rather than running as independents. Because parties have discretion over candidate nominations, mayors remain vulnerable to the interests of central party officials, which usually go against local community interests (Center for Civil Initiatives 2009; Zlokapa 2009).

Mayoral recalls were introduced in 2004 after mayors began to be directly elected. The procedure consists of the following three stages and may not take place during an election year: (1) initiation by a citizen petition signed by 10% of residents or by one-third of municipal councilors; (2) local referendum in which citizens vote in favor or against the recall, determined by a simple majority; and (3) an early election in which citizens vote for a new mayor, elected according to the first-past-the-post system. Until amendments to the RS election law were added in 2011, no specific preconditions to justify mayoral recalls existed in either entity. The RS law affirmed six broad preconditions to justify recall initiatives in this entity alone,[8] while FBiH does not specify any preconditions. As a result of these vague or nonexistent rules, recalls are a highly politicized affair.

A total of 26 mayoral recalls were initiated between 2005 and 2015, and ten of these cases resulted in the removal of the mayor from office. Five recalls failed because the Central Election Commission found recall referenda to be in violation of democratic procedures (Auerbach 2021). Municipal councilors initiated these 26 recalls, and in only one case did a citizen petition reach the 10% threshold. Until the recent RS Law on Local Self Governance in 2016, there were no consequences for municipal councilors if the recall initiation did not result in the removal of the mayor. The new law in the RS gives power to the RS National Assembly to dissolve a municipal council if it initiates a recall against the mayor but the recall referendum fails. There are no penalties for recall failure in FBiH.

Although recalls were designed to increase the ability for citizens to hold mayors accountable for their performance in office, they are rarely initiated to sanction mayors for poor policy performance. In practice, recalls serve as venues for political parties and individual politicians to extend electoral competition for the office of mayor. In most cases, politicians in higher levels of government directly influence recall initiations and referenda. This reflects a political strategy by which strong parties that are dominant at the entity level manipulate recalls to extend partisan control over municipal governments (Auerbach 2021).

Local elections in BiH: combining proportional and majoritarian rules

BiH citizens above the age of 18 are eligible to vote in the municipality where they are registered as permanent residents. Voting in absentia may be done by mailing a ballot or by voting at a BiH diplomatic office abroad. Voting is not compulsory, and there are no provisions in the BiH Election Law for noncitizens to vote.

Each municipality forms a single constituency. Municipalities are then divided into voting districts (*mjesne zajednice*). Municipal councils range in size between 11 and 31 members. The BiH Election Law prescribes that municipalities with fewer than 8,000 registered voters have between 11 and 17 members. Municipalities that have between 8,000 and 20,000 registered voters have between 17 and 25 members, and municipalities with more than 20,000 registered voters have between 25 and 31 members. FBiH and RS regulate the precise number of seats according to the population in their territories. Municipalities in BiH tend to be small in population. One-quarter of municipalities have fewer than 7,000 residents, and the median population is 17,000.

In the local elections held on 2 October 2016, citizens voted in all municipalities except in the city of Mostar. A total of 142 mayoral positions were filled, plus the two city mayors of Sarajevo and East Sarajevo.[9] The total number of council seats filled was 3,135. This number includes 1,803 councilors elected in the Federation, 1,301 in the RS, and 31 in Brčko District. In addition, 28 municipal councilors from four Sarajevo municipalities were appointed to the Sarajevo City Council, and 31 councilors from six municipalities were appointed to the East Sarajevo City Council.

In FBiH and the RS, citizens directly elect mayors by plurality (first-past-the-post), while municipal councilors are elected by PR with semi-open lists.[10] Accordingly, citizens receive two ballots, one for mayor and one for the municipal council. They vote for one mayoral candidate. On the ballot for municipal councils, citizens may vote for one independent candidate, one list of independent candidates, or one party/coalition list. Citizens may also vote for one or more candidates within a single party list, and there are no restrictions on the number of candidate preferences. A system of reserved seats for national minorities was introduced in the 2008 local elections. If national minorities make up more than 3% of the population of a municipality, they are guaranteed at least one seat on the council. National minority candidates form a special list, and any voter may vote for a minority candidate from this list. However, voters cannot vote for both a national minority candidate and another party list. In 2016, 26 national minority candidates were elected to municipal councils in 24 municipalities.

Municipal council seats are allocated by the Sainte-Laguë method, and parties (including independents and lists of independent candidates) must obtain at least 3% of the total vote. Rather than *apparentement*, parties may form preelectoral coalitions, and these coalitions form a single party list. Because parties must register in each municipality where they compete, preelectoral coalitions vary between municipalities. In fact, these coalitions may even differ within the same municipality between the mayoral race and the council race. Seats are allocated to candidates according to the number of personal votes they receive if above 10% of the total party vote. Remaining seats are allocated by the ranking of candidates on the party's list. Before 2016, the threshold of preference votes was 5%, but the BiH Parliament amended the threshold before the 2016 local elections. This move increased the importance of candidate rankings on a list. The amendment has thus been criticized for encouraging greater party leadership control as well as party fragmentation, because high thresholds could lead to party defections and smaller splinter parties (Kapidžić 2016).

Brčko District has a unique administrative status because it is the only municipality that is not part of either entity. From 1999 until 2004, Brčko was governed by an international administrator, who appointed mayors and members of its local assembly. Brčko residents have voted regularly in local elections since 2004 (Bieber 2005: 426), and the mayor of Brčko is indirectly elected by the Brčko Assembly.[11]

The city of Mostar, an ethnically divided municipality in FBiH, is another exception to BiH's system of local elections. Due to political stalemate, Mostar has not held local elections since 2008. Previously, the city experimented with multiple power-sharing arrangements aimed at equalizing representation among Bosniaks, Croats, and Serbs on its city council. In 1996, the international community divided Mostar into six separate municipalities; however, this division unintentionally reinforced the city's ethnic segregation (Bieber 2006). The High Representative of BiH[12] imposed a new system in 2004 that unified Mostar into a single municipal unit and divided the city into six electoral districts with a total of 35 seats on its city council. Voters cast two votes for council members: one vote for candidates from their district and one vote for at-large members. Three members came from each electoral district, and 17 at-large members were elected. This system, however, excluded Mostar's central zone from being designated as an electoral district, so that residents from this area could only vote for at-large members (OSCE/ODIHR Election Observation Mission 2005).

After the 2008 local elections in Mostar, a political crisis ensued in which the leading Croat and Bosniak parties fell into deadlock and could not agree on how to reform Mostar's electoral system. In 2019, the European Court of Human Rights found the situation to be discriminatory and in violation of Article 1 of the European Convention of Human Rights. This decision supported previous judgments issued by the Bosnian Constitutional Court in 2010 and 2012 relating to Mostar's local electoral system, which authorities in Mostar had failed to implement (European Court of Human Rights 2019; Constitutional Court of BiH 2012). In July 2020, leaders of the Party of Democratic Action (SDA) and the Croatian Democratic Union (HDZ) negotiated a political agreement to reform Mostar's election system. The BiH parliament passed this agreement, and Mostar's local elections will take place on 20 December 2020 (Central Election Commission of BiH 2020).

Mostar's city council will again contain 35 members who will elect the mayor. Thirteen councilors will be elected from a citywide electoral district, and 22 will be elected from the six electoral districts that comprise the city of Mostar.[13] The new rules also set up an ethnic quota so that no fewer than four and no more than 15 councilors can be affiliated with each of the three constituent peoples of BiH (Bosniaks, Croats, and Serbs). At least one councilor must come from a different ethnicity.

The requirements for registering candidates in BiH are relatively simple. At least 135 days before the election, political parties and independent candidates need 100 signatures of registered voters in municipalities with fewer than 10,000 registered voters or 200 signatures when the number of registered voters is greater than 10,000. If the total number of registered voters is fewer than 1,000, then candidates need the signatures of 5% of registered voters. If the party or independent candidate is already elected at a higher level of government, then it or he/she is exempt from the signature requirement. In all levels of elections, candidates must declare his or her ethnic affiliation as one of the three constituent peoples (Bosniak, Croat, or Serb) or as 'Other'. No person who has been indicted, is serving a sentence, or who has failed to comply with an order of the International Criminal Tribunal for the former Yugoslavia, a Bosnian court, or a foreign court for serious violations of humanitarian law can vote or be a candidate for election. Mayors may not hold another elected position, but councilors may hold a higher level political position.

Local electoral outcomes within a fragmented party system

Figure 32.2 shows that turnout for local elections has hovered between 50% and 60% in each entity, which has kept pace with turnout for national elections. In the most recent local elections in 2016, turnout was 60% in the whole country. The highest recorded turnout was 86% in Trnovo in the FBiH, while the lowest turnout was 34% in Sanski Most, also in the Federation. There is a negative correlation (−0.4) between turnout and population size, as pictured in Figure 32.3.

Mayoral elections are competitive, although there is a strong incumbency advantage. In the RS, 29 incumbents won in 63 municipalities, equal to a reelection rate of 46%. In FBiH, the rate was even higher at 52 out of 78, or 67%. Given the small size of most municipalities in BiH, a few hundred votes often decide the winner. In 2016, there were two unopposed mayors, in Kupres (RS) and Kresevo (FBiH), who won 100% of the vote.

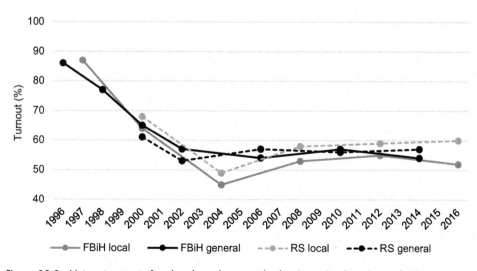

Figure 32.2 Voter turnout for local and general elections in Bosnia and Herzegovina, 1996–2016

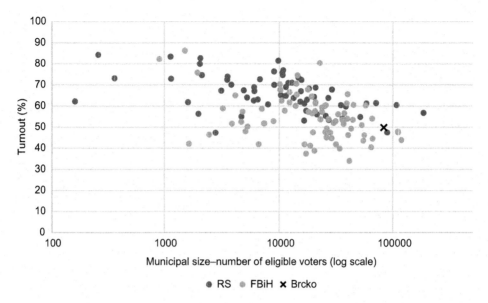

Figure 32.3 Voter turnout for the 2016 local elections in Bosnia and Herzegovina by municipality size

BiH has a highly fragmented party system that is segmented into three subsystems, defined by ethnic group and entity (for a discussion, see Kapidžić 2015). All major parties in BiH have an explicit ethnic affiliation, with the exception of the Social Democratic Party (SDP) and its splinter party, Democratic Front (DF).[14] Political competition is intraethnic, meaning that it takes place within each of the three ethnic pillars rather than between parties representing different ethnic groups. Bosniak and Croat parties mainly compete for power in the Federation, while Serb parties mainly compete in the Republika Srpska. The RS party system is more consolidated than that in FBiH. SNSD is the most powerful Serb party, which has governed since 2006, and SDS is its main opposition. In FBiH, party competition is further regionalized due to its ten cantons, five of which have a clear Bosniak majority and three of which have a Croat majority (Hulsey & Keil 2020). SDA is the most powerful Bosniak party, and HDZ is the most powerful Croat party.

The intraethnic arena of party competition and the regionalization of the party system within the entities and cantons have resulted in a large number of parties that compete in elections. The 2014 BiH parliamentary election results reflect this fragmentation: 19 parliamentary parties (including parties that formed preelectoral coalitions) won mandates in the 42-seat House of Representatives. Most electoral districts, all the way down to municipalities, are dominated by one ethnic group. Scholars note that the territorialization of ethnicity and the lack of electoral incentives for parties to compete across districts create poor linkage across elections at different levels of government and result in low nationalization of the party system (Bochsler 2010; Hulsey 2015).

Table 32.1 shows that national parliamentary parties dominate local politics. SDA and SNSD are the strongest parties in FBiH and RS, respectively. These two parties control the most seats in the BiH parliament and entity parliaments. Column three in Table 32.1 shows that SDA and SNSD are also dominant in local politics as they control the greatest share of municipal council seats (19% and 13%, respectively) and the greatest share of mayors (23% and 24%, respectively). Independent candidates and local lists, however, play an important role in local politics.

Table 32.1 Parliamentary parties and 2016 local election results in Bosnia and Herzegovina

Parties in BiH Parliament (2014–2018)	Percentage of municipalities where running (2016)	Percentage of municipalities where represented (2016)	Percentage of seats on local councils (2016)	Percentage of (aggregate) votes in local elections (2016)	Percentage of mayors affiliated with the party (2016)
Demokratska Fronta (DF)	43.7	32.4	3.0	3.4	0.7
Demokratski Narodni Savez (DNS)	47.2	43.7	5.3	5.1	3.6
Hrvatska Demokratska Zajednica (HDZ)	44.4	30.3	8.2	6.4	13.6
Partija Demokratskog Progresa (PDP)	47.2	40.8	3.8	3.7	0.0
Savez za bolju budućnost Bosne i Herzegovine-Fahrudin Radončić (SBB)	54.9	44.4	4.8	5.2	19.3
Stranka Demokratske Akcije (SDA)	72.5	62.7	18.8	18.8	22.9
Socijaldemokratska Partija (SDP)	63.4	52.1	6.9	8.1	5.7
Srpska Demokratska Stranka (SDS)	45.8	45.1	9.2	5.1	7.9
Savez Nezavisnih Socijalnademokratska-Milorad Dodik (SNSD)	54.2	48.6	13.0	12.3	23.6
Other parliamentary parties	20.3	12.9	14.3	12.4	4.3
Independents and local lists	56.0	42.6	4.5	4.4	15.0

Sources: Data compiled by author from the BiH Central Election Commission, Local Elections 2016 http://izbori.ba/rezultati_izbora_2016; RS Institute of Statistics, "Gradovi i opštine Republike Srpske 2018; "FBiH Agency of Statistics"; and "Lokalni Izbori 2016"

Notes: All values include seats and vote shares won as a local preelectoral coalition. Preelectoral coalitions differ between national elections and local elections, and they also vary between municipalities. At the national level, HDZ was in a preelectoral coalition with the following parties: HSS, HKDU BiH, HSP Dr. Ante Starčević, and HSP Herceg-Bosne. DNS was in a preelectoral coalition at the national level with NS and SRS. PDP was in a preelectoral coalition at the national level with NDP. Other parliamentary parties include A-SDA, BPS Stranka-Sefer Halilović, HDZ 1990, HSS, HSP Dr. Ante Starčević, HSP Herceg-Bosne, HKDU, NDP, NS, and SRS. Columns 1 and 2 are the percentages of municipalities where these parties ran and won at least one seat. Columns 3, 4, and 5 are percentages of seats, votes, and mayors affiliated with these parties in all municipalities, respectively.

Individuals from these groups represent 15% of all mayors and won at least one seat in 43% of municipalities across the country. In the RS, fewer parties and fewer independent candidates compete and win in local elections than in FBiH.

Preelectoral coalitions, in which parties band together to form a single party list, differ at the entity, cantonal, and municipal levels (including between municipalities). For example, in the 2016 elections, SDA captured 27 of its 32 mayoral positions as a coalition partner with SBB. By pooling candidates into a single list, independents and parties from the same ethnic block become more competitive, particularly when they represent the minority population in a municipality. Furthermore, co-ethnic parties that are rivals at the national level often form preelectoral coalitions at the local level as a pragmatic strategy to increase their chances of winning seats on municipal councils. For example, HDZ, the strongest Croat party, ran together with HDZ 1990 in several municipalities.

Gender quotas for candidate lists have existed since 1998; however, Figure 32.4 shows low levels of female representation in locally elected positions. In 2016, the BiH Election Law was amended, requiring women to represent at least 40% of all candidates on a party's list. In addition, one candidate from the underrepresented gender must be ranked among the first two candidates, two candidates from the underrepresented gender among the first five candidates, and three candidates from the underrepresented gender among the first eight candidates.

Although the Central Election Commission must certify that parties meet gender requirements, the law has had limited impact. One of the main reasons is that the open-list system disadvantages women because the distribution of preferential votes for individual candidates tends to favor men (Borić 2004). Female politicians in BiH also report widespread physical and psychological harassment that is most often perpetrated by political parties (including their copartisans), members of the elected bodies on which they sit, voters, the media, and social media users (Miftari 2019). In FBiH, the share of local female politicians has not increased substantially since data on gender representation began to be recorded for the 2000 local elections. In 2016, 16% of the elected municipal councilors in the RS and 20% in FBiH were female. Only one female mayor was elected in FBiH, and five female mayors were elected in the RS.

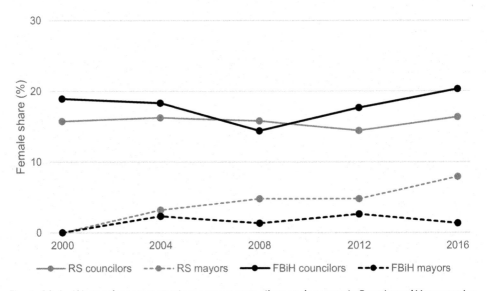

Figure 32.4 Women's representation among councilors and mayors in Bosnia and Herzegovina

Further issues: the dominance of national politics at the local level

Despite gradual reforms that have strengthened local self-government over the past 25 years, Bosnian municipalities lack de facto fiscal and political autonomy. The tension between strengthening local autonomy and maintaining dependence on higher levels relates to the locus of political power within the BiH system and control over political party patronage networks. Moreover, Dayton's power-sharing institutions encouraged ethnic segregation of the population and among political parties. Furthermore, the Dayton system set up a weak central state and concentrated political and economic power in the entities and cantons. The system thus facilitated ethnic parties that function as patronage machines. Political parties in BiH appeal to a particular ethnic group, but beyond ethnicity there are negligible programmatic differences between parties. Most parties win votes by rewarding supporters with public sector jobs (e.g., Hulsey & Keil 2020; Jansen et al. 2016). Therefore, political parties that dominate at the entity and cantonal levels have resisted major reforms that would cede power to the local level for fear of breaking their control over patronage networks (Bojičić-Dželilović 2011).

One way that entity and cantonal governments maintain dominance over municipalities is through fiscal transfers and grants upon which municipalities depend to finance local public services. Higher levels have been criticized for their lack of transparency and discretionary spending toward municipalities, especially in FBiH where cantons share certain competencies (often ill-defined) with municipalities, and each canton has its own unique legislation (Bojičic-Dželilović 2011). To raise additional funding, many municipalities apply directly to international donors for development grants (e.g., Pickering & Jusić 2018).

Politicians at higher levels also use various political strategies to interfere in local politics. They exploit electoral rules, distract voters from local issues, and pressure voters and local politicians with clientelistic incentives. For example, Kapidžić's analysis of the 2016 local elections discusses the impact of a last-minute amendment to the electoral law, in which BiH's parliament raised the intraparty threshold from 5% to 10%. This reform increased the importance of party leaders who rank candidates on the list, because candidates must now win at least 10% of the party's vote to gain a seat. Another example of political interference was the RS-wide referendum held one week before local elections. Pushed onto the agenda by the prime minister of the RS, the referendum concerned a controversial law to establish a national holiday in the RS, a law that the BiH Constitutional Court previously found to be unconstitutional. The contentious issue affected the local elections by mobilizing ethnic divisions between supporters and opponents of the referendum, detracting from local issues, bolstering support for the prime minister's party (SNSD), and weakening the SDS opposition (Kapidžić 2016). Finally, politicians at higher levels have co-opted council members to initiate recalls against mayors who are unfavorable to central party interests. Central party leaders have also punished disloyal, co-partisan mayors by revoking their party membership and/or forcing them to resign from office (Auerbach 2018). These strategies point to multiple pathways by which national politicians and central party organizations maintain political power over municipal governments.

Notes

1 Local elections took place in November 2020, but this chapter covers up to the previous round in 2016.
2 The Constitution of BiH is Annex 4 of the Dayton Peace Agreement.

3 The new law grants legal representation to cities, regulates the number of municipal employees in proportion to the municipality's population, and gives the RS National Assembly the power to dissolve municipal councils for particular offenses.
4 See, for example, USAID (2017) National Survey of Citizens' Perceptions in Bosnia and Herzegovina 2016, *Findings Report* http://measurebih.com/national-survey-of-citizens-perceptions; Analitika-Center for Social Policy (2015) Fakti: Rezultati ankete [Fact Sheet: Survey Results], http://analitika.ba.
5 Tax revenue transfers have decreased due to BiH's debt service payments for an IMF loan taken out in 2009. For example, in 2016 debt servicing 'reduced local government's share of indirect taxes from legally defined 8.42% to 7.1%' (NALAS 2018: 69).
6 An exception is Brčko District, which did not hold elections until 2004.
7 In 2004, RS mayors were selected by first-past-the-post while FBiH used a two-round majority voting system in which the two leading candidates proceeded to a second round (if no candidate won at least 50% in the first round). FBiH changed this system to first-past-the-post in 2008.
8 These preconditions include the following:

> Mayor does not ensure the execution of laws, other regulations, and general acts; does not ensure the implementation of strategic documents of national importance; does not implement the decisions of the municipal assembly and strategic development documents of the municipality; if material damage occurs for the municipality due to the adoption or failure to adopt acts within the competence of the mayor; if he does not submit a report on the work to the assembly; and if he does not propose the municipal budget within the deadline provided by law.
>
> *(Law on changes and amendments to the electoral law of Republika Srpska, Article 16, November 2011)*

9 There were violent incidents at polling stations in the municipality of Stolac, so the Central Election Commission of BiH annulled the electoral results for Stolac. New elections took place in 2017 in Stolac, and these results are included with the electoral data for this chapter.
10 Prior to 2000, municipal council members were elected by a closed-list proportional system. However, the international electoral administration in BiH felt that closed lists gave too much power to party leaders and prevented the rise of more moderate, multiethnic parties (Belloni 2008; Bose 2002). Therefore, an open-list system was adopted in 2000, in which voters could vote for party lists and individual candidates within a list.
11 Brčko residents voted for municipal assembly members in the 1997, 2004, 2008, 2012, and 2016 local elections.
12 Annex 10 of the Dayton Peace Agreement set up the Office of the High Representative. The high representative is an international diplomat charged with civilian implementation of the Peace Agreement. This individual has legal powers that supersede Bosnian institutions, including the president of BiH and the BiH parliament.
13 Voters thus receive two ballots: one ballot for the city-level constituency and one ballot for one of the six electoral districts that comprise the city. Each of Mostar's six electoral districts has a quota for the number of councilors to be elected, ranging from two to seven (Law on amendments to the electoral law of BiH, BiH Official Gazette 41/20: 4).
14 SDP is the successor party to the BiH League of Communists that ruled during the Yugoslavian regime. SDP and DF are officially multiethnic parties but mainly win support from moderate Bosniak voters.

References

Auerbach, K. R. (2021) 'Accountable to whom? How strong parties subvert local democratic institutions', *Party Politics*. doi: 10.1177/13540688211019720.

Auerbach, K.R. (2018). *Partisan Accountability and the Perversion of Local Democracy: Evidence from Bosnia and Herzegovina*. PhD Dissertation, University of North Carolina at Chapel Hill.

Belloni, R. (2008). *State Building and International Intervention in Bosnia*. London: Routledge.

Bieber, F. (2005). Local Institutional Engineering: A Tale of Two Cities, Mostar and Brčko. *International Peacekeeping, 12*(3), 420–433.

Bieber, F. (2006). *Post-War Bosnia: Ethnic Structure, Inequality and Governance of the Public Sector*. London: Palgrave Macmillan.

Bochsler, D. (2010). The Nationalisation of Post-Communist Party Systems. *Europe-Asia Studies, 62*(5), 807–827.

Bojičić-Dželilović, V. (2011). Decentralisation and Regionalisation in Bosnia-Herzegovina: Issues and Challenges. *LSEE Papers on Decentralisation and Regional Policy, Research Paper*.

Borić, B. (2004). *Application of Quotas: Legal Reforms and Implementation in Bosnia and Herzegovina*. Budapest: International Institute for Democracy and Electoral Assistance (IDEA)/CEE Network for Gender Issues Conference.

Bose, S. (2002). *Bosnia after Dayton: Nationalist Partition and International Intervention*. Oxford: Oxford University Press.

Center for Civil Initiatives. (2009). *Odnos nacelnika i skupstina u BiH* [*The Relationship between Mayors and Municipal Councils in BiH*]. www.cci.ba.

Central Election Commission of BiH. (2020). *Odluku o raspisivanju i održavanju lokalnih izbora 2020. godine u gradu Mostaru* [*Decision on Announcement and Holding of 2020 Local Elections in the City of Mostar*]. www.izbori.ba/Documents/Lokalni_izbori_2020/Mostar/Odluka_o_raspisivanju_i_odrzavanju_Lokalnih_izbora_2020_godine-bos.pdf.

Constitutional Court of BiH. Decision. (18 Jan. 2012). BiH Official Gazette 15/09.27 Feb. 2012. www.izbori.ba/Documents/documents/ZAKONI/Rjesenja/DOCU9-9-bos.pdf.

Council of Europe. (29 Nov. 2004). *Report on the Municipal Elections in Bosnia and Herzegovina*. Standing Committee CG/CP (11)13. https://rm.coe.int/1680718c09.

European Court of Human Rights. (29 Oct. 2019). *Case of Baralija v. Bosnia and Herzegovina*. Judgment. Application 30100/18. Strasbourg: Council of Europe. http://hudoc.echr.coe.int/eng?i=001-197215.

Gavrić, S., Banović, D. & Barreiro, M. (2013). *The Political System of Bosnia and Herzegovina Institutions – Actors – Processes*. Sarajevo: Sarajevo Open Centre.

The General Framework Agreement for Peace in Bosnia and Herzegovina, 1995. www.ohr.int/dayton-peace-agreement/.

Heinelt, H. & Hlepas, N. K. (2006). Typologies of Local Government Systems. In H. Bäck, H. Heinelt, & A. Magnier (Eds.), *The European Mayor Political Leaders in the Changing Context of Local Democracy* (pp. 21–42). Baden-Baden: VS Verlag für Sozialwissenschaften.

Hulsey, J. (2015). Party Politics in Bosnia and Herzegovina. In: S. Keil & V. Perry (Eds.), *State-Building and Democratization in Bosnia and Herzegovina* (pp. 41–60). London: Routledge.

Hulsey, J. & Keil, S. (2020). Change Amidst Continuity? Assessing the 2018 Regional Elections in Bosnia and Herzegovina. *Regional & Federal Studies, 30*(3), 1–19.

Jansen, S., Brković, Č. & Čelebičić, V. (Eds.). (2016). *Negotiating Social Relations in Bosnia and Herzegovina: Semiperipheral Entanglements*. London: Routledge.

Kapidžić, D. (2015). Party System of Bosnia and Herzegovina. In: N. Mujagić & S. Arnautović (Eds.), *Political Pluralism and Internal Party Democracy: National Study for Bosnia and Herzegovina* (pp. 35–56). Podgorica: CeMi.

Kapidžić, D. (2016). Local Elections in Bosnia and Herzegovina. *Contemporary Southeastern Europe, 3*(2), 127–134.

Leonardson, G.S. & Mirčev, D. (1979). A Structure for Participatory Democracy in the Local Community: The Yugoslav Constitution of 1974. *Comparative Politics, 11*(2), 189–203.

Miftari, E. (2019). *Violence Against Women in Politics in Bosnia and Herzegovina*. Westminster Foundation for Democracy. www.wfd.org/wp-content/uploads/2019/07/Violence-Against-Women-in-Politics-BiH-WFD2019.pdf.

Network of Associations of Local Authorities of South-East Europe (NALAS). (2018). *Fiscal Decentralization Indicators for South-East Europe: 2006–2017*. NALAS Report. www.nalas.eu/News/FD_2018.

Network of Associations of Local Authorities of South-East Europe (NALAS). (2019). *Local Government Finance Indicators in South-East Europe. Statistical Brief.* www.nalas.eu/.

OSCE/ODIHR Election Observation Mission. (2005). *Final Report: Bosnia and Herzegovina: Municipal Elections in 2004.* Warsaw: OSCE Office for Democratic Institutions and Human Rights. www.osce.org/odihr/elections/bih/41178?download=true.

Pickering, P.M. & Jusić, M. (2018). Making Local Government Work Better: How Local and Internationally Sponsored Institutions Interact to Influence Performance in Bosnia-Herzegovina. *Governance, 31*(4), 665–682.

Zlokapa, Z. (Ed.). (2009). *Načelnik i lokalna samouprava: liderstvo, demokratija, razvoj* [*The Mayor and Local Self-Governance: Leadership, Democracy, Development*]. Banja Luka: Center for Civic Initiatives. www.osfbih.org.ba/.

# 33

Bulgaria
More open local electoral rules

Desislava Kalcheva and Daniela Ushatova

Local government system

In 1991, Bulgaria adopted a new constitution, and the process of reforming the local government and extending the competencies of the municipalities began. Since the democratic transition, the municipalities in Bulgaria have been governed by regularly elected councils. According to the new Constitution of the Republic of Bulgaria, the country's territory is divided into districts (*oblasti*) and municipalities (*obshtini*). The municipality is the main administrative-territorial unit responsible for service delivery. In 1991, the territory of Bulgaria was divided into nine districts and 273 municipalities. Currently, there are 28 districts and 265 municipalities, as several administrative-territorial changes took place: 16 new municipalities were created, and 24 municipalities were merged. As of the end of 2019, the average population of a municipality in Bulgaria is 26,200, but the variation in the population of municipalities is significant (from 815 to about 1.3 million inhabitants). Currently, there are no active discussions regarding mergers of municipalities.

Bulgarian municipalities are equipped with an independent budget and municipal property. Prior to the reforms from the 1990s, the Bulgarian municipalities did not have their own property, separate from the state. Bulgarian municipalities perform their own and delegated tasks (Vladimirova & Naydenov 2011: 64). Since 2003, the responsibilities for public services are clearly divided between the central state and the municipalities, and the sources of their financing are differentiated. Their own tasks include improvement of the settlements, maintenance of local roads and parks, and waste management. The delegated tasks embrace kindergartens, schools, social care, cultural institutions, and security. In general, local authorities have the same powers and obligations related to the performance of the tasks delegated to them by the state, notwithstanding the significant differences between them in terms of territory, population size, or settlement structure.

A moderate level of autonomy characterizes the local government system in Bulgaria. According to Local Autonomy Index data, Bulgaria ranks 13th among 39 European countries on the scale of general local autonomy, which includes organizational, legal, and financial aspects of autonomy, and range of responsibilities (Ladner et al. 2019: 240). It should be noted that Bulgaria is one of the countries in Central and Eastern Europe whose index of local autonomy ranking increased significantly between 1990 and 2014 (the period covered by LAI data). Although Bulgarian municipalities have a long history and traditions, they have been the most viable in recent decades. The autonomy of the municipalities was absent during the time of Communist rule in Bulgaria (1944–1989). During this period, local democracy and free elections were nonexistent. There was only territorial-administrative division. The active processes moving toward real fiscal decentralization of the municipalities started only after 2002.

In Bulgaria, the levels of trust in the mayor and municipal councilors are higher than in the members of the National Assembly (parliament) (Transparency International Bulgaria 2020). According to the recent opinion polls, the only institutions that are more trusted than distrusted are the head of state (59%), the EU (47%), and the local authorities (44%). This is also confirmed by the value of the local integrity index for Bulgaria from 2017. The local government received an average score of 3.29 (compared to a maximum value of 5).[1] The highest rating was ascribed to the role of the mayor (3.89), followed by the municipal administration (3.79), and the municipal council (3.39). In comparison, the score for political parties was 2.99, and for the media it was only 2.78.

Although the municipal council performs local legislative functions, the role of the executive mayor is much more pronounced, as it practically implements the local policies as defined by the council. In certain situations, the municipal council may suspend an administrative act of the mayor and appeal to the respective administrative court. In turn, the mayor has the right to a one-off veto suspending the municipal council's decision. Yet, this is a relatively weak veto, as during the repeat discussion of the contested decision, the municipal council may confirm it.

The type of horizontal power relations at the local level in Bulgaria is closest to the strong mayor model (Heinelt et al. 2018). The 'strength' of the directly elected mayor is usually enforced by the majority supporting his or her proposals on the council. The mayor is the head of the local administration and responsible for human resources. He/she has the right to appoint the deputy mayors and the secretary of the municipality; he/she also submits the draft budget of the municipality. The position is also significantly strengthened by additional prerogatives defined under various national laws (Stefanova 2018: 94–96).

The local elections

Elections of mayors and municipal councilors have been held in Bulgaria since the democratic transition, with the first local elections organized in October 1991 simultaneously with the elections for the 36th National Assembly. Although local elections are held regularly every four years, there was no synchronization between the election cycles at the local and national levels due to the early parliamentary elections. Between 2011 and 2019 in Bulgaria, three early parliamentary elections were held. In this situation, the results of the local elections are perceived as a 'poll' preceding the parliamentary elections, and their outcome can be an indicator of local attitudes toward the main political forces.

Compared to other types of elections, local elections are significant for the citizens. If we compare the average voter turnout for local elections (55.6%) with the average turnout for other elections, it is close to the rates noted in the parliamentary elections (60%) and the presidential elections (55.7%). Local elections attract significantly more voters than European elections (35.3%). According to the opinion polls, citizens believe that it is essential to vote in the local elections because they assume that if the municipal officials are sufficiently responsible and incorruptible, they can significantly influence the development of the locality (Alfaresearch 2003).

Local elections are held simultaneously in all municipalities on the same non-working day (traditionally on Sunday, involving a second round of mayoral elections one week later). A run-off is required in the municipalities if none of the candidates for mayor won more than 50% of the votes in the first round (the two candidates with the highest results participate in the second round). The four-year term of office has not been modified since 1991; there are also no term limits in the case of local elected offices.[2]

The first complex Electoral Code was adopted in Bulgaria in 2011. It consolidated the provisions of the Act on Election of Members of Parliament, Presidential Election Act, Act on Election of Members of the European Parliament from the Republic of Bulgaria, and Local Elections Act. An entirely new code was adopted in 2014, and it follows the recommendations of the Venice Commission to a greater extent. The main changes include the introduction of preferential voting for municipal councilors, optional machine voting, and a new nomination procedure of the Central Election Commission.

Since 2011, the Central Election Commission (CEC) (*Tsentralna izbiratelna komisiya*) has been the independent state body that conducts all types of elections and national and local referendums. The CEC is also responsible for the appointment of the district and municipal election commissions. Any party or coalition registered by the CEC and the particular municipal electoral commissions can participate in the elections for municipal councilors and mayors. Additionally, 'initiative committees' can be set up to nominate independent candidates in local elections. Their registration is carried out only by the municipal election commissions.

The mayoral and council elections, although simultaneous, are loosely linked: there is no requirement for the mayoral candidates to submit a list of municipal councilors or vice versa. It is not unusual for a political party other than the one that supports the mayor to form a majority in the council. Divided local government can have negative consequences for local development, as the council may reject the municipal budget, request changes that do not correspond to the mayor's program, or refuse to agree on the municipality's long-term debt.

There is no procedure for recalling a mayor in Bulgaria. The powers of the mayor may be terminated due to the inability to perform his/her duties for more than six months (caused by illness), effective criminal conviction, or election as an MP. The position of mayor or municipal councilor cannot be combined with the position of MP, minister, deputy minister, district governor, or deputy district governor.

Characteristics of the electoral system in Bulgaria

The electoral system in Bulgaria has undergone changes in recent years, yet its main characteristics remained unchanged – two-round majority voting in mayoral elections and the list proportional representation system in the election of municipal councils. One of the most crucial changes was the introduction of preferential voting in 2014, which 'opened up' the previously used closed-list PR system. The seat allocation formula in municipal council elections has also been changed.

Bulgarian citizens who have reached the age of 18 and have lived for at least six months in the respective settlement prior to the election have the right to elect municipal councilors and mayors (domicile principle). Voters who have changed their address registration to another settlement in Bulgaria within six months before the local elections have the right to vote under their previous address registration, where they have been included on the list of voters. The Election Code does not allow Bulgarian citizens permanently or temporarily residing abroad to vote in local elections. Since 2007, all EU citizens eligible to vote in their home countries may also participate in the local elections in Bulgaria. Since that time, every citizen of an EU member state has had the right to be elected as a municipal councilor if he/she has lived for at least the preceding six months in the respective settlement.

Mayors in Bulgaria are directly elected under a two-round majority system. The candidate who received the absolute majority of votes in the first round is considered elected. When none of the candidates is elected in the first round, a runoff between the two leading contenders is held seven days from the date of the first round. When electing a mayor, local voters are motivated not only by the candidate's political affiliation but to a large extent by his/her personal qualities. The mayor must be known to his/her constituents and be aware of the needs of the local population (Georgiev 2009: 71). According to a survey conducted in September 2019, citizens listed the following qualities that a mayor should possess: honest and correct, not corrupt, knowledge of the people and their needs, and will work for the municipality (Trend 2019).

The number of municipal councilors varies between 11 (in the smallest municipalities) and 61 (in Sofia). It depends on the number of residents of a given municipality (Table 33.1). Due to the decline in the population of Bulgaria in recent years, there has been a decrease in the number of elected municipal councilors. The total number of elected municipal councilors decreased from 6,996 in 1995 to 5,135 in 2019.

Municipal councilors are elected with the use of an open-list PR system (OLPR). The seats are allocated between lists with the Hare method (this method replaced the d'Hondt rule used until 2007; the change aimed to achieve greater proportionality in the allocation of seats). A separate electoral quota is calculated for each municipality by dividing the total number of valid votes by the number of seats on the respective municipal council. The council elections are held at large, that is, the territory of each municipality is one multiseat constituency.

As in other open-list systems, preferential votes cast for candidates are used to allocate seats within each list at the next step. The number of candidates placed on a list of candidates may not exceed the size of the municipal council. Each independent candidate forms a stand-alone candidate list. Coalitions run in the elections with a joint list of candidates; coalition parties may not register their own lists or candidates. Since 2014, voters have been able to indicate their personal preference in the council elections. They may select one candidate from the list of candidates, and the distribution of preferential votes may rearrange the order of the candidates during seat allocation. According to CEC data, during the latest local elections, 44% of the voters cast preferential votes. The opportunity for preferential voting allows citizens to express support not only for a party but also for a particular candidate. The

Table 33.1 Number of municipal councilors by number of residents in a local territorial unit in Bulgaria

Population	Number of municipal councilors
Up to 5,000	11
5,000–10,000	13
10,001–20,000	17
20,001–30,000	21
30,001–50,000	29
50,001–75,000	33
75,001–100,000	37
100,001–160,000	41
>160,000	51
Sofia	61

preference becomes effective when the share of preference votes for an individual candidate is not less than 7%.

The ballots used in local elections include the option 'I do not support anyone', which is analogous to the 'none of the above' (NOTA) option that appears in other electoral systems. The votes cast for this option are considered valid, but practically they do not affect the election results. When election results are reported, these votes are not taken into account for the determination of the electoral quota. The consequences of NOTA votes are slightly different in mayoral elections; in this case, the candidate must receive more than half of all valid votes to win.

Although, according to the Election Code, voting is mandatory in Bulgaria and should be performed in person by the voter, Decision no. 3/2017 of the Constitutional Court declared the sanctions for noncompliance (removal from the voters' register and the requirement to apply for reregistration in the next elections) were unconstitutional.

During recent years in Bulgaria, the idea of introducing remote electronic and/or machine voting[3] has been widely discussed. These voting opportunities are equivalent to voting using a paper ballot. There is a legislative option only for machine voting at this stage, but it has not been used in local elections.

In 2015, a national referendum was held in the country on the following question: 'Do you support the possibility of remote electronic voting in elections and referendums?' This referendum had a turnout of 39.7%. A total of 69.5% of the voters supported the introduction of electronic voting. However, the low voter turnout has not led to the mandatory introduction of electronic voting. According to the CEC's simulations of remote electronic voting, it was found that remote voting is fast and convenient for the voters. The risk of casting an invalid vote is minimized and the votes are processed more quickly. However, the risk of cyberattacks, which could lead to vote rigging, is a serious consideration. Finally, the CEC recommended postponing the introduction of remote electronic voting and providing the opportunity for testing and phased implementation of a remote electronic voting system (Central Election Commission 2017).

Local election outcomes

The citizens' interest in local elections has marked periods of rise and fall. The first democratic local elections in Bulgaria mobilized the citizens, and voter turnout reached 84%. Later, participation rates declined for both national and local elections (Table 33.2). For the period 1991–2019, the average turnout for local elections is estimated to be about 55.6%, while that for national (parliamentary) elections is 62.0%.

In the recent local elections, turnout exceeding 50% is reported when voting is coupled and the stakes are higher. In 2011, both presidential elections and the first round of local elections were held simultaneously, and voter turnout was 51.6%. In 2015, the first round of local elections was held simultaneously with a national referendum; the turnout exceeded 53%.

There is a negative relationship between the population size of a municipality and voter turnout for local elections (Figure 33.1). Participation rates in the largest cities are much lower than those in small municipalities. In the most recent local elections, the 76 smallest Bulgarian municipalities (with a population of up to 6,000 residents) reported an average turnout of 67.8%; the smallest municipality reported one of the highest voter turnouts of 86%. In the cities with a population over 100,000, the turnout was rather low and varied between 39% and 45% (almost 43% in Sofia).

In the 2019 local elections, there was considerable competition in both the council and mayoral races. There were 29,477 registered candidates for councilor (on average 111 per

Table 33.2 Turnout for local and parliamentary elections in Bulgaria during the period 1991–2019

Date	Turnout (parliamentary elections)	Date	Turnout (local elections)
13/10/1991	83.9%	13/10/1991[1]	83.9%
18/12/1994	75.3%	29/10/1995	57.9%
19/4/1997	62.4%	16/10/1999	51.6%
6/17/2001	67.0%	26/10/2003	47.0%
25/6/2005	55.7%	28/10/2007	49.8%
5/7/2009	60.2%	23/10/2011[2]	51.6%
12/5/2013	51.3%	25/10/2015[3]	53.6%
5/10/2014	48.7%	27/10/2019	49.8%
26/3/2017	54.1%		

[1] Held simultaneously with the elections for the 36th National Assembly.
[2] Held simultaneously with presidential elections.
[3] Held simultaneously with a national referendum.

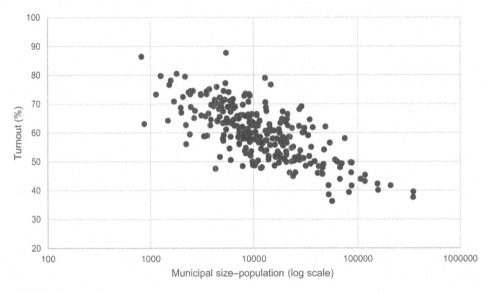

Figure 33.1 Voter turnout for the 2019 Bulgarian local elections by municipality size

municipality) and 1,253 for mayor (4.7 per municipality). The competition was the most intense in the largest cities, where a particularly large number of mayoral candidates was observed (more than 10 candidates). However, the first round was often decisive. In 2019, a runoff was required in 105 municipalities (39.6% of all cases), and there were only five municipalities in which there was only one mayoral candidate.

The data demonstrate that in recent years the number of candidates running for local offices is increasing. The local patterns of party competition are relatively complex, as there are various electoral coalitions, some of which unite parties at the local level that are in opposition to each other at the national level. In the larger municipalities, there is also a visible trend of increased competition within lists and between the individual candidates (CEC 2020).

The incumbency ratio in mayoral elections is relatively high. In 2019, this ratio was 74.3% (197 out of 265 mayors won their second or higher consecutive term of office). One could also find mayors serving seven or eight consecutive terms. Usually, the incumbency advantage is explained by the personal qualities and effectiveness of candidates running for reelection. There are also municipal councilors who have been elected for the eighth time in a row, and council chairpersons who have led the council for six consecutive terms. The incumbency advantage is related to the importance of a personal vote: many long-term incumbents have been supported by different parties during their consecutive terms of office. In many cases, an incumbent who was initially supported by a party ran for reelection and won subsequent terms as an independent candidate (CEC 2020).

The local elections in Bulgaria demonstrate an exceptional variety of candidates – nominees from the main national parties, local initiative committees, and local coalitions and independent candidates. The participation of small nonparliamentary parties is also noticeable. The position of various parties in the 2019 local elections is presented in Table 33.3.

The data show that the party with a majority at the parliamentary level (GERB) also performed the best during the local elections in 2019, receiving more than 30% of the aggregate votes. BSP and DPS, which are in opposition to the ruling majority, ranked second and third. These three are the only national parties that nominated mayoral candidates in more than half of Bulgarian municipalities. Nonetheless, most of the parties represented in the National Assembly nominated candidates for mayor in the larger municipalities, where local party structures are more developed.

In Bulgaria, there are no gender quota regulations aiming to increase the representation of women in the local government. Nonetheless, the gap between the share of male and female councilors and mayors is still large. The situation is similar at the national level: the share of female councilors after the 2019 elections (over 27%) is only slightly higher than the share of

Table 33.3 Share of all seats on the local councils won by the main parties in the last local elections in Bulgaria, 2019

	% of municipalities where running	% of municipalities where represented	% of seats on local councils	% of (aggregate) votes in local elections	% of mayors affiliated with the party
GERB	91.0	96.7	33.9	30.7	46.0
BSP	88.0	87.5	19.0	10.1	10.2
DPS	68.0	54.7	16.0	9.4	14.3
ABV	20.0	6.4	0.7	2.1	0.8
VMRO	42.0	23.0	3.2	1.4	1.9
Volya	60.0	10.2	0.8	n/a	0.0
Ataka	35.0	2.6	0.3	1.8	0.0
LC	65.0	59.0	12.8	n/a	14.4
IC	13.0	1.5	0.1	n/a	7.2
Other parties	94.0	57.0	13.3	n/a	5.3
Total			100.0		100.0

Notes: Local coalitions (LC) may be formed for participation in the elections for municipal councilors and mayors only by parties and coalitions registered with the Central Election Commission. Initiative committees (IC) may propose only one independent candidate for municipal councilor for registration with the municipal election commission. Only the results for single-party lists are included.

Table 33.4 Share of female elected mayors (1999–2019) and municipal councilors (2015–2019) in Bulgaria

	1999		2003		2007		2011		2015		2019	
	Number	%	Number	%	Number	%	Number	%	Number	%	Number	%
Mayors	12	4.6	23	8.8	25	9.5	28	10.6	34	12.8	37	14.0
Councilors	n/a	n/a	n/a	n/a	n/a	n/a	n/a	n/a	1345	26.0	1394	27.2

female MPs elected in 2017 (almost 24%). Although the precise data are scattered, one can observe a gradual increase in women's participation in local politics (Table 33.4)[4] in recent years. The share of female mayors in Bulgaria has increased from 4.6% in 1999 to nearly 14% 20 years later. The presence of women on municipal councils is about double that among mayors. During the last two terms of office, the number of women holding municipal councilor positions increased by nearly 1.2%.

Discussion and summary

The local electoral system in Bulgaria has developed gradually over the last three decades. The most significant changes 'opened' the initial rules in various respects. The lists for council elections were 'opened', as the system switched from CLPR to OLPR in 2014: voters were granted the opportunity to elect councilors with preference votes. Along with this change, the local electoral system also departed from the CLPR system used in the parliamentary elections until 2014. The seat allocation system also changed toward more proportionality – the d'Hondt rule was replaced by use of the Hare quota. The electorate become more numerous: since Bulgaria's accession to the EU, citizens of other member states can run for municipal councilor and vote for mayors and councilors. Nonetheless, the direct mayoral elections, the two-round majority system in mayoral elections, and the proportional rule in council elections remained the stable elements in the institutional context.

Over the years, there has been a decline in voter turnout for local elections. However, relatively high participation rates are observed in small and medium-sized municipalities. In this context, the introduction of electronic and machine voting has been defined as an opportunity to increase turnout. Yet, the discussion on the introduction of new voting methods in Bulgaria remains open.

Notes

1 The local integrity index is the product of an annual comparative survey of the key institutions and social actors that build the system of integrity and accountability at the local level. It provides a comparative overview of the anticorruption capacity and the role and importance of the municipal councils, mayors, local administration, political parties, judiciary, police, media, business, and civil society. The study covers 27 larger municipalities in Bulgaria (district capitals). More information may be found at http://lisi.transparency.bg/.
2 In addition to the mayor of the municipality, there are also other elected executive positions in the Bulgarian local government system. The mayor of an urban district is elected by the residents of only three largest municipalities in Bulgaria – Sofia (includes 24 urban districts), Plovdiv (six urban districts), and Varna (five urban districts). The mayor of a mayoralty (a submunicipal unit) is elected only by the residents of the particular settlement within a larger municipality. Both executive offices have significantly

limited powers. They include implementation of the municipal budget for its part of the respective municipality, organization of public works, infrastructure maintenance, local environment protection, and other functions established by national law or by a decision of the municipal council.

3 Remote electronic voting involves the use of electronic means for the communication and processing of results through a specially designed, secure electronic system, eliminating the need for the voter to visit a polling station. Machine voting means a voting system using special machines to register and count the votes, which requires the voter to visit a polling station.

4 It should be noted that there was no official register for the gender distribution of mayors and municipal councilors before 2015. Part of the data has been assembled from various sources: the websites of individual municipalities and information from the National Association of Municipalities in the Republic of Bulgaria (NAMRB).

References

Alfaresearch (2003). Obshtestveno mnenie (online). Available at: https://alpharesearch.bg/userfiles/file/AlphaResearch2003.pdf (Accessed: 10 September 2020).

Central Electoral Commission for Local Elections (2020). Report: Analysis of the conducted simulations of remote electronic voting. Available at: www.cik.bg/bg/simulation_deg (Accessed: 08 September 2020).

Georgiev, L. (2009). Da badesh kmet. *Ikonomika*, 3, 68–74.

Heinelt, H. et al. (2018). *Political Leaders and Changing Local Democracy The European Mayor*. London: Palgrave Macmillan.

Ladner, A. et al. (2019). *Patterns of Local Autonomy in Europe*. Cham: Palgrave National register of populated places of Republic of Bulgaria (online). Available at: www.nsi.bg/nrnm/index.php?ezik=en&f=4&date1=01.01.1990&date=31.12.1995&unit_kind=4_2&evt_kind=2 (Accessed: 08 September 2020).

Stefanova, M. (2018). Obshtinite v Bulgaria – mestnata vlast i samoupravlenie. *Publichni Politiki.bg*, 2, 84–107.

Transparency International Bulgaria (2020). Mestna sistema za pochtenost (online). Available at: http://lisi.transparency.bg/years/2017/ (Accessed: 10 September 2020)

Trend (2019). *Idealinyat kmet* (online). Available at: https://rctrend.bg/project/%d0%b8%d0%b4%d0%b5%d0%b0%d0%bb%d0%bd%d0%b8%d1%8f%d1%82-%d0%ba%d0%bc%d0%b5%d1%82/ (Accessed: 20 September 2020).

Vladimirova, T. & Naydenov, L. (2011). *Mestni finansi*. Varna: IK Steno.

34
Croatia
Games of local democracy in the shadow of national politics

Mihovil Škarica and Tijana Vukojičić Tomić

Basic features of the local government system

The present system of local government in Croatia was established at the beginning of 1993 and currently comprises 556 municipalities – 128 urban (*gradovi*) and 428 rural municipalities (*općine*) – at the first level and 20 counties (*županije*) at the second level. As it is the capital, the City of Zagreb has been granted dual status as both a municipality and a county. On average, Croatian municipalities are rather small; the average number of inhabitants is 7,706 (the median is 2,983). The establishment and regulation of submunicipal units belong to the prerogatives of municipal councils. As of now, there are 3,809 elected submunicipal councils in 380 local units.

After a period of a centralized and hierarchical system of public governance in the 1990s, the institutional position of local government improved in 2000–2001 when constitutional amendments embraced the modern European concept of local self-government based on subsidiarity, acknowledged the general nature of local competences, and provided guarantees for a wide scope of local government affairs. However, the decentralization wave that followed has been evaluated as limited, confusing, and hesitant because it covered only a small part of the municipalities and did not widen local autonomy at all (Koprić & Đulabić 2018). Asymmetrical decentralization continued in 2005 when larger towns (>35,000) and counties' capital towns (altogether 26 municipalities) were entrusted with some additional competences. Despite the decentralization efforts, Croatia has remained a centralized country with functionally differentiated municipalities in which the share of local government budgets in general government expenditure has remained around 15%, and their share in GDP has stagnated at 6–7%. A recent comparative study (Ladner et al. 2019) ranks Croatia as 24th among 39 European countries according to the Local Autonomy Index for the period 1990–2014, which places Croatia in a group of countries with a medium degree of local autonomy. A collective executive model was in place until 2009, when it was replaced by a strong mayor model of local government systems, following the introduction of the direct election of mayors (Heinelt et al. 2018). Since then, the balance in horizontal power relations has gradually skewed toward mayors, as they acquired complete control over local administration, municipal companies, and other institutions and have been granted a dominant role in the budgetary process (Koprić & Škarica 2017).

Despite enormous disparities among municipalities regarding their size, level of development, and overall capacity, territorial consolidation reforms have not been on the agenda of any government in the past three decades, nor have they been seriously advocated by any major political party. The complementary influence of two circumstances has been of vital importance for this situation: the negative memory of large, bureaucratized, and nonresponsive Socialist municipalities and the reluctance of political elites to substantially reduce the number of available political seats and offices at the local level. Intermunicipal cooperation is underdeveloped and lacking the straightforward support of national policies. It is mostly limited to the joint ownership of municipal companies and other local service-providing organizations (Škarica & Giljević 2016). As a result, the supplementary, supervisory, and coordinating roles of counties toward municipalities have been increasing (Škarica 2020).

According to the 2018 Eurobarometer survey, a low level of public trust characterizes all territorial levels and institutions in Croatia. Only 23% of citizens trust their local and regional authorities, which is significantly lower than the EU average (54%), but even this level of trust is still higher than the trust in national institutions (18% parliament, 19% government; European Commission 2018).

Local elections and their relationship with national elections

The first democratic (multiparty) local elections were held in 1990, more than a year before the proclamation of independence of the state, and, for the first and only time, simultaneously with parliamentary elections. With the introduction of the new, two-tier local government system in 1993, all local government elections take place on the same day, and since 2001 they have been held on the third Sunday of May, every four years. Therefore, the turnout rate has been more or less the same for both tiers of local government, as well as for their representative and executive institutions. In most municipalities, even the elections for submunicipal councils usually take place on the same day. Accordingly, the average voter participates in five different elections at once. Early elections can be called in cases explicitly prescribed by law. The councilors and mayors who take their seats after an early election complete the remaining term of office until the next regular elections. Instances of early local elections have traditionally been quite uncommon, but during the current electoral cycle even more so. There have been only five such cases in the whole of the 2017–2020 period. All elections at all territorial levels (except at the submunicipal level) are organized by the National Electoral Commission, an independent body that appoints and coordinates electoral commissions in each county and municipality.

From 1997 to 2013, local elections took place a year and a half after parliamentary ones, but the recent early parliamentary elections in September 2016 brought them closer together. The previous timing of local elections contributed to their greater recognition, visibility, and media coverage as they were perceived as a midterm test for national parties. Parties of the national opposition often looked at local elections as an opportunity to bounce back and to consolidate their position for the next parliamentary elections. In this regard, they were quite successful, as ruling parties at the national level traditionally scored worse in local elections. Unfortunately, this has led to the dominance of nonlocal and purely ideological topics and issues during the local electoral campaigns, especially in larger municipalities. The current timing of local elections has not affected the mobilization of voters, as the turnout rate has remained the same. It seems that the electoral outcomes of the last local elections deviated much less from the results of the preceding parliamentary elections, as the national ruling party scored similar or even better results locally (Raos 2017). A tentative conclusion may be drawn: the closer in time the local elections are to the parliamentary ones, the more they mirror the results of the latter. The interdependence of local and parliamentary elections also stems from the substantial degree of overlap in personnel between local and national political actors and elites. Mayors and influential councilors have regularly stood as candidates for parliamentary elections, and members of parliament (especially from the opposition) have regularly competed for local political offices. Due to the developments just described, perceptions, and low turnout rates, local elections have remained second-order elections (Reif & Schmitt 1980) throughout the whole period of national independence.

The evolution of the local electoral system and its formal rules

All Croatian citizens above the age of 18 and officially residing in Croatia have the right to vote and to stand as candidates in both national and local elections. In national elections, these rights are expanded to nonresident Croatian citizens worldwide, but to exercise them requires prior registration on electoral rolls. This makes the electorate for national elections bigger than the electorate for local elections, but usually only by 3–4%. In local elections, these rights are exercised by secret ballot and only in the municipality of the voter's or candidate's permanent residence. Voting in either election is not compulsory. Non-Croatian citizens from EU member states residing either permanently or temporarily in a municipality holding an election are able to vote and to stand as candidates for local councils, but not for local executive office, parliament, or the presidency of the Republic. This opportunity has had only a marginal effect on the size of the electorate: in the 2017 elections, only 25 non-Croatian EU citizens officially registered on the electoral rolls.

Since 2013, the number of seats on local councils has been strictly fixed by law. Prior to this, the number of seats was determined by the municipalities themselves but within a legally provided range, which differed according to their size. Although proclaimed as a measure of rationalization of the political system in the midst of economic crisis, this change reduced the total number of seats by only 1.3%. The number of councilors to be elected depends on the population of the municipality, varying from seven in those with fewer than 500 inhabitants to 51 in the City of Zagreb. Naturally, the ratio of the representation of smaller councils is much higher: while in the smallest municipality (Civljane) there are only 34 eligible voters per council seat, in the City of Zagreb this ratio is 13,571 voters per seat. During the last local elections in 2017, a total of 7,501 seats were filled (including minority representatives, this issue will be discussed later).

The local electoral system is uniform and applies equally to all municipalities. While its rules were frequently changed during the 1990s, it has been rather stable since the beginning of the millennium. The first local elections in 1990 applied the same election rules as parliamentary elections – a majority/plurality two-round system.[1] The elections in 1993 and 1997 were conducted according to the parallel mixed electoral system. In 1993, one half of the councilors were elected by proportional representation, while other half were elected in single-member districts (FPTP). In the 1997 local elections, the share of seats allocated by the proportional representation system increased to three-quarters. The full application of proportional representation with closed lists and of municipalities as single electoral units was introduced in 2001, and all subsequent elections have applied the PR system.

The gradual shift to a proportional system suggests the intention to create conditions for smaller and local political parties to win seats and to influence local decision-making. Furthermore, the stabilization of big national parties and their electorates has allowed local party leaders to be less dependent on individually recognizable candidates. In this context, a proportional system with closed lists has allowed for more effective control of candidates and potential councilors by party leaders. Closed lists make it difficult for voters to identify certain candidates and their political programs, which may cause the depersonalization of local politics (Koprić et al. 2015). This is why the introduction of preferential voting has been the subject of public debate in Croatia for some time and has already been introduced in elections for both the European and national parliaments in 2013 and 2015, respectively. Lists that receive more than 5% of the votes may participate in the division of seats (a 5% threshold), while the number of seats allocated to a list is calculated by the d'Hondt method. This method does not favor small parties or independent lists and stimulates coalitions, particularly when combined with the small size of a council. Due to the high natural threshold, in a number of cases, even lists that obtained more than 5% of the votes did not participate in the distribution of seats. Councilors are elected for a four-year term of office with nonimperative mandates, and they cannot be recalled during the term.

The direct election of mayors and county governors was introduced in 2009 following great public and political support for such a reform. Deputy mayors are also directly elected on the same ticket as mayors, but they do not necessarily represent the same political party. Despite their direct legitimacy, they do not have any legally guaranteed competences of their own. In smaller municipalities (<10,000) one deputy is elected, while in larger ones there are two deputies. In the 2017 local elections, a total of 556 mayors and 694 deputies were elected (including minority representatives, see discussion to follow).

Mayors are elected in a majority two-round system. The candidate that has more than 50% of the total votes is elected. If none of the candidates receives more than 50% of votes in the first round, a second round is organized two weeks after the first involving the two most successful candidates from the first round, in which case the candidate who obtains more votes wins. Mayoral candidates are not obliged to present a candidacy list for the council or to affiliate with any of the competing lists, but this rarely happens and usually with nonpartisan candidates (Koprić & Vukojičić Tomić 2013). Legislation provides the possibility of a recall referendum: it can be initiated by either 20% of eligible voters or by the council – a decision that requires a specific, two-thirds majority of all councilors. In the referendum, the mayor is recalled by a majority of valid votes, but only if this majority represents at least one-third of the total number of eligible voters in the municipality. Rather restrictive provisions have contributed to an arguably nonexistent referendum practice: only two recall referenda have been held since 2009, but in neither of them was the mayor in question actually recalled due to low voter turnout. The number of terms of office for mayors is not limited, although public discussions regarding this issue do emerge sporadically. Because mayors usually occupy approximately 15% of seats in the national parliament, any reform aiming to restrict their powers or question their position is unlikely.[2]

As for candidacy, registered political parties may propose a list of candidates. In addition, a group of citizens (voters) may propose a list of candidates, but it must provide a sufficient number of citizens' signatures depending on the size of the municipality, which varies between 25 and 2,500. For the election of mayors and their deputies, political parties and voters are both obliged to collect voters' signatures; the number of signatures again varies depending on the size of the unit, between 25 and 5,000. Candidacy (for both representative and executive offices) is explicitly forbidden for active police or military personnel (including civil servants in the respective ministries) and for those sentenced to at least six months in prison (even if suspended) for a number of specific criminal offenses that are enumerated in the Electoral Code.

Cumul des mandats is only partially restricted, and further restrictions have not been debated nor planned. The office of councilor is incompatible with the same function in another municipality, a civil service or mayoral office in his/her municipality, or a number of national executive offices. On the other hand, councilors may simultaneously be members of representative bodies at higher or lower levels of government or of the national parliament. The same rules apply to the mayor. One may simultaneously perform a representative function at the county and/or national level and a mayoral function. This not only opens up room for a potential conflict of interest and for the channeling of state budget resources into the parent unit of local government (pork-barreling) but also potentially diminishes the quality of the political representation (Raos 2013).

The electoral outcomes: an ongoing process of localization of local politics

In the last 20 years, the turnout rate for local elections has been rather low as it has never exceeded 50% (Table 34.1). Turnout has always been lower for local than for national elections, although the latter have also experienced a significant decrease in citizen participation. With the exception of 2005, the turnout rate for several recent local elections has been surprisingly stable at around 47%. The average turnout rate across eight rounds of local elections is 56.1%, while the average for ten parliamentary elections is 65.8%. Low turnout rates for local elections are not very surprising considering the low level of political decentralization. Direct elections for mayor in 2009 did boost voters' participation in comparison to previous elections, but nowhere near its peak rates in the 1990s.

The size of municipalities is an important predictor of voter turnout as their size is inversely correlated to their turnout rates. Local elections attract a larger proportion of voters in smaller municipalities, as indicated by the turnout rate in groups of municipalities of different size (Table 34.2).

In the 2017 elections, 2,494 lists competed for seats on 556 local councils – 4.5 lists per municipality. There were 35,862 candidates competing for 7,414 seats on local councils – 4.8 candidates per seat. Mayoral elections were less competitive. There were 1,716 candidates in 2017 (3.1 per municipality), but with a significant difference between urban and rural municipalities: 4.2 and 2.8 candidates on average, respectively. Uncontested elections for local councils happen rarely. In 2017, only nine (1.6%) municipalities had only a single list filing candidates for the council. Unopposed mayoral elections occur more frequently, as these elections featured

Table 34.1 Voter turnout for local and national elections in Croatia since 1990

Local elections		Parliamentary elections	
Election date	Voter turnout (%)	Election date	Voter turnout (%)
1990	84.5	1990	84.5
1993	64.0	1992	75.6
1997	71.2	1995	68.8
2001	46.8	2000	74.5
2005	40.8	2003	69.1
2009	47.0	2007	63.1
2013	47.3	2011	61.9
2017	47.0	2015	60.8
		2016	52.6
		2020	47.0

Source: Authors, based on National Electoral Commission data

Table 34.2 Voter turnout in municipalities of different size in Croatia

Size of municipality	Number of municipalities	Turnout %
0–2,999	283	53.4
3,000–4,999	111	51.2
5,000–9,999	88	47.5
>10,000	74	45.0
All municipalities	556	47.0

Source: Authors, based on National Electoral Commission data

Table 34.3 Number of mayoral candidates and candidate lists in the last three cycles of local elections in Croatia

	2009	2013	2017
Average number of mayoral candidates (urban municipalities)	3.8	4.4	4.2
Average number of mayoral candidates (rural municipalities)	3.4	3.3	2.8
Average number of lists (urban municipalities)	6.5	7.5	6.4
Average number of lists (rural municipalities)	4.8	4.8	3.9

Source: GONG (2017: 5)

a single candidate in 45 (8%) municipalities. As can be expected, cases of uncontested elections of mayor happen mostly in rural and rather small municipalities. In general, trends suggest a slight decrease in political competition in local elections in comparison with the previous two electoral cycles (Table 34.3). To a certain extent, this can be explained by negative demographic trends – the total population of the country has been steadily decreasing since the 1990s – and also by the unfulfilled promises of decentralization, which have negatively affected the political engagement of citizens at the local level of government. The described trajectory of political competition is also reflected in the frequency of second rounds in mayoral elections. In 2009, a second round took place in 40% of the municipalities, while in 2017 it was held in 28% of them. Nevertheless, the second round regularly occurs in Croatia's largest cities, so the majority of the population faces two rounds of mayoral elections. The motivation of voters to participate in the second round is considerably lower, as second rounds of mayoral elections have recorded even lower turnout rates: 32% in 2009 and 41% in both 2013 and 2017.

In 2017, 83% of incumbent mayors ran for reelection, and 86% of them won their election. In total, 71.5% of standing mayors were reelected, which is a rather high incumbent ratio. In the 2009 local elections, this ratio stood at 66% (Koprić & Vukojičić Tomić 2013), and it seems that direct elections contributed to successful reelections. Mayors have always been the dominant actors in local politics, and direct elections have only solidified such a position. As a rule, they score better results than their accompanying list for council.

The Croatian political scene is rather fragmented, with a great number of political parties. At the beginning of 2020, there were 167 officially registered parties, 16 of which entered parliament in the 2016 elections. More than 100 competed in the 2017 local elections, and approximately two-thirds are represented on local councils with at least one seat. Coalition lists are quite common and popular, even with the largest parties. In the 2017 local elections, 25% of all lists were coalition lists, 20% were nonpartisan (independent), and 55% were individual party lists. Traditionally, local elections have been dominated by big national parties (Koprić et al.

2015; Koprić 2011; Omejec 2002), although this dominance has been recently challenged by a multitude of local nonpartisan lists and local parties that participated successfully in the 2017 local elections (Table 34.4).[3] However, the established parties still won more than 80% of the votes, council seats, and mayoral offices.

The centralized environment and the dependence of local government on higher levels perpetuate the dominance of the established parties at the local level. National support (political, administrative, and financial) for local plans and projects is more likely when the same party controls all of the positions along the vertical axis of the territorial governance system. Although not proven, this argument has been explicitly used by local members of national ruling parties during electoral campaigns. There is a substantial difference between the results of the two biggest national parties (HDZ and SDP). While HDZ traditionally scores better results locally, the success of SDP in local elections is almost two times worse than in national elections. A couple of older parties with an extensive infrastructure of local branches (HSS and HNS) have scored significantly better results in local than in parliamentary elections.

Although the introduction of the proportional electoral system in 2001 and the direct election of mayors in 2009 were supposed to boost the success of nonpartisan (independent) political actors, their success in council elections has improved only slightly. Their proportion of all council seats recorded in the last two decades is as follows: 2001, 7.9%; 2005, 9.9%; 2009, 10.4%; 2013, 10.8%; 2017, 11.1%. Independent mayoral candidates have been more successful: while in 2009 they won in only 8% of municipalities and in 2013 only 11% of them, in the 2017 local elections they doubled their results of the first direct elections, winning mayoral elections in 16% of municipalities. According to some authors, this is due to the relatively high threshold and weak voter turnout in most Croatian municipalities, as party members and supporters are more easily mobilized and are more reliable (Koprić et al. 2015, 2017). Higher turnout rates are positively correlated with the success of nonpartisan mayoral candidates, but the size of a municipality is not systematically related to the success of independent candidates. Previous research has shown that independent actors have been more successful in coastal and ethnically mixed parts of the country (Koprić 2011). However, independent and local actors put together were the second strongest contenders in the last local elections. Due to rather discriminatory rules on the candidacy procedure, finances, and overall visibility, many local lists have recently been registered as parties but under names of obvious local significance, often containing an 'independent list' or the name of the municipality or leading person.[4] This trend has become particularly frequent in the last decade in which more than 40 such parties were established.

The majority of independent lists and local parties do not affiliate with any ideology and reject being positioned on the right-left political spectrum, preferring to emphasize their focus on local problems 'that know no ideology'. Still, some of them were formed around notable dissidents from major national parties, and their ideology is present and known, at least implicitly. Independent local actors are often perceived as those capable of changing the dynamics of national politics as well, and quite often this perception matches their ambition. In the 2015 parliamentary elections, a platform that connected various local lists and independent candidates (MOST) won 12% of seats in parliament, thus becoming the third largest individual grouping, which led to their short-term participation in a coalition government with HDZ in 2016 and 2017. This platform has advocated a wide array of public sector reforms and has specifically pledged decentralization, anticorruption, and rationalization of the public sector.

The proportion of women on municipal councils has gradually increased over the years (Table 34.5). A gender quota of at least 40% of the underrepresented gender on electoral lists was legally introduced in 2008, and the increase in the women's share is certainly a direct consequence of this obligation. For the first time, this quota was fully achieved in the 2017 local

Table 34.4 Share of all seats on local councils received by parliamentary parties in the last local elections (2017) in Croatia

Parties	% of municipalities where running	% of municipalities where represented	% of seats on local councils	% of (aggregate) votes in local elections	% of mayors affiliated with the party
HDZ (Hrvatska demokratska zajednica)	95.6	95.1	40.4	30.9	46.2
SDP (Socijal-demokratska partija)	64.2	60.4	16.1	18.3	12.0
HSS (Hrvatska seljačka stranka)	38.7	34.0	7.3	4.1	8.1
HNS (Hrvatska narodna stranka)	26.2	18.9	4.6	3.3	5.2
IDS (Istarski demokratski Sabor)	7.9	7.7	3.6	2.3	4.7
SDSS (Samostalna demokratska srpska stranka)	10.8	7.4	2.3	1.0	2.7
MOST (Most nezavisnih lista)	7.7	5.2	1.1	3.5	–
HSLS (Hrvatska socijalno-liberalna stranka)	9.2	5.4	1.1	0.8	1.1
BM365 (Bandić Milan 365 – Stranka rada I solidarnosti)	5.2	4.1	0.6	5.1	0.2
ŽZ (Živi zid)	11.3	5.7	0.5	2.4	–
Reformisti (Narodna stranka-reformisti)	4.5	3.2	0.5	0.5	
HDSSB (Hrvatski demokratski sabor Slavonije I Baranje)	5.6	3.4	0.4	0.6	
HSU (Hrvatska stranka umirovljenika)	7.0	2.7	0.2	0.4	–
HDS (Hrvatska demokršćanska stranka)	2.0	1.4	0.2	0.4	–
HRAST (Hrvatski rast)	1.8	0.5	0.05	0.2	–
Other nonparliamentary national parties[1]	20.0	13.8	4.5	7.0	3.1
Independent and local	69.8	58.8	16.5	19.2	16.7

[1] Parties with national aspirations and coverage and usually ex-parliamentary status.
Source: Authors, based on National Electoral Commission data

Table 34.5 Share (percent) of women among elected councilors (2001–2017) and mayors (2009–2017) in Croatia

Election year	1993	1997	2001	2005	2009	2013	2017
Councilors	4.7	5.2	9.0	11.3	14.8	17.9	25.2
Mayors	n/a	n/a	n/a	n/a	4.9	7	9
Deputy mayors	n/a	n/a*	n/a	n/a	14.1	18.5	24.6

Note: n/a indicates that mayors and deputies were elected by their council.
Source: Authors, based on National Electoral Commission data

elections: the total share of female candidates was 41.7%. Still, 15% of all lists failed to meet this requirement. The share of women elected (25.2%) still does not fully correspond to their share on the lists, because they have been predominantly positioned in the lower sections (e.g., only 15% of women were leaders on the lists). Women are still seriously underrepresented in the local government executive – they hold the mayor's office in only 9% of Croatian municipalities and 24.6% of deputy mayor positions. These numbers largely correspond with women's representation in the national parliament, in which their share was 12.6% and 23.2% in the 2016 and 2020 elections, respectively.

Croatia has a distinctive and refined system of representation of ethnic minorities in local government institutions, which was established in 2002 by a law at the constitutional level. Minorities are guaranteed the right of representation through established quotas. One minority representative on a council is guaranteed in municipalities where the share of the respective minority in the population is between 5% and 15%. The same applies to all those units that autonomously guarantee the right of minority representation even if its share is lower than 5%. In municipalities with a higher proportion of minorities in the population (more than 15%), they are guaranteed a number of seats proportional to their share in the municipal population. These quotas may be, and usually are, fulfilled after the initial distribution of seats among the elected councilors from all lists. If this is not the case, minority representatives are added to the council, which therefore increases its size. These additional representatives are recruited from among the nonelected candidates on the participating lists (the more successful ones have priority) who belong to the minority group in question. Only in cases where the required minority quota on the council is not attained as described (e.g., there are not enough minority members among the remaining candidates on all of the participating lists) are additional elections held, but this has proven to be very unlikely.

In the 2017 local elections, ethnic minorities were guaranteed a total of 262 seats on local councils in 146 municipalities (Table 34.6). In 68 municipalities, a total of 84 additional council seats were needed to fulfill the required quota. Minority representatives are usually recruited by the established parties and incorporated in their candidacy lists. Although minorities may present their own lists, this usually happens only in municipalities where a particular minority represents a majority of the municipal population. Furthermore, in municipalities with a share of an ethnic minority population of more than 15%, an additional deputy mayor is elected as a minority representative in the local executive. The minority deputy mayor is elected on a separate ballot by only members of the minority in question on the basis of a relative majority, one-round system. In the 2017 elections, minority deputy mayors were elected in 49 municipalities, representing Serbs (29), Italians (six), Hungarians (four), Czechs (three), Bosniaks (two), Roma (two), Rusyns (two), and Slovaks (one). The aforementioned rules apply equally to the cases of municipalities in which Croatians are a minority. In 19 municipalities, Croatians were

Table 34.6 Representation of ethnic minorities on municipal councils in Croatia

	Serbs	Italians	Hungarians	Roma	Bosniaks	Czechs	Slovaks	Rusyns	Albanians	Ukrainians
Number of municipalities	104	16	10	10	9	5	3	2	1	1
Number of representatives	165	34	17	12	12	10	7	3	1	1

Source: Authors, based on Ministry of Justice and Public Administration data

guaranteed 50 seats on councils, and in only five cases did this requirement produce additional councilors. Additionally, Croatians elected 14 deputy mayors as minority representatives in the local executive.

Discussion and concluding remarks

As the analysis suggests, local elections in Croatia have proven to be mostly an additional playing field for national political parties and actors: one with less significance and having a secondary, but nevertheless quite important role. Although recent election cycles have recorded the increasing success of independent (genuine) local actors, it seems that their more significant proliferation is systematically limited by the existing framework and is heavily contingent on the further emancipation of local government through decentralization and consolidation reforms. The direct election of mayors has hardly delivered on its promises to boost voter participation and to improve legitimacy in the local government arena. As electoral outcomes have shown, legitimacy problems reflected in low turnout rates mostly pertain to larger municipalities. Higher rates in smaller municipalities indicate the importance of more immediate contact between candidates and the electorate, which can be stimulated through social media and other contemporary platforms. The decreasing trend in political competition, particularly in smaller and rural municipalities, and stagnating rates of voter turnout could result in an even greater incumbency advantage in the future, which increases the risk of personalization of local governance, clientelism, and the politicization of local administration. The necessary revitalization of local elections could be partially sought through the introduction of preferential voting and/or the implementation of an electronic or online voting system, which would presumably increase the rate of participation and the overall legitimacy of local political processes. Preferential voting has been announced, but the chances of it being introduced before the 2021 local elections are slim. Electronic voting is predominantly advocated by the NGO sector, but government officials are not very keen on introducing it, citing the lack of technical prerequisites for such an innovation. Nevertheless, local elections and their problems are inseparable from the generally weak position of local government in the multilevel system of governance. Therefore, any reform aimed at decentralization, territorial consolidation, and/or local capacity building should indirectly lead to more vibrant, more plural, and more important electoral processes and outcomes in the future. However, initial steps toward the full emancipation of local elections could be taken by more restrictive regulation of *cumul des mandats*, which would demarcate the domains of national and local political competition more clearly.

Regarding the research agenda of local elections in Croatia, there is substantial room for further development and improvement. Mainstream output from domestic scholars is limited to either descriptive analyses of electoral outcomes or an institutional analysis of various elements of the electoral system and its rules. There is an evident deficit of empirical research to explain different voting patterns as dependent on various institutional and environmental variables. Future research should fill this gap.

Notes

1 In the 1990 local elections, the electoral system required an absolute majority in the first round and a relative majority in the second round. All candidates who received at least 7% of the votes in the first round – and no fewer than two candidates – were entitled to run in the second round.
2 Currently, 12.6% of MPs are mayors, which has been their lowest share for a while. A total of 30% of the MPs elected in 2016 competed for a mayoral office in the 2017 local elections.
3 Because coalition lists are quite common and official electoral results indicate only the number of votes and seats won by the list and not by individual parties from the list (in the case of coalition lists), Table 34.4 presents the results in the following manner: results are affiliated to a party in the leftmost column in the case of an individual party list *and* in the case of a coalition list *led by* the respective party. Therefore, among the seats presented as won, for example, by HDZ, there is certainly a number of seats belonging to some other party, but there is no fully accurate way of distinguishing these. There are also some seats won by HDZ that are presented as belonging to another party, when that party led the coalition list involving HDZ. Parties in Table 34.4 are ordered according to the number of total seats won.
4 Nonpartisan (independent) lists are legally obliged to use the phrase 'candidacy list of a group of voters' on their ballot. This is another reason for them to register as a party – to point out their identity and affiliation.

References

European Commission (2018). *Standard Eurobarometer 90*. Eurobarometer Surveys. [Online] Available from: https://ec.europa.eu/commfrontoffice/publicopinion/index.cfm/Survey/getSurveyDetail/instruments/standard/yearFrom/1974/yearTo/2018/surveyKy/2215 [Accessed 1 February 2020].

GONG (2017). *Izvještaj o izborima za članove predstavničkih tijela jedinica lokalne i područne (regionalne) samouprave te za općinske načelnike, gradonačelnike, župane i gradonačelnika Grada Zagreba*. [Online] Available from: www.gong.hr/hr/izborni-sustav/izvjestaj-o-lokalnim-izborima-2017/ [Accessed 1 February 2020].

Heinelt, H., Hlepas, N., Kuhlmann, S. & Swianiewicz, P. (2018). Local Government Systems: Grasping the Institutional Environment of Mayors. In: H. Heinelt, A. Magnier, M. Cabria & H. Reynaert (eds.), *Political Leaders and Changing Local Democracy. The European Mayor* (pp. 19–78). London: Palgrave Macmillan.

Koprić, I. (2011). Nezavisni lokalni politički akteri u Hrvatskoj. In: J. Barbić (ed.), *Izbori zastupnika u Hrvatski sabor i referendum* (pp. 87–112). Zagreb: Hrvatska akademija znanosti I umjetnosti.

Koprić, I., Dubajić, D. & Vukojičić Tomić, T. (2015). County Elections in Croatia: On the Path to Genuine Regional Politics. *Hrvatska i komparativna javna uprava*, 15(4), 475–516.

Koprić, I., Dubajić, D., Vukojičić Tomić, T. & Manojlović, R. (2017). Croatia: Elections for Weak Counties When Regionalization Is Not Finished Yet. In: A. H. Schakel (ed.), *Regional and National Elections in Eastern Europe: Territoriality of the Vote in Ten Countries* (pp. 59–81). London: Palgrave Macmillan.

Koprić, I. & Đulabić, V. (2018). Evaluation of the Decentralisation Programme in Croatia: Expectations, Problems and Results. In: I. Koprić, H. Wollmann & G. Marcou (eds.), *Evaluating Reforms of Local Public and Social Services in Europe: More Evidence for Better Results* (pp. 243–260). London: Palgrave Macmillan.

Koprić, I. & Škarica, M. (2017). Evaluacija neposrednog izbora načelnika i župana u Hrvatskoj nakon dva mandata: korak naprijed, dva nazad. In: S. Gongeta & M. Smoljić (eds.), *Zbornik radova 7. međunarodne konferencije 'Razvoj javne uprave'* (pp. 156–172). Vukovar: Veleučilište 'Lavoslav Ružička' u Vukovaru.

Koprić, I. & Vukojičić Tomić, T. (2013). Lokalni politički sustav nakon uvođenja neposrednog izbora načelnika – stanje i prijepori. In: I. Koprić (ed.), *Reforma lokalne i regionalne samouprave u Hrvatskoj* (pp. 155–188). Zagreb: Institut za javnu upravu & Pravni fakultet Sveučilišta u Zagrebu.

Ladner, A., Keuffer, N., Baldersheim, H., Hlepas, N., Swianiewicz, P., Steyvers, K. & Navarro, C. (2019). *Patterns of Local Autonomy in Europe*. London: Palgrave Macmillan.

Omejec, J. (2002). Izborni sustav i rezultati lokalnih izbora održanih 2001. godine. *Hrvatska javna uprava*, 4(1), 115–165.

Raos, V. (2013). Svibanjski lokalni izbori: mnogo staroga, malo novog. *Političke analize*, 4(15), 25–32.

Raos, V. (2017). Lokalni izbori kao međuizbori? *Političke analize*, 8(30), 29–35.

Reif, K. & Schmitt, H. (1980). Nine Second-Order National Elections – a Conceptual Framework for the Analysis of European Election Results. *European Journal of Political Research*, 8(1), 3–44.

Škarica, M. (2020). Interplay between the Tiers in Croatian Local Government: Who Is Winning the Interdependence Game? *Hrvatska i komparativna javna uprava*, 20(2), 207–240.

Škarica, M. & Giljević, T. (2016). Inter-Municipal Cooperation in Local Service Provision: Comparative Trends and Regulatory Frameworks. In: D. Lhomme, A. Musa & S. De La Rosa (eds.), *Good Local Governance: Application of European Standards of Local Public Services in France and Croatia* (pp. 97–122). Bruxelles: Larcier Bruylant.

35
Kosovo
Local elections and ethnic ramifications

Memet Memeti

Overview of the local government system: patterns of reforms

The Republic of Kosovo (Kosovo) declared independence in 2008 and is the newest state in Europe. Kosovo is a republic with a multiparty, parliamentary democracy. The assembly of Kosovo (Kosova) elects the president, the head of state, and the prime minister. Executive power is headed by the prime minister, and legislative power is held by the Assembly. There are two levels of government: central and municipal. At the municipal level, there are currently 38 municipalities. Since the 1999 war, Kosovo has gone through two very important stages in the development of its local and central governments: from 1999 to 2008 under the United Nations Interim Administration Mission in Kosovo (UNMIK) and since 2008 based on the Kosovo Constitution.

Notably, in the period 1999–2008 under UN administration, the central government was UNMIK's administration, which also oversaw the work of municipal administrators. The legal basis for the functioning of local government in this period was UNMIK Regulation 45/2000, with the ultimate authority and power in terms of central-local government relations vested with the UNMIK administration. Accordingly, the Special Representative of the Secretary-General (SRSG) retained all of the powers granted to him under United Nations Security Council Resolution 1244. The SRSG had the authority to annul any municipal decision if it violated Res. 1244, UNMIK Regulations, or other applicable laws and in cases where the rights and interests of the communities living in a given municipal territory were discriminated against.

The second phase was initiated in 2008 with the adoption of the Constitution of Kosovo and the Law on Local Self-Government. The new legislative framework institutionalized the relationship with clearly defined rights and responsibilities of the central and local governments in accordance with the principles of the European Charter of Local Self-Government (Article 123.3 of the Constitution).

The Constitution of Kosovo provides special protection to local self-government in terms of due process. It envisages special procedures in the adoption and amendment of laws that regulate the organization and competencies of the units of local self-government. The constitution requires a double majority[1] for the adoption and amendment of laws that regulate local self-government.

The principles upon which local self-government in Kosovo is developed aim to balance the relationship between the central and local levels of government. According to the constitution, local self-government is exercised by municipal councils elected in general, equal, free, and direct elections based on a secret ballot. The first local elections in the history of Kosovo were held in 2000 when citizens voted for municipal assemblies in 30 municipalities, which were set up on the basis of the administrative boundaries of municipalities in the former Yugoslavia. Accordingly, only these municipal bodies can exercise the functions of local self-government. This constitutional provision is coherent with the European Charter of Local Self-Government. These bodies enjoy constitutional, administrative, and other protections, which can be exercised by judicial redress.

In addition, according to Article 113.4 of the constitution, municipalities are authorized to refer to the Constitutional Court of Kosovo to challenge the constitutionality of laws that violate their jurisdiction and income.

The new administrative system established in 2008 created smaller municipalities, which increased the number of municipalities to 38 and had an impact on municipal economic and administrative capacities and, consequently, on local government finances as well. Outside of the capital Pristina, the bulk of municipalities cover dozens of villages and submunicipal units without any legal or formal standing. There are 1,412 villages (on average 47 villages per municipality) with a total of 453 submunicipal units.

Municipal competencies are determined and regulated by law. However, there are two cases of special treatment in the local self-government of Kosovo. First, there are enhanced competencies[2] exclusively for the ten Serb-dominated municipalities, thus creating an asymmetry of municipal competences and local self-governance powers. The second exception is Kosovo's capital city Pristina, which since 2018 has been granted special status and is no longer subject to the Law on Self-Government. According to the new law, the capital city Pristina retains the competences of a normal unit of local self-governance, is entitled to establish public enterprises without government approval, and receives additional competencies in health care and policing. The financial resources of a municipality consist of its own sources of revenue, local taxes and utilities, operating grants, grants for enhanced competencies, transfers for delegated competencies, extraordinary grants, financial assistance from the Republic of Serbia for Serb-dominated municipalities, and proceeds from municipal borrowing. However, the financial stability and autonomy of municipalities remain problematic, with most municipalities relying on grants and financial transfers from the central government. For instance, in 2017, the municipalities' own resources amounted to less than 20% of their budget, covering just €80 million from a total budget of €421 million (Freedom House 2018). Kosovo is not part of the Local Autonomy Index (LAI) assessment, but an analysis of the local governance system would likely result in lower scores on dimensions such as financial autonomy, political discretion, and noninterference compared to dimensions of legal and organizational autonomy.

The process of decentralization also has ethnic ramifications. For more than two decades, the main focus of the international community and Kosovan institutions has been the utilization of decentralization as an instrument for political integration of its relatively small minorities, granting particular powers to Serb-majority municipalities to govern their own affairs (Stroschein 2008). Immediately after the declaration of independence in 2008, the Kosovan authorities initiated the creation of five new municipalities (Gracanica, Ranilug, Partesh, Mitrovica North, and Klokot) with a Serb majority and the border extension of one other (Novo Brdo), thus bringing the number of Serb-dominated municipalities to 10.

The municipal assembly (legislative) and the mayor (executive) are the key institutions of local government. Dynamics and relations between the mayor and the municipal assembly are a vital component of the quality of policies at the local level (Memeti and Kreci 2016). Elected mayors are key institutional actors of local self-government.

Kosovo has strong mayoral form of government; the municipal assembly operates in the shadow of the mayor as the bulk of executive competences – including the setting up, directing, staffing, and financial management of the municipal administration – are his/her responsibility. Moreover, the law assigns to him/her 'all competencies not explicitly assigned to the municipal assembly or its committees'.

Local government trust levels are nearly double that of national institutions. While only 26% of the population trust the national assembly and government, 42% trust the local government (NDI 2019).

Local elections and their place in the multilevel system

The legal framework for local elections in the 38 municipalities can be found in two different laws. The Law on General Elections regulates the recognition and protection of voting rights and voter eligibility criteria, maintenance of the list of voters, regulation and certification of political parties, coalitions, citizen initiatives and independent candidates, the institutional framework for conducting elections, financial support, and media coverage. The Law on Local Elections regulates the organization and implementation of elections for municipal assemblies and mayors of municipalities.

Local elections for the municipal council and mayor are held every four years. Each municipality is a single electoral district, and the elections are organized by the Central Election Commission (CEC). The CEC is composed of 11 members, and they are responsible for preparing and publishing electoral rules, certifying political entities, maintaining the voter lists, accrediting observers, conducting voter education activities, and certifying and announcing election results. The CEC also establishes the municipal election commissions (MECs) and the polling station committees (PSCs). The MECs are appointed for each election and are responsible for administering the election within their municipality and ensuring the legality, legitimacy, and efficiency of the electoral process. The PSCs are responsible for administering the voting process on election day, opening and closing the polls, and counting the ballots.

The latest local elections were held on 22 October and 17 November 2017. In Kosovo, the electoral cycle at the local level does not correspond with the electoral cycle at the national level.

Assembly elections in the shadow of mayoral elections

In terms of local elections, free, democratic, and multiparty elections have been organized since 2000. Major steps in consolidating local democracy were the 2007 legal changes, which introduced the direct election of mayors, and the 2008 introduction of open lists of candidates for municipal assemblies. The first elections at both the national (2001, 2004) and local levels (2000, 2002) applied a closed-list model, while elections held from 2007 onward have used open lists, shifting the balance of control of candidate selection from party leaders to the voters. These steps strengthened accountability and challenged the embedded political allegiances of political parties who controlled local institutions.

While members of a municipal assembly are elected through an open-list PR system, mayors are elected through a majority system. In Kosovo, each municipality is a single electoral district. The municipal assembly is directly elected by the voters registered in the municipality.

The number of seats on the municipal assemblies is dependent on the number of citizens: municipalities of up to 10,000 citizens have 15 seats; municipalities with 10,001–20,000 citizens have 19 seats; municipalities with 20,001–30,000 citizens have 21 seats; municipalities with 30,001–50,000 citizens have 27 seats; municipalities with 50,001–70,000 citizens have 31 seats; municipalities with 70,001–100,000 citizens have 35 seats; and municipalities with more than 100,000 citizens have 41 seats. The municipal assembly of Pristina has 51 seats (Article 36, Law on Local Self-Government). The formula used for seat allocation at the local (as well as the national) level is Sainte-Laguë (with the divisors 1, 3, 5, 7, 9, etc.).

A voter can cast one vote for the party or a name on the list of candidates. If a ballot is marked for more than one candidate, only the political party, coalition, or citizen initiative indicated is counted, and the vote goes to the leader of the list (IFES 2017). Contrary to national elections, where a 5% threshold applies, there is no formal minimum threshold for the local elections.

Another difference between national and local elections is that the model of reserved seats for nonmajority communities in the parliamentary elections does not apply at the local level. Political parties, coalitions, or citizen initiatives submit a list of candidates for certification for each municipality, and each candidate list comprises at least 30% certified candidates of the other gender. Being a member of a municipal assembly is not a full-time professional position; however, members of the municipal assembly cannot simultaneously hold a position as a member of the Assembly of the Republic of Kosovo. While in office, councilors are excluded from the decision-making and administrative procedures relating to any matter in which he or she, or an immediate family member of his or hers, has a personal or financial interest or a conflict of interest.

There are 1.9 million eligible voters (including Kosovo citizens who live abroad). Every citizen of Kosovo who is 18 or older on election day has the right to vote as long as he or she meets at least one of the following criteria: (1) registered as a citizen of Kosovo on the Central Civil Registry; (2) if residing outside Kosovo – provided he or she meets the criteria for being a citizen – obtained refugee status, as defined in the Convention Relating to the Status of Refugees on or after 1 January 1995, and is eligible to be registered on the Central Civil Registry.

Those serving a sentence imposed by the International Criminal Tribunal for the former Yugoslavia, those who are under indictment and have failed to appear before the Tribunal as ordered, or those who have been declared mentally incompetent by a final court decision are barred from voting (Article 5, Law on General Elections).

In 2017, 11,065 local voters utilized these instruments; this number accounts for 1.36% of the total votes in the election and attests the issue of updating the list of voters in a timely manner. While the Ministry of Internal Affairs is legally responsible for maintaining the civil registry in its electronic form, interoperability with municipalities to update all information in real time, including permanent residence, is lacking (KFOS 2015).

Out-of-country voting is conducted in the local election process. Eligible voters residing outside of Kosovo can apply for out-of-country voting. To vote from outside of Kosovo, a person must prove his or her identity and eligibility. If eligibility is approved, ballots will be sent to the voter prior to the election and must be returned to the CEC by midnight two days before election day. Voters born outside Kosovo vote in the municipality of their origin (Election Regulation No/2013). In the 2017 local elections, 6,570 votes (from those living abroad) or 0.8% of the total were cast by mail.

For the purpose of mayoral elections, each municipality is considered one single-member electoral district. A candidate for mayor must have been a resident of the municipality in which she or he is running for at least three years. Each mayor is directly elected with the use of a two-round system. A candidate is elected mayor of a municipality if he or she receives a majority of valid votes in the first round; if none of the candidates receives the majority of votes, the second round is organized 14 days after the first round (Article 9, Law on Local Elections). In the 2017 local elections, second rounds were organized in slightly more than half of the municipalities. Kosovo legislation introduced the unique legal instrument of suspension of a mayor by a decision of the Government of the Republic of Kosovo if it considers that the mayor has violated the constitution and the applicable laws and simultaneously submits the case to the Constitutional Court. If the Constitutional Court upholds the decision, the government removes the mayor from office (Article 64, Law on Local Self-Government). This legal mechanism has not been applied in practice so far; there are no decisions of the Constitutional Court to serve as a basis for removing a mayor from office in Kosovo for violating the constitution. There are no legislative instruments that allow for a municipal assembly or the voters to remove a mayor from office.

To accommodate the needs of nonmajority communities in the municipalities in which they comprise at least 10% of the citizens, the position of a deputy mayor for communities is allowed (Article 61, Law on Local Self-Government). However, the deputy mayor is not elected in general local elections but is appointed by the mayor with prior approval of the majority of the whole council and the majority of the councilors belonging to the nonmajority community (the principle of double majority).

In addition, party politics is an important variable for building the supremacy of the mayor vs. the assembly. In the last elections, 36 out of the 38 mayors had majority coalitions, implying multiparty coalitions in the assembly after the election process. This is the case due to partisan politics and due to the fact that the focal points of local election campaigns are candidate mayors and not candidate councilors. This had led to criticisms that municipal assemblies are not upholding their role of oversight of the executive at the local level and that they serve as a body to legitimate a mayor's proposals and municipal budget.

Predominance of national party actors

For Kosovo, as a new democracy, a discussion of electoral turnout is of the utmost importance. Figure 35.1 compares voter turnout in the country for local and national elections since 2000. Despite the difference in the time of the electoral cycles' (national vs. local) organization, distinctive patterns have arisen in the two decades of practice of electoral democracy at the national and local levels. First, following global trends, turnout at the local as well as the national level has been decreasing. In the 2000 elections, turnout at the national level was 64.3% and at the local level 79%, while for the latest elections it has dropped to 41.3% and 44.1%, respectively. Second, turnout for local elections is slightly higher than for national elections (in 2000, 79% local vs. 64.3% national; in 2002, 53.9% local vs. 49.5% national; 2013, 46.3% local vs. 42.63% national; and 2017, 42.9% local vs. 41.3% national). An exception to this pattern is the period 2007–2009, the years prior to and following the proclamation of independence (2008), when turnout was slightly higher at the national level: 40% vs. 39.4% (2007) and 45.3% vs. 44.7% (2009). Bearing in mind that 2007–2009 was the period during which the issues of independence and statehood were key topics on the political agenda, higher turnout can be attributed to the mobilization of the electorate during the process of statehood building, among other reasons.

Figure 35.2 disaggregates the turnout percentage for the most recent local elections (2017) by the population size of the municipalities in Kosovo. As mentioned previously, the number of seats differs according to the size of the population. Figure 35.2 demonstrates the inverse correlation between population size and voter turnout: the larger the population size, the lower the

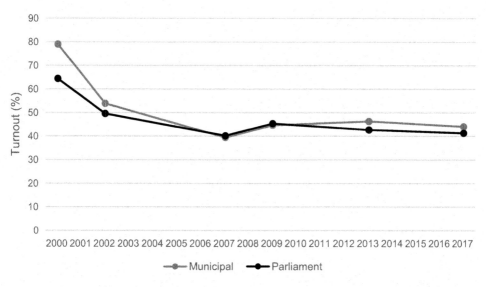

Figure 35.1 Voter turnout for local and national elections in Kosovo, 2000–2017
Source: Central Election Commission of Kosovo

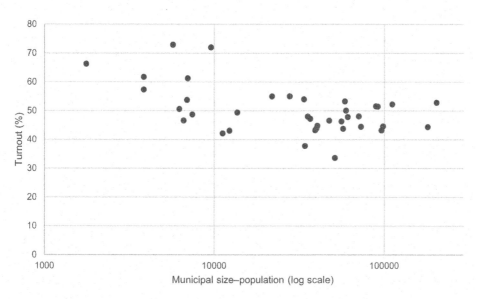

Figure 35.2 Voter turnout for local elections in Kosovo by municipality size

share of eligible voters participating (Pearson's $R = -.460$). Evidently, this relationship is not perfectly linear, as highlighted by the varied range of values in each category of population size. Nevertheless, the data exemplify that the bulk of municipalities with fewer inhabitants show higher voter turnout. It seems that, in smaller municipalities, the dynamics between politicians and voters energizes the electorate to go the polls in greater numbers compared to larger municipalities. However, there are exceptions that require further analysis; for instance, the capital Pristina had higher turnout than many smaller municipalities for the 2017 local elections. Among other things, this is due to the fact that the bulk of the resources of political parties and the attention of the media are focused on Pristina which, in terms of a prize, is more valuable to political parties than any other municipality.

While in some European countries, national candidate lists are only present in a minority of municipalities (due to the difficulties of competing under their label and vying with the perception that politics at the local level is factual and harmonious and thus hostile to partisan conflict) (Steyvers and Hayerick 2017), data from the 2017 elections in Kosovo suggest that local party systems resemble Kosovo's national party system. There is vivid interconnectedness between local party systems and their (supra)system level formed by a national party system (Maškarinec 2015).

Key national parties filed candidacies in most of the municipalities, which resulted in their overrunning of the nonnational alternatives (Table 35.1). In Kosovo, an antecedent predominance of national candidate lists in a certain locality constitutes a barrier to nonnational alternatives. Longitudinal analysis of elections (2000–2017) shows that institutionalization of national actors in local politics makes it difficult for nonnational alternatives to compete due to the lack of financial resources, party infrastructure, and political tradition. Similar to the observation of Reiser and Holtmann (2008) on the impact of national parties on the local election process, empirical evidence in Kosovo attests that antecedent penetration of national lists into the local electoral arena has a strong negative effect on the vote shares of nonnational lists. The presence of national parties in local elections is not correlated with municipal size. In the 2017 elections, only two independent candidates were elected as mayors, and the number of independent councilors elected was insignificant. Election outcomes demonstrate the strong position of the national actors in local politics. Nevertheless, this is not the case in municipalities inhabited by minorities (Serb, Turkish), where nonnational actors compete successfully with the national ones. National parties of different ideological backgrounds have not been successful in building or asking for support from these communities, and at the same time, Serbia's interventions in the Serbian majority municipalities through the parallel structures[3] have been instrumental in entrenching the political organization of Serbians on ethnic lines.

With regard to incumbency, it is worth noting that the pattern of traditional regional and municipality strongholds of the national party system is evolving (2000–2017 elections). This trend is prevalent in terms of both elected mayors and members of the municipal assembly.

Out of 38 elected mayors, 22 incumbent mayors were reelected in the 2017 election, while in five municipalities, the incumbent political party regained the mayoral office after nominating a different candidate. Regarding the municipal assembly, it ought to be highlighted that, in 27 municipalities, the chairperson and majority remained in power after the 2017 local elections.

In terms of gender equality, national legislation stipulates of a gender quota, requiring that at least 30% of the candidates on a list to be of the other gender. In the 2017 elections, of the 1,002 assembly members elected, 356 are women (36%) and 646 are men (64%) (Central Election Commission). In 33 municipalities, the quota requirement of 30% women in the assembly was met, while in five (smaller and rural) municipalities it was not. The only municipality in which more than 50% of assembly members are women is Partesh (with 53.5%).

In terms of ethnicity, Albanian, Serbian, and Turkish men, as well as Serbian and Turkish women, seem to be overrepresented among municipal assembly members (Table 35.2). Meanwhile, Albanian, Bosnian, Turkish, and Gorani women, as well as Ashakali, Egyptian, and Bosnian men, are underrepresented among municipal assembly members. Roma, Ashkali, and Egyptian women and Roma men are not represented in any municipal assemblies (Kosovo Women's Network 2018).

Table 35.1 Party politicization in local elections in Kosovo, 2017

	% of municipalities where running	% of municipalities where represented	% of seats on local councils	Total # of votes in local elections	Total # of mayors affiliated with the party
Kosovo Democratic League	86.8	76.8	21.25	181,917	8
Alliance for Future of Kosovo	76.3	71.0	12.67	103,878	6
Democratic Party of Kosovo	86.8	86.4	21.5	167,434	6
Vetvendosja Movement	81.6	78.0	12.67	119,152	3
Serbian List	44.7	44.7	11.67	3,7416	10
NISMA	73.0	63.0	5.0	40,277	1
Alliance for New Kosovo	81.5	44.7	3.6	28,060	1
Alternativa	13.2	7.9	0.8	8,904	0
Kosovo Turkish Democratic Party	15.8	7.9	1.09	7,626	1
Movement for Unification	36.8	10.5	0.7	5,790	0
Coalition Vakat	5.3	5.3	0.5	5,046	0
Albanian Demo-Christian Party	26.3	5.3	0.4	4,322	0
Party for Equality	26.3	13.6	0.5	3,588	0
New Democratic Party	5.3	2.6	0.2	2,477	0
Independent Liberal Party	18.4	10.5	0.7	2,118	0
Party of Kosovo Serbs	5.3	2.6	0.6	2,111	0
Kosovo Turkish Party of Justice	10.5	2.6	0.7	1,742	0
Fjala	26.3	2.6	0.01	1,458	0
Party of Askali Integration	18.4	5.3	0.20	1,232	0
Progressive Democratic Party	18.4	5.3	0.3	1,116	0
Liberal Party of Egyptians	5.3	2.6	0.01	1,188	0
Unified Gora Party	2.6	2.6	0.2	1,180	0
Organization Balli Kombetar	13.2	2.6	0.01	737	0
Movement for Gora	2.6	2.6	0.01	354	0
Democratic Initiative	2.6	2.6	0.01	343	0
Citizen initiatives	55.3	44.7	4.3	13834	0
Independents and nonnational (local) lists	34.2	5.3	0.3	3519	2

Table 35.2 Members of municipal assemblies in Kosovo by ethnicity and gender, compared to proportion of the population

Ethnicity	% of women in the population	# and (%) of women in assemblies	% of men in the population	# and (%) of men in assemblies	Total % of population	Total # and (%) in assemblies
Albanian	46.1	286 (28.7)	46.8	522 (52.3)	92.9	808 (81.0)
Serbian	0.7	56 (5.6)	0.7	102 (10.2)	1.0	158 (15.8)
Roma	0.3	0 (0)	0.3	0 (0)	0.5	0 (0)
Ashkali	0.4	0 (0)	0.5	2 (0.2)	0.9	2 (0.2)
Egyptian	0.3	0 (0)	0.3	1 (0.1)	0.7	1 (0.1)
Bosnian	0.8	3 (0.3)	0.8	4 (0.4)	1.0	7 (0.7)
Turkish	0.5	7 (0.7)	0.5			18 (1.8)
Gorani	0.3	1 (0.1)	0.3	3 (0.3)	0.6	4 (0.4)
Total	49.4	353 (35.4)	50.2	645 (64.6)	99.8	998 (100)

Only 4% of the 204 mayoral candidates were women, and no woman was elected as mayor in the 2017 elections. Political party representatives claim that women's underrepresentation is due in part to women not being interested in declaring their candidacy in mayoral elections (Kosovo Women's Network 2018).

While quotas exist for minority ethnic groups' participation in the general assembly, these are not a requirement for municipal assemblies. In practice, both in the national parliament and in the municipal assemblies, women from minority ethnic groups have been underrepresented (Kosovo Women's Network 2018).

Discussion

Although elections are far from the sole element of democracy, they are *condicio sine qua non* thereto. In general, since the first local elections in 2000, subsequent local and national elections have been conducted mainly in a fair and democratic manner. It also evident that local democracy has been strengthened over the years due to reforms in the electoral process and growing institutional and societal maturity. Until the election of 2007, responsibility for the preparation and implementation of the electoral process lay with the Organization for Security and Cooperation in Europe (OSCE), which transferred the task to the national institutions, who gradually created the appropriate infrastructure for the electoral process. Nevertheless, isolated irregularities continue to accompany the electoral process, and, in most cases, they have been related to dissatisfaction with the procedures for administering election processes and results, votes by mail for Kosovo citizens living abroad, and others (Balkan Policy Research Group Report 2018).

Lack of political unity or consensus on political aspects of the electoral system has made it impossible to address some easily accessible issues that would directly contribute to a better and more credible election process.

Campaign finance is a gray area of the electoral process in Kosovo. In 2019, 100 civil society organizations protested the draft law on financing of political entities, claiming that it violated Kosovo's Constitution and international party funding regulations. The Venice Commission pointed out that some donations in Kosovo are still being received in (nontrackable) cash, and it is not clear how citizens have made contributions larger than their annual incomes. The country is ranked around the bottom when it comes to perceptions of corruption in Europe, and its Transparency International's (TI) Global Corruption Barometer ranking dropped from 85th place in 2017 to 93rd place in 2018. In its 2018 Report on Kosovo, the European Commission also noted that 'corruption is widespread and remains an issue of concern'. Corruption thrives on the hierarchical patronage-based structure of political parties and their control of the state's institutional framework, and it has an impact on the election process and results (OBC Transeuropa 2020).

In parallel, concerns over the practice of 'family voting'[4] have to be addressed more seriously. In the 2017 local elections, this phenomenon was reported in 845 polling stations (Kosovo Women's Network 2018). This practice threatens women's ability to freely and independently exercise their vote and undermines the principle of secrecy of the vote.

In addition, voter intimidation[5] creates a perception that a certain party knows whether people have voted and for whom they voted. Studies show that this approach is used in smaller municipalities and villages (Democracy for Development D4D 2011).

In parallel, the election turnout has dropped in the past five elections; the political parties and civil society must work together to energize the electorate to practice their fundamental political right to vote.

Local election results more or less resemble national ones as the seats on local assemblies are fragmented among the national parties. In municipal assemblies, which in a majority of cases are represented by the same party or coalition that nominates the mayor, political power is concentrated with the mayor, and the assembly as an elected body has a tendency to relinquish, to some extent, its policymaking power and influence.

In parallel, Kosovo as a multiethnic state with a history of ethnic tensions, especially between the country's Albanian and Serb communities, faces tremendous challenges in terms of integration and social cohesion. Kosovo's ethnic minorities live in their own communities and municipalities, and many Kosovo Serbs retain loyalty to Serbia (USAID 2017). Similarly, the 2013 agreement between Kosovo and Serbia for the creation of an Association of Serbian Municipalities could have transformative implications for the country's governance (ECMI 2016). As originally envisioned in a 2013 agreement between Kosovo and Serbia brokered by the European Union, the association is intended to represent the collective interests of those municipalities in Kosovo with an ethnic Serb majority. Serbs in Kosovo expect it to provide institutional autonomy for their communities and a durable link to Belgrade. However, ethnic Albanians fear that the association will become a de facto state inside Kosovo.

Despite having a substantial level of decentralization compared to other countries in the Western Balkans, Kosovo's persistent interethnic tensions and disagreements, the lack of a political will to reform party financing and the electoral legislation, the monopolization of local politics by national actors, voter apathy, and the very limited capacity of municipalities to generate their own revenues are undermining local autonomy and democracy and represent immanent challenges that national and local policy actors ought to address for a more democratic, fair, and legitimate electoral process.

Notes

1 Double majority: majority of the general assembly and the majority of the MPs belonging to the non-majority ethnic communities.
2 Certain municipalities with Serbian majority populations (Mitrovica North, Gracanica, Strpce) have their own enhanced competences in the areas of secondary health care, university education, culture, and enhanced participatory rights in the selection of local police station commanders, competences which by law in other municipalities are performed by central government institutions.

3 Parallel structures: bodies that have been or still are operational in Kosovo after 10 June 1999 and de facto operate under the authority of the Serbian government.
4 Family voting: where a group of citizens vote in the same voting booth at the same time. In such instances, usually male heads of households vote on behalf of female family members.
5 Voter intimidation: calling the voters who have not voted on election day and asking them why they have not voted.

References

Balkan Policy Research Group (2018) *Kosovo and elections what can be improved*. Available at: https://balkansgroup.org/en/kosovo-elections-what-can-be-improved/ (Accessed:15 February 2020).

Democracy for Development D4D (2011) *Exploring election trends 2000–2010. Prishtina: Democracy for Development*. Available at: https://d4d-ks.org//assets/2012/09/2011-09-22-Election-Deconstructing-Election-Trends-2000-2010.pdf (Accessed:15 February 2020).

Freedom House (2018) *Nations in Transit. Country Report Kosovo*. Available at: www.ecoi.net/en/document/1429162.html (Accessed:15 February 2020).

European Centre for Minority Issues (2016) *The Association/community of Serb -majority municipalities. Breaking the Impasse*. Available at: www.ecmikosovo.org/en/Political-update-and-analysis (Accessed:19 February 2020).

International Foundation for Electoral Systems (2017) *Elections in Macedonia – 2017 Local Elections – Frequently Asked Questions. Arlington*. Available at: www.ifes.org/faqs/elections-macedonia-2017-local-elections (Accessed:19 February 2020).

Kosovo Foundation for Open Society (2015) *Local reform in Kosovo. Final report*. Available at: www.researchgate.net/publication/283504465_Local_reform_in_Kosovo (Accessed: 19 March 2020).

Kosovo Women's Network (2018) *Kosovo Gender Analysis*. Available at: https://womensnetwork.org/publications/kosovo-gender-analysis/ (Accessed:19 February 2020).

Maškarinec, P. (2015) Nationalization of the Czech local party system: Case study of the 2010 local elections in municipalities with extended powers. *Sociológia*, 47(6), 625–656.

Memeti, M., & Kreci, V. (2016, June) Role of municipal council in increasing citizen participation at the local budget process. *The International Public Administration Review*, 14(2–3).

National Democratic Institute (2019) *Kosovo public opinion survey*. Available at: www.ndi.org/publications/ndi-kosovo-public-opinion-poll-2019 (Accessed:19 March 2020).

Osservatoria balcani e caucaso transeuropa (2020) *Kosovo: Corruption, electoral funding and political participation of women*. Available at: www.balcanicaucaso.org/eng/Areas/Kosovo/Kosovo-corruption-electoral-funding-and-political-participation-of-women-202255 (Accessed:17 June 2020).

Reiser, M., & Holtmann, E. (Eds.) (2008) *Farewell to the party model? Independent local lists in East and West European countries*. Wiesbaden: VS Verlag.

Steyvers, K., & Hayerick, A. (2017) Fifty shades of Rokkan? Reconceiving local party system nationalisation in Belgium. *Croatian and Comparative Administration*, 17(4), 509–538.

Stroschein, S. (2008) Making or breaking Kosovo: Applications of dispersed state control. *Perspectives on Politics*, 6(4), 655–674.

USAID. (2017) *Kosovo political economy analysis*. Available at: https://usaidlearninglab.org/library/kosovo-political-economy-analysis (Accessed:19 April 2020).

36

Moldova

Party-shifting mayors within a nationalized local party system

Ion Beschieru

The local government system

Moldova has two tiers of subnational government: on the first tier we find 896 municipalities (named towns, villages, communes, or '*municipii*'[1]), while on the second tier we find 35 territorial units (32 districts, the municipalities of Chisinau and Balti, and the Territorial Autonomous Unit of Gagauzia).[2] The country has undergone two major territorial reforms. The first one in 1998 reduced the number of municipalities from 912 to 662 and merged the 40 districts inherited from the Soviet Union into 10 larger counties (plus Gagauzia), while a counterreform in 2003 more or less reverted the territorial organization back to its starting point (Cornea 2018).[3] As a result of the failed territorial reform, but also in the background of a continuous population decrease,[4] the territorial-administrative structure of the Republic of Moldova is extremely fragmented. Approximately 90% of the municipalities have fewer than 5,000 inhabitants – one-third of all municipalities have fewer than 1,500 inhabitants (Beschieru et al. 2018). In recent years, there have been several attempts to put the topic of territorial reform on the political agenda. However, due to the sensitivity of the matter and the lack of wide popular support, so far this has been unsuccessful.

In Moldova, decentralization is symmetric and all of the territorial units at the first level have the same competences and responsibilities. The competences attributed to the municipal level include powers that are commonly attributed to first-tier local level administration in European countries, such as planning, waste management, water supply, sanitation, construction and maintenance of local roads, street lighting, local transportation, and management of preschool educational institutions, local stations of firefighters and rescuers, and certain social care services.

In 2013–2015, the government conducted an important reform of the local finance system, when a clear and objective formula for equalization (non-earmarked) of transfers was introduced, which greatly alleviated the problem of politicization of the transfers and eliminated the interference of the district administration in the allocation of funds. However, the other elements of local public finance reform foreseen by the national decentralization strategy (2012–2018), such as an increase in the local government's own revenues and improved local financial autonomy, so far have not been addressed. As a result, local budgets are highly dependent on transfers from the state budget: local governments' own revenues in 2018 counted for only 11% of local budgets, and no less than 70% is from transfers from the state budget (while the remaining originates from general state taxes and other sources) (Budianschi 2019). In spite of some reforms and a considerable number of adopted strategies, Moldova continues to face major issues that are noted in the periodic monitoring reports of the Congress of Local and Regional Authorities of the Council of Europe, such as recentralization trends, limited local financial autonomy, the lack of precision of the grounds to activate the mechanism to recall mayors, and the intensive practice of bringing criminal prosecutions against mayors as political pressure (Congress of Local and Regional Authorities 2019). The situation is also reflected by the position of Moldova on the Local Autonomy Index, where Moldova is last in the ranking of all 39 participating countries (Ladner et al. 2015). In spite of this limited decentralization and weak local autonomy, surveys demonstrate that the trust in local authorities among citizens is consistently high, way above the levels of trust in the central government and the president of the Republic of Moldova (Public opinion barometer by Institute for Public Policy 2020).

In terms of horizontal power relations, the municipal councils and the mayors have strong positions, as both authorities are directly elected and both have at their disposal a series of checks and balances. More concretely, the council, as a collective and deliberative body, is mandated to take decisions on the most important matters for the municipality, while the mayor is the executive authority responsible for implementation of the decisions taken by the council. The mayor has to present annual reports to the council regarding the situation in the municipality and, upon request, supplementary information about its activity. In cases where the mayor does not respect the interests of the local community, does not adequately exercise the established powers of a local elected official, or violates moral and ethical norms, the council can initiate a recall election. Alternatively, the mayor can challenge the council's decisions in court if they are considered to be unlawful. As the majority of the Moldovan municipalities are so small and have a very limited staff,[5] the mayor, in addition to being an elected official and head of administration, also fulfills the function of city manager. And, therefore, very often it is the mayor who personally takes care of many routine issues.

Seven rounds of local elections

In 1995, the first democratic (with a universal, equal, and free vote) local elections were held in Moldova. Since then, the voters have cast their ballots for both the council elections and the mayoral elections (in Moldova, the mayor is elected directly). Local elections take place simultaneously for all municipalities every four years. The local elections are synchronized with the elections of councilors to district councils, the upper-level territorial units. The voter receives three ballot papers, one for the mayoral election, one for the municipal council election, and one for the district council election. When it comes to national elections, although the term of office of the president of the Republic of Moldova and of the national legislators is also four years, national and local elections are not synchronized with each other. In fact, none of seven local elections held so far (1995, 1999, 2003, 2007, 2011, 2015, and 2019) has been synchronized with either parliamentary or presidential elections. Also, the elections for the members of the People's Assembly and for the Governor of Gagauzia, an autonomous territorial unit with special legal status situated in the southeastern part of Moldova, take place at different times from the general local elections. The local elections are organized by the Central Electoral Commission, assisted by District Electoral Councils, polling stations, electoral bureaus, and other bodies that also organize national elections.

The electoral law allows local recall referenda only vis-à-vis the mayors. The recall vote, in national legislation called the 'local referendum for the revocation of the mayor', may be initiated one year after the mayor's entry into office or from the date of the previous local referendum for the revocation of the same mayor. The recall vote cannot be initiated during the last six months before the expiration of the mayor's mandate. The recall elections may be initiated only if the mayor does not respect the interests of the local community, does not adequately exercise the powers of a local elected official as foreseen by the law, or violates moral and ethical norms, facts that should be confirmed in the established manner. However, the legislation is not very precise on how or by what authority the respective facts should be confirmed. The lack of precision about the grounds to activate the mechanism of a recall referendum was noted by the Council of Europe's Congress in its last report on Moldova, and in practice, it led to this mechanism being used for political pressure and fights. Recall elections can be initiated by two-thirds of the elected local councilors or by 10% of the number of inhabitants with the right to vote from the relevant municipality. In order for the recall election to be effective, a number of voters equal to or greater than the number of those who voted for the mayor in the local election, but no fewer than half of the number of voters who participated in the referendum, has to vote for the recall. In addition, a mayor's recall election shall be declared invalid if fewer than one-third of voters included on the voters' lists have voted. In the period from 2010 to 2020, seven recall elections took place, but none succeeded, mostly due to low turnout (Central Electoral Commission 2020b).

The local electoral system

Unlike the electoral systems for the national parliament and the president, which were subject to various experiments and considerable changes over recent years, the local electoral system for the mayors and local councilors has remained practically untouched since the first local elections in 1995, and particularly since the adoption of the electoral law in 1997.

In terms of eligibility rules, only the citizens of the Republic of Moldova who have reached the age of 18 have the right to vote in local elections. Voting is not compulsory in Moldova. In addition to the general conditions for eligibility to vote (i.e., to have reached the age of 18 by election day), the electoral code establishes specific restrictions for local elections – active-duty soldiers shall not participate in local elections. The right to stand in local elections is granted to citizens of the Republic of Moldova who are eligible to vote and have reached age 18 for candidates for local councilor and age 25 for candidates for mayoral elections. The restrictions concerning the right to stand in local elections are the same as for the national elections, that is, persons who have been sentenced to imprisonment (deprivation of liberty) by a final court decision and are serving their sentence in a penitentiary institution, persons who have an active criminal record for deliberately committed crimes, and persons deprived of the right to hold decision-making positions by a final court decision (Electoral Code 1997). Independent candidates may stand for both mayoral and council elections, along with the candidates (for mayoral elections) and lists (for council elections) proposed by parties. Political parties and coalitions are not requested to fulfill any special requirements for the registration of their lists for council elections or candidates for the mayoral elections. They only need to ensure the minimum representation quota of 40% for both sexes on their lists. In addition, the number of candidates on their lists for council elections should include a number of candidates no fewer than half of the number of councilor seats on the respective municipal council and no greater than this number plus five. On the other hand, an independent candidate has to collect a number of signatures equal to 2% of the total number of voters from the respective constituency divided by the number of seats on the respective municipal council, but no fewer than 50 signatures. In case of mayoral elections, the independent candidate has to collect a number of signatures equal to 5% of the total number of voters, but no fewer than 150 and no greater than 10,000. The collection of signatures can be a challenging process, especially taking into account the fact that a voter may only support one candidate. The independent candidates are also disfavored in terms of timing, because by the time political parties and their candidates start the electoral campaign, the independent candidates can only start to collect signatures, which negatively affects the equality of campaign opportunities (OSCE/ODIHR 2015). In terms of the openness of the local electoral system, the unequal conditions for the registration of election candidates, by disfavoring independent candidates in large constituencies, and the unduly high requirements for their registration are issues flagged by specialized organizations observing local elections in Moldova (Promo-Lex 2015; OSCE/ODIHR 2015).

A local council's size is determined by the Central Electoral Commission for each local election according to the number of inhabitants of the municipality as of 1 January of the year in which the local elections are to take place. The council size can vary from nine seats in municipalities with a population of fewer than 1,500 inhabitants up to 43 seats for municipalities with more than 200,000 inhabitants. In the last local elections from October 2019, a total number of 898 mayors[6] and 10,472 municipal councilors (ADEPT on the results of 2019 local elections, 2019) were elected. In Moldova, the municipalities are not divided into electoral districts; each municipality forms only one electoral district for the election of local councilors.

The local electoral system in Moldova is uniform for the entire country. For the election of mayors, the two-round system is used, while for the election of councilors to municipal councils, the closed-list proportional representation system is applied. The only asymmetry concerns the elections of the members of the People's Assembly of the Autonomous Territorial Unit of Gagauzia, which is based on single-member electoral constituencies and a two-round system. In terms of ballot structure, the voter has only one vote, in the case of both mayoral and local council elections. The council elections are based on closed lists and *apparentement* is not allowed. The seats for municipal council elections are allocated on the basis of the d'Hondt formula without any legal threshold. In order for the local elections in a specific municipality to be valid, a participation rate of at least 25% of registered voters is necessary. If the local elections in a municipality are declared invalid due to low turnout, new elections will be organized within two weeks with the participation of the same candidates. This time the local election will be considered valid regardless of the number of voters who participate in the voting. In practice, as the turnout threshold is quite low, it is a very rare situation to not reach the required participation rate – in 2011 and 2019, the local elections were valid in all municipalities, while in the 2015 elections, the participation rate was lower than required in only one municipality and new elections were conducted.

In Moldova *cumul des mandats* is not allowed. However, at election times, a person can run for the position of councilor both in the municipal council and in the district council (second tier). A person may run for mayor and local councilor in the same municipality, but he/she may not run for office in more than one constituency. If a person wins both a council seat and a mayorship, the vacant council seat will be will be given to the next person from the list (substitute) if the person ran for councilor on a party list, or the seat will be given to the next candidate in the decreasing series determined according to the d'Hondt formula if the person ran as an independent candidate. Public officials can run in local elections, but they need to be suspended from their office from the moment of their registration as a candidate for local councilor or mayor.[7] A local elected official's position is incompatible with any position in public office, with that of civil servant in the territorial offices of the State Chancellery, with that of civil servant or employee of a local public administration, or with that of head or deputy head of structures subordinate to local public authorities. The incompatibilities for the mayoral position are even more restrictive – the holder of the mayor's office is not allowed to hold any other paid position or job in any entity or organization, be it private or public, national or foreign/international, with the exception of scientific, didactic, or artistic activities.

The electoral outcomes

The participation rate for local elections in Moldova is relatively low. Analysis of the data provided in Table 36.1 shows a decreasing trend in the turnout for both local and national elections. However, the turnout for local elections has been consistently lower than the participation rate for national elections (an average national-local turnout gap of around 10% can be observed across all local and national elections held at comparable times).

The average voter turnout for the seven local elections held in Moldova since 1990 is 53.9%, while the average turnout for parliamentary elections in the nine elections held in the same period (including four snap elections) is 63.2%. Voter turnout has been declining across the globe since the beginning of 1990s (Solijonov 2016), and Moldova, as well as other post-Communist countries, is not an exception. While the phenomenon still remains to be properly understood, several factors that may have had an impact on the turnout trend in Moldova may be noted, including quite massive permanent and temporary emigration (in case of local elections it is not possible to vote from abroad, as there is no electronic voting and no polling stations abroad, as in the case of national elections), nonvoting as a form of protest, disappointment, inaccurate voters' lists, and the political culture. The analysis of participation in local elections by territorial profile shows that voter turnout decreases with increasing municipal size. Figure 36.1 shows that there is a degree of dependence between municipality size and voter turnout using the 2015 local elections as an example. Osoianu et al. (2010) arrived at the same conclusion, noting that the turnout decreases with increasing municipality size, especially in the 500- to 5,000-inhabitant range, which covers most municipalities in Moldova.

Despite extreme territorial fragmentation and, consequently, very small municipalities, continuous depopulation, and relatively low wages for local elected officials, both the mayoral and council elections in Moldova are relatively competitive. In the latest local elections of

Table 36.1 Voter turnout (percent) for local and national elections in Moldova since 1990

Local elections		Parliamentary elections	
Election date	Voter turnout (%)	Election date	Voter turnout (%)
16.04.1995	60.0	**27.02.1994**[1]	79.3
23.05.1999	58.5	**22.03.1998**	69.1
25.05.2003	58.7	**25.02.2001**[1]	67.5
03.06.2007	54.6	**06.03.2005**	64.8
05.06.2011	54.6	**05.04.2009**	57.6
14.06.2015	49.7	**29.07.2009**[1]	58.8
20.10.2019	43.7	**28.11.2010**[1]	63.4
		30.11.2014	57.3
		24.02.2019	50.6

[1] Snap parliamentary elections.
Source: Central Electoral Commission

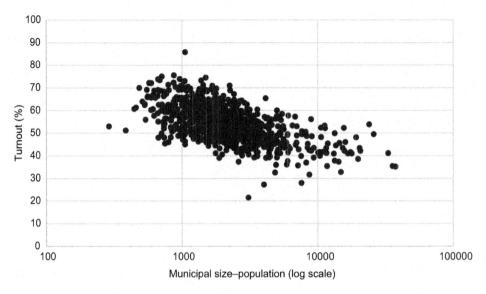

Figure 36.1 Voter turnout for local elections in Moldova in municipalities of different size
Source: Central Electoral Commission and National Bureau for Statistics

October 2019, there were, on average, 4.2 candidates competing for one mayoral office. In the 2011 and 2015 local elections, this ratio was 4.8 and 4.9, respectively, which shows a minor decrease in competitiveness for mayoral elections (Central Electoral Commission 2020b, author calculations). Also, the number of uncontested seats for mayoral elections has been increasing – in the 2011 local elections there were only three cases, in 2015 there were nine, while in 2019 the number reached 19. Regarding council elections, in 2019, for the elections in 896 municipal councils, a total number of 42,181 candidates proposed by 26 political parties and other sociopolitical organizations, along with 893 independent candidates, were registered (ADEPT on the results of 2019 locale elections, 2019). On average, this means a competition of 4.1 candidates per council seat (the total number of municipal councilors elected in 2019 was 10,472). There are also cases of uncontested seats in council elections – in 2019 there were six municipalities where only one party proposed a list of candidates, while in 54 municipalities only two lists were on the ballot (Promo-Lex 2019: 40). On average, in the last local elections there were 5.7 lists/individual candidates[8] competing per local council (Idem, author's calculations).

In Moldova, there are no regional and/or local parties,[9] but the national political parties play a significant role in local elections and politics. For instance, in the 2019 local elections, 28 parties out of 46 registered in Moldova participated in municipal elections. The four parliamentary parties and coalitions won over 80% of the total municipal councilors' seats and 76% of the mayoral offices (ADEPT on general local elections from 2019). Although both independent and party candidates can compete in the mayoral and council elections, the share of mandates obtained by independent candidates is quite small. In the last local elections in October 2019, 332 registered independent candidates won 112 mayoral offices from a total of 898, and 510 independent candidates (out of 893 that registered) won seats as municipal councilor out of a total of 10,472 (ADEPT on general local elections from 2019), which makes roughly 12.5% and 4.9%, respectively. Furthermore, independent candidates frequently join political parties after they are elected, which fuels suspicions of corruption or coercion among citizens (Munteanu

Table 36.2 Aggregate electoral results of the parliamentary (national) parties in the most recent local elections (2019) in Moldova

	% of municipalities where running	% of municipalities where represented	% of seats on local councils	% of (aggregate) votes in local elections	% of mayors affiliated with the party
Socialist Party	86.0	768	28.5	24.7	22.9
Democratic Party	84.7	695	25.2	20.3	29.1
Electoral block 'ACUM Platforma DA și PAS'	84.2	704	23.0	21.3	19.2
'Sor' Party	56.0	226	4.9	6.3	4.8
Independents	30.6	226	4.9	11.4	12.5
Other nonparliamentary parties	n/a	n/a	13.5	16.0	11.5

Source: ADEPT (2019a), http://alegeri.md/w/Rezultatele_alegerilor_locale_generale_din_2019 accessed 10 July 2020

et al. 2017). Political migration at the local level is a widespread phenomenon and a serious issue in Moldova. For instance, between 2015 and 2019, as a result of pressure exerted by the ruling parties and by law enforcement bodies, at least 471 out of the 898 elected mayors changed their political affiliation during this period according to available and verifiable public data; 103 changed their affiliation twice, while two actually changed affiliation three times (ADEPT on the phenomenon of political migration of mayors in 2015–2019, 2020).

In 2016, a 40% quota on the proposed lists of candidates was introduced for both sexes (in practical terms it mainly concerns women, who are consistently underrepresented). To prevent the practice of including women only at the end of the list of candidates, a new provision was introduced in 2019 requiring that there be a minimum of four candidates of the underrepresented sex for every ten positions on the proposed list, starting from the top. As a result, in the 2019 local elections 3,823 women won seats on municipal councils (36.5%) (Central Electoral Commission on the gender profile of the 2019 local elections). While the number of female mayors registered only a minor increase during the last three general elections (2007 and 2011, 18%; 2015, 20.6%; and 2019, 21.8%), the number of female councilors on municipal councils witnessed a greater increase, especially in the last local elections after the introduction of the new rule for positioning women candidates on the lists (at least four for every ten places). More concretely, in the 2007 local elections, 26.5% of councilor seats were won by women: 28.6% in 2011, 30% in 2015, and in 2019, as mentioned previously, 36.5% (Central Electoral Commission 2019). Comparatively, the percentage of female MPs in the Moldovan parliament constitutes 25.7% in the current legislature (after the February 2019 elections[10]), 18.8% in the 2010–2014 legislature, and 20.8% in 2014–2018 (Central Electoral Commission 2020a).

Concerning incumbency in local elections, during the seven general local elections held since 1995, it was established that, in general, more than three-fourths of incumbent mayors run for a new term. These statistics were also reconfirmed in 2019, when 766 out of 898 incumbent mayors registered as candidates for the new election (85.3%), out of which 528 (58.8%) were reelected (ADEPT 2019b). Data on the incumbency rate among local councilors are not available.

Discussion

The local electoral system in Moldova has changed very little since the first democratic local elections in 1995, and even more so since the adoption of the 1997 Electoral Code. For mayoral elections, a TRS is used, where the candidate's image is the most important factor (small municipalities are an important reason: people personally know all the candidates); this is why good mayors and prospective candidates are chased by political parties to participate in elections under their label. This situation results not only in quite a high incumbency rate but also in the higher chances for a larger number of independent mayors (compared to the share of independent councilors, for instance). For municipal council elections a CLPR is used, where people vote mostly for parties' logos and the voters usually know little about the actual composition of the lists; under this system, the independent candidates have fewer chances to succeed.

Local election results almost mirror the results of the national elections – in the 2019 local elections, 82% of local council seats were won by parliamentary parties, while the distribution of local seats aggregate at the national level mainly corresponds with the share of votes received by the parties in the 2019 parliamentary elections. This is why local elections are frequently used as a forecast for national elections, or indeed vice versa, depending on which elections come first (as sometimes snap parliamentary elections change the sequence of the two types of elections). An interesting feature of local elections in Moldova is the geopolitical vote, that is, in cities or regions with a significant Russian-speaking population, such as Balti, municipalities from Gagauzia, or the North tend to vote more for pro-Russia parties and candidates, while municipalities from other regions, such as those closer to Chisinau, the Romanian border, or some specific districts in the South such as Cahul vote more for pro-EU parties and candidates. In terms of the importance the parties attach to local elections, local electoral support is used to assess the support the party is enjoying at the national level (a testing ground). Also, the phenomenon of using administrative resources, including in national elections and political interest, is still prevalent in Moldova, and therefore parties are motivated to compete in as many municipalities as possible, especially bigger ones, in order to be able to use these administrative resources or to prevent other parties from using them.

Unlike the national elections, where recent changes to the electoral system for parliamentary elections attracted a lot of attention and were reflected in many articles,[11] local elections and voting in Moldova is an almost completely unexplored topic in academic papers. With scarce scientific research on the matter, the monitoring reports prepared by various international organizations, missions, and local NGOs[12] for each general local election are an important source of information and analysis, as they not only focus on observation of the electoral process but also often extend the analysis to various features of the local electoral system.

The most important topic related to local elections addressed by specialized NGOs, think tanks, and experts (for instance, IDIS 'Viitorul', Alianta INFONET, ADEPT, Ziarul de Garda, Expert Forum) is the political migration of local elected officials, usually toward the governing parties, which points to weak protection and high financial dependence of municipal budgets on the state budget (for instance, mayors belonging to the governing party are more likely to get funds for capital investments from various national funds). The migration of mayors intensified in an unprecedented way during 2015–2019 as a direct result of political movements at the central level, starting shortly after the parliamentary elections of 30 November 2014 (Fala et al. 2020). Two main tools are usually used by governing parties to 'persuade' mayors and other elected officials to join their teams – different types of pressure, such as more control by various state agencies, criminal cases against them initiated by the law enforcement bodies and courts under their control, and financial incentives.[13] As mentioned earlier, mayors belonging to the ruling party get more funding [for more information on how public finance is used to fuel political clientelism, see Fala et al. (2020)].

At the moment, there are no major debates about changing the electoral rules for local elections, except for specific recommendations to fix concrete issues from organizations and experts in the field who monitor local elections, such as the recommendation to change the discriminatory requirements regarding independent candidates.

Notes

1 The notion of municipality (in Romanian, *municipiu*) has a special meaning in the context of Moldova's legal and territorial-administrative system. According to Moldovan legislation, the municipality is an urban settlement with a special role in the economic, sociocultural, scientific, political, and administrative life of the country, with important industrial and commercial structures and institutions in the fields of education, health care, and culture. The status of municipality (*municipiu*) is granted to only 13 larger cities and towns in Moldova. However, in this chapter the notion is used with its generic and usual meaning, referring to all of the territorial units of the first tier.
2 The territorial-administrative units from the left bank of the Nistru river, also referred to as Transnistria, are not under the control of the Moldovan authorities and will not be included in this analysis.
3 The counterreform was conducted by the Communist Party of Moldova, which came to power after winning a comfortable majority in the national legislature as a result of the 2001 elections. Among the arguments brought by the party were the long distances citizens had to travel to the new administrative centers of the counties (*judet*) in order to benefit from various administrative and social services, the halt of economic and social development of the old district centers after the administration moved, and complaints from the citizens. Many experts and organizations (for instance, Cornea 2018, IDIS Viitorul 2005) claim that the decision to reverse the territorial reform was purely political ambition (reverting back to the old territorial structure was a part of the electoral program of the Communist party), conducted without proper public debates and consultations and without solid research and analysis, and that this led to the waste of public money invested in the amalgamation reform and to an increase in administrative expenditures in the local administrations.
4 According to the data provided by the National Bureau of Statistics, the population decreased from roughly 3.3 million in 2004 to 2.9 million in 2014, while for 2019 the bureau estimates that approximately 2.7 million inhabitants have their usual residence in Moldova. https://statistica.gov.md/news-view.php?l=ro&idc=168&id=6416 (accessed 7 August 2020).
5 The number staff units for each municipality is determined according to the number of inhabitants by central regulation, and the staffing schemes of each municipality have to be endorsed by the central public administration (State Chancellery).
6 The total number of mayors includes 896 mayors of the territorial units of first tier and the mayors (official terminology – 'general mayors') of the Chisinau and Balti municipalities, which are upper (second) level territorial units.
7 It specifically refers to deputy prime ministers, ministers, ex officio members of the government, the heads of the central public authorities, the presidents and vice presidents of the districts, mayors and deputy mayors, and praetors and vice praetors (Electoral Code, 1997).
8 The figure includes both the number of lists of candidates proposed by parties and applications from individual candidates. It also covers 896 councils of first-tier territorial units (municipalities) and 35 councils of administrative-territorial units of the second tier. Disaggregated calculations for each territorial-administrative level are not available.
9 On 25 February 2020, the Constitutional Court declared unconstitutional the provision of the Law on Political Parties no. 294 from 2007 that required, for the registration of a new party, no fewer than 4,000 members who must be domiciled in at least half of the second-level administrative-territorial units of the Republic of Moldova and no fewer than 120 members in each of the just mentioned administrative-territorial units (Constitutional Court Decision no. 5, 2020). The rationale for those requirements and restrictions was linked to the attempt to limit geopolitical influences and was also conditioned by the existence of an uncontrolled territory on the left bank of the Nistru river (Transnistria). The respective provisions, however, were not making it possible for regional or local parties to register. Although the respective restriction was annulled, no regional or local party has registered so far.

10 Elections took place before the new rule for positioning women on the list of candidates was introduced.
11 For instance, Bakken, M., Sorescu, A. (2017), *A. Electoral System Design: Moldova*. Promo-Lex: Chisinau; Cornea, S., Mandaji, E. (2017), The Parliamentary Elections of 24 February 2019 in the Republic of Moldova: Particularities and Consequences of the Mixed Electoral System. *SSRN Electronic Journal* 9(1); Simpson, H. (2019). *Anatomy of a fraud: The Moldovan Parliamentary elections*. Foreign Policy Research Institute; Mogildea, M., Kralova, D. (2018), *Between Theory and Practice: Possible outcomes of the Parliamentary Elections in Moldova under the mixed electoral system*. IPRE: Chisinau.
12 In this context, reports prepared by the OSCE Office for Democratic Institutions and Human Rights (ODIHR), the Congress of the Local and Regional Authorities of the Council of Europe (Congress), the European Network of Election Monitoring Organizations (ENEMO), and Promo-Lex Association and analyses and election profiles prepared by the Association for Participatory Democracy (ADEPT) and other think thanks (normally also available in English) represent a valuable resource.
13 For more information, see, for instance, the last report on the state of local and regional democracy in Moldova of the Congress of Local and Regional authorities and Furdui, V., Osadci, A., Rusu, V. (2018), Local democracy situation and the degree of implementation of policy documents in the field of decentralization in Republic of Moldova. *Monitoring report*. Chisinau, pp. 12–16.

References

ADEPT (2019a), *Alegerile locale generale din 2019 în Republica Moldova*, viewed on 10 July 2020, <http://alegeri.md/w/Alegerile_locale_generale_din_2019_%C3%AEn_Republica_Moldova>

ADEPT (2019b), *Rezultatele alegerilor locale generale din 2019*, viewed on 10 July 2020, <http://alegeri.md/w/Rezultatele_alegerilor_locale_generale_din_2019>

ADEPT (2020), *Fenomenul migrării politice a primarilor între anii 2015–2019*, viewed on 14 July 2020, <http://alegeri.md/w/Fenomenul_migr%C4%83rii_politice_a_primarilor_%C3%AEntre_anii_2015%E2%80%932019>

Beschieru, I. et al (2018), *Administrative-territorial reform scenarios in Moldova*. GIZ: Chisinau.

Budianschi, D. (2019), *Autonomia financiară în Republica Moldova: evoluția veniturilor bugetelor locale*. Expert-Grup: Chisinau, pp. 32–37.

Central Electoral Commission (2019), *2019 Parliamentary elections gender perspective*, viewed on 14 July 2020, <https://a.cec.md/storage/ckfinder/files/Analiza%20de%20gen%20Parlamentare%202019%20Eng.pdf>

Central Electoral Commission (2020a), *Gender profile of the 2019 Local General Elections*, viewed on 14 July 2020, <www.md.undp.org/content/moldova/en/home/library/effective_governance/analiza-din-perspectiva-egalitii-de-gen-a-alegerilor-locale-gene.html>

Central Electoral Commission (2020b), *On the results of local referendums*, viewed on 15 September 2020, <https://a.cec.md/ro/alegeri-si-referendumuri-2830.html>

Congress of Local and Regional Authorities of the Council of Europe (2019), *Local and regional democracy in the Republic of Moldova*. Report CG36(2019)15final, viewed on 14 July 2020, <https://rm.coe.int/local-and-regional-democracy-in-the-republic-of-moldova-monitoring-com/1680939183>

Cornea, S. (2018), *Fundamentele conceptuale ale reformării organizării teritoriale a puterii locale în Republica Moldova*. US 'Bogdan Petriceicu Hasdeu' din Cahul: Cahul, pp. 70–77.

Electoral Code (1997), *Electoral Code of Moldova of 21 November 1997*. Law no. 1381-XIII.

Fala, A., Nemerenco, V., Pintea, D., & Rusu, I. (2020), Study on political clientelism in the management of public funds. *Chisinau*.

Institute for Public Policy (2020), *Barometrul opiniei Publice*, viewed on 14 September 2020, <http://ipp.md/wp-content/uploads/2020/07/BOP_06.2020_prima_parte_finale.pdf>

Ladner, A., Keuffer, N., & Baldersheim, H. (2015), *Self-rule index for local authorities*. European Commission: Brussels.

Munteanu, I., Chiriac, L., Berbeca, V., Vremiș, M., & Znaceni, A. (2017), *Starea democrației locale în Republica Moldofa*. Idis 'Viitorul': Chișinău.

OSCE/ODIHR (2015), *Republic of Moldova – Local elections of 14 and 28 June 2015, OSCE/ODIHR Limited Election Observation Mission. Final Report*. ODIHR: Warsaw.

Osoian, I., Sirodoev, I., Prohnițchi, V., & Veverita, E. (2010), *Analytical study on optimal administrative-territorial structure for Republic of Moldova*. Expert-Grup: Chisinau.

Promo-Lex (2015), *Final report. Monitoring of the general local elections of 14 (28) June 2015*. Promo-Lex: Chisinau.

Promo-Lex (2019), Observation mission – general local elections and new parliamentary elections of 20 October (3 November) 2019. Promo-Lex: Chisinau.

Solijonov, A. (2016), *Voter turnout trends around the world*. International Institute for Democracy and Electoral Assistance: Stockholm.

37
Montenegro
Local elections in the shadow of national politics

Olivera Komar and Slaven Živković

Local governments in Montenegro

As in many other Central and East European countries, the first popularly elected democratic institutions in Montenegro, at both the national and the local level, were established at the beginning of the 1990s, after the fall of Communism and the introduction of multiparty electoral systems. However, at that time, Montenegro was not an independent country, but rather a constituent republic of a war-torn Yugoslavia. After a turbulent war period and two transitions (Darmanovic 2007), Montenegro managed to obtain more autonomy and finally regained its independence in 2006. The process of dissolution began in the late 1990s when, after an internal clash, part of the Montenegrin leadership distanced themselves from the policies of the Serbian leader Slobodan Milošević. After prevailing over their party colleagues who supported a broad plan favoring the continuation of Milošević's politics, the rest of the Democratic Party of Socialists (DPS) negotiated a series of steps that eventually led to the achievement of full independence for Montenegro. The first step was a symbolic change of the name of the union from Yugoslavia to the *Republic of Serbia and Montenegro*. It was then followed by administrative distancing and finally the persuasion of EU leaders to allow the two republics to partake in separate negotiation processes regarding EU accession (Vuković 2015).

Montenegro regained its independence in 2006 after a referendum on the split with Serbia, with 55.5% of voters in favor of independence (55% was the required threshold). However, this narrow result has left the country divided and reopened the cleavage that continues to split the country along the lines of the statehood issue, that is, between proponents and opponents of Montenegrin independence (Komar & Živković 2016).

The DPS stayed in power continuously until the parliamentary election in 2020 when, for the first time since the introduction of the multiparty system, this party and its coalition partners were not able to form a national government. As a result, Montenegro ceased to have a dominant party system (Sartori 2005) and entered a new period of multiparty competition.

As a small country in terms of population (with a total of 620,029 citizens according to the latest census in 2011), which is also relatively new on the European map of independent countries, Montenegro is often missing from comparative political analyses. Research on the organization of local governments is no exception. Literature on how the government is formed at a local level and how it functions is not available, except in the form of various administrative reports. Even the data on the results of local elections are not readily available, so the data set used in this chapter had to be built by collecting data directly from each and every municipality individually.[1]

Montenegro is a unitary republic that is divided into 24 local municipalities. This number includes two municipalities that have special status and whose autonomy and organization are regulated by separate laws – the capital city of Podgorica and the old royal capital of Cetinje. Since the country regained its independence, the number of municipalities has been increased several times, most recently in September 2018 when one part of the capital split administratively and formed the newest, that is the 24th, local municipality in Montenegro – Tuzi.

The country is characterized by a strong inclination toward internal migration to its larger cities, not least among these the capital. According to 2018 population estimates, almost one-third of the country's population live in the capital of Podgorica (199,715 citizens according to 2018 population estimates – almost 30,000 more than in 2000). Additionally, almost two-thirds of the country's population live in the four largest cities. The mean population size of the municipalities is 27,053 citizens (with a median of 18,260), but 18 out of the 24 municipalities have fewer citizens than the mean municipal population.

Vertical power relations can be described in relation to the level of political and fiscal autonomy on the part of the local municipalities, particularly with regard to the national government. When it comes to fiscal autonomy, the authors have described three phases of development. The first was a period of high centralization due to the change of the legal status and unfavorable political, social and economic situation in the country (1992–2003). The second was a period of administrative, political, and fiscal decentralization, which was characterized by a stable legislative environment and an increase in local government revenue (2003–2008), and the third began in 2008 and lasted until 2016 when several centralizing changes were introduced into the legislative framework, thus decreasing the level of fiscal autonomy (Kaluđerović & Jocović 2018: 132).

Politically, local municipalities are autonomous with regard to electing their own local government. The range of local government's competences are prescribed by the *Law on Local Self-governance*.[2] In general, these competences are described as those 'of interest to the local population' (Article 4). A more detailed and comprehensive list is provided in Articles 25–28 of the law, although the majority are related to 'communal and utility services' (Kaluđerović & Jocović 2018: 132). The local governments have no obligations when it comes to health care or education. However, they are in charge of tasks that are not specifically identified as competences of the national government, as well as those that the national governance transfers to the local level (either by law or decision). The main competences of the local government include passage of the local strategic development plan, the local budget, and the urban development plan. Their other competences include maintaining the utilities infrastructure, managing traffic and transport between municipalities, managing local properties, housing, local cultural and historic heritage, environmental protection, and water management.

The correlation between the national and the local levels may be illustrated by the data on public trust in the central government and the municipalities. In a 2020 survey, 42.0% of respondents stated that they entirely or somewhat agree with the statement that the municipal authorities protect the interests of citizens in Montenegro, while 52.8% said they somewhat or entirely disagree. The figures are similar when it comes to the national government – 40.0% of respondents agreed and 55.8% disagreed with this statement.[3] As the numbers show, people's views of the national level of government correspond relatively closely to their views of the local authorities.

In terms of the horizontal dimension, where the distinctiveness is based on differences in the relationship between the mayor and the local council, Montenegro can be classified as a *dualistic system*, with the local council as the legislative body and the mayor heading the executive branch of local government. The mayor or president of the municipality[4] is the most influential figure in local politics and is fully in charge of the local administration. However, his/her position was stronger prior to 2009, when the law was changed and mayors were no longer directly elected; instead, they are now selected by the local councils.[5] The system itself, its nature, and its legal structure were not designed to foster strong mayors. However, due to the longevity of the predominant party in Montenegro, mayors who were members of this party were, in fact, strong. Their power came from the fact that they had the predominant party behind them as a key bastion of support for their political power. With the most recent change in government, following the 2020 national elections, we would expect that the political power of these mayors will be further reduced.

Local elections in Montenegro

Being a unitary state, Montenegro has elections on two tiers –the national and the local level. The national elections are organized in order to elect the national parliament and the president, who is elected directly. Local elections are organized to elect local councilors. Members of both the national parliament and local councils are elected in accordance with the *Law on the Election of Members of the National and Local Parliaments* (Electoral Code, EC).[6] The elections are not concurrent, even though both local councils and the national parliament have four-year electoral cycles. Because the mandate of some local councils was shortened by snap elections, each municipality now follows its own schedule. However, most local elections that are held within the same year are – with some exceptions – scheduled for the same day.

The primary entity in charge of organizing local elections is the local electoral commission. These commissions are selected by the local councils. They have 'permanent' members selected from the local councilors and 'additional' members who are representatives of each confirmed electoral list (under Article 24 of the EC). The work of local electoral commissions is overseen by the Montenegrin State Electoral Commission.

Until the end of 2009, mayors were elected directly by the citizens and held a five-year mandate. The legislation changed that year, so that the indirect election of mayors by local councils was introduced and their mandate was shortened to four years. Currently, mayors are elected by local councils within 30 days of the local council elections.[7] The candidates for this position do not have to be local councilors, but they must come from the local electoral lists.[8] The candidates must be proposed among the councilors by at least one-third of the councilors, while more than half are needed for successful election. Once elected, a mayor ceases to be member of the local council if s/he was a member before. His or her mandate lasts for four years unless s/he is dismissed either by the local council (with a majority of all councilors supporting the dismissal) or by the government of Montenegro or unless s/he resigns for political or personal reasons.

The previous system that included direct elections and a longer term produced several effects, one of which was stronger local politicians and mayors, as directly elected politicians were competing among themselves to best serve the citizens. On the other hand, in several municipalities, unfortunate co-habitations occurred in situations in which elected mayors belonged to one party while the majority on the local councils consisted of other parties. In these situations, the most common outcomes were political stalemates and frequent snap elections.

After the legislation was changed and mayors were elected by the local councils, another interesting change occurred. On several occasions, the voters did not even know who the mayor would be should a party or coalition win the election. Mayors became appointees, who were not even the people listed first on the electoral lists of their coalitions or parties which, as a result, simply emphasized the mayors' dependence on the parties instead of on the votes of citizens.

A local council can be dismissed before the end of its four-year term in cases in which it does not hold sessions for a period of six months or it does not fulfill its duties. In such cases, the government can dismiss the local council and call new elections. The local council can shorten its own term by a simple majority (50% or more) of all councilors. A new election is also to be held if the president of the local council or the president of the municipality cannot be elected within 30 days of the constitution of the local council following a local election.

Features of the local electoral system

According to the EC, in Montenegro, a person is eligible to vote if four conditions are met: s/he is at least 18 years old, is legally competent, holds citizenship, and has been resident in the country for at least two consecutive years. The same rules used to apply for local and national elections, with the only exception being the last of the four conditions – a voter must have been a resident of the given municipality for at least six months prior to the election in order to be able to vote. This meant that if a voter had moved from one municipality to another, s/he could not vote in the new municipality for the first half year of his or her residence. However, the six-month residence rule was overturned by the Constitutional Court (decision U-I-23/17) with the explanation that it is contrary to the Montenegrin Constitution to take away voting rights from people who change their residence within six months of a local election. Voting is not compulsory.

The size of the council depends on the number of registered voters. The minimal size of the council is 30 councilors, with one additional member for each 5,000 registered voters. The smallest councils have 30 councilors, such as the local council in Šavnik, and the largest is in Podgorica with 61 councilors.

The electoral system is a closed-list proportional representation (CLPR) system, and each municipality is one electoral district. The lists are closed, and voters cannot cast a preferential vote – only a vote for the list as a whole. According to the Carey and Shugart classification (1995), CLPR systems are known to attribute low value to personal reputation. Parties offer fixed ballots to the voters, and the voters decide to take it or leave it, as it is.

The number of seats on the council are allocated using the modified d'Hondt method, with special thresholds for parties representing ethnic minorities. Gender quotas were first introduced in 2011, but they were quite ineffective at the time because they did not require fixed positions for female candidates on the list. Currently, the quota rules stipulate that each candidate list must include at least 30% of candidates of each gender and, furthermore, that at least one person in every four consecutive names on the list must be of the less represented gender. This effectively means that at least every fourth candidate on a given list is a woman. All of these requirements have to be met for a party list to be verified by the electoral commission.

The minimal threshold that a party list must receive in terms of votes in order to be able to participate in the distribution of seats is 3%. There is an exception to this rule when it comes to minority parties or coalitions. If no party or coalition that represents a specific ethnic minority passes the threshold, and if they individually receive at least 0.7% of the vote (in the case of ethnic Croat parties, this threshold is set to 0.35%), they are all considered as a one-party list and they jointly receive up to three mandates. The right to use this mechanism is given to any party list that represents an ethnic group that makes up between 1.5% and 15% of the population of the municipality. All of the major ethnic minorities in Montenegro are represented by ethnic parties. However, almost all of the nonethnic parties also include representatives of various ethnic minorities on their party lists. The only exception is found among the Roma and Egyptian communities. Although they are estimated to make up approximately the same percentage of the population that the Croat minority does, they are not allowed to benefit from the special threshold of 0.35%, which is designed specifically for the Croat minority. As a consequence, there is currently no Roma or Egyptian ethnic party in Montenegro.

To compete in the local elections, a party list must be supported by at least 0.8% of the voters registered to vote in the municipality. If the list represents an ethnic minority group, they need to be supported by at least 150 voters. In municipalities where the councilor's mandate in the prior election was allocated on the basis of less than 150 votes, the rule is that the electoral list may be registered if it is supported by one voter less than the number of votes needed for one seat on the local council. The voters that give support to the list so that it may participate in local elections must be residents of the given municipality.

In order to be a candidate on the list, a person needs to have Montenegrin citizenship and be registered as a voter on the Register of Voters at the time of the elections. If elected as mayor, a councilor loses his/her seat on the local council.

High participation, predictable results? The electoral outcomes

Citizens in Montenegro turn out on election day in high numbers. Compared to other European countries that also do not have compulsory voting, Montenegro has seen a stable, high level of turnout which, again in contrast to many European countries, even slightly increased for the parliamentary election in 2020.

Given that, as described previously, local elections do not all happen on the same day or even all in the same year, and different municipalities hold elections in different years, for the purposes of our analysis we have grouped local elections organized in the same year. Figure 37.1 presents the average turnout for local elections for each year, as well as five data points for national parliamentary elections, which are the first-order elections in Montenegro.

As we can see from the graph in Figure 37.1, participation is almost the same in both national (parliamentary) and local elections in Montenegro.

There may be several explanations that lie behind the almost identical levels of turnout for national and local elections. The first parliamentary elections after Montenegro regained independence were held simultaneously with 11 local elections on 10 September 2006 (meaning local elections were held in half of all Montenegrin municipalities at the time). As is often the case, simultaneity with first-order elections boosted turnout rates (Lefevere & Van Aelst 2014). After that, the months for most of the Montenegrin local elections were May 2010, May 2014, and May 2018. On all of these occasions, more than 50% of municipalities voted on the same day. We find Podgorica, the largest city in Montenegro and the country's capital, in this group as it is the municipality with the *highest stakes* among all local elections. The fact that more than half of the country elected their councilors on the same day made the atmosphere around local elections more heated, campaigns more intensive, and citizens more interested, all of which are factors that contribute to explaining the high turnout at the local level. Moreover, the political parties' agendas in local elections, and the most salient campaign issues, often have more to do with national level politics than local problems.

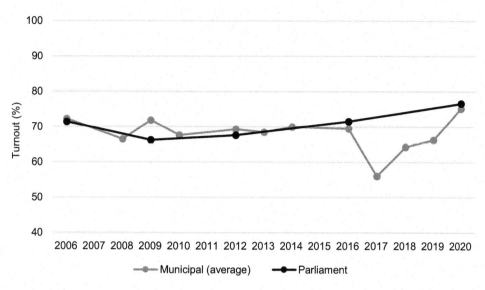

Figure 37.1 Voter turnout for parliamentary and local elections in Montenegro, 2006–2020

The slightly lower turnout rate in the fourth election cycle at the local level can be attributed, at least to some extent, to the 2017 local elections in Nikšić, the second largest municipality in Montenegro. These elections were boycotted by all of the opposition parties, and the turnout rate was as low as 44.3%, which is significantly lower than for the three previous local elections in the same municipality when the turnout was consistently around 70%.

Moreover, one additional factor that may help to explain the relatively high turnout numbers in Montenegro is the size of the country. Previous research suggests that attitudes connected with higher turnout are easier to develop in small countries, where relations between people are closer and more direct (Oliver 2000). The data show that smaller municipalities have higher levels of turnout. For all of the local elections in Montenegro, there is a small negative correlation between the size of the municipality and the turnout level (-0.12, $p < 0.05$). This increases slightly if we take into consideration the most recent elections. We have also split all Montenegrin municipalities into three groups, by size, and plotted turnout across time.[9]

Figure 37.2 shows that only in the third cycle were there no major differences in levels of turnout across municipalities of different size. In all of the others, citizens in the smallest Montenegrin municipalities tended to vote in higher rates compared to others, thus confirming Oliver's theory. Interestingly, only in the most recent cycle of local elections was the mean level of participation higher in medium-sized municipalities compared to large municipalities (although these differences are minor).

When it comes to electoral outcomes, the Montenegrin party system is shaped by the country's main political cleavage – the statehood issue, which corresponds to the existing ethnic division (Džankić 2014). This division was most pronounced in Montenegro at the time of the Independence referendum in 2006, when the two largest ethnic groups in the country formed two competing blocs on the issue: most Montenegrins and minority ethnic groups – Croats, Bosniaks, Muslims, and Albanians – were in favor of an independent Montenegro, while most Serbs were in favor of remaining in the union with Serbia. Although the question of the status of an independent Montenegro was officially resolved 14 years ago, the salience

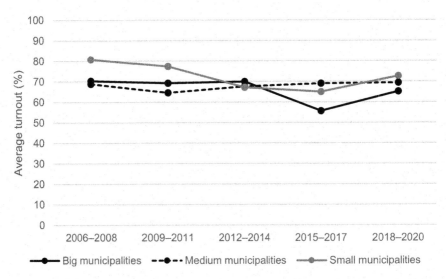

Figure 37.2 Average voter turnout in Montenegrin local elections by size of municipality, 2006–2020

of this ethnically based division has not decreased. In fact, the opposite is true. Most recently, this division reemerged and escalated when the Law on Religious Freedoms was passed by the parliament in late 2019. The law envisaged that religious property, including places of worship, for which religious communities do not have proof of ownership should return to the state and those properties should be made available for all religious communities to use. This law significantly affected the Serbian Orthodox Church, which has had the use of most Orthodox churches and property since 1918, when Montenegro was unlawfully annexed to Serbia (Vuković 2015). As a result, the Serbian Orthodox Church started a wave of protests that completely hijacked the political agenda in the country, instigating a significant Montenegrin-Serb division and forcing all political parties to choose sides.

This cleavage is strongly reflected in local level politics as well, mainly because of the lack of strong local parties and the fact that the national parties are also the key political players at the local level. The majority of the parties in Montenegro can be classified into two camps – either *pro-Montenegrin* or *pro-Serbian*. There is also a camp of parties representing ethnic minorities, which so far has mainly cooperated with the pro-Montenegrin side. Some parties have tried to mend this division and bridge the gap between the two camps in order to attract voters from both sides. These attempts have only been partially successful for a short period of time, as various issues (mostly related to identity) have forced these parties to take specific positions on identity questions, which has been seen as (un)favorable by the different identity groups. The first group (pro-Montenegrin) is perceived as being led by the Democratic Party of Socialists (DPS), the party that won all elections following the introduction of pluralism and that held the office of prime minister and president of Montenegro from 1990 up to the parliamentary election of August 2020, which it lost, resulting in the appointment of a new prime minister representing the pro-Serbian block. The major political entity in the camp pro-Serbian camp is the Democratic Front (DF), a stable political alliance of several parties that have worked closely together in all local and national elections since July 2014. Several parties, such as United Reform Action (URA) or Democratic Montenegro (the Democrats), have tried to position themselves at the center and not to align across the ethnic lines of political cleavage. However, the fact that they have sided with the newly formed government's decisions that favored the Serbian Orthodox Church's position has somewhat brought their 'neutrality' into question.

The largest national parties in Montenegro are crucial players in all of the local elections as well. They are major players in all municipalities in Montenegro, and the mayors are usually member of these parties. Parties, or party lists that are not tied to the most significant national parties, have had very limited success in local elections in Montenegro. In the 82 local elections held since independence, 2,951 councilors were elected in total. Out of this number only 72 councilors were elected from local lists, forming just 2.4% of the total. Only 13 out of the 24 Montenegrin municipalities have, or had at some point, elected councilors not connected to the major national parties.

The dominance of the Democratic Party of Socialists (DPS) in national level politics has also been reflected at the local level. In all 24 Montenegrin municipalities since 2006, 64 out of 87 elected mayors (both indirectly and directly) were members of this political party, which is 73.5% of all mayors. Additionally, in half of the municipalities (12), all of the mayors since 2006 have represented the DPS. These 12 municipalities include, among others, Podgorica, the country's capital and the largest municipality, Nikšić, the second largest municipality in Montenegro, and Cetinje, the old Royal capital with its status as the traditional center of Montenegrin identity.

Plužine, one of the smallest Montenegrin municipalities, is the only one where the DPS has never been part of the governing structure at the local level. This municipality is also the only one that has not changed its mayor since 2006. The locally very popular member of the Socialist Peoples' Party (SNP) has been mayor of the city for 18 years now.

Other mayors, who do not represent the DPS, in most instances are members of one of the ethnic minorities that usually closely cooperate with the DPS at both the local and national levels. As might be expected, this often happens in municipalities where these ethnic minorities actually form a majority at the local level, such as Ulcinj (where the Albanian ethnic minority is dominant locally), Plav, or Rožaje (in which the majority ethnic group at the local level for both is the Bosniaks).

Apart from the already mentioned municipality of Plužine, political parties that were, until recently, in opposition in the national parliament have had some success at the local level in a few municipalities. Currently, they hold the mayoral position in Budva and Herceg Novi, both wealthy costal municipalities. Budva represents a peculiar case, where the two largest opposition parties formed a coalition and agreed to split the term of mayor, so that for the first two years the mayor was a member of one coalition partner (the Democrats) and for the next two years the mayor was from the other (the Democratic Front).

Representation of women and ethnic minorities

Table 37.1 presents the percentage of seats allocated to men and women since 2006 at the national and local levels. First, because the lists are closed, the likelihood of someone winning the election depends on the decision of the party leadership about the sequence and positioning of the candidates on the list. In general, we can observe that the average percentages of women holding seats do not vary significantly when it comes to the National Parliament and the local councils. The most significant change occurred after gender quotas with placement rules were introduced in 2014.[10] The change was visible for the first time in the 2016 national elections, when the percentage of women elected jumped to 23.5%. Because not all local elections are

Table 37.1 Percentage of female councilors and mayors in Montenegro

Election year	2007	2009	2012	2013	2014	2015	2017	2018	2020
Councilors	11.37	12.70	14.26		24.80	26.24		30.03	–
Mayors	4.50	–	4.76		4.76	13.04		8.33	7.2
Members of the National Parliament	11.1	11.1	13.5	14.8		17.3	23.5		22

Note: Some local parliaments are yet to be assembled at the time of writing this chapter.
Source: Series of statistical publications produced by the Statistical Office of Montenegro 'Women and men in Montenegro', 2006–2018, accessed on 4 March 4 2020 at www.monstat.org/cg/publikacije_page.php?id=213&pageid=142

held at the same time, some municipalities experienced the change in 2014, while others did not see the it until 2017.

A woman became mayor only seven times during the previous 87 local elections (around 8%). Two of the female mayors had multiple terms, so thus far only five individual women have at some point been mayors of Montenegrin municipalities. Currently, only two of the 24 municipalities have a female mayor.

Political parties representing ethnic minorities in Montenegro have a special status when it comes to the distribution of MPs and councilors. The lower threshold for minorities and the different method for the transformation of votes into seats (described earlier) has led to an increase in the number of MPs representing minority groups in the national parliament. Additionally, almost all of the major parties have representatives of minorities among their MPs. This is generally replicated at the local level, with one specific difference: in different municipalities, different groups have the status of a minority group, something that is decided on the basis of the census results for that given municipality. Thus, minorities at the national level do not gain that benefit in their local strongholds, where they form the majority of the population (for example, Albanians in Ulcinj or Bosniaks in Rožaje).

Apart from parties that represent only one minority group, some members of various ethnic minorities run not only as part of an ethnic minority list but often also on civic party lists. However, data on the ethnic origins of individuals on party lists are not available. Thus, we cannot know the precise number of councilors of various ethnic origins on either ethnic minority party lists or civic party lists. Other types of minorities, apart from ethnic and religious minorities, do not have a pronounced role in Montenegrin political life.

Conclusion: the dominance of top-down politics

The main features of the Montenegrin political system – the statehood-ethnic cleavage, the longevity of the predominant party in power, and the centralization of resources – strongly affect local politics. However, unlike the national level, where there was no alteration in power for 30 years (from 1990 to 2020), local level politics has been much more dynamic.

Even though parties not belonging to the national level ruling coalition managed to win in local elections, they were still significantly affected by the constellation of power at the national level. In particular, predominant party systems (a feature of the Montenegrin system until the parliamentary elections in 2020) are known as systems in which the ruling party has monopolistic access to public resources, decision making, and adjudication (Magalon, 2006). Those are also systems in which one of the main linkages between parties and voters is clientelism (Kitschelt 1995). Finally, systems with predominant parties tend to exhibit a low level of administrative independence, which is reflected in a lack of accountability and legal certainty. The advantages described here translated directly to local level politics, especially given the size of the country and the fact that it is highly centralized. To understand the effects of the predominant nationalized party system, especially in a situation in which local elections are not all held at the same time, we should consider the example of one or two smaller or medium-sized municipalities that had elections separately from the others. In these situations, the predominant party (Sartori 2005), with its direct link to public resources, can focus all of its resources on a very small number of voters, which gives it a significant advantage.

Furthermore, local election agendas are dominated by national level topics that reflect the main ethnic cleavage – *pro* and *contra* NATO accession, *pro* and *contra* the recognition of Kosovo, or *pro* and *contra* the Law on Religious Freedoms – making the local elections de facto mini referenda on the overarching theme of Montenegrin statehood.

This reflection of the national in the local is amplified by the depersonalized electoral legislation that strengthens the power of the parties vis-à-vis individual candidates. The fact that local councilors and mayors depend completely upon the will of their central party leadership to be placed on the list and subsequently elected discourages accountability toward voters. In some cases, the local councilors or party members ended up in direct conflict with the decisions of the party centers, which led them to defect from their parties and run as individual candidates. Unfortunately, without long-term party support these initiatives are often short-lived. Recently, there have been several initiatives to loosen parties' power over individual candidates by opening up the party lists. Several parliamentary parties supported by some NGOs initiated a campaign to change the electoral code and introduce some sort of preferential voting approach. However, the initiative has not yet been considered in parliament, and the question of whether its benefits would outweigh the disadvantages (for example, in relation to the representation of women, increased corruption due to interparty competition, and invalid ballots) remains.

Notes

1 The authors managed to collect full data on 80 out of the 82 local elections held in Montenegro since 2006. Unfortunately, the data on two elections, those in Rožaje and Plužine in 2006, have been lost from public archives. The authors managed to reconstruct most of the information about these two elections by contacting people who witnessed the election process, but not all.
2 Zakon o lokalnoj samoupravi, Službeni list Crne Gore 2/2018, 34/2019, 38/2020, accessed 7 October 2020.
3 Survey on the Perception of Public administration, March 2020, by De Facto Consultancy (available to the authors).
4 The president of the capital, Podgorica, is officially titled mayor, while the others are called 'presidents of municipality'. Because there are no substantive differences between mayors and presidents of the municipalities when it comes to their authority, election, or dismissal, in this chapter we use the term more appropriate in English– mayor.
5 Zakon o lokalnoj samoupravi, Službeni list Crne Gore 88/09, December 2009, accessed 24 March 2020.
6 Zakon o izboru odbornika i poslanika, accessed 3 March 2020 at http://dik.co.me/wp-content/uploads/2018/07/Zakon-o-izboru-odbornika-i-poslanika.pdf
7 Zakon o Lokalnoj samoupravi, Službeni list br. 2–2018 and 34–2019, accessed on 3 March 2020 at www.paragraf.me/propisi-crnegore/zakon-o-lokalnoj-samoupravi.html
8 This is the official interpretation, which is in line with all of the cases so far. The law is, however, ambiguous when it comes to the question of whether a mayor could be someone who was not on the electoral list.

9 All municipalities are divided into three equal groups, according to the number of registered voters.
10 The gender quotas (30% of the candidates on the list) were first introduced in 2011, but because they had no placement rules they have not been effective.

References

Carey, J. M., & Shugart, M. S. (1995). Incentives to cultivate a personal vote: A rank ordering of electoral formulas. *Electoral Studies, 14*(4), 417–439. https://doi.org/10.1016/0261-3794(94)00035-2

Darmanovic, S. (2007). Montenegro: A miracle in the Balkans? *Journal of Democracy, 18*(2), 152–159. https://doi.org/10.1353/jod.2007.0021

Džankić, J. (2014). Reconstructing the meaning of being "Montenegrin". *Slavic Review, 73*(2), 347–371. https://doi.org/10.5612/slavicreview.73.2.347

Kaluđerović, J., & Jocović, M. (2018). Montenegro: Volatile municipal revenues. In W. Bartlett, S. Kmezić, & Đulić, K. (Eds.), *Fiscal decentralisation, local government and policy reversals in Southeastern Europe* (pp. 123–161). Cham: Palgrave Macmillan.

Kitschelt, H. (1995). Formation of party cleavages in post-communist democracies: Theoretical propositions. *Party Politics, 1*(4), 447–472. https://doi.org/10.1177/1354068895001004002

Komar, O., & Živković, S. (2016). Montenegro: A democracy without alternations. *East European Politics and Societies, 30*(4), 785–804. https://doi.org/10.1177/0888325416652229

Lefevere, J., & Van Aelst, P. (2014). First-order, second-order or third-rate? A comparison of turnout in European, local and national elections in the Netherlands. *Electoral Studies, 35*, 159–170. https://doi.org/10.1016/j.electstud.2014.06.005

Oliver, J. E. (2000). City size and civic involvement in metropolitan America. *American Political Science Review, 94*(2), 361–373. https://doi.org/10.2307/2586017

Sartori, G. (2005). *Parties and party systems: A framework for analysis*. Colchester: ECPR Press.

Vuković, I. (2015). Political dynamics of the post-communist Montenegro: One-party show. *Democratization, 22*(1), 73–91.

38
North Macedonia
Local elections and parliamentary political dynamics

Veli Kreci and Islam Jusufi

Local government system: the adoption of self-government rule

The local government system in North Macedonia was reestablished in 1996 as part of the process of democratic transition. Municipalities (*opštini*), functioning as the administrative units of the lowest tier of government in Socialist Yugoslavia, were granted some autonomy in 1996 with the establishment of the first ever popularly elected local democratic institutions, which included mayors and municipal councils.

North Macedonia possesses two levels of territorially integrated, general-purpose governance: the central and the local (Jusufi 2006). The latter consists of 80 municipalities and the City of Skopje, which has a special two-tier administrative organization covering ten submunicipalities and is regulated by a separate law (Siljanovska-Davkova 2009). The local territorial structure is supplemented by the voluntary submunicipal tier within all municipalities and voluntary institutions of intermunicipal cooperation among some of the municipalities. Throughout the reference period, the number of municipalities has undergone frequent changes: from 124 in 1996 to 85 in 2004 (Swianiewicz 2014; Jusufi 2006; Kreci & Ymeri 2010) to the current 80 plus the City of Skopje as a special local self-government unit (Article 10, Law for Territorial Organization). The changes in the number of municipalities came as a result of municipal splits and mergers in 2004 (Kreci & Ymeri 2010) and mergers in 2013. National debates on local self-government have mainly centered around the territorial reorganization of the municipalities due to the multiethnic composition of the country. Despite the debates about the detrimental consequences of depopulation and economic difficulties, as well as problems with maintaining an adequate level of public services in sparsely populated areas, there have been limited discussions on further systematic amalgamation reform in North Macedonia. Although the median population size for local government units is 15,894, the number of municipalities with a population under 20,000 is around 60%.

All municipalities, including the City of Skopje, in total 81, are equal, and in principle a symmetric decentralization model has been applied. All municipalities have the same political and administrative powers (Maksimovska-Veljanovski 2010). An asymmetric approach has been used only in regard to the fiscal aspects of decentralization (Jusufi 2006).

The system of local government in North Macedonia has featured substantial improvements in the formal autonomy of local government (Kreci & Ymeri 2010), specifically between 2000 and 2005 following the reforms initiated after the Ohrid Framework Agreement of 2001, which led to the acknowledgment of the principle of local self-government. Municipalities in North Macedonia are responsible for basic local infrastructure such as water supply and sewage treatment, child care, primary and secondary education, social welfare, primary health care, and spatial planning (Jusufi 2006). According to the Local Autonomy Index, North Macedonia ranks 25th out of 39 European countries on the scale of overall local autonomy, which includes organizational, legal, and financial dimensions of autonomy, as well as the scope of responsibilities (Ladner et al. 2016). However, fiscal autonomy is limited, as North Macedonia is a country where local borrowing had only been allowed beginning in 2018 (Swianiewicz 2014), the proportion of local government revenues deriving from their own sources is small, and most of the transfers from the central government are conditional (Ladner et al. 2016). The scope of local government functions remains narrow (Swianiewicz 2014), and despite the fact that political decentralization has expanded the potential space available for citizens to participate in local governance, the participation of local communities has not been equitable or effective (Lyon 2015; Memeti & Kreci 2016).

The population of North Macedonia has a stronger attachment to the local communities than the central authorities, as historically the former has been more stable. However, traditions of local self-rule have been limited as this has come as a novelty only since 2004. Citizens attach importance to the local level, where they assess their quality of life in relation to the quality of public services offered by the municipality (Tim Institut 2018). A 2018 survey of public opinion focused on the quality of life demonstrates that municipalities in North Macedonia get the average grade of 3.1 (on a 1–4 scale), which is an increase compared to the numbers from a similar survey conducted in 2017 (Tim Institut 2018; Rating Agency 2017).

The municipalities of North Macedonia are represented by a directly elected mayor, who is the official representative of the municipality vis-à-vis the central government, and whose work is subject to municipal council supervision (Heinelt et al. 2018). Mayors serve as political leaders or interest mediators with the central government. The horizontal power relations in municipalities in North Macedonia, with the introduction of direct mayoral elections in 1996, may be characterized as the strong mayor model. The directly elected mayors are responsible for executive power at the local level, and they are both political leaders and heads of the local administration (Swianiewicz 2014). However, elected mayors who are not affiliated with the ruling party may experience challenges in their interactions with the central government.

Local elections as a contributor to the dynamics of democracy

The voters in North Macedonia vote for two main levels of government: for President of the Republic and members of the parliament at the central level, and for mayors and municipal councilors at the local level (IFES 2017). The elections are governed by the 2006 Electoral Code, which is valid for all elections at all levels of government. The Electoral Code has undergone a series of amendments since its adoption, but generally it provides a sound basis for the conduct of free and fair elections (OSCE 2017; State Election Commission 2017).

The local elections are scheduled to be held in early October every four years (Article 16, Electoral Code). They normally are not held simultaneously with other elections (the exception being the elections in 2009 where the local and presidential elections coincided). The first municipal elections in North Macedonia were held in 1996, followed by elections in 2000, 2005, 2009, 2013, and most recently in 2017. The municipal elections originally scheduled for 2004 were postponed to 2005 due to a referendum that challenged the Law for Territorial Organization of 2004 (OSCE 2005). There are no legal provisions for recall referenda for mayors or municipal councilors.

The local elections tend to be perceived as serving a barometric function for parliamentary and presidential elections. This intermediate character of local elections substantially contributes to the dynamics of democracy in the country. They are interpreted as a popularity test of the sitting government or as a forecast for the upcoming parliamentary or presidential elections.

The municipal elections are administered by a three-level election administration, comprising the State Election Commission (SEC), 80 municipal election commissions (MECs) and the election commission of the City of Skopje, and 3,480 electoral boards (EBs). The EBs consist of five members, three of whom are state, public, or municipal employees who are randomly selected, and the other two are appointed by the main political parties, one from the opposition and one from the ruling party. The SEC is supported by 34 regional offices and a secretariat made up of civil servants (OSCE 2017). It is the body responsible for conducting elections at all levels of government. It is composed of nine members appointed by the parliament for a five-year term. Three members are nominated by the ruling party, three by the opposition, and three are independent experts. The independent experts were added following the agreement signed in 2015 between political parties, known as the Przhino Agreement. With this agreement, the SEC's composition was changed from a political to a mixed model and the number of members increased from seven to nine. The president and deputy of the SEC are selected from the three independent experts (Congress of Local and Regional Authorities – Council of Europe 2018). The independent experts have no political affiliation and are selected through open competition. The nonpartisan members' five-year tenure is reasonably protected (OSCE 2017). The MECs and the election commission of the City of Skopje are responsible for their units of self-government, and EBs oversee the conduction of the elections at the level of the polling stations (Congress of Local and Regional Authorities – Council of Europe 2018).

MECs consist of five members who are employees in the state and municipal administrations and are randomly selected by the SEC. All members of MECs and EBs have deputies (IFES 2017). The SEC is responsible for the accuracy of voters' lists extracted from the permanent civil register kept by the Ministry of Internal Affairs, the publication of results of the elections, and for complaints and appeals.

A uniform system for all municipalities

Citizens who are 18 years old by election day and who have a residence in the municipality in which the election takes place are eligible to vote, unless they have lost their ability to vote through a court decision. Voter registration is given to people who have an official address in North Macedonia, a valid ID card or passport, and who are 18 years of age (IFES 2017). There is no difference in eligibility rules between the parliamentary and municipal elections. However, contrary to the parliamentary and presidential elections, voters residing abroad cannot vote in diplomatic missions for local elections. Noncitizens do not have a right to vote in any of the elections, and voting is not compulsory.

Municipalities have different numbers of councilors depending on the population size: it cannot be fewer than nine if the population is under 5,000 and it cannot be more than 33 if the population is over 100,000. The only exception is the council of the City of Skopje, which comprises 45 members (Congress of Local and Regional Authorities – Council of Europe 2018). These rules for the number of seats on municipal councils are set by the Electoral Code. The total number of elected members of municipal councils in the whole country is 1,336

(State Election Commission 2017). Additionally, 81 mayors are directly elected. There is a uniform system for the conduct of local elections: the same rules apply in all municipalities.

Mayors are elected through a majority two-round system (Reynolds 2008), while municipal councilors are elected through a closed-list PR system (Reynolds 2008). In the City of Skopje, voters elect both the citywide mayor and citywide members of the council of the City of Skopje and the mayor and the members of the municipal councils of the municipalities that fall within the boundaries of the City of Skopje.

In the mayoral election, a candidate must receive more than 50% of the votes to be elected in the first round. For the election to be valid, one-third of registered voters must turn out for the first round (IFES 2017). If none of the candidates receives an absolute majority of votes in the first round, a second round is organized within 14 days between the two candidates who received the most votes in the first round. No minimum turnout for the second round is required. If during the first round of voting for the election of the mayor more than two-thirds of the total number of voters registered on the voters' lists in that municipality fail to vote, the elections (with two rounds) shall be repeated again in that municipality regardless of the number of candidates (IFES 2017), although in practice this does not happen frequently.

Although the mayoral and local council elections are held simultaneously, in principle, there is no formal connection between the two. There is no need for the mayoral candidates to be supported by a list taking part in the municipal council elections.

North Macedonia organizes local elections at large. The candidate lists are the same for the entire territory of the municipality. The municipalities are divided into electoral polling stations (*izbiracko mesto*); however, they all participate in the election of the municipal administration for the whole municipality. The polling stations simply serve as the place where people vote that is normally a place closest to their residence.

The voter receives two ballot cards: one for voting for mayor and another for voting for the members of the municipal council. The voters may make only one choice for mayor, and they may only vote for one closed list for the council. For every type of ballot, there is a separate ballot box (Stockemer 2018).

The seat allocation for each municipal council is determined with the use of the d'Hondt method (IFES 2017), without any minimum turnout or legal threshold requirements. There are no specific seats designated for any candidates or groups.

Any eligible voter residing in the respective municipality may stand for election, except those currently in prison or sentenced to serve a prison term of more than six months. Candidates may be nominated by parties or coalitions of parties, or they may stand as independent candidates who are nominated by groups of voters. The latter are required to support the nomination of a whole list with signatures from 100 to 1,000 voters depending on the number of voters in the municipality, which is equivalent to 0.2–4.8% of eligible voters residing in the respective municipality. In 18 municipalities, the required number of signatures exceeds 2%, and in nine municipalities it is over 3% of all registered voters. This impinges on the equality of citizens' ability to stand for election and goes against good practice developed by the OSCE, which recommends that supporting signatures should not exceed 1% of registered voters (OSCE 2017). On a positive note, voters may now sign in support of more than one candidate for mayor and for more than one list of candidates for local councilors. However, signatures are still to be collected in the presence of a SEC representative. In small communities, such requirements may have a dissuasive or even intimidating effect on some voters.

In the most recent municipal elections of 2017, following a largely inclusive registration process, 19 parties and coalitions and 65 groups of voters fielded a total of 6,630 candidates on 370 lists for the council elections and 258 mayoral candidates, including 19 independents, for the mayoral elections (SEC 2017). There have been no instances of noncompetitive local elections. Contrary to the Electoral Code, in the 2017 elections the SEC held two separate lotteries on candidate order on the ballot: one for parties and coalitions of parties and the other for groups of voters that propose independent candidates. The separate lotteries discriminated against independent candidates, as they were placed at the bottom of the ballots.

To enhance gender equality, the Electoral Code requires candidate lists to include at least 40% of the less represented gender. Also, at least one candidate of each gender must be placed simultaneously within every three spots on the list and an additional one in every ten spots added. However, in the most recent local elections of 2017, after the deadline for nominations and in response to requests by political parties, the SEC amended a regulation detailing how the gender quota should be applied. It contradicted the Electoral Code and undermined the gender quota. MECs registered nine lists with fewer than 40% female candidates, 11 lists did not have a woman in every third place, and six lists did not have one in every tenth spot (OSCE 2017). Although this was noted by observers, it did not cause any controversy and the MECs allowed the registration of the disputed lists.

There are legal restrictions concerning the mayoral candidacy and the effective taking up of a mandate. The position of a mayor is a full-time professional post. The incumbent cannot hold any other post while serving as mayor. At the same time, the municipal councilors are part-time and there are no restrictions on concurrent eligible posts or jobs for them.

The electoral outcomes: stability in voter turnout throughout the years

The first democratic parliamentary elections in North Macedonia were held in 1994. Voter turnout in this very first election in which citizens were given the power to decide on their representatives freely and democratically showed historically the highest voter turnout (77.6%) compared to all elections held since. The first local elections held in 1996 recorded a voter turnout rate of 60.2%, which was highest turnout until the 2013 local elections, which surpassed the record of 1996 and reached the highest ever local electoral participation rate of 67.0% (see Figure 38.1). Nevertheless, the turnout for local elections has been stable throughout the reference period.

When attempting to understand voter turnout trends in North Macedonia, one should bear in mind the conditions surrounding each local election held, which show great variations due to two long-standing arguments. First, there was a series of revisions of municipality boundaries, altering the ethnic composition of municipalities (Kreci & Ymeri 2010). Namely, two major territorial reorganizations of local self-government units took place in 1996 and 2004.[1] The number of municipalities changed from 124 in 1996 to 85 municipalities in 2004. In addition to these changes and prior to the 2013 local elections, a merger of the Kicevo and Struga municipalities took place, bringing the number of municipalities down to 80 and the City of Skopje.[2] The second argument has to do with centralized policymaking influence over local elections; very often voter behavior reflects national politics rather than local considerations. Subsequently, national election outcomes are considered an indicator for the upcoming local elections contest. Therefore, the mobilization of voters for national elections enjoys higher interest by political actors than local elections. Still, local elections often serve as a kind of poll before parliamentary elections.

However, the 2013 local elections were an exception to this rule, as a strong emphasis on 'ethnic politics' played a major role in the mobilization of voters within ethnic lines. Subject to such a political environment was the fact that the merger of the Kicevo and Struga

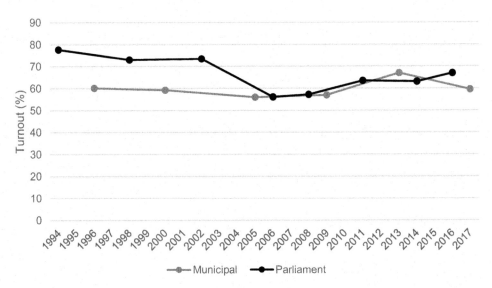

Figure 38.1 Voter turnout for local and parliamentary elections in North Macedonia, 1994–2017

municipalities became a nationwide issue and a mobilizing factor, as it spurred dissatisfaction among the majority of ethnic Macedonians from the concerned municipalities, leading to coalitions of ethnic Macedonian voters, which in turn triggered ethnic sensitivity on the part of ethnic Albanians and all other ethnic groups in the country.[3]

The number of municipal councilors is considered a factor in influencing political participation due to the spirit of community belonging or closeness to policymakers in municipal administration. Thus, the majority of municipalities with relatively few councilors tend to show higher voter turnout. The smaller the population size of the municipality, the higher the voter turnout. The implication in our context is that a municipality's social structure, which may present a competitive advantage to one ethnic group over the other ethnic group(s), directly affects the turnout and impacts the group share of voter turnout, which incorporates group behavior within 'group membership models', as illustrated in the cases of Kicevo and Struga (Ben-Bassat & Dahan 2012).

Therefore, when we analyze voter turnout rate in relation to the population size of a municipality, the evidence from the most recent local election in 2017, as presented in Figure 38.2, suggests higher levels of voter turnout in municipalities with populations of fewer than 20,000, while the voter participation difference is quite variable from municipality to municipality with larger population sizes. No significant differences are evident among the municipalities with populations over 40,000. One potential explanation of this tendency may be understood from the perspective of theoretical models (Harsanyi 1980; Feddersen & Sandroni 2006; Coate & Conlin 2004) that predict that in small-scale elections individuals are motivated to vote by the desire to maximize the aggregate utility of their group. Therefore, the social structure of municipalities measured by relative group size affects political participation, that is, the groups must be large enough relative to the total population to generate realistic voter turnout (Ben-Bassat & Dahan 2012).

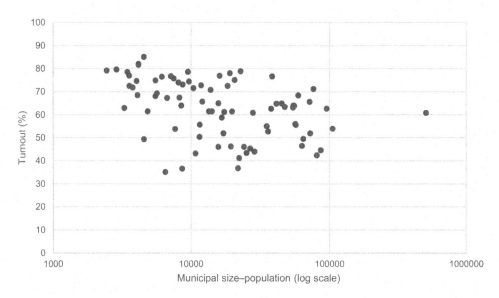

Figure 38.2 Voter turnout in the 2017 North Macedonian local elections by municipality size

In addition, there are a few municipalities with fewer than 5,000 inhabitants in which the turnout rate is lower than the average. Such cases need to be analyzed further prior to contending the argument that municipality size matters.

Since the first democratic elections, political parties in North Macedonia, either independently or through coalitions, have actively competed for seats in both parliamentary and local elections. No cases of uncontested seats have been recorded. Moreover, the degree of electoral competition is relatively high due to the highly fragmented electorate in terms of ethnicity and social status. The political parties, whether for national or local elections, are somehow obliged to form coalitions. For example, in the local elections of 2017, electoral competition was run by 17 political entities, three of which were coalitions of parties that are not necessarily ideologically homogeneous and the remaining 14 were political parties that promoted their candidates for mayors and councilors. However, the three coalitions of parties were formed by 43 political parties in total, who at the same time are active at the parliamentary level and promoted their own candidates for mayor or supported their coalition candidates. As a result of this coalition formation for 80 municipalities and the City of Skopje, 223 candidates ran for mayor and 373 candidate lists for municipal councilors were promoted by 19 political entities in total (Dimeski & Pankovski 2018). Out of this contest, the party coalitions won overwhelmingly in the mayoral elections. Specifically, candidates from the coalition led by the Social Democratic Union of Macedonia (SDSM) won a total of 57 mayoral posts, including the mayor of the City of Skopje, while candidates from other coalitions of parties and individual political parties won a total of 21 mayoral posts. On the other hand, independent candidates won only three mayoral posts.[4] The performance of coalitions of parties, political parties, and independent candidates is similar at the parliamentary level.

Therefore, local elections in North Macedonia are dominated by parliamentary political parties. The role and impact of political parties on local government politics and policymaking are considerable. After all, as shown in Table 38.1, in the 2017 local elections only 3% of councilors

Table 38.1 Party politicization in the 2017 local elections in North Macedonia

	% of municipalities where running	% of municipalities where represented	% of seats on local councils	% of votes in local elections	% of mayors affiliated with the party
Coalition[1] led by the Social Democratic Union of Macedonia (SDSM)	95.1	95.1	41.0	40.9	70.4
Coalition[2] led by the Democratic Party for National Unity (VMRO-DPMNE)	92.5	88.9	32.1	32.8	6.2
Democratic Union of Integration (BDI)	44.0	34.5	9.4	8.7	12.3
Democratic Party of the Albanians (PDSH)	26.6	12.3	1.7	1.6	1.2
BESA Movement	34.5	25.0	4.7	4.5	1.2
Alliance for the Albanians (ASH)	37.0	28.4	4.7	4.8	3.7
Democratic Party of the Turks in Macedonia (TDP)	14.8	9.8	1.3	1.0	1.2
Movement of National Unity of Turks (TBMH)	8.6	3.7	0.2	1.0	0.0
Citizens' Option for Macedonia (GROM)	4.9	2.4	0.2	0.5	0.0
The Left	8.6	2.4	0.2	0.6	0.0
Union of Roma in Macedonia (SRM)	4.9	4.9	0.5	0.3	0.0
People's Movement for Macedonia	8.6	6.1	0.5	0.4	0.0
Coalition 'Alliance for the Albanians'[3]	2.4	2.4	0.0	0.3	0.0
Independents and nonnational (local) lists	71.0	48.1	2.8	2.4	3.7

[1] The coalition is an alliance of 22 political parties.
[2] The coalition is an alliance of 18 political parties.
[3] Political parties BDI, BESA, and ASH in a coalition running in three municipalities – Bitola, Gazi Baba, and Ohrid.

in North Macedonia were not overtly affiliated with a political party, and only three (out of 81) municipalities were won by independent mayors. In North Macedonia, the politics in local government is equated with party politics.

Female representation in politics both nationally and locally has received interventions in legislation by the introduction of mandatory quotas. Specifically, to enhance gender equality, the Electoral Code introduced a 40% gender quota (Congress of Local and Regional

Authorities – Council of Europe 2018; Haxhijaha-Imeri 2017). Although enforcement of the quota provisions became an issue of concern in the 2017 municipal elections,[5] female representation reached its highest level historically in local elections, with an increase from 8.4% in 2000 to 33% in 2017. The female representation in parliament stands at 37.5% in 2016, which is ten times higher than the rate achieved in the 2000 national elections (see Table 38.2). Moreover, in both types of elections – local and national – female representation has shown a significant increase particularly since 2005. On the other hand, it is evident that the participation of women at the mayoral level is lacking or is 'virtually absent where no quota laws exist' (Haxhijaha-Imeri 2017: 2). In terms of the political representation of women by statistical regions, it is well balanced, with the highest representation in the Eastern region with 36.6% and the lowest in the Polog region with 28.1%, where the share of the rural population is the highest in the country; overall female representation in local government administration is 37%, whereas there is a significant lack of representation within managerial positions.[6]

North Macedonia's constitution and laws include several key provisions regarding representation of minorities in the local administrations, but not specifically regarding local elected officials. Persons without the citizenship of North Macedonia have no right to be represented at the local level. The representation of minorities is built around the understanding that there should be nonterritorial opportunities for representation of minorities in the country's central or local governance. There are no specific provisions regarding the representation of minorities in the local electoral system. The system of minority representation at the local level includes other elements. One element is that any language other than Macedonian that is spoken by at least 20% of the population in a municipality (practically, it mainly refers to the Albanian language) is also an official language in the respective municipality. Another element of minority representation is the special procedure of double majority voting, also called the 'Badinter Majority', as it was proposed by the French Senator Robert Badinter in 2001. At both the central (parliament) and local levels (municipal council), the double majority voting applies to matters concerning the rights of minorities. It means that a proposal may be accepted only if a majority of all members of the Parliament/Municipal Council votes for it, as well as a majority of the representatives of the ethnic minorities in the parliament and municipal council that need to declare to which minority they belong (Article 69, Constitution; Article 41, Law for Local Self-Government). This voting pattern has also been adopted as a rule in adopting the Law for Local Self-Government, which regulates the rights and obligations of the municipalities (Article 114, Constitution; Friedman 2005).

The incumbency advantage in local elections in North Macedonia is limited due to high electoral volatility. It is particularly visible in the case of mayoral elections: mayoral posts won by leading parties or coalitions of parties, which shared over 75% of mayoral posts in the last two election cycles, alternated between those political parties or coalitions of parties. For an illustration, in the 2013 local elections, VMRO-DPMNE and its coalition won 57 mayoral posts against its major competitor – the coalition led by the SDSM, which won only four

Table 38.2 Female representation at the local and national levels in North Macedonia

Election year	1996		2000	2005	2009		2013	2017
Councilors	n/a		8.4%	22.3%	27.0%		30.0%	33.0%
Mayors	0,0%		2.4%	3.6%	0.0%		4.7%	7.4%
Election year	1990	1994	1998	2002	2006	2008	2011	2014	2016
MPs	4%	3%	7.5%	17.5%	28.3%	32.5%	34.1%	34.9%	37.5%

mayoral posts. However, in the subsequent 2017 local elections, the ratio of mayoral positions between two biggest coalitions reversed in favor of SDSM, with 57 mayoral posts, whereas VMRO-DPMNE won only five mayoral posts. Similar tendencies were observed for municipal councilors seats in the last two election cycles of 2013 and 2017.

Decoupling of local electoral dynamics from the dominance of parliamentary politics is yet to emerge

North Macedonia lacks systematic academic studies and research on local elections as indicators of voter behavior versus local or national politics. Also, local election voter surveys and comparative analysis of the results focusing on recent local elections are yet to emerge.

The local electoral system in North Macedonia is under the dominance of national party politics. Rarely does a candidate with a nonnational political party affiliation win a mayoral post. This is also the case for municipal councilors. Generally, political parties primarily focus on seizing positional power in national parliamentary elections, quantified by the number of seats won by political party representatives in the parliament. This tendency is evident for all existing and newly formed political parties. As the number of representatives of the political party in the parliament increases, vote swapping for the parties expands in local elections. Voters' behavior in favoring a less preferable candidate in their district in order to get better results for their party in the overall local election may well be observed in several electoral districts with highly competitive party candidates. On the other hand, the insignificant influence of independent candidates on local elections further accelerates competition among coalitions of parties. The remaining independent candidates or smaller and newer political parties tend to form coalitions with the national political parties, thus further consolidating the existing large party coalitions. The number of municipal councilors is considered a factor influencing political participation across municipalities. In addition, due to North Macedonia's social structure, there is a strong influence of group share on voter turnout. The expectation that further devolution of powers and resources to municipalities would lead to decoupling of local electoral political dynamics from the national political dynamics is yet to happen.

The dominance of national political party competition over the local elections is further exacerbated by the centralization tendencies in vertical accountability mechanisms, such as media and civil society. These two have increasingly adopted a nationalized frame when reporting on or advocating for issues that relate to local politics or local development. Although candidate recruitment for mayoral posts mainly happens through a predominantly local process; the candidates with former national political experience tend to have more leverage over the local political candidates. The dominance of national party politics over the local electoral politics has not left the space for emergence of serious debates as regards the local electoral system.

Notes

1 See Article 10 from the Law on Territorial Organization of the Local Self-Government.
2 149/2014 amendments to the Law on Territorial Organization of the LSG by merging four rural municipalities (Vranestica, Drugova, Zajas, and Oslomej) with the Kicevo and Struga municipalities.
3 For illustration, voter turnout in Kicevo municipality in the 2013 elections reached 71.7% whereas in the 2017 local elections it was merely 56.0%
4 For more information on the State Election Commission website: www.sec.mk

5 Among mayoral candidates, only 16 were women (6%), and 14% of lists for councils were headed by women. MECs registered nine lists with fewer than 40% female candidates and 17 lists that did not place women in the required spots.
6 http://rodovreactor.mk/subject/politics/

References

Ben-Bassat, A. & Dahan, M. (2012). Social Identity and Voting Behavior. *Public Choice*, 151(1–2), 193–214.
Coate, S. & Conlin, M. (2004). A Group Rule – Utilitarian Approach to Voter Turnout: Theory and Evidence. *American Economic Review*, 94(5), 1476–1504.
Congress of Local and Regional Authorities – Council of Europe. (2018). *Observation of municipal elections in the former Yugoslav Republic of Macedonia*. CPL34(2018)02prov. Strasbourg.
Dimeski, J. & Pankovski, M. (2018). *The Republic of Macedonia's 2017 Local Elections Handbook* (Second Updated Edition). Skopje: Konrad Adenauer Foundation & Institute for Democracy "Societas Civilis".
Electoral Code, Official Gazette of the Republic of North Macedonia, No.42/20.
Feddersen, T. & Sandroni, A. (2006). A Theory of Participation in Elections. *American Economic Review*, 96(4), 1271–1282.
Friedman, E. (2005). Electoral System Design and Minority Representation in Slovakia and Macedonia. *Ethnopolitics*, 4(4), 381–396.
Harsanyi, J.C. (1980). Rule Utilitarianism, Rights, Obligations and the Theory of Rational Behavior. *Theory and Decision*, 12(2), 115–133.
Haxhijaha-Imeri, A. (2017). *Enhancing Women Participation In Electoral Processes*. Policy brief (unpublished).
Heinelt, H., Hlepas, N., Kuhlmann, S., & Swianiewicz, P. (2018) Local Government Systems: Grasping the Institutional Environment of Mayors. In: H. Heinelt, A. Magnier, M. Cabria, H. Reynaert (eds) *Political Leaders and Changing Local Democracy. Governance and Public Management* (pp. 19–78). Cham: Palgrave Macmillan.
IFES. (2017). *Elections in Macedonia – 2017 Local Elections – Frequently Asked Questions*. Arlington.
Jusufi, I. (2006). Policy Shift in the Fiscal Equalization in Macedonia: Yet to Be Implemented. In: *Fiscal Equalization in Southeast Europe*. Budapest: Fiscal Decentralization Initiative for Central and Eastern Europe.
Kreci, V. & Ymeri, B. (2010). The Impact of Territorial Re-Organisational Policy Interventions in the Republic of Macedonia. *Local Government Studies*, 36(2), 271–290.
Ladner, A., Keuffer, N. & Baldersheim, H. (2016). Measuring Local Autonomy in 39 Countries (1990–2014). *Regional and Federal Studies*, 26(3), 321–357.
Law on Local Self-Government, Official Gazette of the Republic of Macedonia, No.5/02.
Law on Territorial Organization of the Local Self-Government in the Republic of Macedonia, Official Gazette of the Republic of Macedonia, No.55/2004, 12/2005,98/2008,106/2008 and 149/2014.
Lyon, A. (2015). Political Decentralization and the Strengthening of Consensual, Participatory Local Democracy in the Republic of Macedonia. *Democratization*, 22(1), 157–178.
Maksimovska-Veljanovski, A. (2010). The Model of the Asymmetric Fiscal Decentralisation in the Theory and the Case of Republic of Macedonia. *Iustinianus Primus Law Review*, 1(1), 1–11.
Memeti, M. & Kreci, V. (2016). Role of Municipal Council in Increasing Citizen Participation at the Local Budget Process. *Central European Public Administration Review*, 14(2–3), 53–73.
OSCE. (2005). *Former Yugoslav Republic of Macedonia – Municipal Elections – 2005*. Final Report. Warsaw: OSCE.
OSCE. (2017). *Former Yugoslav Republic of Macedonia – Municipal Elections – 2017*. Final Report. Warsaw: OSCE.
Rating Agency. (2017). *Research of Citizens' Satisfaction from the Local Government Services*. Skopje: Rating Agency.
Reynolds, A., Reilly, B. & Ellis, A. (2008). *Electoral System Design: The New International IDEA Handbook*. Stockholm: IDEA.

Siljanovska-Davkova, G. (2009). Local and Institutional Framework of Local Self-Government in the Republic of Macedonia. *Lex Localis-Journal of Local-Self Government*, 7(2), 107–127.

State Election Commission. (2017). *Report – Municipal Elections – 2017*. Skopje.

Stockemer, D. (2018). Gender Equality and Electoral Corruption: Some Insights from the Local Elections in Macedonia. *Journal of Contemporary Central and Eastern Europe*, 26(2–3), 267–275.

Swianiewicz, P. (2014). An Empirical Typology of Local Government Systems in Eastern Europe. *Local Government Studies*, 40(2), 292–311.

Tim Institut. (2018). *Survey Report on Citizen's Satisfaction with Local Public Services*. Skopje.

39
Romania
A case of national parties ruling local politics

Cristina Stănuș and Andrei Gheorghiță

Introduction

Democratic local elections were organized in post-Communist Romania for the first time in February 1992, following the adoption in 1991 of a new constitution and subsequent legislation. They were part of a wider and prolonged effort to reconstitute local self-government and the first democratic local elections organized on Romanian territory since 1937. The February 1992 founding local elections preceded the first legislative elections by eight months. This set a pattern in which local and legislative elections usually take place in the same year, with local elections occurring first. The combination of timing and electoral rules makes Romanian local elections an important predictor of the strength of parties in the upcoming legislative elections. Hence, they are attributed great importance by political actors and fiercely contested. They have, however, received less attention in the field of Romanian electoral studies.

There are two tiers of local government in Romania. The first tier comprises municipalities, grouped into three categories: 103 *municipia* (urban settlements of socioeconomic, historical, and/or cultural importance and/or county capitals, which can also include neighboring villages), 216 towns (*orașe*, the rest of the urban settlements, can also include neighboring villages), and 2,862 communes (*comune*, rural settlements grouping one or more villages). The current territorial structure is the result of the 1968 compulsory amalgamation reform implemented by the Communist regime and the reforms of the early 2000s (de-amalgamations and status upgrades). The second tier comprises 41 counties. The capital city of Bucharest has a somewhat special organization, similar to a county, as it comprises six sectors governed by first-tier local governments (Coman et al. 2001; Preda & Soare 2008). First-tier local governments are rather small. The average size, excluding Bucharest, was 6,331 in 2016 (79,320 for *municipia*, 10,826 for towns, and 3,388 for rural municipalities). Municipalities are a decentralized level of policymaking, with elected authorities that have full legal power and own property, are entitled to their own financial resources, and able (with limited discretion) to impose local taxes (for details, see Coman et al. 2001; Ladner et al. 2015).

Vertical power relations are defined by the concomitant implementation of decentralization and deconcentration reforms. Decentralization was a slow, multistage, stop-and-go process (Profiroiu & Profiroiu 2006), while deconcentration was focused upon and has proceeded at a much faster (Preda & Soare 2008), yet chaotic (Baba et al. 2007) pace. While asymmetrical decentralization was introduced in 2016, very little has happened in terms of implementation. The decentralization of tasks has not been accompanied by full fiscal decentralization; the central government continues to control local financial management and does not provide sufficient resources for local governments to match the decentralized responsibilities (Profiroiu & Profiroiu 2006; Profiroiu et al. 2017). The central government supervises the activity of local governments for legality and compliance with financial regulations, without subordinating them. However, central government representatives sometimes overstep their mandate and instead of the legality control, focus on the policy appropriateness (see Stănuș & Pop 2011). The overall degree of local autonomy is quite similar to other countries in the region, though much lower than in the older democracies of Western Europe (Ladner et al. 2015).

Horizontal power relations are shaped by electoral rules and wider political system variables. Romania presents a dualist system, with mayors exercising executive functions and councils exercising legislative functions. Mayors are directly elected: their terms in office are independent of the term of the council, they usually control a majority in the council, they can be recalled by referendum, they co-define the council agenda, and they control the bureaucratic apparatus of the local government. This is further reinforced by mayors being full-time officials, while councilors are part-time officials. Moreover, mayors in major cities are important political figures, with significant influence outside the local government going far beyond the legal limits of their mandates (Ștefan et al. 2004). Broadly, Romania fits the strong mayor model of local government as discussed in the literature (Heinelt & Hlepas 2006). This, in turn, shapes the electoral environment, as the directly elected mayors become the most visible figures of local politics and drivers of the votes for national political parties in both local and national elections (Comșa 2008; Gheorghiță 2010).

Local elections and a nationally managed electoral process

Local elections for both tiers of local government are organized every four years on a Sunday in June, on a date set by the central government. They are managed by an ad hoc nested structure of electoral bureaus (one national, 41 counties, one for Bucharest) comprising judges, representatives of the Permanent Electoral Authority (*Autoritatea Electorală Permanentă*, AEP), and representatives of political parties and national minority organizations holding seats in parliament. They coordinate lower level electoral bureaus at the municipal or polling station levels comprising representatives of the AEP and the competitors. The electoral bureaus manage every aspect of the election, from registering candidates, through the entire process, to declaring the results.

Local officials are elected for a fixed four-year term, which can only be prolonged by the central government in extreme situations such as war, natural disasters, or officially declared states of siege or emergency. To date, this has only happened in 2020 in the context of the COVID-19 pandemic, when local elections that were to be held on 28 June were postponed to 27 September.

This choice of a nationally managed electoral process has been accompanied by a series of provisions aimed at avoiding by-elections. Thus, unsuccessful candidates on party lists for councils become substitutes for colleagues leaving office before the end of their term. To ensure that substitutes are always available, the law allows lists to include 25% more candidates than the number of seats on the respective council. If a mayoral seat becomes vacant, an interim mayor is appointed by the council, and by-elections are organized to elect a person to serve the remainder of the term. Sometimes local governments can go on for months with an interim mayor, because setting the date for a by-election is not compulsory, but rather a question of opportunity to be determined by the central government (Autoritatea Electorală Permanentă 2017).

Sometimes interim mayors serve until the end of the term, not least due to the fact that the law does not allow for by-elections to be organized within a year of the regular local elections.

Local elections cannot be concurrent with parliamentary elections. An attempt by the government in 2011 to push through parliament the cumulation of the 2012 local and parliamentary elections was deemed unconstitutional. The Constitutional Court cited difficulties with expressing a citizen's right to vote (because of the high number of ballot papers required, the procedures would take too long with the consequence that not all citizens willing to vote would manage to do it in on election day) and restrictions on a citizen's right to be elected (because a citizen not elected in local elections would be deprived of the chance to run in parliamentary elections, as concomitant candidacies of the same individual were not allowed) (Curtea Constituțională a României 2012).

A strict separation of offices between and within different tiers of government is in place. Thus, one local elected official cannot simultaneously hold another elective or appointed political office at any level of government. For example, a mayor cannot be a member of the local or county council, a member of parliament, a member of the cabinet, or a holder of an appointed political position at central government level.

The law provides for the symmetrical mechanism of recall by electorate (Whitehead 2018). Mayors and local councils as groups may be recalled by citizens via referendum. A total of 25% of the citizens eligible to vote in a municipality (overall and, previously, also in each of the localities) must sign a motivated request to recall the mayor or the council. If this condition is met a recall referendum is organized, which must meet a 30% turnout threshold to be valid. This is a seldom-used provision and none of the attempts so far has been successful, as either there were not enough signatures to start the procedure (see the cases of Corni or Fărcășești) or the referendum turnout threshold was not met (Pungești, while a higher 50% threshold applied). The situation of recall from above (see Whitefield 2006) is much more widespread. Thus, councilors are automatically removed from office if they are no longer members of the political party on whose list they were elected, 'as they would no longer meet the representation and legitimacy conditions necessary to fulfil the political program for which citizens voted' (Curtea Constituțională a României 2013). Councilors may either resign from the party or be expelled from it, with the latter giving significant discretion to party organizations. In both cases, it falls to the party to initiate the procedure to replace the councilor. Actual replacement can only happen if the local council votes with a simple majority to vacate and the fill the seat. The provision has been introduced in response to the political and organizational consequences of party-switching by elected officials at all levels of government. Mayors can lose their position only if they resign from the party who supported their candidacy (Parlamentul României 2004). This allows for a higher degree of party control over elected officials in collective bodies. A recall of any local elected official from above is also possible for incompatibility, change of residence, missing three council meetings in a row without justification, inability to exercise their mandate for six months, sentencing to a prison term, interdiction by the court, or loss of electoral rights. Most frequently invoked in procedures to recall local elected officials are incompatibilities and sentencing to prison terms (Agenția Națională de Integritate 2019).

The electoral system: the simplicity of proportional representation

Romania has a uniform system for the election of local officials, with the same set of rules and procedures applicable throughout the country. In what follows, the rules applicable to the latest local elections, those of 2020, are discussed. A closed-list proportional representation system has been used since 1992. Mayors have been directly elected using a plurality system since 2012, as the majoritarian system with runoff was abolished in 2011 in a controversial move. The change was formally justified by making references to reducing the financial burden of municipalities during the economic crisis, but it is widely believed that the center-right governing party was seeking to maximize its chances in the local elections. In 2020, the matter was again on the agenda as the rules applicable to the September local elections were debated, with a notable reversal of positions: some parties and politicians who supported the change in 2011 wanted a reversal to the runoff system, while some of those opposing the 2011 change preferred the plurality system.

For council elections, each municipality is a single, multimember constituency, theoretically ensuring a high degree of proportionality. The size of the local council is based on the size of the municipality, as determined by the National Institute for Statistics at the beginning of the respective year. Local councils have between nine and 31 members, and the Bucharest council has 55. The total number of seats varies from one election to the next, depending on variations in the population of local governments; it stood at 40,066 for the 2020 municipal elections.

All Romanian citizens over the age of 18 are eligible to vote in the local government in which they reside. Formal registration of residence with the authorities prior to the election is required, which leads to automatic inclusion on the electoral register maintained by local governments with assistance from the AEP and central government structures in charge of population records. A similar procedure applies to EU citizens whose residence status is confirmed by immigration authorities (Autoritatea Electorală Permanentă 2017). Some citizens may have their right to vote restricted by a court in very specific conditions (mental illness or criminal conviction). Voting is not compulsory and may only be exercised if proper identification is provided.

Romanian and EU citizens residing in Romania over the age of 23 can run for office in the local government in which they reside. The only exception is made for the residents of Bucharest, who may run for a council seat in any of the six first-tier local governments (sectors) in the city. Until 2012, EU citizens were only allowed to run for council seats. According to constitutional provisions, judges sitting on the Constitutional Court, the ombudsman, magistrates, active members of the military and the police, and certain categories of civil servants cannot run in elections. Moreover, courts can place interdictions on individuals in specific cases (mental illness, criminal convictions, and violations of incompatibility regulations).

Citizens may run as independents or as part of a list of candidates supported by a political party, a political alliance, an electoral alliance, or an organization of citizens belonging to a national minority. One party can only be part of a single alliance, and one citizen can only be included on a single list of candidates at the same tier of local government. The same individual may run at the same time for mayor, county council president, the local council, and the county council. Lists of candidates must include both genders, without quotas being applied. However, there have been isolated cases in which lists of candidates were accepted without this provision being enforced. Candidacies (lists, mayors, independent candidacies for council or mayor) need to be supported by the signatures of residents. This should include 1% of the total number of voters, but no fewer than 100 for communes, 500 for small and medium-sized urban settlements, and 1,000 for large urban settlements, counties, and the capital city and its subdivisions.

Some provisions concerning candidacies induce some distortion specific to proportional representation systems (Farrell 1997). Thus, the electoral law restricts the participation of organizations of the national minorities (other than political parties). The organizations already represented in parliament can freely submit lists of candidates. Any other minority organization may run in local elections if it is accepted at the national level by the Central Electoral Bureau.

To be accepted, it must submit a list of members that includes at least 15% of the number of people who declared at the last census that they belong to the respective minority. If the 15% correspond to a number larger than 25,000 citizens, the list needs to include a minimum of 300 persons per at least 15 counties and Bucharest. The latter provision would effectively apply, on the basis of data from the 2011 census, to organizations representing the two largest minorities, Hungarians and Roma.

On election day, citizens cast four ballots: for mayor, the local council, the county council, and the county council president. The ballot structure for council elections is simple: the citizen gets one vote, which he or she may give to a list or to an independent candidate. The lists are closed, giving a high degree of control over who gets elected to the parties, alliances, or minority organizations proposing them. Elections are valid no matter the turnout. Before 2008 a turnout threshold applied, but it was abolished to simplify the electoral process.

Simple ballot structure translates into easy counting procedures and a relatively straightforward determination of the election results. The candidate who has received a plurality of valid votes becomes mayor. The results of local council elections are determined in two stages:

1. A combination of an electoral threshold with a simple Hare quota is applied. First, it is determined which parties, alliances, or minority organizations have met the electoral threshold (since 2004, 5% of the valid votes in the constituency for parties or minority organizations, 7% for alliances with two members, and 8% for alliances with three or more members). The electoral threshold is the key component in the efforts of national parties to maintain their dominance of local politics. Second, a simple Hare quota (Farrell 1997) is calculated. With the use of the quota, seats are allocated to all lists that passed the threshold, as well as to independent candidates who met the quota.
2. All remaining seats (if any) are distributed using the largest remainder method to all competitors who have passed the threshold. However, if no minority organization other than one representing the Hungarians has received a seat in the previous stage, then the organization with the highest number of votes that has passed the threshold takes precedence over other competitors and gets a seat. An analogous procedure applies for minority organizations representing Hungarians. The first provision was introduced for the 2004 elections, while the second was applied for the first time in 2016. If these provisions are applied, all other minority organizations are excluded from seat allocation under the largest remainder method.

The electoral law also includes provisions for special circumstances. If no party or alliance meets the threshold, seats are first allocated to the independents meeting the quota (if the case) and then to the first three parties in decreasing order of the total number of votes. To address likely center-periphery issues in urban or rural municipalities that include several localities, an artifice of representation is introduced. If a village is not represented by a resident in the newly elected council, a village representative (*delegat sătesc*) is elected by residents for the duration of the council's term. He or she participates in local council meetings debating issues related to that village, without voting rights.

Turnout, competitiveness, and the dominance of national parties

Given the established time pattern in which local elections and national elections take place in the same year and in this specific order, the former were largely perceived as a 'poor relative' of the latter (Radu 2012), raising less public interest, but similar passions from political actors.

Consequently, turnout for local elections was systematically lower compared to the national elections for the first four electoral cycles (1992–2004), with a maximum gap of almost 20% (see Table 39.1). This trend reversed after the separation of the parliamentary elections from the presidential ones in 2008 (due the constitutional reform of 2003 extending the president's term in office from four to five years). Stripped of the public attention raised by the presidential competition, parliamentary elections generated much lower turnout in 2008, and since then local turnout has been larger than parliamentary turnout.

Data from the 2016 local elections[1] suggest a negative relation between turnout and municipality size (an overall Pearson's correlation coefficient of $-.32$ between turnout rate and the number of adults included on the electoral register). This negative relation becomes more straightforward when tested inside groups of municipalities that are more homogeneous in size: $-.53$ for *municipia*, $-.41$ for towns, and $-.48$ for communes.

Local elections tend to be highly competitive in Romania. The competition is stronger in larger municipalities. Parliamentary parties are expected to run lists of candidates for all local councils. In 2016, the average number of candidates per mayoral seat was 4.4, while the average number of council lists per municipality was 5.6 (see Table 39.2). Unopposed local elections are quite rare: in 2016, in only 2.2% of municipalities was there a single candidate for the mayoral office, and only in 0.7% of the municipalities, the council election was uncontested with only one list running. The voting process still takes place, even if the election is uncontested. Most of the unopposed elections occur in rural municipalities inhabited by a large majority of Hungarians, where the Democratic Alliance of Hungarians in Romania (UDMR/RMDSZ) has a quasi-monopoly of representation. Overall, competitiveness in local elections appears to be on a negative trend, reflecting the consolidation of the national party system, with one big party on the left (Social Democrats, PSD) and one big party on the right (National Liberals, PNL).

Table 39.1 Voter turnout for local and national elections in Romania, 1992–2020

Date of first round of elections:	1992 February 9	1996 June 2	2000 June 4	2004 June 6	2008 June 1	2012 June 10	2016 June 5	2020 September 27
Turnout for local elections (%) – second tier, first round of elections (when applicable)	65.0[1]	56.5	50.9	54.2	48.8	56.3	48.2	45.6
Turnout for parliamentary elections (%) – lower chamber	76.3	76.0	65.3	58.5	39.2[2]	41.8[2]	39.8	Dec. 2020
% difference in turnout for local elections compared to previous	–	–8.5	–5.6	+3.3	–5.4	+7.5	–8.1	–2.6
% difference in turnout for parliamentary elections compared to previous	–	–0.3	–10.7	–6.8	–19.3	+2.6	–2.0	–

[1] *Source*: Iațu et al. (2013)
[2] Mixed electoral system in use. All other parliamentary elections used PR. Turnout for the second round of presidential elections after the constitutional reform: 2019, 54.9%; 2014, 64.1%; 2009, 58%.

Table 39.2 Competitiveness of local elections in Romania, 2004–2016

Election	Competitiveness/Year	2004	2008	2012	2016
Mayoral election	Number of mayoral candidates	25,568	19,156	14,138	14,039
	Average number of candidates per mayoral seat	8.2	6.0	4.4	4.4
	Uncontested mayoral seats	44 (1.4%)	28 (0.9%)	37 (1.2%)	70 (2.2%)
Local council election	Number of local council lists (independents included)	29,021	25,188	19,865	17,765
	Average number of lists per municipality	9.3	7.9	6.2	5.6
	Uncontested local council elections	10 (0.3%)	4 (0.1%)	12 (0.4%)	21 (0.7%)

Local elections in Romania are dominated by national parties: for their local branches, better results are rapidly converted into heavier influence on party decisions and more eligible positions on the parliamentary lists. Over the years, the relevance of local leaders for the two most important national parties followed an ascending trend. While the Social Democrats are frequently labeled as 'dominated by local barons', the National Liberals are sometimes addressed as 'the party of mayors'. The landscape of Romanian local politics after the 2016 local elections was described as imperfectly bipartite (Radu & Buti 2016) given the absolute domination of the two largest parties: PSD and PNL cumulated nationally more than 86% of the mayors and more than 74% of the local councilors. This is an underestimation of the real state of fact, as in some municipalities the local branches of the two parties (especially the PSD) also won mayoral and council seats as part of local alliances.

Parliamentary parties (at the moment of the local elections) in 2016 won more than 96% of the mayorships and 92% of the seats on local councils (see Table 39.3). Among these, the clear winner was the Social Democratic Party (PSD), governing party at the time and main representative of the left, with a strong appeal in rural areas and small and medium-sized urban municipalities. Second was the National Liberal Party (PNL), coagulated under a valued historical brand after the recent merger (2014–2015) of the former National Liberal Party (PNL, liberal) with the Democrat Liberal Party (PDL, conservative). The third party in terms of votes was the Alliance of Liberals and Democrats (ALDE), of liberal orientation, a new party founded from the merger of the Liberal Reformist Party (PLR, liberal, a breakaway party from PNL) with the Conservative Party (PC, social liberal) under the leadership of the former Prime Minister Călin Popescu-Tăriceanu. Fourth came the Democratic Alliance of Hungarians in Romania (UDMR/RMDSZ), the main political organization of the Hungarian minority, with strong support in Transylvania and formally affiliated with the EPP. Two other new parties of recent intraparliamentary origin are also relevant for the 2016 local elections: the National Union for the Progress of Romania (UNPR, social democratic) and the People's Movement Party (PMP, Christian democratic).

Nonnational lists were largely irrelevant in the 2016 local elections, as their success was limited to 1.5% of the mayoral seats and 2.4% of the council seats. One could say that irrelevant is too soft a term if we consider that most of these local lists are actually local alliances of the big parliamentary parties, typically PSD+ALDE and PSD+UNPR. Still, a special mention is needed for the local Save Bucharest Union, who achieved the second highest number of votes

Table 39.3 Electoral performance of the parliamentary parties, independent candidates, and nonnational lists in the 2016 local elections in Romania

Competitors	% of municipalities where running	% of municipalities where represented	% of seats on local councils	% of (aggregate) votes in local elections	% of mayors affiliated with the party
PSD (Social Democratic Party)	95.4	94.0	41.4	33.7	52.7
PNL (National Liberal Party)	95.3	93.9	32.8	29.6	33.9
ALDE (Alliance of Liberals and Democrats)	71.9	45.3	6.2	6.5	2.0
PMP (People's Movement Party)	57.3	27.8	3.3	4.3	0.6
UNPR (National Union for the Progress of Romania)	50.9	23.8	3.0	2.9	0.8
UDMR/RMDSZ (Democratic Alliance of Hungarians in Romania)	15.9	14.3	5.7	4.7	6.1
Independents	30.8	8.7	0.8	3.1	1.7
Nonnational lists (local alliances may or may not include the parties above)	n/a	8.8	2.4	7.2	1.5

Note: Small national nonparliamentary parties competing in local elections are not included.

in three sectors of Bucharest and the third highest number of votes in two other sectors. Soon after, the Union converted into a national party, the Save Romania Union (USR, liberal, progressive), hoping to channel voter discontent with the two large parties. Independent candidates were widespread in the 2016 local elections, especially for local council seats, but their success was limited to 1.7% of mayors and 0.8% of councilors.

There is a strong incumbency effect in mayoral elections, as shown in Table 39.4, with almost one-third of the mayoral election winners in 2016 winning their fourth term in office. The incumbency effect is particularly strong in rural municipalities. A typical rural mayor has a longer office tenure than an urban mayor.

Romanian legislation requests that lists include female candidates, but it does not impose quotas or obligations to have female candidates in eligible positions. Thus, the gender gap is enormous in local elections: after the 2016 elections, women only won 4.6% of the mayoral offices and 12.3% of the council seats (see Table 39.5). The share of female mayors is on a very feeble growing trend, with changes over time being far from significant. It is surprising

Table 39.4 Electoral success of incumbents in mayoral elections in Romania, 2004–2016

Mayors elected for a …	% of total municipalities			% of rural municipalities			% of urban municipalities		
	2016	2012	2008	2016	2012	2008	2016	2012	2008
second consecutive term	23.5	25.0	66.4	22.1	24.9	66.0	27.0	25.8	61.0
third consecutive term	17.3	45.7	-	18.5	46.9	-	15.6	34.7	-
fourth consecutive term>	30.9	-	-	32.4	-	-	17.8	-	-

Note: The year of reference is 2004. Terms prior to 2004 are not considered.

that female mayors are twice as frequent in rural municipalities than in urban ones. Female representation among councilors is slightly higher, but still very far from a balanced distribution. For the 2016 local elections, the share of women among councilors was greater in urban municipalities (17.3%) than in rural ones (11.5%). Consequently, local politics in Romania appears to be highly masculinized. As local key politicians also function as gatekeepers in the internal recruitment process conducted by the main political parties for the parliamentary elections, it is no surprise that the natural effect of such a masculinized recruitment base is a similar underrepresentation of women in national politics (Băluță 2017). After the 2016 legislative elections, women represented only 18.9% of the members of the Romanian Parliament (Agenția Națională pentru Egalitatea de Șanse între Femei și Bărbați 2016).

Romania is the extreme case of minority parliamentary inclusiveness (King & Marian 2012); however, it does not present a significant degree of inclusiveness in local government, despite the apparently favorable legal framework just described. The introduction of the electoral threshold, as well as a 2004 tightening of rules concerning candidacies, has reduced the presence of minority organizations and parties in local elections. The threshold for entering the race has become too high for minority organizations, and non-Hungarian organizations slowly disappeared from local elections, as illustrated by data for the second tier. From 2000 to 2016 the number of minority organizations running in county elections dropped from 25 (with three gaining seats) to four (only one gained seats).

Minority representation on county councils in the 2016 elections was reduced to three Hungarian organizations or parties and one organization representing Germans. The same organizations were most successful at the first tier (see Table 39.6). The UDMR/RMDSZ maintained its status as the representative of Hungarians, despite being challenged by other organizations; challengers were only successful in enclave conditions as Hungarian voters preferred to avoid factionalization (Stroschein 2011). The change in electoral formula for the election of mayors seems to have advantaged Hungarian organizations, as together they went from 195 mayors elected using a majority formula in 2008 to 210 mayors elected using a plurality formula in 2012. Like in national elections (Protsyk & Matichescu 2010), and despite being half the size of the Hungarian population, the Roma are the main losing group in terms of proportionality of representation in local elections due to factionalization within the Roma community. The Democratic Forum of Germans in Romania (FDGR) is overrepresented due to its ability to attract the votes of Romanians; in the 2016 election it obtained 42,652 votes, despite the 2011 census registering only 36,042 ethnic Germans. An examination of the effects of the special provisions for minority representation (other than the Hungarians) has shown them to have little effect. In 2004, there were eight municipalities in which minority organizations won a seat on the basis of these rules, while in five others they lost seats they would have won had they

Table 39.5 Share of women among elected mayors (2004–2016) and local councilors (2016) in Romania

Election year		2004	2008	2012	2016
Mayors	% overall	3.6	3.8	3.9	4.6
	% urban	1.9	2.5	2.2	2.5
	% rural	3.8	4.0	3.9	4.8
Councilors	% overall	n/a	n/a	n/a	12.3
	% urban	n/a	n/a	n/a	17.3
	% rural	n/a	n/a	n/a	11.5

Table 39.6 The electoral success of minority organizations and parties in Romanian municipalities, 2016

	Mayors	Councilors
Number of minority organizations/parties running	15.0	21.0
Minority seats – % of total seats	6.8	7.5
Seats won by Hungarian organizations/parties – % of minority seats	96.3	89.0
Seats won by German organizations/parties – % of minority seats	2.3	2.8
Seats won by Roma organizations/parties – % of minority seats	0.5	5.3
Seats won by other minority organizations/parties – % of minority seats	0.9	2.9

been treated like political parties; in 2008, seats were won in four municipalities and lost in five municipalities (Székely 2008).

Given the short time since Romania joined the European Union, there is a very small presence of EU citizens in local elections (58 candidates out of a total of 267,242 in 2016). Most of these candidates (14) were put forward by the organization representing ethnic Germans.

Discussion and conclusion

The previous sections illustrate a slow and steady process leading to a dominance of national political parties over local politics in Romania. The process starts with setting the timing of local elections so that they precede the parliamentary elections by a couple of months. This leads to local elections being perceived by both competitors and voters as a litmus test for the results of parliamentary elections. Thus, voters maintain a steady interest in these elections, as showcased by a rather stable turnout compared to that for parliamentary elections.

National political parties seek to shape the rules to gain advantage. Key to this are the nationally managed electoral process and rules concerning candidacies, turnout, and thresholds. The electoral law is usually modified before each round of local elections. Changes in electoral formula appear for the two executive positions – mayor and president of the county council. These reflect the important status of the holders of these positions in both local and national politics. There are ongoing debates about whether a majority or a plurality formula is better suited for the election of mayors, with major political parties generally endorsing the formula they perceive to suit their electoral interests better. The formula used for the election of councils remained the same. However, smaller changes (the threshold and provisions concerning minority organizations) have slightly affected proportionality and competition. These changes reflect a power preservation approach [similar to the power maximization approach discussed in the literature; see Renwick (2010)] employed by national political parties and the national minority organizations already represented in parliament in their approach to electoral reform.

Furthermore, Romanian local politics, and some of the rules detailed earlier, were shaped by the phenomenon of party-switching. Generally justified by the involved officials in relation to their ability to obtain more funds for their community if they belong to the governing party, the practice became controversial and was forbidden by law. The extent of the phenomenon is visible if we examine the results of a temporary 45-day suspension of these provisions granted by a governmental emergency ordinance in 2014. It was estimated then that 17.4% of the mayors, 13.8% of the local councilors, and 11.5% of the county councilors switched party, mostly toward the governing parties.[2] Empirical data do suggest a linkage between the political affiliation of local leaders and the receipt of central government funds via two causal mechanisms: (1) sharing merit between central and local leaders of the same party, especially the more experienced ones, and (2) exchange of perks (local electoral mobilization versus funds from central government, which enhance the status and increase the reelection chances of local leaders) (Coman 2018).

The analysis of electoral outcomes suggests that national parties are rather unchallenged by local actors. This even reflects into the realm of minority representation (except for the Hungarian minority), where there is a slow but constant decrease in the number of organizations competing in elections and gaining seats. Alongside the declining minority representation, a gender gap persists.

Notes

1 By the time this chapter was finalized, the AEP had not made publicly available the full data set concerning the 2020 local elections. Hence, the analysis of electoral outcomes is based on the last full data set available, which is from the 2016 elections.
2 See data at https://expertforum.ro/en/migration-of-local-elected-officials/, accessed 25 April 2020.

References

Agenția Națională de Integritate (2019). *Raport de activitate anual 2019*. București: Agenția Națională de Integritate.
Agenția Națională pentru Egalitatea de Șanse între Femei și Bărbați (2016). *Reprezentarea femeilor și a bărbaților în alegerile parlamentare din 2016*. București: Agenția Națională pentru Egalitatea de Șanse între Femei și Bărbați.
Autoritatea Electorală Permanentă (2017). Alegerile locale parțiale – 11 iunie 2017. *Expert Electoral*, 2(15), 49–59.
Băluță, O. (2017). Alegerile locale și reprezentarea politică parlamentară. Trambulină pentru bărbați, obstacol pentru femei? *Sfera Politicii*, 25(193–194), 12–21.
Baba, A., Balogh, M., Dragoș, D., Marian, C., Pop, D., Renert, C. & Suciu, A.M. (2007). *Impactul serviciilor deconcentrate ale ministerelor asupra politicilor publice locale*. București: Fundația Soros.
Coman, E.E. (2018). Local elites, electoral reform and the distribution of central government funds: Evidence from Romania. *Electoral Studies*, 53, 1–10.
Coman, P., Crai, E., Rădulescu, M. & Stănciulescu, G. (2001). Local government in Romania. In E. Kandeva (ed.) *Stabilization of Local Governments: Local Governments in Central and Eastern Europe* (pp. 351–416). Budapest: OSI/LGI.
Comșa, M. (2008). Clujul alege Boc. In G. Teodorescu (ed.) *Alegeri 2008. Continuitate și schimbare* (pp. 131–160). Iași: Polirom.
Curtea Constituțională a României (2012). *Decizia Nr. 51 din 25 ianuarie 2012*. Monitorul Oficial, Partea I, nr. 90.
Curtea Constituțională a României (2013). *Decizia Nr. 280 din 23 mai 2012*. Monitorul Oficial, Partea I, nr. 431.

Farrell, D.M. (1997). *Comparing Electoral Systems*. London: Macmillan Education UK.
Gheorghiță, A. (2010). *Lideri politici și construcția deciziei de vot*. Iași: Institutul European.
Heinelt, H. & Hlepas, N.-K. (2006). Typologies of local government systems. In H. Bäck, H. Heinelt, & A. Magnier (eds) *The European Mayor* (pp. 21–42). Baden-Baden: VS Verlag für Sozialwissenschaften.
Iațu, C., Boamfă, I., Alupului, C., Năstuță, S., Grecu, S.P., Asiminei, R., Horea-Șerban, R.I., Bodocan, V., Giugăl, A. & Timofciuc, C. (2013). *Atlasul electoral al României*. Iași: Editura Universității 'Al.I. Cuza' din Iași.
King, R.F. & Marian, C.G. (2012). Minority representation and reserved legislative seats in Romania. *East European Politics and Societies*, 26(3), 561–588.
Ladner, A., Keuffer, N. & Baldersheim, H. (2015). *Self-rule Index for Local Authorities. Final Report*. Luxembourg: Publications Office of the European Union.
Parlamentul României (2004). *Lege nr. 393 din 28 septembrie 2004 privind Statutul aleșilor locali*. Monitorul oficial Nr. 912 din 7 octombrie 2004.
Preda, C. & Soare, S. (2008). *Regimul, partidele și sistemul politic din România*. București: Nemira.
Profiroiu, C.M. & Profiroiu, A.G. (2006). Decentralization process in Romania. *Transylvanian Review of Administrative Sciences*, 2(16), 115–123.
Profiroiu, C.M., Profiroiu, A.G. & Szabo, S.R. (2017). The decentralization process in Romania. In J.M. Ruano & M. Profiroiu (eds) *The Palgrave Handbook of Decentralization in Europe* (pp. 353–387). Cham: Springer International Publishing.
Protsyk, O. & Matichescu, L.M. (2010). Electoral rules and minority representation in Romania. *Communist and Post-Communist Studies*, 43(1), 31–41.
Radu, Alexandru. (2012). Mecanisme ale alegerilor locale în România. Continuitate vs. schimbare. *Sfera Politicii*, 20(171), 3–16.
Radu, A. & Buti, D. (2016). Alegeri locale 2016. Sub semnul "revoluției politice"? *Sphere of Politics/Sfera Politicii*, 188(2), 5–12.
Renwick, A. (2010). *The Politics of Electoral Reform: Changing the Rules of Democracy*. Cambridge: Cambridge University Press.
Stănuș, C. & Pop, D. (2011). Romania. In H. Heinelt & X. Bertrana (eds) *The Second Tier of Local Government in Europe: Provinces, Counties, Départements and Landkreise in Comparison* (pp. 223–241). London: Routledge.
Ștefan, L., Grecu, R., Todor, A. & Cristescu, R. (2004). Local elections 2004: A turning point in Romanian politics. *Romanian Journal of Society and Politics*, 4(2), 66–126.
Stroschein, S. (2011). Demography in ethnic party fragmentation: Hungarian local voting in Romania. *Party Politics*, 17(2), 189–204.
Székely, I.G. (2008). *Reprezentarea politică a minorităților naționale în România/The political representation of national minorities in Romania*. Cluj-Napoca: Institutul pentru Studierea Problemelor Minorităților Naționale.
Whitefield, S. (2006). Mind the representation gap: Explaining differences in public views of representation in postcommunist democracies. *Comparative Political Studies*, 39(6), 733–758.
Whitehead, L. (2018). The recall of elected officeholders the growing incidence of a venerable, but overlooked, democratic institution. *Democratization*, 25(8), 1341–1357.

40
Serbia
Three phases of local electoral politics after 1990

Aleksandar Marinković and Novak Gajić

The heritage of local self-government

Local self-government in the Republic of Serbia is enshrined in the country's 2006 Constitution, which defines it not as a tier of government but as the right of citizens to limit the power of the state. The Law on Territorial Organization prescribes that Serbia is subdivided into municipalities, cities, and the City of Belgrade (as local self-government units) and the two autonomous provinces of Voivodina and Kosovo-Metochia. Local elections in the latter are not part of this chapter, because Serbia has had no effective control over this disputed territory since 1999, although in this period some of the municipal elections there have been organized under Serbian law.

The current territorial organization is almost unchanged since the 1960s, with only two new municipalities established since then (both before 1990). At the moment, there are 145 local self-government units in Serbia (without Kosovo-Metochia): the City of Belgrade, which has the special status regulated by the Law on the Capital City, 27 cities (*grad* – usually larger local governments that are de facto regional centers, typically with more than 50,000 citizens), and 117 municipalities (*opština*).

In addition to the local self-government units, the cities are entitled to further subdivide their territories into boroughs (*gradska opština*) and to decide which competences should be delegated to them, but usually not the key ones. Currently there are 25 boroughs: Belgrade is divided into 17, Niš into five, and another three cities (Požarevac, Užice, and Vranje) gave this status to a part of their territory. Elections in boroughs are, however, not part of this chapter.

The average population of a Serbian local self-government unit is currently around 48,000 inhabitants, but the average is fewer than 37,000 if Belgrade is excluded, as its sheer size significantly distorts the mean. The City of Belgrade numbers just under 1.7 million inhabitants (this is the metropolitan area that constitutes the City of Belgrade as a local self-government unit, rather than just the urban settlement), while the smallest municipality, Crna Trava, only has 1,219 inhabitants. This places Serbian local self-governments among the larger ones in Europe, but on the other hand, more than 75% of them have fewer than 30,000 inhabitants and almost half have fewer than 20,000 (Statistical Office of the Republic of Serbia 2019).

During the Communist era, municipalities in Yugoslavia (of which Serbia was a part) functioned as administrative units of the lowest tier. Although their councils had not been elected in free multiparty elections, they had considerable autonomy and competencies, as Communist Yugoslavia was quite a decentralized country, in line with its official ideology of self-management. In addition to competences in public utilities and communal infrastructure, Yugoslav local authorities had a huge influence on education, health care, and social welfare, but also even on public safety and the police. Unlike in most former Communist countries in Europe, the process of reintroduction of the multiparty system was not followed by the transfer of more responsibilities to the local level: quite the opposite because there was a move toward centralization. It was not until after the democratic changes in 2000 that a process of decentralization started with a transfer (i.e., return) of more responsibilities to the local level, strengthening the autonomy of the local tier. In this process, the property that was taken away by the central government in the 1990s was returned to municipalities.

The Law on Local Self-Government (adopted in 2007) defines the responsibilities as well as the rights of local authorities, while the Law on Local Self-Government Finance (adopted in 2007 and amended in 2012 and 2016) includes regulatory provisions on the financing of local self-government units.

The system of local government in Serbia is among the most autonomous of the countries in Southeastern Europe. And, according to Local Autonomy Index data, Serbia is ranked 13th among 39 European countries on the scale of overall local autonomy, which includes organizational, legal, and financial dimensions of autonomy, as well as the scope of responsibilities (Ladner et al. 2019: 240). Municipalities are responsible for the basic local infrastructure (including water supply and sewage treatment, waste management, roads, and local public transport), child care, social care, and spatial planning. Serbia also has had relatively long-standing traditions of self-rule at the local level since independence in the early nineteenth century (with roots in medieval Serbian states and even during the Ottoman rule, when local self-rule actually served as the infrastructure of the Serbian Revolution of 1804–1815), yet developing differently during the twentieth century.

The horizontal power relations in Serbian municipalities belong to the collective form (Heinelt and Hlepas 2006), with the municipal executive elected by the council (*skupština*) and accountable to the councilors. The executive consists of the mayor (*predsednik opštine* in municipalities and *gradonačelnik* in cities) and the executive council (*veće*), where the former has more legal and political power than the latter. The executive councils number between five and 11 members, depending on the size of the municipality (as per the Law on Local Self-Government), with the exception of Belgrade which has 15 members (as per the Law on Capital City). Legally, the main power at the local level is vested in municipal councils, but in practice it is usually accumulated by the mayors. Municipal administration in theory is independent from political officeholders but in reality is heavily influenced by them (which is corroborated by the reports of the State Audit Institution; see State Audit Institution 2009–2019).

Frequent discontinuities in the electoral system and rules

Once in four years, the Speaker of the National Assembly of the Republic of Serbia (*Narodna skupština Republike Srbije*) calls the 'general' local elections, which take place on the same day in all municipalities. Exempted are those local self-government units where snap elections have been called by the speaker, usually due to loss of a majority on the council and inability to form a new ruling coalition or because the council did not hold a session in three months (since 2009, around 20 local self-governments have had snap elections, including the capital Belgrade);

elections in these municipalities and cities take place on different dates, four years after the expiry of the mandates of the councils elected in snap elections. Elections are organized by the local electoral commissions, budgeted by local councils, and supported organizationally by municipal administrations, with the representation of all political groups on each municipality's council.

An electoral list is approved to participate in local elections if it submits 30 signatures of support per candidate from eligible voters from that municipality (for instance, a list with 20 candidates must be supported by at least 600 voters). An exemption is made for municipalities with a population of under 20,000, where a total of 200 signatures is needed for a list to run. The minimal number of candidates on a list is set to one-third of the number of seats in the municipal council for which they run.

Direct mayoral elections were introduced in 2002 with the adoption of new Laws on Local Self-Government and on Local Elections, but they were used only once in 2004. This model was abandoned, because it resulted in situations in which the mayor and the council majority belonged to opposing political parties. In less than two years, more than 25 mayoral recall procedures were launched by the councils (at the request of one-third of councilors), and in almost half of those cases the recall was successful. Although there was no threshold for the recall of a mayor, in many cases there were more than 50% of registered voters who voted. As these recalls in almost every case resulted from political deadlock in many municipalities, all major political parties agreed to change the system and return to the indirect election of mayors.

The electoral system at the local level

The eligibility rules have been the same since the first post-World War II local multiparty elections in 1992: all citizens of the Republic of Serbia aged 18 or more are entitled to vote. Residents without Serbian citizenship cannot vote, and for subnational elections, contrary to the presidential and parliamentary elections, Serbian citizens residing abroad cannot vote either.

The size of the municipal councils in Serbia – unlike in most other European countries – does not depend on the size of the population and is determined by the Law on Local Self-Government. The number of councilors is determined by municipal statutes, in line with the Law on Local Self-Government. The current law adopted in 2007 defines that the number of councilors on local councils cannot be fewer than 19 nor more than 75 (each municipality defines it by its statute) (39 on average). The only exception is the City of Belgrade with 110 councilors, as defined by the Law on the Capital City.

The local electoral system is uniform for all local self-governments in the Republic of Serbia. In the first three elections, Serbia used a majoritarian electoral system. In the first two elections, 1992 and 1996, Serbs elected local councilors in single-member districts in a two-round system (also known as the second ballot), where if no candidate received enough votes (50% + 1) in the first round, a second round of voting was held with just the top two candidates (see Table 40.1).

Expecting that the opposition would remain divided, the ruling Socialist Party of Serbia (SPS) changed the electoral system for local elections in 2000 to the first-past-the-post (FPTP) system. This proved not to be a smart decision for the party, as the Democratic Opposition of Serbia (DOS) – a coalition of 18 parties – ended up winning the elections in most of the municipalities, including all major cities. In Belgrade, for example, the Democratic Opposition of Serbia achieved a landslide victory, winning no fewer than 105 out of 110 seats.

The local electoral system changed again in 2002 to the closed-list proportional system (CLPR) where every local self-government represents a single electoral district. One of the

Table 40.1 Main parameters of the local electoral system in Serbia, 1992–2016

Election year	Voting system for council members
1992	Two-round system
1996	Two-round system
2000	FPTP
2004	CLPR, Hare-Niemeyer, threshold 3%
2008	CLPR, d'Hondt, threshold 5%
2012	CLPR, d'Hondt, threshold 5%
2016	CLPR, d'Hondt, threshold 5%
2020	CLPR, d'Hondt, threshold 3%

Source: Jovanović (2020)

most important reasons for the change was that the majoritarian system was marked by widespread gerrymandering favoring the ruling party, often by giving more gravity to rural and suburban votes that were more inclined toward the SPS. The legal threshold was set to 3%, with the Hare-Niemeyer method for seat allocation. This was done in the interest of the plethora of small parties in the DOS coalition. The DOS was at that point already on its way to disintegration and this was the only way in which the small parties could enter municipal councils. In 2007 the threshold was changed to 5%, and the d'Hondt rule for the allocation of seats was introduced (the same as in parliamentary elections since 2000), except for party lists representing national minorities for which there is no threshold. Both the national and local thresholds were lowered from 5% to 3% in early 2020. The government introduced this change for the sake of minimizing the effects of most of the opposition's boycott of parliamentary and local elections originally scheduled for 26 April 2020, but postponed to 21 June 2020 due to the COVID-19 pandemic.[1]

In 2002, the Law on Local Elections introduced a gender quota. In 2020, the obligatory minimal participation of candidates belonging to the less represented gender (practically, women) on each list was increased from one-third to 40%. The provision stipulates that at least two candidates of the less represented gender must be placed among each five candidates in the order of the list (the first five places, the second five places, and so on until the end of the list). This, however, does not guarantee that at least 40% of the seats will be taken by the less represented gender, once the final allocation of mandates is complete.

The right to stand for the local council elections is granted to all adult voters. Serbian law excludes *cumul des mandats*, and mayors are specifically barred from holding any office on the national or provincial levels. Councilors are, however, allowed to be members of the National Assembly, and during the past decade there were several notable cases of MPs with some political gravity resigning from a mayoral post and taking over the position of municipal council speaker, using this to circumvent the prohibition and to informally yet effectively keep running their local self-governments.

The results of the local elections

Out of the seven local elections held since 1992, the citizens of Serbia only once (in 2004) elected the local council members exclusively. All other local elections were held in parallel

is also, in general, higher in municipalities with a population of a more mixed ethnic background, because in these municipalities both nationwide and minority parties compete.

Nowadays, local elections in Serbia are dominated by nationwide parties, and the number of local independent lists that are not affiliated with them is relatively small. At the beginning of the post-Communist era, local elections were not so much dominated by the nationwide parties

Table 40.2 Voter turnout (percent) for local and national elections in Serbia since 1990

Election date	Voter turnout (%)		Notes
	Local elections	National elections (parliamentary and presidential)	
9 December 1990		Parliamentary: 71.5 Presidential: 65.2	The first multiparty elections in Serbia after World War II.
31 May 1992		56.0	The first multiparty Federal Assembly election – boycotted by the opposition; in addition to boycott, there were an unusually high number of void ballot papers (12%).
20 December 1992	No data available	67.4	The first multiparty local elections after World War II and repeated Federal Assembly elections (uncontested by the opposition).
19 December 1993		61.3	Parliamentary election in Serbia.
3 November 1996	67.0	60.3	Local and Federal Assembly elections. The outcome of local elections (opposition victory in almost all major cities) was contested by the government, which triggered three-month-long protests. After OSCE mediation headed by former Spanish prime minister Felipe González, the government acknowledged the results.
21 September 1997		57.4	Parliamentary election in Serbia – boycotted by most of the opposition.
23 September 2000	74.7	71.5 (Federal President) 74.4 (Federal Assembly)	Local and federal (parliamentary and presidential) elections.
23 December 2000		57.6	Parliamentary election in Serbia.
28 December 2003		56.8	Parliamentary election in Serbia.

(Continued)

Table 40.2 (Continued)

Election date	Voter turnout (%)		Notes
	Local elections	National elections (parliamentary and presidential)	
19 September 2004	40.6		Local elections in Serbia – the only ones not held simultaneously with elections for other levels of government.
21 January 2007		60.6	Parliamentary election in Serbia.
11 May 2008	61.2	61.4	Local, parliamentary, and presidential elections in Serbia.
6 May 2012	57.9	57.8	Local, parliamentary, and presidential elections in Serbia.
16 March 2014		53.1	Parliamentary election in Serbia.
24 April 2016	56.4	56.1	Local and parliamentary elections in Serbia.
14 February 2017		54.4	Presidential election in Serbia.
21 June 2020	No data available	48.9	Not all data from the outcome of the June 2020 elections were available at the time of finalizing this chapter. These elections were marked by the boycott by most of the opposition and by the government's attempt to diminish its effect by lowering the threshold from 5% to 3%, which did motivate a minority within the opposition to abandon the boycott.

Notes: National elections include both the elections for the authorities of the Republic of Serbia (since 1990) and of the Federal Republic of Yugoslavia (1992–2000). In the case of federal elections, only turnout in Serbia is counted and does not include the turnout in Montenegro.
Sources: Goati (2001) and Statistical Office of the Republic of Serbia (2016)

(on the same day, in the same voting posts) with national elections (or federal elections like those in 1996 and 2000 for the then-Federal Republic of Yugoslavia). This has led to centralized, mainly leader-led campaigns, where themes and messages have mainly been of national significance, thus putting local themes behind. The low voter turnout for the 2004 local elections proves their lesser significance compared to the national elections (see Table 40.2).

Electoral participation in both types of elections differs significantly between municipalities of different sizes. The usual pattern in the previous electoral cycles was that the voter turnout in general – in both local and parliamentary elections – was negatively correlated with the population size. Even more interesting, the highest turnout was in the southern part of the country, which is economically the least developed.

Competitiveness in local elections is very high (with an average of over eight party lists per local self-government) with the larger ones having the most competitive elections. Competitiveness

as there was higher participation of independent candidates, as the multiparty system was still in its beginnings (see Table 40.3).

Local elections since the reintroduction of the multiparty system evolved through three phases. The *first phase* (1990–2000) was characterized by the rule of Slobodan Milošević and the dominance of his post-Communist successor the Socialist Party of Serbia (SPS), as well as

Table 40.3 Share of all seats on local councils received by the main (parliamentary) parties in the latest local elections (2016) in Serbia

Parties	% of municipalities where running	% of municipalities where represented	% of seats on local councils	% of (aggregate) votes in local elections	% of mayors affiliated with the party
Serbian Progressive Party (SNS, *Srpska napredna stranka*) **and SNS-dominated local lists**	97.9	97.9	37.4	41.6	80.0
Socialist Party of Serbia (SPS, *Socijalistička partija Srbije*) **and United Serbia (JS,** *Jedinstvena Srbija*)	89.7	89.0	18.7	11.4	3.4
Democratic Party (DS, *Demokratska stranka*) **and DS-dominated local lists**	53.1	51.7	6.9	7.9	1.4
Coalition: Social Democratic Party (SDS, *Socijaldemokratska stranka*)**, Liberal Democratic Party (LDP,** *Liberalno-demokratska partija*)**, and League of Social Democrats of Vojvodina (LSV,** *Liga socijaldemokrata Vojvodine*)	63.4	26.2	2.1	5.5	0.0
Serbian Radical Party (SRS, *Srpska radikalna stranka*)	29.6	28.3	3.8	6.0	1.4

(Continued)

Table 40.3 (Continued)

Parties	% of municipalities where running	% of municipalities where represented	% of seats on local councils	% of (aggregate) votes in local elections	% of mayors affiliated with the party
Coalition: Democratic Party of Serbia (DSS, *Demokratska stranka Srbije*) and Serbian Movement Dveri (*Srpski pokret Dveri*)	31.0	21.4	2.2	4.6	1.4
Parties of ethnic minorities	38.7	31.9	6.8	4.8	4.8
Independent lists	51.7	48.3	11.1	12.7	6.2
Other smaller and regional parties	31.7	24.8	11.0	5.5	1.4

Note: The latest local elections were held in June 2020, but not all data on their outcome were available at the time this chapter was finalized. These elections were marked by the boycott by most of the opposition and by the government's attempt to diminish the effect of it by lowering the threshold from 5% to 3%, which did motivate a minority within the opposition to abandon the boycott, yet without much success. The major outcome was that the dominance of the SNS grew even bigger.
Source: Statistical Office of the Republic of Serbia (2016).

by the majoritarian electoral system at the local level. SPS was the successor of the League of Communists (SK), which had ruled the country for decades since the end of World War II. SPS therefore had the most developed party infrastructure at the local level, which gave it a stronger influence over the electorate, while the newly formed opposition parties were only starting to develop theirs. Another impediment for the opposition was the Yugoslav Civil War on Serbia's borders, which the regime used for political mobilization in which the opposition was regularly labeled as treacherous. The main event of this period related to local elections was the November 1996 victory of the opposition in most major Serbian local self-governments (combined containing more than 60% of the population), which SPS attempted to prevent by claiming procedural reasons and filing thousands of complaints to annul the election results. The opposition refused to participate in the rerun, which triggered three-month-long demonstrations from which it emerged victorious, paving the way for the final ousting of Milošević in 2000. The OSCE mediated in this crisis and dispatched a special mission to Serbia headed by former Spanish prime minister Felipe González.

The *second phase* (2000–2012) was an era of democratization, which started with the toppling of Milošević by DOS and the country's exit from international isolation. It was also an era of continued instability, with the assassination of prime minister Zoran Đinđić (2003) as a culminating event, followed by the state of emergency and a massive crackdown on organized crime, the dissolution of the union with Montenegro (2006), and the unilateral declaration of independence by the ethnic Albanian Provisional Institutions of Self-Government in UN-administered Kosovo. The second phase was characterized by the dominance of political parties that emerged from DOS – primarily the Democratic Party (DS), the Democratic Party of Serbia (DSS), and to a lesser degree United Regions of Serbia (URS) – and also by the gradual recovery of SPS, which joined the government in 2008. The main opposition during this period was the Serbian Radical Party (SRS), which split in 2008. The SRS defectors formed the Serbian Progressive Party (SNS), which in 2012 became the dominant party in Serbia.

The closed-list proportional electoral system was introduced during this period (in 2004) and has been in use ever since. As described, the 2004 election was the only one in which the mayors were elected directly by the voters. The second phase is also characterized by the success of numerous local groups and leaders who were not affiliated with the national-level political parties.

The current, *third phase* (since 2012) is characterized by the dominance of SNS. After its first leader Tomislav Nikolić narrowly and somewhat surprisingly defeated the incumbent Boris Tadić (DS) in the presidential election, SPS and URS defected from DS to form a governing coalition with SNS, which soon became the overwhelmingly dominant partner. One of the first manifestations of this dominance was the process euphemistically called 'recomposition of power', during which SNS forced its new allies (in the meantime quite marginalized) to break up all municipal coalitions with DS and other opposition parties and to form coalitions with SNS. Over time, SNS has achieved such a dominance that, as of 2016, it was in power – directly or through coalitions – in all but one city, two municipalities and two boroughs. This dominance is reflected in all aspects, reaching the levels often described as state capture, so most of the opposition decided to boycott the 2020 elections, claiming the conditions in which they took place undemocratic. This phase is symbolized by the personal rule of Aleksandar Vučić, who sidelined Nikolić very soon and became president in 2017.

There was a significant increase in female representation among the elected officials at the local level due to the introduction of a gender quota (see Table 40.4). The share of female councilors elected in the last local elections amounted to 31.2%, which is still lower than the share in the National Assembly (37.2 %), but more than three times higher than it was in the local elections held 20 years earlier when there were no quotas. However, a large gap still exists between representation the legislative body and the executive at the local level. Only 12 out of 170 mayors (7.1%) in Serbia are women. In the only elections in which mayors were elected directly (2004), only six (3.6%) women became mayors.

Political parties of the minorities – most notably Hungarian, Bosniak, and Albanian, but sometimes also Bulgarian, Roma, Croat, Slovak, etc. – regularly compete in elections at all levels, while members of Serbia's minorities also participate in nationwide parties and as independents. There are currently eight mayors from the minorities' parties (three Hungarians, three Bosniaks, and two Albanians) and four other mayors belong to ethnic minorities (two Bulgarians, one Hungarian, and one Slovak). The political parties of the minorities rule or participate in ruling coalitions in about one-third of Serbia's local self-governments. The 2009 Law on Political Parties recognizes them as a special category. While registration of a nationwide party requires the endorsement (by signature) of 10,000 voters, registration of a minority political party requires 1,000 and that its manifesto states that it promotes the interests of a certain minority. In this process, the ethnic background of the said thousand citizens is not checked, based on the rationale that every citizen is free to declare his or her ethnicity. As stated earlier, there is no

Table 40.4 Share of women among elected councilors in Serbia, 1990–2016

Election year	1996	2000	2004	2008	2012	2016
% of female councilors	4.8	6.6	21.4	21.2	28.6	31.2

Source: Statistical Office of the Republic of Serbia (2016)

threshold for minority parties, neither in national nor in local elections. This rule is colloquially called 'natural threshold', since minority parties can win a seat with a percentage of votes that corresponds with the percentage of that one seat in a council (e.g., in a 50-seat council one seat is 2% of all seats, so a minority party can enter that council by winning approximately 2% of the votes). Another preferential mechanism was introduced in 2020: that the number of votes won by ethnic minorities' parties is multiplied by 1.35 before the d'Hondt formula distributes the seats. While originally designed to give an advantage to minorities and encourage their political participation, the rule has sometimes also been exploited by others. The simple procedure for registering a minority's party motivated some groups that do not really represent minorities, contrary to the purpose, to win seats in an easier way.

Discussion

Although the choice of proportional representation eased Serbia's transition to democracy, the closed-list single-district proportional system did not help to consolidate democracy and develop it further, because it distanced the councilors from the electorate and made them overdependent on the national-level parties and their leadership. The outcome is a highly depersonalized electoral system, and the problem is magnified by the fact that local elections almost as a rule happen simultaneously with national elections, which overshadow them. Many citizens, political leaders, and experts believe that the current system should be modified to reduce some of the following problems with the current electoral system:

- Because the councilors are not elected from electoral districts, it is almost impossible for the residents of a given geographic area or community to hold individual councilors accountable for their performance on behalf of the community.
- Because the councilors cannot be held individually accountable for their performance, they have few incentives to learn about the particular needs of local communities or to address these needs.
- Furthermore, because the councilors do not represent the residents of a defined geographic area, they are not easily accessible to members of the public. This is particularly true for rural populations, because most councilors reside in the municipal center.

This is, however, not a prime topic of current political debates. Some momentum for changing toward a more personalized system seemed to have existed a decade ago when it was promoted by the last DS Minister of Public Administration & Local Self-Government, but he did not succeed in convincing the upper echelon of his own party, let alone create a wider political consensus. The idea is nowadays, in principle, supported by the opposition, but so far it has failed to set it on the main political agenda, concentrating rather on electoral conditions in general. To change the electoral system toward a more personalized one is not in the interest of SNS, which has very few local leaders able to mobilize support on their own and which draws its electoral success at all levels from the popularity of its leader. In the 2020 local elections SNS did not even run under its name; it was Vučić's name in the title of all municipal lists.

In sum, the current electoral system weakens the vital links between the government and the public that are the essence of democracy, thus making local electoral politics in Serbia strongly partisan and depersonalized. This is reflected not only by the degradation of formal rules of procedural democracy but also by contextual factors, such as the long-lasting (and quite overwhelming) domination of certain nationwide political parties.

Note

1 Not all data on the outcomes of the 2020 local elections were available at the time this chapter was finalized, so it refers to the 2016 elections as the latest.

References

Goati, V. (2001) *Izbori u SRJ od 1990. do 1998: Volja građana ili izborna manipulacija. Dodatak: Izbori 2000.* [*Elections in the FRY 1990–1998: Citizens' Will or Electoral Manipulation. Addendum: 2000 Elections*]. Belgrade: CESID.

Heinelt, H. & Hlepas, N. (2006). 'Typologies of Local Government Systems'. In: Bäck, H., Heinelt, H. & Magnier, A. (eds.), *The European Mayor. Political Leaders in the Changing Context of Local Democracy*. Wiesbaden: VS Verlag für Sozialwissenschaften, pp. 21–33.

Jovanović, M. (2020) Локални избори у Србији 1992–2016. године [Local Elections in Serbia 1992–2016]. In: Jovanović, M. (ed.) *Приручник за спровођење локалних избора* [*Handbook for Conducting Local Elections*], 2nd Edition. Belgrade: SKGO, pp. 21–41.

Ladner, A., Keuffer, N., Baldersheim, H., Hlepas, N., Swianiewicz, P., Steyvers, K., & Navarro, C. (2019). *Patterns of Local Autonomy in Europe*. London: Palgrave Macmillan.

State Audit Institution (2009–2019) Извештаји о ревизији [*Audit Reports*]. [online] Available at: www.dri.rs/%D1%80%D0%B5%D0%B2%D0%B8%D0%B7%D0%B8%D1%98%D0%B5/%D0%BF%D0%BE%D1%81%D0%BB%D0%B5%D0%B4%D1%9A%D0%B8-%D0%B8%D0%B7%D0%B2%D0%B5%D1%88%D1%82%D0%B0%D1%98.135.html [Accessed 10 December 2020].

Statistical Office of the Republic of Serbia (2016) Локални избори [*Local Elections*]. [online] Available at: www.stat.gov.rs/sr-Cyrl/oblasti/izbori/lokalni-izbori [Accessed 24 August 2020].

Statistical Office of the Republic of Serbia (2019) Општине и региони у Републици Србији 2019. [*Municipalities and Regions in the Republic of Serbia 2019*]. [online] Available at: https://publikacije.stat.gov.rs/G2019/Pdf/G201913046.pdf [Accessed 10 September 2020].

41
Slovenia
Where strong, nonpartisan mayors are reelected many times over

Simona Kukovič and Miro Haček

Local self-government in Slovenia: evolution of a one-tier system

The Constitution of the Republic of Slovenia, adopted in 1991 after the country gained independence from former socialist Yugoslavia, ensured local self-government for all Slovenian citizens, thereby joining modern states in Europe and beyond that recognize the right of citizens to participate in the management of local public affairs (Haček, Kukovič & Brezovšek 2017). The next crucial step was the adoption of the umbrella Law on Local Self-Government in December 1993. The basis for the implementation of the reestablishment of local self-government was laid with the adoption of the Law on Referenda for the Establishment of Municipalities and the conduct of the first democratic local elections in 1994 (Brezovšek & Kukovič 2012). Reformed and modernized local self-government finally became operational in January 1995.

Slovenia consists of 212 municipalities,[1] which were gradually established between 1994[2] and 2014 when, for the first time, local representatives were elected in the youngest Slovenian municipality. Municipalities are the only decentralized unit of government, as Slovenia decided to adopt a one-tier system of local self-government until there is enough political will in the National Assembly to also establish regions.

Because local self-government is still relatively young in Slovenia, the most well-known typologies of the vertical dimension of power relations (see, e.g., Page & Goldsmith 1987; Hesse & Sharpe 1991; Goldsmith 1992), as well as the horizontal dimensions of power relations within the local community, failed to detect Slovenia, similar to the local systems of other post-Communist countries of Central and Eastern Europe.[3] The initial typology developed by Heinelt and Hlepas (2006; i.e., 2004 POLLEADER typology) did not include Slovenia; however, on the basis of this typology, researchers (see Kukovič 2015) did a simulation on the case of Slovenia, placing it in the subsequently added Central and Eastern European group of countries for the vertical dimension and into the model of a strong mayor for the horizontal dimension of Mouritzen and Svara (2002).[4] This was later confirmed by international research (see Heinelt et al. 2018: 38).

Although municipalities in Slovenia represent the only autonomous level of local self-government, their financial autonomy does not reflect that at all, as they hardly have any of their own resources (Ladner, Keuffer & Baldersheim 2016: 335). The system of municipal funding is mainly linked to the transfer of funds from the national to the local governments through the system of *per capita* financing (Kukovič, Haček & Bukovnik 2016), the amount of which heavily depends on the political will of ruling coalitions. Therefore, if we follow the arguments of many theorists (see, e.g., Page 1991: 31) who posit that it is precisely the field of financing that is crucial for the status of local communities and the degree of their actual autonomy, we can say that the autonomy of Slovenian local self-government is among the weakest in Europe, which is also reflected in its score on the Local Autonomy Index (see Ladner, Keuffer & Baldersheim 2016).

Normative framework of local elections

Slovenian local elections are held every four years and are not tied to any other elections in the country. Until the most recent local elections, which took place on 18 November 2018, the voting date was flexible and was moving backward to an earlier date.[5] However, the Law on Amendments to the Law on Local Elections 2017 set the exact timing for holding local elections to the second Sunday in November, mainly because of the greater predictability and stability of the local electoral system.

Local elections are held simultaneously across the country (polling stations open at 7:00 a.m. and close at 7:00 p.m.), with the 212 different individual local elections being held at the same time. In each municipality, the electorate directly elects the mayor, municipal councilors, and representatives of the sublocal communities.[6] Therefore, elections of mayors, municipal councilors, and representatives of the sublocal communities are held at the same time, but they are not systematically connected, as ballot cards are separated. The term of office of the mayor begins and ends at the same time as the term of office of the municipal council, which is also the case when, for various reasons, it is necessary to hold mayoral by-elections. The term of office of a by-elected mayor expires with the term of office of the municipal council (Kukovič 2020). The term of office for the mayor, municipal councilors, and representatives of the sub-local communities is four years, which is the exactly same length as the term of national MPs. The legislation does not provide any recall instrument for either the mayor, the municipal councilors, or any other local representative of the voters. However, in the most extreme cases of abusive behavior, the mayor or municipal council may be removed from their positions following the proposal of the national government and with absolute majority support in the National Assembly, although there have been no such examples so far. Elections are organized by municipal electoral commissions under the control of the national election commission and are announced by the president of the National Assembly.

Despite the fact that the current regulation determines the direct election of the mayor, the analysis of the previous legal framework shows that this was not always the case when establishing Slovenian local government. The entire draft of the original Law on Local Self-Government (1993) was based on the dominant role of the representative body (municipal council), which was to elect a mayor from among its members. Although the idea of indirect mayoral election was very vivid and already enshrined in the proposed legislation, the legislative process was dominated by the idea of direct mayoral election, and legislation portraying this idea was finally adopted before the first local elections were held in 1994. In addition to positive consequences (such as direct voter influence on candidate selection, greater legitimacy, and mayoral responsibility to the voters), such arrangements can also lead to problems in cases of divided government. However, practical examples show that when cohabitation does happen, the mayor and municipal councilors usually reach an agreement (though often not ideal) and lead the municipality away from a standstill. The complete standstill of a municipal operation is rare as local administrators know that this would cause stagnation in the municipality, which certainly diminishes its basic role, that is, to satisfy the basic needs of citizens and to enable participation in the implementation of municipal policy (Kukovič 2020).

Acta non verba: direct voter influence

Mayors, councilors, and members of the sublocal communities are elected on the basis of universal and equal suffrage in free and direct elections by secret ballot (Law on Local Elections 2007, Article 2). Article 5 of the Law on Local Elections stipulates that every citizen who has reached the age of 18 on the day of the elections has both the right to vote and the right to be elected mayor and/or municipal council member. An active and passive right to vote for a mayor and municipal council member also extends to citizens of another EU member state who have a permanent residence permit and a registered permanent residence in the Republic of Slovenia. Non-EU citizens only have the right to vote (but not to run) for mayor and municipal council members. For the election of the Italian or Hungarian national minority representatives, members of each community have the right to vote; the same applies to the election of the Roma community representative (more about special arrangements for minorities in the next section). The voting right is linked with permanent residence, as both active and passive voting rights can be exercised only in the municipality in which the individual has registered permanent residence with the general municipal electoral register.[7] Voting is not compulsory.

The legal basis for determining the number of municipal council members is determined in Article 38 of the Law on Local Self-Government (2007), which stipulates that a municipal council has seven to 45 members. This article gives municipalities the sovereign right to determine the number of municipal council members by its own statute within the statutory framework. The number of municipal council members is dependent on the number of inhabitants in a municipality: (1) 7–11 councilors in the municipalities of up to 3,000 inhabitants; (2) 12–15 councilors in municipalities of up to 5,000 inhabitants; (3) 16–19 councilors in municipalities of up to 10,000 inhabitants; (4) 20–23 councilors in a municipalities of up to 15,000 inhabitants; (5) 24–27 councilors in municipalities of up to 20,000 inhabitants; (6) 28–31 councilors in municipalities of up to 30,000 inhabitants; (7) 32–35 councilors in municipalities with more than 30,000 inhabitants; and (8) 36–45 councilors in municipalities with more than 100,000 inhabitants.

There are two basic voting principles that are implemented for Slovenian municipal council elections. If the municipal council has fewer than 12 members, the municipal councilors are elected by plurality vote; if there are 12 councilors or more on the municipal council, they are elected on the basis of a proportional principle (Law on Local Elections 2007, Article 9). In municipalities in which municipal councilors are elected by a plurality principle, the dominant system used is bloc vote, but it is also possible that an individual municipality can decide to establish a 'limited vote' system or an SNTV system, although only 18 municipalities are using those systems at the moment (16 limited vote, two SNTV). At proportional elections, voters cast their votes on the candidate lists for the constituency. Each voter is allowed to vote for only one candidate list. A voter may also mark one candidate on the ballot of the candidate list for which s/he casts a vote, giving that candidate an advantage over other candidates on the list (preferential vote, closed list). Preferential votes are only considered if at least one-quarter of voters that have cast votes for the list have also cast preferential votes. If the candidate lists are voted on in a municipality as one constituency, the mandates are allocated to the candidate lists according to the d'Hondt rule (Law on Local Elections 2007, Articles 13, 14, and 15).

Candidates for municipal council who are elected by majority vote and lists of candidates for municipal council who are elected on a proportional basis are determined by political parties and voters in the constituency, which requires a minimum of 1% of voter signatures in a constituency, but no fewer than 30 and no more than 1,000.[8] Each individual may run in only one constituency and on only one list of candidates, and each candidature requires the written consent of the candidate, which is irrevocable (Law on Local Elections 2007, Articles 48, 54, 65, and 68). When a candidate list is compiled, a gender quota of 40% of a single gender must be taken into account (Law on Local Elections 2007, Article 70a);[9] candidates must be placed alternately by gender at least on the first half of the candidate list ('zipper' system).[10] Candidate nominations must be submitted to the municipal electoral commission no later than 30 days before the day of voting (Law on Local Elections 2007, Article 74).

The provisions of the law are in the case of a mayoral candidacy similar to those of a municipal councilor candidacy. Political parties and voters may propose candidates for mayor. When voters are proposing a candidate for mayor, the number of voter signatures required is at least 2% of the number of votes cast in the first round in the most recent previous regular mayoral election, but no fewer than 15 and no more than 2,500 voter signatures (Law on Local Elections 2007, Article 106). The mayor is elected directly by a two-round majority voting system. The candidate who receives the absolute majority of the votes cast is elected. If no candidate wins an absolute majority in the first round, exactly two weeks after the first round a second round is held between the two candidates who received the most votes in the first round (Kukovič 2019a).

The Law on Local Self-Government (2007, Article 37b) determines several other issues related to the positions of mayor and municipal councilor, in particular the incompatibility of their positions with other positions. The position of mayor is not compatible with the position of a member of the municipal council (and vice versa), membership on the municipal supervisory board, positions in the municipal administration, and several other political functions on the national level of government, such as prime minister, member of parliament, minister, or state secretary. The positions of mayor and member of the municipal council are also incompatible with the positions of senior civil servants in state administration, as well as with any position in the state administration where civil servants exercise their powers in connection with control over the municipal bodies.

Local elections: well-oiled machine for the selection of representatives

Voter turnout for local elections in the early period after the reestablishment of local self-government (1994–2002) was higher than in the latter period (2006–2018), although it should be noted that the 2002 local elections were held simultaneously with the presidential election, which undoubtedly had a positive effect on turnout. The turnout for local elections in the last decade has consolidated at about 50%, with a negative bottom in 2014 and a fairly unexpected 6% turnout increase for the most recent local elections in 2018[11] (Haček 2019a). Turnout has traditionally been higher in smaller municipalities (see Table 41.1).

In the most recent local elections in 2018, there were a total of 22,314 candidates for the available 3,334 council seats;[12] on average, 6.7 candidates competed for one council seat (Haček 2019b). The most successful national political parties were center-right political parties (SDS, NSi and SNS) with a total of 713 municipal councilors, compared to center-left political parties (SD, SMC, DeSUS, LMŠ, Left, SAB) with a total of 660 municipal councilors (Kukovič & Haček 2018; Haček 2019b).[13] The most successful political party is SDS, which has at least one representative in 143 out of 147 municipalities with proportional principle, followed by the SD,

Table 41.1 Voter turnout (percent) for local elections in the period 1994–2018 with details regarding the size of municipalities in the 2018 local elections in Slovenia

Year of local elections	Voter turnout (%, first round of local elections)		
1994	62.7		
1998	58.3		
2002	72.1		
2006	58.2		
2010	51.0		
2014	45.2		
2018	51.2	Fewer than 3,000 inhabitants	60.8
		3001–5,000 inhabitants	59.1
		5,001–10,000 inhabitants	54.5
		10,001–20,000 inhabitants	51.4
		More than 20,000 inhabitants	46.8

Source: Data of the State Electoral Commission (in Haček 2019a) and data for the 2018 local elections (Kukovič & Haček 2019)

which has at least one municipal councilor in 119 municipalities (see Table 41.2). We should also mention an array of nonpartisan lists and candidates, cumulatively representing the strongest 'political' force with 34.2% of municipal councilors.

In 65 municipalities with a majority electoral system, there were 594 elected councilors, with 251 (42.3%) nonpartisan councilors being elected. The dominance of center-right political parties (44.8%) over center-left political parties (8.8%) is even more daunting here.

We can observe a similar pattern in the mayoral elections. A total of 794 candidates competed in mayoral races in the most recent local elections in November 2018; on average, 2.6 candidates ran for mayor. It should also be pointed out that in 35 municipalities there was only single candidate, so (s)he needed only one vote to be elected. Nonparty candidates were also victorious in the mayoral elections, beating politically affiliated opponents in 123 municipalities (58%). As with the municipal council elections, the center-right parties were more successful with a total of 53 elected mayors; generally, those parties were more successful in smaller municipalities. Among the center-left political parties, the SD stood out with 16 elected mayors, but four other center-left parties were unsuccessful with just three elected mayors in total. Generally, center-left parties were more successful in municipalities with a larger population. It should be observed that partisan electoral success in the local elections is more closely related to the left-right cleavage than the coalition-opposition divide in national politics (Kukovič & Haček 2018; Haček 2019a).

However, when analyzing Slovenian election results, one should not overlook gender representation in elected local government bodies. An analysis of the nominations shows that there were 102 female mayoral candidates in the local elections in 2018. Women ran for mayor in 83 municipalities in total and were victorious in 22 municipalities; female candidates are most successful in smaller municipalities (Kukovič 2019b: 118). Table 41.3 shows the statistics for female mayoral candidates in local elections in the period 1994–2018.

Table 41.2 Success of political parties and local lists in the Slovenian 2018 municipal council elections in municipalities with the proportional principle

Political party	% of municipalities where running	% of municipalities where represented	% of seats on local councils	% of (aggregate) votes in local elections
SDS (Slovenian Democratic Party)	99.3 (146 out of 147)	97.3 (143 out of 147)	19.6 (537 out of 2,740)	16.7
SD (Social Democrats)	88.4 (130 out of 147)	81.0 (119 out of 147)	12.2 (335 out of 2,740)	10.1
NSi (New Slovenia-Christian People's Party)	100 (147 out of 147)	70.7 (104 out of 147)	6.4 (175 out of 2,740)	6.4
DeSUS (Pensioners' Party)	81.6 (120 out of 147)	61.9 (91 out of 147)	4.9 (133 out of 2,740)	4.8
SMC (Party of Modern Center)	71.4 (105 out of 147)	37.4 (55 out of 147)	3.3 (91 out of 2,740)	4.1
Left	32.6 (48 out of 147)	20.4 (30 out of 147)	1.5 (41 out of 2,740)	3.1
LMŠ (List of Marjan Šarec)	23.8 (35 out of 147)	19.0 (28 out of 147)	1.9 (53 out of 2,740)	2.5
SNS (Slovenian National Party)	28.6 (42 out of 147)	8.8 (13 out of 147)	0.5 (14 out of 2,740)	1.1
SAB (Party of Alenka Bratušek)	9.5 (14 out of 147)	4.8 (7 out of 147)	0.3 (7 out of 2,740)	0.8
Nonpartisans and local lists	93.2 (137 out of 147)	91.2 (134 out of 147)	34.2 (940 out of 2,740)	31.7

Note: The table shows only data for municipal council elections voted on a proportional basis in 147 municipalities with a total of 2,740 municipal councilors. The State Electoral Commission does not include data for the 65 municipalities with 594 municipal council seats that use a majority electoral system for municipal council elections.
Source: Authors' calculations using State Electoral Commission data (2020)

The number of women is also steadily increasing on the municipal councils; in the most recent local elections, 1,120 female municipal councilors[14] were elected, representing a share of 33.2%. The increase in female council representatives in 2006 is most likely a result of the 2005 legislative change that introduced a clause on equal opportunities for both genders in the electoral legislation (Kukovič & Haček 2018; Kukovič 2019b). In 65 municipalities with a majority electoral system, a total of 594 municipal councilors were elected, of which 136 (22.9%) were women. There are four municipalities with the majority principle that have exclusively male representatives on the council; however, there are no municipalities with exclusively female representatives. In 147 municipalities with proportional elections, there are 2,740 municipal councilors in total, of which 974 (35.5%) are female and 1,766 (64.5%) are male. The latter confirms the thesis that the proportional electoral principle gives women greater opportunity for election. Compared to municipalities with a majority electoral principle, the proportion of women elected in municipalities with a proportional electoral principle is higher by 12.6% (Kukovič 2019b). If we compare these data with the share of women elected to the national parliament in the most recent parliamentary elections in 2018 (24.4%),[15] we can observe that the share of female councilors on municipal councils is substantially higher.

Table 41.3 Number of female mayoral candidates in local elections in Slovenia, 1994–2018

	1994	1998	2002	2006	2010	2014	2018
Number of municipalities	147	192	193	210	211	212	212
Number of all mayoral candidates	635	750	724	847	783	811	794
Number of female mayoral candidates	31	53	77	91	94	108	102
Percentage of female candidates	4.9	7.1	10.6	10.7	12.0	13.3	12.8
Number of elected female mayors (%)	2 (1.4)	8 (4.2)	11 (5.7)	7 (3.3)	10 (4.7)	16 (7.5)	22 (10.4)
Percentage of female municipal councilors elected at local elections	10.7	11.9	13.1	21.5	22.0	31.7	33.2

Source: Authors' calculations based on data from the State Electoral Commission (Kukovič 2019b)

Positive discrimination has been introduced in some Slovenian municipalities, which means that voters also elect local representatives of the Italian and Hungarian national minorities and the Roma community, slightly increasing the size of the council. Nineteen candidates ran for nine local representatives of the Italian national minority in four coastal municipalities. For seven local representatives of the Hungarian national minority in five municipalities in Pomurje, there have been 12 candidates in total. The number of candidates for the local representative of the Roma community has been slowly declining since 2006 and has reached the bottom in the most recent local elections in 2018 (26 candidates for 20 council seats in 20 municipalities) (Haček 2019b).

Two major peculiarities: reelection and nonpartisanship

In the Slovenian system of local self-government, the mayor plays a central role and is largely recognized by the public as the most important actor in local government, who at the same time also bears the greatest responsibility for the development of the municipality as well as for the provision of local public services. The first peculiarity that the researchers (Kukovič & Haček 2013, 2016; Kukovič 2015, 2019a) have discovered is the mayors' perception of their own position: they see their position as a long-term career and (in the absence of any term-related limit) they repeatedly enter successive mayoral elections. On the other hand, voters favor the stability of local leadership, and this stance allows incumbent mayors to continue their careers through multiple reelections. For example, 184 incumbent mayors (from 212) decided to run again in the most recent local elections in 2018, and 144 were reelected for another term, marking the electoral success rate[16] of incumbent mayors at 78.3%. In Table 41.4, we can observe that, at the end of their term, a large proportion of mayors develop static ambitions (Schlesinger 1966: 10; Kjaer 2006: 94) and run for reelection. The percentage of incumbent candidates was above 80% in all six previous local elections; it should be noted that the number of incumbent candidates is steadily increasing.[17]

A closer analysis of the aggregate data reveals several interesting facts. There is not a single municipality in which a different candidate would be victorious in each local election. In all municipalities, at least one incumbent mayor was also reelected at least once. Moreover, there are currently nine mayors who have been running in their municipalities since 1994 without interruption; in addition to these nine 'veterans', there are also 16 municipalities that were established after 1994 that have had the same mayor ever since (for more details see Kukovič 2019a: 95–96, 2020).

Table 41.4 Incumbency of mayors in local elections in Slovenia, 1998–2018

	1998	2002	2006	2010	2014	2018
Number of municipalities	192	193	210	210	212	212
Incumbency of mayors (%)	133 out of 147 (90.5)	168 out of 192 (87.5)	163 out of 193 (84.5)	179 out of 210 (85.2)	177 out of 211 (83.9)	184 out of 212 (86.8)
Number of reelected mayors in total	103	133	133	148	149	144
Electoral success (%)	77.4	79.2	81.6	82.7	84.2	78.3

Source: Kukovič (2020)

Another interesting feature is the ever-increasing success of nonpartisan mayors and the ever-decreasing influence of political parties. Currently, as many as 123 municipalities are run by a nonpartisan mayor.[18] The electoral success of nonpartisan mayoral candidates is no surprise, given that political parties in Slovenia face great distrust and given the fact that local elections are the only place where nonpartisan candidates have a realistic chance for election, because the same is basically impossible in the parliamentary elections due to the demanding rules of registration and hard-to-reach formal thresholds. Nonpartisan candidates thus represent a viable alternative to the established partisan elite, which is strongly anchored at the national level but its position is slowly degrading in Slovenian municipalities. On the one hand, such an outcome could be seen as positive, because at the local level the focus shifts to public services and development of the local community, but on the other hand, it also drives a wedge between the local and the national levels, as an important connection[19] that would represent the local community on the national level is slowly being lost.

Over the past decade, there have been some (later unsuccessful) initiatives about legislative change in terms of limiting the mayoral mandate, both on the issue of reelection of mayors and increasingly strong nonpartisan candidates. The discussion showed that most experts are not in favor of this change, as it is believed such change could establish so-called 'shadow mayors', where the incumbent mayor would mentor a personal favorite, who would formally replace him or her as the mayor. This could certainly prove harmful, as currently transparent municipal leadership could turn into stories of political sponsorship and evasion of responsibility.

Notes

1 There are currently 201 rural and 11 urban municipalities in Slovenia. The average size of a Slovenian municipality is 9,683 inhabitants (January 2020) with 53 municipalities having more and 159 having fewer inhabitants. The median municipality has 4,604 inhabitants.
2 With the process of local government reform in 1994, which brought about substantive organizational and territorial changes, Slovenia initially established 136 rural and 11 urban municipalities or 147 in total. After that, many municipal splits emerged, that is, there were 192 municipalities (1998), 193 (2002), 210 (2006 and 2010), and 212 municipalities (2014 and 2018).
3 In 2014, an empirical typology of local government systems in new democracies of Central and Eastern Europe was developed. Slovenia was categorized as type III (see Swianiewicz 2014).
4 According to the calculated index of mayoral strength (see Heinelt & Hlepas 2006: 38; Kukovič 2015), Slovenian mayors reach 11 points and share second place with their Spanish counterparts. Slovenian mayors are directly elected executives who have the power of political mayors of the Mediterranean countries within the institutional framework (see Kukovič 2018).

5 Dates of previous local elections were set by the President of the National Assembly for 4 December 1994, 22 November 1998, 10 November 2002, 22 October 2006, 10 October 2010, and 5 October 2014.
6 Sublocal communities are envisaged as an optional form of internal division in the municipality, for which there must be expressed interest among the citizens. They represent a form of territorial organization and ensure the active participation of inhabitants in decision-making on local issues. They may be established in any municipality, regardless of its size; the municipal council of each municipality is free to decide on their autonomy and finances. The sublocal communities have a representative body that is elected in local elections.
7 In local elections, it is possible to vote by post or upfront, but only for voters who registered in advance to do so. However, in local elections it is impossible to vote from abroad; on the other hand, it is possible in the case of parliamentary or presidential elections.
8 A minimum of 15 voter signatures must be collected for a representative of the Italian or Hungarian national minorities. Candidates for the representative of the Roma community must collect at least 15 voter signatures or they may also be proposed by the body of the Roma social organization in the municipality (Law on Local Elections 2007, Article 49).
9 This is slightly higher than the 35% gender quota for elections to the National Assembly.
10 Slovenia introduced the provision on equal opportunities for candidates of both genders into the Law on Local Elections in 2005.
11 As a comparison, we add voter turnout for parliamentary elections in the period 1992–2018: 85.6% (1992); 73.7% (1996); 70.1% (2000); 60.6% (2004); 63.1% (2008); 65.6% (2011); 51.7% (2014) (Haček, Kukovič & Brezovšek 2017: 144); and 52.6% (2018) (State Electoral Commission 2020).
12 There were an additional 60 candidates for 35 seats of Italian and Hungarian national minorities and Roma community representatives.
13 Center-right political parties received 36 MPs (out of 90) at the most recent parliamentary elections in 2018, while center-left parties received 52 MPs. Two additional MPs represent national minorities.
14 Ten out of 1,120 female councillors are female representatives of Italian and Hungarian national minorities and the Roma community.
15 Since independence, the gender structure of the National Assembly has changed quite a bit as follows: election year 1992 (14 female MPs), 1996 (7), 2000 (12), 2004 (11), 2008 (12), 2011 (29), 2014 (31) (see Haček, Kukovič & Brezovšek 2017: 39).
16 Electoral success rate is calculated as a quotient of the number of municipalities in which incumbent mayors have been reelected and the overall number of proposed candidacies of incumbent mayors in all municipalities.
17 During the period 1998–2018, a total of 154 incumbent mayors decided not to run again. The largest share (45.5%) of these mayors chose to retire; 33.1% moved to another job incompatible with the position of the mayor, usually at the national level; and 21.4% of incumbent mayors decided not to enter the race for personal reasons. Sadly, nine mayors also passed away while in office (Kukovič 2020).
18 The number of nonpartisan mayors: 29 out of 147 (1994); 46 out of 192 (1998); 60 out of 193 (2002); 67 out of 210 (2006); 71 out of 212 (2010); and 115 out of 212 (2014) (Haček 2020).
19 The latter phenomenon is particularly noticeable from 2011 onward after the amendment of the legislation stipulating that the position of mayor is incompatible with the position of member of national parliament (MP).

References

Brezovšek, M. & Kukovič, S. (2012). *Organizacija lokalne oblasti v Sloveniji [Organisation of local government in Slovenia]*. Ljubljana: Faculty of Social Sciences.

Constitution of the Republic of Slovenia [Ustava Republike Slovenije, URS]. Official Gazette of the Republic of Slovenia 33/91 & further changes. Available at: www.pisrs.si/Pis.web/pregledPredpisa?id=USTA1 (28 August 2020).

Goldsmith, M.J. (1992). Local Government. *Urban Studies*, 29(3/4), 393–410.

Haček, M. (2019a). Kdo je torej zmagovalec lokalnih volitev? [Who is then the Winner of Local Elections?]. In S. Kukovič (Ed.), *Lokalna demokracija v Sloveniji: značilnosti lokalnih volitev 2018 [Local Democracy in Slovenia: Patterns of Local Elections 2018]* (pp. 137–153). Ljubljana: Faculty of Social Sciences.

Haček, M. (2019b). Uresničevanje pasivne volilne pravice na slovenskih lokalnih volitvah [Implementation of Passive Voting Right at Slovenian Local Elections]. In S. Kukovič (Ed.), *Lokalna demokracija v Sloveniji: značilnosti lokalnih volitev 2018 [Local Democracy in Slovenia: Patterns of Local Elections 2018]* (pp. 11–31). Ljubljana: Faculty of Social Sciences.

Haček, M. (2020). Lokalna demokracija v Sloveniji: prvih petindvajset let [Local Democracy in Slovenia: The First Twenty-five Years]. In S. Kukovič & M. Haček (Eds.), *Petindvajset let lokalne samouprave v Republiki Sloveniji [Twenty-five Years of Local Self-Governemnt in Slovenia]* (pp. 9–31). Ljubljana: Faculty of Social Sciences.

Haček, M., Kukovič, S. & Brezovšek, M. (2017). *Slovenian Politics and the State*. Lanham, Boulder, New York & London: Lexington books.

Heinelt, H. & Hlepas, N.-K. (2006). Typologies of Local Government Systems. In H. Bäck, H. Heinelt & A. Magnier (Eds.), *The European Mayor, Political Leaders in the Changing Context of Local Democracy* (pp. 21–42). Wiesbaden: VS Verlag für Sozialwissenschaften.

Heinelt, H., Hlepas, N., Kuhlmann, S. & Swianiewicz, P. (2018). Local Government Systems: Grasping the Institutional Environment of Mayors. In H. Heinelt, A. Magnier, M. Cabria & H. Reynaert (Eds.), *Political Leaders and Changing Local Democracy, The European Mayor* (pp. 19–78). Cham: Springer International Publishing AG.

Hesse, J.J. & Sharpe, L.J. (1991). Local Government in International Perspective: Some Comparative Observations. In J.J. Hesse & L.J. Sharpe (Eds.), *Local Government and Urban Affairs in International Perspective; Analyses of Twenty Western Industrialised Countries* (pp. 603–621). Baden-Baden: Auflage.

Kjaer, U. (2006). The Mayor's Political Career. In H. Bäck, H. Heinelt & A. Magnier (Eds.), *The European Mayor, Political Leaders in the Changing Context of Local Democracy* (pp. 75–98). Wiesbaden: VS Verlag für Sozialwissenschaften.

Kukovič, S. (2015). *Lokalno politično vodenje: slovenski župani v primerjalni perspektivi [Local Political Leadership: Slovenian Mayors in Comparative Perspective]*. Ljubljana: Faculty of Social Sciences.

Kukovič, S. (2018). Unique Type of Slovenian Local Leaders: Where Executive Mayors Have Mediterranean Strength. *Studia politica: Romanian Political Science Review*, 18(2), 173–192.

Kukovič, S. (2019a). Fenomen ponovne izvoljivosti: nekdanji-sedanji župani [The Phenomenon of Re-election: Former-current Mayors]. In S. Kukovič (Ed.), *Lokalna demokracija v Sloveniji: značilnosti lokalnih volitev 2018 [Local Democracy in Slovenia: Patterns of Local Elections 2018]* (pp. 79–103). Ljubljana: Faculty of Social Sciences.

Kukovič, S. (2019b). Ženske v igri za prestol [Women in a Game for the Throne]. In S. Kukovič (Ed.), *Lokalna demokracija v Sloveniji: značilnosti lokalnih volitev 2018 [Local Democracy in Slovenia: Patterns of Local Elections 2018]* (pp. 105–136). Ljubljana: Faculty of Social Sciences.

Kukovič, S. (2020). Župani v slovenskem sistemu lokalne samouprave: kot riba v akvariju [Mayors in the Slovenian Local Self-government System: Like a Fish in a Bowl]. In S. Kukovič & M. Haček (Eds.), *Petindvajset let lokalne samouprave v Republiki Sloveniji [Twenty-five Years of Local Self-governemnt in Slovenia]* (pp. 83–103). Ljubljana: Faculty of Social Sciences.

Kukovič, S. & Haček, M. (2013). The Re-election of Mayors in the Slovenian Local Self-government. *Lex localis*, 11(2), 87–99.

Kukovič, S. & Haček, M. (2016). Continuity of Leadership in Slovenian Local Government. *Annales*, 23(1), 97–108.

Kukovič, S. & Haček, M. (2018). *Lokalno politično vodenje: glas svetnikov [Local Political Leadership: The Voice of Councillors]*. Ljubljana: Faculty of Social Sciences.

Kukovič, S. & Haček, M. (2019). *Analiza volilne udeležbe na lokalnih volitvah 2018, baza podatkov [Analysis of Voter Turnout at Local Elections 2018, Database]*. Ljubljana: Centre for the Analysis of the Administrative-Political Processes and Institutions.

Kukovič, S., Haček, M. & Bukovnik, A. (2016). The Issue of Local Autonomy in the Slovenian Local Government System. *Lex Localis*, 14(3), 303–320.

Ladner, A., Keuffer, N. & Baldersheim, H. (2016). Measuring Local Autonomy in 39 Countries (1990–2014). *Regional & Federal Studies*, 26(3), 321–357.

Law on amendments to the Law on local elections [Zakon o spremembah in dopolnitvah Zakona o lokalnih volitvah, ZLV-J]. Official Gazette of the Republic of Slovenia 68/2017. Available at: www.uradni-list.si/glasilo-uradni-list-rs/vsebina/2017-01-3192?sop=2017-01-3192 (28 August 2020).

Law on local elections [Zakon o lokalnih volitvah, ZLV-UPB3]. Official Gazette of the Republic of Slovenia 94/2007 & further changes. Available at: www.uradni-list.si/1/objava.jsp?urlurid=20074693 (28 August 2020).

Law on local self-governemnt [Zakon o lokalni samoupravi, ZLS]. Official Gazette of the Republic of Slovenia 72/93. Available at: www.pisrs.si/Pis.web/pregledPredpisa?id=ZAKO307 (28 August 2020).

Law on local self-governemnt [Zakon o lokalni samoupravi, ZLS-UPB2]. Official Gazette of the Republic of Slovenia 94/2007 & further changes. Available at: www.uradni-list.si/1/objava.jsp?urlid=200794&stevilka=4692 (28 August 2020).

Law on Referenda for the Establishment of Municipalities [Zakon o referendumu za ustanovitev občin, ZRUO]. Official Gazette of the Republic of Slovenia 5/94. Available at: http://pisrs.si/Pis.web/pregledPredpisa?id=ZAKO312 (28 August 2020).

Mouritzen, P.E. & Svara, J.H. (2002). *Leadership at the Apex. Politicians and Administrators in Western Local Governments*. Pittsburgh: University of Pittsburgh Press.

Page, E.C. (1991). *Localism and Centralism in Europe: The Political and Legal Bases of Local Self-government*. Oxford: Oxford University Press.

Page, E.C. & Goldsmith, M. (1987). *Central and Local Government Relations: A Comparative Analysis of West European Unitary States*. Beverly Hills: Sage.

Schlesinger, J.A. (1966). *Ambition and Politics: Political Careers in the United States*. Chicago: Rand McNally.

State electoral commission [Državna volilna komisija]. 2020. *Lokalne volitve 2018 [Local Elections 2018]*. Available at www.dvk-rs.si/index.php/si/arhiv-lokalne-volitve/lokalne-volitve-leto-2018 (28 August 2020).

Swianiewicz, P. (2014). An Empirical Typology of Local Government Systems in Eastern Europe. *Local Government Studies, 40*(2), 292–311.

Part 8
Conclusions

42
'Happily ever after'? Comparing local elections and voting in 40 European countries

Adam Gendźwiłł, Ulrik Kjaer, and Kristof Steyvers

Comparing 40 countries

Local elections and voting have long been considered the 'perennial bridesmaids' of behavioral research. Largely understudied, particularly from a cross-national perspective, the existing assertions denote these as either lower rank ('second order') or of a different kind. Meanwhile, the local layer has often been neglected in multilevel studies of elections and voting (Gendźwiłł & Steyvers 2021). This *Handbook* helps to fill this gap.

First, it builds on a more contemporary conception of the local level as 'second tier'. This recognizes the importance of vertical integration and horizontal variation when theoretically refining and empirically substantiating the answer to a question that is also central in this *Handbook*: how *local* are these elections and voting (Kjaer & Steyvers 2019)? Second, it develops a rationale to further engage with the local tier, as both a means and an end. More systematic evidence on this level is needed when drawing on the treasure trove of the political actors, institutions, and processes it represents. Embracing its importance for the multilevel study of elections and voting fosters a more comprehensive and integrated understanding of various key topics in the study of (local) political systems. Third, as an attempt to clear away the underbrush, the body of this book consists of a cross-country account of first tier local elections and voting (from situating these in local government systems to patterns and dynamics in electoral outcomes). An unprecedented number of cases and units have been paired; these are assessed in no fewer than 40 European states.

Wedding the accumulated evidence of the country chapters with the framework developed in the Introduction, this conclusion aims to determine the current state of affairs. The comparison has two complementary aims: first, to summarize the main findings from the country chapters; second, to analyze their subsequent insights along the integration-variation dimensions. Evidently, both are based on the empirical material (i.e., country chapter descriptions and data versus the common template), and their ultimate goal is to classify cases in theoretically relevant types or along pertinent continua. However, the first remains closer to the material while drawing on existing characterizations in the literature. Still, it adds empirical breadth by providing an updated and/or geographically extended account for a wide array of cases. The second builds on this, adding depth while pursuing the aim of enriching this literature more theoretically. We posit both have merit and treat them in a two-step process.

To summarize the rich material from the country assertions can be done from various angles. In the first part of the conclusion, we will advance two classic takes: comparison across space and over time. For the former, a cross-national picture is drawn, structured by an adapted version of the categories discerned in the frequently cited *Oxford Handbook of Local and Regional Democracy* (Loughlin et al. 2012). Referring to state traditions and modes of local democracy, these amended categories were also used to organize the country chapters in our *Handbook* (i.e., Nordic, Rhinelandic, the British Isles, Southern European, and New Democracies). We prepend one subdivision and sustain another. In the Rhinelandic group, we further distinguish federal from unitary states.[1] The federal tradition usually influences local government systems. Most federations display an (often remarkable) internal variation – for example, concerning the design of local electoral rules.[2] In most instances, subnational subsystems should be considered as the proper point of reference. This often renders an overall account of local elections and voting in such contexts highly complex (compounded by the discretion in choosing to apply and adhere to certain rules locally). In the New Democracies, we maintain the division between Central and Eastern and Southeastern states (Swianiewicz 2014).[3] The temporal comparison focuses on critical junctures in the evolution of local elections and voting and on the subsequent path dependencies stemming from these (Pierson 2004). They include more incremental continuity and change in the dynamics of local electoral systems, participation, politicization, and representation but also deliberate instances of electoral reform and the discourses thereon (such as the proliferation of the direct election of mayors or alterations of local electoral systems).

Analysis of the integration-variation dimensions adds a vertical and horizontal angle to the comparison in the second part of this chapter. Vertical integration structures the between-level comparison. Here, local elections and voting are assessed against their national counterparts.[4] Given their default linkage, the interconnection between various aspects in both arenas can be estimated in terms of divergence or similarity. This provides a first perspective on the *localness* of municipal elections and voting. It should be noted that in countries where mayors are directly elected, there is also room to compare local legislative (i.e., council) and executive elections and voting.

Horizontal variation shapes the between-jurisdictions differentiation. Multiple entities stand for sets of contests in separate constituencies. Diversity in elections and voting between local authorities should be conceded as the second perspective on their *localness*. This renders estimates on the heterogeneity or homogeneity across locations. In this, size appears to be the main factor, since previous research has demonstrated that small and large communities differ: size stands for variation in the urban nature or population heterogeneity of the locality, affecting the societal context of local elections and voting (Denters et al. 2015). In some cases, there are institutional corollaries because size is often used in national legislation to differentiate the rules of local elections and voting across municipalities.

In what follows, we attempt to develop these four comparative angles. We will elaborate on this along the four themes central in this volume: (1) local electoral systems; (2) local electoral participation; (3) local party politicization; and (4) local political representation. Our ultimate goal is to combine these angles and establish an explorative typology based on the analysis of the 40 countries in this book. We presume that more (vertical) divergence and (horizontal) heterogeneity signal more *localness* in elections and voting. We close with a brief overall summary and state an agenda for future research: how can the scholarly community further commit to the study of local elections and voting? With the perennial bridesmaids now fully fledged spouses, how can the couple live 'happily ever after'?

Local electoral systems

This section focuses on the set of rules that determines who gets elected in local democracy and how? The *who* refers to the offices subject to direct elections. Whereas this nearly universally includes the members of the local legislature – the council – there is more variation as to whether it also applies to those in the local executive, notably mayors. This distinction primarily organizes the discussion of our findings. The *how* pertains to their mode and the configuration of these systems, namely, the way in which the vote is expressed and translated into seats. This will subdivide the section.

Direct council elections

Councils are an essential part of local democracy. As established in the *European Charter*, local self-government 'shall be exercised by councils or assemblies composed of members freely elected by secret ballot on the basis of direct, equal, universal suffrage' (Article 3). Their central position in representative democracy is rooted in the layman's rule (Mouritzen & Svara 2002). Therein, all citizens (i.e., nonprofessional politicians) meeting the eligibility criteria can aspire to the allegedly most important decision-making body of the local authority, as long as they are mandated by their fellow citizens, who are themselves unable to authoritatively decide on every political issue all of the time. The layman's rule thus reconciles popular sovereignty (political equality) with managing democratization (an extension of political rights). Therefore, 'all European countries have local government systems that are either entirely based on representative democracy or . . . possess significant components of it' (Lidström et al. 2016: 288). The latter refers to countries such as Switzerland where, in the bulk of municipalities, citizen assemblies substitute legislative organs, and only the executive is directly elected. In other instances, this equally applies to the local council (Egner et al. 2013).

Local council sizes

In any case, the mere number of local councilors is impressive. Based on the latest electoral cycle included in this *Handbook*, the countries cover contests in about 89,000 municipalities. These comprise around 1.1 million directly elected councilors.[5] This number can hardly be filled with professional politicians, and the sheer number of seats reinforces the necessity of the layman's rule. Local elections and voting are thus extensive and complex exercises in recruiting and selecting political elites – much more so than at the national level, where a comparable aggregate would only amount to a few thousand members of parliament. By default, councils are relatively small representative bodies, where single mandatories have more numerical weight than in the average national parliament. In addition, their representative ratio (i.e., the number of eligible voters they stand and act for) remains lower. However, differences are not limited to those general ones between levels. They also pertain between countries and/or municipalities. Table 42.1 summarizes some key statistics on local council size. For each country, the average (in ascending order), minimal, and maximal number of seats is displayed.

Table 42.1 demonstrates that the average council in the countries covered has about 20 members. This average is lowest in Hungary (about a one quarter of the total average) and highest in Sweden (more than double the total average). It also suggests some relationship with state traditions. The average council size is highest for the two countries representing the British Isles (Ireland and the United Kingdom), while it is lowest for the three unitary Rhinelandic

Table 42.1 Local council size by country

Country	Local council size (number of seats)		
	Average	Min	Max
Hungary	5.3	2	32
Iceland	7.0	5	23
Slovakia	7.1	3	45
Spain	8.4	3	57
Portugal (*parishes*)	8.7	7	21
Liechtenstein	9.5	7	13
Czech Republic	9.5	5	65
Luxembourg	11.0	7	27
Andorra	11.4	10	12
Italy	11.7	10	40
Moldova	11.7	9	43
Cyprus	12.3	8	26
Romania	12.6	9	31
Croatia	13.3	7	51
Latvia	13.6	9	60
France	14.3	7	163
Slovenia	15.9	7	45
Poland	16.0	15	60
North Macedonia	16.6	9	45
Austria	19.0	9	100
Bulgaria	19.4	11	61
Estonia	21.9	7	79
Bosnia and Herzegovina	22.1	11	31
Belgium	23.2	7	55
Lithuania	24.0	15	51
Netherlands	24.3	9	45
Ukraine	24.6	22	120
Denmark	24.8	9	55
Albania	26.1	15	61
Norway	26.2	11	77
Kosovo	26.4	15	51
Greece	28.8	13	49
Finland	30.5	13	85
Ireland	30.6	18	63
Portugal (*municipalities*)	31.0	15	123
Montenegro	35.3	30	61
United Kingdom	36.3	18	99
Serbia	39.7	19	110
Sweden	43.8	21	101
Total (*average*)	**19.8**	**10.9**	**59.8**

Notes: A few countries were excluded: Germany (no reliable data), Switzerland, and Spanish open-council municipalities. Partial information in the case of nonsimultaneous elections: 72.3% municipalities in England, 65.1% municipalities in Italy, 54.2% in Montenegro, 89.6% in Serbia. Singular off-cycle elections in other countries were excluded.

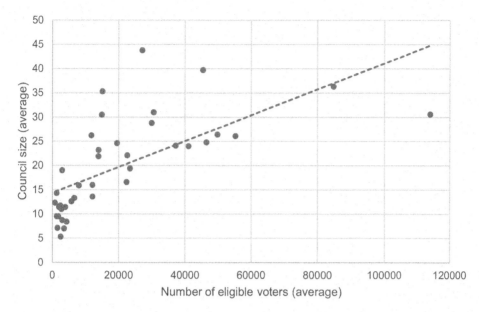

Figure 42.1 Council size by eligible voters (country averages)

states (Liechtenstein, Luxembourg, and The Netherlands). Evidently, in many groupings there is also substantial internal variation (as cases do not appear by group in the table).

We also find that territorial fragmentation matters. Figure 42.1 plots the average council size against the average number of eligible voters in the municipalities of the countries included. It suggests that in countries where municipalities have relatively few voters, councils also tend to have fewer members.[6] At the same time, the picture is not entirely linear. In particular, in countries where typical municipalities appear to represent relatively few voters, average council sizes vary (first below and then above the trend line). These findings are in accordance with representativeness research in the field of legislative studies, in which a (nonlinear) relationship between the size of the electorate and that of the assembly has been equally observed (Kjaer & Elklit 2014).

Council size also varies within countries. On average, the range is somewhere between 11 and 60 members. In the minimum range, Hungary again scores lowest and Montenegro highest. Regarding the maximum, we find the lowest scores in Andorra and the highest in France. The description in the country chapters shows that the number of seats in the council is invariably related to the population size of the municipality (larger ones having more). The exact number is either predetermined by national law (by categories of population size) or left open (within limits) to the discretion of the local council. It should be noted that the largest cities (particularly capitals) can have sizable councils. With more than 100 councilors, they gravitate toward the magnitude of national parliaments. The record 163 members of the *Conseil de Paris* in France are a case in point.

Over time, instances where the overall number of councilors has decreased can be found. Here, the case of Hungary is noteworthy. As part of the 2010 electoral reform, the number of obtainable mandates diminished by around one third of all seats. In Slovakia, councils were able to become smaller in size after the minimal number of members had been lowered. Also, Finland reformulated recommendations for council size (further upon local discretion).

Local council electoral systems

The local electoral system concerns 'the kinds of information voters are asked to provide during the election . . . and regulates the translation of this information into an allocation of seats' (van der Kolk 2007: 161). As stated in the introduction to this *Handbook*, we asked the country experts to start by considering its uniformity. Is the system the same throughout the country or do various subsystems exist? Each was then situated in the larger families of plurality/majority, proportional, or mixed considering the possibility to cultivate a preference vote. These siblings were further scrutinized along the dimensions central to many classification schemes (Rae 1969): the *electoral formula* (how votes are translated into seats), the *districting* (whether votes are at large or in single- or multi-member constituencies) and the *ballot structure* (the effective choice of the voter between parties and/or candidates, and nominating one or several of these versus ordering them). For each of these dimensions, some additional considerations were included (see introduction). Values might differ on the various aspects of these dimensions which in turn are distinct but not unrelated. The subsequent configuration therefore determines the local electoral system (van der Kolk 2007; Cole 2019).

A synthetic overview of our findings can be found in Table 42.2, which reports the local electoral systems in their general families (with the number of cases where these are found) and is organized along the state traditions of the countries included. For the latter, different subsystems might be discerned. The specific branches of these systems are denominated along the International IDEA typology (Reynolds et al. 2005). Table 42.8 placed at the end of this chapter provides a more extensive description of the aspects considered. The discussion to follow will draw on elements from both tables and proceed along the aforementioned dimensions. Thereby, it provides a timely update of van der Kolk's earlier scheme, widening its geographical and thematic scope.

Table 42.2 demonstrates that, in most countries (28 cases, or 70%), the family membership of local electoral systems is uniform throughout. Where variation occurs, this is mostly due to differences between smaller and larger municipalities, often based on a population threshold established by law. There is a tendency for smaller municipalities to elect their representatives via non proportional means versus larger ones via a proportional system. In the United Kingdom, differences appear along the devolved entities, the Anglo-Saxon core being nonproportional and the Celtic Fringe proportional. It is noteworthy that in federal polities (such as those in the Rhineland), the electoral system appears relatively homogenous, at least where general family is concerned (notice Austria or Switzerland in this respect). A further look at the tables shows that, here, variation occurs along more specific aspects of the system (such as the possibility of preference voting – see Germany).[7]

Local councils in Europe are predominantly composed using a proportional electoral formula. Variants of the principle that the distribution of seats should approximate that of the vote can be found in all but two countries (38 cases, or 95%). The finding that most cases are situated in this category holds regardless of state tradition. Within this family, list systems are the most popular. Again, in all but two countries (36 cases) in this branch, parties (or their equivalents) publish lists of candidates and receive seats in proportion to their share of the vote (which is primarily directed at those lists).

Among list systems, the open variant (OLPR) is the most common (27 cases). Here, the number of preference votes received by each candidate co-determines who gets elected (up to

Table 42.2 Local electoral systems by state tradition (synthetic overview)

	Plurality/majority (10 cases)	Mixed (1 case)	Proportional (38 cases)
Nordic	Iceland/small (BV)		Denmark (OLPR), Finland (OLPR), Iceland/large (OLPR), Norway (OLPR), Sweden (OLPR)
British Isles	UK/England (FPTP), UK/Wales (FPTP)		Ireland (STV), UK/Scotland (STV), UK/Northern Ireland (STV)
Rhinelandic: federal			Austria (OLPR), Belgium (OLPR), Germany/10 states (OLPR), Germany/3 states (CLPR), Switzerland (mostly OLPR)
Rhinelandic: unitary	Luxembourg/small (BV)		Liechtenstein (OLPR), Luxembourg/large (OLPR), Netherlands (OLPR)
Southern European	France/small (TR-BV), Spain/small (LV)		Andorra (CLPR/MBS), Cyprus (OLPR), France/large (CLPR/MBS), Greece (OLPR), Italy (OLPR/MBS), Portugal (CLPR), Spain/large (CLPR)
New democracies: Central and Eastern European	Hungary/small (BV), Poland/small (FPTP), Slovakia (BV), Ukraine/small (LV)	Hungary/large (MMP)	Czech Republic (OLPR), Estonia (OLPR), Latvia (OLPR), Lithuania (OLPR), Poland /large (OLPR), Ukraine/large (OLPR)
New democracies: Southeastern European	Slovenia/small (BV, LV, SNTV)		Albania (CLPR), Bosnia and Herzegovina (OLPR), Bulgaria (OLPR), Croatia (CLPR), Kosovo (OLPR), Moldova (CLPR), Montenegro (CLPR), North Macedonia (CLPR), Romania (CLPR), Serbia (CLPR), Slovenia/large (OLPR)

the share of the list). Elsewhere, the list is closed (CLPR) implying that preference voting is not possible, and/or the order on the list decides who proceeds to elected office.[8] With the exception of a few states in Germany, this closed format seems to be concentrated in Southern and Southeastern Europe (a wider parallel between the Franco tradition and local government systems in the Balkans has already been drawn by Swianiewicz 2014). It reflects a strong embedding of partisan politics at the local level (see below). CLPR can be combined with a majority bonus (MBS). Such systems are more difficult to classify. Nominally proportional, the bonus rewards the winners (mainly the list with the most votes) of the election (often reinforced proportionally). This variant can be found in Andorra, France (larger municipalities),

Table 42.3 Directly elected mayors and local state traditions

	Direct mayoral elections	
	Yes	No
Nordic		Denmark, Finland, Iceland, Norway, Sweden
British Isles	UK (England)[1]	UK (England, Wales, Scotland, Northern Ireland), Ireland
Rhinelandic: federal	Austria (six states), Germany (13 states),[3] Switzerland[4]	Belgium, Austria (three states)[2]
Rhinelandic: unitary	Liechtenstein	The Netherlands, Luxembourg
Southern European	Cyprus, Greece, Italy, Portugal[5]	Andorra, France, Spain[6]
New democracies: Central and Eastern European	Hungary, Lithuania, Poland, Slovakia, Ukraine	Estonia, Czech Republic, Latvia
New democracies: Southeastern European	Albania, Bosnia and Herzegovina,[7] Bulgaria, Croatia, Kosovo, Moldova, North Macedonia, Romania, Slovenia	Montenegro, Serbia

[1] Only in selected municipalities.
[2] Including Vienna.
[3] Excluding smaller municipalities in Schleswig-Holstein; city states (Bremen, Hamburg, Berlin) have indirectly elected executives.
[4] Collective executives.
[5] Directly elected executives at both the municipal and parish levels (municipal executives are collective, with mayors elected as the winning list leaders).
[6] Directly elected executive only in the smallest municipalities with an open-council system.
[7] Excluding Brčko District.

and Italy. Table 42.8 (at the end of this chapter) shows that when it comes to the specific method of seat allocation, the logic of the highest average dominates (e.g., d'Hondt), complemented by the largest remainder (e.g., Hare-Niemeyer). Formal thresholds are rare and never amount to more than 5% of the vote.

As an alternative to the list system, the single transferable vote (STV) can only be found in local elections in the British Isles (notably Ireland, Scotland, and Northern Ireland). Here, seats are determined by a quota based on a formula and a series of counts of the vote (which ranks candidates). STV and OLPR are considered more personalized than CLPR and create incentives for intraparty competition (Carey & Shugart 1995).

Members of the nonproportional family are clearly in the minority. A system where seats are allocated according to plurality, or the majority of the votes, can only be found for local council elections in ten cases (or 25%). In all but one case (Slovakia), this system applies only to part of the country, notably its smaller municipalities (but sometimes also along regional lines, as in the United Kingdom). Here, the nontransferable variant is the most popular (with differences according to the number of representatives to be elected in the constituency). It is noteworthy that in Slovenia, smaller municipalities may decide on the variant of the plurality formula to be applied.

Meanwhile, mixed systems are absent in all but one case. In the larger municipalities of Hungary, a mixed member proportional system can be found. It appears that in local elections and voting, the choice for an electoral system is more clear-cut. There is less need for two electoral circuits where the balance between territorial and partisan representation can be sought and/or aligned. However, the distinction between both principles (and which to prioritize) is equally somewhat visible in the division into subsystems along the population size of the municipality.

Along with the default of proportional list systems, districting is not very popular in local council elections. Most are held at large, where the municipality in its entirety is one constituency (and councilors are expected to represent the entire locality). A further territorial delineation into distinct geographical areas is thus avoided. However, deviations from the standard model can be established, even in list systems (see some of the new democracies in Central and Eastern Europe in Table 42.8). In some instances of the latter, districting relates to size. This might occur in larger cities with clear internal divisions at the submunicipal level. Examples can be found in Estonia (in the capital Tallin), France (in the capital, Paris, and in Lyon and Marseille), Slovenia (upon the discretion of the council), and Sweden. Districting also appears where a recent amalgamation has taken place (e.g., Estonia). Here, the mechanism is a means to prevent the overall domination of the biggest local community in the newly created jurisdiction. In other systems and countries, districting is more common. The plurality model of first-past-the-post (FPTP) operates within single-member constituencies. Other nonproportional subtypes (such as bloc vote or limited vote) have multiple-member districts. The latter also holds in STV systems. Poland could be noted as an extreme case: as smaller municipalities use FPTP, districting is innate to the system, but distinct constituencies also appear in their larger counterparts with OLPR, which means that the electoral system becomes territorially fragmented.

Where districting transpires from single-member constituencies (found in parts of Hungary, Poland, Slovakia, Slovenia, and the United Kingdom), it comes with different but usually small magnitudes (see also Table 42.8 at the end of this chapter). This ranges from two (small municipalities in Ukraine) to 12 (Slovakia) in non-list systems, and in list systems, from two (Estonia) to 43 (a few municipalities in Sweden that have exceptionally large districts). When small, the informal electoral threshold raises and forms a natural barrier against party system fragmentation. In such cases, the electoral system may turn out to be de facto majoritarian.

When it comes to the ballot structure in local elections, voters usually dispose of one vote either to a party (think of closed list systems) or a candidate (as in plurality or majority systems). Combinations are also possible. Sometimes, multiple preferences can be expressed up to the number of seats to be filled in the constituency. This is found in several instances of OLPR and in STV. The latter is also the only system in which an ordering occurs instead of a nominal vote for one or more candidates. When the object of the vote is primarily partisan, the electorate must usually remain with(in) one list. However, panachage appears in the list systems of five countries (the Czech Republic, Germany, Liechtenstein, Luxembourg, and Norway). Cumulation therein is even more exceptional and comes about in two cases (Germany and Luxembourg).

The electoral system for the local council has also been subject to reform over time, albeit to a different degree. There are examples where the alterations were extensive and/or consecutive. Ukraine is a case in point. Almost each electoral cycle brought new electoral rules. As the country has two subsystems, the changes mainly pertained to the larger and urban municipalities (with their smaller and rural counterparts largely sticking with plurality). Here, different variants of the list system appeared after the turn of the century (with a move from a closed to an open system). Around that time, Serbia also shifted from majority toward a (closed) list system.

The dynamics in these more extreme cases point to the tendencies found where reform and change so far have been more incremental and irreversible. That is the move to more proportional and/or personalized systems. Croatia first experimented with plurality and mixed formulas before fully turning to proportional representation. Scotland and Wales recently swapped their plurality system for the single transferable vote. In other cases, the list system became open. There are also occurrences of more specific changes. Some countries modified the precise method of seat allocation in list systems (e.g., Bulgaria, Hungary, and Liechtenstein). Others moved the threshold that distinguishes large from small municipalities, thereby affecting the distribution of authorities in various subsystems. Poland has done so no less than four times since the 1990s; France only once at the beginning of the century.

Direct mayoral elections

Sometimes, the scope of local elections widens and not only councils but also mayors are directly elected. Instead of relying exclusively on the support of the majority in the council, the directly elected mayor also has a separate mandate (Back 2005: 82–83). This local variant of presidentialism is usually associated with the strong mayor form of local government (Mouritzen & Svara 2002). Nevertheless, horizontal power relations at the local level vary between countries. Therefore, the directly elected mayor does not always hold very strong executive functions (Heinelt et al. 2018; see their mayoral strength index in particular). Sweeting (2017) notices that directly elected executives have been traditional features of local political systems in many countries (such as the United States, Canada, and Japan). In Europe, this institution has been introduced more recently as part of a reform agenda, aimed at improving legitimacy, leadership, and accountability in local authorities.

The spread of direct mayoral elections can be traced back to the post-war period in Germany, with Bavaria and Baden-Wuerttemberg paving the way (Wollmann 2005). After reunification, the country largely mainstreamed this model. The proliferation of directly elected mayors accelerated in the 1990s, with several countries also experimenting with singular local executives. Italy broke with its consensual model of local democracy, turning toward a directly elected strong mayor, after the dramatic collapse of the first republic. The biggest numerical surge came when many new democracies adopted direct election in the frameworks of their reconstructed local government systems. In many instances, based on an anti-Communist sentiment, the introduction drove the reconfiguration of the newly emerging party system, and at the same time, left variable room for independent lists and candidates. Only Serbia and Montenegro moved back to an indirect election. A recurring theme in the debates on direct mayoral elections is the impact of this institution on the stability of the mayoral office: while mayors became less dependent on fragile local coalitions, an excessive incumbency advantage was also noticed.

The experiences with directly elected mayors are only concisely discussed in the chapters of this *Handbook*, but one can find a more nuanced evaluation of this institutional arrangement in existing cross-national comparisons (Elcock 2009; Sweeting 2017). Here, we attempt to summarize how mayoral elections are organized in Europe. In the 40 countries included in this *Handbook*, there are 22 (or 55%) where local voters elect mayors, at least in some of the municipalities (Table 24.3). There is some regional variation in this respect. None of the Nordic countries introduced direct mayoral elections, traditionally building their local government systems on the principles of collective leadership, which are well-embedded also at the national level. Directly elected executives are also very rare on the British Isles. Only a dozen English local authorities decided to change the form of government into a model with direct election (Copus 2006; Sweeting & Hambleton 2020).

The procedure to become a mayor in Rhinelandic countries varies. In three Austrian states, mayors are elected by the council, while in the other six Austrian states, most of the German states, and Liechtenstein, mayors are directly elected. The Belgian and Dutch mayors are appointed (yet this is to a large extent dependent on the composition of the council and Luxembourgish).[9] In Germany, in three city states (Berlin, Bremen, and Hamburg) local/state executives are elected by the local parliaments, as in other states. Switzerland is a separate case, internally diversified: usually, the collegial executive has three to seven members and is elected under majoritarian rule, but the situation differs both between and within cantons.

Southern European countries predominantly fall in the strong mayor category of local government, yet not always with the typical direct election of the executive. There is a considerable gray zone between direct and indirect mayoral elections, investigating not only the 'rules-in-form' but also those 'in use'. For example, in Belgium there has been an informal practice (recently formalized in Wallonia), indicating that the person who obtains the most preference votes of the largest list in the majority is automatically designated as the mayor of the municipality (Verstraete et al. 2018). In France, mayors are formally elected by the municipal council, but in fact the municipal council always chooses the list's leader as mayor. As Dolez and Laurent argue in Chapter 18, this common practice reverses the chain of representation and local elections primarily serve to elect mayors. While formally it is the council majority who endorses the mayor, in practice mayoral candidates carefully construct their lists, pre-selecting councilors before election day. In Spain, mayors are indirectly elected during the first council meeting. If none of the candidates reaches the majority, the councilor heading the winning list becomes the mayor. This model is more flexible than the one in place in Portuguese municipalities, where the leader of the winning list automatically becomes the mayor (the other members of the municipal executive are directly elected from party lists in proportional elections). Such a strong interdependence between council and mayoral elections appears as an indicator of a quasi-directly elected executive. It is worth noting that in both Portugal and Spain, council elections are held under the party-centered electoral system of CLPR. However, in these cases, the focus on mayoral candidates leading the lists is an additional incentive for the personalization of electoral races.

Mayoral races almost always take place simultaneously with council elections. The exceptions are in some of the German states, where terms of office differ (see Chapter 11). Simultaneity increases the stakes, giving the voters direct influence on the local executive, but it also increases the complexity of the vote choice. Although simultaneity of council and mayoral elections allows for split-ticket voting, the joint campaign efforts and a common programmatic platform of candidates for legislative and executive offices decreases the likelihood that a divided local government emerges as an election outcome. This could produce tensions between the local legislative and executive and result in a decision-making gridlock. Most often, mayoral candidates are endorsed by the same parties (or local lists) as those running for seats in the council. In many countries there is an explicit legal requirement in this respect.

As Table 42.4 demonstrates, European mayors are mostly elected via FPTP plurality vote or a two-round system (TRS) requiring an absolute majority. The latter can be achieved in the first or the second round (runoff), which takes place one or (most often) two weeks later. The two-round system is more popular among the analyzed countries than FPTP. In Italy and

Table 42.4 Electoral systems in mayoral elections

FPTP	Hungary, Slovakia, Cyprus, Portugal (parishes), Spain (open council), Albania, Bosnia and Herzegovina (RS and FBiH), Romania, Italy (under 15,000), Ukraine (under 75,000)
TRS	Lithuania, Poland, Austria (six states), Germany (13 states), Greece, Liechtenstein*, Bulgaria, Croatia, Kosovo, Moldova, North Macedonia, Slovenia, Ukraine (over 75,000), Italy (over 15,000)
SV	England (few municipalities only)

In Liechtenstein, all candidates can participate in the second round and the plurality of votes decides upon the winner.

Ukraine, both systems are used, but determined by different population thresholds. Mayors of smaller municipalities are elected under FPTP, while in larger municipalities with more complex political arenas, TRS is used. Only in England is a supplementary vote (SV) method used (for the first time to elect the London mayor in 2000). As van der Kolk et al. (2006) describe, this is similar to the two-round system, yet instead of two separate elections, SV uses the second preferences expressed by the voters to conclude the election in one round.

FPTP incentivizes the consolidation of local electoral arenas around the strongest candidates and the formation of preelectoral coalitions. However, it does not assure the strong electoral legitimacy of the TRS, in which the winner receives the majority of votes – if not in the first, then in the second ballot. Some authors provide evidence that this difference in the local electoral system has profound consequences for the national arena. Recently, O'Dwyer and Stenberg (2021) compared Hungary and Poland, two European countries experiencing democratic backsliding, arguing that the FPTP system in Hungarian mayoral elections helped to consolidate the dominant party regime, while the TRS system in Poland hampered a similar process, instead being instrumental in consolidating the dispersed resources of the opposition. With TRS being the default, in some countries a shift over time towards FPTP can be noticed (Hungary and Romania).

Local electoral participation

Local turnout: the cross-national picture

Broad popular participation in elections fuels representative democracies, as it provides legitimacy for elected representatives and inputs for directing public policies. These general considerations, which stress the importance of mass electoral participation, apply also to local democracy, even if the local level is frequently used as a space for democratic innovations that attempt to overcome the deficiencies of the representative model, and a space where traditional institutions of direct democracy are still practiced (as in small Swiss municipalities). An important measure of local political participation is local turnout, namely the share among eligible and registered citizens who turn up at the ballot box on election day.

The general picture of voter turnout in local elections, emerging from previous studies and the chapters in this *Handbook*, conforms to a large extent with Reif and Schmitt's (1980) second-order election model. Local voter turnout is almost always lower than in national elections. It also depends on the placement of local elections within the main electoral cycle (Vetter 2015). However, there is a substantial variation in turnout both between and within countries.

Looking at the cross-national variation in voter turnout observed in local elections, it is worth keeping in mind the 'vertical' dimension, which suggests comparing turnout rates in local elections with those reported in first-order elections (Reif & Schmitt 1980). For the sake of simplicity, we may assume that, in Europe, elections for the national parliaments establish a baseline of 'standard' electoral participation. Therefore, drawing attention to the 'turnout gap' between the two levels makes it possible to focus on the specificity of local elections, and find out their *relative* intensity of voter mobilization. This analytical approach is well grounded in the study of regional (Schakel & Dandoy 2014) and local elections (Gendźwiłł 2019; Gendźwiłł & Kjaer 2021).

Figure 42.2 plots average voter turnout rates for local elections against those for parliamentary elections, with dots and crosses, respectively (see also Table 42.9 at the end of this chapter). This picture orders all 40 countries presented in the *Handbook* by the magnitude of the national-local turnout gap, namely, the difference between the national and local turnout. Most of the cases confirm the expectation derived from the second-orde relection model that lower stake elections,

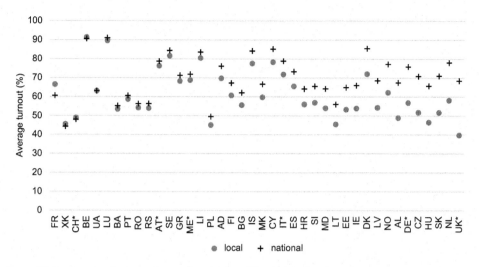

Figure 42.2 Average turnout for national (+) and local (●) elections
* Averaged turnout in non-simultaneous local elections (details described in Table 42.9)

which do not decide the control of national executive power, mobilize fewer voters.[10] This is in line with the existing evidence (Morlan 1984; Blais 2000; Gendźwiłł 2019). One of the few exceptions – France – is a very specific case, as in the French model of strong semi-presidentialism, it is not parliamentary but rather presidential elections that should be considered first order. If we use the average turnout rate from 1995 to 2017, with presidential elections as a benchmark instead of turnout in parliamentary elections, the national-local turnout gap in France changes from -6.0 p.p. to +11.7 p.p. and places this country well above the European median. In four other cases (Kosovo, Switzerland, Belgium, and Ukraine), the values of the national-local turnout gap were just below 0, indicating only slightly higher turnout rates for local elections.

Although voter turnout for local and national elections is highly correlated, the size of the national-local turnout gap differs substantially – from values around 0 (indicating a similar level of participation) to 19.7 p.p. in The Netherlands and 28.6 p.p. in the United Kingdom. A small turnout gap is systematically reported even in Sweden, where local and national elections have taken place simultaneously since the 1970s. Among the EU countries, turnout for local elections is almost always higher than for the European elections (excluding simultaneous ones). This pattern of voter turnout supports the idea that second orderness is not a binary trait. Heath et al. (1999: 391), who compared national, European, and local elections in the UK, even labeled the latter as 'one and three-quarters order'.

The variation of voter turnout in local elections generally reproduces the systematic differences between old and new European democracies (the latter displaying lower turnout rates), known also from the comparative studies of participation in parliamentary elections (Kostadinova 2003; Pacek et al. 2009). There is no country of Eastern Europe among the top ten countries with the highest local turnout; at the same time, eight out of the bottom ten countries with the lowest local turnout are new democracies established after the collapse of the Eastern bloc or after the Yugoslav war. There are two notable exceptions from Western Europe in this group: Switzerland and the UK. Switzerland notes very low turnout rates for both local and national elections (this is usually explained by the consensus system and the importance of direct democracy). The United Kingdom, with its asynchronous electoral cycles, is an extreme case of low voter turnout for local elections (usually around 40% in England, Wales, and Scotland,

and just above 50% in Northern Ireland). Such a low level of participation results in a relatively large national-local turnout gap, ranging up to more than 25 p.p. (Rallings & Thrasher 2007).

Nonetheless, there are some caveats that complicate interlevel comparisons of the aggregate voter turnout. First, the electorates in local elections are of – sometimes considerably – different sizes compared with the electorates in the national (parliamentary) elections. Generally, suffrage rules are more permissive in local elections (Seidle 2015). In most countries described in this *Handbook*, citizenship is not required to have the right to vote in local elections. Noncitizens who are permanent residents, usually with a required minimum period of residence, can also elect their local representatives and/or run for local offices. More permissive rules (i.e., a shorter period of required residence) apply within the European Union or among citizens of the Nordic countries. In the EU, the Maastricht Treaty introduced the principle that EU nationals can vote and stand as candidates in local elections under the same conditions as nationals of the country where they live. Yet some restrictions apply to the direct mayoral elections or elections of local councils that simultaneously perform the function of regional parliaments – for example, German city states or Vienna. In the latter case, the suffrage for nonnationals was heavily limited by a ruling of the Constitutional Court.

Still, in many EU countries registration of nonnationals on the electoral roll is not automatic, which constrains participation; yet, in such cases the turnout rate is not deflated by the increased denominator. In Luxembourg, which is a case with an exceptionally high share of nonnationals in the electorate, only 23% of non-Luxembourgers registered to vote in the 2017 elections. In Cyprus, voters' registration is required in all types of elections, and pertains to both citizens and residents. Only a relatively small fraction of the eligible population is registered (in the 2016 local elections only 12%). In contrast to the parliamentary elections, out-of-country voting in local elections is generally not allowed. Also, postal voting, if applicable, tends to be more restricted in local than in parliamentary elections. These formal regulations stress the role of residency in constituting the 'local citizenry' and additionally emphasize the place-bound character of local elections.

Electorates also tend to be more inclusive in local elections because, in some cases, they have been used as an experimental field for lowering the voting age below 18. The group of countries that have extended franchise to 16- and 17-year-olds includes the majority of German states (which pioneered this electoral reform in the 1990s), Austria (the first states lowered the voting age in 2000; the whole country at all levels of government in 2007), Scotland (2015), Estonia (2017), and Wales (2019). In Greece, the voting age in local elections was lowered to 17 in 2016. Existing studies usually report that the turnout among the youngest first-time voters is somewhat higher than in the slightly older age cohort but well below the general average (Leininger & Faas 2020).

The complexity of suffrage rules may lead to situations in which, within the same jurisdiction, the population entitled to vote in local elections is considerably larger than in national elections. The smaller size of local electorates may even lead to paradoxical situations, where foreigners with local residency outnumber local citizens, as in small Spanish coastal municipalities where British retirees play a decisive role in local electorates (Muñoz 2018). Furthermore, paradoxes questioning voters' equality and the 'one (wo)man one vote' principle are possible. Austria is an exemplary case in this respect, as secondary residencies (e.g., weekend houses) in certain states are not carefully scrutinized in searches for duplicate entries in voter registers. Practically, this allows voters to cast a ballot in local elections in two different municipalities, as happens in Lower Austria. It is suggested that this practice is beneficial for the Christian Democrats (ÖVP), traditionally holding a strong position in this region.

The extant research suggests that election timing – the placement of local elections within the main national electoral cycle – influences voter turnout to a greater degree. According to theory, when local elections are horizontally simultaneous (i.e., all municipalities elect their authorities on the same day) and vertically simultaneous (i.e., held concurrently with elections of other types: European, regional, presidential, etc.), the stakes are higher, and voters are more willing to turn out (Blais 2000; Vetter 2015; Gendźwiłł 2019; Schakel & Dandoy 2014 on regional elections). The most pronounced, yet rare, are the simultaneity effects when local and national elections are held concurrently – in such cases, the 'boost' is clearly visible, and the turnout gap temporarily disappears (Figure 42.3 provides examples from the 2001 elections in Denmark and the 1994 elections in North Rhine-Westphalia). Although several EU countries have decided to hold local and European elections on the same day (in 2019, these were nine German states, Greece, Ireland, Spain, and parts of Italy), or combine local and regional elections, the simultaneity effects in these cases seem to be weak and not systematic (Gendźwiłł 2019). It should be noted that the lack of horizontal simultaneity co-occurs with relatively large national-local turnout gaps in the UK and Germany. However, the cases of Switzerland and Italy, also holding local elections on various dates, do not follow this pattern.

Trends in local voter turnout

Decreasing participation rates in national elections have been diagnosed in the vast majority of democracies. This phenomenon is usually related to democratic consolidation and post-democratization disenchantment (Wattenberg 2002; for a more nuanced approach, see Kostelka 2017). The data documenting participation in local elections in the recent decades display a similar declining trend as the one observed in the national (parliamentary) elections. Trends presented in Figure 42.4 are based on the turnout rates, which have been relativized to the first post-1990 elections in each country. Such a simple transformation allows us to ignore the turnout gap

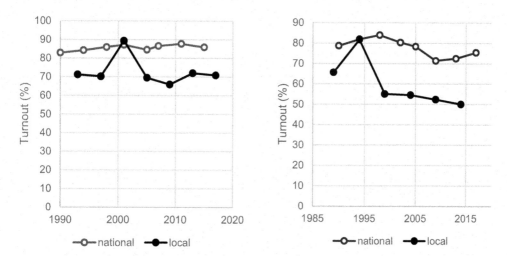

Figure 42.3 Examples of elections' simultaneity effects on voter turnout: (A) Denmark and (B) North Rhine-Westphalia, Germany

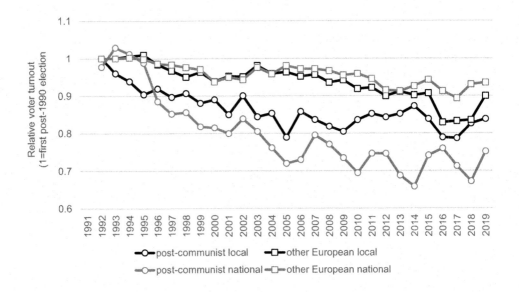

Figure 42.4 Post-1990 changes in voter turnout in 30 European countries

Source: IDEA Turnout Database, statistical offices, authors of the country chapters

and better visualize the aggregate picture of trends that emerges from the data collected by the authors of the country chapters.

The decline in voter turnout is much sharper in post-Communist countries than in the older European democracies, particularly in the first decade after the transition. After 2000, the turnout in national elections in this group decreases at a much slower pace, while the voter turnout in local elections is more or less stable (at above 0.8 of the baseline turnout). The baseline level of voter turnout in the post-Communist countries includes a turnout boost, typical for the first founding elections held after the collapse of electorally mobilized dictatorships (Kostelka 2017). Such a boost is visible in both national and local elections, yet much stronger in the former, which corresponds to the extraordinary salience of the first national elections under democratic rule. In the older European democracies (i.e., democratized before 1990), the electoral participation trends at the national and local levels were almost identical (i.e., slowly decreasing) for many years, and started to diverge after 2000. Yet here the observed pattern is different from the post-Communist countries: the decline of electoral participation has become more intense recently in the case of local elections.

Local voter turnout: horizontal differences

When it comes to horizontal variation in local electoral participation, almost all chapters report a systematic negative relationship between municipal population size and local voter turnout, yet of different intensity. These findings extend the existing evidence on the size-turnout nexus (Cancela & Geys 2016; Gendźwiłł & Kjaer 2021). They appear to suggest that, in small units, local electoral mobilization is galvanized by the existence of closer bonds between politicians and voters, despite the assumption of harmonious nonpartisan decision-making. This holds even if in larger units something more might be at stake in local elections, and ideologically driven political conflict could be enhanced by the presence of renowned partisan and civic actors (Kjaer & Steyvers 2019).

Another feature of local electoral arenas, which correlates with municipal size – and is reported in the preceding chapters, is the supply of candidates and the occurrence of uncontested seats (in council as well as mayoral elections). This pertains particularly to the countries with a high level of territorial fragmentation. A limited supply of candidates and the lack of electoral competition also influence participation. It may weaken the negative relationship between voter turnout and size, as weak electoral competition (or, in an extreme case, the lack of competition) usually depresses voter turnout. Some of the chapters explicitly mention low and decreasing levels of electoral competition as one of the factors contributing to the lower relevance of local elections in some of the localities.

Local party politicization

The presence and success of political parties in local politics is one of the most important themes in the study of local elections and voting. By taking part in elections at different levels, national parties become important links between various electoral arenas. Similar patterns of national parties' competition reproduced in various municipalities homogenize local elections.

What drives parties to colonize local politics? Harmel and Janda (1994) enumerated four main goals of political parties: maximizing votes, maximizing offices, advocating policy, and maximizing intraparty democracy. The involvement in local politics may help to achieve each of these. First, local elections provide an additional opportunity for campaigning and the mobilization of party supporters, particularly when they are held before national elections and have the additional barometric function. Second, local government is an important part of state resources. Local elections provide access to numerous offices, and party patronage. The presence of parties in the field increases the efficiency of state resources' exploitation (Van Biezen & Kopecký 2007). Third, local politics provides room for introducing some of the preferred policies locally, regardless of the composition of the national government and its agenda. Local discretion in important domains – for example, social policies, education, child care, economic development, and planning – may be used to align local policies with the political program of a party. Finally, taking part in local elections is a complex organizational endeavor and requires more decentralized and robust organizational infrastructure – an infrastructure that can be exploited also in parliamentary election campaigns. Thus, it may be assumed that access to local offices develops multilevel party organizations and strengthens the position of midlevel party elites.

In a similar vein, Kjaer (2012) argued that the multilevel structure of the political system allows parties to use the offices available at the subnational level as 'respirators' or 'incubators'. In the former, local offices sustain party structures and the party's access to power after a failure to secure seats at the national level. In the latter, a presence at the local level serves as a stepping-stone to the national party system.

As the *Handbook* demonstrates, in many European countries, national and regional parties are accompanied by independent candidates and local independent lists (Reiser & Holtmann 2008). Their presence, far from marginal in many countries, is the visible sign of dissimilarity between local and national arenas. The nationalization of local party systems has been frequently presented as a process in which national parties gradually penetrate local electoral arenas and take over local offices (Rokkan 1970). In strongly nationalized contexts, the national patterns of party competition are reproduced locally, which strengthens the ties between local and national electoral arenas. Nationalization tends to limit intermunicipal differences, as larger parties run for offices in multiple municipalities. For Rokkan (1970), this proliferation of national parties and patterns of party competition, labeled party politicization, was the last stage of democratic consolidation, and typical for mature representative democracies. Yet it seems that local politics in many European countries, including old Western democracies, shows at least some resistance against national parties' colonization efforts (Kjaer & Elklit 2010; Copus et al. 2012; Egner et al. 2018). Some authors even argue that the process of party politicization is sometimes reversed through local independent lists (Aars & Ringkjøb 2005). The ideal fully nationalized party system, and homogeneous patterns of party competition at all levels of government, is challenged. Copus et al. (2012: 225) argue that the continuous presence of nonnationwide parties and local lists is generally advantageous for democracy:

> "Non-partisans and smaller parties open up local democracy, provide a range of alternative voices for local citizens, enhance democratic accountability, provide space for public political discourse, present challenges to the major parties, refocus local politics on local issues, and can provide a challenge to notions of party loyalty superseding loyalty to the electorate."

So far, genuine cross-national evidence on these issues is lacking. Table 42.5 compares the level of party politicization in the European countries studied in this *Handbook*. Our classification is based on two indicators, reported in the country chapters (in some cases only one was available): (1) the share of votes cast for local independent lists, local parties, and independents, and (2) the share of independents among all local councilors. On the basis of the empirical distributions of these indicators, three categories were constructed:

- Countries with *high party politicization* of local governments, where either the share of votes cast for independent local lists is lower than 10% or the share of independents among elected councilors is lower than 10%.
- Countries with *low party politicization* of local governments, where either the share of votes cast for independent local lists is higher than 50% or the share of independents among elected councilors is higher than 50%.
- All other countries are classified as having a *medium level of party politicization*.

This classification in Table 42.5 aligns to a large extent with accounts from the previous surveys of European local councilors (Egner et al. 2013) and mayors (Heinelt et al. 2018), which provided rough estimates of reported party membership. One could argue that the categorization in this study is based on more accurate data, namely, official election results, and instead of focusing on the larger municipalities, it includes all municipalities within each country.

The presence of national political parties is very high in Nordic countries, with the exception of Iceland, the smallest country in this group and the one with the most fragmented local government. It is among the Nordic countries that the smallest share of votes for local independent lists is observed: only 2.1% in Finland, 4.2% in Denmark, and 4.7% in Sweden. Political parties traditionally dominate local politics in the UK and Ireland also, but in these cases, the presence of local independents and small local parties is not as marginal as in the Nordic countries. This caveat pertains particularly to Ireland, Wales, and Scotland, where the STV electoral system (one with strong incentives to cultivate a personal vote) is used to elect local councils.

The Rhinelandic countries are grouped mainly in the mid-category, with the exceptions of Luxembourg and Liechtenstein, where party politicization is high, and with the caveat that the position of France and Switzerland is an approximation based on the qualitative descriptions from the respective chapters. The picture is even more complicated in the federal countries, for

Table 42.5 Party politicization and local state traditions

	Degree of party politicization		
	Low (5 cases)	Medium (20 cases)	High (14 cases)
Nordic		Iceland	Sweden, Norway, Denmark, Finland
British Isles		Ireland, UK	
Rhinelandic: federal		Germany,[1] Austria,[2] Switzerland[3]	
Rhinelandic: unitary		Belgium,[4] The Netherlands, France[5]	Luxembourg, Liechtenstein
Southern European	Andorra, Italy	Greece, Spain	Cyprus, Portugal
New democracies: Central and Eastern European	Czech Republic, Hungary, Poland	Estonia, Lithuania Slovakia, Ukraine	Latvia
New democracies: Southeastern European		Bulgaria, Croatia, Kosovo, Serbia, Slovenia	Albania, Bosnia and Herzegovina, Moldova, North Macedonia, Romania

[1] Three out of 13 German lands analyzed in the handbook's chapter qualify as highly party politicized; if one adds Berlin, Hamburg, and Bremen (city states dominated by national parties) to this group, it would result in six highly party politicized Länder plus ten in the medium category.
[2] Vienna + three lands classify as highly party politicized, five lands as medium.
[3] The situation differs across cantons; classification was based upon the aggregate picture discussed in the chapter on Switzerland.
[4] Walloon – low level, Flanders – high level, Brussels – medium level.
[5] France: the classification is based on the share of independent mayors; precise data on councilors are missing.

which we have more fine-grained data: Germany, Austria, and Belgium are internally diversified in this respect (see notes to Table 42.5).

Southern European countries are dispersed among three categories. Italy, with its convoluted local electoral system and nonsimultaneous local elections, is an example of a country with a remarkably high presence of local independent lists, particularly in the small municipalities. Andorra is another country with a low level of party politicization. In this microstate, parties were formally nonexistent before 1993, and the current rules still encourage local elites to change party labels and create personal platforms. A medium level of party politicization is observed in Greece and Spain. Yet in the latter case, the specific feature is the presence of well-institutionalized regional parties in local elections. The most intense entrenchment of national parties is observed in Portugal (at the municipal level) and Cyprus.

The post-Communist countries of Central and Eastern Europe are the group with the lowest level of party politicization at the local level. In these countries, the reenactment of local democracy has been taking place simultaneously with profound party system changes. In most countries in this group, electoral rules are very permissive for independent candidates. Local independent lists dominate in Poland, the Czech Republic, and Hungary – pioneers of democratic transition in the region. Slovakia and Ukraine are in the mid-category, accompanied by the post-Soviet Baltic states Estonia and Lithuania. Latvia has recently moved toward the group of countries with a high presence of parties, along with the progress of territorial consolidation and a decreasing number of local governments. Larger municipalities are more intensely colonized by parties, and since the 2020 territorial reform in Latvia, only parties will be entitled to compete in future local elections.

The post-Communist countries of Southeastern Europe share a similar historical background, and their local government systems are also relatively new. Yet they display a generally higher level of party politicization, with five countries (Albania, Bosnia and Herzegovina, Moldova, North Macedonia, and Romania) placed in the highest category, and five countries (Bulgaria, Croatia, Kosovo, Serbia, and Slovenia) placed in the middle category.

Several chapters in this *Handbook* report difficulties in assessing the level of party politicization accurately – not only due to data unavailability but also due to the fact that some of the local lists are actually parties 'in disguise'. Candidates closely related to parties establish their local committees and try to hide their affiliations in order to garner more support.

Another issue reported in various countries with fragmented or more volatile party systems is the presence of electoral coalitions, often composed of several parties and local lists. For example, in the 2017 North Macedonian local elections, two main electoral alliances were composed of 22 and 18 parties, respectively. Sometimes the territorial heterogeneity of coalition agreements (i.e., when two or more parties cooperate in one municipality, but run separately in another) blurs the picture even more. Nonetheless, most chapters notice the increasing presence of local independent lists and small extraparliamentary parties, particularly in Western Europe – although in most countries, they clearly still play a supplementary role.

Although the list labels appearing locally usually allow for distinct identification of the political party they belong to, and local alliances between parties are frequently a reflection of the coalitions organized at national level (as in France, where local coalitions represent either the center-left or center-right bloc), the polarization of local electorates is not necessarily organized along the national issues, but instead along local ones.

For most of the countries included in the *Handbook*, we were able to compare the share of independents among councilors and mayors (executives), respectively. The results are presented in Figure 42.5. Not surprisingly, the indicators are highly correlated. The graph presents

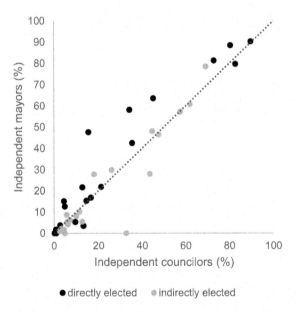

Figure 42.5 Share of independent mayors and councilors in local elections (the graph includes only countries for which both figures were available)

countries with directly and indirectly elected mayors separately, and the main difference is that, in the former group, the share of independents among mayors tends to be higher than among councilors. This relationship suggests that the personalization of mayoral elections creates opportunities for political entrepreneurs who can win local elections without a recognized party label (it could even be a burden in some local races). Nonetheless, in countries with high shares of independent mayors, many were initially endorsed and supported by a party and became independent while running for reelection. This suggests that there is a systematic relationship between incumbency and independence in mayoral elections.

The original formulation of the second-order elections model (Reif & Schmitt 1980) assumed several effects pertaining to party support in second-order elections: better performance of the parties remaining in opposition at the national level, and better performance of the small, new, and fringe parties. The main challenge with the empirical verification of these hypotheses is related to the aforementioned limited and scattered presence of parties in local elections.

Based on the tables reporting various indicators of party politicization in European countries included in each country chapter, we notice that there are only a limited number of examples of national parties running for offices in *all* municipalities in the country. Among the 40 countries, there are about a dozen such 'omnipresent' parties, including Swedish and Danish Social Democrats, Fianna Fail, Fine Gael, and Sinn Fein in Ireland, and the three main parties in Albania. Generally, in Western countries 'old' traditional parties (Christian Democrats, socialists and liberals) have stronger local anchorage than their newer counterparts (greens, regionalists, or the radical right).

The largest parliamentary parties usually run for office in most municipalities, but if the territorial fragmentation of the local tier is high in a given country, parties are visible in larger municipalities, while smaller municipalities remain the domain of independent local lists. The exceptions in this respect may be some of the agrarian parties (e.g., Polish Peasants Party in Poland) that are present mainly in smaller, rural municipalities, or regional parties, running for office only in a particular region.

As we lack precise fine-grained data on intermunicipal differences in party supply and support, we must rely on approximations and qualitative assessments when assessing the horizontal variation of voting patterns. Large differences between shares of party votes, and shares of councilors representing some of the parties, indicate that the electorates of such parties are concentrated in larger municipalities (mainly cities). Such a biased geographical presence is particularly visible in the case of liberal, green, and radical left parties.

Local political representation

The final section summarizes aspects of local political representation, understood here in a descriptive manner. This refers to the extent to which those present in public office resemble the characteristics of their constituents. From a normative point of view, it is often argued that political institutions should comprise a society in miniature. Representatives should act *and* stand for the diversity of those represented. Empirically, however, political recruitment and candidate selection often progress as in a game of musical chairs, in which, from the many, the few are chosen. The chances of occupying a seat are not randomly distributed. They often have a social base, and certain groups therefore remain underrepresented. Even though local politics is commonly considered as a more open arena compared with other tiers of governance, the findings above also hold for the local level (Steyvers & Verhelst 2012; Steyvers & Medir 2018). Our synthesis focuses on two of the key features related to descriptive representation: gender and ethnicity, the first being more systematically assessed than the second, due to data availability.

Female representation

The underrepresentation of women as elected councilors remains a well-known fact of local political life. This gender gap is often explained by an interaction of the supply of and demand for women candidates. The former refers to an engendered division of (political) labor, limiting the time, energy, and networks of (potential) female candidates. The latter to the combination of an outgroup effect among (party) selectors and the (preference) voting of the electorate (Crowder-Meyer 2013; Navarro & Medir 2016). It also pertains to the base office of councilor. A comparison of 16 European countries in the previous decade found an average of about 30% female councilors (Verhelst et al. 2013). Here, we update and extend these findings. Figure 42.6 shows the share of female councilors by country. The data are displayed in ascending order. The country percentages can be compared with the total average.

The figure reveals that on average about one-third of all councilors (32%) in the 40 countries covered are women. The gender imbalance thus persists largely in line with the earlier findings. The range varies, however, from the lowest score in (the 'masculinized' local politics of) Romania (12%) to the highest one in Iceland, nearing parity (47%). As the ordering of the countries suggests, some relationship with state traditions exists. The share of female councilors is lowest in the federal states of the Rhinelandic group (about 28%). It is highest in the Nordic countries (about 41%) with their often-ascribed concern for gender equality. It should be noted that in some country groups there is a relatively large internal variation. In particular, this holds for Southern Europe and the new democracies in Southeastern Europe. Here, cases are found with 20% or fewer female councilors (e.g., Romania and Greece), as well as cases harboring 40% or more (e.g., Andorra). In each group, specific country deviations can be discerned.

Remarkably, the representation of women appears almost unaffected by the existence of a legal gender quota at the local level. Such a quota is explicitly mentioned in 17 country chapters (or 43% of all cases). With two exceptions, these are concentrated in Southern Europe and in the new democracies. The average share of female councilors in cases with a gender quota is less than 1% higher than elsewhere (the difference being insignificant). Explanations can be

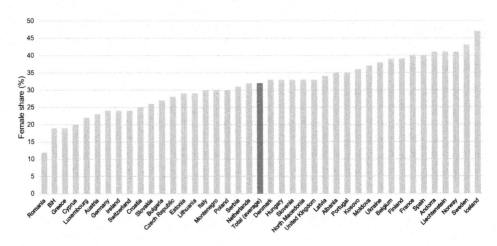

Figure 42.6 Female councilors by country (% in ascending order)

multiple. For one thing, quotas are limited to local elections with a proportional formula and/ or multi-member districts (particularly list systems). In that respect, the reform of the French local electoral system (limiting majoritarianism) was in part motivated by a concern with gender parity. In addition, their form can be varied (and our comparison considers their mere existence). The most common one reserves a share of candidacies for the underrepresented gender (evidently females). This share may (but must not) extend to near parity. In several instances, a gendered ordering is taken into consideration as well, trying to ensure that females are among the leading candidates presented to the voter. The combination of assigned numbers and positions seems to reduce the gap most concretely. It should further be noted that several authors refer to the existence of a legal gender quota at the national level (which does not apply locally but may have a contagious effect) or to more informal variants, adopted by (specific) parties (which can but must not include their local chapters). Over time, the number of female councilors has increased in almost all countries, albeit not always in a spectacular or linear manner. It is often asserted that the introduction or entwining of legal gender quotas accelerated this societal evolution (see country chapters).

To better assess female representation across the 40 countries, we add two points of reference to the equation. The first compares the share of female councilors in the country with that of female mayors. An earlier assessment of 23 countries in Europe showed an average of around 14% mayoral offices won by women (Steyvers & Medir 2018). Here, the analysis is limited to local political systems with directly elected mayors (see the section on local electoral systems). The comparison for the 18 countries included is visualized in Figure 42.7. It allows us to further

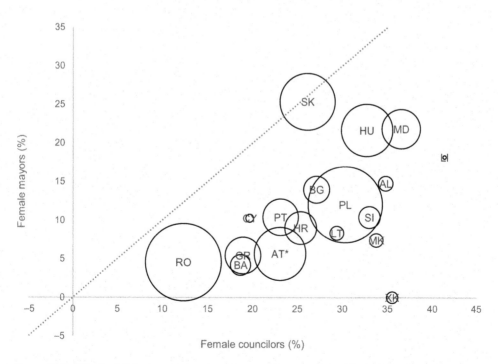

Figure 42.7 The legislative-executive gender gap (18 countries with directly elected mayors); the entry for Austria (AT*) represents the six states with direct elections. Where different subsystems exist, data are aggregated at the country level.

determine the legislative-executive gender gap at the local level. The dotted line in the figure represents a situation where the share of females in the local legislative body equals that of those in the executive. The size of the circles is proportional to the total number of councilors and mayors in the country. Country codes are explained at the bottom of Table 42.2.

Figure 42.7 shows that the legislative-executive gender gap at the local level is rather universal. All cases are ultimately situated below the dotted line, indicating that they have relatively more female councilors than mayors. The average share of the latter in the countries included is about 11%. Consequently, the legislative-executive gap here amounts to about 17%. It is lowest in Slovakia (only 1%) and largest in Kosovo (where not a single female mayor was elected despite the relatively large share of councilors of this gender). Overall, these findings confirm the glass ceiling also being present at the local level – the higher in the political hierarchy, the less room for female office holders. A combination of supply and demand is likely to be at play again but seems to have a stronger gender effect when the local top job is at stake. This drop aligns with the notion of 'intra-polity women attrition' (Kjaer & Kosiara-Pedersen 2019). One specificity is that direct mayoral elections are oriented by default on single candidates. For these, males more often come forward and/or have higher chances to be (s)elected.

The figure also suggests a correlation between female councilors and female mayors at the country level (but this is more obvious where the critical mass of the first is already fairly large). In their discussions of the share of female councilors and mayors, several authors probe into the variations between certain types of local authorities. Opposing patterns can be discerned. In some contexts, the share of female councilors is larger in smaller and/or rural municipalities (which tend to adopt nonproportional electoral systems). Here, the local arena opens up for hitherto underrepresented groups, as less appears to be at stake (Hungary is an example). In other circumstances, the percentage rises in larger and/or urban contexts (with predominantly proportional systems). The acknowledgment of societal diversity and/or the wider district magnitude enlarge recruitment and selection to females (Slovenia is an example).

The second point of reference touches upon another type of gender gap: that between local and national office. Local politics often serves as a platform for entering office and provides a stepping-stone to move up the political ladder. Putting women in the proverbial pipeline, it is often assumed that female representation is higher at the local than at the national level. The decrease in women's representation moving up the representative pyramid can alternatively be termed as 'inter-polity women attrition'. However, 'recent studies challenge this perceived pattern' and introduce 'alternative patterns of inter-level gender gaps' (Kjaer 2019: 53). An earlier exploration of 27 European countries found that in most cases the gap existed as expected, but in the remainder, more or less equal representation, or the opposite pattern, was upheld (Kjaer 2011). These modes have later been termed as a 'woman's place is in the council', the 'copycat', and the 'old boys' local network' (Kjaer 2019). Figure 42.8 updates and extends the insights for the 40 countries included in the *Handbook*. The percentage of female members of parliament is correlated with that of female councilors. Country codes explained are explained at the bottom of Table 42.2.

Compared with the previously discussed gap, the national-local one displays more dispersion. In only half of all cases does the classic pyramid apply. Here, there are more female councilors than members of parliament. In the other half, the opposite holds true. With relatively more female members of parliament, the pattern is rather that of a funnel. On average, the national-local gap amounts to about 2%. Hence, by default, there are slightly more female councilors than members of parliament (the latter averaging about 30%). To the advantage of the local level, the gap is largest in Liechtenstein (about 29 p.p. more female councilors); to that

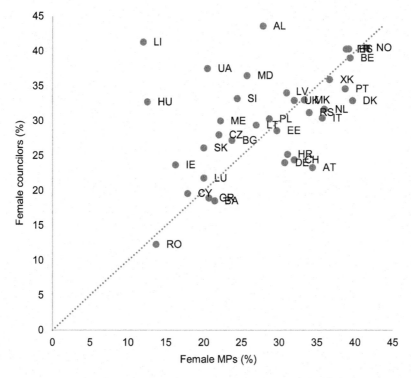

Figure 42.8 The local-national gender gap. The data for female MPs have been derived from the *World Bank* and the *Interparliamentary Union*. They refer to the most recent parliamentary elections for which information was available.

of the national, in Austria (about 11 p.p. more female MPs). Taking a 2 p.p. difference on either side of the gap as a benchmark, 14 cases (or 35%) can be denoted as being of the 'woman's place is in the council' type (more female councilors than MPs in the country); and twice there are 13 cases (each about 33%) of the 'copycat' (difference 2 p.p. or less) and 'old boys' local network' type (more female MPs than councilors).[11]

Ethnic minority representation

Next to gender, ethnicity is a dimension very often included in studies of political representation (Bird et al. 2015). In this *Handbook* and section, it refers to local mandate-holding by members of cultural minorities and people with a foreign origin (i.e., nonnationals). Whereas the political representation of such individuals only steadily increases at the national level, evidence suggests this inclusion to have come around more easily in the local realm (Saalfeld & Lucas 2018).[12] The local political level is characterized by a closer proximity between voters and politicians and a larger influence of social networks or perceptions of shared interests on the political mobilization of specific groups. A common ethnic or migration history contributes to the shaping of group awareness and collective connectedness, stimulating social capital and political participation. Locally, the effect of geographical concentration may also materialize more straightforwardly (Bloemraad & Schönwälder 2013). This is enhanced by the extended voting rights at the local level, notably regarding nonnational (EU) citizens.[13]

Ethnic minority representation at the local level has been treated less comprehensively in the *Handbook*. We did request the authors of the country chapters to explore the issue wherever pertinent. Based on their reflections, some general conclusions can be drawn. First, the underrepresentation of ethnic minorities in politics can also be confirmed at the local level (even though ethnic minorities in some local units constitute a significant share of the population). Also, when requirements of citizenship and eligibility are taken into consideration, the share of voters with a minority background undeniably exceeds that of electoral candidates and surely of elected representatives. This point is made in many country chapters. However, exceptions to the rule exist. In Kosovo, certain minorities appear overrepresented (whilst others are not). Moreover, and over time, the ethnicity gap seems to decrease in many contexts.

A second observation is that ethnic minority representation takes on various forms. The default model is one where no specific legal provisions exist; therefore, the minorities take part in the regular local electoral process. A standard pathway within this model is that ethnic minorities are recruited and selected by established party lists (national or not) or as (their) candidates. The minority background might then be an element in the production of a balanced ticket and/or a personal vote-earning attribute (i.e., in ethnic voting), ultimately leading to representation (Dancygier 2017). Alternatively, this happens through the upswing of ethnic minority parties and/or when minority candidates run in constituencies with a concentration of like-minded voters. Examples can be found in Albania (for the Greek minority), Austria (for the Slovene minority), Croatia (for several minorities), Slovakia (for the Hungarian or Roma minority), and the United Kingdom (some councils). Romania is a case where the tightening of electoral rules over time has diminished the chances of becoming represented through the alternative mode for some minorities but not for others (e.g., the Hungarian minority). It also shows that some ethnic parties may extend their reach to non-co-ethnic voters (e.g., those of the German minority). Along the two former paths, Bosnia and Herzegovina is an extreme case where ethnicity and territoriality are entangled from the regional down to the municipal level. As the country chapter indicates, ethnic parties are very common, maintaining power in ethnic enclaves (often through patronage). This is encouraged by the power-sharing institutions in place after the Dayton Agreements.

Third, in some countries legal provisions exist. There, local electoral systems are specifically adapted to facilitate the incorporation of ethnic minorities in local decision-making. At times, this occurs on a discretionary and nonbinding basis. In one Austrian region, local authorities may set up migrant advisory boards (elected alongside the council). Elsewhere these provisions are obligatory. Their design often aims at reducing or resolving local tensions based on ethnicity. This is mostly visible in the new democracies of Southeastern Europe, notably states belonging to the former Yugoslavia. Croatia is a case in point. It has a 'distinctive and refined system' at the local level where 'minorities are guaranteed the right of representation through established quota'. This seat (or the share thereof, depending on the part of the minority population) can be distributed after the overall allocation, and may increase the size of the council (if additional representatives are to be designated). This system also extends to the local executive. If the share of certain ethnic minorities in the population is large enough, an elected deputy mayor of that minority will be representing it (see country chapter for more details). A comparable form of 'positive discrimination' can be found in some municipalities in Slovenia. In Montenegro, parties acknowledged to represent ethnic minorities have a special status (facing lower electoral thresholds and a different electoral formula). A similar situation can be found in Serbia (lower registration, no electoral thresholds, and a multiplication of their vote share before seat allocation). Where ethnic parties have such rights, political maneuvering can be discerned to own the concomitant label. In North Macedonia, a provision for ethnic minority representation can be found beyond the electoral politics of presence. Here, double majority voting applies in council matters concerning minority rights.

Between integration and variation: toward a typology capturing the *localness* of elections and voting

This section probes into the second angle of comparison in these concluding remarks: the analysis along integration-variation dimensions. In an attempt to answer the question of 'how local are local elections and voting in Europe', the second-tier model (Kjaer & Steyvers 2019) invites us to examine the vertical integration between national and local electoral arenas, as well as the horizontal variation between local electoral arenas, each having their own place-bound context. Linked by default, the extent and mode of integration between the national and the local level imply some degree of similarity in elections and voting between both tiers. Less similarity is a sign of limited nationalization and a more localized pattern of multilevel electoral politics (vertical dissimilarity). At the same time, more variation between municipalities belonging to the same tier, both in terms of institutional settings and voting behavior, is also a sign of a more localized pattern (horizontal variation). These two vectors, without assuming their orthogonality, decide upon the 'localness' of local elections. Such an approach disentangles two variants of what Reif and Schmitt's model of second-order elections originally labeled as the 'arena-specific dimension'.

Vertical integration and horizontal variation, discussed already in the introduction, help to organize the rich empirical material in this *Handbook*. In this concluding section, we use them to develop a typology of local elections and voting in Europe. Each dimension is made operational through a set of three indicators. Conceding that these may not fully cover all aspects of each dimension, the typology should not be conceived of as a final or comprehensive assessment of the localness of local elections and voting. However, the typology does provide a novel and systematic exploration of key issues, placing local elections in Europe in a comparative framework, based on the angles that helped define and organize the country chapters included in the *Handbook*.

When assessing vertical dissimilarity, namely, the separation from the national electoral arena, we focus on three indicators:

1 Dissimilarities in the design of electoral systems used in local (council) and national (parliamentary) elections. The scores are based on Table 42.2, in which we assess whether electoral systems at both levels belong to a different category – if so, dissimilarity is high (++); if not, dissimilarity is low (0); cases where only part of local councils are elected in a similar manner to national parliaments were assigned to the middle category (+).
2 Lack of simultaneity with upper-tier elections (simultaneity could distract the focus of the electorates from local politics). The scores are based on the information provided by country experts on whether local elections are held concurrently with the elections of upper-tier authorities. For Sweden, being the extreme case of simultaneity across levels, warranted constitutionally, the value of this indicator is zero. All cases where local elections are held concurrently with county (upper local), regional, or European elections are placed in the middle category (+). The same value was assigned to Andorra and Estonia, due to the specific constitutional provisions guaranteeing the impact of local authorities on national politics. All cases in which local elections are not regularly coupled with elections at other tiers have high values of this indicator (++).

3   Dominance of local lists and/or independent candidates within elected local authorities – we assume that this indicator is of crucial importance because it refers to the main interface linking electoral arenas (and, more broadly, politics) in multilevel polities, namely national political parties.[14] The more intense the presence of independents and local lists, having no equivalents at the national level, the less integration between local and national arenas. The scores are based on Table 42.5, which classifies countries by the level of party politicization; yet here the indicator is reversed: high party politicization means that local lists and/or independents are of marginal significance (0), while low party politicization indicates their prevalence in local elections (++).

When assessing horizontal variation, namely, the degree to which place-bound local electoral arenas differ from each other, we also refer to three indicators approximating this internal variation:

1   Horizontal differences in electoral systems – based on the descriptions of local electoral systems, we assess whether various electoral systems are used to elect local councils in various regions of a country or subsets of municipalities (often distinguished on the basis of population size). This indicator has only two possible values: countries with a uniform electoral system are marked with 0; countries using various electoral systems are marked with +.
2   Nonsimultaneous local elections – a lack of horizontal simultaneity introduces a temporal component to the local context: local elections in various municipalities occur at various moments of the main electoral cycle. The role of place-specific factors may increase as long as local elections cannot be perceived as a nationwide political event. This indicator is also binary: countries with nonsimultaneous local elections are marked with +, while the rest, having local elections the same day throughout the country, with 0.
3   Lack of national cues in local party competition. Due to the lack of fine-grained data, it is very difficult to assess the specific diversity of local party systems emerging after local elections. This would probably be the best indicator of horizontal variation. To overcome this difficulty, we refrain from making an approximation and focus on the cues brought to the local level by the largest national parties running for office. Yet here we are not interested in their overall electoral fortunes; instead, we investigate whether at least two competing national parties are widely present in the electoral arenas. If so, that could act as an important homogenizing factor, reducing differences between local arenas. Based on the data provided by the authors of the country chapters, we assigned low values (0) for the countries where at least two national parties run lists and/or candidates in at least 80% of municipalities. Medium values (+) were assigned to countries where one national party run their lists and/or candidates in at least 80% of all municipalities, and at least one other party in at least 60% of all municipalities. High values (++) are assigned to remaining countries. In some cases, in the absence of precise data, the only available option was a qualitative assessment based on the respective chapters.

The matrix with scores assigned to each country is displayed in Table 42.6 (specific cases, requiring arbitrary decisions or approximations are explained in the footnotes).

Based on the scores in the table and to develop our typology, we place each country in a 3 × 3 matrix that assembles the two analytical dimensions, each covered by three indicators. We applied the following rules to delineate categories.

Table 42.6 Local elections and voting in Europe: indicators of vertical dissimilarity and horizontal variation

Country	Vertical dissimilarity			Horizontal variation		
	Dissimilar electoral system at local and national levels	Local elections not simultaneous with upper-level elections	Share of local lists/ independents in local government	Horizontal differences in electoral systems	Nonsimultaneous local elections	Lack of national cues in local party competition
Albania	0	++	0	0	0	0
Andorra	++	+[1]	++	0	0	++
Austria	0	++	+	+	+	+[2]
Belgium	0	++	+	0	0	+[3]
BiH	0	++	0	0	0	++
Bulgaria	0	++	+	0	0	0
Croatia	0	+	+	0	0	+
Cyprus	0	++	0	0	0	0
Czech Republic	0	++[4]	++	0	0	++
Denmark	0	+	0	0	0	0
Estonia	0	+[5]	+	0	0	+
Finland	0	++	0	0	0	0
France	+	++	+	+	0	++[6]
Germany	++	+	+	+	+	+[6]
Greece	0	+	+	0	0	++[6]
Hungary	+	+	++	+	0	++
Iceland	+	++	+	+	0	++
Ireland	0	+	+	0	0	0
Italy	++	++[7]	++	0	+	++
Kosovo	0	++	+	0	0	0
Latvia	0	++	0	0	0	++
Liechtenstein	0	++	0	0	0	0
Lithuania	++	++	+	0	0	0
Luxembourg	+	++	0	+	0	0
Moldova	++	+	0	0	0	0
Montenegro	0	++	0	0	+	0[6]
Netherlands	0	++	+	0	0	0
North Macedonia	0	++	0	0	0	0
Norway	0[8]	+	0	0	0	0
Poland	+	+	++	+	0	++
Portugal	0	+	0	0	0	0
Romania	0	+	0	0	0	0
Serbia	0	+	+	0	0	0
Slovakia	++	++	+	0	0	++
Slovenia	+	++	+	+	0	0
Spain	0	+	+	+	0	+[6]
Sweden	0	0	0	0	0	0

(Continued)

Table 42.6 (Continued)

Country	Vertical dissimilarity			Horizontal variation		
	Dissimilar electoral system at local and national levels	Local elections not simultaneous with upper-level elections	Share of local lists/ independents in local government	Horizontal differences in electoral systems	Nonsimultaneous local elections	Lack of national cues in local party competition
Switzerland	+[9]	++	+	+	+	++[6]
Ukraine	++	+	+	+	0	++
United Kingdom	+	++	+	+	+	+[10]

Notes: (1) Andorra – constitutional "coupling" of the national and local level (quasi-federal polity). (2) High interregional differences, some regions (states) more diversified. (3) Regional differences (Wallonia more differentiated than Flanders and Brussels). (4) Czech Republic – one-third of the senate is elected along with the local elections. (5) Local officials take part in the indirect presidential elections – it increases the stake and nationalizing pressure. (6) Qualitative assessment based on the respective country chapters. (7) Simultaneous only in a small part of municipalities (depending on the cycle). (8) Norway having a open-list system at the parliamentary level is mostly in the formal sense, since preferential votes seldom affects who gets elected. (9) Mostly similar electoral systems (open-list PR). (10) Regional differences: weaker presence of main parties in Scotland and Wales, yet even in England only Conservatives pass the 80% threshold.

For *vertical dissimilarity*:

- High – all cases with a low level of party politicization, namely, countries with a dominance of local lists and/or independent candidates (either more than 50% of council seats or more than 50% of total vote share received), irrespective of the scores received on the two other dimensions; we assume that the presence of parties (along with centralized campaign efforts orchestrated by party organizations) and party cues for the vote choice are crucial to establish vertical ties between the levels.
- Low – all countries with a medium or high level of party politicization and receiving no more than one '+' for the two other indicators.
- Medium – the remaining cases.

For *horizontal variation*:

- High – all countries where a lack of national cues in electoral competition was identified (++) jointly with at least one other symptom, and all countries with medium presence of national cues (+) combined with the presence of two other symptoms.
- Low – cases for which values of all three indicators are low (marked as '0').
- Medium – the remaining cases.

Table 42.7 presents the typology. As always, the logic behind such an endeavor is to classify cases that are *relatively* alike on the criteria developed (more so than in comparison with other cases in different categories). At least when it comes to the combination of positions on the indicators discussed above, the differences between the groups are larger than those within. Of course, that is not to say that the latter are absent.

As the table demonstrates, seven countries score low on both dimensions of localness. Here, the national and local arenas mostly have similar features in terms of elections and voting. Both levels use the same family of electoral systems. They also tend to organize at least some elections simultaneously with those for the local level. Sweden is an case extreme in that respect, as since

Table 42.7 Typology of local elections in Europe: horizontal variation and vertical dissimilarity

		Horizontal variation		
		Low	Medium	High
Vertical dissimilarity	**Low**	Denmark, Ireland, Norway, Portugal, Romania, Serbia, Sweden	Croatia, Estonia, Greece, Spain	
	Medium	Albania, Bulgaria, Cyprus, Finland, Kosovo, Liechtenstein, Lithuania, Moldova, The Netherlands, North Macedonia	Belgium, Bosnia and Herzegovina, France, Iceland, Latvia, Luxembourg, Montenegro, Slovakia, Slovenia, Ukraine	Austria, Germany, Switzerland, United Kingdom
	High		Andorra, Czech Republic, Hungary, Poland	Italy

the 1970s, there is a constitutional provision coupling subnational (local and regional) elections with the parliamentary ones. In these countries, the share of local lists and/or independent candidates is rather limited. There is also relative uniformity between local authorities in elections and voting. Here, all municipalities adopt the same electoral system, hold elections on one day and are driven by national party cues. Taken together, this induces a strongly nationalized frame on local elections and voting. The patterns and dynamics at both tiers are thus more likely to mirror or mimic one another. The core of the Nordic group is placed in this category. The remaining countries come from different state traditions.

For only one country found in Southern Europe is the localness high on both dimensions: Italy displays differences between the national and local arena, and within the latter, between authorities. It can be considered as somewhat the opposite of a country like Sweden. Local electoral systems differ (within the national arena but also between localities). Local elections are organized in different (within the country) and separate (from other levels) cycles. Non-national lists and independent candidates have a larger share of the vote, and there is a clear limit on national cues. This clearly implies a very localized setting.

Some countries score high on one of the dimensions but medium on the other. For vertical dissimilarity, this holds for four cases (including three Visegrád countries). This means that either there are different electoral systems between levels, decoupled elections, and/or successful local lists or independent candidates. For horizontal variation, it applies to four cases. This includes three federations in the Rhineland and the devolved United Kingdom (where differences appear between the Anglo-Saxon core and the Celtic Fringe). Here, local authorities use various electoral systems, have different electoral cycles, and/or limited national party cues.

All remaining 24 cases are in the medium category on either both (ten countries) or one (14 countries) of the dimensions (low on the other for the latter subgroup). It is also noteworthy that no cases appear where localness is high on one but low on the other dimension (either dissimilarity or variation). This suggest that the two dimensions are not entirely unrelated.

'Happily ever after'? Avenues for future research

The preceding sections thematically summarized the main findings from the country chapters and analyzed their insights along integration – variation dimensions. By doing so we moved beyond the 'encyclopedic' assemblage of country profiles, explaining the complexities of local electoral systems and specificities of voting behavior in local elections. The result is a rich comparative account of local elections and voting in 40 European countries on key topics such as electoral systems, electoral participation, party politicization, and political representation. The sections also demonstrate the added value of disentangling specific electoral arenas in contemporary multilevel polities of contrasting levels and jurisdictions. We argue that the *localness* of place-bound elections and voting can be asserted in terms of vertical dissimilarity and horizontal variation. Indicators pertaining to electoral systems, electoral cycles, and party politicization allowed seven real-world *types* to be discerned that appear to stand for different configurations of local elections and voting. Such further engagement renders the *perennial* local *bridesmaids* as more *fully fledged spouses* in the multilevel study of elections and voting. However, the wedding celebrations in this conclusion provide not only a momentum in glancing back but equally in looking forward. In the remainder, we therefore suggest some avenues for future research.

First, our assessment of local electoral systems showed that more than one million councilors in Europe come to office in bodies of different sizes and mainly through proportional means. In directly elected local councils, (open) list systems dominate. Nevertheless, variation exists (often on a more specific level). Population size explains some of the variation in council size and diversifies electoral systems (nonproportional variants are mainly used for elections in smaller municipalities). We also discern the ascent of the direct election of the local executive, notably mayors. Here, the two-round majority system prevails over first-past-the-post.

The choice of the local electoral system, usually made at the upper tier, comes with underlying conceptions of local governance. It may 'be interpreted as indicative of the democratic values and assumptions' (Cole 2019: 14ff). The system affects the likelihood of single or multi-party majorities, and thus the broader capacity for radical or incremental local policy alteration. It further influences the balance between territorial, partisan, and personal representation and accountability. This conditions the extent and mode of linkage with voters, and how choice discretion and distributive fairness of the vote can be achieved. Introducing directly elected mayors may in turn legitimize strong leadership in a singular executive mandate (countervailing the traditional layman's rule embodied by the council with legislative powers). We invite scholars to probe deeper into these more normative concerns and to falsify their alleged implications with empirical evidence.

Furthermore, the evidence gathered opens room for a more systematic study of electoral reform. Local government is often conceived of as a laboratory of institutional change. Alterations of electoral systems tend to be discussed or implemented first and foremost at the local level. Many of the country chapters reflect such a discourse. In some instances, the rules are negotiated and adapted instrumentally in an attempt to solve pressing political issues. These may pertain to municipal amalgamations, ethnic tensions, or debates on the extension of the suffrage. The mere variety of rules displayed in the *Handbook* offers inspiration for assertions of electoral reform. Processes and outcomes of alternative electoral systems can be exemplified and compared. This offers opportunities for quasi-experimental designs, especially where differences over time and/or space occur within one country. Evidently, this requires a constant and fine-grained monitoring of the evolving electoral rules-in-form and in use.

Second, addressing local political participation generally confirmed one of the long-held assumptions of second-order elections. With some exceptions, local voter turnout falls below that for national elections. The gap decreases by concurring electoral cycles (around the main arena). Comparing levels is somewhat complex because of differences in eligibility rules (locally, these are often more open), which have even increased in recent decades. Furthermore, substantial variation in local voter turnout exists between and within countries. Broadly speaking, it tends to be lower in new than old democracies. Over time, turnout also diminishes (again especially in the new democracies but more evidently so at the national level). Between localities, size has a fairly universal and expected effect: in smaller municipalities, more citizens turn out to vote. Future research can refine our macro- and micro-level insights in the national-local turnout gap (Gendźwiłł & Kjaer 2021; Gorecki & Gendźwiłł 2021). It can also extend the comparison with other subnational or European elections to provide a more precise account of the potential ordering of elections, as evidently not all second-order elections are characterized by similar lower stakes. Such endeavors should equally probe into the causal mechanisms producing the ranking at the level of the individual voter (thus, beyond aggregate effects). In addition, localities can be contrasted to systematically test the assumption that context matters for voter turnout. If contextual factors matter, they should be most pronounced in place-bound local elections. Local elections offer a setting to investigate whether differences in factors such as the socioeconomic or ethnic makeup and/or metropolitan status of local authorities affect electoral participation.

Third, our study exhibits varying degrees of local party politicization. In about one-third of all country cases, the predominance of national political parties is high. Here, room for nonnational lists and/or independent candidates is limited. In a handful, the latter stand for more than half of all votes or seats. The remaining half is more balanced. There, the tendency is for national parties to be mainstream, with their nonnational or independent counterparts in niches. Where mayors are directly elected, the overall share of independent mayors aligns with that found for the councilors in the country.

Of course, the picture now pertains to country aggregates and the juxtaposition of national and nonnational/independent parties or candidates. Future research must attempt to disentangle these broad categories. Are all national parties equally successful in the local arena and why (not)? Does the answer to the previous question depend on the characteristics of the locality (and which)? Do local branches of the nationwide parties provide linkage with national politics and how? To what extent and by which means are nonnational lists or independent candidates the functional equivalent of (national) parties (Copus et al. 2012; Scarrow et al. 2017)? How do they operate in mobilizing voters (i.e., local party on the ground/in the electorate), building an extra-council or -executive organization (i.e., local party central office), and in representing or governing (local party in public office)? What fosters their institutional survival, and their carving out of a sustainable electoral share, hindering them from becoming ephemeral or flash phenomena? More evidence is also needed regarding the local vote choice (Gendźwiłł & Steyvers 2021). Few countries conduct regular surveys to probe into the motives and actions of the individual municipal voter. The formation of party and candidate preferences in local elections therefore remains understudied. In that, resolving choice dilemmas appears of particular interest. To what extent and how are place-bound considerations confronted with pre-existing national party loyalties and images? What are the considerations standing behind the *sincere* and *strategic* vote in local elections? To what extent is local voting either *retrospective* (as some kind of referendum on the governance of the sitting majority) or rather *prospective* (about future plans for the locality)?

Fourth, the focus on local political representation displays the persistence of a gender imbalance in local politics. About one-third of all laymen in the various councils of Europe are actually lay*women*. Despite an increase over time in the share of female councilors, few countries approach parity. The share also appears to be unrelated to the existence of formal quotas at the local level. Where mayors are directly elected, a nearly universal legislative-executive gap can be established (with relatively fewer women breaking through the local glass ceiling). Such intrapolity attrition is not always matched by an interpolity counterpart. The national-local gender gap shows more cross-national dispersion (dividing the country cases in half, with more

Table 42.8 Local electoral systems by state traditions (extensive description)

State tradition Country	Subsystem	Electoral formula			District structure		Ballot structure			
		System family	Seat allocation	Threshold	Districts	DM	Number of votes	Panachage (in list systems)	Cumulation (in list systems)	Ordering
Nordic										
Denmark		OLPR	d'Hondt, apparentement	–			1			
Finland		OLPR	d'Hondt	–			1			
Iceland	Proportional system	OLPR	d'Hondt	–			1			
	Personal vote system	BV					5			
Norway		OLPR	Modified Sainte-Laguë	–			1 (party) + several preference votes [1]	Yes		
Sweden		OLPR	Modified Sainte-Laguë	2–3%[2]	No/Yes[3]	13–43	1			
British Isles										
Ireland		STV			Yes	3–7	from 1 to N			Yes
United Kingdom England		FPTP			Yes	1	1			
Wales		FPTP			Yes	1	1			
Northern Ireland		STV			Yes	5–7	from 1 to N			Yes
Scotland		STV			Yes	3–4	from 1 to N			Yes

'Happily ever after'

Rhinelandic: federal

Austria	Burgenland, Carinthia, Lower Austria, Upper Austria, Salzburg, Styria, Tirol, Vorarlberg	OLPR	d'Hondt	–		1
	Vienna	OLPR	d'Hondt	5%		1
Belgium	Flemish Region, Walloon Region, Brussels Capital Region	OLPR	Imperiali	–		1 (party) + N seats (candidates)
Germany	Baden-Württemberg	OLPR	Sainte-Lague	–	n/a	N seats	Yes	Yes
	Nordrhein-Westfalen	CLPR	Sainte-Lague	–	n/a	1	Yes	
	Bayern	OLPR	Sainte-Lague, apparentement	–	n/a	N seats	Yes	Yes
	Brandenburg	OLPR	Hare-Niemeyer, apparentement	–	n/a	3	Yes	Yes
	Hessen	OLPR	Hare-Niemeyer	–	n/a	N seats	Yes	Yes
	Mecklenburg-Vorpommern	OLPR	Hare-Niemeyer, apparentement	–	n/a	3	Yes	Yes
	Niedersachsen	OLPR	Hare-Niemeyer	–	n/a	3	Yes	Yes
	Rhineland-Pfalz	OLPR	Sainte-Lague, apparentement	–	n/a	N seats	Yes	Yes
	Schleswig-Holstein	CLPR	Sainte-Lague	–	n/a	from 1 to N seats	Yes	
	Saarland	CLPR	d'Hondt, apparentement	–	n/a	1		
	Sachsen	OLPR	d'Hondt, apparentement	–	n/a	3	Yes	Yes
	Sachsen-Anhalt	OLPR	Hare-Niemeyer, apparentement	–	n/a	3	Yes	Yes

(Continued)

523

Table 42.8 (Continued)

State tradition Country	Subsystem	Electoral formula			District structure		Ballot structure		
		System family	Seat allocation	Threshold	Districts	DM	Number of votes	Panachage (in list systems)	Cumulation (in list systems)	Ordering
	Thüringen	OLPR	Hare-Niemeyer, apparentement	-	n/a		3	Yes	Yes	
Rhinelandic: unitary										
Liechtenstein		OLPR	Hagenbach-Bischoff	-			N seats	Yes		
Luxembourg	small municipalities	BV		-			N seats			
	large municipalities	OLPR	d'Hondt	-			N seats	Yes	Yes	
The Netherlands		OLPR	d'Hondt/Hare [4]	- [5]			1			
Southern Europe										
Andorra		PR MBS	Hare	-			1			
Cyprus		OLPR	Hare	-			from 1 to 7			
France	>1000 inh.	PR MBS	d'Hondt	5%		[6]	1			
	<1000 inh.	TR-BV	majority, plurality				from 7 to 15			
Greece		OLPR	Hare-Niemeyer	-			from 1 to 3			
Italy		PR MBS	d'Hondt	3% [7]			1 (mayor) + 1 (party) + up to 2 (candidates)			
Portugal	municipal	CLPR	d'Hondt	-			1			
	sub-municipal	CLPR	d'Hondt	-			1			

'Happily ever after'

Spain[8]	>250 inh.	CLPR	d'Hondt	5%			1
	<250 inh.	LV					from 2 to 4
New democracies: Central and Eastern Europe							
Czech Republic		OLPR	d'Hondt	5%			N seats	Yes
Estonia		OLPR	d'Hondt	5%	Yes	2–8	1
Hungary	< 10,000 inh.	BV					N seats
	> 10,000 inh.	MMP (FPTP + compensation)	Sainte-Lague	5%	Yes	1	1
Latvia		OLPR	Sainte-Lague	5%			1 (party) + up to N positive or negative pref.
Lithuania		OLPR	Hare-Niemeyer	4%			1
Poland	> 20,000 inh.	OLPR	d'Hondt	5%	Yes	5–8	1
	< 20,000 inh.	FPTP			Yes	1	1
Slovakia		BV			Yes	1–12	N seats
Ukraine	< 10,000 voters	SNTV			Yes	2–4	1
	> 10,000 voters	OLPR		5%			1
New democracies: Southeastern Europe							
Albania		CLPR	d'Hondt	3%			1
Bosnia and Herzegovina	RS, FBH, Brčko District	OLPR	Sainte-Lague	3%			N seats
Bulgaria		OLPR	Hare-Niemeyer	–			1
Croatia		CLPR	d'Hondt	5%			1
Kosovo		OLPR	Sainte-Laguë	–			1
Moldova		CLPR	d'Hondt	–			1
Montenegro		CLPR	d'Hondt	3%			1

(Continued)

Table 42.8 (Continued)

State tradition Country	Subsystem	Electoral formula				District structure		Ballot structure			
		System family	Seat allocation	Threshold		Districts	DM	Number of votes	Panachage (in list systems)	Cumulation (in list systems)	Ordering
North Macedonia		CLPR	d'Hondt	-				1			
Romania		CLPR	Hare	5%				1			
Serbia		CLPR	d'Hondt	5%				1			
Slovenia	large municipalities	OLPR	d'Hondt	-				1			
	small municipalities	BV/LV/SNTV				Yes/No[9]	1–5	from 1 to N			

Notes:

[1] A list vote + preference votes (up to N from the selected party list + up to 0.25N from lists of other parties).
[2] 3% in the municipalities with districts, 2% in other municipalities.
[3] Electoral districts have been established only in ca. 8% of municipalities.
[4] Hare method for councils with less than 19 seats, d'Hondt method for larger councils.
[5] Municipalities using the Hare system have a formal threshold defined as 75% of the electoral quotient.
[6] Electoral districts only in Paris, Lyon and Marseille.
[7] No formal threshold for municipalities under 15,000 inhabitants.
[8] Open-council system not reported in the table.
[9] Depending on the decision of the local council.

Table 42.9 Turnout (gap) for local and national elections by country

Country	Code	Local elections		National elections		National-local turnout gap (p.p.)
		Average voter turnout (%)	Years	Average voter turnout (%)	Years	
France	FR	66.5	1995–2014	60.5	1993–2017	−6.0
Kosovo	XK	45.6	2002–2017	44.3	2004–2019	−1.3
Switzerland[1]	CH	48.9	2017	48.0	2015–2019	−0.9
Belgium	BE	91.4	1994–2018	90.5	1991–2019	−0.9
Ukraine	UA	63.1	1994–2015	63.0	1994–2019	−0.1
Luxembourg	LU	89.6	2005–2017	90.9	2004–2018	1.3
Bosnia and Herzegovina	BA	53.5	2004–2016	55.1	2002–2018	1.6
Portugal	PT	58.7	1993–2017	60.5	1991–2019	1.8
Romania	RO	54.3	1992–2016	56.3	1990–2020	2.0
Serbia	RS	54.0	2004–2016	56.3	2007–2020	2.3
Austria[2]	AT	76.3	1997–2020	78.6	2002–2019	2.3
Sweden	SE	81.6	1991–2018	84.3	1991–2018	2.7
Greece	GR	68.2	1990–2019	71.1	1993–2019	2.9
Montenegro[3]	ME	68.8	2006–2020	71.8	2006–2020	3.0
Liechtenstein	LI	80.5	1991–2019	83.9	1993–2017	3.4
Poland	PL	45.2	1990–2018	49.5	1991–2019	4.3
Andorra	AD	69.7	1995–2019	76.0	1993–2019	6.3
Finland	FI	60.7	1992–2017	67.1	1991–2019	6.4
Bulgaria	BG	55.6	1991–2019	62.0	1991–2017	6.4
Iceland	IS	77.6	1990–2018	84.1	1991–2017	6.6
North Macedonia	MK	59.8	1996–2017	66.5	1990–2016	6.7
Cyprus	CY	78.3	1991–2016	85.1	1991–2016	6.8
Italy[4]	IT	71.8	2001–2019	78.7	2001–2018	6.9
Spain	ES	65.6	1991–2019	73.2	1993–2019	7.6
Croatia	HR	56.1	1990–2017	64.1	1990–2020	8.0
Slovenia	SI	57.0	1994–2018	65.5	1992–2018	8.5
Moldova	MD	54.0	1995–2019	64.1	1994–2019	10.2
Lithuania	LT	45.5	1995–2019	56.0	1990–2020	10.5
Estonia	EE	53.3	1993–2017	64.9	1990–2019	11.5
Ireland	IE	54.0	1991–2019	66.0	1992–2020	12.0
Denmark	DK	72.0	1993–2017	85.5	1990–2019	13.5
Latvia	LV	54.3	1994–2017	68.5	1990–2018	14.1
Norway	NO	62.3	1991–2019	77.1	1993–2017	14.8
Albania	AL	49.0	1992–2019	67.4	1991–2017	18.4
Germany[2]	DE	56.9	1990–2019	75.8	1990–2017	18.9
Czech Republic	CZ	51.8	1990–2018	70.7	1990–2017	18.9
Hungary	HU	46.6	1990–2019	65.6	1990–2018	19.0
Slovakia	SK	51.8	1990–2018	70.9	1990–2020	19.1
Netherlands	NL	58.2	1990–2018	77.9	1994–2017	19.7
UK[5]	UK	39.8	2016–2019	68.4	2017–2019	28.6

(Continued)

Table 42.9 (Continued)

¹ Local turnout in Switzerland is estimated on the basis of a 2017 survey of local secretaries as an unweighted average across cantons (details in the country chapter).
² Turnout figures for Germany and Austria are computed as unweighted averages across states (without the city states Vienna, Hamburg, Bremen, and Berlin).
³ Turnout in Montenegrin local elections is an average of yearly turnout rates reported in the country chapter.
⁴ Turnout in Italian local elections is an average of yearly turnout rates reported in the country chapter.
⁵ Turnout in the UK is computed as an average of turnout rates in 2017 local elections in Wales, 2017 local elections in Scotland, 2019 local elections in Northern Ireland, and four consecutive waves of local elections in England held between 2016 and 2019.
Sources: Data from national electoral commissions, statistical offices, and other sources assembled by the country experts, International IDEA Voter Turnout database.

national than local female representatives, or the other way around). Councilors from ethnic minorities remain equally underrepresented. In most instances, representation occurs without formal provisions. Candidates from such backgrounds run for established parties or form ethnic minority counterparts, coming forward in targeted electoral districts (where concurring minorities concentrate). In some countries, specific rules exist to ensure ethnic minority representation (e.g., by quota). These binding arrangements often aim to reduce tensions with an ethnic foundation.

Such findings on descriptive representation can advance the investigation of the local level as an arena of political recruitment and selection (Guérin & Kerrouche 2008; Steyvers & Medir 2018). As a relatively large number of seats must be filled, to what extent is the local tier more open to and inclusive of the diversity that characterizes contemporary society? To what extent does the composition of the local political elite differ from that of the national, and how? As with voter turnout, a specific focus on the gender and ethnicity gap (between tiers and authorities) seems particularly promising. In addition, local arenas offer the potential to probe the microfoundations of underrepresentation. A particular niche in the literature can be advanced where experimental studies assess the occurrence and contingency of gender or ethnic stereotypes in the eyes of voters, and how these can affect local political representation (Devroe 2020; Van Trappen 2021).

Fifth and finally, our typology shows patterns in vertical integration and horizontal variation. These dimensions of localness are clearly not unrelated. In some instances, municipal elections and voting are thus more local than others. This happens when electoral systems, cycles, and partisan cues differ between levels and jurisdictions. Many cases show intermediate levels of dissimilarity and heterogeneity. There, the local arena in part stands on its own but also transcends specific tiers and places. The origin and relevance of these configurations for the comparative study of local government systems should further be scrutinized. To what extent, why, and how do the delineated types affect other aspects of local elections and voting (think of motivations and actions of local choice)? The types can also be refined or challenged by adding information on other comparable indicators. Perhaps, sometimes, they can even be supplemented by positions on more discrete continua of local elections and voting.

In conclusion, these avenues do not provide an encompassing road map but rather an explorative global positioning of guiding questions. We hope to have paved the way for other researchers to follow our steps and develop additional directions. We trust the scholarly community to commit to the above and wider agendas. If that happens the comparative approach and electoral research will marry, and the comparative study of local elections and voting will be able to thrive and live 'happily ever after'.

Notes

1 These are Austria, Belgium, Germany, and Switzerland versus Liechtenstein, Luxembourg, and The Netherlands.
2 The more recent and holding-together federalism in Belgium being the exception.
3 These are the Baltics, the Visegrád states, and Ukraine versus the Balkan states (including the republics established after the collapse of former Yugoslavia).
4 Within the scope of this volume, our comparison thus makes abstraction of alternative points of multilevel reference, such as the regional or the European level.
5 This is an underestimation of the actual number of local councilors in the 40 countries. It excludes Germany (no reliable data), part of Spain (the open-council municipalities) and Switzerland (mostly citizen assemblies). It provides only partial information in the case of non-simultaneous elections (England, Italy, Montenegro, and Serbia). It also makes abstraction of singular off-cycle elections in other countries.
6 Pearson's correlation coefficient (average council size versus average number of eligible voters) = .66 (significant at the .01 level).
7 Switzerland is not included in Table 42.8 as information on the specific aspects of electoral systems differs, not only between the cantons but also within them (despite the tendency toward open-list systems). Often, municipalities dispose of a large amount of discretion when determining the configuration of their own electoral system. Hence, no accurate aggregate information is available.
8 To be more precise, a hybrid form can be discerned where the list system is semi-open. This means that both the list position (through a transfer of list votes) and the number of preference votes have an impact on who gets elected. Belgium is an example. These forms have been classified as open. It can be noted that Greece recently moved from MBS/OLPR to OLPR.
9 In Belgium, this appointment is a central rubber stamp of a local political decision, in which the office of mayor is designated to an elected mandatory in the process of majority formation (usually to the person with the most preference votes of the largest party in the majority). In the Netherlands, the council makes up a profile in case the position of mayor is vacant and advises (largely with success) the appointment by central government.
10 It is usually argued that the control of national executive power is what makes elections first-order: legislative elections in parliamentary systems and elections for the head of the state in presidential systems. It is more problematic in semi-presidential systems. Although Reif (1985) considered that both presidential and parliamentary elections are first-order in semi-presidential systems, exemplified by the French Fifth Republic, Freire (2004) notes that, in reality, semi-presidential regimes vary considerably in this respect.
11 The 2% benchmark is based on the total average of the gap. This empirical criterion operationalizes a pattern termed by Kjaer (2019: 60) as one where female representation is '*more or less equal*'. Evidently, it is more of a rule of thumb. A different range would produce other ratios of the categories.
12 See the comparative project: http://pathways.eu/.
13 Although this may be compensated for by the impossibility to vote and/or stand as a candidate for those living abroad (as might be possible for national elections).
14 This pertains also to regional parties active in the national arena.

References

Aars, J., & Ringkjøb, H. E. (2005). Party Politicisation Reversed? Non-partisan Alternatives in Norwegian Local Politics. *Scandinavian Political Studies*, 28(2), 161–181.
Bäck, H. (2005). The institutional setting of local political leadership and community involvement. In M. Haus, H. Heinelt & M. Stewart (Eds.), *Urban Governance and Democracy. Leadership and Community Involvement* (pp. 80–86). London: Routlegde.
Bird, K., Saalfeld, T., & Wüst, A. (Eds.) (2015). *The Political Representation of Immigrants and Minorities. Voters, Parties and Parliaments in Liberal Democracies*. London: Routledge.
Blais, A. (2000). *To Vote or Not to Vote? The Merits and Limits of Rational Choice Theory*. Pittsburgh: University of Pittsburgh Press.
Bloemraad, I., & Schönwälder, K. (2013). Immigrant and Ethnic Minority Representation in Europe. Conceptual Challenges and Theoretical Approaches. *West European Politics*, 36(3), 564–579.

Cancela, J., & Geys, B. (2016). Explaining Voter Turnout: A Meta-analysis of National and Subnational Elections. *Electoral Studies*, *42*, 264–275.

Carey, J., & Shugart, M. (1995). Incentives to Cultivate a Personal Vote: a Rank Ordering of Electoral Formulas. *Electoral Studies*, 14(4), 417–439.

Cole, M. (2019). Local Electoral Systems. In R. Kerley, P. Dunning, & J. Liddle (Eds.), *The Routledge Handbook of International Local Government* (pp. 13–24). London: Routledge.

Copus, C. (2006). *Leading the Localities. Executive Mayors in English Local Governance*. Manchester: Manchester University Press.

Copus, C., Wingfield, M., Steyvers, K., & Reynaert, H. (2012). A Place to Party? Parties and Nonpartisanship in Local Government. In K. Mossberger, S. E. Clarke, & P. John (Eds.), *The Oxford Handbook of Urban Politics* (pp. 210–230). Oxford, UK: Oxford University Press.

Crowder-Meyer, M. (2013). Gendered Recruitment Without Trying: How Local Party Recruiters Affect Women's Representation. *Politics and Gender*, 9(4), 390–413.

Dancygier, R. (2017). *Dilemmas of Inclusion. Muslims in European Politics*. Princeton: Princeton University Press.

Denters, B., Goldsmith, M., Ladner, A., Mouritzen, P.-E., & Rose, L. (2015). *Size and Local Democracy*. Cheltenham: Edward Elgar Publishing.

Devroe, R. (2020). Stereotypes, Who to Blame? Exploring Individual-level Determinants of Flemish Voters' Political Gender Stereotypes. *Political Studies* (online first). https://doi.org/10.1177/0032321720924808.

Egner, B., Gendźwiłł, A., Swianiewicz, P., & Pleschberger, W. (2018). Mayors and Political Parties. In H. Heinelt, A. Magnier, M. Cabria, & H. Reynaert (Eds.), *Political Leaders and Changing Local Democracy. The European Mayor* (pp. 327–358). London: Palgrave Macmillan.

Egner, B., Sweeting, D., & Klok, P.-J. (Eds.) (2013). *Local Councillors in Europe*. Wiesbaden: Springer VS.

Elcock, H. (2009). Elected Mayors. Lesson Drawing from Four Countries. *Public Administration*, 86(3), 795–811.

Freire, A. (2004). Second-Order Elections and Electoral Cycles in Democratic Portugal. *South European Society and Politics*, 9(3), 54–79.

Gendźwiłł, A. (2019). Local Autonomy and National – Local Turnout Gap: Higher Stakes, Higher Turnout? *Regional & Federal Studies* (online first). https://doi.org/10.1080/13597566.2019.1706496.

Gendźwiłł, A., & Kjaer, U. (2021). Mind the Gap, Please! Pinpointing the Influence of Municipal Size on Local Electoral Participation. *Local Government Studies*, 47(1), 11–30.

Gendźwiłł, A., & Steyvers, K. (2021). Comparing Local Elections and Voting in Europe: Lower Rank, Different Kind . . . or Missing Link? *Local Government Studies*, 47(1), 1–10.

Gorecki, M., & Gendźwiłł, A. (2021). Polity Size and Voter Turnout Revisited: Micro-level Evidence from 14 Countries of Central and Eastern Europe. *Local Government Studies*, 47(1), 31–53.

Guérin, É., & Kerrouche, É. (2008). From Amateurs to Professionals: The Changing Face of Local Elected Representatives in Europe. *Local Government Studies*, 34(2), 179–201.

Harmel, R., & Janda, K. (1994). An Integrated Theory of Party Goals and Party Change. *Journal of Theoretical Politics*, 6(3), 259–287.

Heath, A., McLean, I., Taylor, B., & Curtice, J. (1999). Between First and Second Order: A Comparison of Voting Behaviour in European and Local Elections in Britain. *European Journal of Political Research*, 35(3), 389–414.

Heinelt, H., Hlepas, N., Kuhlmann, S., & Swianiewicz, P. (2018). Local Government Systems: Grasping the Institutional Environment of Mayors. In H. Heinelt, A. Magnier, M. Cabria, & H. Reynaert (Eds.), *Political Leaders and Changing Local Democracy. The European Mayor* (pp. 19–78). London: Palgrave Macmillan.

Kjaer, U. (2011). Women in Politics: The National-Local Gap in Comparative Perspective. In M. Edinger, & W. Patzelt (Eds.), *Politik als Beruf* (pp. 334–351). Wiesbaden. VS Verlag.

Kjaer, U. (2012). Local Politics: Incubator or Respirator for Political Parties? In J. Blom-Hansen, Ch. Green-Pedersen, & S.-E. Skaaning (Eds.), *Democracy, Elections, and Political Parties. Essays in Honour of Jørgen Elklit* (pp. 201–209). Aarhus: Politica.

Kjaer, U. (2019). Patterns of Inter-Level Gender Gaps in Women's Descriptive Representation. *Lex Localis – Journal of Local Self-Government,* 17(1), 53–70.

Kjaer, U., & Elklit, J. (2010). Party Politicization of Local Councils: Cultural or Institutional Explanations for Trends in Denmark, 1966–2005. *European Journal of Political Research,* 49(3), 337–358.

Kjaer, U., & Elklit, J. (2014). The Impact of Assembly Size on Representativeness. *The Journal of Legislative Studies,* 20(2), 156–173.

Kjaer, U., & Kosiara-Pedersen, K. (2019). The Hourglass Pattern of Women's Representation. *Journal of Elections, Public Opinion and Parties,* 29(3), 299–317.

Kjaer, U., & Steyvers, K. (2019). Second Thoughts on Second-Order? Towards a Second-Tier Model of Local Elections and Voting. In R. Kerley, P. Dunning, & J. Liddle (Eds.), *The Routledge Handbook of International Local Government* (pp. 405–417). London: Routledge.

Kostadinova, T. (2003). Voter Turnout Dynamics in post-Communist Europe. *European Journal of Political Research,* 42(6), 741–759

Kostelka, F. (2017). Does Democratic Consolidation Lead to a Decline in Voter Turnout? Global Evidence Since 1939. *American Political Science Review,* 111(4), 653–667.

Leininger, A., & Faas, F. (2020). Votes at 16 in Germany: Examining Subnational Variation. In J. Eichhorn & J. Bergh (Eds.), *Lowering the Voting Age to 16: Learning from Real Experiences Worldwide* (pp. 143–166). London: Palgrave.

Lidström, A., Baldersheim, H., Copus, C., Hlynsdóttir, E., Kettunen, P., & Klimovský, D. (2016). Reforming Local Councils and the Role of Councillors: A Comparative Analysis of Fifteen European Countries. In S. Kuhlmann & G. Bouckaert (Eds.), *Local Public Sector Reforms in Times of Crisis* (pp. 287–300). London: Palgrave Macmillan.

Loughlin, J., Hendriks, F., & Lidström, A. (Eds.) (2012). *The Oxford Handbook of Local and Regional Democracy in Europe.* Oxford: Oxford University Press.

Morlan, R. L. (1984). Municipal vs. National Election Voter Turnout: Europe and the United States. *Political Science Quarterly,* 99(3), 457–470.

Mouritzen, P. E., & Svara, J. (2002). *Leadership at the Apex: Politicians and Administrators in Western Local Governments.* Pittsburgh: Pittsburgh University Press.

Muñoz, R. D. (2018). International Retirees at the Polls: Spanish Local Elections 2015. *RIPS: Revista de Investigaciones Políticas y Sociológicas,* 17(1), 27–54.

Navarro, C., & Medir, L. (2016). Patterns of Gender Representation in Councils at the Second Tier of Local Government: Assessing the Gender Gap in an Unexplored Institutional Setting. In X. Bertrana, B. Egner, & H. Heinelt (Eds.), *Policy-Making at the Second Tier of Local Government in Europe* (pp. 111–133). London: Routledge.

O'Dwyer, C., & Stenberg, M. (2021). Local-Level Democratic Backsliding? The Consolidation of Aspiring Dominant-Party Regimes in Hungary and Poland. *Government & Opposition,* 12, 1–24.

Pacek, A. C., Pop-Eleches, G., & Tucker, J. A. (2009). Disenchanted or Discerning: Voter Turnout in post-communist Countries. *The Journal of Politics,* 71(2), 473–491.

Pierson, P. (2004). *Politics in Time. History, Institutions and Social Analysis.* Princeton: Princeton University Press.

Rae, D. (1969). *The Political Consequences of Electoral Laws.* New Haven: Yale University Press.

Rallings, C., & Thrasher, M. (2007). The Turnout 'Gap' and the Costs of Voting – a Comparison of Participation at the 2001 General and 2002 Local Elections in England. *Public Choice,* 131(3), 333–344.

Reif, K. (1985). Ten Second-order Elections. In K. Reif (Ed.), *Ten European Elections* (pp. 1–36). Gower: Aldershot.

Reif, K., & Schmitt, H. (1980). Nine Second-Order National Elections – a Conceptual Framework for the Analysis of European Election Results. *European Journal of Political Research,* 8(1), 3–44.

Reiser, M., & Holtmann, E. (Eds.) (2008). *Farewell to the Party Model? Independent Local Lists in East and West European Countries.* Wiesbaden: Springer.

Reynolds, A., Reilly, B., & Ellis, A. (Eds.) (2005). *Electoral System Design: The New International IDEA Handbook.* Stockholm: International IDEA.

Rokkan, S. (1970), *Citizens, Elections, Parties.* Oslo: Universitetsforlaget.

Saalfeld, T., & Lucas, G. (2018). *Analyzing the Representation of Citizens of Immigrant Origin in Eight Contemporary European Democracies*. Bamberg: University of Bamberg.

Scarrow, S., Webb, P., & Poguntke, T. (Eds.) (2017). *Organizing Political Parties. Representation, Participation, and Power*. Oxford: Oxford University Press.

Schakel, A. H., & Dandoy, R. (2014). Electoral Cycles and Turnout in Multilevel Electoral Systems. *West European Politics*, 37(3), 605–623.

Seidle, F. L. (2015). Local Voting Rights for Non-Nationals: Experience in Sweden, the Netherlands and Belgium. *Journal of International Migration and Integration*, 16(1), 27–42.

Steyvers, K., & Medir, L. (2018). From the Few Are Still Chosen the Few? Continuity and Change in the Social Background of European Mayors. In H. Heinelt, A. Magnier, M. Cabria, & H. Reynaert (Eds.), *Political Leaders and Changing Local Democracy. The European Mayor* (pp. 79–108). London: Palgrave Macmillan.

Steyvers, K., & Verhelst, T. (2012). Between Layman and Professional? Political Recruitment and Career Development of Local Councillors in Comparative Perspective. *Lex Localis – Journal of Local Self-Government*, 10(1), 1–17.

Sweeting, D. (Ed.) (2017). *Directly Elected Mayors in Urban Governance. Impact and Practice*. Bristol: Polity Press.

Sweeting, D., & Hambleton, R. (2020). The Dynamics of Depoliticisation in Urban Governance: Introducing a Directly Elected Mayor. *Urban Studies*, 57(5), 1068–1086.

Swianiewicz, P. (2014). An Empirical Typology of Local Government Systems in Eastern Europe. *Local Government Studies*, 40(2), 292–311.

Van Biezen, I., & Kopecký, P. (2007). The State and the Parties: Public Funding, Public Regulation and Rent-seeking in Contemporary Democracies. *Party Politics*, 13(2), 235–254.

van der Kolk, H. (2006). The Effective Use of The Supplementary Vote in Mayoral Elections: London 2000 and 2004. *Representation. Journal of Representative Democracy*, 42(4), 91–102.

van der Kolk, H. (2007). Local Electoral Systems in Western Europe. *Local Government Studies*, 33(2), 159–180.

Van Trappen, S. (2021). Steered By Ethnicity and/or SES Cues? An Examination of Party Selectors' Stereotypes About Ethnic Minority Aspirants. *Journal of Ethnic and Migration Studies*. Published online: https://doi.org/10.1080/1369183X.2021.1874319.

Verhelst, T., Reynaert, H., & Steyvers, K. (2013). Political Recruitment and Career Development of Local Councillors in Europe. In B. Egner, D. Sweeting, & P.-J. Klok (Eds.), *Local Councillors in Europe* (pp. 27–49). Wiesbaden: Springer VS.

Verstraete, D., Devillers, S., Dandoy, R., Dodeigne, J., Jacquet, V., Niessen, C., & Reuchamps, M. (2018). *Les rôles, fonctions et choix politiques des bourgmestres en Wallonie et à Bruxelles*. Bruxelles: CRISP.

Vetter, A. (2015). Just a Matter of Timing? Local Electoral Turnout in Germany in the Context of National and European Parliamentary Elections. *German Politics*, 24(1), 67–84.

Wattenberg, M. P. (2002). *Where Have All the Voters Gone?* Boston: Harvard University Press.

Wollmann, H. (2005). The Directly Elected Executive Mayor in German Local Government. In R. Berg, & N. Rao (Eds). *Transforming Local Political Leadership* (pp. 29–41). London: Palgrave.

Index

Note: Page numbers in *italics* indicates figures and page numbers in **bold** indicates tables.

advance (early) voting 29n7, 32, 53, 63, 99, **102**, 190, 284; *see also* postal voting
Albania 8–9, 363–373, **492, 495, 499, 507**–510, 514, **517, 519, 525, 527**
Andorra 8–9, 187–196, **492**–493, **495**–**496, 507**, 510, 515, **517, 519, 524, 527**
apparentement 13, 65, 165, **330**–331, 367, 378, 422, **522**–524
Austria 8–9, 97–113, 140, **492**, 494–**496**, 498–**499**, 502, 506–**507**, 513–514, **517, 519, 523, 527**

Belgium 8–9, 114–125, **492, 495**–**496**, 498–**499**, 501, 506–**507, 517, 519, 523, 527**
bloc vote system (BV) 15n11, 48, 154, 295–298, 299, 330, 339, 478, **495**, 497, **522**–**526**; *see also* two-round bloc vote system (TR-BV)
Bosnia and Herzegovina (BiH) 8–9, 374–386, **492, 495**–**496, 499, 507**–508, 514, **517, 519, 525, 527**
Bulgaria 8–9, 387–395, **492, 495**–**497, 499, 507**–508, **517, 519, 525, 527**

closed-list proportional representation system (CLPR) 130–131, **218**–219, 250, 255, 319, 349–350, 366–367, 372, 389, 394, 398–399, 410, 422, 426, 433, 444, 455, 467–**468**, 473–474, 478, **495**–**496**, 499, **523**–**526**
compulsory voting 12, 100, **102**, 104, 116, 118, 123, 153–154, 159n4, 166, 177, 200, 201, 225, 235, 391
council size (number of seats) 12, 23, 33, 43, 53, 64, 75–76, 86, 100, 116, 130, 153, 162, 177, 190, 200–201, 212, 225–**226**, **228**, 236, 249–251, 261, 272, 274, 285, 296, 308, 318, 330, 340, 350, **365**–366, 377, 398, 411, 422, 433, 443, 456, 467, 478, 491–494, 520
Croatia 8–**9**, 396–407, **492, 495**–**497, 499, 507**–508, 514, **517, 519, 525, 527**

cumulative vote 13, 100, **102**–103, 128–129, 136, 137n3, 154, 178, 295, 319, 367, 497, **522**–**526**
cumul des mandats 13, 23, 33, 44, 54, 66, 77, 80, 103, 114, 159, 166, 178, 190, 225, 260, 286, 296, 308, 331, 339, 367, 399, 405, 422, 468
Cyprus 8–9, 197–208, **492, 495**–**496, 499**, 502, **507, 517, 519, 524, 527**
Czech Republic 8–9, 271–281, 317, **492, 495**–497, 507, **517, 519, 525, 527**

Denmark 8–9, 15n5, 21–30, 52–53, 174, 210, 289, 303, **492, 495**–**496**, 503, 506–**507, 517, 519, 522, 527**
disproportionality 251, 255, 324, 330–331
district magnitude 13, 87, 153, 213, 330–332, 335, 340, 497, 512
dual mandate *see cumul des mandats*

early voting *see* advance (early) voting
electoral cycle 4, 11–12, 22, 32, 39n1, 43, 52, 75, 85, 98, **101**, 118, 122, 152, 176, 189, 199, 201, 211, 224, 243, 267, 272, 283, 294, 296, 305, 318, 328, 388, 397, 410, 412, 432, 453, 462, 477, 500–501, 503, 516, 519–520, 528
electoral threshold 13, 44, 53, 103, 109, 128, 130, **131**, 136, 141–142, 148, 165, 178, 190, 227, 236–**237**, 250, 261, 274, 285, 287, 296, 307, 310, 313, 319, **330**–331, 349–350, 357, 368, 372, 377, 399, 411, 422, 433–434, 444, 457, 461–462, **468**, **470, 472**, 474, 496–497, 514, **522**–**526**
electronic voting (e-voting) 28, 69, 76, 284, 287, 291, 391, 394, 405
Estonia 8–9, 282–292, 317, **492, 495**–**496**, 497, 502, **507**, 515, **517, 519, 525, 527**
ethnic quota 378, 404, 416, 514, 528
e-voting *see* electronic voting

female representation 14, *27*, **37**, *47*, *57*, **68**, *79*, **91, 109**, *122*, **135**, *147*, **157**, *169*, **181, 194**, *205*, **218**, 229, 242, **255**, 266, *278*, **288, 299**,

Index

312, 323, **334**, **345**, 356, 366, *382*,
394, **404**, **416**, 425, 438, **449**, **462**,
473, **482**, 510–513, 521
Finland 8–9, 15n5, 31–40, 52–53, **492**, 494,
495–496, 506–**507**, **517**, **519**, **522**, **527**
first-past-the-post system (FPTP) 15n11, 86,
87, 189, 194, 199, 201, 295–296, 330–331,
334–335, 339, 348–351, 358, 364, 366,
376–377, 398, 467–**468**, **495**, 497, 499–500,
520, **522–526**
France 8–9, 15n5, 187–188, 190, 209–221, 234,
271, **492**–493, **495**–499, 501, 506–508, 511,
517, **519**, **524**, **527**

gender quota 14, 27, 34, 37, 46–47, 57, 67,
79–80, 107, 117, 120, 135–136, 144, 148,
157, 194, 205, 218, 226, 229, 242, 255, 266,
278, 287, 323, 331, 334–335, 341, 351, 370,
382, 393, 402, 414, 421, 425, 433, 437, 445,
448–449, 456, 460, 468, 473, 479,
510–511, 521
Germany 8–**9**, 15n5, 126–139, 174, 247, 494,
495–499, 502–503, 506–**507**, **517**, **519**,
523–524, **527**
Greece 8–9, 210, 222–232, 247, **492**, **495–497**,
499, 502–503, **507**, 510, **517**, **519**, **524**, **527**

horizontal variation 5–6, 14, 58–59, 207,
489–490, 504, 509, 515–516, **517–519**, 520
Hungary 8–9, 210, 289, 293–302, 304, 491–493,
495–497, **499**, 500, **507**, 512, **517**, **519**,
525, **527**

Iceland 8–9, 23, 33, 41–50, 53, 64, 267n1, **492**,
495–496, 506–**507**, 510, **517**, **519**, **522**, **527**
incumbency advantage 38, 329, 332, 339, 379,
393, 405, 449, 498, 509
Ireland 8–9, 73–83, 491–**492**, **495–496**, 503,
506–**507**, 509, **517**, **519**, **522**, **527**
Italy 8–9, 233–245, **492**, **495–496**, 498–499, 503,
507, **517**, **519**, **524**, **527**

Kosovo 8–9, 408–418, 439, 465, 472, **492**,
495–496, **499**, 510, **507**–508, 512, 514, **517**,
519, **525**, **527**

Latvia 8–9, 303–315, 317, **492**, **495–496**, 507,
517, **519**, **525**, **527**
Liechtenstein 8–9, 11, 140–150, **492**–493,
495–499, 506–**507**, 512, **517**, **519**, **524**, **527**
limited vote system (LV) 478, 497, **524–526**
Lithuania 8–9, 316–326, **492**, **495–496**, **499**, 507,
517, **519**, **525**, **527**
local (independent) list 13, 25–26, 35–38, 46, 48,
67, 90, 120, 128–129, 134–137, **155**, 167–170,
189, 192–193, 204, 219, 225, 239, **241**, 243,
262, 276–277, 279, 329–330, 332–335, 342,
351, 380–381, 402, **415**, 437, **448**, 459, 469,
471, **481**, 499, 505–509, 516–519
Luxembourg 8–9, 151–160, **492**–493, **495**–498,
502, 506–**507**, **517**, **519**, **524**, **527**

majority bonus system (MBS) 189–190, 192, 194,
212–214, 219, 226, 235–237, 266, **495**, **524**
mandatory voting *see* compulsory voting
mixed-member majoritarian system (MMM)
15n11, 300n4, 324, 358n4, 370, 398
mixed-member proportional system (MMP)
15n11, 295–300, 366, **495–496**, **524**
Moldova 8–9, 74, 419–429, **492**, **495**, **499**,
507–508, **517**, **519**, **526–527**
Montenegro 8–9, 430–440, 472, **492**–493, 495,
498, 514, **517**, **519**, **526–527**

Netherlands, the 8–9, 15n5, 161–173, 317,
492–493, **495–496**, 498, 501, **507**, **517**, **519**,
524, **527**
North Macedonia 8–9, 441–452, **492**, **495–496**,
499, **507**–508, 515, **517**, **519**, **526–527**
Norway 8–9, 23, 33, 51–61, 64, 247, 267n1, **492**,
495–496, 497, **507**, 514, **517**, **519**, **522**, **527**

open-list proportional representation system
(OLPR) 23–24, 33, 53, 64, 99, 109, 129, **130**,
143, 154, 165, 177, 201, 235, 261, 237, 274,
285, 305, 307, 319, 330–333, 357, 372, 377,
382, 390, 394, 410, 494–497, 520, **522–526**,
529n8

panachage 13, 59n9, 65, 103, 117, 154,
178, 212, 219, 226, 243n9, 319, 367,
497, **522–526**
parallel voting system *see* mixed-member
majoritarian system (MMM)
party politicization *see* political parties
Poland 8–9, 247, 327–336, **492**, **495**–500, **507**,
509, **517**, **519**, **525**, **527**
political parties 13, **26**, **36**, **47**, **56**, **67**, **80**, **90**,
108, **121**, **134**, **144**–145, **155**, **168**, **180**, **193**,
204, **217**, **230**, **241**, **254**, **264**–266, **277**, **289**,
297, **311**, **322**, **334**, **344**, **353**–357, **369**, **381**,
393, **403**, **415**, **425**, **437**, **448**, **460**, **471**–472,
481, 505–509
Portugal 8–9, 158, 210, 246–257, **492**, **495–496**,
499, **507**, **517**, **519**, **524**, **527**
postal voting 29n7, 53, 98–99, 142, 176–177, 227,
484n7, 502; *see also* advance (early) voting

Romania 8–9, 317, 426, 453–464, **492**, **495–496**,
499–500, **507**–508, 510, 514, **517**, **519**,
526–527
runoff system *see* two round system (TRS)

seat-allocation method: D'Hondt 13, 24, 34, 39n1, 44, 98–99, 103, 117, 130–**131**, 143, 154, 165, 213, 236–**237**, 250, 260–261, 275, 285, **330**–331, 367, 390, 394, 399, 422, 433, 444, **468**, 474, 478, 496, **522**–**526**; Droop 76, 87; Hagenbach-Bischoff 143, 154, 177, **524**; Hare (Hare-Niemeyer) 130–**131**, 165, 189–190, 201, 351, 390, 394, 457, **468**, 496, **523**–**526**; Imperiali 13, 117, **523**; modified Sainte-Laguë 53, 65, **330**, **522**; Sainte-Laguë 13, 66, 130–**131**, 296, 307, 331, 378, 411, **523**–**526**
second-order elections 4, 23, 38, 59, 79, 81, 88, 121, 167, 175–176, 181, 206, 215, 286, 296, 398, 500–501, 509, 515, 520–521
Serbia 8–**9**, 317, 409, 414, 417, 430, 435–436, 465–475, **492**, **495**–498, **507**–508, 514, **517**, **519**, **526**–527
single non-transferable vote (SNTV) 478, **495**, **525**–**526**
single transferable vote (STV) 15n11, 76, 81, 86–89, 92, **495**–**497**, 506, **522**
Slovakia 8–**9**, 271, 289, 337–346, **492**–493, **495**–**497**, **499**, **507**, 512, 514, **517**, **519**, **525**, **527**
Slovenia 8–**9**, 317, 476–486, **492**, **495**–**497**, **499**, **507**–508, 512, 514, **517**, **519**, **526**–**527**
Spain 8, **10**, 187–188, 210, 247, 258–268, **492**, **495**–**496**, 499, 503, **507**, **517**, **519**, **524**, **527**
supplementary vote system (SV) 86–87, 499–500
Sweden 8, **10**, 53, 62–70, 491–**492**, **495**–**496**, **497**, 501, 506–**507**, 509, 515, **517**–518, **519**, **522**, **527**

Switzerland 8, **10**–11, 140, 174–184, 188, 491, 494, **495**–**496**, 498, 500–501, 503, 506–**507**, **518**–**519**, **527**

timing *see* electoral cycle
two-round bloc vote system (TR-BV) 177, 212, 214, 218–219, **495**, **522**–**526**
two round system (TRS) 15n11, 100, 129, 177, 189, 212, 218–219, 226, 231, 235, **237**, 318–319, 329, 335, 339, 351, 358, 384n7, 389–390, 394, 398–399, 422, 426, 444, 467–**468**, 479, 499–500, 520

Ukraine 8, **10**, 347–359, **492**, **495**–**497**, **499**–501, **507**, **518**, **519**, **525**, **527**
United Kingdom (UK) 8, **10**, 74, 84–94, 304, 491, **492**, 494, **495**–**497**, 501, 503, 506–**507**, 514, **518**–**519**, **522**, **527**

vertical dissimilarity 515, **517**–**519**, 520
vertical integration 4–6, 14, 58–59, 206, 489–490, 515, 528; *see also* vertical dissimilarity
voter turnout 4, 6–7, 13, 24–25, 28, 34–35, 45, 54–56, 58, 66–67, 78, 87–89, 103–105, 110, 118–119, 130, 132–133, 136, 145–146, 154–155, 166–167, 177–180, 182, 191–193, 201–203, 206, 213–215, 227–228, 237–239, 252–254, 262–263, 267, 275–277, 286–287, 296–297, 309–310, 320, 331–333, 341–342, 351–352, 358, 366–368, 379–380, 388, 391–392, 400–402, 412–414, 423–424, 434–436, 445–447, 457–458, 469–470, 479–480, 500–505, 520–521, **527**–**528**

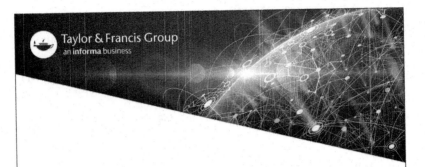